AA Lifestyle Gui
Best Western H
30 Getaway Break ... vo

in 6 Free Prize Draws

see overleaf for terms & conditions

Discover Britain at its best with Best Western Hotels. For a refreshingly different experience Getaway Breaks offer you guaranteed value and excellent service. Try one of the exciting special activity breaks for a leisure break with a difference. With over 370 hotels across the UK, we're bound to be your best bet!

Best Western Donnington Manor Hotel, Sevenoaks.

For more information on Best Western Hotels or for a copy of the Getaway Breaks in Britain brochure call: 08457 74 74 74 quoting 'AA Lifestyle Guides'.

HOW TO ENTER

Just complete (in capitals please) and send off this card or alternatively, send your name and address on a stamped postcard to the address overleaf (no purchase required). Entries limited to one per household and to residents of the UK and Republic of Ireland over the age of 18. This card will require a stamp if posted in the Republic of Ireland. **Closing date 26 October 2001.**

MR/MRS/MISS/MS/OTHER, PLEASE STATE: ______

NAME: ______

ADDRESS: ______

______

______

POSTCODE: ______

TEL. NOS: ______

Are you an AA Member? Yes/No

Have you bought this or any other AA Lifestyle Guide before? Yes/No

If yes, please indicate the year of the last edition you bought:

The AA Hotel Guide	____	AA Camping & Caravanning (Britain & Ireland)	____
AA Bed and Breakfast Guide	____	AA Camping & Caravanning (Europe)	____
AA Restaurant Guide	____	AA Hotels in France	____
AA Pub Guide	____	AA Bed & Breakfast in France	____
AA Britain Guide	____	AA France: Where to Stay	____

If you do not wish to receive further information or special offers from

AA Publishing ☐ **Best Western Hotels** ☐ **please tick the box(es)** BB00

Terms and Conditions

1. Five winners will be drawn for each of the six prize draws to take place on 29 December 2000 and 23 February, 27 April, 29 June, 31 August, 26 October 2001.

2. Closing date for receipt of entries is midday on the relevant draw date. **Final close date for receipt of entries is 26 October 2001.**

3. Entries received after any draw date other than the final one will go forward into the next available draw. Entries will be placed in one draw only. **Only one draw per household accepted.**

4. Winners will be notified by post within 14 days of the relevant draw date. Prizes must be booked within 3 months of the relevant draw date. Prizes are not transferable and there will be no cash alternative.

5. This offer cannot be used in conjunction with any other discount, promotion or special offer.

6. Each prize consists of two nights' accommodation, full traditional breakfast and a complimentary champagne and flowers on arrival, for two adults sharing a standard twin/double room at participating Best Western Hotels. Supplements may be charged for feature and family rooms. All offers of accommodation are made subject to availability.

7. All hotel accommodation, services and facilities are provided by Best Western Hotels and AA Publishing is not party to your agreement with Best Western in this regard.

8. The prize draw is open to anyone resident in the UK or the Republic of Ireland over the age of 18 other than employees of the Automobile Association or Best Western Hotels, their subsidiary companies or their families or agents.

9. For a list of winners, please send a stamped, self addressed envelope to AA Lifestyle Guides Winners, AA Publishing, Fanum House (4), Basingstoke, Hants, RG21 4EA.

10. If this card is posted in the Republic of Ireland it must have a stamp.

BUSINESS REPLY SERVICE
Licence No BZ 343

PLEASE NOTE: Requires a stamp if posted in Republic of Ireland

AA Lifestyle Guide 2001 Prize Draw

AA PUBLISHING
FANUM HOUSE (4)
BASING VIEW
BASINGSTOKE
HANTS RG21 4EA

AA

The Britain Guide 2001

AA Lifestyle Guides

Produced by AA Publishing
Maps prepared by the Cartographic Department of The Automobile Association
Maps © The Automobile Association 2000
Directory generated by the AA Establishment Database, Information Research, AA Hotel Services
Design by Nautilus Design UK Ltd, Basingstoke, Hampshire
Cover artwork by Sue Climpson, Whitchurch, Hampshire
Main Picture: Elton Hall. AA Photo Library/M. Birkitt
'The Glory of the Garden' feature by Julia Hynard

Typeset/Repro by Microset Graphics, Basingstoke, Hampshire, UK

Printed in Italy by Rotolito Lombarda SpA

The contents of this book are believed correct at the time of printing. Nevertheless, the Publisher cannot be held responsible for any errors or omissions or for changes in the details given in this guide or for the consequences of any reliance on the information provided in the same. We have tried to ensure accuracy in this guide but things do change and we would be grateful if readers would advise us of any inaccuracies they may encounter.

A CIP catalogue record for this book is available from the British Library

Published by AA Publishing, which is a trading name of Automobile Association Developments Limited whose registered office is Norfolk House, Priestley Road, Basingstoke, Hampshire RG24 9NY, Registered number 1878835.

ISBN 0 7495 2531 2

Contents

In this edition of the guide we are highlighting gardens, with a special feature, 'The Glory of the Garden' (p8), and a list of gardens in the guide that are open to visitors (p10).

How to Use *this Guide*

THE DIRECTORY

The directory is arranged in country, then county order, then in alphabetical location order within each county. The Scottish Islands have their own section. Each county has an introductory page which may mention places, landmarks or streets that do not have an entry in the directory.

OPENING TIMES quoted in the guide are inclusive - for instance, where you see Apr-Oct, that place will be open from the beginning of April to the end of October.

PRICES quoted for the majority of entries are current. If no price is quoted, you should check with the establishment concerned before you visit. Places which are open 'at all reasonable times' are usually free, and a number of the places which do not charge admission at all may ask for a voluntary donation.

DIRECTIONS are given after the address of each establishment or attraction and where shown have been provided by the places of interest themselves. Map references for establishments can be found in the index. These are based on the National Grid, and can be used with the Atlas at the back of this book, or with any AA Atlas of Britain. As the atlas section is prepared before the gazeteer late entries may not be identified on the maps.

See page 7 for a key of Symbols and Abbreviations used in this guide.

CREDIT & CHARGE CARDS are now taken by a number of establishments for admission charges. To indicate which accept credit cards we have used this symbol at the end of the entry.

For the hard of hearing induction loops are indicated.

PHOTOGRAPHY is restricted in some places and there are many where it is only allowed in specific areas. Visitors are advised to check with places of interest on the rules for taking photographs and the use of video cameras.

SPECIAL EVENTS are held at many of these establishments, and although we have listed a few of the more important ones on the county introduction pages, we cannot hope to give details of them all, so please ring the places of interest for details of exhibitions, themed days, talks, guided walks and more.

TELEPHONE NUMBERS have the STD code shown before the telephone number. (If dialling Northern Ireland from England use the STD code, but for the Republic you need to prefix the number with 00 353).

VISITORS WITH DISABILITIES should look for the wheelchair symbol showing where all or most of the establishment is accessible to the wheelchair-bound visitor. We strongly recommend that you telephone in advance of your visit to check the exact details, particularly regarding access to toilets and refreshment facilities. Guide dogs are usually accepted where the establishments show the 'No Dogs' symbol - unless stated otherwise.

Sample entry

ANY TOWN

ANY PLACE

ZE17 5ZE (off A14 at junc with B760 signed Old Weston)

☎ 01002 293002 📠 01002 293007

e-mail: anyplace@demon.co.uk

A wildlife breeding centre, dedicated to the practical conservation of endangered species including gibbons, marmosets, lemurs, wildcats, meerkats, Britain's only group of breeding sloths and many more. There is also a large and varied bird collection, with several species unique to this location. Over 120 species in all. Other attractions include a children's play area, and undercover viewing of many mammals.

Times: summer daily 10.30-6; winter daily 10.30-4. (Closed Xmas)

P ✕ ♿ toilets for disabled, shop ⊗

Key to SYMBOLS AND ABBREVIATIONS

SYMBOLS

In order to give you as much information as possible in the space available, we have used the following symbols in the guide:

	ENGLISH	FRANÇAIS	DEUTSCH	ITALIANO	ESPAÑOL
☎	Telephone number	Numéro de téléphone	Telefonnummer	Numero telefonico	Número telefónico
	Fax number				
♿	Suitable for visitors in wheelchairs	Les invalidens fauteuils roulants pourrant y accéder	Für Rollstuhltahrer zugänglich	Accessibile agli handicappeti	Acondicionado para visitantes en silla de reudas
P	Parking at Establishment	Stationnement à l'établissement	Parken an Ort und Stelle	Parcheggio in loco	Aparcamiento en el establecimiento
P	Parking nearby	Stationnement tout près	Parken in der Nähe	Parcheggio nelle vicinanze	Aparcamiento cerca del
	Refreshments	Rafraîchissements	Erfrischungen	Snack-bar	Refrescos
✕	Restaurant	Restaurant	Restaurant	Ristorante	Restaurante
	No dogs	Chiens non permis	Hundeverbot	Cani non accettati	Se prohiben los perros
	No coaches	Les groupes en cars pas admis	Keine Reisebusgesellschaften	Non si accettano comitive in pullman	Non se admiten los grupos de viajeros en autobús
	Cadw (Welsh Historic Monuments)	Cadw Monument ancien (Pays de Galles)	Cadw Historiches Gebaude (Walisland)	Cadw Monumento storico (Galles)	Cadw Monumento histórico (Gales)
#	English Heritage	English Heritage	English Heritage	English Heritage	English Heritage
	National Trust	National Trust	National Trust	National Trust	The National Trust
	National Trust for Scotland	National Trust en Ecosse	National Trust in Schottland	National Trust per la Scozia	The National Trust de Escocia
	Historic Scotland				

ABBREVIATIONS

In the same way, we have abbreviated certain pieces of information:

	ENGLISH	FRANÇAIS	DEUTSCH	ITALIAN	ESPAÑOL
BH	Bank Holidays	Jours fériés	Bankfeiertage	Festività nazionale	Días festivos (bancos y comercio)
PH	Public Holidays	Jours fériés	Feiertage	Festività nazionale	Días festivos
Etr	Easter	Pâques	Ostern	Pasqua	Semana Santa
ex	except	sauf	ausser	eccetto	excepto
IR£	Irish punts	Punts irlandais	Punts Irisch	Punts irlandesi	Punts irlandeses
Free	Admission free	Entrée gratuit	Freier eintritt	Ingresso gratuito	Entrada gratuita
£1	Admission £1	Entrée £1	Eintritt £1	Ingresso £1	Entrada £1
ch 50p	Children 50p	Enfants 50p	Kinder 50p	Bambini 50p	Niños 50p
ch 15 50p	Children under 15 50p	Enfants de moins de 15 ans 50p	Kinder unter 15 Jahren 50p	Bambini sotto i 15 anni 50p	Los niños de menores de 15 años 50p
Pen	Senior Citizens	Retraites	Rentner	Pensionati	Jubilados
Party	Special or reduced rates for parties booked in advance	Tarifs spéciaux ou réduits pour groupes réservés d'advance	Sondertarife oder Ermässigungen für im voraus bestellte Gesellschaften	Tariffe speciali o ridotte per comitive che prenotano in anticipo	Tarifas especiales o reducidas para los grupos de viajeros que reserven de anternano
Party 30+	Special or reduced rates for parties of 30 or more booked in advance	Tarifs spéciaux ou réduits pour groupes de 30 ou plus réservés d'advance	Sondertarife oder Ermässigungen für im voraus bestellte Gesellschaften von wenigstens 30 Personen	Tariffe speciali o ridotte per comitive di 30 o più persone che prenotano in anticipo	Tarifas especiales o reducidas para grupos de 30 viajeros, o más, que reserven de anternano

The Glory of *The Garden*

By Julia Hynard

On a fine day there's nothing more edifying than a visit to one of our Great British or Irish gardens. Whether you're in need of quiet contemplation, creative stimulation, or a brisk walk in the fresh air, a beautiful garden will always be a delight to the senses. If you've lost the plot with your own small acreage, it's a chance to dream of all you'd achieve with a little time, imagination … and perhaps a couple of under gardeners.

Sanctuary in the city

There are so many gardens open to the public that, wherever you happen to be, there should be one within easy striking distance. If you're looking for an antidote to the urban jungle, from London head for the Royal Botanical Gardens at Kew, which cover some 300 acres, including woodland, arboretum and formal gardens. Closer to the city centre are Kensington Gardens, which form part of Hyde Park, and the ancient Chelsea Physic Garden, begun in 1673, famed for its rare and unusual plants and still used today for botanical and medicinal research. Up river, Hampton Court has 60 acres of gardens including the famous hedge maze.

Other major cities with botanical gardens are Belfast, Birmingham, Dublin, Edinburgh and Glasgow. As well as providing a haven of peace for the city-dweller, these gardens are centres of education, research and conservation, amassing impressive collections of plant species from all over the world.

In Manchester, two National Trust properties with lovely gardens are Tatton Park, a 1,000-acre estate at Knutsford, 11 miles from Manchester, and Dunham Massey Hall at Altrincham, eight miles from the city. Temple Newsam House and Park, off the A63 near Leeds, is set in 1,200 acres of parkland landscaped by 'Capability' Brown. Dyffryn Gardens, six miles west of Cardiff on the A48, are among the finest landscaped gardens in Wales.

Getting away from it all

If you seriously want to get away from it all, gardens to get lost in include Leonardslee at Lower Beeding, West Sussex, which has 240 acres in a sheltered valley with walks around seven lakes. It's one of the last great private gardens in England, dating from the early 1800s. The famously Lost Gardens of Heligan, in Cornwall, unchanged since the outbreak of World War 1, have become the largest garden restoration project in Europe, capturing forever a period of horticultural history. New on the scene is the National Botanic Garden of Wales, a Millennium Commission development set in the Towy valley, Carmarthenshire. It has a number of 21st-century features including the Bioverse, an interactive exhibition on the role of plant life.

Including the kids

With kids in tow you'll need something to keep them amused while you sniff the roses and contemplate paradise. Paradise Park at Newhaven, East Sussex combines a Planet Earth and Dinosaur Exhibition with a wonderful variety of gardens including a history trail. Wilton House in Wiltshire, with 21 acres of landscaped parkland, is home to the Wareham Bears and has an adventure play area in the grounds. Muncaster Castle, Gardens and Owl Centre at Ravenglass, Cumbria, offer something for everyone, including an adventure playground.

Specialist gardens

For gardens to inspire you check out the National Garden Exhibition Centre at Kilquade, Co Wicklow in Southern Ireland. It has a whole range of gardens to suit a variety of lifestyles and environmental factors – the shady secrets garden, the family garden, budget garden and sensory garden – plus tips on how to conceal your washing line or oil tank. Another specialist attraction is the Japanese Gardens at Tully, Co Kildare, believed to the finest of their kind in Europe.

Those who enjoy the drama, perspective and sheer scale of the 18th-century landscaped garden, will not want to miss Stourhead in Wiltshire, Stowe in Buckinghamshire, and Painshill in Surrey. All have artfully placed architectural features to create a certain mood or set off a particular scene - a Turkish tent here and a Gothic temple there.

For sheer spectacle visit Exbury Gardens, Hampshire, in spring, for its unrivalled collection of rhododendrons, azaleas, magnolias and camellias; in May, the glorious Laburnum Arch at Bodnant, Tal-y-cafn; and in early June the remarkable Inverewe Garden at Poolewe, where rare and sub-tropical plants grow courtesy of the North Atlantic Drift. If roses are your passion, the Garden of the Rose at St Albans, home of the Royal National Rose Society, has over 30,000 roses on display, and in June or July the old-fashioned roses in the walled garden at Mottisfont Abbey, Hampshire are a picture. Finally, no serious plantsperson will want to miss Vita Sackville-West's exquisite garden at Sissinghurst Castle, Kent, regarded by many as the finest example of a garden for all seasons.

Gardens of Britain

This is a list of the gardens in this book that are open to visitors. See the individual entries for more details.

England

BEDFORDSHIRE
Wrest Park House & Gardens, SILSOE

BERKSHIRE
Savill Garden (Windsor Great Park), WINDSOR

BUCKINGHAMSHIRE
Stowe Gardens, STOWE

CAMBRIDGESHIRE
University Botanic Garden, CAMBRIDGE

CHESHIRE
Cholmondeley Castle Gardens, CHOLMONDELEY

Hare Hill, MACCLESFIELD

Stapeley Water Gardens, NANTWICH

Liverpool University Botanic Gardens, NESTON

CORNWALL & ISLES OF SCILLY
Trengwainton Garden, MADRON

Glendurgan, MAWNAN SMITH

Trebah Garden, MAWNAN SMITH

The Lost Gardens of Heligan, PENTEWAN

Trelissick Garden, TRELISSICK GARDEN

CUMBRIA
Acorn Bank Garden, TEMPLE SOWERBY

DEVON
Marwood Hill Gardens, BARNSTAPLE

Coleton Fishacre House & Garden, KINGSWEAR

Babbacombe Model Village, TORQUAY

DORSET
Mapperton Gardens, BEAMINSTER

Compton Acres Gardens, CANFORD CLIFFS

Minterne Gardens, MINTERNE MAGNA

Knoll Gardens & Nursery, WIMBORNE

EAST SUSSEX
Groombridge Place Gardens & Enchanted Forest, GROOMBRIDGE

Sheffield Park Garden, SHEFFIELD PARK

ESSEX
The Beth Chatto Gardens Ltd, COLCHESTER

GLOUCESTERSHIRE
Barnsley House Garden, BARNSLEY

Kiftsgate Court Garden, MICKLETON

Painswick Rococo Garden, PAINSWICK

Westbury Court Garden, WESTBURY-ON-SEVERN

GREATER LONDON
Kew Gardens (Royal Botanic Gardens), KEW

HAMPSHIRE
Spinners, BOLDRE

Exbury Gardens, EXBURY

West Green House Gardens, HARTLEY WINTNEY

Braxton Gardens, LYMINGTON

HEREFORDSHIRE
Hergest Croft Gardens, KINGTON

The Weir Gardens, SWAINSHILL

The Gardens of The Rose (Royal National Rose), ST ALBANS

ISLE OF WIGHT
Ventnor Botanic Garden, VENTNOR

KENT
Great Comp Garden, BOROUGH GREEN

Emmetts Garden, BRASTED

Sissinghurst Castle Garden, SISSINGHURST

LEICESTERSHIRE
University of Leicester Harold Martin Botanic, LEICESTER

LINCOLNSHIRE
Springfields Gardens, SPALDING

Spalding Tropical Forest, SPALDING

LONDON
Chelsea Physic Garden, LONDON SW3

NORTH YORKSHIRE
Parcevall Hall Gardens, PARCEVALL HALL GARDENS

OXFORDSHIRE
University of Oxford Botanic Garden, OXFORD

SHROPSHIRE
Hodnet Hall Gardens, HODNET

SHROPSHIRE
The Dorothy Clive Garden, WILLOUGHBRIDGE

SOMERSET
Hadspen Garden & Nursery, CASTLE CARY

East Lambrook Manor Garden, EAST LAMBROOK

STAFFORDSHIRE

Biddulph Grange Garden, BIDDULPH

SURREY

Claremont Landscape Garden, ESHER
RHS Garden Wisley, WISLEY

WEST SUSSEX

Wakehurst Place Garden, ARDINGLY
Holly Gate Cactus Garden, ASHINGTON
Denmans Garden, FONTWELL
Nymans Garden, HANDCROSS
Borde Hill Garden, HAYWARDS HEATH
Leonardslee Gardens, LOWER BEEDING
West Dean Gardens, WEST DEAN

WILTSHIRE

The Courts, HOLT
Heale Gardens, Plant Centre & Shop, MIDDLE WOODFORD
Stourton House Flower Garden, STOURTON

WORCESTERSHIRE

Stone House Cottage Gardens, STONE

JERSEY

Flying Flowers, ST LAWRENCE

Scotland

Cruickshank Botanic Garden, ABERDEEN, ABERDEEN CITY
Kildrummy Castle Gardens, KILDRUMMY, ABERDEENSHIRE
Storybook Glen, MARYCULTER, ABERDEENSHIRE
Pitmedden Garden, PITMEDDEN, ABERDEENSHIRE
Arduaine Garden, ARDUAINE, ARGYLL & BUTE
Benmore Botanic Garden, BENMORE, ARGYLL & BUTE
Achamore Gardens, GIGHA ISLAND, ARGYLL & BUTE
Crarae Gardens, MINARD, ARGYLL & BUTE
Ardencraig, ROTHESAY, ARGYLL & BUTE
Malleny Garden, BALERNO, CITY OF EDINBURGH
Royal Botanic Garden Edinburgh, EDINBURGH, CITY OF EDINBURGH
Glasgow Botanic Gardens, GLASGOW, CITY OF GLASGOW
Greenbank Garden, GLASGOW, CITY OF GLASGOW
Ardwell House Gardens, ARDWELL, DUMFRIES & GALLOWAY
Threave Garden & Estate, CASTLE DOUGLAS, DUMFRIES & GALLOWAY
Logan Botanic Garden, PORT LOGAN, DUMFRIES & GALLOWAY
Castle Kennedy Gardens, STRANRAER, DUMFRIES & GALLOWAY
Inveresk Lodge Garden, INVERESK, EAST LOTHIAN
Inverewe Garden, POOLEWE, HIGHLAND
Kinross House Gardens, KINROSS, PERTH & KINROSS
Drummond Castle Gardens, MUTHILL, PERTH & KINROSS
Branklyn Garden, PERTH, PERTH & KINROSS
Priorwood Garden & Dried Flower Shop, MELROSE, SCOTTISH BORDERS
Harmony Garden, MELROSE, SCOTTISH BORDERS
Bargany Gardens, OLD DAILLY, SOUTH AYRSHIRE

Wales

Dyffryn Gardens, CARDIFF, CARDIFF
National Botanic Garden of Wales, LLANARTHNE, CARMARTHENSHIRE
Bodnant Garden, TAL-Y-CAFN, CONWY
Colby Woodland Garden, AMROTH, PEMBROKESHIRE
Glansevern Hall Gardens, BERRIEW, POWYS

Northern Ireland

Botanic Gardens, BELFAST, CO BELFAST

Republic of Ireland

Garnish Island, GLENGARRIF, CO CORK
Rowallane Garden, SAINTFIELD, CO DOWN
Howth Castle Rhododendron Gardens, DUBLIN, CO DUBLIN
National Botanic Gardens, DUBLIN, CO DUBLIN
Japanese Gardens/Irish National Stud, KILDARE, CO KILDARE
Lismore Castle Gardens, LISMORE, CO WATERFORD
Johnstown Castle Gardens, WEXFORD, CO WEXFORD
National Gardens Exhibitions Centre, KILQUADE, CO WICKLOW

Bedfordshire

One of England's smallest counties, Bedfordshire contains the picturesque villages of Woburn and Old Warden, and the large towns of Luton and Bedford. There's plenty of countryside to explore on foot or by bike, and plenty to see and do in Bedfordshire's towns and villages.

For many travellers, Luton is the gateway to London and Eastern England. London Luton Airport offers an increasing number of international flights, but that's not all there is to this bustling town. Once a centre for hat manufacture, Luton has a variety of attractions including gardens, museums, parks and a unique collection of horse-drawn carriages. Not far from the town there stands the magnificent Luton Hoo, a 19th-century house with 1,500 acres of Capability Brown garden and a notable collection of art connected with the Russian royal family.

The county has some charming sights, set among its many small villages. Woburn is one of these, and is known not only for its Abbey and Safari Park, but also its fine Georgian houses and antique shops. Not far from Old Warden, the Swiss Garden is an ideal place for a quiet afternoon. In its ten acre spread there are trees and shrubs from all over the world, as well as islands and ponds and a tiny thatched Swiss cottage.

There is also plenty of history on view. Dunstable boasts the Norman Church of St Peter, with medieval additions that include a 15th-century chancel screen. Ampthill, between Luton and Bedford, is full of fascinating architecture, including Avenue House, and the 14th-century Church of StAndrew, which houses a cannon-ball monument to Richard Nicolls, a local citizen who became the first Governor of Long Island, USA.

EVENTS & FESTIVALS

March
3-10 Bedfordshire Festival of Music, Speech & Drama

May
1 Ickwell May Festival, The Maypole, Ickwell Green

June
tbc Great British Picnic Air Show, Shuttleworth

July
tbc PFA International Air Rally & Exhibition, Cranfield
tbc Summer Air Show, Shuttleworth

August
tbc Proms in the Park, Bedford Park
tbc Military Pageant & Vintage Transport Day, Shuttleworth

September
15-16 Bedfordshire Steam & Country Fayre, Shuttleworth

October
tbc Bedford Beer Festival, Bedford Corn Exchange
tbc National Apple Day at Bromham Mill

November
tbc Bedford Fireworks Display

December
tbc Bedford Victorian Fayre, Bedford town centre

Top: the picturesque Green of Ickwell.

AMPTHILL

Houghton House

(1m NE off A421)

Now a ruin, the mansion was built for Mary Countess of Pembroke, the sister of Sir Philip Sidney. Inigo Jones is thought to have been involved in work on the house, which may have been the original 'House Beautiful' in Bunyan's *'Pilgrim's Progress'*.

Times: Open all reasonable times.

Fee: Free.

BEDFORD

Bedford Museum

Castle Ln MK40 3XD (close to town bridge)

01234 353323 01234 273401

Times: Open all year, Tue-Sat 11-5, Sun 2-5. (Closed Mon ex BH Mon afternoon, Good Fri & Xmas).

(50 mtrs) (lift available on request, subject to staff availability) toilets for disabled shop *Details not confirmed for 2001*

Cecil Higgins Art Gallery & Museum

Castle Ln MK40 3RP (in the centre of the town, just off the Embankment)

01234 211222 01234 327149

A recreated Victorian mansion, with the rooms arranged as though the house was lived in. Includes bedroom with furniture designed by Victorian architect William Borges. The adjoining gallery has an outstanding collection of ceramics, glass and changing exhibition of prints, drawings and watercolours.

Times: Open all year, Tue-Sat 11-5, Sun & BH Mon 2-5. (Closed Mon, Good Fri & 25-26 Dec).

Fee: £2 (concessions free)

(50 yds) toilets for disabled shop (ex guide dogs)

ELSTOW

Moot Hall

(signposted off Elstow Road)

01234 266889 01234 228531

Times: Open 2 Apr-Oct, Tue-Thu, Sat, Sun & BH's 2-5 (Closed Mon ex BH's & Fri). Phone to confirm.

shop *Details not confirmed for 2001*

LEIGHTON BUZZARD

Leighton Buzzard Railway

Pages Park Station, Billington Rd LU7 8TN (0.75m SE on A4146 signposted in and around Leighton Buzzard)

01525 373888 01525 377814

e-mail: info@buzzrail.co.uk

Built in 1919 to serve the local sand industry, this railway has run a steam passenger service since 1968. With the largest collection of narrow gauge locomotives in Britain, the Leighton Buzzard Railway is an important part of Britain's railway heritage.

Times: Open Mar-Oct, Sun & BH wknds; Jun-Jul, Wed; Aug, Tue-Thu, Sat & BH wknds.

Fee: Return ticket £5 (ch 2-15 £1.50, pen £4 & ch under 2 free). Party 10+.

(platform & train access for wheelchairs) toilets for disabled shop

LUTON

John Dony Field Centre

Hancock Dr, Bushmead LU2 7SF (signposted from rdbt on A6, at Barnfield College on New Bedford Rd)

01582 486983 01582 422805

e-mail: tweent@luton.gov.uk

The John Dony Field Centre is a purpose built study centre for exploring the landscapes, plants and animals of the Luton area. Featuring permanent displays of local archaeology, natural history and the management of the local nature reserve, it explains how ancient grasslands and hedgerows are conserved and follows 4000 years of history from Bronze Age to modern times.

Times: Open all year, Mon-Fri 9.30-4.45, Sun 9.30-1. Closed BHs.

Fee: Free.

toilets for disabled (ex guide dogs)

Luton Museum & Art Gallery

Wardown Park, Old Bedford Rd LU2 7HA (1m N of Luton town centre)

01582 546722 & 546739 01582 546763

e-mail: burgessl@luton.gov.uk

A Victorian mansion, with displays illustrating the natural and cultural history, archaeology and industries of the area, including the development of Luton's hat industry, and the Bedfordshire and Hertfordshire Regimental Collections. Due to refurbishment, some galleries may be affected during 2000-2001, telephone 01582 546722 for further details.

Times: Open all year, Tue-Sat 10-5, Sun 1-5 (Closed Xmas, 1 Jan & Mon).

Fee: Free.

(parking adjacent to entrance, lift to 1st floor) toilets for disabled shop (ex guide dogs & hearing dogs)

Stockwood Craft Museum & Gardens

Stockwood Country Park, Farley Hill LU1 4BH (signposted from M1 junct 10 and from Hitchin and Dunstable)

01582 738714 & 546739 01582 546763

e-mail: burgess@luton.gov.uk

The Museum is set in period gardens which incorporate the Ian Hamilton Finlay Sculpture Gardens. The Mossman collection of horse-drawn vehicles traces the history of transport from Roman times to the 1940s. Craft demonstrations are held at weekends in the summer. Please telephone for details of special events.

Times: Open all year; Mar-Oct, Tue-Sat 10-5, Sun & BH Mons 10-6; Nov-Mar, weekends 10-4. (closed Xmas & 1 Jan)

Fee: Free.

licensed (stair lift, parking, induction loop, automatic door) toilets for disabled shop (ex guide & hearing dogs)

OLD WARDEN

The Shuttleworth Collection

Old Warden Aerodrome SG18 9EP (2m W from rdbt on A1, Biggleswade by-pass)

☎ 01767 627288 ▯ 01767 627745

Times: Open all year, daily 10-4 (3pm Nov-Mar). Closed 10 days at Xmas, up to and including 1 Jan.

P ✕ licensed ♿ (passageways between hangars are ramped) toilets for disabled shop ✗ *Details not confirmed for 2001*

SANDY

RSPB Nature Reserve

The Lodge SG19 2DL (1m E, on B1042 Potton Rd)

☎ 01767 680541

The headquarters of the Royal Society for the Protection of Birds. The house and buildings are not open to the public, but there are waymarked paths and formal gardens, and two species of woodpecker, nuthatches and woodland birds may be seen, as may muntjac deer. Another feature is the specialist wildlife garden created in conjunction with the Henry Doubleday Association.

Times: Open daily dawn-dusk. Visitor Centre 9-5.15.

Fee: Members free. Non-members £2.50 (ch 50p, concessions £1.50) Family £5.

P ♿ (partial access) toilets for disabled shop ✗

SILSOE

Wrest Park House & Gardens

MK45 4HS (three quarters of a mile E off A6)

☎ 01525 860152

The formal gardens designed over 150 years ago form a serene and beguiling setting for this elegant 19th-century mansion.

Times: Open Apr-Sep, wknds & BH's 10-6 (Oct 10-5).

Fee: £3.40 (ch 5-15 £1.70, under 5's free). Personal stereo tour included in price.

P ✗ (in certain areas) #

WHIPSNADE

Whipsnade Wild Animal Park

LU6 2LF (signposted from M1 junct 9 & 12)

☎ 01582 872171 ▯ 01582 872649

Set in 600 acres of countryside, Whipsnade is home to over 2,500 creatures, and is one of the largest wildlife conservation centres in Europe. Visitors can see tigers, elephants, penguins, giraffes, bears, chimps, hippos and more. Free daily demonstrations include the Elephant Walk, Birds of the World and penguin feeding.

Times: Open all year, daily. (Closed 25 Dec). Telephone 01582 872171 for opening times.

Fee: £9.90 (ch 3-15, pen & student £7.50). Car entry £8.

P (charged) ♿ (free entry for disabled cars) toilets for disabled shop ✗

WOBURN

Woburn Abbey

MK17 9PQ

☎ 01525 290666 ▯ 01525 290271

e-mail: woburnabey@aol.com

Standing in 3000 acres of parkland, this palatial 18th-century mansion was originally a Cistercian Abbey, and the Dukes of Bedford have lived here since 1547. The art collection includes works by Canaletto, Rembrandt, Van Dyck, and Gainsborough. 14 state apartments are on view, and the private apartments are shown when not in use. Special events are held during the year, including a Craft Fair and a De-Havilland Tiger Moth Fly-In.

Times: Open Jan-25 Mar; Abbey Sat & Sun only 11-4, Deer park 10.30-3.45; 26 Mar-1 Oct; Abbey weekdays 11-4, Sun & BH 11-5; 2-31 Oct Sat & Sun only; Deer Park weekdays 10-4.30, Sun & BH 10-4.45.

Fee: Abbey & Deer Park £7.50 (ch over 12yrs £3.00, pen £6.50). Family ticket £19-£21.50. Deer Park only car & passengers £5. Motorcycles & passengers £2.

P ♿ (wheelchairs accommodated by prior arrangement) toilets for disabled shop ✗

Woburn Safari Park

Woburn Park MK17 9QN (Signposted from M1, junc 13)

☎ 01525 290407 ▯ 01525 290489

e-mail: wobsafari@aol.com

Set in the 3000 acres of parkland belonging to Woburn Abbey, Woburn Safari Park has an extensive collection of many species. The safari road passes through an African plains area stocked with eland, zebra, hippos and rhinos, then through well-keepered tiger and lion enclosures and on past bears and monkeys. Animal encounters, sea lion and parrot shows, and elephant displays, are all popular attractions. The large leisure complex also offers a boating lake, adventure playgrounds, railway train, walk-through aviary, squirrel monkey exhibit and `Friends in the Forest', with deer and wallabies.

Times: Open daily, 11 Mar-Oct, 10-5.

Fee: £12 (ch3-17 £8.50, pen £9). Ch under 3 free. From 15 Jul-4 Sep prices increase by extra 50p during Bedfordshire School Holidays)

P ✕ licensed ♿ toilets for disabled shop ✗ (guide dogs in leisure area)

Berkshire

Berkshire is a narrow county of wide variety, reaching from the edge of London on its eastern boundary to the relative isolation of the Lambourn Downs in the west, containing towns as diverse as Reading and Hungerford, Newbury and Windsor.

Waterways play an important part in Berkshire's character and history, not least the River Thames which forms the county's border with Oxfordshire. The Kennet, a tributary of the Thames that was partially converted into the Kennet and Avon Canal, had a major role in the growth and success of both Reading and Newbury, and flows the length of the county from Reading until it peters out somewhere in Wiltshire. Both of these rivers, as well as The Bourne and the River Pang, flow through some of England's prettiest countryside. Part of the charm of these scenes has been preserved in one of Britain's best-loved children's books. Kenneth Graham used the river banks around Cookham as the setting for The Wind in the Willows in 1908. Cookham is also known as the birthplace of eccentric artist, Sir Stanley Spencer (1891-1959), whose work includes Christ Carrying the Cross and various religious murals.

Newbury, the county's largest town after Reading, has seen its share of history. Its most famous citizen, Jack of Newbury, (JohnWinchcombe) established the first true factory in England with 200 looms and 1000 employees. In 1513 he led 150 men against the Scots at Flodden in Northumberland. The town saw fighting during the Civil War, when Donnington Castle was ruined. Today, the town is better known for the more peaceful, if no less noisy, sport of horseracing.

EVENTS & FESTIVALS

March
Shrove Tuesday - Great Newbury Pancake Race

May
7 Crafty Craft Race, Kennet & Avon Canal
9-13 Royal Windsor Horse Show
tbc Newbury International Spring Festival

July
Bracknell Festival
20-21 Kennet Valley Kite Festival, Thatcham
tbc Cartier International Polo, Windsor Great Park
tbc Kennet & Avon Canal Trust Water Carnival
tbc WOMAD World Music & Arts Festival, Reading

August
tbc International Orchid Fayre, Jarvis Elcot Park Hotel
tbc Reading Rock Festival

September
22-23 The Ascot Festival of Racing
22 Sep-6 Oct Windsor Festival
tbc Newbury & Royal County of Berkshire Show

October
22 Sep-6 Oct Windsor Festival
tbc Michaelmas Fair, Northcroft, Newbury
tbc Royal Windsor Half Marathon

Top: Windsor Castle

BASILDON

Basildon Park

Lower Basildon RG8 9NR (7m NW of Reading on W side of A329)

☎ 0118 984 3040 0118 984 1267

e-mail: tbdgan@smtp.ntrust.org.uk

This 18th-century house, built of Bath stone, fell into decay in the 20th century, but has been beautifully restored by Lord and Lady Iliffe. The classical front has a splendid central portico and pavilions, and inside there are delicate plasterwork decorations on the walls and ceilings. The Octagon drawing room has fine pictures and furniture, and there is a small formal garden.

Times: House open 1 Apr-31 Oct, Wed-Fri 1-5.30; Sat, Sun & BH Mon 1-5.30 (Closed Good Fri). Park & garden 1 Apr-31 Oct, 12-5.30. **Fee:** House & grounds £4.20, family ticket £10.50; Grounds only £1.80, family ticket £4.50. (driven buggy) toilets for disabled shop (ex on lead in grounds)

Beale Park

Lower Basildon RG8 9NH (signposted from M4 junc 12)

☎ 0118 984 5172 0118 984 5171

Times: Open daily, Mar-Sep 10-6. Last admission 5pm. Oct-Dec 10-5. Last admission 4pm.

(wheelchair available, parking) toilets for disabled shop

Details not confirmed for 2001

ETON

Dorney Court

Dorney SL4 6QP (signposted from M4 exit 7, via B3026)

☎ 01628 604638 01628 665772

e-mail: palmer@dorneycourt.co.uk

An enchanting brick and timber manor house (c1440) in a tranquil setting. With tall Tudor chimneys and a splendid great hall, it has been the home of the present family since 1510.

Times: BH Mons in May and preceding Sun 1-4.30 Jul & Aug, Mon-Thu 1-4.30. **Fee:** £5 (ch £2.80, under 9's free)

garden centre (ex guide dogs)

MAIDENHEAD

Courage Shire Horse Centre

Cherry Garden Ln, Maidenhead Thicket SL6 3QD (off A4 0.5m W of A4/A423/A423M jct)

☎ 01628 824848 01628 828472

You are free to wander around and meet the horses, or take a free tour with a guide who will explain the care and history of these gentle giants of the equestrian world. Dray rides are also available.

Times: Open Mar-Oct, daily 10.30-5. Last admission 4pm.

Fee: £3 (ch & pen £2). Party 10+.

(wheelchair available) toilets for disabled shop

NEWBURY

West Berkshire Museum

The Wharf RG14 5AS (M4 junct 13, then Southbound on A34 for 3m, follow signs for town centre.)

☎ 01635 30511 01635 38535

e-mail: hentage@westberks.gov.uk

Situated in two historic buildings in the centre of Newbury, the Cloth Hall built in 1627, and the Granary built in 1720. Apart from local history and archaeology, birds and fossils, the museum displays costume and other decorative art.

Times: Open all year: Apr-Sep, Mon-Fri (Wed during school hols only) 10-5, Sat 10-4.30. Oct-Mar, Mon-Sat (Wed during school hols only) 10-4. (Closed Sun & BHs). **Fee:** Free. P (15yds) shop (ex guide dogs)

READING

Museum of English Rural Life

University of Reading, Whiteknights Park RG6 6AG (2m SE on A327)

☎ 0118 931 8660 0118 975 1264

e-mail: info@rhc.ac.uk

This museum houses a national collection of agricultural, domestic and crafts exhibits, including wagons, tools and a wide range of other equipment used in the English countryside over the last 150 years. Special facilities such as videos and teaching packs are available for school parties. The museum also contains extensive documentary and photographic archives, which can be studied by appointment.

Times: Open all year, Tue-Sat, 10-1 & 2-4.30. (Closed BH's & Xmas-New Year). **Fee:** £1 (ch free & pen 75p). shop

The Museum of Reading

The Town Hall, Blagrave St RG1 1QH

☎ 0118 939 9800 0118 939 9881

Times: Open all year, Tue-Sat 10-5, Sun & BH 2-5.

P (200m) licensed (lifts parking space) toilets for disabled shop (ex guide dogs) *Details not confirmed for 2001*

RISELEY

Wellington Country Park

RG7 1SP (signposted off A33)

☎ 0118 932 6444 0118 932 6445

contd.

350 acres of woodland and meadows, set around a lake in peaceful countryside. The Thames Valley Time Trail traces the development of earth and mineral resources in the area, and there's a collection of farm animals, a deer park and a miniature steam railway. You can also fish, sail, windsurf and row here.
Times: Open Mar-Oct, daily 10-5.30. **Fee:** £4 (ch £2) (fishing platform & nature trail for disabled) toilets for disabled shop

WINDSOR

Frogmore House

Home Park SL4 1NJ (entrance from B3021 between Datchet & Old Windsor)
☎ 01753 831118 (recorded info)
01753 832290

The present building dates back to 1618, and residents have included Charles II's architect, Hugh May, who built it, Queen Charlotte, Queen Victoria and Queen Mary. An original mural, discovered only recently during redecoration, can be seen on the stairway.
Times: Open:16,17 & 18 May 10-7 (last admission 6), 24 May (mausoleum only) 11-4 (last admission 3.30), 26-28 Aug 10-5.30.
Fee: May, house: £3.40 (ch £1.20, pen £2.40), grounds: £2.50 (ch free, pen £2.50). 29-31 Aug guided tours £6.50. shop

Household Cavalry Museum

Combermere Barracks, St Leonards Rd SL4 3DN
☎ 01753 755203

One of the finest military museums in Britain, with comprehensive displays of the uniforms, weapons, horse furniture (tack, regalia, etc) and armour used by the Household Cavalry from 1600 to the present day.
Times: Open all year Mon-Fri (ex BH) 9-12.30 & 2-4.30.
Fee: Free admission, however a donation would be appreciated.
shop

Legoland Windsor

Winkfield Rd SL4 4AY (on B3022 Windsor to Ascot road well signposted from M3 junct 3 & M4 junct 6)
☎ 0990 040404 01753 626300
e-mail: www.legoland.co.uk
Times: Open daily 13 Mar-Oct
licensed toilets for disabled shop (ex guide dogs)
Details not confirmed for 2001

St George's Chapel

SL4 1NJ
☎ 01753 865538 01753 620165

Begun in 1475 by Edward IV, and completed in the reign of Henry VIII, the chapel is a fine example of Perpendicular architecture, with large windows adding to the effect of light and spaciousness. The fan vaulting on the ceiling is magnificent, and the chantries, and intricate carving on the choir stalls, all add to this superb building.
Times: Open Mon-Sat 10-4. (Closed 26 & 27 Apr, 16-19 Jun, 24-25 Dec & occasionally at short notice). Closed Sun worshippers very welcome.
Fee: Free entry to the Chapel is included in the price of entry to Windsor Castle. shop

Savill Garden (Windsor Great Park)

Wick Ln, Englefield Green SL4 2HT (Signposted off A30 between Egham & Virginia Water)
☎ 01753 847518 01753 847536

The 35 acres include woodland plantings, rhododendrons and azaleas, magnificent rose beds and herbaceous borders, dry gardens and temperate houses, fiery autumn colour and winter interest.
Times: Open all year, daily 10-6 (10-4 Nov -Feb). (Closed 25-26 Dec)
Fee: £5 (ch 6-16 £2, pen £2.50) Apr & May; £4 (ch 6-16 £1, pen £3.50) Jun-Oct; £3 (ch 6-16 £1, pen £2.50) Nov-Mar. Ch 1-5 free.
licensed (wheelchairs available) toilets for disabled shop (& plant centre) (ex in the garden)

Windsor Castle

SL4 1NJ
☎ 01753 831118 01753 832290
e-mail: information@royalcollection.org.uk

Covering 13 acres, this is the official residence of HM The Queen and the largest inhabited castle in the world. Begun as a wooden fort by William the Conqueror, it has been added to by almost every monarch since. The Upper Ward includes the State Apartments, magnificantly restored following the fire of 1992, and the Lower Ward where St George's Chapel is situated. The Doll's House designed for Queen Mary in the 1920s by Lutyens, is also on display.
Times: Open all year, daily except 21 April, 19 June & 25-26 Dec. Nov-Feb 10-4 (last admission 3), Mar-Oct 10-5.30 (last admission 4). As Windsor Castle is a royal residence the opening arrangements may be subject to change.
Fee: £10.50 (ch 17 £5, under 5's free, over 60's £8) Family ticket £25.50 (2 adults & 2 under 17's)
(400yds) (except The Gallery) toilets for disabled shop 

Bristol

Bristol was once one of the South of England's major ports but is now perhaps better known for its contributions to contemporary art and music. It is an ancient city with a modern outlook, and centuries of history are waiting, ready to be explored by the curious visitor

For centuries ships sailed from Bristol to every part of the known world in search of new produce and markets, opening up international trade routes. In 1497 John Cabot (Giovanni Caboto), a Genoese pilot set sail from Bristol and within months had discovered North America. Four centuries later the Cabot Tower was built in commemoration. In 1843 Brunel launched his SS Great Britain, the largest iron ship then built. She now sits, rescued and restored, in the dock where she was built.

The city's cathedral was founded as an Augustinian monastery and contains examples of Norman, early-English, Gothic and Victorian architecture. Other important church buildings include St Mary Redcliffe, which was built and extended in the Middle Ages and carries a massive tower with a 285ft spire.

Post-war rebuilding of the blitz-damaged city centre means that Bristol's current identity is less defined by its history than by its recent contributions to popular culture and art. Redevelopment of the disused dockland has led to the creation of art spaces such as the Arnolfini and the Watershed, which are at the forefront of uncovering new talent. In music the city has left its mark in the shape of innovative dance acts such as Massive Attack, Roni Size, Tricky and Portishead (the last of which are named after a nearby resort overlooking the Bristol Channel).

EVENTS & FESTIVALS

March
3-10 Bedfordshire Festival of Music, Speech & Drama

May
1 Ickwell May Festival, The Maypole, Ickwell Green

June
tbc Great British Picnic Air Show, Shuttleworth

July
tbc PFA International Air Rally & Exhibition, Cranfield
tbc Summer Air Show, Shuttleworth

August
tbc Proms in the Park, Bedford Park
tbc Military Pageant & Vintage Transport Day, Shuttleworth

September
15-16 Bedfordshire Steam & Country Fayre, Shuttleworth

October
tbc Bedford Beer Festival, Bedford Corn Exchange
tbc National Apple Day at Bromham Mill

November
tbc Bedford Fireworks Display

December
tbc Bedford Victorian Fayre, Bedford town centre

SS Great Britain

BRISTOL

Blaise Castle House Museum

Henbury Rd, Henbury BS10 7QS (4m NW of city)
☎ 0117 950 6789 📠 0117 959 3475
e-mail: general-museum@bristol-city.gov.uk

Built in the 18th century for a Quaker banker, this mansion is now Bristol's Museum of Social History. Nearby Blaise Hamlet is a picturesque estate village.
Times: Open Apr-Oct, Sat-Wed, 10-5. **Fee:** Free. P ♿ shop

Bristol City Museum & Art Gallery

Queen's Rd BS8 1RL
☎ 0117 922 3571 📠 0117 922 2047
e-mail: general-museum@bristol-city.gov.uk

Regional and international collections, representing ancient history, natural sciences, and fine and applied arts. Displays include dinosaurs, Bristol ceramics, silver, Chinese and Japanese ceramics.
Times: Open all year, daily 10-5. **Fee:** Free.
P (NCP 400 yds) ♿ (lift) toilets for disabled shop

Bristol Industrial Museum

Prince's Wharf, Prince St, City Docks BS1 4RN
☎ 0117 925 1470 📠 0117 729 7318
e-mail: general-museum@bristol-city.gov.uk

The museum is housed in a converted dockside transit shed. Motor and horse-drawn vehicles from the Bristol area are shown, with locally built aircraft and aero-engines. Railway exhibits include the industrial locomotive Henbury. The steam tug *Mayflower* also takes trips around the harbour weekends in summer.
Times: Open Apr-Oct, Sat-Wed 10-5; Nov-Mar, Sat & Sun 10-5.
Fee: Free. P (charged) ♿ toilets for disabled shop

Bristol Zoo Gardens

Clifton BS8 3HA (M5 junct 17 or 18. Follow signs)
☎ 0117 973 8951 📠 0117 973 6814
e-mail: information@bristolzoo.org.uk

Over 300 species of wildlife in beautiful gardens. Seal and penguin coasts with underwater viewing and favourites such as Gorilla Island, Bug World, Twilight World and Reptile House. There is a popular 'hands-on' Activity Centre, special events and feeding time talks.
Times: Open all year, daily (ex 25 Dec) from 9am. Closing times approx 5.30pm (summer) 4.30pm (winter).
Fee: £8.20 (ch 3-13 £4.60, pen £7.20). Party.
P (charged) ✕ licensed ♿ toilets for disabled shop

Georgian House

7 Great George St, off Park St BS1 5RR
☎ 0117 921 1362 📠 0117 922 2047
e-mail: general-museum@bristol-city.gov.uk

A carefully preserved example of a late 18th-century merchant's town house, with many original features furnished to illustrate life both above and below stairs. Small display recounting Bristol's involvement in the slave trade.
Times: Open Apr-Oct, Sat-Wed, 10-5. **Fee:** Free. P

Harveys Wine Museum

12 Denmark St BS1 5DQ (City Centre)
☎ 0117 927 5036 📠 0117 927 5001

Explore a world of wine at Harveys 13th-century cellars, and discover the delights of tasting from a range of sherries, ports, wines and champagnes. The Cellars depict Bristol's history as a trading port.
Times: Open all year, Mon-Sat 10-5. (Closed Sun & BH).
Fee: £5 (concessions £4). Family ticket £10.
P (5 mins walk) (parking meters) ✕ licensed shop

John Wesley's Chapel(The New Room)

36 The Horsefair, Broadmead BS1 3JE
☎ 0117 926 4740
e-mail: newroom@lineone.net

The oldest Methodist chapel in the world, built in 1739 and extended in 1748. Above the chapel are the preacher's rooms where John Wesley, Charles Wesley and the early Methodist preachers stayed.
Times: Open all year, Mon-Sat 10-4. **Fee:** Free.
P (250yds) ♿ shop (ex guide dogs)

Maritime Heritage Centre

Gas Ferry Rd BS1 6UN (follow brown tourist signs)
☎ 0117 926 0680 📠 0117 925 5788
e-mail: commerical@ss-great-britain.com

Exploring 200 years of Bristol shipbuilding, with special reference to Charles Hill & Son, and their predecessor, James Hillhouse. At the Great Western Dock the museum forms part of the *SS Great Britain* and John Cabot's *Matthew* experience.
Times: Open all year, 10-5.30, 4.30 in winter. (Closed 24 & 25 Dec).
Fee: Admission for museum, SS Great Britain & Matthew £6.25 (ch £3.75, pen £5.25). Family ticket (2 adults & 2 ch) £16.50.
P (charged) ♿ toilets for disabled shop

Red Lodge

Park Row BS1 5LJ
☎ 0117 921 1360 📠 0117 922 2047
e-mail: general-museum@bristol-city.gov.uk

The house was built in 1590 and then altered in 1730. The garden has recently been laid out in Elizabethan style.
Times: Open Apr-Oct, Sat-Wed 10-5. **Fee:** Free. P (NCP, adjacent)

SS Great Britain

Great Western Dock, Gas Ferry Rd BS1 6TY
☎ 0117 926 0680 📠 0117 925 5788

Built and launched in Bristol in 1843, the *SS Great Britain,* designed by Isambard Kingdom Brunel, was the first ocean-going, propeller-driven, iron ship in history. After life as a passenger liner, troop transport and cargo carrier, she was abandoned in the Falkland Islands in 1886. In 1970 she was towed back to Bristol and is now in the dock where she was built.
Times: Open all year 10-5.30, 4.30 in winter. (Closed 24 & 25 Dec).
Fee: £6.25 (ch £3.75, pen £5.25). Family ticket (2+2) £16.50.
P (charged) ♿ shop

Buckinghamshire

Visitors to Buckinghamshire cannot fail to be enchanted by the majestic sweep of the Chiltern Hills, and fascinated by the history and heritage of the county's many attractive towns and villages.

Richly wooded in the west but mainly windswept and bare near Ivinghoe in the east, the Chilterns extend in a line from Goring in the Thames Valley, across the breadth of Buckinghamshire, to a point near Hitchin in Hertfordshire. Its highest point is the 835ft Coombe Hill near Wendover. Many of the chalk downs are crowned with ancient beech groves. Walkers can get to grips with the Chilterns by walking the North Bucks Way - 30 miles from Wolverton to Chequers near Great Missenden.

Chequers Court plays an important role as the official country residence of the British Prime Minister. It was given to the nation by Lord Lee of Fareham in thanksgiving for the end of World War I. It sits in acres of parkland and fittingly, contains some valuable Cromwellian relics.

Buckinghamshire is famous for its pretty villages and any one of them would make a visit here worthwhile. Not only are they pretty, but many have strong historical connections. Jordan is the site of the most famous of all Quaker Meeting Houses, which was built in 1688. British Prime Minister, Benjamin Disraeli, lived at Hughenden Manor in Hughenden; John Milton, author of Paradise Lost, lived in a cottage near Chalfont St Giles; Florence Nightingale lived at Claydon House near Buckingham; and in the 17th century, Charles II visited his mistress, Barbara Palmer, Countess of Castlemaine, at Dorney Court near Windsor.

EVENTS & FESTIVALS

March
Shrove Tuesday Olney Pancake Day Race

May
7 Marlow Spring Regatta, Higginson Park, Marlow
7 Milton Keynes Garden Show
tbc Elizabeth Cullum Memorial Challenge, Princes Risborough

June
6 Coombe Hill Run, Wendover
24 Milton Keynes City Spectacular & Carnival
29 Jun-1 Jul Milton Keynes International Festival
tbc Marlow Regatta, Higginson Park, Marlow

July
tbc North Bucks Show, Buckingham
tbc Jazz Festival, Marlow
tbc Buckingham Festival

August
10 Bucks County Show, Weedon Park, Aylesbury

September
9 Thames Valley Grand Prix Raft Race, Marlow
15 Marlow Carnival, Marlow

November
tbc Milton Keynes Free Firework Display, central Milton Keynes

Top: Bletchley Park, HQ of the Enigma code-breaking operation in WWII

BEACONSFIELD

Bekonscot Model Village

Warwick Rd HP9 2PL (2.7m junc 2 M40, 4m junc 16 M25)

☎ 01494 672919 01494 675284

e-mail: bekonscot@dial.pipex.com

A miniature world, depicting rural England in the 1930s. A Gauge 1 model railway meanders through six little villages, each with their own tiny population.

Times: Open 19 Feb-29 Oct, daily 10-5.

Fee: £4.50 (ch £2.50, pen & students £3). Party 13+.

(wheelchair loan) toilets for disabled shop (ex guide dogs)

CHALFONT ST GILES

Chiltern Open Air Museum

Newland Park, Gorelands Ln HP8 4AD (M25 junct 17, M40 junct 2. Follow brown signs)

☎ 01494 871117 & 875542 01494 872774

Saved from demolition and moved brick by brick to Newland Park, this collection of old buildings includes barns, granaries and even a tin chapel. Step back in time and get a feel of the 1940s in a fully furnished Prefab, or experience 50AD at the Iron Age House. Demonstrations and regular living history re-enactments.

Times: Open Apr-29 Oct, daily 10-5.

Fee: £5.50 (ch 5-16 £3, concessions £4.50) Family ticket (2 adults & 2 ch) £15.

(Braille guide books & taped guides available, wheelchairs) toilets for disabled shop (ex on lead)

Milton's Cottage

Dean Way HP8 4JH (0.5m W of A413. 3m N of M40 junct 2)

☎ 01494 872313

e-mail: pbirger@clara.net

A timber-framed, 16th-century cottage, with a charming garden, the only surviving home in which John Milton lived and worked. He completed *Paradise Lost* and started *Paradise Regained* here. First editions of these works are among the many rare books and artefacts on display.

Times: Open Mar-Oct, Tue-Sun 10-1 & 2-6. Also open Spring & Summer BH. **Fee:** £2 (ch 15 £1). Party 20+.

(special parking area closer to cottage) shop

CHICHELEY

Chicheley Hall

MK16 9JJ (A422 between Newport Pagnell and Bedford)

☎ 01234 391252 01234 391388

Built for Sir John Chester between 1719 and 1723, this is one of the finest and least-altered 18th-century houses in England, with wonderful Georgian craftsmanship in its brickwork, carving, joinery and plasterwork. It has a naval museum, English sea pictures and furniture, and an 18th-century dovecote.

Times: Open all year by appointment only.

Fee: £6 (ch £1.50). Parties 20+.

CLIVEDEN

Cliveden

SL6 0JA (2m N of Taplow)

☎ 01628 605069 01628 669461

e-mail: tclest@smtp.ntrust.org.uk

The 375 acres of garden and woodland overlook the River Thames, and include a magnificent parterre, topiary, lawns with box hedges, and rose and water gardens. The palatial house, home of the Astors, is now a hotel, 3 rooms only of the house can be visited on certain afternoons.

Times: Open Grounds 15 Mar-31 Oct daily 11-6, Nov-Dec daily 11-4 (Woodlands open all year 11-6). House Apr-Oct, Thu & Sun 3-6 by timed ticket. (Last admission 5.30)

Fee: Grounds: £5. House: £1 extra. Family ticket £12.50.

licensed powered vehicle & wheelchairs available, parking near house toilets for disabled shop (ex in woodland)

HIGH WYCOMBE

Wycombe Local History & Chair Museum

Castle Hill House, Priory Av HP13 6PX

☎ 01494 421895 01494 421897

e-mail: enquiries@wycombemuseum.demon.co.uk

Times: Open all year, Mon-Sat 10-5, Sun (seasonal-please telephone for details). Closed on BHs except special events - ring for details.

toilets for disabled shop (ex guide dogs) *Details not confirmed for 2001*

HUGHENDEN

Hughenden Manor

HP14 4LA (1.5m N of High Wycombe, W of A4128)

☎ 01494 755573 01494 463310

Benjamin Disraeli, later Earl of Beaconsfield and twice Prime Minister, bought the house in 1847 and lived there until his death in 1881. It still has many of his books and other possessions. The gardens are a recreation of the colourful designs of Disraeli's wife, Mary-Anne.

Times: House open 1-30 Mar, Sat & Sun only. Apr-Oct, Wed-Sun & BH Mon 1-5. Last admission 4.30. Gardens same dates as house 12-5. Park open all year. (closed on Good Friday)

Fee: £4.20. Family ticket £10.50. Garden only £1.50 (ch 75p). Park free. licensed (braille leaflet and taped guide) toilets for disabled shop (ex in park & car park only)

LONG CRENDON

COURTHOUSE

HP18 9AN (2m N of Thame, via B4011)

☎ 01494 528051 📠 01494 463310

Probably built as a wool store in the early 1400s, but also used as a manorial courthouse until the late 19th century, this timber-framed building stands out, even in this picturesque village. Although the windows and doors have been altered and the chimney stack is Tudor, the magnificent timber roof is original.

Times: Open, Upper storey Apr-Sep, Wed 2-6, Sat, Sun & BH Mons 11-6. **Fee:** £1 P (street)

MIDDLE CLAYDON

CLAYDON HOUSE

MK18 2EY (off A413, entrance by North drive only).

☎ 01296 730349 📠 01296 738511

e-mail: tcdgen@smtp.ntrust.org.uk

The rather sober exterior of this 18th-century house gives no clue to the extravagances that lie inside, in the form of fantastic rococo carvings. Ceilings, cornices, walls and overmantels are adorned with delicately carved fruits, birds, beasts and flowers by Luke Lightfoot. The Chinese room is particularly splendid.

Times: Open 4 Apr-Oct: Sat-Wed 1-5pm, Closed Good Friday. Last admission 4.30pm. **Fee:** £4.20. Family ticket £10.50.

P ♿ (Braille guide) toilets for disabled (ex park)

QUAINTON

BUCKINGHAMSHIRE RAILWAY CENTRE

Quainton Rd Station HP22 4BY (Off A41 Aylesbury to Bicester Road. 7miles NW of Aylesbury)

☎ 01296 655720 & 655450 (info)

📠 01296 655720

The Centre houses an interesting and varied collection of about 20 locomotives with 40 carriages and wagons from places as far afield as South Africa, Egypt and America. Items date from the 1800s up to the 1960s. Visitors can take a ride on full-size and miniature steam trains and stroll around the 20-acre site to see locomotives and rolling stock. The Centre runs locomotive driving courses for visitors.

Times: Open with engines in steam Apr-Oct, Sun & BH Mon; Jul-Aug, Wed; 10.30-5.30. Dec Sat & Sun Santa's Magical Steamings-advanced booking recommended. Also open for static viewing Sun Jan-Mar 11-4 & Sat Apr-Oct 11-4.

Fee: Steaming Days; £3.50 (ch & pen £2.50). Family ticket £10. BH wknds £5 (ch & pen £4). Family ticket £15. Static viewing; £2 (ch & pen £1). P ♿ toilets for disabled shop

STOWE

STOWE GARDENS

MK18 5EH (3m NW of Buckingham)

☎ 01280 822850 📠 01280 822437

e-mail: tstmca@smtp.ntrust.org.uk

One of the supreme creations of the Georgian era, the first, formal layout was adorned with buildings by Vanbrugh, Kent and Gibbs. In the 1730s Kent designed the Elysian Fields in a more naturalistic style, and it's one of the earliest examples of the reaction against formality, which lead to the evolution of the landscape garden.

Times: Open 29 Mar-2 Jul (closed 27 May) & 10 Sep-29 Oct, Wed-Sun; 4 Jul-10 Sep Tue-Sun; 2-23 Dec Wed-Sun. Open all BH' Mons. Mar-Oct 10-5.30 (last admission 4). Dec 10-4 (last admission 3)

Fee: £4.60 (ch £2.30). Family ticket £11.50

P ✕ licensed ♿ (unsuitable manual wheelchairs,powered batricars available) toilets for disabled shop

STOWE HOUSE

MK18 5EH

☎ 01280 818282 📠 01280 818186

e-mail: sses@stowe.co.uk

Set in the National Trust's landscaped gardens, Stowe is a splendid 18th-century mansion. The leading designers of the day were called in to lay out the gardens, and leading architects - Vanbrugh, Gibbs, Kent and Leoni - commissioned to decorate them with garden temples. The house is now a major public school.

contd.

Times: Open 29 Mar-20 Apr & 3 Jul-10 Sep. Daily 2-5pm, 12-5pm Sun. May occasionally be closed if booked for private functions. Please ring for confirmation. **Fee:** £2 (ch £1). P ♿ shop (ex guide dogs)

WADDESDON

Waddesdon Manor

HP18 OJH (gates off A41, 6m NW of Aylesbury)
☎ 01296 653211 01296 653212
e-mail: twmjhn@smtp.ntrust.org.uk

Designed by the French architect Destaileur in the 1870s for Baron Ferdinand de Rothschild, this Renaissance style château was concieved as a showcase for the Baron's collection of works of art, which includes portraits by Gainsborough and Reynolds and works by Dutch and Flemish masters of the 17th century. The wine cellars, which house more than 15,000 bottles of Rothschild wine, are also open to the public. The garden includes a Rococo-style aviary, shrubberies and woodland.
Times: Open, Grounds & Aviary only, Mar-24 Dec, Wed-Sun & BH Mon 10-5. House 30 Mar-29 Oct, Thu-Sun & BH Mon 11-4, also open Wed in Jul & Aug. Entrance by timed ticket.
Fee: Grounds & Aviary £3 (ch £1.50). Family ticket £7.50. Nov-24 Dec free. House - £7 (ch £6). Tickets bookable in advance at booking charge of £3 per transaction (tel 01296 651226).
P ✕ licensed ♿ (wheelchairs available, braille guide) toilets for disabled shop (ex guide dogs in grounds)

WEST WYCOMBE

West Wycombe Caves

HP14 3AJ (on A40)
☎ 01494 524411 (office) & 533739 (caves)
01494 471617

The entrance to West Wycombe caves is halfway up the hill that dominates the village. On the summit stands the parish church and the mausoleum of the Dashwood family. The caves are not natural but were dug on the orders of Sir Francis Dashwood between 1748 and 1752. Sir Francis, the Chancellor of the Exchequer, was also the founder of the Hell Fire Club, whose members were reputed to have held outrageous and blasphemous parties in the caves, which extend to approximately half a mile underground. The entrance consists of a large forecourt, from which a brick tunnel leads into the caves, where tableaux and curiosities are exhibited.
Times: Open all year, Mar-Oct, daily 11-6; Nov-Feb, Sat & Sun 1-5.
Fee: £3.50 (ch & pen £2, students £2.50). Party 20+.
P ♿ toilets for disabled shop garden centre (ex guide dogs)

West Wycombe Park

HP14 3AJ (S of A40)
☎ 01628 488675

Set in 300 acres of beautiful parkland, the house was rebuilt in the Palladian style, between 1745 and 1771, for Sir Francis Dashwood. Of particular note are the painted ceilings by Borgnis. The park was laid out in the 18th century and given an artificial lake and classical temples.
Times: Open, House & grounds Jun-Aug, Sun-Thu 2-6. Grounds only Apr-end May, Sun & Wed 2-6 & Etr, May Day & Spring BH Sun & Mon 2-6. Last admission 5.15. Entry by timed tickets on wkdays. Parties must book in advance.
Fee: House & grounds £4.60. Grounds only £2.60. Family ticket £11.50. P ♿ (partial access to ground floor & gardens) (ex on lead in car park)

WING

Ascott

LU7 0PS (0.5m E, on S side of A418)
☎ 01296 688242 01296 681904
e-mail: www.nationaltrust.org.uk

This house contains houses a collection of French and Chippendale furniture, pictures by Hogarth, Gainsborough and Rubens, and an outstanding collection of Oriental porcelain. Outside there are 260 acres of grounds, with many unusual trees, thousands of naturalised bulbs, and a formal garden.
Times: Open: Apr, 29 Aug-4 Oct; house & gardens daily except Mon, 2-6; May-28 Aug garden only Wed & last Sun 2-6.
Fee: House & Garden £5.60.
P ♿ (wheelchairs available) toilets for disabled

Cambridgeshire

The City of Cambridge is the place that most visitors will want to visit most, and who can blame them? It's ancient colleges, air of learning and rich history are guaranteed to be of interest to anyone looking for a special taste of England. Yet there is much more to the county.

Much of Cambridgeshire remains unspoilt and is ideal for exploration. Many of the peat-black Fens have been reclaimed over the centuries, and beautiful rivers such as the Ouse and the Nene, as well as miles of canal, are all perfect for visitors looking for a relaxed pace of life. 750 acres of undrained fenland at Wicken Fen have been retained by the National Trust as a nature reserve.

Walkers are well catered for, with over 3,000 miles of public footpaths to explore. Routes include the Fen Rivers Way, the Hereward Way, and the Nene Way.

But Cambridgeshire isn't all peace and quiet. Peterborough has modern arcades as well as lots of old streets that have been pedestrianised. Huntingdon, Ely, Wisbech, St Neots and St Ives have all retained something of the atmosphere of the English market town, complete with family-run shops and busy market days.

The county also has many connections with important historical figures. Katherine of Aragon is buried in Peterborough's Norman cathedral, Wisbech is home to the Octavia Hill Birth Place Museum, commemorating the life and work of one of the founders of the National Trust, and Lord High Protector Oliver Cromwell was born in Huntingdon.

EVENTS & FESTIVALS

January
13 Whittlesey Straw Bear Festival

March
17-18 National Shire Horse Show, Peterborough
31 Mar-1 Apr Daffodil Weekend, Thriplow

May
7 Stilton Cheese Rolling,
tbc Duxford Air Show,
tbc St Neots Folk Festival

June
15-17 East of England Show, Alwalton
26-29 Charles Wells Cambridge Folk Festival
30 Jun-1 Jul Hemingford Abbots Open Gardens & Flower Festival Weekend

July
2 July-end Aug Cambridge Shakespeare Festival
4-8 Wisbech Rose Fair
tbc Ely Folk Week, Cresswells Lane Site, Ely

August
tbc Peterborough Beer Festival

September
tbc Duxford Air Show

October
14 The World Conker Championships, Ashton, Peterborough

Top: Peterborough Cathedral

CAMBRIDGE

Cambridge & County Folk Museum

2/3 Castle St CB3 0AQ

☎ 01223 355159 01223 576301

This timber-framed inn houses items covering the everyday life of the people of Cambridgeshire from the 17th century to the present day. There are also temporary exhibitions. Special exhibitions and children's activity days take place throughout the year.

Times: Open all year, Apr-Sep, Mon-Sat 10.30-5, Sun 2-5. Oct-Mar, Tue-Sat 10.30-5, Sun 2-5. (Last admissions 30 mins before closing) Closed 1 Jan, Good Fri, 24-31 Dec.

Fee: £2 (ch 5-16 50p, concessions £1)

P (300 yds) (pay and display on street parking) ♿ (braille & tape guides) shop (ex guide dogs)

Fitzwilliam Museum

Trumpington St CB2 1RB

☎ 01223 332900 01223 332923

Times: Open all year Tue-Sat 10-5, Sun 2.15-5 plus Etr Mon, Spring & Summer BH. (Closed Good Fri, May Day & 24 Dec-1 Jan).

P (400 yds) (2hr max, metered) ♿ (preferably pre-arranged) toilets for disabled shop *Details not confirmed for 2001*

Scott Polar Research Institute Museum

Lensfield Rd CB2 1ER (1km S of City Centre)

☎ 01223 336540 01223 336549

e-mail: rkh10@cam.ac.uk

An international centre for polar studies, including a museum featuring displays of Arctic and Antarctic expeditions, with special emphasis on those of Captain Scott. Other exhibits include Eskimo work and other arts of the polar regions, as well as displays on current scientific exploration. Public lectures run from October to December and February to April.

Times: Open all year, Mon-Sat 2.30-4. Closed for some public & university hols.

Fee: Free. P (400mtrs) ♿ shop (ex guide dogs)

University Botanic Garden

Cory Lodge, Bateman St CB2 1JF (1.5m S of city centre)

☎ 01223 336265 01223 336278

e-mail: gardens@cam.ac.uk

Founded in 1762, and transferred to its present site in 1846, the Garden covers 40 acres, with collections of trees and shrubs; botanical groups of herbaceous perennials, and a lake. Features include a Scented Garden and collection of native British plants. The Gardens hold nine National Collections.

Times: Open all year daily 10-6 (summer), 10-5 (autumn & spring), (10-4) winter. Glasshouses 10-12.30 & 2-3.45. (Closed 25-26 Dec). Entry by Bateman St and Station Rd gates on weekdays & by Bateman Street gate only at weekends & BH.

Fee: £2 (ch & pen £1.50).

P (0.25m) (on street parking bays-pay & display) ♿ (scented garden for the visually impaired) toilets for disabled shop (Gilmour Building, open Mar-Oct, 11-4) (ex guide dogs)

University Museum of Archaeology & Anthropology

Downing St CB2 3DZ

☎ 01223 337733 01223 333517

Times: Open all year Tues-Sat 2-4.30.(Closed 1 wk Etr, Aug BH & 24 Dec-2 Jan)

P (100yds) (severely limited short-term parking) ♿ (lift available) shop *Details not confirmed for 2001*

DUXFORD

Duxford Airfield

CB2 4QR (off junc 10 of M11 on A505)

☎ 01223 835000 01223 837267

e-mail: aclover@iwm.org.uk

This former Battle of Britain fighter station, with hangars dating from WWI, is home to most of the Imperial War Museum's collection of military aircraft, armoured fighting vehicles, midget submarines and other large exhibits. Also on display is the Duxford Aviation Society's collection of civil aircraft.

Times: Open all year, mid Mar-mid Oct daily 10-6; mid Oct-mid Mar daily 10-4. (Closed 24-26 Dec)

Fee: £7.40 (pen £5.20 & concessions £3.70). Ch under 16yrs free.

P ✕ licensed ♿ (wheelchair available-phone in advance) toilets for disabled shop (ex guide dogs)

ELY

Oliver Cromwell's House

29 St Mary's St CB7 4HF (adjacent to St Mary's church)

☎ 01353 662062 01353 668518

e-mail: elytic@compuserve.com

Cromwell inherited the house and local estates from a maternal uncle and moved here in 1636, along with his mother, sisters, wife and eight children. There are displays and period rooms dealing with Cromwell's life, the Civil War and domestic life in the 17th century, as well as the history of The Fens and the house itself, from its medieval origins to its role as an inn in the 19th century.

Times: Open all year: Apr-Sep, daily 10-5.30; Oct-Mar, Mon-Sat 10-5. Winter, Sun, 11-3 **Fee:** £2.80 (concessions £1.80). Family ticket £7.

P (100yds) ♿ shop (ex guide dogs)

Ely Cathedral

CB7 4DL (A10 or A142, 15m from Cambridge)

☎ 01353 667735 01353 665658

The Octagon Tower of Ely Cathedral can be seen for miles as it rises above the surrounding flat fenland. A monastery was founded on the site by St Etheldreda in 673, but the present cathedral church dates from 1083 and is a magnificent example of Romanesque architecture.

Times: Open daily, Summer 7am-7pm, Winter 7.30-6 (5pm Sun).

Fee: £4 (concessions £3.50). Ch free in family group.

P (walking distance) (no charge) ✕ licensed ♿ (touch tour for blind/partally sighted) toilets for disabled shop (ex guide dogs)

The Stained Glass Museum

The Cathedral CB7 4DN (situated inside Ely Cathedral)

☎ 01353 660347 01223 327367

Times: Open daily, Mon-Fri 10.30-4.30, Sat & BH 10.30-5 & Sun 12-6.

P 400yds shop (ex guide dogs) *Details not confirmed for 2001*

HAMERTON

Hamerton Zoo Park

PE17 5RE (off A14 at junct with B660 signed Old Weston/Kimbolton)

☎ 01832 293362 01832 293677

e-mail: office@hamertonzoopark.com

A wildlife breeding centre, dedicated to the practical conservation of endangered species including gibbons, marmosets, lemurs, wildcats, meerkats, sloths and many more. There is a large bird collection, with several species unique to Hamerton. Other attractions include a children's play area, and new "creature contact" sessions.

Times: Open Summer 10.30-6; winter 10.30-4. (Closed 25 Dec)

Fee: £5.45 (pen £4.95 & ch 3-12 £3.95).

toilets for disabled shop

LINTON

Chilford Hall Vineyard

Chilford Hall, Balsham Rd CB1 6LE (signposted from A1307 and A11)

☎ 01223 892641 01223 894056

e-mail: simonalper@chilfordhall.co.uk

Taste and buy award-winning wines from the largest vineyard in Cambridgeshire. See the grapes growing in the 18-acre vineyard and take a winery tour to learn how English wine is made and appreciate the subtle difference between each of the Chilford quality wines.

Times: Open Apr-24 Dec.

Fee: Guided tours £4.50 (ch free). Party 15+. Includes wine to taste, tour of the vineyards & a souvenir glass to take home.

toilets for disabled shop

Linton Zoological Gardens

Hadstock Rd CB1 6NT (exit M11 at junct 9/10, situated on B1052 off A604/A1307, signposted)

☎ 01223 891308 01223 891308

The perfect place for school or family trips, this breeding centre houses many rare creatures. Wildlife includes zebras, tapir, tigers, monkeys, parrots, snakes, tortoises and insects.

Times: Open daily 10-6 or dusk (ex 25 Dec).

Fee: £5 (ch 2-13 £4, pen £4.75).

toilets for disabled shop

LODE

Anglesey Abbey

CB5 9EJ (6m NE of Cambridge on B1102)

☎ 01223 ~~811200~~ 01223 811200

e-mail: aayus@smtp.ntrust.org.uk

A medieval undercroft has survived from the priory founded here in 1135, but the house dates mainly from

1600. Thomas Hobson of *Hobson's Choice* was one of the owners. A later owner was Lord Fairhaven, who amassed the huge collection of pictures, and laid out the beautiful gardens.

Times: Open House: 25 Mar-22 Oct, Wed-Sun & BH Mon 1-5. Garden: 6 Jan-24 Mar, 26 Oct-23 Dec & 4 Jan-25 Mar Thu-Sun, 10.30-dusk; 25 Mar-2 Jul & 20 Sep-22 Oct, Wed-Sun & BH Mon 10.30-5.30.3 Jul-17 Sep, daily 10.30-5.30. Lode Mill: 9 Jan-19 Mar, wknds 11-4; 25 Mar-22 Oct, Wed-Sun & BH Mons 1-5; 26 Oct-17 Dec wknds 11-4. Last admission to House, Garden & Mill 4.30, during 25 Mar-22 Oct.

Fee: £6.10 (£7.10 Sun & BH Mon). Garden & Mill only £3.75 (£3 in winter). Family & party discounts available.

licensed (electric buggy, braille guide) toilets for disabled shop garden centre (ex guide dogs)

PETERBOROUGH

Longthorpe Tower

PE1 1EP

☎ 01733 268482

The main attractions of this medieval fortified house are the rare wall paintings of religious and educational subjects, which are the finest in Northern Europe.

Times: Open Apr-Sep, daily 10-6 (Oct 10-5). Nov-Mar wknds 10-4. Closed 24-26 Dec & 1 Jan.

Fee: £1.90 (ch 5-15 £1, under 5's free).

Peterborough Cathedral

PE1 1XS (access from A1 juncts with A605 or A47)
01733 343342 01733 52465

Behind the huge Early English arches and Perpendicular porch of the West Front is one of the finest examples of Norman architecture in the country, with superb examples of early rib-vaulting and a Norman apse. The painted wooden ceiling dates from 1220.

Times: Open all year, daily 8.30-5.15 (8pm summer)
Fee: Free - donations towards the cost of upkeep are requested.
P (300yds) (no parking within cathedral precincts) (touch & hearing centre, braille guide, ramps to grnd floor) shop (ex guide dogs or in grounds)

RAMSEY

Abbey Gatehouse

Abbey School PE17 1DH (SE Ramsey, where Gatteris Road leaves B1096)
01263 733471 (East Anglia Regional Office)

The ruins of this 15th-century gatehouse, together with the 13th-century Lady Chapel, are all that remain of the abbey. Half of the gatehouse was taken away after the Dissolution. Built in ornate late-Gothic style, it has panelled buttresses, and friezes around both the doorway and the oriel window above it.

Times: Open Apr-Oct, daily 10-5 (or dusk). **Fee:** Free.

WANSFORD

Nene Valley Railway

Wansford Station, Stibbington PE8 6LR (A1 west of Peterborough)
01780 784444 01780 784440

Seven-and-a-half miles of track through the picturesque Nene Valley, with locomotives and rolling stock from Europe and the UK. There's a museum and engine shed, and facilities for the disabled at Wansford, as well as a specially adapted carriage on each train. Home of 'Thomas' the children's favourite engine.

Times: Open end Feb-Etr, Sun; Apr-June, Sep-end Oct, wknds; May, June & Jul, Wed; Aug, daily ex Mondays, (but inc BH Mondays). Some midweek days at other times.
Fee: £8 (ch £4, other concessions £6). Family ticket £19.50.
(disabled access to trains) toilets for disabled shop 

WIMPOLE

Wimpole Hall

SG8 0BW (M11 junct 12, 8 miles SW of Cambridge off A603)
01223 207257 01223 207838
e-mail: aweusr@smtp.ntrust.org.uk

Wimpole Hall is one of the grandest mansions in East Anglia, and has 360 acres of parkland devised and planted by no less than four celebrated landscape designers, Charles Bridgeman, 'Capability' Brown, Sanderson Miller and Humphrey Repton. The house dates back to 1640, but was altered into a large 18th-century mansion with a Georgian façade. The chapel has a painted trompe l'oeil ceiling, and the garden has two restored parterres.

Times: Open 18 Mar-22 Oct, Tue-Thu, Sat-Sun & Good Fri 1-5, BH Mon 11-5. Open Fri in Aug 1-5. 25 Oct-5 Nov, Wed, Sat & Sun 1-5.
Fee: £5.90 (ch £2.70). Party. Joint ticket with Home Farm £7.50. Garden only £2 (ch free).
licensed (braille guide, battery operated vehicle, stairlift) toilets for disabled shop (ex park only)

Wimpole Home Farm

SG8 0BW (M11 junct 12 8m SW of Cambridge off A603)
01223 208987 01223 207838
e-mail: awensr@smtp.ntrust.org.uk

When built in 1794, the Home Farm was one of the most advanced agricultural enterprises in the country. The Great Barn, now restored, holds a display of farm machinery and implements. On the farm there are rare breeds of domestic animals.

Times: Open 18 Mar-5 Nov, Tue-Thu & Sat-Sun 10.30-5; Jul & Aug Tue-Sun, also open Good Fri & BH Mons; 6 Nov-17 Mar Sat & Sun 11-4 (open Feb half-term week). (Closed Xmas & New Year).
Fee: £4.70 (ch £2.70). licensed (braille guide) toilets for disabled shop (ex guide dogs)

WISBECH

Peckover House & Garden

North Brink PE13 1JR (Leave A47 & take town centre signs, then follow brown signs)
01945 583463 01945 583463
e-mail: aprigx@smtp.ntrust.org.uk

Peckover House is a fine Georgian town house, and is named after a banker who purchased the house in 1777. The interior has Rococo decoration in plaster and wood. The two-acre garden is a colourful example of Victorian planting, and in the kitchen garden there are orange trees still bearing fruit after 250 years.

Times: House, Garden & Tearoom Apr-Oct, wknds, Wed & BH Mon 12.30-5.30pm. Garden open: Apr-Oct, Mon & Tue & Thu 12.30-5.30.
Fee: House & garden £3.80 (ch £1.50). Garden £2.50 on days when only garden is open.
P (400yds) (Batricar & wheelchair available on loan) toilets for disabled

Wisbech & Fenland Museum

Museum Square PE13 1ES (on A47)
01945 583817 01945 589050

Purpose-built in 1847, this museum retains almost all of its original cases and fittings, and contains a fine collection of ceramics and *objets d'art*, as well as local and natural history displays.

Times: Open all year, Tue-Sat 10-5 (4pm Oct-Mar). Closed Xmas.
Fee: Free. (Museum libraries & archives available by appointment only). P (100 yds) shop

Cheshire

Bordered by Wales and the metropoli of Liverpool and Manchester, Cheshire has a rich history that can be seen in its wealth of Roman heritage, black and white buildings, and industrial waterways. The county also boasts some beautiful countryside and a strong tradition of floral excellence.

From the invasion of the Romans who made Chester one of their major garrisons, to skirmishes with Norsemen during the Dark Ages, Cheshire has been the scene of many conflicts. The area was also the base for Hugh the Wolf's violent reign in the 11th century, and the setting for the some of the fiercest battles of the Civil War, including the seige of Chester. Clearly, life is less stressful now, but the history of the county is far from forgotten.

Cheshire's canals, part of which form a ring of around 100 miles (151km) of waterways, are the ideal way to explore by foot or by boat. The county has over 200 miles (302 km) of man-made waterways - more than any other county in England - and is a centre for boating holidays. Ellesmere Port has a Boat Museum which has preserved many of the vessels used for both inland and sea travel, from a small weedcutter to a 300-ton coaster. Cheshire's canals also played in important part in the salt and silk industries which contributed to the county's success. The museums detailing these industries are in Northwich and Macclesfield respectively.

Cheshire is full of gardens. From the acres of orangeries and Japanese gardens surrounding the stately homes, to the town parks of Crewe and Congleton, the county is a feast of flowers, lawns and landscaping. Even many private gardens are showpieces of gardening expertise.

EVENTS & FESTIVALS

May
16-19 Alderley Edge Music Festival
tbc Knutsford Royal May Day

June
19-20 Cheshire County Show, The Showground, Tabley, nr Knutsford
30 World Worm Charming Championship, Willaston Primary School, Willaston (provisional)

July
18-22 Royal Horticultural Society Flower Show, Tatton Park, Knutsford
tbc Macclesfield Carnival

August
25 Poynton Show
tbc Family Fun Day, West Park, Macclesfield

October
Macclesfield Festival for the Performing Arts, Ryles Park High School (Autumn Half Term)
27-28 Chrysanthemum Show, Wilmslow Royal British Legion

Top: Bridestones chambered tomb, Congleton

BEESTON

Beeston Castle

Tarporley CW6 9TX (on minor road off A49 or A41)
☎ 01829 260464

This 13th-century stronghold was built by the Earl Ranuf of Chester on a steep and inaccessible hillside. The remains of the inner and outer wards, can still be seen and there is an exhibition of the castle's history.
Times: Open all year, Apr-Sep, daily 10-6 (Oct 10-5); Nov-Mar daily 10-4/ Closed 24-26 Dec & 1 Jan. **Fee:** £2.80 (ch £1.40, under 5's free).
P shop (in certain areas) #

CAPESTHORNE

Capesthorne Hall

SK11 9JY (On A34 between Congleton and Wilmslow)
☎ 01625 861221 & 861779 📠 01625 861619

Capesthorne has been the home of the Bromley-Davenport family and their ancestors since Domesday times. The present house dates from 1719, altered by Edward Blore in 1837 and after a disastrous fire in 1861 the whole of the centre portion was rebuilt. It now contains a great variety of sculptures, paintings and a collection of American Colonial furnishings.
Times: Open Apr-Oct, Wed-Sun & BH's (Closed Xmas & New Year). Park & Garden 12-5.30, Hall 1.30-3.30.
Fee: Park, Garden & Chapel £3.50 (ch £1.50). Park, Gardens, Chapel & Hall £6 (ch £2.50 & pen £5.50). Family ticket £12. Party 25+
P ✕ licensed ♿ (ramp access to ground floor of hall & gardens) toilets for disabled (ex guide dogs & in gardens)

CHESTER

Cheshire Military Museum

The Castle CH1 2DN (follow signs to Military Museum)
☎ 01244 327617 📠 01244 403933

Exhibits from the history of the Cheshire Regiment, Cheshire Yeomanry, 5th Royal Inniskilling Dragoon Guards, and 3rd Carabiniers. Display of the work of George Jones, Victorian battle artist, and an exhibition of life in barracks in the 1950s. Research available by written appointment and donation.
Times: Open all year, daily 10-5 (last entry 4.30pm). (Closed 22 Dec-2 Jan). **Fee:** £1 (ch & pen 50p). P (within 400yds) ♿ shop

Chester Cathedral

Saint Werburgh St CH1 2HU (opposite the town hall)
☎ 01244 324756 📠 01244 341110
e-mail: office@chestercathedral.org.uk

Founded as a Benedictine monastery in 1092 on the sites of earlier churches, in 1541 it became the cathedral of the newly created Diocese of Chester and is a good example of a medieval monastic complex. Restored in the 19th century, the building contains work by Gilbert Scott, Clayton, Pugin and Kempe. There are daily services and visitors are welcome.
Times: Open daily 7.30-6.30 (subject to alteration).
Fee: Donation of £2 per person requested.
P (multi-storey) ✕ licensed ♿ (induction loop, tactile model) toilets for disabled shop (ex guide dogs)

Chester Visitor Centre

Vicars Ln CH1 1QX (opposite Roman Amphitheatre)
☎ 01244 402111 📠 01244 403188
e-mail: tis@chestercc.gov.uk

Among the attractions at this visitor information centre are guided walks of Chester, brass rubbing, candle-making, World of Names which explores the history of family and first names.
Times: Open May-Oct Mon-Sat 9-5.30, Sun & BHs 10-4; Nov-Apr Mon-Sat 10-5, Sun 10-4. **Fee:** Free.
P (200yds) (short stay visitor parking) ♿ (ramped access from Vicars Lane) toilets for disabled shop

Chester Zoo

Upton-by-Chester CH2 1LH (2m N of city off A41)
☎ 01244 380280 📠 01244 371273
e-mail: marketing@chesterzoo.co.uk

The largest zoological gardens in the UK, with 6000 animals in 525 species. There are large outdoor islands for chimps, orang-utans and monkeys, a children's farm, penguin pool, and birds of prey. The Bat Cave is the largest enclosure in the world for endangered bat species. New features include a Komodo Dragon, an extension to the elephant paddock, and a new 'Noah's Ark' area for children.
Times: Open all year, daily from 10. Last admission varies with season from 5.30pm high summer to 3.30pm winter. (Closed 25 Dec).
Fee: £10 (ch 3-15 £7.50 & pen £8). Family ticket (2 adults & 3 ch) £36.
P ✕ licensed ♿ (electric scooters-prebooked, audio guide for blind) toilets for disabled shop (ex guide & sensory dogs)

Deva Roman Experience

Pierpoint Ln, (off Bridge St) CH1 1NL (city centre)
☎ 01244 343407 📠 01244 347737

Stroll along reconstructed streets experiencing the sights, sounds and smells of Deva (the Roman name for Chester) and then on an extensive archeological 'dig', you can discover the substantial Roman, Saxon and medieval remains beneath modern Chester.
Times: Open daily 9-5. (Closed 25-26 Dec).
Fee: £3.95 (ch £2.25, under 5's free, pen £3.50, student £3.50). Family ticket £11. Party. P (200yds) ♿ shop (ex guide dogs)

"ON THE AIR" THE BROADCASTING MUSEUM
42 Bridge St Row CH1 1NN
☎ 01244 348468 📠 01244 348468
e-mail: steve@ontheair.free-online.co.uk
Times: Open Jan-Etr, Tue-Sat 10-5; Etr-Xmas Mon-Sat 10-5. (Closed Sun ex BH's) P (100yds) ♿ shop 🐕 (ex guide dogs) *Details not confirmed for 2001*

CHOLMONDELEY

CHOLMONDELEY CASTLE GARDENS
SY14 8AH (off A49/A41)
☎ 01829 720383 📠 01829 720383

Dominated by a romantic Gothic Castle the gardens are laid out with fine trees and water gardens, with rhododendrons, azaleas, cornus, and acer. There is also a rose and lavender garden, lakeside and woodland walks, and rare breeds of farm animals.
Times: Open 2 Apr-28 Sep, Wed-Thu, Sun & BH 11.30-5. (Closed Good Fri). **Fee:** £3 (ch £1, pen £2.50).
P ☕ ♿ (disabled car park near tearoom) toilets for disabled shop garden centre

DISLEY

LYME PARK
SK12 2NX (off A6, 6.5m SE of Stockport)
☎ 01663 762023 📠 01663 765035

Home of the Legh family for 600 years and the largest house in Cheshire, Lyme Park featured as Pemberley in the BBC's production of *Pride and Prejudice*. Parts of the original Elizabethan house remain, with 18th and 19th century additions. Set in extensive historic gardens with a lake and also a 1,400 acre park, home to red and fallow deer.
Times: 25 Mar-5 Nov, Wed-Sun (open BH Mon) 11.30-5 or dusk if earlier; mid Nov-mid Dec, Sat & Sun 11.30-4 (access restricted to ground floor, garden, shop and restaurant only)
P ☕ ✕ licensed ♿ (by arrangement) toilets for disabled shop 🐕 (ex park on lead) *Details not confirmed for 2001*

ELLESMERE PORT

BOAT MUSEUM
South Pier Rd CH65 4FW (M53 junct 9)
☎ 0151 355 5017 📠 0151 355 4079

Occupying a historic dock complex at the junction of the Shropshire Union and Manchester Ship Canals, this museum has the world's largest collection of floating craft. Boat trips are also available. There are indoor exhibitions together with period worker's cottages, a blacksmith's forge and working engines.
Times: Open Summer daily 10-5. Winter daily (ex Thu & Fri) 11-4. (Closed 25 & 26 Dec).
Fee: £5.50 (ch £3.70, pen £4.30, student £4.20). Family ticket £16.50.
P ☕ ♿ (resources pack for blind & deaf) toilets for disabled shop

GAWSWORTH

GAWSWORTH HALL
SK11 9RN (2.5m S of Macclesfield on A536)
☎ 01260 223456 📠 01260 223469
e-mail: gawsworth@lineone.net

This fine Tudor black-and-white manor house was the birthplace of Mary Fitton, thought by some to be the 'Dark Lady' of Shakespeare's sonnets. Pictures and armour can be seen in the house, which also has a

contd.

tilting ground - now thought to be a rare example of an Elizabethan pleasure garden.
Times: Open daily, 20 Apr-1 Oct, 2-5pm. Closed Sat – May & Sep (ex BH) **Fee:** £4.20 (ch £2.10). Party 20+.
(disabled parking in front of house) shop (guide dogs in garden only)

JODRELL BANK SCIENCE CENTRE & ARBORETUM

Jodrell Bank Science Centre, Planetarium & Arboretum

SK11 9DL (M6 junct 18, A535 Holmes Chapel to Chelford road)
☎ 01477 571339 🖷 01477 571695
e-mail: visitorcentre@jb.man.ac.uk

The Lovell telescope is one of the largest fully-steerable radio telescopes in the world, and the Science Centre features exhibitions on space, energy, astronomy and space art. Outside, there are 35 acres of tree-lined walkways in the Arboretum.
Times: Open summer 3rd weekend in Mar-last weekend in Oct, 10.30-5.30: winter Nov-mid Mar. Tue-Sun 11-4.30. (closed 18-22, 25, 26 Dec 1, 8-12 Jan)
Fee: £4.60 (ch £2.30, pen £3.30) includes Exhibition, Planetarium, Arboretum & Environmental Discovery Centre. Family ticket £13.50. Children under 5 not admitted to the Planetarium.
(Audio loop, wheelchair loan, audio guide & tactile guide) toilets for disabled shop (ex guide dogs)

KNUTSFORD

Tabley House

WA16 0HB (leave M6 junct19 onto A556 S towards Chester. Entrance for cars off A5033, 2m W of Knutsford)
☎ 01565 750151 🖷 01565 653230

Home of the Leicester family since 1272, the present magnificent 18th-century mansion has the first great collection of English pictures, furniture by Chippendale, Gillow and Bullock, and fascinating family memorabilia. Friendly stewards are available to talk about the Leicester's 700 years at Tabley.
Times: Open daily, inc BH, Apr-Oct, 2-5 (last entry 4.30).
Fee: £4 (ch & students £1.50)
(Phone administrator in advance for help) toilets for disabled shop

Tatton Park

WA16 6QN (5m from M6, junc 19, or M56 junc 7)
☎ 01625 534400 🖷 01625 534403

Tatton is one of England's most complete historic estates, with gardens and a 1000-acre country park. The centrepiece is the Georgian mansion, with gardens laid out by Humphry Repton and Sir Joseph Paxton. More recently, a Japanese garden with a Shinto temple was created.
Times: Open Apr-Sep, daily except Mon; Oct Sat & Sun, opening times vary telephone to check. Gardens all year daily except Mon. Park Apr-Oct daily; Nov-Mar daily except Mon.
(charged) (Old Hall & areas of Farm not accessible) toilets for disabled shop garden centre (ex in Park) *Details not confirmed for 2001*

MACCLESFIELD

Hare Hill

SK10 4QB (4m N off B5087)
☎ 01625 828981

The beautiful parkland at Hare Hill also features a pretty walled garden and pergola. There are woodland paths and ponds, and, in late spring, a brilliant display of rhododendrons and azaleas.
Times: Open Apr-Oct Wed, Thu, Sat, Sun & BH Mons 10-5.30. 10 May-30 May daily 10-5.30; (Closed Nov-Mar).
(charged) (wheelchair available braille guides) (ex guide dogs) *Details not confirmed for 2001*

Macclesfield Silk Museum

Heritage Centre, Roe St SK11 6UT (follow brown signs)
☎ 01625 613210 🖷 01625 617880
e-mail: postmaster@silk-macc.u-net.com

The story of silk in Macclesfield, told through a colourful audio-visual programme, exhibitions, textiles, garments, models and room settings. The Silk Museum is part of the Heritage centre, a restored Georgian Sunday school.
Times: Open all year, Mon-Sat 11-5, Sun & BH Mon 1-5. (Closed Good Fri, 24-26 Dec & 1 Jan)
Fee: £2.80 (concessions £1.95). Family ticket £7.50 Joint ticket with Paradise Mill £4.95 (concessions £2.80). Family ticket £10.80.
(50m) licensed (ramps & chairlift) toilets for disabled shop (ex guide dogs)

Paradise Mill

Park Ln SK11 6TJ (follow brown signs)
☎ 01625 618228

A working silk mill until 1981, with restored jacquard hand looms in their original location. Knowledgeable guides, many of them former silk mill workers, illustrate the silk production process with the help of demonstrations from weavers. Exhibitions and room settings give an impression of working conditions at the mill during the 1930s.

Times: Open all year, BH Mon & Tue-Sun 1-5 (1-4 in winter). (Closed Good Fri, 24 Dec-3 Jan).

Fee: £2.80 (concessions £1.95). Family ticket £7.50. Joint ticket with Macclesfield Silk Museum £4.90 (concessions £2.80). Family ticket £10.80. P (400 yds) (care needed on uneven floors) shop (ex guide dogs)

MOULDSWORTH

Mouldsworth Motor Museum

Smithy Ln CH3 8AR (6m E of Chester, off B5393, close to Delamere Forest & Oulton Park Racing Circuit)

01928 731781

Housed in an amazing 1937 large Art Deco building close to Delamere Forest, this is a superb collection of over 60 motor cars, motorcycles and bicycles. There is also a massive collection of automobilia - old signs, pumps, tools, mascots and badges, Dinky cars and pedal cars all complimented by a motoring art gallery. School parties are encouraged for a guided tour and structured talk.

Times: Open Feb-Nov (Sun only), Etr weekend, early May BH Mon, Spring BH Sun-Mon & Aug BH wknd; Sun, Feb-Nov; also Wed, Jul-Aug, noon-5.

Fee: £2.50 (ch £1, reductions for pensioners Wed only Jul-Aug £2)
(hands on items) shop

NANTWICH

Stapeley Water Gardens

London Rd, Stapeley CW5 7LH (off junc 16 M6, 1m S of Nantwich on A51)

01270 623868 & 628628 01270 624919
e-mail: stapeleywg@btinternet.com

Stapeley Water Gardens consists of three main areas. The Palms Tropical Oasis is a glass pavilion which is home to Koi carp, Giant Amazon water-lilies, sharks, piranhas, parrots and exotic flowers, whilst the two-acre Water Garden Centre houses the National Collection of water-lilies.

Times: Open Summer: Mon-Fri 9-6, Sat & BHs 9-6, Sun 11-5, Wed 10-8; Winter: Mon-Fri 9-5, Sat & BHs 10-5, Sun 11-5, Wed 10-7. The Palms Tropical Oasis open from 10am.

Fee: The Palms Tropical Oasis £3.65 (ch £1.85, pen £2.85).
licensed (free wheelchair loan service) toilets for disabled shop garden centre (ex guide dogs)

NESTON

Liverpool University Botanic Gardens (Ness Gardens)

Ness Gardens L64 4AY (off A540 near Ness-on-Wirral)

0151 353 0123 0151 353 1004
e-mail: ejs@liv.ac.uk

A long association with plant collectors ensures a wide range of plants, providing interest for academics, horticulturists and amateurs alike. There are tree and shrub collections, water and rock gardens, herbaceous borders and glasshouses. A regular programme of lectures, courses and special events take place throughout the year for which tickets must be obtained in advance.

Times: Open all year, Nov-Feb, daily 9.30-4; Mar-Oct, daily 9.30-5. Closed 25 Dec.

Fee: £4.50 (ch free admission when accompanied with an adult, concessions £4)
licensed (wheelchair route, induction loop in lecture theatre) toilets for disabled shop garden centre (ex guide dogs)

NETHER ALDERLEY

Nether Alderley Mill

Congleton Rd SK10 4TW (1.5m S of Alderley Edge on E side of A34)

01625 523012 68045 527139

Built in the 15th century, this water-mill is much larger inside than it looks. Inside there are tandem overshot water-wheels, original Elizabethan timber work, and Victorian machinery which was restored to full working order in the 1960s after being derelict for 30 years. Wheat is ground occasionally for demonstration purposes, water permitting.

Times: Open Apr-May & Oct, Wed, Sun & BH Mon 1-4.30; Jun-Sep, Tue-Sun & BH Mon 1-5. Parties by arrangement.
Details not confirmed for 2001

NORTHWICH

Arley Hall & Gardens

Great Budworth CW9 6NA (5m N of Northwich)
☎ 01565 777353 & 777284 📠 01565 777465
e-mail: enquires@arleyestate.zuunet.co.uk

Owned by the same family since medieval times, the present Arley Hall is a good example of the early Victorian Jacobean style and contains fine furniture, plasterwork, panelling and family portraits. The gardens include a walled garden, unique clipped Ilex avenue, herb garden, scented garden and a woodland garden with rhododendrons, azaleas and exotic trees.

Times: Open Etr-end Sep, Tue-Sun & BH 11-5. Hall open Tue & Sun only.

Fee: Gardens, Grounds & Chapel £4.40 (ch 6-16 £2.20, pen £3.80) Family ticket £11 Hall £2.50 (ch 6-16 £1.60,pen £2). Party 15+.

P ☕ ✕ ♿ (ramps parking by entrance) toilets for disabled shop garden centre 🐕 (ex in gardens on lead)

Salt Museum

162 London Rd CW9 8AB (signposted from A556)
☎ 01606 41331 📠 01606 350420
e-mail: cheshiremuseums@cheshire.gov.uk

Britain's only Salt Museum tells the fascinating story of Cheshire's oldest industry. Models, reconstructions, original artefacts and audio-visual programmes throw new light on something we all take for granted.

Times: Open Tue-Fri 10-5, wknds 2-5. Open BH Mons.

Fee: £2.10 (ch £1.10).

P ☕ ♿ (inductory video with induction loop facilities) toilets for disabled shop 🐕 (ex guide dogs)

RUNCORN

Norton Priory Museum & Gardens

Tudor Rd, Manor Park WA7 1SX (from M56 junct 11 in direction of Warrington, signposted)
☎ 01928 569895

Thirty-eight acres of peaceful woodland gardens are the setting for the medieval priory remains, museum and Walled Garden. Displays tell the story of the transformation of the priory into a Tudor manor house and then into an elegant Georgian mansion.

Times: Open all year, Apr-Oct, Mon-Fri 12-5; Sat, Sun & BHs 12-6; Nov-Mar daily 12-4. (Closed 24-26 Dec & 1 Jan). Walled Garden open Mar-Oct.

P ☕ ♿ (wheelchairs available, Braille guide, audio tapes, parking) toilets for disabled shop garden centre (guide dogs only wall garden)

SCHOLAR GREEN

Little Moreton Hall

Newcastle Rd CW12 4SD (4m SW of Congleton on A34)
☎ 01260 272018

One of the best examples of half-timbered architecture in England, and was used for the recent TV production of *Moll Flanders*. By 1580 the house was much as it is today, and the long gallery, chapel and the great hall are very impressive. The garden has a knot garden, orchard and herbaceous borders.

Times: Open mid Mar-early Nov, Wed-Sun 11.30-5 or dusk if earlier, BH Mon 11.30-5; early Nov-mid Dec, weekends 11.30-4.

P (charged) ✕ licensed ♿ (wheelchair & electric vehicle available, Braille guide) toilets for disabled shop 🐕 *Details not confirmed for 2001*

STYAL

Quarry Bank Mill & Styal Country Park

Quarry Bank Mill SK9 4JQ (M56 junct 5, signposted)
☎ 01625 523012 📠 01625 539267

Quarry Bank Mill is a Georgian cotton mill that is now a museum of the cotton industry and powered by a waterwheel. Galleries illustrate all aspects of the textile process and the role of factory pioneers. Other attractions include the factory 'colony' nearby with its shop, cottages and chapels, and the apprentice house. The garden is laid out in Victorian utilitarian style.

Times: Mill open all year, Apr-Sep daily 11-6 (last admission 4.30); Oct-Mar Tue-Sun 11-5 (last admission 3.30). Apprentice House & Garden, as Mill opening times during school hols, daily 2-4.30; Sun & Aug 11.30-6.(Closed Mon all year ex BH Mon).

P (charged) ☕ ✕ licensed ♿ toilets for disabled shop 🐕 (ex in Park) *Details not confirmed for 2001*

WIDNES

Catalyst: The Museum of the Chemical Industry

Mersey Rd WA8 0DF (signed from jnct 7 of M62 and jnct 12 of M56)
☎ 0151 420 1121 📠 0151 495 2030
e-mail: info@catalyst.org.uk

Times: Open all year, BH Mon, Tue-Fri daily 10-5, wknds 11-5. (Closed Mon ex BH's, 24-26 Dec & 1 Jan).

P ☕ ♿ toilets for disabled shop 🐕 (ex guide dogs) *Details not confirmed for 2001*

Cornwall & Isles of Scilly

Cornwall is one of Britain's most striking and majestic counties, and is also a land of contrasts. While small coastal towns like Mousehole, Mevagissey and Polperro remain largely untouched by time, the resort of Newquay is at the forefront of the European surfing scene.

Unsurprisingly, Cornwall's history is tied to the sea and seafaring, surrounded as it is by the Atlantic on three sides. For a long time the county was a centre for smuggling operations. The seclusion of its many coves and caves were ideal for the shady machinations of customs dodgers right up until the 20th century.

The isolation and ruggedness of the coastal landscape and its inhabitants has offered the perfect challenge for many religious groups and individuals. Some of Britain's earliest Christian churches and communities were started in Cornwall, including St Pirran's Church in Perranporth which was founded in the 6th century by the patron saint of tinners. Like many other missionaries of this time he came from Ireland and local tales claim, was not the most sober of ministers. St Columba was another, perhaps more important influence on Christianity in England

As legend has it, Cornwall was once the site of fabled Camelot. High on the cliffs near Tintagel is the ruined castle most strongly connected to the ancient hero, although its remains post-date Arthurian lore by some seven centuries. Some local legends state that nearby Camelford was once Camelot.

EVENTS & FESTIVALS

March
31 Mar-1 Apr Falmouth Spring Flower Show

May
1 Padstow 'Obby 'Oss
11-20 Daphne du Maurier Festival of Arts & Literature
12-13 Second Jazz 2000, Looe
25 May-2 Jun Calstock Festival

June
7-9 Royal Cornwall Show, Wadebridge
14-24 Golowan Festival, Penzance

July
16 Stithians Show
31 Jul-10 Aug St Endellion Summer Festival, Port Isaac

August
31 Jul-10 Aug St Endellion Summer Festival, Port Isaac
12-18 Falmouth Regatta Week
24-27 Wadebridge Folk Festival
25 Aug-1 Sep Angling Festival, Looe

September
1 Cornish Gorsedd, Perranzabuloe
10-22 St Ives Festival
24-30 Tamarisk Festival, Newquay

October
17-21 Lowender Peran, Perranporth

Top: Polperro

BODMIN

Military Museum

The Keep PL31 1EG (on B3268 beside steam railway)
01208 72810 01208 72810

The history of a famous County Regiment with fascinating displays of uniforms, weapons, medals, badges and much more.
Times: Open all year Mon-Fri, Sun during Jul & Aug 9-5. (Closed Etr & Xmas).
Fee: £2 (ch 50p). Parties 10+.
P shop

Pencarrow

Washaway PL30 3AG (4m NW, signposted off A389 & B3266)
01208 841369 01208 841369
e-mail: pencarrow@aol.com

Still a family home, this Georgian house has a superb collection of pictures, furniture and porcelain. The 50 acres of formal and woodland gardens include a Victorian rockery, a lake, 700 different rhododendrons and an acclaimed conifer collection. There is also a craft centre and a children's play area.
Times: Open 2 Apr-15 Oct, Sun-Thu, 1.30-4.30; BH Mon & Jun-10 Sep 11-4.30. Gardens open daily.
Fee: House & Garden £5 (ch £2.50). Gardens only £2.50 (ch free).
P toilets for disabled shop (ex in gardens)

CALSTOCK

Cotehele

St Dominick PL12 6TA (2m E of St Dominick)
01579 351346 01579 351222
e-mail: cctlce@smtp.ntrust.org.uk

A 15th-century house that contains tapestries, embroideries, furniture and armour; and outside, a beautiful garden on different levels, including a formal Italian style garden, medieval stewpond, dovecote, and an 18th-century tower with lovely views. There is a restored water mill in the valley below, and an outstation of the National Maritime Museum.
Times: Open 27 Apr-Oct, House, daily (ex Fri) 11-5; (11-4.30 Oct). Mill, daily (ex Fri) 1-5.30 (4.30 Oct) - open Fri in Jul & Aug (4.30 Oct). Garden & Shop daily 11-5 (4.30 Oct). Last admission 30 mins before closing. Nov-Mar garden & woodland open daylight hours.
licensed (limited access in garden, braille guide) toilets for disabled shop (ex guide dogs) *Details not confirmed for 2001*

CHYSAUSTER ANCIENT VILLAGE

Chysauster Ancient Village

TR20 8XA (2.5m NW of Gulval, off B3311)
07831 757934

This fascinating ancient Celtic village, 2000 years old, includes 9 drystone houses ranged along the oldest known village street in England.
Times: Open Apr-Oct, daily 10-6 (5pm Oct).
Fee: £1.60 (ch 5-15 80p, under 5's free).
P

DOBWALLS

Dobwalls Family Adventure Park

PL14 6HD (0.5m N of A38)
01579 320325 & 321129
e-mail: dobwallsadpk@aol.com

Plenty to do here, with stretches of miniature American railroads to ride - there are steam and diesel locos, and visitors can take the Rio Grande ride through the forests or the Union Pacific route over the prairies. Adventureland - action-packed areas filled with adventure play equipment - is another attraction.
Times: Open 12 Apr-10 Sep, daily 10.30-5.30 (10am in high season); 11 Sep-29 Sep, Sat-Thu; 1-22 Oct, Sat-Wed; 23-29 Oct, daily.
Fee: £6 (pen & disabled £4.50) Family ticket (2 persons) £11.25, (3 persons) £16.75, (4 persons) £22.
P (motorised & manual wheelchairs available) toilets for disabled shop

FALMOUTH

Pendennis Castle

TR11 4LP (1m SE)
01326 316594

The well preserved granite gun fort and outer ramparts testify to the strength of the coastal fortresses erected in the Tudor period by Henry VIII. It was eventually besieged and captured from the land during the Civil War.
Times: Open all year, Apr-Jun & Sep, daily 10-6 (Oct 10-5); Jul-Aug, daily 9-6; Nov-Mar, daily 10-4. Closed 24-26 Dec & 1 Jan.
Fee: £3.80 (ch 5-15 £1.90, under 5's free).
P shop (in certain areas)

FOWEY

St Catherine's Castle

(three quarters of a mile along footpath off A3082)

The ruined stronghold (restored in 1855) was one of the many castles built by Henry VIII to defend the coast.
Times: Open all year, any reasonable time.
Fee: Free.

GODOLPHIN CROSS

Godolphin House

TR13 9RE (situated off A303 between Townshend and Godolphin)
01736 762409 01736 763194

The former home of the Earls of Godolphin dates from the 15th century, but is most notable for the colonnade added in 1635. Inside is Wootton's painting, Godolphin Arabian, one of the three Arab stallion ancestors of all British bloodstock. The gardens are Tudor, with some areas even earlier. Due to extensive repair works, please telephone for details of areas open to the public.
Times: Open May & Jun, Thu 2-5; Jul-Sep, Tue & Thu 2-5; Aug, Tue & Thur 2-5. Open BH Mons. Parties by arrangement at anytime throughout the year including Sun (refurbishment in progress, contact in advance).

Fee: £3 (ch £1). Party 20+. Garden costs extra. Prices may vary according to repair programme & what is available for viewing.
(telephone prior to visit) toilets for disabled shop (ex guide dogs)

GOONHAVERN

WORLD IN MINIATURE

Bodmin Rd TR4 9QE (on B3285)
01872 572828 01872 572829

There are six major attractions for the price of one at this theme park. Visitors can stroll amongst famous landmarks such as the Taj Mahal and the Statue of Liberty, all in miniature scale, set in spectacular gardens. Then there is Tombstone, a wild-west town complete with saloon, bank, shops, livery stable and jail. The Adventure Dome is the original super cinema 180 direct from the USA which shows two exciting films. The gardens are 12 acres of beautifully landscaped grounds with over 70,000 plants and shrubs. See Jurassic Adventure World, Super X Simulator and childrens fairground rides.

Times: Open 9 Apr-29 Oct, daily 10-4 (5pm Jul-Aug).
Fee: £5 (ch under 3 free, ch 4-13 £3.50, pen £4). Family ticket (2 adults & 2 ch) £15
toilets for disabled shop garden centre 

GWEEK

NATIONAL SEAL SANCTUARY

TR12 6UG (pass RNAS Culdrose & take A3293 & then B3291 to Gweek, the sanctuary is signposted from village)
01326 221361 & 221874 01326 221210

Britain's largest seal rescue facility - offering a unique opportunity to learn more about these beautiful creatures. Every year it rescues, rehabilitates and releases around 30 sick or abandoned seal pups.

Times: Open all year, daily from 9am. (Closed 25 Dec).
Fee: Please call for admission prices.
(wheelchair available) toilets for disabled shop 

HELSTON

FLAMBARDS VILLAGE THEME PARK

Culdrose Manor TR13 0QA (0.5m SE of Helston on A3083)
01326 573404 01326 573344
e-mail: info@flambards.co.uk

Three award-winning, all-weather attractions can be visited on one site here. Flambards Victorian Village is a recreation of streets, shops and houses from the turn of the century, including a chemist's shop. Britain in the Blitz is a life-size wartime street featuring shops, a pub and a living room with Morrison shelter; and Cornwall Aero Park covers the history of aviation. The Exploratorium, is a science playground for the whole family. There are many rides from the gentle to the daring, including the Hornet Rollercoaster, Flambards

Family Log Flume, Balloon Race and play areas for the very young.

Times: Open 15 Apr-Oct 10.30-5. Extended opening 24 Jul-Aug 10-6pm. Closed some Fri/Mon in low season.
Fee: £7.95 (ch 4-11 £6.50; pen £5) Family ticket (4 persons) £27. Over 80's & ch under 4 free.
(free loan of wheelchairs, route guides) toilets for disabled shop garden centre (ex guide dogs)

LANHYDROCK

LANHYDROCK

PL30 5AD (2.5m SE of Bodmin, signposted from A30, A38 & B3268)
01208 73320 01208 74084
e-mail: clhan@smtp.ntrust.org.uk

Part-Tudor, part-Victorian building that gives a vivid picture of life in Victorian times. The `below stairs' sections have a huge kitchen, larders, dairy, bakehouse, cellars, and servants' quarters. The long gallery has a moulded ceiling showing Old Testament scenes, and overlooks the formal gardens with their clipped yews and bronze urns. The higher garden, famed for its magnolias and rhododendrons, climbs the hillside behind the house.

Times: Open Apr-Oct: House daily (ex Mon), but open BH Mon 11-5.30 (11-5 in Oct). Gardens daily from 1st Mar, last admission half hour before closing. Winter Gardens Nov-Feb during daylight hours.
Fee: House & Grounds £6.60 (ch £3.30). Grounds £3.60 (ch £1.80). Family ticket £16.50. Party £5.50.
licensed (house accessible ex 2nd floor, small lift to 1st floor) toilets for disabled shop garden centre (ex on lead in park)

LANREATH

LANREATH FARM & FOLK MUSEUM

Churchtown PL13 2NX (A390 from Liskeard, then B3359 for Looe/Polperro, signposted)
01503 220321

A hands on Countryside Museum reflecting bygone times in Cornwall. Implements and equipment from the farmhouse, dairy and farmyard are displayed, together with mill workings rescued from a derelict mill house. Demonstrations of local crafts are given on weekday

contd.

afternoons from 2-4pm. Play phones, pets, and models to operate make it a fun place as well as educational.
Times: Open Etr-May & Oct, daily 11-5; Jun-Sep, daily 10-6.
Fee: £2.50 (ch £1.25, under 5 free). Party.
P shop

LAUNCESTON

LAUNCESTON CASTLE
01566 772365

Dominating this old market town is the ruin of the 12th-and 13th-century castle. Built in the early years of the Norman Conquest, it soon became a symbol of the authority of the Earls of Cornwall.
Times: Open Apr-Sep, daily 10-6; Oct, daily 10-5; Nov-Mar, Fri-Sun 10-1 & 2-4. (Closed 24-26 Dec & 1 Jan).
Fee: £1.80 (ch 90p, concessions £1.40)
(outer bailey only)

LAUNCESTON STEAM RAILWAY
St Thomas Rd, Newport PL15 8DA (from A30 well signposted)
01566 775665

The Launceston Steam Railway links the historic town of Launceston with the hamlet of New Mills. Tickets are valid for unlimited travel on the day of issue and you can break your journey at various points along the track. Launceston Station houses railway workshops, a transport museum, gift shop and book shop.
Times: Open Good Fri-Etr Mon, then Tue & Sun until 31 Oct. Open daily (ex Sat) spring BH-Sep, 10.30-4.30.
Fee: £5.20 (ch £3.50, pen £4.70). Family ticket £17. Dogs 50p.
P shop

LAWRENCE HOUSE
Castle St PL15 8BA (in centre of town, near Launceston Castle)
01566 773277 & 774518

Housed in a well-preserved red brick Georgian house, Launceston's local history museum was once used as a prison for French officers. The displays and artefacts all relate to the history and social history of Launceston. A programme of exhibitions takes place throughout the year.
Times: Open Apr-early Oct, Mon-Fri 10.30-4.30. Other times by appointment. Closed BH's.
P (50yds) (public parking with small charge) (ex guide dogs)
Details not confirmed for 2001

LOOE

MONKEY SANCTUARY
St Martins PL13 1NZ (4m E off B3253)
01503 262532 01503 262532
e-mail: monkey-sanctuary-uk.@compuserve.com

Visitors can see a colony of Amazonian woolly monkeys in extensive indoor and outdoor territory. There are also conservation gardens, childrens' play area, and activity room. Vegetarian cafe.
Times: Open 16 Apr-Sep, Sun-Thu 11-4.30.
Fee: £4 (ch £1.50 & concession £3).
P (disabled toilets in car park) toilets for disabled shop

MADRON

TRENGWAINTON GARDEN
Penzance TR20 8RZ
01736 363021 01736 368142

Rhododendrons and magnolias grow in profusion at Trengwainton, along with many plants that are difficult to grow in Britain. The mild climate means that seed collected on expeditions to the Far East and southern hemisphere have flourished to produce a magnificent display in this 20th-century garden.
Times: Open 1 Mar-29 Oct, Sun-Thu also Good Fri 10-5.30. (Mar & Oct 11-5). Last admission 30 mins before closing.
P (braille guide) toilets for disabled shop garden centre *Details not confirmed for 2001*

MARAZION

ST MICHAEL'S MOUNT
TR17 0HT (0.5m S of A394)
01736 710507 & 710265 01736 711544

Reached on foot by causeway at low tide, or by ferry at high tide in the summer only, St Michael's Mount rises dramatically from the sea, a medieval castle to which a magnificent east wing was added in the 1870s. It is home to Lord St Leven, whose ancestor St John Aubyn aquired it in the 17th century.
Times: Open Apr-30 Oct, Mon-Fri 10.30-5.30. Last admission 4.45. Mar-May special educational visits by prior arrangement, Tue only. The Castle and grounds are open most weekends during the summer season. These are special charity open days and NT members are also asked to pay.
P (on mainland) licensed shop (Apr-Oct) *Details not confirmed for 2001*

MAWNAN SMITH

GLENDURGAN
TR11 5JZ (4m SW of Falmouth. 0.5m SW of Mawnan Smith on road to Helford Passage)
01812 862090 01872 865808

This delightful garden, set in a valley above the River Helford, was started by Alfred Fox in 1820. The informal landscape contains trees and shrubs from all over the world, including the Japanese loquat and tree ferns from New Zealand. There is a laurel maze, and a Giant's Stride which is popular with children. The house is not open.
Times: Open 22 Feb-28 Oct, Tue-Sat & BH Mon 10.30-5.30 (last admission 4.30). (Closed Good Fri).
Fee: £3.50 (ch £1.75). Family ticket £8.75.
P (braille guide, limited access to gardens/ground floor) toilets for disabled shop garden centre (ex guide dogs)

TREBAH GARDEN
TR11 5JZ (signposted at Trelieve Cross roundabout at junction of A39/A394)
☎ 01326 250448 📠 01326 250781
e-mail: mail@trebah-garden.co.uk

A 25-acre wooded ravine garden, descending 200 feet from the 18th-century house down to a private cove on the Helford River. The cascading Water Garden has pools of giant koi and exotic water plants, winding through two acres of blue and white hydrangeas to the beach. There are glades of sub-tropical tree ferns and palms, as well as rhododendrons and many other trees and shrubs. The beach is open to visitors and there are children's trails and activities all year.
Times: Open daily 10.30-5 (last admission).
Fee: Mar-Oct £3.50 (pen £3.20, ch & disabled £1.75, ch under 5 free); Nov-Feb £1.50 (concessions £1.20). Party 12+.
(2 wheelchair routes) shop garden centre (only on leads)

NEWQUAY

DAIRY LAND FARM WORLD
Summercourt TR8 5AA (Signposted from A30 at exit for Mitchell/Summercourt)
☎ 01872 510246 📠 01872 510349
e-mail: farmworld@yahoo.com

Visitors can watch while the cows are milked to music on a spectacular merry-go-round milking machine. The life of a Victorian farmer and his neighbours is explored in the Heritage Centre, and a Farm Nature Trail features informative displays along pleasant walks. Children will have fun getting to know the farm animals in the Farm Park. They will also enjoy the playground, assault course and indoor play areas.
Times: Open daily, late Mar-Oct 10.30-5. Xmas opening telephone for details.
Fee: £4.95 (ch 3-15 £3.95, pen £4.75). Family £14.95. Party.
(wheelchairs for loan; disabled viewing gallery - milking) toilets for disabled shop

NEWQUAY ZOO
Trenance Gardens TR7 2LZ (off A3075)
☎ 01637 873342 📠 01637 851318
e-mail: info@newquayzoo.co.uk

Education and conservation are the key issues at this exciting Zoological Centre. Apart from attractions such as the Monkey enclosures, penguin pool, tropical house and lion house, the park also boasts a Maze, an Oriental Garden, an activity Play Park, a Tarzan Trail Assault Course, and a tortoise enclosure.
Times: Open Etr-Oct, daily 9.30-6; Nov-Etr 10-4. (Closed 25 Dec)
Fee: £5.50 (ch 5-15 £3.50, ch 2-4 £1.20, pen £4).Family ticket £16.50.
toilets for disabled shop (no exceptions)

PENTEWAN

THE LOST GARDENS OF HELIGAN
PL26 6EN (signposted from A390 & B3273)
☎ 01726 845100 📠 01726 845101
e-mail: info@heligan.com

The largest garden reclamation project in Britain, covering 80 acres. Four walled gardens are being restored to their former glory including the re-planting of Victorian varieties of fruit and vegetables. Various events are held throughout the year including walks, horticultural events, theatre workshops and educational courses.
Times: Open daily 10-6 (last admission 4.30pm): winter 10-dusk. Closed 24-25 Dec.
Fee: £5.50 (ch 5-15 £2.50, pen £5, ch under 5 free). Family £15.
(free loan of wheelchairs) toilets for disabled shop garden centre

POOL

CORNISH MINES & ENGINES
East Pool TR14 7AW (2m W of Redruth on A3047)
☎ 01209 315027 📠 01209 315027

Impressive relics of the tin mining industry, these great beam engines were used for pumping water from 2000ft down and for lifting men and ore from the workings below ground. The mine at East Pool has been converted into the Cornwall Industrial Heritage Centre.
Times: Open Engine Houses, Apr-Oct, daily 11-5. Museum Mon-Fri 9-5. Discovery Centre daily.
shop (ex guide dogs) *Details not confirmed for 2001*

PROBUS

TREWITHEN
Grampound Rd TR2 4DD (on A390 between Truro & St Austell)
☎ 01726 883647 📠 01726 882301
Times: Open Apr-Jul & Aug BH, Mon & Tue 2-4.
toilets for disabled garden centre *Details not confirmed for 2001*

RESTORMEL

Restormel Castle

PL22 OBD (1.5m N of Lostwithiel off A390)
☎ 01208 872687

Perched on a high mound surrounded by a deep moat, the huge circular keep of this splendid Norman castle is remarkably well preserved and commands the Fowey Valley.

Times: Open Apr-Sep, daily 10-6(Oct 10-5).
Fee: £1.60 (ch 5-15 80p, under 5's free).

ST AUSTELL

Charlestown Shipwreck & Heritage Centre

Quay Rd, Charlestown PL25 3NJ (1.25m SE A3061)
☎ 01726 69897 01726 68025

Times: Open Mar-Oct, daily 10-5 (later in high season). Last admission 1 hour before closing.
(charged) licensed (ramps) toilets for disabled shop
Details not confirmed for 2001

Wheal Martyn China Clay Heritage Centre

Carthew PL26 8XG (2m N on B3274)
☎ 01726 850362 01726 850362
e-mail: whmartyn@aol.com

This museum tells the story of Cornwall's most important present-day industry: china clay production. The open-air site includes a complete 19th-century clayworks, with huge granite-walled settling tanks, working water-wheels and a wooden slurry pump. There is a short audio-visual programme, a working pottery, nature trails, and a children's adventure trail.

Times: Open Apr-Oct, 10-6 (last admission 5pm).
Fee: £4.25 (ch £2, pen/student £3.50)
shop

ST IVES

(Park your car at Lelant Station and take advantage of the park and ride service. The fee includes parking and journeys on the train between Lelant and St Ives during the day).

Barbara Hepworth Museum & Sculpture Garden

Barnoon Hill TR26 1AD (M5 to Exeter, A30 onto Penzance & St Ives)
☎ 01736 796226 01736 794480

Dame Barbara Hepworth lived here from 1949 until her death in 1975, and the house is now a museum displaying sculptures and drawings, photographs, documents and other memorablia. Visitors can also visit her workshops, which house a selection of tools and some unfinished carvings.

Times: Open all year, Tue-Sun (Mon Jul/Aug) 10.30-5.30, BHs 10.30-5.30 (Closed 24-26 Dec).
Fee: £3.50. (concessions £1.80)
(880 yds) (accessible with assistance) shop (ex guide dogs)

Tate St Ives

Porthmeor Beach TR26 1TG (M5 to Exeter, then A30 onto Penzance & St Ives)
☎ 01736 796226 01736 794480

Tate Gallery St Ives offers a unique introduction to modern art, where over 200 works can be seen at any one time in the surroundings and atmosphere which inspired them. The gallery presents changing displays from the Tate Gallery's Collections, focusing on the post-war modern movement St Ives is so famous for.

Times: Open all year, Tue-Sun (Mon in Jul-Aug) 10.30-5.30. BHs 10.30-5.30 (Closed 24-25 Dec).
Fee: £3.90 (concessions £2.30)
(800yds) licensed toilets for disabled shop (ex guide dogs)

ST MAWES

St Mawes Castle

TR2 3AA (on A3078)
☎ 01326 270526

Part of the coastal-defence system built in the reign of Henry VIII, the castle guarded the Fal estuary, together with Pendennis Castle (see Falmouth). A fine example of military architecture, it is of particular interest to military historians, and a further attraction are the delightful gardens surrounding it.

Times: Open Apr-Sep, daily 10-6 (Oct 10-5); Nov-Mar, Fri-Tues 10-4 (closed 1-2pm). Closed 24-26 Dec & 1 Jan.
Fee: £2.50 (ch 5-15 £1.30, under 5's free)
shop

SANCREED

Carn Euny Ancient Village

(1.25m SW, off A30)

Four courtyard houses and several round houses dating from the 1st century BC can be seen at this site. There is also an impressive 'fogou', a subterranean passage leading to a circular chamber which may have served as a hiding place.

Times: Open any reasonable time.
Fee: Free.

TINTAGEL

Tintagel Castle

PL34 0HE (on Tintagel Head, half a mile along uneven track from Tintagel, no vehicles)
☎ 01840 770328

These romantic ruins make a dramatic sight on the edge of the towering cliffs. Associated in popular legend with King Arthur and the magician, Merlin, theories as to its origins abound: a Celtic monastery, the stronghold of Cornish Kings of the Dark Ages, the Durocornovium of the Romans? Whatever the true answer, it remains one of the most spectacular sites in Britain.

Times: Open all year, Apr-Sep, daily 10-6 (9 Jul-26 Aug 7pm, Oct 10-5); Nov-Mar, daily 10-4. Closed 24-26 Dec & 1 Jan. (Please note there is a steep climb up steps to reach the castle)

Fee: £2.80 (ch 5-15 £1.40, under 5's free).

P (in village) shop

TORPOINT

ANTONY HOUSE

PL11 2QA (2m NW, off A374 from Trerulfoot rdbt, 2m from Torpoint Ferry)

☎ 01752 812191

A fine, largely unaltered mansion, built in brick and Pentewan stone for Sir William Carew between 1711 and 1721. The stable block and outhouses remain from an earlier 17th-century building. Most of the rooms in the house contain contemporary furniture and family portraits. The grounds include a dovecote and the Bath Pond House.

Times: Open Apr-29 Oct, Tue-Thu & BH Mons (also Sun Jun-Aug), 1.30-5.30. Last admission 4.45.

P (braille guide) toilets for disabled shop *Details not confirmed for 2001*

TREDINNICK

SHIRES FAMILY ADVENTURE PARK

Trelow Farm PL27 7RA (signposted off A39)

☎ 01841 540215

The Dragon Kingdom is large undercover adventure zone, with slides, ball pools, ropes and bridges. Also of interest in the Enchanted Forest, animal electronic shows with talking and singing wildlife. Train rides around the woods and lakes can be taken.

Times: Open Good Fri-Oct daily 10-5.

Fee: £5.95 (ch 2-14 £4.55, pen £5)

P licensed (most areas are ramped) toilets for disabled shop

TRELISSICK GARDEN

TRELISSICK GARDEN

TR3 6QL (Trelissick is located 4m S of Truro on both sides of the B3289, King Harry Ferry Road)

☎ 01872 862090 01872 865808

Set amidst more than 500 acres of park and farmland, with panoramic views down the Carrick Roads to Falmouth and the sea. The garden is well known for its large collection of hydrangeas, camellias, rhododendrons and exotic and tender plants. The Cornish Apple Orchard contains the definitive collection of Cornish apple varieties and is particularly lovely in the spring.

Times: Open 19 Feb-31 Oct, Mon-Sat 10.30-5.30, Sun 12.30-5.30. Park & woodland walks open all year.

Fee: £4.30 (Family ticket £10.75).Party rate 15+ £3.60. Car park charge £1.50 (refundable on admission).

P (charged) licensed braille/audio guide, wheelchairs, batricar, induction loops toilets for disabled shop (open 11-4.30) garden centre (ex in garden)

TRERICE

TRERICE

TR8 4PG (3m SE of Newquay off A3058 at Kestle Mill)

☎ 01637 875404 01637 879300

Built in 1571 for Sir John Arundell, this picturesque Elizabethan house has unusual curved and scrolled gables, which may have been influenced by Sir John's stay in the Netherlands. The hall has an imposing window with 576 panes. Throughout the house are plasterwork ceilings, fine furniture and a large clock collection. Ring for details of special events.

Times: Open daily 2 Apr-Oct 11-5.30 (ex Tue & Sat), Open every day from 24 Jul-9 Sep.

P (braille/large print guides & tape tour) toilets for disabled shop (ex guide dogs) *Details not confirmed for 2001*

TRURO

ROYAL CORNWALL MUSEUM

River St TR1 2SJ (follow A390 towards town centre)

☎ 01872 272205 01872 240514

Interesting displays on the history of the county, a world-famous collection of minerals, and paintings and drawings, including a number of Old Masters. Other galleries house displays of archaeology, Cornish history, and Egyptian artefacts. Recently completed galleries of Cornish wildlife, fashion and textiles.

Times: Open all year, Mon-Sat 10-5. Library closes 1-2. (Closed BHs).

Fee: £3 (unaccompanied ch 50p, pen & students £2)

P (200 yds) licensed (lift, ramps to main entrances) toilets for disabled shop (ex guide dogs)

WENDRON

POLDARK MINE AND HERITAGE COMPLEX

TR13 0ER (on B3297)

☎ 01326 573173 01326 563166

e-mail: info@poldark-mine.co.uk

Times: Open Etr-Oct, daily 10-5.30 (last admission 4pm)

P licensed shop (ex grounds) *Details not confirmed for 2001*

ZENNOR

WAYSIDE FOLK MUSEUM

TR26 3DA (4m W of St Ives, on B3306)

☎ 01736 796945

Founded in 1937, this museum covers every aspect of life in Zennor and District from 3000BC to the 1930s. Over 5000 items are displayed in 14 workshops and rooms covering wheelwrights, blacksmiths, agriculture, fishing, wrecks, mining, domestic and archaeological artefacts. A photographic exhibition entitled People of Past Zennor tells the story of the village.

Times: Open Apr & Oct Sun-Fri 11-5, May-Sep Sun-Fri 10-6, also Sat during school & Bank holidays.

Fee: £2.20 (ch £1.50, over 60's £2). Party rates 10+.

P (50 yds) (not suitable for wheelchair users) shop (ex guide dogs)

Cumbria

EVENTS & FESTIVALS

March
24-31 Mary Wakefield Westmorland Festival, Lambrigg, Kendal

April
tbc Ulverston Walking Festival

May
7 Carlisle & Borders Spring Flower Show
18-20 Jennings Keswick Jazz Festival

June
2-3 La'al Cumbrian Beer Festival, Seascale
tbc Appleby Horse Fair, Appleby-in-Westmorland
tbc Edwardian Festival, Grange-over-Sands

July
21 Cumberland County Show, Carlisle
28-29 Cumbria Steam Gathering, Flookburgh

August
10 Cartmel Show, Cartmel
12 Yorkshire Dales & English Lakes Historic Vehicle Event
tbc Grasmere Lakeland Sports & Show, Stock Lane, Grasmere, Ambleside

September
15 Egremont Crab Fair & Sports (including gurning competition)

Top: Blea tarn

The heart of Cumbria is the massive and majestic Lake District National Park, approximately 1,200 square miles of woodland, hills, lakes, mountains, rivers, and small villages. This means that a visit to Cumbria is basically a visit to some of Britain's finest landscapes.

The highest of the Lake District's peaks is Scafell Pike, which at 3,210ft (978m) is also the highest point in England. Other notable peaks include Scafell itself, Helvellyn towering above Ullswater, Skiddaw looming in the north above Bassenthwaite Lake and the impressive Langdale Pikes towering above the fertile greenery of the Great Langdale valley. In all, there are more than 60 summits above 2,500ft (762m).

At the foot of the mountains are the lakes the district takes its name from. These were scooped out millions of years ago by Ice Age glaciers, and are mostly called 'mere' (Old English) or 'water'. Derwent Water is commonly regarded as the most beautiful of these, and is studded with islands that provide a haven for wildlife. Wast Water is much more sombre, hemmed in by grim mountains and scree slopes, while long and winding Ullswater is perhaps the most spectacular. Windemere is certainly the busiest as well as the biggest at 10.5 miles (17km) long.

It wasn't until the 18th century that the Lake District began to be appreciated, and it wasn't until the 19th century, that people came in large numbers to see it. Now, those wishing to visit may want to come in the spring or autumn, as the area can get very crowded in summer. Fell walking, rock climbing, pony trekking, and fishing are major Lake District activities.

ALSTON

SOUTH TYNEDALE RAILWAY

The Railway Station, Hexham Rd CA9 3JB (0.25m N, on A686)

☎ 01434 381696 & 382828 (timetable)
e-mail: jy40@dial.pipex.com

Running along the beautiful South Tyne valley, this narrow-gauge railway follows the route of the former Alston to Haltwhistle branch. At present the line runs between Alston and Kirkhaugh.

Times: Open Etr-Oct, wknds & BH's; Jul-Aug, daily. Please enquire for times of trains.

Fee: Please enquire for fare details.

(railway carriage for wheelchairs-pre-booking required) toilets for disabled shop

AMBLESIDE

ARMITT MUSEUM

Rydal Rd LA22 9BL (beyond Bridge House opposite main car park)

☎ 015394 31212 015394 31313
e-mail: almc@armitt.com

A chronicle of the Lakes from Roman times to the 20th century. Talk to John Ruskin, watch your own lantern slide show, explore Lakeland scenery with photographer Herbert Bell. Talk to Oscar Gnospelius the early seaplane pioneer and admire the treasury of Beatrix Potter's original natural history watercolours.

Times: Open all year, daily 10-5 (last entrance 4.30pm). Closed 25 Dec.

Fee: £2.50 (ch, students, pen £1.80) Family ticket £5.60.

P 100 yds (chairlift to upstairs library) toilets for disabled shop

APPLEBY-IN-WESTMORLAND

APPLEBY CASTLE

CA16 6XH (on A66, castle is top of the main street)

☎ 017683 51402 017683 51082

The grounds of beautiful Castle provide a natural setting for wildlife. The fine Norman Keep and the Great Hall of the house are open to the public. Clifford family portraits and part of the Nanking Cargo are on display in the Hall. An added attraction is the introduction of a Nursery Garden in the old walled kitchen garden.

Times: Open 4 Apr-Oct, daily 10-5 (last admission); Oct, daily 10-4.

Fee: not confirmed

(assistance available) toilets for disabled shop garden centre (ex on lead, guide dogs)

BARROW-IN-FURNESS

FURNESS ABBEY

LH13 0TJ (1.5m NE on unclass road)

☎ 01229 823420

Founded by the wealthy Cistercian Order in the 12th century, the red sandstone abbey is an impressive ruin. Its setting is the beautiful 'Glen of Deadly Nightshade' near Barrow. Fine stone carving is displayed in the site museum.

Times: Open all year, Apr-Sep, daily 10-6 (Oct 10-5); Nov-Mar, Wed-Sun 10-4 (closed 1-2). Closed 24-26 Dec & 1 Jan.

Fee: £3 (ch 5-15 £1.50, under 5's free). Personal stereo tour included in admission.

(in certain areas)

BIRDOSWALD

BIRDOSWALD ROMAN FORT

CA8 7DD (signposted off A69 between Brampton & Hexham)

☎ 016977 47602 016977 47605
e-mail: birdoswald@dial.pipex.com

This unique section of Hadrian's Wall overlooks the Irthing Gorge, and is the only point along the Wall where all the components of the Roman frontier system can be found together. Birdoswald isn't just about the Romans, though, it's also about border raids in the Middle Ages, and recent archaeological discoveries.

Times: Open Mar-Nov 10-5.30. Reduced hours in winter.

Fee: £2.50 (ch £1.50, pen & students £2). Family ticket £6.50

(ramp outside, disabled parking) toilets for disabled shop (not in tea room)

BRAMPTON

LANERCOST PRIORY

CA8 2HQ (2.5m NE)

☎ 016977 3030

The Augustinian priory was founded around 1166. The nave of the church has survived and is now used as the local parish church, providing a striking contrast with the ruined chancel, transepts and priory buildings.

Times: Open Apr-Sep, daily 10-6 (Oct 10-5).

Fee: £2 (ch 5-15 £1, under 5's free).

BROUGH

BROUGH CASTLE

(S of A66)

☎ 0191 261 1585

Standing on the site of the Roman Verterae, the castle, of which the keep and curtain wall remain, was built in the 12th and 13th centuries to replace an earlier stronghold. The later castle also fell into ruin, but was restored in the 17th century.

Times: Open any reasonable time.

Fee: Free.

BROUGHAM

BROUGHAM CASTLE

CA10 2AA (1.5m SE of Penrith on minor road off A66)

☎ 01768 62488

On the banks of the River Eamont lie the ruins of one of the strongest castles in the region, founded in the 13th century and restored in the 17th by the strong-minded Lady Anne Clifford.

Times: Open Apr-Sep, daily 10-6 (Oct 10-5).

Fee: £2 (ch 5-15 £1, under 5's free)

(ex keep)

CARLISLE

Carlisle Castle & Border Regiments Museum

CA3 8UR (north side of Carlisle city centre, close to station)

☎ 01228 591992

This medieval castle has a long history of warfare. An exhibition marks the Jacobite Rising of 1745, when Bonnie Prince Charlie took the castle. It is also the home of the Museum of the King's Own Border Regiment.

Times: Open all year, daily Apr-Sep 10-6; (Oct 10-5); Nov-Mar 10-1 & 2-4. Closed 24-26 Dec & 1 Jan.

Fee: £3 (ch 5-15 £1.50, under 5's free).

P (400 yds) ♿ (parking for disabled at Castle) shop

Carlisle Cathedral

Castle St CA3 8TZ (M6 Junct 42,43 or 44)

☎ 01228 535169 & 548151 01228 547049

e-mail: office@carlislecathedral.org.uk

Founded in 1122 as a Norman Priory for Augustinian canons. The chancel roof is magnificently decorated and the cathedral features an exquisite east window. Special event for 2001 : (13-14 October) Border Cathedrals Festival, a musical festival featuring the choirs of Carlisle, Edinburgh and Newcastle cathedrals.

Times: Open daily throughout the year, Mon-Sat 7.30-6.15, Sun 7.30-5, summer BHs 9.45-6.15, winter BHs, Xmas & New Year 9.45-4.

Fee: Suggested donation of £2 per adult.

P (5 mins walk) (2xdisabled only at establishment) licensed ♿ (disabled parking, ramped entrance, loop system) toilets for disabled shop (ex guide dogs)

Guildhall Museum

Green Market CA3 8JE (near Town Centre, opposite The Crown & Mitre Hotel)

☎ 01228 534781 01228 810249

e-mail: barbaral@carlisle-city.gov.uk

The Guildhall was once the meeting place of Carlisle's eight trade guilds, and it still has an atmosphere of medieval times. It is an early 15th-century building with exposed timber work and wattle and daub walls. The displays include items relating to the guilds, and other reminders of life in medieval Carlisle.

Times: Open Good Fri-Sep, Tue-Sun 1-4. Winter by arrangment.

Fee: Free.

P (500yds) (disc parking on street, 1 hr limit) shop (ex guide dogs)

Tullie House Museum & Art Gallery

Castle St CA3 8TP (M6, Junct 42, 43 or 44 follow signs to City Centre. Car park located in Devonshire Walk)

☎ 01228 534781 01228 810249

e-mail: barbaral@carlisle-city.gov.uk

Travel back into the mists of time and explore Luguvalium (Roman Carlisle), climb part of Hadrian's turf Wall and experience a land inhabited by eagles and peregrines. Peep into Isaac Tullie's study as it might have been when he sat down to record in his diary how the Roundheads laid siege to his Royalist city in 1644, or sit in the 1st-class compartment of a railway carriage and recall the days of steam locomotion.

Times: Open all year, Mon-Sat 10-5, Sun 12-5. (Closed 25-26 Dec & 1 Jan).

Fee: Ground floor (including Art Gallery & Old Tullie House) - Free. Upper floors - £3.75 (concessions £2.75/£2.25) Family ticket (2 adults 3 ch) £12.

P (5mins walk) (disabled parking on site by request) licensed ♿ (chair lift) toilets for disabled shop (ex guide dogs)

COCKERMOUTH

Jennings Brewery Tour

The Castle Brewery CA13 9NE

☎ 01900 821011 01900 827462

e-mail: brewery@globalnet.co.uk

Jennings Brothers have been brewing traditional beers for 160 years and still use today the methods used by the founder in 1828. Situated in the shadow of Cockermouth Castle, the water for the brewing process is still drawn from the well which supplied the Castle with pure water.

Times: Tours: 16-20 Feb & 23 Mar-30 Oct, Mon-Fri 11 & 2; 13 Jul-28 Aug, extra tour at 12.30; 4 Apr-19 Sep, Sats at 11; BHs 11 & 2. (Closed Sun).

Fee: £3 (ch 12-18 £1.50).

P shop

Lakeland Sheep & Wool Centre

Egremont Rd CA13 0QX (M6 junct 40, W on A66 to rdbt at Cockermouth on A66/A586 junction)

☎ 01900 822673 01900 822673

Come face to face with 19 different breeds of live sheep. Stage show with *'One Man and his Dog'* demonstration and sheep-shearing. Shows four times daily, mid Feb-mid Nov. All indoors.

Times: Open all year, daily 9-6 (Closed 4-14 Jan 2001).

Fee: £3 (ch £2).

P licensed ♿ (hearing loop system) toilets for disabled shop (ex guide/hearing dogs)

Wordsworth House

Main St CA13 9RX (W end of Main Street)

☎ 01900 824805 01900 824805

William Wordsworth was born here on 7th April 1770, and happy memories of the house had a great effect on his work. The inside staircase, panelling and other features are original. Portraits and other items connected with the poet are displayed. Please ring for details of concerts and other events during the season.

Times: Open 27 Mar-27 Oct, Mon-Fri 10.30-4.30. Also Sats in Jun, Jul & Aug.

Fee: £3 (ch £1.50). Family ticket £7.50. Party. Ask for details of discount with Dove Cottage,the Wordsworth Museum and Rydal Mount.

P shop

CONISTON

Brantwood

LA21 8AD (2.5m SE off B5285, unclass road. Regular ferry services from Coniston Pier)

☎ 015394 41396 📠 015394 41263

e-mail: josie@brantwood.org.uk

Brantwood, home of John Ruskin, is a beautifully situated house with fine views across Coniston Water. Inside, there is a large collection of Ruskin paintings and memorabilia, and visitors can enjoy delightful nature walks through the Brantwood Estate.

Times: Open mid Mar-mid Nov, daily 11-5.30. Winter, Wed-Sun 11-4.30. (Closed 25-26 Dec).

Fee: House & Estate £4 (ch £1, student £2.80). Family ticket £9.50. Estate only £2.

P licensed toilets for disabled shop (ex guide dogs & on grounds)

Ruskin Museum

The Institute, Newdale Rd LA21 8DU (In centre of Coniston)

☎ 015394 41164 📠 01539 441132

e-mail: museum@coniston.org.uk

John Ruskin (1819-1900) was one of Britain's most versatile and important political thinkers and artists. The museum contains many of his watercolours, drawings, letters, sketchbooks and other relics. The geology, mines and quarries of the area, Arthur Ransome's *Swallows and Amazons* country, and Donald Campbell's *Bluebird* are also explored in the Museum.

Times: Open Apr/Etr (whichever earlier)-mid Nov, daily 10-5.30. Phone for details of winter opening.

Fee: £3 (ch £1.75). Family ticket £8.50: Joint ticket to include museum, Brantwood and lake cruise on S.Y. Gondola £9.50 (ch £5). Family ticket £28.

P (audio guide) toilets for disabled shop (ex guide dogs)

Steam Yacht Gondola

Pier Cottage LA21 8AJ

☎ 015394 36003

Launched in 1859, the graceful Gondola worked on Coniston Water until 1936. She came back into service in 1980, and visitors can once again enjoy her silent progress and old-fashioned comfort.

Times: Open Apr-Oct to scheduled daily timetable. Trips commence 11 at Coniston Pier; 12 on Sat. Piers at Coniston, Park-a-Moor at SE end of lake & Brantwood. (Not NT).

Fee: Ticket prices on application.

P shop (ex guide dogs)

DALEMAIN

Dalemain

CA11 0HB (between Penrith & Ullswater on A592)

☎ 017684 86450 📠 017684 86223

e-mail: admin@dalemain.com

Originally a medieval pele tower, Dalemain was added to in Tudor times, and the imposing Georgian façade was completed in 1745. It has oak panelling, Chinese wallpaper, Tudor plasterwork and fine period furniture. The tower contains the Westmorland and Cumberland Yeomanry Museum, and there is a countryside collection in the Great Barn. The gardens include a collection of old fashioned roses and in early summer a magnificent display of blue Himalayan poppies.

Times: Open 2 Apr-8 Oct, Sun-Thu. 10.30-5, Gardens, Medieval Hall and agricultural & countryside collections. House 11-4.

Fee: House £5 (ch £3) Family ticket £13. Gardens £3. (ch free when accompanied). Party.

P licensed (ramp access at entrance, setting down & collection point) toilets for disabled shop garden centre (ex guide dogs)

DALTON-IN-FURNESS

South Lakes Wild Animal Park

Crossgates LA15 8JR (M6 junct 36, A590 to Dalton-in-Furness, signed)

☎ 01229 466086 📠 01229 466086

e-mail: office@wildanimalpark.co.uk

This zoo park is a unique safari on foot, with many animals wandering free in natural surroundings. Animals include tigers, rhino, giraffes, apes and monkeys, kangaroo and many other species.

Times: Open all year, daily 10-6, during Winter 10-dusk. (Closed 25 Dec).

Fee: £6.50 (ch/pen £3.20). Family ticket £17.

P (Sound system, wheelchair users may need help) toilets for disabled shop

GRASMERE

Dove Cottage & The Wordsworth Museum

LA22 9SH (S, off A591, immediately before Grasmere village)

☎ 015394 35544 & 35547 015394 35748

e-mail: enquires@wordsworth.org.uk

Dove Cottage was the inspirational home of William Wordsworth for over eight years, and it was here that he wrote some of his best-known poetry. The cottage has been open to the public since 1891, and is kept in its original condition. The museum displays manuscripts, works of art and items that belonged to the poet.

Times: Open daily 9.30-5.30, last admission 5pm. (Closed 8 Jan-4 Feb & 24-26 Dec).

Fee: £4.70-£5 (ch £2.35-£2.50). Reciprocal discount offer with Rydal Mount, Ambleside & Wordsworth House, Cockermouth.

licensed (ramps) toilets for disabled shop (ex guide dogs)

HARDKNOTT CASTLE ROMAN FORT

Hardknott Castle Roman Fort

(at W end of Hardknott Pass)

Hair-raising hairpin bends on a steep hill are a feature for which Hardknott Pass is famous, and this astonishing Roman fort commands its western end, looking down over Eskdale.

Times: Open any reasonable time. Access may be hazardous in winter.

Fee: Free.

HAWKSHEAD

Beatrix Potter Gallery

Main St LA22 0NS

☎ 015394 36355 015394 36118

An annually changing exhibition of Beatrix Potter's original illustrations from her children's storybooks, housed in the former office of her husband, solicitor William Heelis.

Times: Open 2 Apr-29 Oct & Good Friday Sun-Thu 10.30-4.30 (last admission 4). Admission is by timed ticket including NT members.

Fee: £3 (ch £1.50) Family ticket £7.50

(300metres) (braille guide) shop

HOLKER

Holker Hall & Gardens

Cark in Cartmel, Grange over Sands LA11 7PL (from M6 junct 36, on A590, signposted)

☎ 015395 58328 015395 58776

Dating from the 16th century, the new wing of the Hall was rebuilt in 1871 after a fire. It has notable woodcarving and many fine pieces of furniture which mix happily with family photographs from the present day. There are magnificent gardens, both formal and woodland, and the Lakeland Motor Museum, exhibitions, deer park and adventure playground are further attractions.

Times: Open 2 Apr-30 Oct Sun-Fri 10-6. Last entry to grounds, hall & motor museum 4.30pm.

Fee: £3.50 (ch over 6 £2, ch under 6 free). Family ticket £10.35.

(ramps, handrails) toilets for disabled shop (ex guide dogs & in grounds)

KENDAL

Abbot Hall Art Gallery

LA9 5AL (M6 junct 36, follow signs to Kendal)

☎ 01539 722464 01539 722494

e-mail: info@abbothall.org.uk

The ground floor rooms of this splendid house have been restored to their former glory, with original carvings and fine panelling. The walls are hung with paintings by Romney, Gardner, Turner and Ruskin. The gallery has a fine collection of 18th-and 19th-century watercolours of the Lake District, and 20th-century British art, including works by Hepworth, Frink, Nicholson, and Sutherland.

Times: Open mid Feb-22 Dec, Mon-Sun 10.30-5 (reduced hours in Feb, Mar, Nov & Dec) please telephone for details.

Fee: £3 (ch & students £1.50, pen £2.80). Family ticket £7.50.

(chair lifts in split level galleries, large print lables) toilets for disabled shop (ex guide dogs)

Kendal Museum

Station Rd LA9 6BT (opposite railway station)

☎ 01539 721374 01539 737976

e-mail: enquires@kendalmuseum.org.uk

The archaeology and natural history of the Lakes is explored in this popular museum which also features a world wildlife exhibition and a gallery devoted to author Alfred Wainwright, who was honorary clerk to the museum.

Times: Open Feb-Dec, Mon-Sat 10.30-5. Reduced hours Feb, Mar. Nov & Dec, 10.30-4. Closed Sun.

Fee: £3 (ch, students £1.50, pen £2.80). Family tickets £7.50. Groups 10+. Seasonal tickets available. Ticket provides reduced entry to Abbot Hall Art Gallery & Museum of Lakeland life & Industry.

(chair lift) toilets for disabled shop (ex guide dogs)

Museum of Lakeland Life & Industry

LA9 5AL (M6 junct 36, follow signs to Kendal)

☎ 01539 722464 01539 722494

e-mail: info@lakelandmuseum.org.uk

The life and history of the Lake District is captured by the displays in this museum, housed in Abbot Hall's stable block. The working and social life of the area are well illustrated by a variety of exhibits including period rooms, a Victorian Cumbrian street scene and a farming display. One of the rooms is devoted to the memory of Arthur Ransome, another to John Cunliffe's *Postman Pat*.

Times: Open mid Feb-22 Dec, daily 10.30-5. Reduced hours Feb, Mar, Nov & Dec, please telephone for details.

Fee: £3 (ch & students £1.50 pen £2.80). Family ticket £7.50.

(listening posts, large print lables) shop (ex guide dogs)

KESWICK

Keswick Museum & Gallery

Fitz Park, Station Rd CA12 4NF (M6 junct 40, follow tourist signs for Museum & Art Gallery when in Keswick)

☎ 017687 73263 📠 017687 80390
e-mail: hazeldavison@allerdale.gov.uk

Keswick's surprising past, from industrial mining centre to peaceful tourist town, is revealed in this fine example of a late Victorian museum. Set in the beautiful Fitz Park, the collections cover local and natural history, famous inhabitants and visitors, including the Lake Poets, and houses the work of many artists who have been captivated by the local landscape and history.

Times: Open Good Fri-Oct, daily 10-4.
Fee: £1 (ch, pen, students, UB40's & disabled 50p). Party 10+.
P (on road outside) (2 hour limit) ♿ (ramp at front entrance, with handrails) shop (ex guide & hearing dogs)

Mirehouse

CA12 4QE (3m N of Keswick on A591)

☎ 017687 72287 📠 017687 72287
e-mail: info@mireho.freeserve.co.uk

Visitors return to Mirehouse for many reasons: the spectacular setting of mountain and lake, the varied gardens, changing displays on the Poetry Walk, free childrens nature notes, four woodland playgrounds, connections with many writers and artists, live classical piano music in the house, generous Cumbrian cooking in the tearoom, and a relaxed, friendly welcome.

Times: Open Apr-Oct. House: Wed, Sun, (also Fri in Aug) 2-last entry 4.30. Grounds: daily 10.30-5.30. Parties by arrangement Mar-Nov.
Fee: House & grounds £4 (ch £2). Grounds only £1.70 (ch £1). Family ticket £11.50 (2 adults & up to 4 children)
P ♿ (notes available listing facilities) toilets for disabled (ex in grounds on lead)

LAKESIDE

Aquarium of the Lakes

LA12 8AS (M6 junct 36, take A590 to Newby Bridge. Turn rignt over bridge, follow Hawkshead Road to Lakeside)

☎ 015395 30153 📠 01539 530152

Discover the magic of the lakes at Britain's award winning freshwater aquarium. Over 30 displays, featuring the UK's largest collection of freshwater fish as well as mischievous otters and diving ducks. Walk on Windemere's re-created lakebed in the Lake Districts only underwater tunnel, and come face to face with sharks and rays from around our coast in the fascinating Morecambe Bay displays.

Times: Open all year, daily from 9am. Closed 25 Dec.
Fee: £5.25 (ch £3.95). Family ticket (2 adults & 3 ch) £16.95.
P (charged) ♿ (lift to first floor) toilets for disabled shop (ex guide dogs)

LEVENS

Levens Hall

LA8 0PD (M6 junct 36. 5m S of Kendal, on A6)

☎ 015395 60321 📠 015395 60669
e-mail: levens.hall@farmline.com

An Elizabethan mansion, built onto a 13th-century pele tower, with fine plasterwork and panelling. The topiary garden, laid out in 1694, has been little changed. There is also a steam engine collection.

Times: Open: House & gardens 2 Apr-12 Oct, Sun-Thur. Gardens 10-5. House 12-5. Last admission 4.30. Steam collection 2-5.
Fee: House & garden £5.50 (ch £2.80), garden only £4 (ch £2.10).
P ♿ (ramps within garden) toilets for disabled shop (ex guide dogs)

MUNCASTER

Muncaster Castle, Gardens & Owl Centre

CA18 1RQ (on the W coast of Cumbria, 1m S of Ravenglass on A595)

☎ 01229 717614 & 717393 (owl centre)
📠 01229 717010
e-mail: information@muncastercastle.co.uk

Muncaster Castle has been home to the Pennington family for 800 years. Treasures include a Gainsborough painted for a bet, John of Bologna's Alabaster Lady, and Henry VI's drinking bowl. The Castle stands in 77 acres of woodland and gardens, which also houses 50 species of owl in the World Owl Trust.

Times: Open Castle; 19 Mar-5 Nov, Sun-Fri 12-5. Garden & Owl Centre, all year, daily 11-6. Parties by arrangement.
Fee: Castle, Gardens & Owl Centre £6 (ch £4) Family £17. Season & party tickets available.
P licensed ♿ (wheelchair loan, induction loop, tape for partially sighted) toilets for disabled shop garden centre (ex on a lead)

NEAR SAWREY

Hill Top

LA22 0LF (2m S of Hawkshead in Near Sawrey, behind The Tower Bank Arms)

☎ 015394 36269 📠 015394 36118

Beatrix Potter wrote many Peter Rabbit books in this little 17th-century house, which contains her furniture and china.

Times: Open 7 Mar-31 Oct, Sat-Wed & Good Friday 11-5. Last admission 4.30pm.
Fee: £4 (ch £2) Family ticket £7.50.
P (200 metres) (no parking for coaches) (braille guide, handling items, accessibility by arrangment) shop

PENRITH
See Dalemain

Wetheriggs Country Pottery
Clifton Dykes CA10 2DH (approx 2 miles off A6 S from Penrith, signposted)
☎ 01768 892733 📠 01768 892722
e-mail: info@wetheriggs-pottery.co.uk

Wetheriggs is the UK's only remaining steam-powered pottery. The Pots of Fun Studio is an interactive craft experience where you can throw a pot, paint a figurine, make candles or work with mosaics. Also of interest are rare breeds, newt pond and nature area.
Times: Contact establishment for details of opening times.
Fee: Free.
P ☕ ♿ toilets for disabled shop (ex guide dogs & dogs on lead)

RAVENGLASS

Ravenglass & Eskdale Railway
CA18 1SW (close to A595)
☎ 01229 717171 📠 01229 717011
e-mail: rer@netcomuk.co.uk

A narrow gauge steam railway, laid in the 19th century to carry iron ore from the mines at Boot. It began to carry passengers and then other freight once the mines were closed, and is now a passenger line. The railway runs through beautiful countryside for the seven mile journey from Ravenglass, on the coast, up to Dalegarth.
Times: Open: trains operate all year. Apr-Oct & between Xmas & New Year, daily; some winter weekends, please enquire . Limited service Jan & Feb except school hols.
Fee: Return fare £6.80 (ch 5-15 £3.40). Family ticket £16.
P (charged) ☕ ✕ licensed ♿ (special coaches - prior notice advisable) toilets for disabled shop

RYDAL

Rydal Mount
LA22 9LU (1.5m, from Ambleside on A591 to Grasmere)
☎ 015394 33002 📠 015394 31738
e-mail: rydalmount@aol.com

The family home of William Wordsworth from 1813 until his death in 1850. The house contains important family portraits, furniture, and many of the poet's personal possessions, together with first editions of his work. In a lovely setting overlooking Windermere and Rydal Water, the gardens were designed by Wordsworth himself. Evening visits for groups can be organised.
Times: Open Mar-Oct daily 9.30-5; Nov-Feb daily (ex Tue) 10-4 (Closed 8 Jan-1 Feb).
Fee: £3.75 (ch £1.25, pen £3.25 & student £3). Garden only £1.75. Party 10+ (pre booked groups £3.25). Reciprocal discount ticket with Dove Cottage and Wordsworth House.
P ♿ shop (ex guide dogs & garden)

SEDBERGH

National Park Centre
72 Main St LA10 5AS
☎ 015396 20125 📠 015396 21732

At the north-western corner of the Yorkshire Dales National Park, Sedbergh is set below the hills of the Howgill Fells. The rich natural history of the area and the beautiful scenery created a need for this Visitor Centre; maps, walks, guides, local information and interpretative displays can be found here, and there is a full tourist information service.
Times: Open Apr-Oct, daily 10-5. Nov-Mar open 2 days a week.
Fee: Free.
P (charged) ♿ (accessible with help Radar key scheme) toilets for disabled shop

SELLAFIELD

The Sellafield Visitors Centre
CA20 1PG (off A595, signposted)
☎ 019467 27027 📠 019467 27021

Enter the Sellafield Visitors Centre, and computerised technology takes you into the 21st century. Designed to inform and entertain the whole family, it features 'hands-on' interactive scientific experiments, intriguing shows and fascinating displays of technology.
Times: Open all year, Apr-Oct, 10-5; Nov-Mar daily 10-4. (Closed 25 Dec).
Fee: Free.
P ☕ ♿ (induction loop) toilets for disabled shop (ex guide dogs)

SHAP

Shap Abbey
(1.5m W on bank of River Lowther)

Dedicated to St Mary Magdalene, the abbey was founded by the Premonstratensian order in 1199, but most of the ruins are of 13th-century date. The most impressive feature is the 16th-century west tower of the church.
Times: Open any reasonable time.
Fee: Free.
P ♿ #

SIZERGH

Sizergh Castle
LA8 8AE (3.5m S of Kendal)
☎ 015395 60070 📠 015395 61621

The castle has a 60-foot high pele tower, built in the 14th century, but most of the castle dates from the 15th to the 18th centuries. There are panelled rooms with fine carved overmantles and adze-hewn floors, and the gardens, laid out in the 18th century, contain the National Trust's largest limestone rock garden.
Times: Open 28 May-Oct, Sun-Thu 1.30-5.30; Garden open 23 Apr-31 Oct, 12.30. Last admission 5pm.
Fee: £4.60 (ch £2.30). Family ticket £11.50, Garden £2.30, Party 15+.
P ☕ ♿ (wheelchair and powered buggy for use, braille guide etc) toilets for disabled shop

SKELTON

Hutton-in-the-Forest

CA11 9TH (6m NW of Penrith on B5305 to Wigton, 2.5m from M6 junct 41)

☎ 017684 84449 📠 017684 84571

e-mail: hutton-in-the-forest@talk21.com

A beautiful house, set in woods which were once part of the medieval forest of Inglewood. The house consists of a 14th-century pele tower with later additions, and contains a fine collection of furniture, portraits, tapestries and china, a 17th-century gallery and cupid staircase. The walled garden has a large collection of herbaceous plants, and there are 19th-century topiary terraces, a 17th-century dovecote and a woodland walk with impressive specimen trees.

Times: Open, House; 12.30-4 20 Apr-1 Oct, Thu, Fri, Sun,& BH Mons. Grounds daily (ex Sat) 11-5. Groups any day booked in advance from Apr-Oct.

Fee: £4.50 (accompanied ch 7 free, ch £2.50, students £3.50). Family ticket £12. Grounds £2.50 (ch free & students £1.50).

(electric wheelchair available) shop (ex in grounds on leads)

TEMPLE SOWERBY

Acorn Bank Garden

CA10 1SP (6m E of Penrith on A66)

☎ 017683 61893 📠 017683 61467

A delightful garden of some two and a half acres, which is used to grow an extensive collection of over 180 varieties of medicinal and culinary herbs. Scented plants are grown in the small greenhouse, and a circular walk runs beside the Crowdundle Beck. Please ring for details of special events.

Times: Open Apr-Oct, daily 10-5 (last admission 5pm).

Fee: £2.30 (ch £1.20). Family ticket £5.80. Party 15+.

toilets for disabled shop

TROUTBECK

Townend

LA23 1LB (3m SE of Ambleside at S end of Village)

☎ 015394 32628

The house is one of the finest examples of a `statesman' (wealthy yeoman) farmer's house in Cumbria, built in 1626 for George Browne, whose descendents lived here until 1943. Inside is the original home-made carved furniture, with domestic utensils, letters and papers of the farm.

Times: Open 2 Apr-Oct, Tue-Fri, Sun & BH Mon 1-5 or dusk if earlier. Last admission 4.30pm.

Fee: £3 (ch £1.50). Family ticket £7.50.

WINDERMERE

Lake District Visitor Centre at Brockhole

LA23 1LJ (on A591, between Windermere and Ambleside)

☎ 015394 46601 & 01539 73126(minicom)

📠 015394 45555

e-mail: infodesk@lake-district.gov.uk

Set in 32 acres of landscaped gardens and grounds, on the shore of Lake Windermere, this house became England's first National Park Visitor Centre in 1969. It offers exhibitions, audio-visual programmes, lake cruises, an adventure playground and an extensive events programme.

Times: Open Etr-Oct, 10-5 daily. Grounds & gardens open all year.

Fee: Free admission but parking charge £4 full day, £3 half day.

(charged) licensed (wheelchairs with accessable trails & routes, lifts) toilets for disabled shop

Windermere Steamboat Museum

Rayrigg Rd LA23 1BN (0.5m N of Bowness-on-Windermere on A592)

☎ 015394 45565 📠 015394 48769

A unique collection of Victorian and Edwardian steamboats and vintage motorboats, including the oldest steamboat in the world - the *S L Dolly* of 1850. Displays tell the social and commercial history of England's largest lake, and there are steamboat trips daily, weather permitting.

Times: Open 18 Mar-29 Oct daily, 10-5. Steamboat trips subject to availability & weather.

Fee: £3.25 (ch £2) Family ticket £8

toilets for disabled shop

Derbyshire

The natural features of this central English county range from the modest heights of the Peak District National Park, where Kinder Scout stands at 2,088 ft (636 m), to the depths of its remarkable underground caverns, floodlit to reveal exquisite Blue John stone.

These underground explorations may extend as far as a mile by boat at Speedwell Cavern, or half a mile by foot at Peak Cavern. Walkers and cyclists will enjoy the High Peak Trail which extends from the Derwent Valley to the limestone plateau near Buxton.

The county is richly endowed with stately homes. Most notably Chatsworth, the palatial home of the Duke and Duchess of Devonshire, with its outstanding collections of paintings, statuary and decorative art. Other gems include Haddon Hall, a well preserved medieval house; the splendid Elizabethan Hardwick Hall, and Kedleston Hall, an exemplary Adam creation.

The spa town of Matlock is the county's administrative centre. Other major towns are industrialised Derby, home of Royal Crown Derby china, and the old coal mining town of Chesterfield, symbolised by the crooked spire of St Mary and All Saints Church. Bargain hunters will enjoy a browse around the huge open air market in Chesterfield on a Monday, Friday and Saturday, or the Flea Market on a Thursday.

Around the villages of Derbyshire, look out for the ancient tradition of well dressing, the decorating of springs and wells - the precious sources of life-sustaining water - with pictures formed from flowers.

EVENTS & FESTIVALS

May-September
Welldressings throughout the county

April
27-28 April & 5 May Buxton Music, Speech & Drama Festival

May
28 Derbyshire Steam Fair, Hartington Moor Showground
12-13 Chatsworth Horse Trials

July
12-22 Buxton Festival, Opera Festival
15 Ashbourne Highland Gathering

August
1-2 Bakewell Show, The Showground, Bakewell
18 Ashbourne Show, Osmaston Polo Ground
25 Aug-27 Oct Matlock Bath Illuminations
27 Chesterfield Evening Fireworks

September
1-2 Chatsworth Country Fair
8-9, 15-16 & 22-23 Wirksworth Festival, various locations
8-9 Buxton Country Music Festival

October
17 Ilkeston Charter Fair

November
4 Dovedale Dash, Thorpe

Top: Derby Cathedral

BOLSOVER

Bolsover Castle

Castle St S44 6PR (on A632)
☎ 01246 823349

An enchanting and romantic spectacle, situated high on a wooded hilltop dominating the surrounding landscape, this 17th-century mansion was built on the site of a Norman castle. The keep displays elaborate fireplaces, panelling and wall paintings and there is also an impressive indoor Riding School, also of the 17th century.

Times: Open all year, Apr-Sep, daily 10-6 (Oct 10-5); Nov-Mar, Wed-Sun 10-4. Closed 24-26 Dec & 1 Jan.
Fee: £4.20 (ch 5-15 £2.10, under 5's free). Personal stereo tour included in admission.
P ♿ (keep not accessible) shop ✖ #

BUXTON

Poole's Cavern (Buxton Country Park)

Green Ln SK17 9DH (from A6 or A515 follow Tourist signs)
☎ 01298 26978 📠 01298 73563
e-mail: info@poolescavern.co.uk

Limestone rock, water and millions of years created this natural cavern containing thousands of crystal formations. A guided tour lasting 45 minutes leads the visitor through chambers used as a shelter by Bronze-Age cave dwellers, Roman metal workers and as a hideout by the infamous robber Poole. Attractions include the underground source of the River Wye, the 'Poached Egg Chamber', Mary Queen of Scots Pillar, the Grand Cascade and underground sculpture formations.

Times: Open Mar-Oct, daily 10-5. (Open in winter for groups only).
Fee: £4.75 (ch £2.50, concessions £3.50). Family ticket £12.50. Party.
P ☕ ♿ toilets for disabled shop ✖ (ex in woodland) 💳

CALKE

Calke Abbey

DE73 1LE (9m S of Derby, on A514)
☎ 01332 863822 📠 01332 865272
e-mail: eckxxx@smtp.ntrust.org.uk

This fine baroque mansion dating from the early 18th century was built for Sir John Harpur. Among its treasures are an extensive natural history collection, a magnificent Chinese silk state bed, and a spectacular red and white drawing room. The house stands in extensive wooded parkland and also has walled flower gardens.

Times: Open 27 Mar-1 Nov Sat-Wed (incl BH Mon); House & church 1-5.30 Gardens from 11am. Last admission 5pm. Park open all year, Apr-Oct closes 9pm or dusk if earlier, Nov-Mar closes at dusk. House, church & garden closed Sat 12 Aug. Admission to house for all is by timed ticket, obtained on arrival.
Fee: £5.10 (ch £2.50). Family ticket £12.70.
P ✕ licensed ♿ (braille guide, hearing system, buggy/wheelchair available) toilets for disabled shop ✖ (ex guide dogs) 🍃

CASTLETON

Blue-John Cavern & Mine

Buxton Rd S33 8WP
☎ 01433 620638 & 620642 📠 01433 621586

A remarkable example of a water-worn cave, over a third of a mile long, with chambers 200ft high. It contains 8 of the 14 veins of Blue John stone, and has been the major source of this unique form of fluorspar for nearly 300 years.

Times: Open all year daily 9.30-6 (or dusk). Guided tours of approx 1hr every 10 mins tour.
Fee: £6 (ch £3, pen & student £4) Family ticket £16. Party.
P ☕ shop 💳

Peak Cavern

S33 8WS (on A6187, in centre of Castleton)
☎ 01433 620285 📠 01433 623229
e-mail: info@peakcavern.co.uk

One of the most spectacular natural limestone caves in the Peak District, with an electrically-lit underground walk of about half a mile. Ropes have been made for over 500 years in the `Grand Entrance Hall', and traces of a row of cottages can be seen. Rope-making demonstrations are included on every tour.

Times: Open Etr-Oct, daily 10-5. Nov-Etr wknds only 10-5
Fee: £4.75 (ch £2.75, other concessions £3.75). Family ticket £13.
P (charged) shop 💳

Peveril Castle

Market Place SW33 8WQ (on S side of Castleton)
☎ 01433 620613

William Peveril, one of William the Conqueror's trusted knights, guarded the King's manors in the Peak from this natural vantage point which commands spectacular views of the Hope Valley. The area is designated a Site of Special Scientific Interest.

Times: Open all year, Apr-Sep, daily 10-6 (Oct 10-5); Nov-Mar, Wed-Sun 10-4. Closed 24-26 Dec & 1 Jan.
Fee: £2.20 (ch 5-15 £1.10, under 5's free)
shop ✖ #

Speedwell Cavern

Winnats Pass S33 8WA (off A625, (A625 becomes A6187 at Hathersage) 0.5m W of Castleton)
☎ 01433 620512 📠 01433 621888
e-mail: info@speedwellcavern.co.uk

Descend 105 steps to a boat which will take you on a one-mile underground exploration of the floodlit cavern.

Times: Open all year, Etr-Oct daily 9.30-6, Nov-Etr 10-5. (Closed 25 Dec).
Fee: £5.25 (ch £3.25)
P (charged) shop 💳

Treak Cliff Cavern

S33 8WP (0.75m W of Castleton on A6187)
☎ 01433 620571 📠 01433 620519

An underground world of stalactites, stalagmites, flowstone, rock and cave formations, minerals and fossils. There are rich deposits of the rare and beautiful Blue John Stone, and the show caves include the Witch's Cave, Aladdin's Cave and Fairyland Grotto.

Times: Open all year, Mar-Oct daily 9.30-last tour 4.45. Nov-Feb daily 10-last tour at 3.20. All tours are guided & last about 40 mins.
Fee: Adults £5 (ch 5-15 £3). Family ticket £14.
P shop

CHATSWORTH

Chatsworth

DE45 1PP (8m N of Matlock on B6012)
☎ 01246 582204 📠 01246 583536
e-mail: visit@chatsworth-house.co.uk

Home of the Duke and Duchess of Devonshire, Chatsworth contains a massive private collection of fine and decorative arts. There is is a splendid painted hall, and a great staircase leads to the chapel, decorated with statues and paintings. There are pictures, furniture and porcelain, and a trompe l'oeil painting of a violin on the music room door. The park was laid out by `Capability' Brown, but is most famous as the work of Joseph Paxton, head gardener in the 19th century.

Times: Open 15 Mar-29 Oct, House & garden 11-4.30, Farmyard 10.30-4.30
Fee: House & Garden £6.75 (ch £3, students & pen £5.50). Family ticket £16.75. Garden only £3.85 (ch £1.75, students & pen £3). Family ticket £9.50. Farmyard & Adventure Playground £3.50. Car park £1.
P (charged) ✕ licensed ♿ (3 electric wheelchairs available for garden) toilets for disabled shop garden centre (ex park & gardens on lead)

CRESWELL

Creswell Crags Visitor Centre

off Crags Rd S80 3LH (1m E off B6042)
☎ 01909 720378

A deep narrow gorge, pitted with caves and rock shelters, used as seasonal camps by Stone Age hunter-gatherers. Unusual finds from the caves include pieces of decorated animal bone and the remains of extinct animals like woolly mammoth and hyena. Guided cave tours are organised throughout the year.

Times: Open all year, Feb-Oct, daily, 10.30-4.30; Nov-Jan, Sun only 10.30-4.30.
P ♿ (wheelchair loan) toilets for disabled shop *Details not confirmed for 2001*

CRICH

National Tramway Museum

DE4 5DP (off B5035)
☎ 01773 852565 📠 01773 852326

A mile-long scenic journey through a Period Street to open countryside with panoramic views. You can enjoy unlimited vintage tram rides, and the exhibition hall houses the largest collection of vintage electric trams in Britain. Ring for details of special events.

Times: Open Apr-Oct, daily 10-5.30 (6.30pm wknds Jun-Aug & BH wknds). Winter, open Sun & Mon, 10.30-4.
Fee: £6.70 (ch 4-15 £3.30, pen £5.80). Family ticket (2 adults & 3 ch) £18.20.
P ♿ (Braille guidebooks, converted tram, talktype facility) toilets for disabled shop

CROMFORD

Arkwright's Cromford Mill

Mill Ln DE4 3RQ (off A6, 3m S of Matlock)
☎ 01629 824297 & 823256 📠 01629 823256
e-mail: info@cromfordmill.co.uk

Sir Richard Arkwright established the world's first successful water-powered cotton spinning mill at Cromford in 1771. The Arkwright Society are involved in a major restoration to create a lasting monument to an extraordinary genius. Guided tours are available, and there is a programme of lectures and visits - ring for details.

Times: Open all year, daily 9-5 (Closed 25 Dec). Guided tours 10-4.
Fee: Guided tour & exhibitions £2 (ch & pen £1.50). Mill site Free.
P ✕ ♿ toilets for disabled shop

DENBY

Denby Pottery Visitor Centre

Derby Rd DE5 8NX (8m N of Derby, on B6179, 2m S of Ripley)
☎ 01773 740799 📠 01773 740749

Tours of the factory take place daily and include lots of hands-on activities including pot throwing. Cookery demonstrations take place alongside the extensive Cookery Emporium, and a huge range of discounted seconds are available in the Denby Factory Shop.

Times: Open all year. Full factory tours, Mon-Thu 10.30 & 1. Craftroom tour only, daily 10-3.15. Visitors Centre Mon-Sat 9.30-5, Sun 10-5.
Fee: Free.
P ✕ licensed ♿ (lift) toilets for disabled shop garden centre (ex guide dogs)

DERBY

Derby Museum & Art Gallery

The Strand DE1 1BS
☎ 01332 716659 & 716669 📠 01332 716670
e-mail: enquire@derbymuseum.freeserve.co.uk

The museum has a wide range of displays, notably of Derby porcelain, and paintings by the local artist Joseph Wright (1734-97). Also antiquities, natural history and militaria, as well as many temporary exhibitions.

Times: Open all year, Mon 11-5, Tue-Sat 10-5, Sun & BHs 2-5. (Closed Xmas, telephone for details).

Fee: Free.

P (50yds) ♿ (lift to all floors, portable mini-loop, large print labels) toilets for disabled shop (ex guide dogs)

Industrial Museum

The Silk Mill, Silk Mill Ln, off Full St DE1 3AR (From Derby inner ring road, head for Cathedral & Assembly Rooms car park. 5 mins walk from here)
☎ 01332 255308 📠 01332 716670

The museum is set in an early 18th-century silk mill and adjacent flour mill. Displays cover local mining, quarrying and industries, and include a major collection of Rolls Royce aero-engines from 1915 to the present. There is also a section covering the history of railway engineering in Derby.

Times: Open all year, Mon 11-5, Tue-Sat 10-5, Sun & BHs 2-5. (Closed Xmas telephone for details).

Fee: Free.

P ♿ (lift to all floors) toilets for disabled shop (ex guide dogs)

Pickford's House Museum of Georgian Life & Costume

41 Friar Gate DE1 1DA (from A38 into Derby, follow signs to City Centre)
☎ 01332 255363 📠 01332 255527

The house was built in 1770 by the architect Joseph Pickford as a combined workplace and family home. It now shows domestic life at different periods, with Georgian reception rooms and service areas and a 1930s bathroom. Other galleries are devoted to temporary exhibitions. There is also a display on the growth of Georgian Derby, and on Pickford's contribution to Midlands architecture.

Times: Open all year, Mon 11-5, Tue-Sat 10-5, Sun & BHs 2-5. (Closed Xmas, telephone for details).

Fee: Free.

P ♿ (tape guides, video with sign language subtitles) shop (ex guide dogs)

Royal Crown Derby Visitor Centre

194 Osmaston Rd DE23 8JZ (10 mins walk from bus & rail stations & Derby City Centre)
☎ 01332 712800 & 712841 (tours) 📠 01332 712863
e-mail: sjbirks@royal-doulton.com

This museum traces the history of the company from 1750 to the present day, while the factory tour

demonstrates the making of Royal Crown Derby in detail from clay through to the finished product. A demonstration studio gives you the opportunity to watch craftspeople at close quarters and try out a variety of different skills.

Times: Open all year, daily. Factory tours twice daily, booking strongly advised.

Fee: Visitor centre £2.75 (ch/pen £2.25). Family £7. Factory tour £5.50 (ch/pen £4.75). Family £16.

P ☕ ✕ licensed ♿ (visitor entry accessible but not factory tour) toilets for disabled shop (ex guide dogs)

EYAM

Eyam Hall

S32 5QW (in village centre)
☎ 01433 631976 📠 01433 631603
e-mail: nicwri@globalnet.co.uk

Times: Open: House 31 Mar-Oct, Wed,Thu,Sun & BH: first tour 11am, last tour 4.30pm. Craft centre open allyear Tue-Sun 10.30-5.30.

P ☕ ✕ licensed ♿ (disabled may enter by special gate, avoiding steps) toilets for disabled shop (ex guide dogs) *Details not confirmed for 2001*

HADDON HALL

HADDON HALL

DE45 1LA (1.5m S of Bakewell off A6)

☎ 01629 812855 01629 814379

e-mail: haddonestate.fsnet.co.uk

Originally held by the illegitimate son of William the Conqueror, Haddon has been owned by the Manners family since the 16th century. Little has been added since the reign of Henry VIII, and, despite its time-worn steps, few medieval houses have so successfully withstood the ravages of time.

Times: Open Apr-Sep, 10.30-5, Oct, Mon-Thu 10.30-4.30. Closed 16 July.

Fee: £5.75 (ch £3 & pen £4.75). Family ticket £15. Party 15+.

P (charged) licensed (access is impossible for those in wheelchairs) shop (ex guide dogs)

HARDWICK HALL

HARDWICK HALL

Doe Lea S44 5QJ (2m S M1 Junct 29)

☎ 01246 850430 01246 854200

e-mail: hwxxx@smtp.ntrust.org.uk

Hardwick Hall is celebrated as the creation of Bess of Hardwick, who began the building at 70, after the death of her husband, the Earl of Shrewsbury. The house has a vast area of windows, which become taller from the ground floor up. The High Great Chamber and the long gallery are hung with tapestries and Cavendish portraits. Some of the needlework is by Mary, Queen of Scots, who was a prisoner here for 15 years.

Times: Open Apr-31 Oct Wed, Thu, Sat, Sun & BH Mon 12.30-5. (Closed Good Fri). Last admission 4.30pm. Garden Apr-31 Oct daily 12-5.30. Park all year daily dawn-dusk. Car park gates close 6pm.

Fee: House & garden £6 (ch £3). Family ticket £15. Garden only £3.20 (ch £1.60, family £8)

P licensed (hearing scheme, wheelchair if prebooked, braille guides) toilets for disabled shop (ex in park on leads)

ILKESTON

AMERICAN ADVENTURE THEME PARK

DE7 5SX (off M1 junct 26, signposted)

☎ 01773 531521 (switchboard) 535301 (bookings) 01773 716140

e-mail: info@adventureworld.co.uk

This is one of Britain's few fully themed parks, based on the legend of a whole continent. The experiences here are widely varied, from the Missile Rollercoaster in Spaceport USA, to the wet and wild excitement of the Rocky Mountain Rapids ride and the Nightmare Niagara log flume. Fort Adventure is an action packed challenge and the driving school is great for kids to find out if they've got what it takes to be an advanced driver. There's also a Mississippi paddle steamer, a horse-show in Silver City, and glamorous Lazy Lil's Saloon Show.

Times: Open 15 Apr-29 Oct from 10.

Fee: £13.50 (ch under 1m free, otherwise £10.50, pen £2.99). Family ticket (2 adults & 2 ch £39.99, each additional person £9.99)

P licensed (free wheelchair hire, must pre book, call 01773 531521) toilets for disabled shop (ex guide dogs)

KEDLESTON HALL

KEDLESTON HALL

DE22 5JH (5m NW of Derby)

☎ 01332 842191 01332 841972

e-mail: ekdxxx@smtp.ntrust.org.uk

Kedleston has been the Derbyshire home of the Curzon family for over eight centuries. The original house was demolished at the end of the 17th century. In 1760 Robert Adam built the south front and designed most of the interior including the marble hall. There are pictures, furniture and china displayed in the house together with an Indian Museum containing the collection accumulated by Lord Curzon, Viceroy of India.

Times: Open - House; 1 Apr-31 Oct, Sat-Wed 12-4.30, last admission 5pm, (closed Good Fri). Garden; same as house but open 11-6. Park; 1 Apr-31 Oct, daily 11-6, Nov-17 Dec, Sat & Sun 12-4 (entry charge £2 on Thu/Fri for park only).

Fee: £5 (ch £2.50). Family ticket £12.50.

P licensed (braille guide, wheelchair, self-drive vehicle) toilets for disabled shop (ex in park, must be on leads)

MATLOCK

RIBER CASTLE WILDLIFE PARK

DE4 5JU (A615 to Tansley, via Alders Lane and Carr Lane to Riber)

☎ 01629 582073 01629 582073

Times: Open all year, daily from 10am. (Summer last admission 5pm, winter 3-4.30pm). Closed 25 Dec.

P (ramp to cafe and bar. Wide mainly flat paths) toilets for disabled shop (in animal section) *Details not confirmed for 2001*

MATLOCK BATH

The Heights of Abraham Country Park & Caverns

DE4 3PD (On A6, signposted from M1 junct 28 & A6. Base station next to Matlock Bath railway station)
☎ 01629 582365 ▯ 01629 580279
e-mail: info@h-of-a.co.uk

High on a hill above the village of Matlock Bath are the Grounds of the Heights of Abraham. Until recently the climb to the summit was only for the very energetic, but now alpine-style cable cars provide a leisurely and spectacular way of reaching the top. There are two show caverns, plenty for children to do, and, naturally, superb views.

Times: Open daily Etr-Oct 10-5 (later in high season) for Autumn & Winter opening telephone for details.

Fee: £6.50 (ch £4.50, pen £5.50). Under 5's free - one per adult.

P (300m) licensed toilets for disabled shop

Peak District Mining Museum

The Pavilion DE4 3NR (off A6)
☎ 01629 583834

A large display explains the history of the Derbyshire lead industry from Roman times to the present day. The geology of the area, mining and smelting processes, the quarrying and the people who worked in the industry, are illustrated by a series of static and moving exhibits. The museum also features an early 19th-century water pressure pumping engine.

Times: Open all year, daily 11-4 (later in summer season). (Closed 25 Dec).

Fee: Museum & Mine: £4 (ch, students, disabled & pen £2.50). Family £9. Museum only or mine only £2.50 (ch, students, disabled £1.50). Family £6. Party rates.

P (charged) shop

Temple Mine

Temple Rd DE4 3NR (off A6)
☎ 01629 583834

In the process of being restored to how it was in the 1920s and 1930s, this old lead and fluorspar workings makes interesting viewing. A self-guided tour illustrates the geology, mineralisation and mining techniques.

Times: Open all year, Summer 12-4, Winter timed visits during afternoon.

Fee: Museum & Mine: £4 (ch, pen, disabled £2.50). Family ticket £9. Museum only or mine only: £2.50 (ch, pen, disabled £1.50), Family £6. Party rates.

P shop (ex guide dogs)

MELBOURNE

Melbourne Hall

DE73 1EN (9m S of Derby on A514)
☎ 01332 862502 ▯ 01332 862263

Sir John Coke (Charles I's Secretary of State) bought the lease of Melbourne Hall in 1628 and the house has been home to two Prime Ministers: Lord Melbourne and Lord Palmerston. The glorious formal gardens are among the finest in Britain.

Times: Open, house daily throughout Aug only (ex first three Mons) 2-5 (last admission 4.15). Prebooked parties by appointment in Aug. Gardens Apr-Sep, Wed, Sat, Sun & BH Mon 1.30-5.30.

Fee: House Tue-Sat (guided tour) £3 (ch £1.50, pen £2.50), Sun & BH Mon (no guided tour) £2.50 (ch £1, pen £2). House & Garden (Aug only) £5 (ch £3, pen £4). Garden only £3 (pen £2). Family £8.

P (200 yards) (ramp at garden entrance) shop (ex guide dogs)

MIDDLETON BY WIRKSWORTH

Middleton Top Engine House

Middleton Top Visitor Centre DE4 4LS (0.5m S from B5036 Cromford/Wirksworth road)
☎ 01629 823204 ▯ 01629 825336

A beam engine built in 1829 for the Cromford and High Peak Railway, and its octagonal engine house. The engine's job was to haul wagons up the Middleton Incline, and its last trip was in 1963 after 134 years' work. The visitor centre tells the story of this historic railway.

Times: Open: Information Centre, daily, wknds only winter. Engine House Etr-Oct 1st wknd in month (engine in motion).

Fee: Static Engine 50p (ch 25p). Working Engine £1 (ch 50p).

P (charged) (ex Engine house) toilets for disabled shop

OLD WHITTINGTON

Revolution House

High St S41 9LA (on B6052 off A61, signposted)
☎ 01246 453554 & 345727 ▯ 01246 345720

Originally the Cock and Pynot alehouse, this 17th century cottage was the scene of a meeting between local noblemen to plan their part in the Revolution of 1688. The house is now furnished in 17th-century style. A video relates the story of the Revolution and there is a small exhibition room.

Times: Open 21 Apr-29 Oct, daily 10-4. Xmas opening 16-24 Dec & 27 Dec-1 Jan, daily 10-4.

Fee: Free.

P (100yds) shop (ex guide dogs)

RIPLEY

Midland Railway Centre

Butterley Station DE5 3QZ (1m N of Ripley on B6179)
☎ 01773 747674 & 749788 01773 570721
e-mail: info@midlandrailwaycentre.co.uk

A regular steam-train passenger service runs here, to the centre where the aim is to depict every aspect of the golden days of the Midland Railway and its successors. Exhibits range from the steam locomotives of 1866 to an electric locomotive. There is also a large section of rolling stock spanning the last 100 years.
Times: Open Apr-Oct, every wknd, Wed & most school holidays.
Fee: £7.95 (ch 5-16 £4, pen £6.50) children under 5 free. Party 15+.
P ♿ (special accommodation on trains) toilets for disabled shop

ROWSLEY

The Wind in the Willows

Peak Village DE4 2NP (at junct of A6 & B6012)
☎ 01629 733433 01629 734850

Based on the charming book written by Kenneth Grahame and illustrated by E H Shepard, this new attraction brings to life the characters Mole, Ratty, Toad and Badger in an indoor recreation of the English countryside. Designed by the same team that created The World of Beatrix Potter.
Times: Open Apr-Sep, daily 10-5.30; Oct-Mar, daily 10-4.30. (Closed 25 Dec & 1 Jan).
Fee: £3.50 (ch £2, under 4's free).
P ♿ toilets for disabled shop (ex guide dogs)

SUDBURY

Sudbury Hall

DE6 5HT (6m E of Uttoxeter)
☎ 01283 585305 01283 585139
e-mail: esuxxx@smtp.ntrust.org.uk

This country house was started in 1664 by Lord George Vernon. It has unusual diapered brickwork, a carved two-storey stone frontispiece, a cupola and tall chimneys. The interior features work by craftsmen including Edward Pierce and Grinling Gibbons. The Museum of Childhood contains a Victorian schoolroom, collections of toys, and displays on working children.
Times: Open 1 Apr-31 Oct, Wed-Sun + BH Mon (closed Good Fri) 1-5.30pm or sunset if earlier. Last admissions 30 mins before closing. Gardens open 12-6pm.
Fee: House £3.70 (ch £1.80). Family ticket £9.20. Museum of Childhood £3.70. Joint ticket £5.90. Joint Family ticket £14.60.
P ♿ (wheelchair available. braille guide. hearing system) toilets for disabled shop (ex in grounds)

WIRKSWORTH

Wirksworth Heritage Centre

Crown Yard DE4 4ET (on B5023 off A6 in centre of Wirksworth)
☎ 01629 825225
e-mail: www.gilkin.demon.co.uk

The Centre has been created in an old silk and velvet mill. The three floors of the mill have interpretative displays of the town's past history as a prosperous lead-mining industry. Each floor offers many features of interest including a computer game called 'Rescue the injured lead-miner', a mock-up of a natural cavern, and a Quarryman's House. If you visit Wirksworth during Spring Bank Holiday, you can also see the famous Well Dressings.
Times: Open mid Feb-Etr & Nov Wed-Sat 11-4, Sun 1-4; Etr-mid Jul & mid Sep-Oct Tue-Sat 10.30-4.30, Sun 1-4.30; mid Jul-mid Sep daily 10-5. Also BH Sun & Mon. Last admission 40 mins before closing.
Fee: £2 (ch & pen £1) Party 20+.
P (80yds) (pay & display) ✕ licensed shop (ex guide dogs)

Devon

A county of great contrasts, Devon encompasses wild moorland terrain and rolling farming country dotted with delightful villages. Exmoor extends to the spectacular northern coastline with England's highest cliffs, where there are excellent walks on the hills and coastal footpath.

In the south, stretching from Dartmoor to the seaside resorts of Torbay, is the area alluringly dubbed the 'English Riviera'. The major resorts are Torquay, Paignton and Teignmouth on the south coast, and Ilfracombe on the north. Perhaps more interesting to explore however, are the estuaries of Kingsbridge and Dartmouth, Sidmouth with its elegant seafront, and Salcombe with its flotilla of yachts.

Both Dartmoor and Exmoor have National Park status which preserves them from encroachment. Exmoor is home to the hardy little Exmoor pony and is the only remaining habitat in England for the native red deer. Dartmoor is the largest expanse of untamed country in Southern England, with Dartmoor Forest at its heart.

Devon's main towns are Exeter and Plymouth. The former was badly damaged in World War II, but the cathedral survives. Plymouth has been closely associated with naval history since Sir Francis Drake played his legendary game of bowls before facing the Spanish Armada, but as a centre for shipbuilding and a military base, it was also doomed to devastation by Luftwaffe bombing.

Local products to look out for while visiting Devon, are seafood, cider, clotted cream, Honiton lace and Dartington glass.

EVENTS & FESTIVALS

May
17-19 Devon County Show, Clyst St Mary
tbc Brixham Heritage Festival

June
29 Jun-15 Jul Exeter Festival

July
9-15 Okehampton Arts Music Festival
tbc Aquaculture Festival of Music & Arts, Torquay (street theatre, live music, exhibitions)

August
3-10 Sidmouth International Festival (various venues, folk music, dance & song)
4-5 Dartmoor Folk Festival
9 Okehampton Agricultural Show
16 Chagford Agricultural Show
24-26 West Country Hot Air Balloon Festival, Tavistock
tbc The Children's Festival, Paignton Green, Paignton

September
11 Widecombe Fair, Widecombe-in-the-Moor

November
24th Plymouth American Thanksgiving

Top: Dartmoor

APPLEDORE

North Devon Maritime Museum

Odun House, Odun Rd EX39 1PT

☎ 01237 422064

Appledore's history of boat-building and fishing are the subject of this museum. Each room shows a different aspect of North Devon's maritime history, including steam and motor coasters. There is also a full-size reconstruction of an Appledore kitchen of around 1900. A Victorian schoolroom is available for school parties. There are also video showings, a research room, and a large collection of photographs and documents (by appointment only).

Times: Open Etr-Oct, daily 2-5; also May-Sep, Mon-Fri 11-1.

Fee: £1 (ch 30p & pen 70p).

P (opposite) ♿ (hands-on items for visually impaired) toilets for disabled shop (ex guide dogs)

ARLINGTON

Arlington Court

EX31 4LP (7m NE of Barnstaple, on A39)

☎ 01271 850296 01271 850711

Built in 1822, Arlington Court is filled with a fascinating collection of objets d'art: pewter, shells and model ships as well as 19th-century furniture and costumes. The biggest attraction is the collection of carriages and horsedrawn vehicles. Around the house is a landscaped park grazed by Shetland ponies and Jacob sheep.

Times: Open 2 Apr-10 Sep, Sun-Fri, 11-5.30; also Sat of BH wknds. 11 Sep-Oct, Mon-Fri, 11-4.30 & Sun 11-5.30. Footpaths and woods open 2 Apr-Oct, Sun-Fri 11-5.30; Nov-Mar open during daylight hours.

Fee: House & grounds £5.30. Grounds only £3.30. Parties 15+

P ✕ licensed ♿ (wheelchairs available - ramped steps at house) toilets for disabled shop (ex in park)

BARNSTAPLE

Marwood Hill Gardens

EX31 4EB (signposted off A361)

☎ 01271 342528

The gardens with their three small lakes cover 18 acres and have many rare trees and shrubs. There is a large bog garden and a walled garden, collections of clematis, camellias and eucalyptus. Alpine plants are also a feature, and there are plants for sale.

Times: Open daily dawn to dusk.

Fee: £3 (ch 12 free if accompanied).

P ♿ garden centre

BEER

Pecorama Pleasure Gardens

Underleys EX12 3NA (from A3052 take B3174, Beer road, signed)

☎ 01297 21542 01297 20229

The gardens are high on a hillside, overlooking Beer. A miniature steam and diesel passenger line offers visitors a stunning view of Lyme Bay as it runs through the Pleasure Gardens. Attractions include an aviary, crazy golf, children's activity area and the Peco Millennium Garden. The main building houses an exhibition of railway modelling in various small gauges. There are souvenir and railway model shops, plus full catering facilities.

Times: Open Etr-Sep (plus Autumn Half Term), Mon-Fri 10-5.30, Sat 10-1. Also Sun at Etr & 28 May-3 Sep.

Fee: £4.25 (ch 4-14 £2.75, pen £3.75, over 80's, under 4's & disabled helpers free).

P ✕ licensed ♿ (wheelchair available, some areas of garden steep) toilets for disabled shop (ex guide dogs)

BICKLEIGH

Bickleigh Castle

EX16 8RP (off A396 follow signs from Bickleigh Bridge)

☎ 01884 855363

The `castle' is really a moated and fortified manor house that was home to the heirs of the Earls of Devon and later the Carew family. The small chapel is said to be the oldest complete building in Devon, and dates from the early Norman period. The Carew family acquired the house in the 16th century, and it was Admiral Sir George Carew who commanded the Mary Rose on her first and last voyage.

Times: Open Etr wk (Sun-Fri), then Wed, Sun & BH to late May BH, then daily (ex Sat) to 1st Sun in Oct.

Fee: £4 (ch 5-15 £2). Family ticket £10. Party 20+.

P ♿ (specially arranged tours with experienced guide) shop garden centre (ex guide dogs)

BICTON

Bicton Park

East Budleigh EX9 7BJ (2m N of Budleigh Salterton on B3178)

☎ 01395 568465 & 568374 01395 568465

Times: Open all year 10 Jan-May 10-4, May-Oct 10-6, Oct-24 Dec 10-4.

P ✕ licensed ♿ (adapted carriage on woodland railway, wheelchairs) toilets for disabled shop garden centre (ex on lead)

Details not confirmed for 2001

BLACKMOOR GATE

Exmoor Zoological Park

South Stowford, Bratton Fleming EX31 4SG (off A399)
☎ 01598 763352 01598 763352
e-mail: exmoorzoo@fsb.dial.co.uk

These landscaped gardens cover 12.5 acres with a waterfall, streams and a lake with penguins, swans and other water birds. There are aviaries with tropical and exotic birds, and many animal enclosures containing lemurs, marmosets, capybara, rabbits, pigs, tamarins and many more. The zoo specializes in close encounters, handling sessions, and keepers' talks.
Times: Open daily, Apr-Oct 10-6; Nov-Mar 10-4. (Closed 1 Dec-31 Jan)
Fee: £4.55 (ch 3-16 £2.95, under 3 free, pen £3.95), Family £13.
toilets for disabled shop (ex guide dogs)

BUCKFASTLEIGH

Buckfast Abbey

TQ11 0EE (off A38 on A384 Dartbridge turn off, follow tourist signs for 0.5m)
☎ 01364 645530 01364 645533

The Abbey, founded in 1018, was dissolved by Henry VIII in the 16th century. Restoration began in 1907, when four monks with little building experience began the work. The church was built on the old foundations, using local blue limestone and Ham Hill stone. The precinct contains several medieval monastic buildings, including the 14th-century guest hall which contains an exhibition of the history of the Abbey.
Times: Open all year daily 5.30am-9.30pm. (visitor facilities 9-5 (summer) 10-4.30 (winter) **Fee:** Free.
licensed (level site, braille plan, wheelchair available) toilets for disabled shop (ex guide dogs)

Buckfast Butterfly Farm & Dartmoor Otter Sanctuary

TQ11 0DZ (off A38, at Dart Bridge junct, follow tourist signs)
☎ 01364 642916 01364 642916
e-mail: info@ottersandbutterflies.co.uk

Visitors can wander around a specially designed, undercover tropical garden, where free-flying butterflies and moths from around the world can be seen. The otter sanctuary has large enclosures with underwater viewing areas.
Times: Open Good Fri-end Oct, daily 10-5.30 or dusk (if earlier).
Fee: £4.95 (ch £3.50, pen £4.50). Family ticket £15.
(wheelchair ramps) shop (ex guide dogs)

BUCKLAND ABBEY

Buckland Abbey

PL20 6EY (off A386 0.25m S of Yelverton, signed)
☎ 01822 853607 01822 855448

Originally a prosperous 13th-century Cistercian Abbey, and then home of the Grenville family, Buckland Abbey was sold to Sir Francis Drake in 1581, who lived there until his death in 1596. Several restored buildings house a fascinating exhibition about the abbey's history. Among the exhibits is Drake's drum, which is said to give warning of danger to England.
Times: Open Apr-Oct, daily (ex Thu) 10.30-5.30. Nov-end Mar, Sat & Sun 2-5. (Closed 25-26 Dec & 3 Jan-18 Feb). Last admissions 45mins before closing.
(charged) licensed (wheelchairs & motorised buggy available) toilets for disabled shop (ex guide dogs) *Details not confirmed for 2001*

CHITTLEHAMPTON

Cobbaton Combat Collection

Cobbaton EX37 9RZ (signed from A361 & A377)
☎ 01769 540740 01769 540141
e-mail: info@cobbatoncombat.co.uk

World War II British and Canadian military vehicles, war documents and military equipment can be seen in this private collection. There are over fifty vehicles including tanks, one a Gulf War Centurian, and a recent Warsaw Pact section. There is also a section on 'Mum's War' and the home front. The children's play area includes a Sherman tank.
Times: Open Apr-Oct, daily 10-6. Winter, most weekdays, phone for details.
Fee: £4 (ch £2.50, pen £3.50)
toilets for disabled shop (ex guide dogs)

CHUDLEIGH

Canonteign Falls

EX6 7NT (off A38 at Chudleigh/Teign Valley junction onto B3193 and follow tourist signs for 3m)
☎ 01647 252434 01647 52617

Times: Open all year, mid Mar-mid Nov, daily 10-5.30; Feb Half Term & Winter, Sun only 11-4.
licensed shop *Details not confirmed for 2001* 

CLOVELLY

The Milky Way Adventure Park

EX39 5RY (on A39, 2m from Clovelly)
☎ 01237 431255 01237 431735
e-mail: info@themilkyway.co.uk

One of the West Country's leading attractions offers you a day in the country that's simply out of this world. Attractions include Clone Zone - Europe's first interactive adventure ride featuring a suspended roller coaster; Time Warp indoor adventure play area; daily displays from the North Devon Bird of Prey and Sheepdog Centres; archery centre; golf driving nets; railway; pets corner and more.

Times: Open Etr-Oct, daily 10.30-6. Telephone for winter opening.
Fee: £6 (ch, pen & students £5, under 3 free). Family tickt (2 adults & 2 ch) £21-extra ch £4 each.
(ramps) toilets for disabled shop (ex on leads in certain areas)

CLYST ST MARY

Crealy Adventure Park

Sidmouth Rd EX5 1DR (leave M5 junct 30 onto A3052 Exeter to Sidmouth road)
☎ 01395 233200 01395 233211
e-mail: fun@crealy.co.uk

Crealy Adventure Park offers indoor adventures including the River Raiders' Challenge and the Children's Magical Kingdom. Go-karts, bumper boats and train rides, plus lots of friendly animals.

Times: Open Apr-Oct, daily 10-6; Nov-Mar 10-5. (Closed 24-26 Dec & 1 Jan).
Fee: £5.50 (pen £4.25, under 2's free). Party 20+. Annual ticket £23.50.
licensed (Carers admitted free) toilets for disabled shop

COMBE MARTIN

The Combe Martin Motorcycle Collection

Cross St EX34 0DH (adjacent to the main car park, behind beach)
☎ 01271 882346
e-mail: combemartin@motorcycle-collection.co.uk

The collection contains over 60 motorcycles, scooters and motorised invalid carriages displayed against a background of old petrol pumps, signs and garage memorabilia.

Times: Open Etr then 20 May-29 Oct, daily 10-5.
Fee: £2.90 (ch & pen £1.90, ch 10 and under accompanied free). The £2.90 ticket includes a draw ticket for the 1st prize of a motorcycle.
P (adjacent to site) (public car parks have charges) toilets for disabled shop

Combe Martin Wildlife Park & Dinosaur Park

EX34 0NG (M5 jct 7 then A361 towards Barnstaple and turn onto A399)
☎ 01271 882486 01271 882486

Twenty acres of woodland complete with streams, cascading waterfalls, ornamental gardens, tropical plants and rare trees make this the most natural wildlife park in Britain. Visitors can see otters, and Meerkats, living in the largest enclosure in Europe. The Domain of the Dinosaurs has partially animated life-size dinosaurs set in prehistoric woodland.

Times: Open Etr-1 Nov, daily 10-4 (last admission)
Fee: £6.95 (ch & disabled £3.95, ch under 3 free, pen £4.95).
shop (ex guide dogs)

COMPTON

Compton Castle

TQ3 1TA (off A381 Newton Abbot road. 4m W of Torquay)
☎ 01803 875740 01803 875740
e-mail: dpaset@smtp.ntrust.org.uk

A fortified house of the 14th to 16th centuries, Compton has been the home of the Gilbert family for 600 years. The Great Kitchen still has its bread ovens and knife-sharpening marks, and the withdrawing room has squints through which occupants could watch services in the chapel. Defensive measures were added in the 16th century, when there were French raids in the area.

Times: Open 3 Apr-26 Oct Mon, Wed & Thu 10-12.15 & 2-5.
Fee: Castle & garden £2.80 (ch £1.40) Party 15+.
(ex guide dogs)

DARTMOUTH

Bayard's Cove Fort

TQ6 9AT (on riverfront)

Built by the townspeople to protect the harbour, the remains of the circuar stronghold still stand at the southern end of the harbour.

Times: Open at all reasonable times. **Fee:** Free.
(in certain areas)

Dartmouth Castle

Castle Rd TQ6 0JN (1m SE off B3205, narrow approach)
☎ 01803 833588

The castle dates from 1481 and was one of the first to be designed for artillery. It faces Kingswear Castle on the other side of the Dart estuary, and a chain could be drawn between the two in times of war.

Times: Open all year, Apr-Sep, daily 10-6 (Oct 10-5); Nov-Mar, daily 10-4. Closed 24-26 Dec & 1 Jan.
Fee: £2.90 (ch 5-15 £1.50, under 5's free).
shop

Woodland Leisure Park

Blackawton TQ9 7DQ (W, off A3122)
☎ 01803 712598 01803 712680
e-mail: fun@woodlands-leisure-park

A full day of variety for all the family in a beautiful setting. Three water coasters, Toboggan Run and impressive playzones sit alongside the new Seadragon's Empire, a massive indoor playcentre on five floors. There is also a falconry centre and animals galore.

Times: Open 26 Mar-5 Nov daily, also wknds & school holidays.
Fee: £5.95 (ch £5.40, pen £3.50). Family ticket (2 adults & 2 ch) £20.95.
(ramps) toilets for disabled shop (ex guide dogs) 

DREWSTEIGNTON

Castle Drogo

EX6 6PB (4m S of A30)
☎ 01647 433306 01647 433186
e-mail: dcdpjj@smtp.ntrust.org.uk

The granite castle is one of the most remarkable designs of Sir Edwin Lutyens, and was built between 1910 and 1930 for Julius Drewe. It is a fascinating combination of medieval might and 20th-century luxury, with its own telephone and hydro-electric systems. The castle stands on a rocky crag overlooking the gorge of the River Teign.

Times: Open Apr-Oct, daily (ex Fri but open Good Fri) 11-5.30. Garden open all year, daily 10.30-5.30 (or dusk if earlier).
Fee: Castle £5.46. Garden & grounds only £2.60
licensed (wheelchairs available, lift to lower ground floor) toilets for disabled shop garden centre (ex guide/hearing dogs)

EXETER

Guildhall

High St EX4 3EB
☎ 01392 665500 01392 665949

This is one of the oldest municipal buildings still in use. It was built in 1330 and then altered in 1446, and the arches and façade were added in 1592-5. The roof timbers rest on bosses of bears holding staves, and there are portraits of Exeter dignitaries, guild crests, civic silver and regalia.

Times: Open when there are no mayoral functions. Times are posted outside weekly. Special opening by arrangement. **Fee:** Free.
(200yds) toilets for disabled (ex guide dogs)

St Nicholas' Priory

Mint Ln, off Fore St EX4 3AT
☎ 01392 665858 01392 421252
e-mail: ramm-events@exeter.gov.uk

The Benedictine priory was founded in 1087, and its remains include unusual survivals such as the Norman undercroft, a Tudor room and a 15th-century kitchen.

contd.

Some fine plaster decoration can be seen, and there are displays of furniture and wood carving.
Times: Open Etr-Oct, Mon, Wed & Sat 3-4.30pm
Fee: £1.25 (concessions 75p). Family ticket £2.50.
P (200yds) shop (ex guide dogs)

EXMOUTH

The World of Country Life

Sandy Bay EX8 5BU (M5 junct 30, take A376 to Exmouth. Follow signs to Sandy Bay.
☎ 01395 274533 01392 273457

All-weather family attraction including falconry displays, and a safari train that rides through a forty acre deer park. Kids will enjoy the friendly farm animals, pets centre and animal nursery. There are also a Victorian street, working models and thousands of exhibits from a bygone age, including steam and vintage vehicles.
Times: Open Etr-Oct, daily 10-5.
Fee: £5.50 (ch 3-18 £4.30, pen £5). Family ticket £19 Wheelchair plus escort £3.50.
P (all parts accessible ex 'safari train') toilets for disabled shop (ex guide dogs)

GREAT TORRINGTON

Dartington

Linden Close EX38 7AN (follow brown tourist signs)
☎ 01805 626262 01805 626263
e-mail: enquiries@dartington.co.uk

Tours of the factory are conducted from the safety of viewing galleries, where you can watch the craftsmen carrying out the age-old techniques of glass manufacture and processing. The Visitor Centre has a permanent exhibition tracing the history of glass and crystal over the past 2000 years.
Times: Open all year. Factory & Visitor centre: Mon-Fri 9.30-3.15. (Closed 16 Dec-2 Jan)
Fee: £3.50 (ch 6-16 £1, pen £2.50). Party.
P licensed (special tours available, book in advance) toilets for disabled shop (ex guide dogs)

RHS Garden Rosemoor

EX38 8PH (1m SE of town on A3124)
☎ 01805 624067 01805 624717
e-mail: roseadmin@rhs.org.uk

Rosemoor is the Royal Horticultural Society's first Regional Garden and Centre, second only to Wisley. The Formal Garden includes 200 varieties of roses, and there is a herb garden, potager, cottage garden, winter garden, alpine terrace and extensive herbaceous borders.
Times: Open: Gardens all year; Visitor Centre Apr-Sep 10-6, Oct-Mar 10-5. **Fee:** £4 (ch 6-16 £1). Party 10+.
P licensed (Herb garden for disabled) toilets for disabled shop garden centre (ex guide dogs)

HONITON

Allhallows Museum

High St EX14 1PG (next to parish church of St Paul)
☎ 01404 44966 & 42996 01404 46591
e-mail: dyateshoniton@insh.com

The museum has a display of Honiton lace, and there are lace demonstrations from June to August. The town's history is also illustrated, and the museum is interesting for its setting in a chapel built in about 1200.
Times: Open Mon before Easter to end of Sep, Mon-Fri 10-5& Sat 10-2. Oct, Mon-Sat 10-4. Winter opening by special arrangement.
Fee: £2 (ch 50p, pen £1.50)
P (400 yds) shop (ex guide dogs)

ILFRACOMBE

Ilfracombe Museum

Runnymede Gardens, Wilder Rd EX34 8AF
☎ 01271 863541
e-mail: ilfracombe@devonmuseums.net

Ilfracombe was an important trading port from the 14th to the 16th centuries and during the Napoleonic Wars became a popular resort. The history, archaeology, geology, natural history and maritime traditions of the area are illustrated here, along with Victoriana, costumes, photographs and china.
Times: Apr-Oct, daily 10-5.30; Nov-Mar Mon-Fri 10-12.30.
Fee: £1 (ch & students 50p, under 5 free, pen 85p). Disabled & booked school groups free.
P (10yds) (ramp to front door, wide aisles) shop (ex guide dogs)

Watermouth Castle

EX34 9SL (3m NE off A399, midway between Ilfracombe & Combe Martin)
☎ 01271 863879 01271 865864
Times: Open Apr-Oct, closed Sat & Fri in off season. Ring for further details.
P (special wheelchair route) toilets for disabled shop (ex guide dogs) *Details not confirmed for 2001*

KILLERTON HOUSE & GARDEN

Killerton House & Garden

EX5 3LE (off B3181)
☎ 01392 881345

Elegant 18th-century house set in an 18 acre garden with sloping lawns and herbaceous borders. A majestic avenue of beech trees runs up the hillside, past an arboretum of rhododendrons and conifers. The garden has an ice house and rustic summer house where the family pet bear was once kept.
Times: Open: House, daily (ex Tue), Mar & Oct, Wed-Sun, Aug daily. Gardens open all year, daily from 10.30.
Fee: House & grounds £5.10. Grounds only £3.60.
P licensed (wheelchairs & motorised buggy available) toilets for disabled shop garden centre (ex in park)

KINGSBRIDGE

Cookworthy Museum of Rural Life

The Old Grammar School, 108 Fore St TQ7 1AW
☎ 01548 853235

Times: Open all year, Apr-Sep Mon-Sat 10-5; Oct Mon-Fri 10.30-4. Nov-Mar groups by arrangement. Local history room Tue-Thu 10-12 & Wed also 2-4, other times by appointment.

P (100yds) ♿ (Braille labels on selected exhibits) toilets for disabled shop (ex guide dogs) *Details not confirmed for 2001*

KINGSWEAR

Coleton Fishacre House & Garden

Brownstone Rd TQ6 0EQ (3m from Kingswear. Take Ferry Road and turn off at Toll House)
☎ 01803 752466 01803 753017
e-mail: dcfdmx@smtp.ntrust.org.uk

The house, set in a stream fed valley on a beautiful stretch of South Devon coastline, was designed in the 1920s for Rupert and Lady D'Oyly Carte (of Gilbert & Sullivan fame) reflecting the Arts & Crafts tradition. A luxuriant garden was created around it, and has year round interest with a wide variety of rare and exotic plants.

Times: Open 7-21 Mar, Sun only 2-5; 27 Mar-Oct, Wed-Fri, Sun & BH Mon 11-4.
Fee: £4.70 (ch £2.35). Family ticket £11.75.

P ♿ (wheelchair available, braille guides) toilets for disabled shop garden centre (ex guide dogs)

KNIGHTSHAYES COURT

Knightshayes Court

EX16 7RQ (2m N of Tiverton off A396)
☎ 01884 254665 & 257381 01884 243050

This fine Victorian mansion, a rare example of William Burges' work, offers much of interest to all ages. The garden is one of the most beautiful in Devon, with formal terraces, amusing topiary. Pool garden and woodland walks.

Times: House & garden open Apr-Oct 11-5.30. House closed Fri, plus Tues in Oct.
Fee: House & garden £5.30 (ch £2.65). Party.

P licensed ♿ (wheelchairs available, lift, braille & audio guide) toilets for disabled shop garden centre (ex guide dogs & in park/woods

LYDFORD

Lydford Castle

EX20 4BH (off A386)

The great square stone keep dates from 1195. It is not built on a mound, as it seems to be, but had earth piled against the walls. The upper floor was a Stannary Court, which administered local tin mines, and the lower floor was used as a prison.

Times: Open all reasonable times.
Fee: Free.

P #

Lydford Gorge

EX20 4BH (off A386, between Okehampton & Tavistock)
☎ 01822 820441 & 820320 01822 822000

The spectacular gorge has been formed by the River Lyd, which has cut into the rock and caused swirling boulders to scoop out potholes in the stream bed. This has created some dramatic features, notably the Devil's Cauldron close to Lydford Bridge. At the end of the gorge is the 90ft-high White Lady Waterfall.

Times: Open Apr-Sep, daily 10-5.30; Oct, daily 10-4. (Nov-Mar, waterfall entrance only, daily 10.30-3).
Fee: £3.50 (ch £1.75) Party.

P shop

MORWELLHAM

Morwellham Quay

PL19 8JL (4m W of Tavistock, off A390. Midway between Gunnislake & Tavistock. Signed)
☎ 01822 832766 & 833808 01822 833808

Morwellham was the greatest copper port in Queen Victoria's empire. Once the mines were exhausted the port area disintegrated into wasteland, until 1970, when a charitable trust was set up for its restoration. Visitors can ride by electric tramway underground into a copper mine, last worked in 1869. Staff wear Victorian costume, and visitors can try on replica costumes.

Times: Open all year (ex Xmas wk) 10-5.30 (4.30 Nov-Etr). Last admission 3.30 (2.30 Nov-Etr).
Fee: £8.60 (ch 5-16 £6, pen & students £7.50).

P licensed ♿ (smooth paths, but difficult areas in Victorian village) toilets for disabled shop (ex on lead)

See advert on p67.

NEWTON ABBOT

Bradley Manor

TQ12 6BN (on A381)
☎ 01626 354513

A National Trust property of 70 acres, the 15th-century house and chapel are surrounded by woodland. The River Lemon and a millstream flow through the estate.

Times: Open Apr-Sep, Wed only 2-5; also some Thu in Apr & Sep.

P *Details not confirmed for 2001*

Hedgehog Hospital at Prickly Ball Farm

Denbury Rd, East Ogwell TQ12 6BZ (1.5m from Newton Abbot on A381 towards Totnes, follow brown tourist signs)
☎ 01626 362319 & 330685 01626 330685
e-mail: hedgehog@hedgehog.org.uk

See, touch and learn about this wild animal. In mid-season see baby hogs bottle feeding. Find out how to encourage hedgehogs into your garden and how they are put back into the wild. Talks on hedgehogs throughout the day, short basic video information about hedgehogs available.

contd.

Times: Open 26 Mar-Sep, 10-5. Last admission 1hr before closing.
Fee: £5.25 (ch 4-14 £3.95, pen £4.50, ch under 4 free). Wheelchair users free.
P (large print menu, use of wheelchair, Braille menu) toilets for disabled shop (ex guide dogs)

Tuckers Maltings

Teign Rd TQ12 4AA (follow brown tourist signs from Newton Abbot rail station)
☎ 01626 334734 01626 330153

The only working malthouse in England open to the public, producing malt from barley for over 30 West Country breweries. Learn all about the process of malting - and taste the end product at the new in-house brewery. Guided tours last over an hour.
Times: Open Etr-Oct, daily 10-4 (Jul-Aug open to 5pm) for guided tours. Speciality bottled beer shop open throughout the year.
Fee: £4.35 (ch 5-15 £2.75, 16-17 £3.50, pen £3.95). Family ticket £12.25.
P toilets for disabled shop (open all year)

OKEHAMPTON

Museum of Dartmoor Life

3 West St EX20 1HQ
☎ 01837 52295

The West Devon Tourist Information Centre and working craft studios are in the courtyard of this three storey mill. There is a display of Victorian life, and reconstructions of local tin and copper mines are complemented by a geological display of the moor. Local history, prehistory, domestic life, industry and environmental issues are explored.
Times: Open Etr-Oct, Mon-Sat 10-5 (also Sun, Jun-Sep). Winter opening times, telephone for details.
Fee: £2 (ch 5-16 & students £1, pen £1.80). Family ticket £5.60. Party 10+.
P

Okehampton Castle

Castle Lodge EX20 1JB (1m SW of town centre)
☎ 01837 52844

The chapel, keep and hall date from the 11th to 14th centuries and stand on the northern fringe of Dartmoor National Park.
Times: Open all year, Apr-Sep, daily 10-6 (Oct 10-5).
Fee: £2.30 (ch 5-15 £1.20, under 5's free). Personal stereo tours included in admission.
P #

OTTERTON

Otterton Mill Centre

EX9 7HG (between North Poppleford & Budleigh Salterton on A3572)
☎ 01395 568521 01395 568521

Mentioned in the Domesday Book, this water-powered mill grinds wholemeal flour used in the baking of bread and cakes sold on the premises. A gallery houses exhibitions through the summer and autumn, and there are sculpture, pottery, weaving, basket-making and spinning studios. There is a co-operative craft shop, and an annual exibition of furniture from West Country workshops.
Times: Open all year, daily, summer 10.30-5.30; winter 11-4.
Fee: £1.75 (ch 90p). Party.
P licensed (free entry to ground floor) shop garden centre

OTTERY ST MARY

Cadhay

EX11 1QT (near jct of A30 & B3167)
☎ 01404 812432 01404 812432
Times: Open Jul-Aug Tue, Wed & Thu. Also Sun & Mon of late spring & late summer BH's. 2-5.30.
P (ex guide dogs) *Details not confirmed for 2001*

PAIGNTON

Paignton & Dartmouth Steam Railway

Queens Park Station, Torbay Rd TQ4 6AF (in Paignton follow brown tourist signs)
☎ 01803 555872 01803 664313

Steam trains run for seven miles from Paignton to Kingswear on the former Great Western line, stopping at Goodrington Sands, Churston, and Kingswear, connecting with the ferry crossing to Dartmouth. Combined river excursions available.
Times: Open Jun-Sep daily 9-5.30 & selected days Oct & Apr-May.
Fee: Paignton to Kingswear £6.40 (ch £4.40, pen £5.80). Family £20. Paignton to Dartmouth (including ferry) £7.50 (ch £5, pen £6.90). Family £23.
P (5mins walk) (wheelchair ramp for boarding train) toilets for disabled shop

Paignton Zoo Environmental Park

Totnes Rd TQ4 7EU (1m from town centre on A385)
☎ 01803 527936 01803 523457
e-mail: info@paigntonzoo.demon.co.uk

Times: Open all year, daily 10-6 (5pm in winter). Last admission 5pm (4pm in winter). (Closed 25 Dec).
P licensed (some steep hills wheelchair loan-booking advisable) toilets for disabled shop (ex guide dogs) *Details not confirmed for 2001*

PLYMOUTH

City Museum & Art Gallery

Drake Circus PL4 8AJ

☎ 01752 304774 🖷 01752 304775

Times: Open all year, Tue-Fri 10-5.30, Sat 10-5, BH Mon 10-5. (Closed Good Fri & 25-26 Dec).

P ♿ (wheelchair available) toilets for disabled shop ex guide dogs *Details not confirmed for 2001*

Merchant's House Museum

33 St Andrews St PL1 2AX

☎ 01752 304774 🖷 01752 304775

Times: Open Apr-Sep, Tue-Fri 10-5.30, Sat 10-5, BH Mon 10-5 (summer), (closed 1-2)

P (400 yds) ♿ shop *Details not confirmed for 2001*

Plymouth Dome

The Hoe PL1 2NZ

☎ 01752 603300 & 600608 (recorded message) 🖷 01752 256361

Times: Open all year, daily, 4 Apr-24 May 9-6; 25 May-13 Sept 9-7.30; 14 Sep-1 Nov 9-6; 3 Nov-Mar 9-5.30. (Closed 25 Dec). Last admission one hour before closing.

P (200 yds) ♿ (audio descriptions, induction loop, wheelchairs available) toilets for disabled shop ex guide dogs *Details not confirmed for 2001*

Prysten House

Finewell St PL1 2AD (immediately behind St Andrews Church, in city centre)

☎ 01752 661414 (Mon-Fri 9-1) 🖷 01752 661414

Times: Open Apr-Oct, Mon-Sat 10-4 (last admission 3.30pm). Other times by appointment.

P (100 yds) (ex guide dogs) *Details not confirmed for 2001*

Royal Citadel

(at the end of Plymouth Hoe)

☎ 01752 775841

Probably designed by Sir Thomas Fitz, this magnificent gateway was built for the stronghold begun by Charles II in 1666. Some buildings remain, notably the Guardhouse, Governor's House and Chapel.

Times: Open for guided tours only May-Sep, daily. For security reasons tours may be suspended at short notice.

Fee: £3 (ch £2, concessions £2.50). Tickets from Plymouth Dome below Smeaton Tower.

PLYMPTON

Saltram

PL7 1UH (2m W between A38 & A379)

☎ 01752 336546 🖷 01752 336474

This magnificent George II house still has its original contents. The collection of paintings was begun at the suggestion of Reynolds and includes many of his portraits. The saloon and dining room were designed by Robert Adam and have superb decorative plasterwork and period furniture.

Times: Open 27 Mar-Oct, Sun-Thu; House 12-5. Garden & Great Kitchen 10.30-5.

P (charged) licensed ♿ (wheelchairs available, lift, braille & audio guides) toilets for disabled shop (ex designated areas) *Details not confirmed for 2001*

POWDERHAM

Powderham Castle

EX6 8JQ (signposted off A379 Exeter/Dawlish road)

☎ 01626 890243 🖷 01626 890729

e-mail: castle@powderham.co.uk

Built between 1390 and 1420, this ancestral home of the Earls of Devon was damaged in the Civil War. The house was restored and altered in later times and is set in beautiful rose gardens with views over the deer park to the Exe Estuary.

Times: Open Apr-4 Nov, 10-5.30 (last admission 5pm). (Closed Sat).

Fee: £6.15 (ch £3.10, pen £5.65). Family ticket £15.40. Party 10+.

P licensed ♿ (ramps) toilets for disabled shop (open 364 days a year) garden centre (open 364 days a year)

See advert on p61.

SALCOMBE

Overbecks Museum & Garden

Sharpitor TQ8 8LW (2.5m SW of Salcombe and 2m S of Malborough)

☎ 01548 842893 🖷 01548 844038

e-mail: dovrcx@smtp.ntrust.org.uk

The garden is on the most southerly tip of Devon, and allows many exotic plants to flourish. The Edwardian house displays toys, dolls and a natural history collection, and there is a `secret room' for children in which they can search for "Fred" the friendly ghost.

Times: Open Apr-Jul Sun-Fri 11-5.30; Aug daily 11-5.30; Sep Sun-Fri 11-5.30; Oct Sun-Thu 11-5. Gardens open all year, 10-8 (or sunset if earlier).

P (charged) ♿ (ramp from garden, braille guide) shop *Details not confirmed for 2001*

SOUTH MOLTON

Quince Honey Farm

EX36 3AZ (3.5m W of A361)

☎ 01769 572401 🖷 01769 574704

Times: Open daily, Apr-Sep 9-6; Oct 9-5; Shop only Nov-Etr 9-5. (Closed 25 Dec-4 Jan).

P ♿ toilets for disabled shop *Details not confirmed for 2001*

STICKLEPATH

Finch Foundry

EX20 2NW

☎ 01837 840046 🖷 01837 840046

Finch Foundry was, in the 19th century a water-powered factory for making sickles, scythes, shovels and other hand tools. Although no longer in production, three waterwheels can still be seen driving huge hammers, shears, grindstone and other machinery, with daily working demonstrations.

Times: Open Apr-Oct, daily ex Tue, 11-5.30.

Fee: £2.80 (ch £1.40). P ♿ shop

TAVISTOCK
See Morwellham

TIVERTON
Tiverton Castle
EX16 6RP (M5 junct 27, then 7m on A361 towards Tiverton to roundabout where Castle is signposted)
☎ 01884 253200 & 255200 01884 254200

The original castle, built in 1106 by order of Henry I, was rebuilt late 13th/14th century. It resisted General Fairfax during the Civil War and fell to him when a lucky shot hit the drawbridge chain. Now a private house, with gardens and a Civil War armoury.
Times: Open Etr-Jun & Sep, Sun,Thu & BH Mon's only 2.30-5.30; Jul & Aug, Sun-Thu 2.30-5.30.
Fee: £3 (ch 7-16 £2, under 7 free). Disabled half price if accessing ground floor only.
P toilets for disabled shop (ex guide dogs)

Tiverton Museum
Saint Andrew St EX16 6PH
☎ 01884 256295
e-mail: su7711@eclipse.co.uk

This large and comprehensive museum consists of eight galleries and is housed in a restored 19th-century school. The numerous local exhibits include a Heathcote Lace Gallery featuring items from the local lacemaking industry. There is also an agricultural section with a collection of farm wagons and implements. Other large exhibits include two waterwheels and a railway gallery.
Times: Closed through 2000 for major alterations. Telephone for opening times for 2001 .
P (100 yds) shop

TORQUAY
Babbacombe Model Village
Hampton Av, Babbacombe TQ1 3LA (follow brown tourist signs from outskirts of town)
☎ 01803 328669 & 315315 01803 315173
e-mail: ss@babbacombemodelvillage.co.uk

Set in four acres of beautifully maintained, miniature landscaped garden, the village contains over 400 models and 1200ft of model railway. City Lights, a new evening illuminations feature, depicts Piccadilly Circus in miniature. At the end of your visit, enjoy the new facility with breathtaking views over the model village.
Times: Open all year, Good Fri-Jun, 9.30-10; Jul-Aug, 9-10; Sep, 9.30-10; Oct, 9.30-9; Nov-Good Fri, 10-dusk. Closed Xmas day.
Fee: £4.80 (ch £3.10, pen £3.90). Family ticket £13.75.
P (charged) (push button audio information) toilets for disabled shop

'Bygones'
Fore St, St Marychurch TQ1 4PR (follow tourist signs into Torquay and St Marychurch)
☎ 01803 326108 01803 326108
Times: Open all year, Jun-Aug 10am-10pm, (Fri & Sat 10-6); Sep, Oct, Mar, Apr & May 10-5; Nov-Feb 10-4, Sat & Sun 10-5. (Last admission 1 hour before closing). (Closed 25 Dec). Extended opening during school holidays.
P (50 yds) shop (ex guide dogs) *Details not confirmed for 2001*

Kents Cavern
The Caves, 91 Ilsham Rd, Wellswood TQ1 2JF (1.25m NE off B3199, follow brown & white tourist signs)
☎ 01803 294059 & 215136 01803 211034
e-mail: mail@kents-cavern.co.uk

Recognised as one of the most important archaeological sites in Britain. this is not only a world of spectacular natural beauty, but also a priceless record of past times, where a multitude of secrets of mankind, animals and nature have become trapped and preserved over the last 350,000 years. One hundred and seventy years after the first excavations and with over 70,000 remains already unearthed, modern research is still discovering new clues to our past.
Times: Open daily (ex 25 Dec). Oct-Mar 10-last tour 4pm; Apr-Jun & Sep 10-last tour 4.30pm; Jul-Aug 9.30-last tour 5pm. Evenings: Jul-Aug (Mon-Thu) 6-9.30.
Fee: Daytime: £4.75 (ch 4-15 £3) Family £14.30. Ghost evening tour: £5.50 (ch £3.75) Family £17.
P toilets for disabled shop (ex guide dogs)

Torre Abbey Historic House & Gallery
The Kings Dr TQ2 5JE (on Torquay seafront, next to Riviera Centre)
☎ 01803 293593 01803 215948
e-mail: michael.rhodes@torbay.gov.uk

The Abbey was founded in 1196 as a monastery and later adapted as a country house. It contains mementoes of crime writer Agatha Christie, paintings, sculpture, antiques, and Torquay terracotta pottery. The medieval monastic remains, which include the great barn, guest hall, gatehouse and undercrofts, are the most complete in Devon and Cornwall.
Times: Open daily Apr-1 Nov, 9.30-6. (Last admission 5pm).
Fee: £3 (ch 15 £1.50, under 8 free, pen & students £2.50). Family ticket £7.25.
P (100 yds) shop (ex guide dogs)

TOTNES
Bowden House Ghostly Tales & The British Photographic Museum
TQ9 7PW
☎ 01803 863664

Parts of the house date back as far as the 12th century, but most of it was built in 1510 by John Giles, supposedly the wealthiest man in Devon. The Grand Hall is decorated in neo-Classical Baroque style, and the Great Hall is adorned with 18th-and 19th-century

weaponry. The museum has a large collection of vintage cameras, a replica Victorian studio, Edwardian darkroom, shops, and the Les Allen movie pioneer display. Ghostly Tales Tours are at 2, 3 and 4 o'clock.
Times: Open Etr-end Sep from noon. Bowden House & Museum Mon-Fri.
Fee: £4.95 (ch 9-13 £3.40, ch 6-8 £2.20, ch 2-5 £1).
(museum only suitable) toilets for disabled shop

Guildhall
Rampart Walk, off High St TQ9 5QH (behind St Mary's Church on the main street)
☎ 01803 862147 01803 864275
e-mail: totnestowncouncil@talk21.com

Originally the refectory, kitchens, brewery and bakery for the Benedictine Priory of Totnes (1088-1536), the building was established as the Guildhall in 1553 during the reign of Edward VI. A magistrates court and a prison opened in 1624, and the council chamber is still used today.
Times: Open Apr-Oct, Mon-Fri 10.30-1 & 2-4; Other times by appointment.
Fee: £1 (ch 50p).
P (50 yds) shop

Totnes Castle
TQ9 5NU (on hill overlooking town)
☎ 01803 864406

A classic example of the Norman motte-and-bailey castle, Totnes dates from the 11th, 13th and 14th centuries. The circular shell-keep, protected by a curtain wall, gives marvellous views.
Times: Open all year, Apr-Sep, daily 10-6 (Oct 10-5); Nov-Mar, Wed-Sun 10-4, (closed 1-2). Closed 24-26 Dec & 1 Jan.
Fee: £1.60 (ch 5-15 80p, under 5' free)
P (70yds)

Totnes Museum
70 Fore St TQ9 5RU (town centre)
☎ 01803 863821
Times: Open Etr-30 Oct, Mon-Fri & BHs 10.30-5, Sat group bookings only.
P (440yds) Personal guided tours available shop (ex small dogs) *Details not confirmed for 2001*

UFFCULME
Coldharbour Mill Working Wool Museum
Coldharbour Mill EX15 3EE (2m from M5 J27, off B3181. Follow signs to Willand, then brown signs to Working Wool Museum)
☎ 01884 840960 01884 840858
e-mail: info@coldharbourmill.org.uk

Originally an important centre for the wool trade, the Culm Valley now has only one working woollen mill. This was built as a grist mill in 1753, but was converted to a wool mill in 1797 by a Somerset woollen manufacturer, Thomas Fox. The mill closed in 1981 but was reopened as a Working Wool Museum. There are

contd.

displays of machinery and artefacts connected with the wool trade, plus a weaver's cottage, and dye and carpenters' workshops.

Times: Open Apr-Oct, daily 10.30-5. Last tour 4pm. Nov-Mar, Mon-Fri (please telephone for times).

Fee: £5.50 (ch 5-16 £2.50). Family ticket £15. Party 20+.

P ✕ licensed ♿ (helpful guides) toilets for disabled shop (ex guide dogs)

YEALMPTON

NATIONAL SHIRE HORSE CENTRE

PL8 2EL (On A379, Plymouth to Kingsbridge)

☎ **01752 880268** 📠 **01752 881014**

Times: Open 1 May-31 Sep.

P ☕ ✕ licensed ♿ toilets for disabled shop *Details not confirmed for 2001*

YELVERTON

YELVERTON PAPERWEIGHT CENTRE

4 Buckland Ter, Leg O'Mutton PL20 6AD (off A386, Plymouth to Tavistock road at Yelverton)

☎ **01822 854250** 📠 **01822 854250**

e-mail: paperweightcentre@btinternet.com

This unusual centre is the home of the Broughton Collection - a glittering permanent collection of glass paperweights of all sizes and designs. The centre also has an extensive range of modern glass paperweights for sale. Prices range from a few pounds to over £1000. There is also a series of oil and watercolour paintings by talented local artists.

Times: Open Apr-Oct, daily 10-5; 1-24 Dec, daily; Nov & Jan-Mar wknds only or by appointment.

Fee: Free.

P (100yds) ♿ (ramp on request) shop

Dorset

One of England's most picturesque counties, Dorset has such a wealth of history, stunning scenery and coastal attractions on offer that one is spoilt for choice when writing about it, and it seems a shame that so many people simply drive through it on their way somewhere else.

Possibly the county's most famous landmark is the Cerne Abbas giant, a 180-foot high depiction of a naked man with a club, visible for miles around. However, those visiting this important remnant of Dorset's distant past shouldn't pass by Cerna Abbas itself, which contains a centuries-old church, and the remains of a 10th-century Abbey.

Rural Dorset has retained a great deal of the charm and tranquility of England before the Industrial Revolution. All of the market towns in this area (Gillingham, Blandford Forum, Stalbridge, Shaftesbury and Sturminster Newton) are well worth seeing. Shaftesbury is one of England's oldest towns and is the site of an abbey founded by Alfred The Great. The area around these towns, - known as 'Hardy Country', after Thomas Hardy, the 19th-century novelist, - has been designated an Area of Outstanding Natural Beauty, and includes Cranborne Chase, Blackmore Vale and the Dorset Downs.

The major coast resorts, - Weymouth, Poole and Bournemouth - offer a wide range of activities, combined with some beautiful scenery, and yet more of historic interest. The best example of the latter is probably Corfe Castle, which sits on the Isle of Purbeck. The keep was built by the Normans, and the whole thing was completed by 1300. Unfortunately for future generations, the castle was ruined during a Civil War siege.

EVENTS & FESTIVALS

January
1 Annual Bath Race, Poole

May
6-7 Weymouth International Beach Kite Festival
27 Dorset Tour, Vintage & Classic Vehicle Rally, Weymouth
28 Trawler Race & Water Carnival, Weymouth

June
16-22 Fifth Annual Military & Veterans Festival, Weymouth Pavilion Complex, Weymouth Seafront
24 Weymouth Long Distance Swimming Championships
8-10 Wimborne Folk Festival

July
13-15 Weymouth Sailing Regatta, Weymouth Bay
15 Tolpuddle Martyrs Memorial Rally & Festival

August
6, 15, 21, 27 Free International Firework Festival, Weymouth Beach
15 Weymouth Carnival

September
1-7 Weymouth Speed Week, 16th Beaulieu to Weymouth Vintage & Classic Car Rally

Top: Gold Hill

ABBOTSBURY

Abbotsbury Swannery

New Barn Rd DT3 4JG (9m from Weymouth on B3157 coastal road to Bridport)

☎ 01305 871684 & 871858 📠 01305 871092

e-mail: info@abbotsbury-tourism.co.uk

Abbotsbury is the breeding ground of the only managed colonial herd of mute swans. The swans can be seen safely at close quarters, and the site is also home or stopping point for many wild birds. The highlight of the year is the cygnet season, end of May to the end of June, when there may be over 100 nests on site.

Times: Open Etr-Oct, daily 10-6, last admission 5pm.

Fee: £5 (ch £3 & pen £4.70). Family ticket £15.

licensed (wheelchair loan, herb garden for blind) toilets for disabled shop

ATHELHAMPTON

Athelhampton House & Gardens

DT2 7LG (off A35 5m E of Doncaster, Northbrook junct)

☎ 01305 848363 📠 01305 848135

e-mail: pcooke@athelhampton.co.uk

Athelhampton, one of the finest 15th-century houses in England, contains magnificently furnished rooms including The Great Hall of 1485 and the library. The glorious Grade I gardens contain the world-famous topiary pyramids, fountains, and collections of tulips, magnolias, roses, clematis and lilies in season.

Times: Open Mar-Nov, daily 10.30-5. Also Sun in winter. (Closed Sat).

Fee: House & Garden £5.40 (ch £1.50, pen £4.95, student & disabled £3.50), Family ticket £12 (2 adults & 4 children). Garden only £3.80 (ch free).

licensed toilets for disabled shop (ex assistance dogs)

BEAMINSTER

Mapperton Gardens

DT8 3NR (2m SE off A356 & B3163)

☎ 01308 862645 📠 01308 863348

e-mail: office@mapperton.com

Surrounding a manor house dating back to the 16th century are several acres of terraced valley gardens, with specimen trees and shrubs, and formal borders. There are also fountains, grottoes, stone fishponds and an orangery, and the garden offers good views and walks. The Mapperton Courtyard Fair is held annually (in August) with craft demonstrations, stalls, house tours and local displays.

Times: Open Mar-Oct, daily 2-6.

Fee: Gardens £3.50 (ch 5-18 £1.50, under 5 free).

shop (ex guide dogs)

Parnham

DT8 3NA (1m S on A3066)

☎ 01308 862204 📠 01308 863444

This fine Tudor manor house is most famous as the home of John Makepeace and his furniture-making workshop. The workshop is open to visitors, and completed pieces are shown in the house. There are also continuous exhibitions by living designers and craftsmen. Surrounding the house are 14 acres of restored gardens, formal terraces and woodlands.

Times: Open Apr-Oct, Sun, Tue-Thu & BH's 10-5.

Fee: £5 (ch £2, under 5 free)

licensed toilets for disabled shop

BLANDFORD FORUM

Royal Signals Museum

Blandford Camp DT11 8RH (signposted off B3082 Blandford/Wimborne road)

☎ 01258 482248 📠 01258 482084

e-mail: royalsignalssmuseum@army.mod.uk

The Royal Signals Museum depicts the history of military communications, science and technology from the Crimea to the Gulf. As well as displays on all major conflicts involving British forces, there are the stories of the ATS, the Long Range Desert Group, Air Support, Airborne, Para and SAS Signals. For children there are trails and interactivities.

Times: Open Mar-Oct, Mon-Fri 10-5, Sat-Sun 10-4. Closed 10 days over Xmas & New Year

Fee: £4 (ch 5-16 £2, pen £3). Family £9

(ramps & chair lift) toilets for disabled shop (ex guide dogs)

BOURNEMOUTH

Oceanarium

Pier Approach BH2 5AA (from A338 Wessex Way, follow the Oceanarium tourist signs)

☎ 01202 311993 📠 01202 311990

e-mail: oceanarium@reallive.co.uk

A voyage of global discovery during which the visitor visits many of the world's oceans and sees them in an entirely new way. The hidden beauty and drama of underwater life along and beyond these shores will be revealed as never before.

Times: Open all year, daily from 10am. (Closed 25 Dec).

Fee: Telephone for admission charges.

(100mtrs) (wheelchair for hire) toilets for disabled shop (ex guide dogs)

BOVINGTON CAMP

Clouds Hill

BH20 7NQ (4m SW of Bere Regis)

☎ 01929 405616

T E Lawrence *('Lawrence of Arabia')* bought this cottage in 1925 when he was a private in the Tank Corps at Bovington. He would escape here to play records and entertain friends to feasts of baked beans and China tea. Lawrence's sleeping bag, together with other memorabilia. Three rooms only are on show.

Times: Open 2 Apr-29 Oct, Wed-Fri & Sun, also BH Mon, 12-5, or dusk if earlier.

Fee: £2.30.

(Braille guide)

The Tank Museum
BH20 6JG (off A352 or A35, follow brown tank signs from Bere Regis & Wool)
☎ 01929 405096 📠 01929 405360
e-mail: admin@tankmuseum.co.uk

The Tank Museum houses the world's finest international collection of Armoured Fighting Vehicles. Tanks in Action displays are held every Thursday at noon during July-September and every Friday in August. Armoured vehicle rides are available throughout the summer, and various special events take place - please telephone for details.

Times: Open all year, daily 10-5 (Closed from 21-26 Dec).
Fee: £6.90 (ch £4.50, pen £6). Family ticket £18.30. Group rates available.
P ✕ licensed ♿ (wheelchairs available, Braille & audio tours) toilets for disabled shop (ex guide dogs)

BROWNSEA ISLAND

Brownsea Island
BH15 7EE (located in Poole Harbour)
☎ 01202 707744 📠 01202 701635

Visitors to this 250-acre nature reserve managed by the Dorset Trust for Nature Conservation can take advantage of a guided tour. The island is most famous as the site of the first scout camp, held by Lord Baden-Powell in 1907. Scouts and Guides are still the only people allowed to stay here overnight.

Times: Open Apr-1 Oct, daily 10-5 (10-6 Jul & Aug)
Fee: £2.60 (ch £1.30). Family ticket £6.50. Party.
✕ ♿ (Braille guide, 2 selfdrive vehicles- booking advisable) toilets for disabled shop

CANFORD CLIFFS

Compton Acres Gardens
Canford Cliffs Rd BH13 7ES (on B3065, follow brown & white tourist signs)
☎ 01202 700778 📠 01202 707537
e-mail: groups@comptonacres.co.uk

The ten acres of Compton Acres incorporate Japanese, Roman and Italian gardens, rock and water gardens, and heather gardens. There are fine views over Poole Harbour and the Purbeck Hills, and a collection of bronze and marble statuary. Two of the gardens have recently been themed to create an Egyptian Court Garden and a Spanish Water Garden.

Times: Open Mar-Oct, daily 10-6 (last entry 5.15)
Fee: £4.95 (ch £2.45, student & pen £3.95). Party 20+
P ✕ licensed ♿ (level paths and ramps into shops and cafe) toilets for disabled shop garden centre (ex guide & hearing dogs)

CHRISTCHURCH

Christchurch Castle & Norman House
(near Christchurch Priory)

All that remain of the castle buildings are a ruined keep and an interesting, well preserved Norman house, believed to have been the home of the castle constable.

Times: Open any reasonable time.
Fee: Free.
#

Red House Museum & Gardens
Quay Rd BH23 1BU
☎ 01202 482860 📠 01202 481924

Times: Open all year, Tue-Sat 10-5.30, Sun 2-5.30 (Closed Mon ex BH).
P (200yds) ♿ shop *Details not confirmed for 2001*

CORFE CASTLE

Corfe Castle
BH20 5EZ (on A351)
☎ 01929 481294
e-mail: wcfgen@smpt.ntrust.org.uk

Built in Norman times, the castle was added to by King John. It was defended during the Civil War by Lady Bankes, who surrendered after a stout resistance. Parliament ordered the demolition of the castle, and today it is one of the most impressive ruins in England. Ring for details of special events.

Times: Open daily: 5-25 Mar 10-4.30; 26 Mar-29 Oct 10-5.30; 30 Oct-3 Mar 11-3.30. (Closed 25-26 Dec & 2 days end of Jan).
Fee: £4 (ch £2). Family ticket £10 (2 adults & 3 ch) or £6 (1 adult & 3 ch). Party.
P (charged) ✕ licensed (Braille guide & menu) shop

Corfe Castle Museum
West St BH20 5HE
☎ 01929 480415

The tiny, rectangular building was partly rebuilt in brick after a fire in 1780, and is the smallest town hall building in England. It has old village relics, and dinosaur footprints 130 million years old. A council chamber on the first floor is reached by a staircase at one end. The Ancient Order of Marblers meets here each Shrove Tuesday.

Times: Open all year, Apr-Oct, daily 9.30-6; Nov-Mar, wknds and Xmas holidays 10-5.
Fee: Free.
P (200 yds) ♿ toilets for disabled

DORCHESTER

Dinosaur Museum
Icen Way DT1 1EW (In centre of town, just off main High East St)
☎ 01305 269880 📠 01305 268885

Britain's only museum devoted to dinosaurs has an appealing mixture of fossils, skeletons, life-size reconstructions and interactive displays such as the 'feelies'. There are audio-visual presentations, and the idea is to provide an all-round family attraction with new displays each year.

Times: Open all year, daily 9.30-5.30 (10-4.30 Nov-Mar). (Closed 24-26 Dec).
Fee: £4.25 (ch £2.95, pen & student £3.50, under 4's free). Family ticket £11.95.
P (50yds) ♿ (Many low level displays) shop 

Dorset County Museum

High West St DT1 1XA
☎ 01305 262735 📠 01305 257180
e-mail: dorsetcountymuseum@dor-mus.demon.co.uk

Displays cover prehistoric and Roman times, including sites such as Maiden Castle, and there's a gallery on Dorset writers with sections on the poet William Barnes, Thomas Hardy (with a reconstruction of his study), and twentieth century writers.

Times: Open May-Oct, daily 10-5. (Closed Sun Nov-Apr, Good Fri & 25 Dec).
Fee: £3.30 (concessions £2.20, ch £1.60) . Family ticket £8.20.
P (150 yds) ♿ shop (ex guide dogs)

Hardy's Cottage

Higher Bockhampton DT2 8QJ (3m NE of Dorchester, 0.5m S of A35)
☎ 01305 262366

Thomas Hardy was born in this thatched house in 1840. It was built by his great-grandfather and has not changed much in appearance since. The inside can only be seen by appointment with the tenant.

Times: Open 2 Apr-Oct daily execpt Fri & Sat, 11-5 or dusk if earlier. Open Good Fri.
Fee: £2.60.
P ♿ (car parking by arrangement with custodian)

Maiden Castle

DT1 9PR (2m S, access off A354, N of bypass)

The Iron Age fort ranks among the finest in Britain. It covers 47 acres, and has daunting earthworks, with a complicated defensive system around the entrances. One of its main purposes may well have been to protect grain from marauding bands. The first single-rampart fort dates from around around 700BC and by 100BC the earthworks covered the whole plateau. It was finally overrun by Roman troops in AD43.

Times: Open any reasonable time.
Fee: Free.
P #

The Military Museum of Devon & Dorset

The Keep, Birdport Rd DT1 1RN (near the top of High West St)
☎ 01305 264066 📠 01305 250373

Three hundred years of military history, with displays on the Devon Regiment, Dorset Regiment, Dorset Militia and Volunteers, the Queen's Own Dorset Yeomanry, and Devonshire and Dorset Regiment (from 1958). The Museum uses modern technology and creative displays to tell the stories of the Infantry, Cavalry and Artillerymen.

Times: Open all year, Mon-Sat 9-5 (also in Jul & Aug Sun 10-4). (Closed Xmas & New Year).
Fee: £3 (ch, student & pen £2). Family ticket £9
P ♿ (lift avalible to 3 floors) toilets for disabled shop (ex guide dogs)

Teddy Bear House

Antelope Walk, Cornhill DT1 1BE (in the centre of Dorchester near Tourist Information Centre)
☎ 01305 263200 📠 01305 268885

A visit to Teddy Bear House is in fact a visit to the home of Mr Edward Bear and his large family of human-sized teddy bears! Join the bears as they relax around the house. Below in the large cellars is the new Dorset Teddy Bear Museum which displays hundreds of bears in atmospheric and evocative settings. The shop contains hundreds of teddy bears of all kinds.

Times: Open daily 9.30-5. (Closed 25-26 Dec)
Fee: £2.95 (ch £1.50, under 4's free). Family £7.95.
P (500 metres) shop (ex guide dogs)

Tutankhamun Exhibition

High West St DT1 1UW (In centre of town)
☎ 01305 269571 📠 01305 268885

The exhibition recreates the excitement of one of the world's greatest discoveries of ancient treasure. A reconstruction of the tomb and facsimiles of its contents are displayed. The superbly preserved mummified body of the boy king can be seen, wonderfully recreated in every detail. Special exhibitions include `The Jewels of Tutankhamun', `The Discovery of the Tomb of Tutankhamun' and `The Curse of Tutankhamun'.

Times: Open daily, 9.30-5.30; Nov-Mar 9.30-5, wknds 10-4.30. (Closed 24-26 Dec).
Fee: £4.25 (ch £2.95, pen & student £3.50, under 5's free). Family ticket £11.95.
P (200yds) ♿ shop (ex guide dogs)

MINTERNE MAGNA

Minterne Gardens

DT2 7AU (2m N of Cerne Abbas on A352 Dorchester-Sherbourn road)
☎ 01300 341370 📠 01300 341747

Lakes, cascades, streams and many fine and rare trees will be found in these lovely landscaped gardens. The 18th-century design is a superb setting for the spring shows of rhododendrons, azaleas and spring bulbs, and the autumn colour.

Times: Open 28 Mar-10 Nov, daily 10-7.
Fee: £3 (accompanied ch free).
P (ex on lead)

POOLE

Poole Pottery

The Quay BH15 1RF (head towards Poole Town Centre, follow signs for Poole Quay, situated on the front)
☎ 01202 666200 📠 01202 682894

Founded in 1873, this well-known company has been producing its distinctive Poole Pottery since 1921. There is a display of past and present pottery manufacture, factory tour and shop.

Times: Open all year factory tours, daily 10-4. (Closed 22 Dec-2 Jan). Shop open 9-5 (out of season), 9-5.30 & later (in season). Telephone for details.
Fee: Factory tours £2.50 (ch & pen £1.50). Party 10+.
P (100 yds) licensed (wheelchairs available, ask a member of staff) toilets for disabled shop (ex guide dogs)

WATERFRONT MUSEUM & SCAPLEN'S COURT
4 High St BH15 1BW (off Poole quay)
☎ 01202 683138 01202 660896
e-mail: c.fisher@poole.gov.uk

The museum tells the story of Poole's seafaring past. Learn of the Roman occupation, hear the smuggler tell his tale and see material raised from the Studland Bay wreck. Scaplen's Court, just a few yards from the museum, is a beautifully restored domestic building dating from the medieval period. There is a Victorian school room, a kitchen and scullery.
Times: Museum: open Apr-Oct, Mon-Sat 10-5, Sun noon-5; Nov-Mar, Mon-Sat 10-3, Sun noon-3. Scaplen's Court: Aug, Mon-Sat 10-5, Sun noon-5.
P (250meters) (ex Town Cellars & Scaplen's Court) toilets for disabled (ex guide dogs) *Details not confirmed for 2001*

PORTLAND

PORTLAND CASTLE
Castleton DT5 1AZ (overlooking Portland harbour)
☎ 01305 820539

One of the best preserved of Henry VIII's coastal forts, built of white Portland stone and originally intended to thwart attack by the Spanish and French. The castle was much fought over in the Civil War.
Times: Open Apr-Sep, daily 10-6 (Oct 10-5).
Fee: £2.90 (ch 5-15 £1.50, under 5's free). Personal stereo tour included in admission.
P shop

PORTLAND MUSEUM
217 Wakeham DT5 1HS (A354, through Fortuneswell to Portland Heights hotel, then English Heritage signs)
☎ 01305 821804 01305 761654
e-mail: tourism@weymouth.gov.uk

Avice's cottage in Thomas Hardy's book *'The Well-Beloved'*, this building is now a museum of local and historical interest, with varied displays. Regular temporary exhibitions are held. The adjoining Marie Stopes cottage houses the shop and a display of maritime history.
Times: Open: Etr-Oct, Fri-Tue (ex school holidays when open everyday), 10.30-5 (Closed 1-1.30 everyday).
Fee: £1.80 (ch & students free, pen £1).

SHAFTESBURY

SHAFTESBURY ABBEY MUSEUM & GARDEN
Park Walk SP7 8JR
☎ 01747 852910 01747 852910

The Abbey at Shaftesbury was part of a nunnery founded by King Alfred in 888. It became one of the wealthiest in the country but was destroyed during the Dissolution in 1539. The excavated ruins show the foundations of the abbey church. A museum on the site displays carved stones, decorated floor tiles and other artefacts found during the excavations and information panels tell the story of the life of the Abbey.
Times: Open Apr-Oct, daily, 10am-5pm.
Fee: £1.50 (ch 60p, pen & concessions £1).
P (250yds) toilets for disabled shop

SHERBORNE

SHERBORNE CASTLE
New Rd DT9 5NR (off A30, 0.5m E of Sherborne)
☎ 01935 813182 01935 816727
e-mail: enquires@sherbornecastle.com

This 16th-century house, built by Sir Walter Raleigh, has been the home of the Digby family since 1617. Built beside the ruins of the old castle, the house contains fine furniture, paintings and porcelain; and the grounds were designed by 'Capability' Brown in the 18th century. Ring for details of special events.
Times: Open Apr-Oct. Castle open Tue, Thu, Sat, Sun & BH Mon 12.30-5 (last admission 4.30). Gandens, shop & tea room open Thu-Tue 12.30-5 (last admission 4.30).
Fee: £5 (ch £2.50, pen £4.50). Family ticket £12.50. Grounds only £2.50 (ch £1.25). Party 15+.
P shop (ex guide dogs & in garden) 

Sherborne Museum

Abbey Gate House, Church Ln DT9 3BP
☎ 01935 812252

The museum features a model of Sherborne's original Norman castle, as well as a fine Victorian doll's house and other domestic and agricultural bygones. There are also items of local geological, natural history and archeological interest, including Roman material.

Times: Open Apr-Oct, Tue-Sat 10.30-4.30, Sun 2.30-4.30; BH Mon 2.30-4.30
Fee: £1 (ch & students free)
P (400yds) ♿ toilets for disabled shop (ex guide dogs)

Sherborne Old Castle

Castleton D19 3SA (0.5m E off B3145)
☎ 01935 812730

The 12th-century castle was built by Roger, Bishop of Salisbury. In Elizabethan times it belonged to Sir Walter Raleigh, but was largely destroyed by Cromwell in the Civil War. The ruined Norman buildings remain.

Times: Open Apr-Sep, daily 10-6 (Oct 10-5); Nov-Mar, Wed-Sun 10-4, (closed 1-2pm).
Fee: £1.60 (ch 5-15 80p, under 5's free)
P ♿

SWANAGE

Swanage Railway

Station House BH19 1HB (Park & ride Station at Norden, signposted from A351)
☎ 01929 425800 📠 01929 426680

The railway from Swanage to Wareham was closed in 1972, and in 1976 the Swanage Railway took possession and have gradually restored the line, which now runs for 6 miles, passing the ruins of Corfe Castle. Ring for details of special events.

Times: Open every weekend throughout the year, daily Apr-Oct.
Fee: Swanage-Corfe £5.50 return, £3 single. Swanage-Norden £6 return, £3.60 single. (ch 5-15 & pen 50% reduction in price). Family ticket £17. Day Rover £10 (ch & pen £5).
P licensed ♿ (special disabled persons coach) toilets for disabled shop (shop at Swanage Station)

TOLPUDDLE

Tolpuddle Martyrs Museum

DT2 7EH (on A35, 7m E of Dorchester, 4.5m W of Bere Regis)
☎ 01305 848237 📠 01305 848237

Times: Open all year, Apr-Oct, Tue-Sat 10-5.30, Sun 11-5.30; Nov-Mar, Tue-Sat 10-4, Sun 11-4. Open BH Mon. (Closed 24 Dec-1 Jan).
P (outside museum) ♿ toilets for disabled shop *Details not confirmed for 2001*

WEST LULWORTH

Lulworth Castle

BH20 5QS (from Wareham, W on A352 for 1 mile, left onto B3070 to E Lulworth, follow tourist signs)
☎ 01929 400352 📠 01929 400563
e-mail: paul@lulworth.com

Glimpse life below stairs in the restored kitchen, and enjoy beautiful views from the top of the tower of this historic castle set in beautiful parkland. The 18th-century chapel is reputed to be the first Catholic chapel built in England after the Reformation. Children will enjoy the animal farm and play area.

Times: Open 26 Mar-29 Oct, 10-6; 30 Oct-26 Mar 10-4, daily (ex Sat). Closed 24-25 Dec. Lulworth Castle House open Apr-Sep, Wed 1-4.30.
Fee: Free.
P ♿ (limited in castle due to grade one listing) toilets for disabled shop

Lulworth Cove Heritage Centre

Lulworth Cove BH20 5RQ (From A352 to Wool, then onto B3071 and follow brown signs)
☎ 01929 400587

Times: Open daily Nov-Mar 10-4; Apr-Oct 10-6 (Closed 25 Dec)
P (charged) ♿ toilets for disabled shop *Details not confirmed for 2001*

WEYMOUTH

Deep Sea Adventure & Sharky's Play Area

9 Custom House Quay, Old Harbour DT4 8BG
☎ 01305 760690 📠 01305 760690

A fascinating attraction telling the story of underwater exploration and marine exploits. Discover the history of Weymouth's Old Harbour, compelling tales of shipwreck survival, explore the Black Hole and search for Ollie the Oyster. Also a unique display telling the gripping tale of the *Titanic* disaster. Sharky's Play Area is four floors of fun-packed adventure where children can jump, swing, slide and climb in a safe padded play area. Separate toddler area for the under fives.

Times: Open all year, daily 9.30-7 (high season 9.30-9). Closed 24-26 Dec.
Fee: Sharky's Play Area: Adults free (ch £2.75). Deep Sea Adventure: £3.75 (ch 5-15 £2.75, pen/student £3.25). Family ticket £11.95. Combined ticket for both attractions, ch £4.75.
P (100yds) licensed ♿ (lift & sign language for deaf) toilets for disabled shop (ex guide dogs)

RSPB Nature Reserve Radipole Lake
The Swannery Car Park DT4 7TZ (within the town, close to seafront & railway station)
☎ 01305 778313 🖷 01305 778313

Covering 222 acres, the Reserve offers firm paths, hide and a visitor centre. Several types of warblers, mute swans, gadwalls, teals and great crested grebes may be seen, and the visitor centre has viewing windows overlooking the lake. Phone for details of special events.
Times: Open daily 9-5
P (concessions for members from centre) ♿ shop

Sea Life Park
Lodmoor Country Park DT4 7SX (on A353)
☎ 01305 788255 🖷 01305 760165

Set in the beautiful Lodmoor Country Park. Marvel at the mysteries of the deep and discover amazing sea creatures from around our own shores in spectacular marine displays.
Times: Open all year, daily from 10am. (Closed 25 Dec).
Fee: £5.95 (ch & pen £3.95)
P (charged) ♿ toilets for disabled shop

WIMBORNE

Kingston Lacy House, Garden & Park
BH21 4EA (1.5m W of Wimborne B3082)
☎ 01202 883402 (Mon-Fri) & 842913 (wknds) 🖷 01202 882402

Kingston Lacy House was the home of the Bankes family for over 300 years. The original house is 17th century, but in the 1830s was given a stone façade. The Italian marble staircase, Venetian ceiling, treasures from Spain and an Egyptian obelisk were also added. There are outstanding pictures by Titian, Rubens, Velasquez, Reynolds and Van Dyck. No photography is allowed in the house.
Times: Garden & Park; Apr-29 Oct daily ex 18 Aug 11-6; Nov & Dec open Fri-Sun 11-4. House; Apr-29 Oct daily ex Thu & Fri 12-5.30. Last admission 4.30pm.
Fee: £6 (ch £3). Family ticket £15. Park & Gardens only: £2.50 (ch £1.25). Party 15+
P licensed ♿ (parking by arrangement) toilets for disabled shop (ex on leads in park & wood)

Knoll Gardens & Nursery
Stapehill Rd, Hampreston BH21 7ND (3m E between Wimborne and Ferndown off A31, at Canford Bottom rdbt, into B3073 Ham Lane)
☎ 01202 873931 🖷 01202 870842
e-mail: enquiries@knollgardens.co.uk

Over 6000 plant species from all over the world thrive here, within a six-acre site. There are water gardens with waterfalls, pools and a stream, herbaceous borders, and many other features. A wide range of plants, mainly propagated in the Nursery, can be bought here, and there is a tearoom and visitor centre with shops.
Times: Open Mar, Oct & Nov Wed-Sun 10-4.30; Apr-Sep daily 10-5; Jan & Feb wknds 10-4 (or dusk if earlier).
Fee: £3.75 (ch 5-15 £1.80, student £2.75, pen £3.25). Party 15+.
P licensed ♿ toilets for disabled shop garden centre (ex guide dogs)

Priest's House Museum and Garden
23-27 High St BH21 1HR
☎ 01202 882533 🖷 01202 882533

An award-winning local history museum, set in an historic house with a Victorian kitchen where regular cooking demonstrations are held (fourth Saturday of the month, 2pm-5pm). There are nine other rooms to see, along with regular special exhibitions, and a beautiful 300ft-long walled garden.
Times: Open Apr-Oct, Mon-Sat, 10.30-5. Also every Sun 2-5 Jun-Sep. Special Christmas season.
Fee: £2.20 (ch £1, pen & students £1.75). Family ticket £5.50. Season ticket £5.50.
P (200 yds) ♿ (hands on archaeology gallery, audio tapes) shop

Stapehill Abbey
Wimborne Rd West BH21 2EB (2.5m E of Wimborne, off A31)
☎ 01202 861686 🖷 01202 894589

This early 19th-century abbey, home for nearly 200 years to Cistercian nuns, is now a busy working crafts centre with many attractions under cover. There are award-winning landscaped gardens, parkland and picnic spots, and the Power to the Land exhibition. Telephone for details of special events.
Times: Open Etr-Sep, daily 10-5; Oct-Etr Wed-Sun 10-4. (Closed 22 Dec-2 Feb).
Fee: £7 (ch 4-16 £4.50, students & pen £6.50). Family ticket (2 adults & 2 ch) £18.50.
P ♿ toilets for disabled shop garden centre (ex guide dogs)

Top: Durham Castle

County Durham

The Durham Dales lie between the Northumberland National Park and the Yorkshire Dales, and form around a third of the county's area. This huge expanse of waterfalls, meadows, heath and river valleys contains some beautiful scenery.

There are two record-breaking geographic features in the area, which should make an afternoon's ramble more interesting. One is the road from Killhope to Nenthead in Cumbria, which rises to over 2,000 feet, making it the highest classified road in England. The other is the waterfall at High Force, where the River Tees falls 70 feet onto rocks, making it the highest waterfall in England.

The history of the area is as rich as the scenery. In the middle ages the Prince Bishops ruled the County Palatine with a unique blend of political and ecclesiastic power. This power extended into Northumberland and Yorkshire, and provided the first line of defence against the marauding Scots. These unusual figures maintained their own armies, had their own courts and nobility, and minted their own coins. Essentially they were the rulers of virtually independant states. The best expression of this dual worldly and heavenly power is Durham's own cathedral, once described as "Half Church of God, half Castle 'gainst the Scot."

In the 19th century the area around Weardale was the centre of the world lead-mining industry. The industry has long since disappeared, and the 34-foot waterwheel and mine at the Killhope Lead Mining Centre are among the few reminders that this massive undertaking ever took place.

EVENTS & FESTIVALS

May
4-6 Teesdale Thrash - concerts, ceilidhs, music sessions and morris dancing in Barnard Castle

June
8-9 Durham Regatta, River Wear, Durham (provisional)
tbc Morgan Car Meet, Beamish, North of England Open Air Museum

July
7-8 Summer Festival, Durham city centre
tbc Durham County Show, Lambton Park, nr Chester-le-Street

August
26-27 Durham Light Infantry Vehicle Rally, DLI Museum & Durham Art Gallery
25-26 Weardale Agricultural Show, Showfield, St John's Chapel
11-18 Billingham International Folklore Festival, Billingham, Stockton-on-Tees

September
1-2 Wolsingham & Wear Valley Agricultural Show
8-9 Stanhope Agricultural Show & Country Fair

December
1-2 Victorian Christmas Festival, Durham city centre

BARNARD CASTLE

Barnard Castle

DL12 8NP
☎ 01833 638212

The town's name comes from Bernard Baliol, who built the castle in 1125. The impressive ruins cling to the steep banks of the River Tees.

Times: Open all year, Apr-Sep 10-6 (Oct 10-5); Nov-Mar, Wed-Sun 10-4. Closed 1-2pm & 24-26 Dec & 1 Jan)
Fee: £2.30 (ch £1.20, under 5's free) P ♿ shop ⌗

The Bowes Museum

DL12 8NP (on outskirts of town)
☎ 01833 690606 📠 01833 637163

This splendid château-style mansion was built in 1869 by John Bowes, who made his fortune in Durham coal and married a French actress. They amassed an outstanding collection of works of art, and built the flamboyant château to house them. The museum contains paintings by El Greco, Goya and Canaletto among others; porcelain and silver, furniture, ceramics and tapestries.

Times: Open daily 11-5.
Fee: £3.90 (concessions £2.90). Family ticket £12.
P ☕ ♿ (lift, ramped entrance, reserved parking) toilets for disabled shop ✗ (ex guide dogs) 💳

Egglestone Abbey

DL12 8QN (1m S on minor road off B6277)

The remains of this Premonstratensian abbey make a picturesque sight on the bank of the River Tees. A large part of the church can be seen, as can remnants of monastic buildings.

Times: Open any reasonable time. **Fee:** Free. P ♿ ⌗

BEAMISH

Beamish, The North of England Open-Air Museum

DH9 0RG (off A693 & A6076 signed off A1(M) junc 63)
☎ 01207 231811 📠 01207 290933
e-mail: museum@beamish.org.uk

Set in 200 acres of countryside, Beamish recreates a 20th-century Northern town complete with shops, dentist's surgery, pub and sweet factory. Various exhibits show how pitmen and their families lived. Other aspects of this period museum include a Methodist chapel, a school and a farmyard.

Times: Open all year: Summer, Apr-end Oct, daily from 10am. Winter visits centred on The Town & tramway, other areas closed, Nov-Mar from 10am but closed Mon & Fri. Closing times vary according to season it is advisable to check. Also check for Christmas times.
Fee: Summer £10 (ch £6, pen £7). Winter £3 (ch £3, pen £3).
P ☕ ♿ (free admission for essential helpers) toilets for disabled shop 💳

BISHOP AUCKLAND

Auckland Castle

DL14 7NR
☎ 01388 601627 📠 01388 605264
e-mail: auckland.castle@zetnet.co.uk

Serving as the principal county residence of the Prince Bishops since the 12th century, Auckland Castle is now the home of the Bishop of Durham. Built on a promontory overlooking the River Wear and the Roman Fort of Binchester, the Castle has been added to and adapted over the centuries. St Peter's Chapel houses many of the treasures of past Bishops.

Times: Open May-16 Jul & Sep, Fri, Sun & BH Mon 2-5: 17 Jul-Aug daily ex Sat, 2-5. **Fee:** £3 (ch & over 60's £2)
P ♿ toilets for disabled shop ✗ (ex guide dogs)

BOWES

Bowes Castle

DL12 9LD (on A66)

Built inside the earthworks of the Roman fort of `Lavatrae', the castle dates from the 12th century and its great ruined Norman keep still stands to a height of three storeys.

Times: Open any reasonable time. **Fee:** Free. 🚫🚗 ⌗

COWSHILL

Killhope Lead Mining Centre

DL13 1AR (beside A689 midway between Stanhope & Alston)
☎ 01388 537505 📠 01388 537617
e-mail: killhope@durham.gov.uk

Times: Open Apr-Oct, daily 10.30-5. Last entry 4.30pm. Nov, Sun 10.30-4.
P ☕ ♿ toilets for disabled shop *Details not confirmed for 2001* 💳

DARLINGTON

Darlington Railway Centre & Museum

North Rd Station DL3 6ST (0.75m N off A167)
☎ 01325 460532

Times: Open daily 10-5 (closed Jan); Last admission 4.30pm. May be subject to amendment.
P ☕ ♿ (guide tape for visually handicapped) toilets for disabled shop ✗ (ex guide dogs) *Details not confirmed for 2001*

DURHAM

Durham Cathedral

DH1 3EH (A1(M) to Durham turn off at A690 into city take turning into the market place & follow signs)
☎ 0191 386 4266 🖷 0191 386 4267
e-mail: enquiries@durhamcathedral.co.uk

Founded in 1093 as a shrine to St Cuthbert, whose bones still rest in the Feretory. The cathedral is a remarkable example of Norman architecture, set in an impressive position high above the River Wear. St Cuthbert's Day Procession (phone for details).

Times: Open daily, 27 May-Sep 9.30-8. Oct-7 Apr, Mon- Sat, 9.30-6, (Sun 12.30-5). Cathedral is closed to visitors during evening recitals & concerts.
Fee: £2.50 Donation requested.
P (in city centre) (very poor parking) licensed (braille guide touch & hearing centre) toilets for disabled shop (ex guide dogs)

Durham Light Infantry Museum & Durham Art Gallery

Aykley Heads DH1 5TU (0.5m NW, turn right off A691)
☎ 0191 384 2214 🖷 0191 386 1770

Times: Open all year, Tue-Sat 10-4.30 & Sun 2-4.30 (Closed Mon, ex BHs).
P (wheelchair available, lift, ramps) toilets for disabled shop *Details not confirmed for 2001*

Finchale Priory

Brasside, Newton Hall DH1 5SH (3m NE)
☎ 0191 386 3828

This lovely setting was the refuge chosen by St Godric in 1110 for his years of solitary meditation, and the priory, used by monks from Durham Cathedral, was founded in 1180. Remains of the 13th-century church can be seen.

Times: Open Apr-Sep, daily 10-6 (Oct 10-5).
Fee: £1.30 (ch 5-15 70p, under 5's free) P (charged) #

Oriental Museum

University of Durham, Elvet Hill DH1 3TH (signposted from A167 & A177)
☎ 0191 374 7911 🖷 0191 374 7911
e-mail: oriental.museum@durham.ac.uk

The museum has a remarkable collection of Oriental artefacts, ranging from Ancient Egypt to Japan.

Times: Open Mon-Fri 10-5, wknds 12-5. (Closed Xmas-New Year).
Fee: £1.50 (ch, pen & students 75p) P shop

HARTLEPOOL

Hartlepool Historic Quay

Maritime Av TS24 0XZ (from A19 take A179 and follow signs for marina then historic quay)
☎ 01429 860077 🖷 01429 867332

Times: Open daily 10-5 (10-7 in summer). Closed 25 Dec & 1 Jan.
P licensed (all areas ramped or lift access) toilets for disabled shop *Details not confirmed for 2001*

HMS Trincomalee

Jackson Dock TS24 0SQ (From A19 take A689 or A179, follow signs for Hartlepool Historic Quay)
☎ 01429 223193 🖷 01429 864385
e-mail: office@hms-trincomalee.co.uk

HMS *Trincomalee*, launched in 1817, is the oldest British warship afloat, undergoing magnificent resoration by skilled local craftsmen.

Times: Open all year, Summer: 10-4, Winter: 11-3. Closed Fri in winter, Xmas & New Year (inc Boxing day).
Fee: £3.75 (ch, students & disabled £2, pen & unemployed £2.75. Family ticket (2 adults & 3 ch) £10.50. Group & seasonal tickets available. P

Museum of Hartlepool

Jackson Dock, Maritime Av TS24 0XZ (Historic Quay & Museum towards the Marina)
☎ 01429 860077 🖷 01429 523477

This museum tells the story of Hartlepool from prehistory to the present day and includes many original artefacts, models, computer interactives and hands-on exhibits. See how iron and steel ships were built and climb aboard the Humber ferry *Wingfield Castle*, a paddle steamer built in Hartlepool in 1934.

Times: Open all year, daily (closed 25-26 Dec & 1 Jan).
Fee: £4.95 (ch £2.50, under 5's free) Family ticket (2 adults & 3 ch)
P toilets for disabled shop (ex guide dogs)

STAINDROP

Raby Castle

P O Box 50 DL2 3AH (1m N, off A688)
☎ 01833 660202 🖷 01833 660169
e-mail: rabyestate@rabycastle.com

The castle was built during Saxon times but is substantially 14th century, with many later additions. It has an impressive gateway; nine towers; a vast medieval hall; and a splendid restored Victorian octagonal drawing-room which has re-emerged as one of the most striking interiors from the 19th century.

Times: Open May & Sep, Wed & Sun only. Jun-Aug, Sun-Fri. Castle open 1-5. Park & gardens 11-5.30, (last admission 4.30pm).
Fee: Castle, Gardens & Carriage Collection £5 (ch £2 & pen £4). Family ticket (2 adults & 3 ch) £12. Park, Gardens & Carriage Collection £3 (ch & pen £2). Party 20+.
P toilets for disabled shop (ex in Park)

TANFIELD

Tanfield Railway

Old Marley Hill NE16 5ET (on A6076 1m S of Sunniside)
☎ 0191 388 7545 🖷 0191 387 4784
e-mail: tanfield@ingsoc.demon.co.uk

Times: Open all year, summer daily 10-5; winter daily 10-4. Trains: Sun & Summer BH's weekends; also Thu & Sat mid Jul-Aug. Santa's Specials Sat & Sun in Dec (booking essential).
P (all trains carry ramps for wheelchair access) toilets for disabled shop *Details not confirmed for 2001*

Essex

Essex and its inhabitants have for some time been the butt of jokes that imply financial acuity but a lack of taste, discernment and sophistication. This might be due to the county's proximity to London, which has led to the development of commuter towns and changed the nature of an area once rural to something suburban.

However, moving northeast into East Anglia there are some fine country towns and villages, and, approaching the Suffolk border, all the scenic delights of Constable country around the Stour Valley.

The big resorts of Southend and Clacton are the best known on the Essex coast, but by contrast there are pretty places on the Tendring Peninsula, the sailing centres of Burnham-on-Crouch and Maldon, the marshy headland of the Naze, and the birdlife of Maplin Sands.

From medieval times to the 18th century, Saffron Walden was the centre of the saffron crocus industry. It was saffron wealth that bought the town the largest parish church in Essex, and the streets around the church reflect this historic prosperity.

Colchester lays claim to being England's oldest town, and is a fascinating place to visit. There is evidence of a settlement from the fifth century BC, and the town was King Cymbeline's capital in the first century AD. The Romans also made it their capital in 43 AD and the town prospered despite being burnt by Boudicca/Boadicea in 60 AD. The Roman walls are largely intact, and there are the remains of the Norman castle to be seen.

EVENTS & FESTIVALS

May
20 Essex Young Farmers Show, Essex County Showground, Great Leighs
tbc Southend Airshow
tbc Tour de Tendring Cycle Ride, Tendring

June
2-3 Thaxted Morris Ring Meet (various venues), annual meeting of morris men
15-17 Essex County Show, Essex County Showground, Great Leighs

July
tbc Tendring Hundred Show, Lawford
8 Clacton Classic Vehicle Show, West Road Car Park, Clacton

August
23-24 Clacton Air Show, Clacton Seafront
tbc Clacton Jazz Festival
tbc Southend Water Festival
tbc Clacton Carnival

September
8 Clacton Sci-fi Convention, Town Hall, Clacton
tbc Maldon Town Regatta
tbc Old Leigh Regatta

Top: Middle Street, Clavering

AUDLEY END

Audley End House & Gardens

CB11 4JF (1m W of Saffron Walden on B1383)

☎ 01799 522399

Built on a grandiose scale by Thomas Howard, Earl of Suffolk, to entertain King James I, Audley End House was gradually reduced in size over the next century, but what we see today is still impressive in scale and the 30 rooms open to the public display a stunning collection of art, as well as period furnishings. Gardens and a landscaped park surround the mansion.

Times: Open Apr-Sep, Wed-Sun & BH's 11-6 (or dusk if earlier). Park and gardens open from 10am. Last admissions 5pm.

Fee: £6.50 (ch 5-15 £3.30 under 5's free). Grounds £3 (ch £1.80, concessions £2.70)

P (charged) shop

BRAINTREE

The Working Silk Mill

New Mills, South St CM7 3GB (follow brown tourist signs)

☎ 01376 553393 01376 330642

The Working Silk Museum is the country's last remaining handloom. Silk weavers using 150 year old handlooms. Full production can be seen from processing the raw silk to the finished cloth.

Times: Open Mon-Fri, 10-12.30 & 1.30-5. Last admission to mill 12 noon and 4pm.

Fee: £3.30 (ch £1.75, pen/students £2.10). Family ticket £8.90. Party.

P (ramps) toilets for disabled shop (ex guide dogs)

CASTLE HEDINGHAM

Colne Valley Railway & Museum

Castle Hedingham Station CO9 3DZ (4m NW of Halstead on A1017)

☎ 01787 461174

The old Colne Valley and Halstead railway buildings have been rebuilt here. Stock includes seven steam locomotives plus sixty other engines, carriages and wagons, in steam from Easter to December. Visitors can dine in style in restored Pullman carriages while travelling along the line.

Times: Open all year, daily 10-dusk. Steam days, rides from 12-4. (Closed 23 Dec-1 Feb). Steam days every Sun and BH from Mothering Sunday to end Oct, Tue-Thu of school summer holidays & special events. Phone 01787 461174 for timetable information.

Fee: Steam days £6 (ch £3 pen £5); Family ticket £15. Non-steam days (to view static exhibits only) £3 (ch £1.50); Family ticket £7.50.

P licensed (ramps for wheelchairs to get onto carriages) shop (ex guide dogs)

Hedingham Castle

CO9 3DJ (on B1058, 1m off A1017 Colchester/Cambridge. Follow brown tourist signs)

☎ 01787 460261 01787 461473

e-mail: hedinghamcastle@aspects.net

This impressive Norman castle was built in 1140. It was besieged by King John, and visited by Henry VII, Henry VIII and Elizabeth I, and was home to the de Veres, Earls of Oxford, for over 500 years. Please telephone for details civil ceremony weddings and special events.

Times: Open wk before Etr-Oct, daily 10-5.

Fee: £3.50 (ch £2.50). Family ticket £10.50.

P shop (ex in grounds)

COGGESHALL

Paycocke's

West St CO6 1NS (Signposted from A120, on S side of West Street)

☎ 01376 561305

This timber-framed house is a fine example of a medieval merchant's home. It was completed in about 1505 and has interesting carvings on the outside timbers, including the Paycocke trade sign. Inside there are further elaborate carvings and linenfold panelling. Behind the house is a pretty garden.

Times: Open 2 Apr-15 Oct Tue, Thu, Sun & BH Mon 2-5.30.

Fee: £2.20, joint ticket with Coggeshall Grange Barn £3.

P (400yds)

COLCHESTER

Beth Chatto Gardens

Elmstead Market CO7 7DB (5m E of Colchester on A133)

☎ 01206 822007 01206 825933

Begun almost 40 years ago, when Beth Chatto and her late husband began working on acres of wasteland. Today this has become a garden of three distinctive areas. The south-west facing dry garden is on gravel, and has plants such as yucca and pineapple broom. It faces a group of oaks which shade the second area, with woodland and other shade-loving plants. Lastly,

there is the wetland garden, with five large pools filled with fish and surrounded by swathes of bog plants.
Times: Open all year, Mar-Oct, Mon-Sat 9-5; Nov-Feb, Mon-Fri 9-4. (Closed BHs & Sun). **Fee:** £3 (accompanied ch under 14 free)
(access to parts of garden may be difficult) toilets for disabled garden centre

COLCHESTER CASTLE MUSEUM
Castle Park, High St CO1 1TJ (at E end of the High St)
01206 282931 & 282932 01206 282925

The largest Norman castle keep in Europe - built over the remains of the magnificent Roman Temple of Claudius which was destroyed by Boudicca in AD60. Colchester was the first capital of Roman Britain, and the archaeological collections are among the finest in the country.
Times: Open all year, Mon-Sat 10-5, Sun (from Mar) 1-5 & (from Jun) 11-5.
Fee: £3.80 (ch & concessions £3.50). Family ticket (2 adults & 2 ch or 1 adult & 3 ch) £10.20.
P (town centre) (ramps to all areas & lift) toilets for disabled shop

COLCHESTER ZOO
Stanway, Maldon Rd CO3 5SL (S of Colchester from A12)
01206 331292 01206 331392
e-mail: colchester.zoo@btinternet.com

One of England's finest zoos, Colchester zoo has over two hundred types of animals. Visitors can meet the elephants, handle a snake, and see parrots, seals, penguins and birds of prey. New enclosures include Spirit of Africa, Elephant Kingdom, Penguin Shores, the Wilds of Asia for orangutans, and Chimp World. There is also an undercover soft play complex, road train, four adventure play areas, eating places and gift shops.
Times: Open all year, daily from 9.30. Last admission 5.30pm (1hr before dusk out of season). (Closed 25 Dec).
Fee: £8.50 (ch 3-13 & pen £5.50, disabled £3.50).
licensed toilets for disabled shop

HADLEIGH

HADLEIGH CASTLE
(0.75m S of A13)
01536 402840

The subject of several of Constable's paintings, the castle has fine views of the Thames estuary. It is defended by ditches on three sides, and the north-east and south-east towers are still impressive.
Times: Open any reasonable time. **Fee:** Free.
#

HARLOW

HARLOW MUSEUM
Passmores House, Third Av CM18 6YL
01279 454959 01279 626094

Harlow is best known as a new town, but the museum tells its story from Prehistoric and Roman to modern times, with a section on the Harlow Potters and the New Town. It is housed in an early Georgian building set in gardens. Part of the medieval moat from an earlier house can be seen.
Times: Open all year, Tue-Fri 9.30-4.30 & Sat 10-12.30 & 1.30-4.30. Last admission 4.15pm.
Fee: Free. shop

HARWICH

HARWICH REDOUBT FORT
CO12 3TE (behind 29 Main Rd)
01255 503429
e-mail: theharwichsociety@quista.net

The 180ft-diameter circular fort was built in 1808 in case of invasion by Napoleon. It has a dry moat and 8ft-thick walls, with 18 rooms for stores, ammunition and quarters for 300 men. The Redoubt is being restored by the Harwich Society, and contains three small museums. Ten guns can be seen on the battlements.
Times: Open May-Aug, daily 10-5; Sep-Apr, Sun only 10-5.
Fee: £1 (accompanied ch free).
P (200yds) shop

HEDINGHAM

See Castle Hedingham

LAYER MARNEY

LAYER MARNEY TOWER
CO5 9US (off B1022 Colchester to Maldon road, signposted)
01206 330784 01206 330784
e-mail: nicholas@layermarvey.demon.co.uk

The tallest Tudor gatehouse in the country, intended to be the entrance to a courtyard which would have rivalled Hampton Court Palace. The death of Henry, 1st Lord Marney in 1523, and of his son in 1525, meant that the building work ceased before completion. The parish church of St Mary the Virgin in the grounds contains fine Italianate terracotta. The Tower may be climbed, for stunning views of the surrounding countryside.
Times: Open Apr-Sep, Mon-Fri 12-5, Sun 12-5 & BHs 11-5.
Fee: £3.50 (ch £2). Family ticket £10. Guided tour £4.75. Party 20+.
(ramps in garden and farm) toilets for disabled shop (ex guide dogs)

MISTLEY

MISTLEY TOWERS
CO11 1NJ (on B1352, 1.5m E of A137 at Lawford)

All that remains of the grand hall and church, designed by Robert Adam, are the lodges built in 1782 for the hall, and two square towers, topped with drums and domes which came from an earlier church.
Times: Open all reasonable times. Key available from Mistley Quay Workshops & Teashop.
Fee: Free.
(exterior only) (in certain areas) #

NEWPORT

MOLE HALL WILDLIFE PARK

Widdington CB11 3SS (between Stansted & Saffron Walden, off B1383)

☎ 01799 540400 01799 540400

e-mail: enquires@molehall.co.uk

Times: Open all year, daily 10.30-6 (or dusk). (Closed 25 Dec). Butterfly House open mid Mar-Oct.

(Difficult in wet weather for wheelchairs) toilets for disabled shop garden centre (ex guide dogs) *Details not confirmed for 2001*

SAFFRON WALDEN

SAFFRON WALDEN MUSEUM

Museum St CB10 1JL (take B184 & follow signs to Saffron Walden)

☎ 01799 510333 01799 510334

e-mail: museum@uttesford.gov.uk

Built in 1834, this friendly museum lies near the castle ruins in the centre of town. Its collections include local archaeology, natural history, ceramics, glass, costume, furniture, toys, an ancient Egyptian room, a new natural history gallery and Discovery Centre. This museum has won awards for disabled access.

Times: Open all year, Mar-Oct, Mon-Sat 10-5, Sun & BHs 2-5; Nov-Feb, Mon-Sat, 10-4.30, Sun & BHs 2-4.30. (Closed 24 & 25 Dec).

Fee: £1 (concessions 50p & ch under 18 free).

(ramped entrance,spare wheelchairs,stairlift to upper floor) toilets for disabled shop (ex guide dogs)

SOUTHEND-ON-SEA

CENTRAL MUSEUM & PLANETARIUM

Victoria Av SS2 6EW (take A127 or A13 towards town centre, museum adjacent to Southend Victoria Railway Station)

☎ 01702 215640 & 215131 01702 215631

Times: Open - Central Museum Tue-Sat 10-5 (Closed Sun-Mon & BH); Planetarium Wed-Sat, shows at 11, 2 & 4.

(0.50m) (disabled only behind museum) (planetarium not accessible) shop *Details not confirmed for 2001*

STANSTED

HOUSE ON THE HILL MUSEUM ADVENTURE

CM24 8SP (off B1383)

☎ 01279 813237 01279 816391

e-mail: gold@enta.net

A large, privately-owned toy museum, housed on two floors covering 7,000 sq. ft. A huge variety of toys, books and games from the late Victorian period up to the 1970s. There is a train room, space display, Teddy Bears' picnic, Action Men, Sindy, Barbie, military displays and much more.

Times: Open daily, 10-5; (closed for a few days over the Xmas period)

Fee: £3.50 (ch under 14's £2.50 & student £3.20). Party 15+.

(charged) shop (ex guide dogs)

MOUNTFITCHET CASTLE & NORMAN VILLAGE

CM24 8SP (off B1383, in centre of village)

☎ 01279 813237 01279 816391

e-mail: gold@enta.net

Norman motte and bailey castle and village reconstructed as it was in Norman England of 1066, on its original historic site. A vivid illustration of village life in Domesday England, complete with houses, church, seige tower, seige weapons, and many types of animals roaming freely. Animated wax figures in all the buildings give historical information to visitors.

Times: Open daily, 11 Mar-11 Nov, 10-5.

Fee: £4.50 (ch under 14's £3.50, pen £4). Party 15+.

(charged) (laser commentaries) toilets for disabled shop (ex guide dogs)

TILBURY

TILBURY FORT

No 2 Office Block, The Fort RM18 7NR (0.5m E off A126)

☎ 01375 858489

The largest English example of 17th-century military engineering, the fort originally dates from the earlier Tudor period, and is most famous for Queen Elizabeth I's review of her troops before the defeat of the Spanish Armada. It defended the country again in the 17th century against the Dutch and the French.

Times: Open all year, Apr-Sep, daily 10-6 (Oct 10-5); Nov-Mar, Wed-Sun 10-4. Closed 24-26 Dec & 1 Jan.

Fee: £2.60 (ch 5-15 £1.30, under 5's free). Personal stereo tours included in admission price.

shop (in certain areas)

WALTHAM ABBEY

LEE VALLEY PARK FARMS

Stubbings Hall Ln, Crooked Mile EN9 2EG (off B194)

☎ 01992 892781 & 892291 01992 893113

Two different views of farming methods. Hayes Hill Farm has a traditional-style farmyard and you can also look round Holyfield Hall Farm, a working commercial dairy and arable farm of some 700 acres. There are 140 Friesian cows, and milking takes place at 2.45pm every day. Booked guided tours are available.

Times: Open all year, Mon-Fri 10-4.30, wknds & BH 10-5.30pm.

Fee: £3 (concessions £2).

(graded concrete paths, signed routes) toilets for disabled shop

WALTHAM ABBEY GATEHOUSE, BRIDGE & ENTRANCE TO CLOISTERS

Beside the great Norman church at Waltham are the slight remains of the abbey buildings - bridge, gatehouse and part of the north cloister. The bridge is named after King Harold, founder of the abbey.

Times: Open any reasonable time. **Fee:** Free.

Gloucestershire

Most of the Cotswolds lie in the county of Gloucestershire; limestone hills dotted with picturesque villages built from the local stone, varying in hue from honey gold to silver grey. The large churches and substantial manor houses are a legacy from the wealth of the medieval wool trade.

The bits of Gloucestershire outside the Cotswolds include the county town of Gloucester, the Regency spa town of Cheltenham and the countryside around the Severn estuary, the site of the Slimbridge wildfowl reserve. The county's other major natural feature is the Forest of Dean, a mining area from Roman times until the 20th century.

In redbrick Gloucester there is plenty to see and do. The Victorian docks have been redeveloped to provide offices, shops, cafés and museums, while the canal, opened in 1827 in an attempt to reverse the decline of trade via the Severn, is busy now with pleasure craft.

Nearby Cheltenham is rather more upmarket with its elegant Regency architecture and exclusive boutiques. The mineral spring was discovered there in 1715 through the observation of pigeons coming and going. Pigeons are incorporated into the town's crest to this day, though Cheltenham is probably better known for its horse-racing.

South of Cheltenham is the charmingly old-fashioned and rather less self-conscious Cirencester, the 'capital of the Cotswolds'. It was once an immensely powerful town known as Corinium by the Romans, and in those days second only to Londinium. However, little of its Roman heritage remains.

EVENTS & FESTIVALS

May
28 Coopers Hill Cheese Roll tbc
Badminton Horse Trials

June
1 Robert Dover's Cotswold Olympic Games, Chipping Campden
15 Jun-2 July Cirencester Festival of Music & the Arts
22 Jun-14 Jul Longborough Festival Opera
tbc Winchcombe Carnival Parade & Party in the Park

July
tbc The Cotswold Country Fair, Cirencester Park
tbc International Kite Festival, Tewksbury
tbc Tewkesbury Medieval Festival

August
tbc Three Choirs Festival, Gloucester Cathedral

September
1 Moreton Show, Moreton-in-Marsh
tbc The Malvern Autumn Show, Three Counties Showground, Malvern

October
tbc Cheltenham Festival of Literature

Top: Gloucester Cathedral

BARNSLEY

Barnsley House Garden

GL7 5EE (3m NE of Cirencester on B4425 Barnsley House is on right on entering village)

☎ 01285 740561 🖷 01285 740628

e-mail: cverey@barnsleyhouse.freeserve.co.uk

Home of renowned plantswoman, gardener and author Rosemary Verey. A lovely garden, with herb and knot garden, and a vegetable garden planted as a French 'potager orné', here small paths form a chequerboard around fruit trees trained as pyramids, ornamental brassicas and other decorative kitchen plants. Other features include a laburnum walk and a lime walk.

Times: Open all year, Mon, Wed, Thu & Sat 10-5.30; Parties & guided tours by appointment only. (Closed Xmas-end Jan). House not open.

Fee: £3.75 (ch free, pen £3).

P ♿ shop garden centre

BERKELEY

Berkeley Castle

GL13 9BQ (on B4509 1.5m W of A38)

☎ 01453 810332

Home of the Berkeleys for almost 850 years, the castle is a rambling great place surrounded by 14ft thick walls, with a Norman keep, a great hall, medieval kitchens, and the dungeon where Edward II was murdered gruesomely. Outside there are Elizabethan terraced gardens and an extensive park.

Times: Open: Tue-Sun, 2-5 Apr-May. Tue-Sat 11-5, Sun 2-5, Jun & Sep. Mon-Sat 11-5, Sun 2-5 Jul & Aug. Sun only 2-5 Oct. BH Mon 11-5.

Fee: Castle & Gardens: £5.40 (ch £2.90, pen £4.40). Gardens only £2 (ch £1). Party 25+

P shop

Jenner Museum

Church Ln, High St GL13 9BH (follow tourist signs from A38 to town centre, turn left into High St & left again into Church Ln)

☎ 01453 810631 🖷 01453 811690

e-mail: jennermuseum@berkeley19.freeserve.co.uk

This beautiful Georgian house was the home of Edward Jenner, the discoverer of vaccination against smallpox. The house and the garden, with its Temple of Vaccinia, are much as they were in Jenner's day. The displays record Jenner's life as an 18th-century country doctor, his work on vaccination and his interest in natural history.

Times: Open Apr-Sep, Tue-Sat 12.30-5.30, Sun 1-5.30. Oct, Sun 1-5.30. (Closed Mon, ex BH Mon 12.30-5.30).

Fee: £2.50 (ch £1, students & pen £1.70). Family ticket £6.50. Party 20+.

P ♿ (level wide access, hand rails) toilets for disabled shop (ex guide dogs)

BOURTON-ON-THE-WATER

Birdland Park & Gardens

Risssington Rd GL54 2BN (on A429)

☎ 01451 820480 🖷 01451 822398

e-mail: sb.birdland@virgin.net

Set in seven acres of natural woodland, landscaped gardens, lakes and waterways, Birdland is home to over 500 birds from around the world. Attractions/Facilities include: Tropical, temperate and desert houses; cafe; disabled access throughout; picnic areas; children's play area; gift shop. Dogs are admitted on leads.

Times: Open all year, Apr-Oct, daily 10-6; Nov-Mar, daily 10-4. Last admission 1hr before closing. (Closed 25 Dec).

Fee: £4.25 (ch 4-14 £2.50, pen £3.25). Party 10+.

P (adjacent) ♿ toilets for disabled shop

Model Village

Old New Inn GL54 2AF

☎ 01451 820467 🖷 01451 810236

e-mail: old_new_inn@compuserve.com

The model is built of Cotswold stone to a scale of one-ninth, and is a perfect replica of the village. It includes a miniature River Windrush, a working model waterwheel, churches and shops, with tiny trees, shrubs and alpine plants.

Times: Open all year 9-6.30 (summer), 10-dusk (winter). (Closed 25 Dec).

Fee: £2.50 (ch £1.75, pen £2).

P licensed shop

CHEDWORTH

Chedworth Roman Villa

Yanworth GL54 3LJ (3m NW of Fossebridge on A429)

☎ 01242 890256 🖷 01242 890544

e-mail: chedworth@smtp.ntrust.org.uk

The remains of a Romano-British villa, excavated 1864-66. Set in a beautiful wooded combe, there are fine 4th-century mosaics, two bath houses, and a temple with spring. The museum houses the smaller finds and there is a 9-minute video programme. Telephone for further details of special events.

Times: Open 2 May-Sep, Tue-Sun & BH Mon 10-5; Mar-Apr & 4 Oct-mid Nov, Wed-Sun & Etr Mon 11-4.

Fee: £3.60. Family ticket £9.

P ♿ (Braile guide & audio tour) toilets for disabled shop

CHELTENHAM

Art Gallery & Museum

Clarence St GL50 3JT (close to town centre and bus station)

☎ 01242 237431 🖷 01242 262334

e-mail: artgallery@cheltenham.gov.uk

The museum has an outstanding collection relating to the Arts and Crafts Movement, including fine furniture and exquisite metalwork. The Art Gallery contains Dutch and British paintings from the 17th century to the present day. The Oriental Gallery features pottery, costumes and treasures from the Ming Dynasty to the reign of the last Chinese Emperor. There is also a

display about Edward Wilson who journeyed with Captain Scott in 1911-12.
Times: Open all year, Mon-Sat 10-5.20. (Closed BHs).
Fee: Free.
P (500 metres) ☕ ♿ (handling tables; speech reinforcement system) toilets for disabled shop 🐕 (ex guide dogs)

HOLST BIRTHPLACE MUSEUM

4 Clarence Rd, Pittville GL52 3JE (just off Evesham Rd)
☎ 01242 524846 📠 01242 262334
e-mail: artgallery@cheltenham.gov.uk

Times: Open Tue-Sat 10-4.20 (Closed Mon & BHs). From Apr 2000, please telephone for opening details.
P (100 yds) shop 🐕 (ex guide dogs) *Details not confirmed for 2001*

CIRENCESTER

CORINIUM MUSEUM

Park St GL7 2BX (in centre of Cirencester)
☎ 01285 655611 📠 01285 643286
e-mail: simone.clark@cotswold.gov.uk

Cirencester was the second largest town in Roman Britain and the Corinium Museum brings the period to life with full-scale reconstructions. There's a Cotswold Prehistory gallery, a Medieval Cotswolds gallery, and galleries on Roman military history, the Roman town of Corinium, and the Civil War in the Cotswolds.
Times: Open all year, Mon-Sat 10-5, Sun 2-5. Also open BHs. (Closed Xmas).
Fee: £2.50 (ch 80p, students £1, pen £2). Family ticket £5. Party. Fri after 3.30pm free admission.
P (440yds town centre) ☕ ✖ licensed ♿ (Braille guide for exhibits) toilets for disabled shop 💳

CLEARWELL

CLEARWELL CAVES ANCIENT IRON MINES

GL16 8JR (1.5m S of Coleford town centre, off B4228)
☎ 01594 832535 📠 01594 833362
e-mail: jw@clearwellcaves.com

The mines have been worked since the Iron Age, and the industry grew under the Romans. Over half a million tons of ore were extracted in the 19th century, and mining continues today. Nine large caverns can be explored, with deeper trips for the more adventurous. There are engine rooms, a blacksmith's shop, and exhibits of local mining and geology.

Times: Open Mar-Oct daily 10-5. Jan-Feb Sat-Sun 10-5. Christmas Fantasy 1-24 Dec, daily 10-5.
Fee: £3.50 (ch £2.20, concessions £3)
P ☕ ♿ ("Hands-on" exhibits, contact in advance) toilets for disabled shop 🐕 (ex guide & hearing dogs) 💳

CRANHAM

PRINKNASH ABBEY AND POTTERY

GL4 8EX (on A46 between Cheltenham & Stroud)
☎ 01452 812066 📠 01452 812529
e-mail: bjnicholls@prinknash.fsnet.co.uk

Set in a large park, the old priory building is a 12th to 16th-century house, used by Benedictine monks and guests of Gloucester Abbey until 1539. It became an abbey for Benedictine monks from Caldey in 1928. Rich beds of clay were discovered when foundations were being dug for the new abbey building, and so the pottery was established, employing local craftspeople.

Times: Open all year. Abbey Church: daily 5am-8pm. Pottery: Mon-Sat 11-4.30 (Sun pm). Pottery shop & tearoom 9-5.30. (Closed Good Fri, 25 & 26 Dec).
Fee: Guided tour fee £2 (ch £1) Family ticket £5.
P ☕ ♿ toilets for disabled shop

Prinknash Bird & Deer Park

GL4 8EX (M5 junct 11a, A417 Cirencester. Take 1st exit signposted A46 Stroud. Follow brown tourist signs)
☎ 01452 812727

Nine acres of parkland and lakes make a beautiful home for black swans, geese and other water birds. There are also exotic birds such as white and Indian blue peacocks and crown cranes, as well as tame fallow deer and pygmy goats. The Golden Wood is stocked with ornamental pheasants, and leads to the reputedly haunted monks' fishpond, which contains trout. An 80-year old, free-standing, 16ft tall Wendy House in the style of a Tudor house has recently been erected near the picnic area.
Times: Open all year, daily 10-5 (4pm in winter). Park closes at 6pm (5pm in winter). (Closed 25-26 Dec, 1 Jan & Good Fri).
Fee: £3.40 (ch £1.80, pen £2.40). Party 10+. Prices under review.
P shop

DEERHURST

Odda's Chapel

(off B4213 near River Severn at Abbots Court SW of parish church)

This rare Saxon chapel was built by Earl Odda and dedicated in 1056. When it was discovered, it had been incorporated into a farmhouse. It has now been carefully restored.
Times: Open any reasonable time.
Fee: Free.
#

DYRHAM

Dyrham Park

SN14 8ER (8m N of Bath)
☎ 0117 937 2501
e-mail: wdycjc@smtp.ntrust.org.uk

Dyrham Park is a splendid William and Mary house, with interiors which have hardly altered since the late 17th century. It has contemporary Dutch-style furnishings, Dutch pictures and blue-and-white Delft ware. Around the house is an ancient park with fallow deer.
Times: Open - House: 1 Apr-29 Oct; daily ex Wed & Thu, 12-5.30. Garden open same as house except 11-5.30 or dusk if earlier. Park open all year daily 12-5.30 or dusk if earlier, opens 11 when garden opens. Winter: domestic rooms open 4 Nov-17 Dec, Sat & Sun 12-4. Closed Xmas day. Property closed 7, 8 & 9 of Jul for concerts.
Fee: £7.50 (ch £3.70) Family £18.50. Grounds only £2.60 (ch £1.20) Family £6.50. Park only ticket on days when house & gardens closed: £1.80 (ch 90p). Winter: park & domestic rooms £3.80 (£1.90 ch). Party
P ✕ licensed ♿ (Braille & audio guides, stairclimber, free bus from carpark toilets for disabled shop (ex in dog walk area).

GLOUCESTER

City Museum & Art Gallery

Brunswick Rd GL1 1HP
☎ 01452 524131 01452 410898
Times: Open all year, Mon-Sat 10-5. (Also Jul-Sep, Sun 10-4).
P (adjacent) ♿ (lift suitable only for manual wheelchairs) toilets for disabled shop *Details not confirmed for 2001*

Folk Museum

99-103 Westgate St GL1 2PG
☎ 01452 526467 01452 330495
e-mail: irenez@gloscity.gov.uk
Times: Open all year, Mon-Sat 10-5. (Also Jul-Sep, Sun 10-4). Open BH Mon.
P (200yds) ♿ (parking on request, ramps) shop (ex guide dogs)
Details not confirmed for 2001

National Waterways Museum

Llanthony Warehouse, The Docks GL1 2EH (follow signs for historic docks off M5 and also within the city, situated to the south of the city)
☎ 01452 318054 01452 318066
e-mail: info@nwm.demon.co.uk

Based in Gloucester Docks, this museum takes up three floors of a seven-storey Victorian warehouse, and documents the 200-year history of Britain's water-based transport. The emphasis is on hands-on experience, including working models and engines, interactive displays, actual craft, computer interactions and the national collection of inland waterways.
Times: Open all year, daily 10-5 (Closed 25 Dec).
Fee: £4.75 (ch & pen £3.75). Family tickets £11-£13.
P (charged) ♿ (wheelchair, lifts, limited access to floating exhibits) toilets for disabled shop (ex guide dogs)

Nature in Art

Wallsworth Hall, Tewkesbury Rd, Twigworth GL2 9PA (on A38, from village follow tourist signs)
☎ 01452 731422 01452 730937
e-mail: ninart@globalnet.co.uk

Nature is the theme at this gallery, and there are many outstanding exhibits including sculpture, tapestries and ceramics. There is a comprehensive `artist in residence' programme for ten months of the year, and events include regular monthly talks, film showings and a full programme of temporary exhibitions and art courses.
Times: Open all year, Tue-Sun & BH's 10-5. Mon by arrangement. (Closed 24-26 Dec).
Fee: £3.10 (ch, pen & students £2.40, ch under 8 free). Family ticket £9.50. Party 15+
P ♿ (lift & ramps at entrance) toilets for disabled shop (ex guide dogs)

Robert Opie Collection-Museum of Advertising & Packaging

Albert Warehouse, Gloucester Docks GL1 2EH (follow signs for 'Historic Docks')

☎ 01452 302309 01452 308507

e-mail: sales@robertopie.telme.com

Robert Opie has been collecting old and new advertisements, packs, comics, newspapers, games, toys and other artefacts of our everyday life for the past 37 years, and is still adding to this remarkable collection almost on a daily basis. It forms the country's only Museum of Advertising and Packaging.

Times: Open all year, daily, 10-6; winter Tue-Fri 10-5, Sat & Sun 10-6. (Closed 25-26 Dec).

Fee: £3.50 (ch £1.25, pen & students £2.30). Party 10+.

P (charged) shop (ex guide dogs)

GREAT WITCOMBE

Witcombe Roman Villa

(off A417, 0.5m S of reservoir in Witcombe Park)

Several mosaic pavements and evidence of a hypocaust have been preserved in the remains of this large Roman villa.

Times: Open any reasonable time. Guided tours may be available contact 01451 862000.

Fee: Free.

P #

GUITING POWER

Cotswold Farm Park

GL54 5UG (signposted off B4077 from M5 junct 9)

☎ 01451 850307 01451 850423

At the Cotswold Farm Park there are nearly 50 breeding flocks and herds of the rarest British breeds of sheep, cattle, pigs, goats, horses, poultry and waterfowl. Set on the very top of the Cotswold Hills, this is the perfect opportunity to get to know a Bagot goat, cuddle a Cotswold lamb, stroke a mighty Longhorn ox, and admire generations of our living agricultural heritage. New born lambs and goat kids can be seen from April to May, spring calves in May, foals and sheep shearing in June and piglets throughout the year.

Times: Open Apr-1 Oct, daily 10.30-5. (10.30-6, Sun, BH)

Fee: £4.50 (ch £2.30, pen £4). Family ticket £12.

P (ramps, wheelchair to let) toilets for disabled shop (only guide dogs inside)

HAILES

Hailes Abbey

(2m NE of Winchcobme off B4632)

☎ 01242 602398

This Cistercian abbey was, in the Middle Ages, one of the main centres of pilgrimage in England because it possessed a phial reputed to contain some of Christ's blood. Good medieval sculpture and floor tiles are displayed in the museum.

Times: Open Apr-Sep, daily 10-6; Oct, daily 10-5; Nov-Mar, Sat & Sun 10-4. (Closed 24-26 Dec & 1 Jan).

Fee: £2.60 (ch £1.30 & concessions £2).

P shop #

LITTLEDEAN

Littledean Hall

GL14 3NR

☎ 01594 824213 01594 824213

The largest known Roman temple in rural Britain was unearthed here in 1984 and the manor itself is Norman. The house has always been lived in, and has been relatively untouched since the 19th century. Inside there are interpretive displays and the grounds offer beautiful walks. There are fish pools in the walled garden, and, of course, the Roman excavations.

Times: Open - House, Grounds & Archaeological site, Apr-Oct, daily 11-5.

Fee: £3.50 (ch £1.50, pen £2.50)

P (ex in grounds)

LYDNEY

Dean Forest Railway

Norchard Railway Centre, New Mills, Forest Rd GL15 4ET (1m N of Lydney-Parkend Rd, on B4234, signed from A48)

☎ 01594 845840 & (843423 recorded info)

01594 845840

e-mail: mike@cornick.8.freeserve.co.uk

Just north of Lydney lies the headquarters of the Dean Forest Railway where a number of steam locomotives, plus lots of coaches, wagons and railway equipment are on show and guided tours are available by prior arrangement. Standard gauge passenger service Norchard to Lydney Junction.

Times: Open all year, daily for static displays. Steam days: Sun from Etr-Oct; Wed & Sat, Jun-Aug (Aug also open Tue & Thu). Lydney Road & Rail show 3rd Sun in Oct. Santa special Dec (Additional days & school holidays telephone 01594 843423 for details).

Fee: No entry fee on non passenger opening days. Fares on standard Steam days £4.20 (ch 5-16 £2.20 & pen £3.20, under 5's free on standard days only). Various fares during Special events.

P (specially adapted coach for wheelchairs) toilets for disabled shop

MICKLETON

Hidcote Manor Garden

Chipping Campden GL55 6LR (1m E of B4632)

☎ 01386 438333 01386 438817

One of the most delightful gardens in England, created by the horticulturist Major Laurence Johnston and comprising a series of small gardens within the whole, separated by walls and hedges of different species.

Times: Open, Gardens only 1 Apr-Sep, daily (ex Tue & Fri) 11-7; also open Tue in Jun & July only 11-7; Oct-1 Nov, daily (ex Tue & Fri) 11-6. Last admission 1hr before closing.

Fee: £5.60.(ch £2.80) Family ticket £14. Parties by prior written arrangement.

P licensed (limited due to stone paths) toilets for disabled shop garden centre

Kiftsgate Court Garden

Mickleton GL55 6LW (0.5m S off A46, adjacent Hidcote NT garden)

☎ 01386 438777 📠 01386 438777

e-mail: kiftsgte@aol.com

Kiftsgate Garden is spectacularly set on the edge of the Cotswold Escarpment, with views over the Vale of Evesham. It contains many rare plants collected by three generations of women gardeners, including the largest rose in England, the R. Filipes Kiftsgate.

Times: Open Apr-May & Aug-Sep; Wed, Thu, Sun & BH Mon 2-6. Jun-Jul Wed, Thu, Sat & Sun 12-6.

Fee: £4 (ch £1)

P ☕ garden centre 🐕 (ex guide dogs)

MORETON-IN-MARSH

Batsford Arboretum

Admissions Centre, Batsford Park GL56 9QB (1.5m NW, off A44 from Moreton-in-Marsh)

☎ 01386 701441 📠 01386 701827

e-mail: batsarb@batsfound.freeserve.co.uk

One of the largest private collections of woody plants in Great Britain. Of particular note are the oaks, maples, magnolias and cherries. Many other rare and unusual trees, shrubs and bamboos also feature. Spring is a procession of colour with masses of naturalised bulbs, particularly daffodils and narcissi, followed by magnolias and cherries. Autumn is equally impressive, with the fiery oranges and reds of the Japanese maples.

Times: Open Feb (wknds only); Mar-mid Nov daily, 10-5.

Fee: £3.30 (ch under 16 free, pen £3). Party 12+.

P ☕ ♿ (some steep & slippery paths not suited to wheelchairs) toilets for disabled shop garden centre

Cotswold Falconry Centre

Batsford Park GL56 9QB (1m W of Moreton-in-Marsh on A44)

☎ 01386 701043

Conveniently located by the Batsford Park Arboretum, the Cotswold Falconry gives daily demonstrations in the art of falconry. The emphasis here is on breeding and conservation, and eagles, hawks, owls and falcons can be seen.

Times: Open Mar-Nov, 10.30-5.30. (Last admission 5pm).

Fee: £3.50 (ch 4-15 £1.50). Joint ticket with Batsford Arboretum £5.50.

P ♿ (no steps, wide doorways) toilets for disabled shop garden centre 🐕 (ex on leads in car park) 🎫

Sezincote

GL56 9AW (1.5m out of Moreton-in-Marsh on A44 Evesham road)

The Indian-style house at Sezincote was the inspiration for Brighton Pavilion; its charming water garden adds to its exotic aura and features trees of unusual size.

Times: Open: House, May-Jul & Sep, Thu & Fri 2.30-6. Garden only, all year (ex Dec) Thu, Fri & BH Mon 2-6 or dusk if earlier.

Fee: House & garden £4.50. Garden only £3 (ch £1 under 5 free). Children not allowed in the House. Groups by appointment only.

P 🐕 (ex guide dogs in garden)

NEWENT

The National Birds of Prey Centre

GL18 1JJ (1m SW on unclass Clifford's Mesne Road follow brown tourist signs)

☎ 01531 820286 & 821581 📠 01531 821389

e-mail: jpj@nbpc.demon.co.uk

Trained birds can be seen at close quarters in the Hawk Walk and the Owl Courtyard and there are also breeding aviaries, a gift shop, bookshop, picnic areas, coffee shop and children's play area. Birds are flown three times daily in Summer and Winter, giving an exciting and educational display. There are over 110 aviaries on view with 85 species. The centre leads the world in the field of captive breeding.

Times: Open Feb-Nov, daily 10.30-5.30 or dusk if earlier. Also open in Dec for evening events.

Fee: £5.50 (ch £3.25). Family ticket £15.50. Party 12+.

P ☕ ♿ (special tours available, pre-booking required) toilets for disabled shop 🐕 (inc guide dogs) 🎫

The Shambles

Church St GL18 1PP (close to town centre near church)

☎ 01531 822144 📠 01531 821120

A museum of cobbled streets, alleyways, cottages and houses set in over an acre with display shops and trades, even a tin chapel and cottage garden all helping to recreate the feel and atmosphere of Victorian life.

Times: Open 15 Mar-Xmas, Tue-Sun & BH's 10-5 (or dusk).

Fee: £3.50 (ch £1.95, pen £2.95).

P (100 yds) ☕ ♿ toilets for disabled shop

NORTHLEACH

Cotswold Heritage Centre

Fosseway GL54 3JH (12m E of Cheltenham on A429 at Northleach crossroads)

☎ 01451 860715 01451 860091

e-mail: simone.clark@cotswold.gov.uk

The story of everyday rural life in the Cotswolds is told here, in the remaining buildings of the Northleach House of Correction. There's a unique collection of Gloucestershire harvest-wagons; a `below stairs' gallery showing a dairy, kitchen and laundry; and the work of local craftsmen and artists is promoted through exhibitions, workshops and demonstrations.

Times: Open Apr-Oct, Mon-Sat 10-5, Sun 2-5 & BHs 10-5. Open at other times by prior arrangement.

Fee: £2.50 (ch 80p, pen £2 & student £1). Family ticket £5. Party.

(wheelchair available, parking at entrance) toilets for disabled shop

Keith Harding's World of Mechanical Music

Oak House, High St GL54 3ET (at crossroads of A40 & A429)

☎ 01451 860181 01451 861133

e-mail: keith@mechanicalmusic.co.uk

A fascinating collection of antique clocks, musical boxes, automata and mechanical musical instruments, restored and maintained in the world-famous workshops, displayed in a period setting, and played during regular tours. There is an exhibition of coin operated instruments which visitors can play.

Times: Open all year, daily 10-6. Closed 25-26 Dec.

Fee: £5 (ch 16 £2.50, under 3 free, pen & students £4). Family ticket £12.50. Disabled-helpers Free.

toilets for disabled shop (ex guide dogs)

OWLPEN

Owlpen Manor

GL11 5BZ (3m E of Dursley off B4066, follow brown tourist signs)

☎ 01453 860261 01453 860819

e-mail: sales@owlpen.com

A romantic Tudor manor house, with unique 17th-century painted cloth wallhangings, furniture, pictures and textiles. The house is set in formal terraced gardens, and is part of a picturesque Cotswold manorial group including a Jacobean Court House, a Victorian church and medieval tithe barn.

Times: Open Apr-15 Oct, Tue-Sun & BH Mon, 2-5.

Fee: £4.25 (ch £2). Party 30+

licensed

PAINSWICK

Painswick Rococo Garden

GL6 6TH (on B4073 0.5m NW of Painswick)

☎ 01452 813204 01452 813204

e-mail: painsguard@aol.com

This beautiful Rococo garden (a compromise between formality and informality) is the only one of its period to survive complete. There are ponds, woodland walks, a maze, kitchen garden and herbacious borders, all set in a Cotswold valley famous for snowdrops in the early spring. Ring for details of special events.

Times: Open Jan-Nov, Wed-Sun, 11-5. (Daily May-Sep).

Fee: £3.30 (ch £1.75, pen £3)

licensed shop

SLIMBRIDGE

WWT Slimbridge

GL2 7BT (off A38, signed from M5 junct 13 & 14)

☎ 01453 890333 01453 890827

e-mail: enquiries@wwt.org.uk

Slimbridge is home to the world's largest collection of exotic wildfowl - and the only place in Europe where all six types of flamingo can be seen. Up to 8,000 wild birds winter on the 800-acre reserve of flat fields, marsh and mudflats on the River Severn.

Times: Open all year, daily from 9.30-5.30 (winter 4pm). (Closed 25 Dec).

Fee: £5.75 (ch £3.50). Family ticket £15. Party 10+.

licensed (wheelchair loan, tapes for blind, hearing pads & loops) toilets for disabled shop

SNOWSHILL

Snowshill Manor

WR12 7JU (3m SW of Broadway, off A44)
☎ 01386 852410 01386 852410
e-mail: snowshill@smtp.ntrust.org.uk

A traditional Cotswold manor house, best known for Charles Paget Wade's collections of craftmanship and design, including musical instruments, clocks, toys, bicycles, weavers' and spinners' tools, and Japanese armour.

Times: Open Apr-29 Oct, Wed-Sun & BH Mon (also Mon in Jul-Aug). Gardens 11-5.30; Manor 12-5. Last admission to manor 45 mins before closing.
Fee: £6 (ch £3). Family ticket £15. Grounds only £3 (ch £1.50).
(Braille guides) toilets for disabled shop (ex guide dgos)

SOUDLEY

Dean Heritage Centre

Camp Mill GL14 2UB (on B4227)
☎ 01594 822170 01594 823711
e-mail: deanmuse@btinternet.com

The Centre tells the story of this unique area with museum displays which include a reconstructed cottage, coal mine and waterwheel. There are also nature trails (one of which is level), and picnic areas. Charcoal burning takes place twice a year.

Times: Open all year, daily, Apr-Sep 10-6, Oct-Mar 10-4. (Closed 24-26 Dec).
Fee: £3.30 (ch £2, pen & concessions £2.80). Family ticket £9.50. Under 5's free.
(help from establishment staff) toilets for disabled shop (ex guide dogs)

TETBURY

Chavenage House

GL8 8XP (2m NW of Tetbury signposted off B4014. 1m SE of Stroud off A46)
☎ 01666 502329 & 01453 832700
01453 836778
e-mail: caroline@chavenage.com

Built in 1576, this unspoilt Elizabethan house contains stained glass from the 16th-century and earlier, and some good furniture and tapestries. The owner during the Civil War was a Parliamentarian, and the house contains Cromwellian relics. In more recent years, the house has been the location for *Grace and Favour, Poirot, The House of Elliot, Berkeley Square, Casualty* and *Cider with Rosie*. Tours of the house are enlivened by ghost stories.

Times: Open May-Sep, Thu, Sun & BHs 2-5. Also Etr Sun & Mon. Other days by appointment only.
Fee: £4 (ch £2).

ULEY

Uley Tumulus

(3.5m NE of Dusrley on B4066)

This 180ft Neolithic long barrow is popularly known as Hetty Pegler's Tump. The mound, surrounded by a wall, is about 85ft wide. It contains a stone central passage, and three burial chambers.

Times: Open any reasonable time.
Fee: Free.

WESTBURY-ON-SEVERN

Westbury Court Garden

GL14 1PD (9m SW of Gloucester on A48)
☎ 01452 760461
e-mail: westbury@smtp.ntrust.org.uk

This formal water garden with canals and yew hedges was laid out between 1696 and 1705. It is the earliest of its kind remaining in England and was restored in 1971 and planted with species dated pre-1700, including apple, pear and plum trees.

Times: Open Apr-Oct, Wed-Sun & BH Mon 11-6. Other months by appointment only.
Fee: £2.80 (ch £1.40)
(braille guide, wheelchair available) toilets for disabled shop (ex guide dogs)

WESTONBIRT

Westonbirt Arboretum

GL8 8QS (3m S Tetbury on A433)
☎ 01666 880220 01666 880559

Begun in 1829, this arboretum contains one of the finest and most important collections of trees and shrubs in the world. There are 18,000 specimens, planted from 1829 to the present day, covering 600 acres of landscaped Cotswold countryside. Magnificent displays of Rhododendrons, Azaleas, Magnolias and wild flowers.

Times: Open all year, daily 10-8 or sunset. Visitor centre & shop all year. (Closed Xmas & New Year)
Fee: £4.50 (ch £1, pen £3.50).
(electric & manual wheelchair for loan, telephone to book) toilets for disabled shop garden centre

WINCHCOMBE

Sudeley Castle & Gardens

GL54 5JD (B4632 to Winchcombe, Castle is signposted from town)

☎ 01242 603197 & 602308 01242 602959
e-mail: marketing@sudeley.org.uk

Sudeley Castle was home to Katherine Parr, who is buried in the Chapel. Henry VIII, Anne Boleyn, Lady Jane Grey and Elizabeth I all stayed or visited here; and it was the headquarters of Prince Rupert during the Civil War. The Queens Garden is famous for its rose collection, and there is a wildfowl sanctuary, exhibition centre, and children's adventure playground.

Times: Open daily: 4 Mar-Oct, Grounds, Gardens, exhibition, shop & plant centre 10.30-5.30. Apr-Oct, Castle apartments & Church 11-5.
Fee: Castle & Gardens £6.20 (ch £3.20 & concessions £5.20). Gardens only £4.70 (ch £2.50 & concessions £3.70). Family ticket £17. Party 20+ licensed (some parts unaccessible to disabled) shop garden centre (by request on arrival)

Greater Manchester

An urban conurbation in the northwest of England, Greater Manchester incorporates the towns of Bolton, Oldham, Rochdale, Salford, Stockport and Wigan, with the city of Manchester as its administrative headquarters.

Manchester was founded in Roman times, and developed during the 17th century as a textile town, becoming the centre of the English cotton industry. Magnificent Victorian Gothic public buildings are reminders of Manchester's prosperous heyday. These include the town hall designed by Alfred Waterhouse which takes up one side of Albert Square. Other gems to look out for are the recently restored Royal Exchange, - which was damaged in the Manchester bombing of 1996 - the Athenaeum, The Theatre Royal, and the Free Trade Hall. The Castlefield area, 15 minutes' walk southwest of the town hall, has been redeveloped in recent times to include a reconstruction of the Roman fort that once stood on the site.

Another impressive feature is the Manchester Ship Canal, completed in 1894, linking with the Mersey and the sea, bringing ocean-going vessels into Manchester and enabling the city to compete with its major rival, Liverpool.

The city of Manchester is alive with a vibrant youth culture (it has England's largest student population), a flourishing club scene, and a whole range of multi-cultural festivals and events. To take in the atmosphere, take a stroll around Britain's biggest Chinatown (between Charlotte Street and Princess Street), or wander down to Rusholme to take in the tempting aromas of the curry houses, and browse among the sari shops, Asian grocers, and Indian sweet shops.

EVENTS & FESTIVALS

January
tbc Winter Ales Festival, Manchester

February
tbc Chinese New Year Celebrations, parade from Town Hall to Chinatown

May/June
tbc Manchester Jazz Festival

June
tbc Greater Manchester Youth Games, Robin Park Stadium, Wigan
tbc Lord Mayor's Parade, Manchester
tbc Woodford Air Show

July
tbc Chadkirk Festival

August
11th Bramhall Horticultural Show
tbc Mardi Gras, Manchester

September
tbc Castlefield Carnival, Manchester

Top: Dobcross

ALTRINCHAM

Dunham Massey Hall

WA14 4SJ (3m SW of Altrincham (off A56), junct 19 off M6 or junct 7 off M56, then follow brown signs)
☎ 0161 941 1025 🖷 0161 929 7508

A fine 18th-century house and park, home of the Earls of Stamford until 1976. It contains fine furniture and silverware, and some thirty rooms, including the library, billiard room, fully-equipped kitchen, butler's pantry and laundry.

Times: Open: Apr-end Sep, Sat-Wed 12-5 (11-5 BH Sun & Mon). Garden Apr-Oct, 11-5.30 (closes 4.30 in Oct). End Sep-early Nov by guided tour only.
P (charged) ✕ licensed ♿ (batricar & wheelchairs for loan, lift to restaurant) toilets for disabled shop (ex on lead in Park) *Details not confirmed for 2001*

ASHTON-UNDER-LYNE

Museum of The Manchester Regiment

The Town Hall, Market Place OL6 6DL (in town centre, follow signs for museum)
☎ 0161 342 3078 & 0161 342 3710 🖷 0161 343 2869
e-mail: portland.basin@mail.tameside.gov.uk

The social and regimental history of the Manchesters is explored at this museum, tracing the story back to its origins in the 18th century. The Manchesters fought in both World Wars, the Boer War, and the Crimea.

Times: Open all year, Mon-Sat, 10-4. (Closed Sun).
Fee: Free.
P (50yds) (pay & display) ♿ toilets for disabled shop (ex guide dogs)

BRAMHALL

Bramall Hall & Park

SK7 3NX (from A6 turn right at Blossoms public house through Davenport village then turn right - signposted)
☎ 0161 485 3708 🖷 0161 486 6959

This large timber-framed hall dates from the 14th century, and is one of the finest black-and-white houses in the North West. It has rare 16th-century wall paintings and period furniture, and was the home of the Davenport family for 500 years. Much of the house is open to the public and available for hire. Open air concerts and plays are a feature in summer.

Times: Open all year, Good Fri-Sep Mon-Sat 1-5, Sun 11-5; Oct-New Year's Day Tue-Sat 1-4, Sun 11-4; 2 Jan-Good Fri Sat & Sun 12-4. Closed 25-26 Dec.
Fee: £3.50 (concessions £2). Family ticket £8.50.
P (charged) ♿ (access for wheelchair users) toilets for disabled shop (ex guide dogs)

MANCHESTER

City Art Gallery

Mosley St/Princess St M2 3JL
☎ 0161 234 1456 🖷 0161 236 7369
e-mail: cityart@mcrl.poptel.org.uk

The Mosley Street Galleries have permanent displays of European art, ceramics and silver, displayed with furniture in an elaborate decorative scheme. There's a superb collection of Victorian art, including some major Pre-Raphaelite paintings. Decorative and applied arts, including porcelain, furniture and sculpture can also be seen.

Times: Whole gallery closed until 2001 for major expansion scheme.

Gallery of Costume

Platt Hall, Rusholme M14 5LL (situated in Platt Fields Park, access from Wilmslow Rd. 2m S of city centre)
☎ 0161 224 5217 🖷 0161 256 3278

Times: Open all year, daily 10-5.30 (Nov-Feb 10-4).
P ♿ shop (ex guide dogs) *Details not confirmed for 2001*

Granada Studios Tour

Water St M60 9EA
☎ 0161 832 9090 & 0161 833 0880 🖷 0161 834 3684

Times: Open all year, daily summer 9.45-7 (last entry 4); winter 9.45-5.30 weekdays (last entry 3), 9.45-6.30 weekends & BH's (last entry 4). Closed Mon & Tue first half of Feb, Mar, Apr (except Etr), first half of Oct, Nov & Dec (except 28 & 29 Dec). Closed Mon May-Sep (except BH's). Closed 19-25 Dec. Open 1 & 2 Jan and weekends only.
P (charged) ✕ licensed ♿ (ramps & lift throughout) toilets for disabled shop *Details not confirmed for 2001*

John Rylands Library

150 Deansgate M3 3EH
☎ 0161 834 5343 🖷 0161 834 5574

Founded as a memorial to Manchester cotton-magnate and millionaire John Rylands, this is the Special Collections Division of the John Rylands University Library of Manchester. Internationally renowned, it extends to two million books, manuscripts and archival items representing some fifty cultures and ranging in date from the third millennium BC to the present day.

Times: Open all year, Mon-Fri 10-5.30, Sat 10-1. (Closed BH & Xmas-New Year).
Fee: Free.
P (400yds) shop (ex guide dogs by arrangement)

Manchester Museum

The University, Oxford Rd M13 9PL (S of city centre on B5117)
☎ 0161 275 2634 🖷 0161 275 2676
e-mail: dot.fenton@man.ac.uk/museum

Times: Open all year. Some galleries closed for refurbishment until June 2000. Ring for details.
P (350m) ♿ (Provision for disabled telephone in advance) shop (ex guide dogs) *Details not confirmed for 2001*

MANCHESTER MUSEUM OF TRANSPORT

Boyle St, Cheetham M8 8UW (1.5m N of Victoria Station)

☎ 0161 205 2122 & 0161 205 1082 📠 0161 205 2122

Times: Open all year, Wed, Sat, Sun & BH 10-5. Parties at other times by arrangement.

P ☕ ♿ toilets for disabled shop *Details not confirmed for 2001*

MANCHESTER UNITED MUSEUM & TOUR CENTRE

Sir Matt Busby Way, Old Trafford M16 0RA (2m from city centre, off A56)

☎ 0161 868 8631 📠 0161 868 8861

This Museum was opened in 1986 and is the first purpose-built British football museum. It covers the history of Manchester United in words, pictures, sound and vision, from its inception in 1878 to the present day.

Times: Open daily 9.30-5. (Closed 25 Dec & 1 Jan - when this is a day of a home game).

Fee: Stadium tour & Museum: £8 (ch & pen £5.50) Family ticket £22. Museum only: £5 (ch & pen £3.50) Family ticket £14.

P ☕ ✕ ♿ (scripts of all audio visuals available) toilets for disabled shop 🐕 💳

THE MUSEUM OF SCIENCE AND INDUSTRY IN MANCHESTER

Liverpool Rd, Castlefield M3 4FP (follow brown tourist signs from city centre)

☎ 0161 832 2244 0161 832 1830 📠 0161 833 2184

e-mail: marketing@msim.org.uk

Located in the buildings of the world's oldest passenger railway station. You can walk through a reconstructed Victorian sewer, or try the Super X flight simulator. Fibres, Fabrics & Fashion follows the story of Manchester's cotton industry. Warehouse for the World is a sound and light experience detailing the working life of the world's oldest railway building.

Times: Open all year, daily 10-5. Last admission 4.30. (Closed 24-26 Dec).

Fee: £5 (ch 5-18 free ex £2 admission to certain exhibitions, concessions £3) group rates & season tickets available.

P (charged) ☕ ♿ (lifts, hearing system) toilets for disabled shop 🐕 (ex guide dogs) 💳

WHITWORTH ART GALLERY

University of Manchester, Oxford Rd M15 6ER (follow brown tourist signs)

☎ 0161 275 7450 📠 0161 275 7451

e-mail: whitworth@man.ac.uk

The gallery houses an impressive range of modern and historic drawings, prints, paintings and sculpture, as well as the largest collection of textiles and wallpapers outside London and an internationally famous collection of British watercolours.

Times: Open Mon-Sat 10-5, Sun 2-5. (Closed Good Fri & Xmas-New Year).

Fee: Free.

P ✕ licensed ♿ (wheelchair available, induction loop, Braille lift buttons) toilets for disabled shop 🐕 (ex guide dogs)

PRESTWICH

HEATON HALL

Heaton Park M25 2SW

☎ 0161 773 1231 or 0161 234 1456 📠 0161 236 2880

Designed by James Wyatt for Sir Thomas Egerton in 1772, the house has magnificent period interiors decorated with fine plasterwork, paintings and furniture. Other attractions include a unique circular room with Pompeian-style paintings, and the original Samuel Green organ still in working order.

Times: Open Etr-end Oct, but phone for time details on 0161-234 1456.

Fee: Free.

P (charged) ♿ (occasional 'touch tours'. Phone for details) toilets for disabled shop 🐕 (ex guide dogs)

SALFORD

THE LOWRY

Pier Eight, Salford Quays M5 2AZ

☎ 0161 876 2000 📠 0161 876 2001

e-mail: info@thelowry.com

The Lowry is a waterfront home for the arts, entertainment and innovation, housing two theatres, art galleries, bars, shops and restaurants. The Lowry galleries re-present the works of LS Lowry alongside fresh, new exhibitions from major European and international artists.

Times: Open from 28 Apr, daily 9.30-midnight. (Closed 25 Dec).

Fee: Lowry galleries - free. Artworks - £3.75 (under 4's free).

P (charged) ☕ ✕ licensed ♿ toilets for disabled shop 🐕 (ex guide dogs) 💳

Salford Museum & Art Gallery

Peel Park, Crescent M5 4WU (on A6)

☎ 0161 736 2649 📠 0161 745 9490

e-mail: salford.museum@salford.gov.uk

The museum features a reconstruction of a 19th-20th century northern street with original shop fronts. Upstairs in the galleries there are temporary exhibitions, Victorian paintings and decorative arts, and displays featuring local scenes by LS Lowry, and Royal Lancastrian pottery.

Times: Open all year, Mon-Fri 10-4.45, Sat & Sun 1-5. (Closed Good Fri, Etr Sat, 25 & 26 Dec, 1 Jan).

Fee: Free.

(Braille & large print labelling, hearing loop, parking bay) toilets for disabled shop (guide dogs)

UPPERMILL

Saddleworth Museum & Art Gallery

High St OL3 6HS (on A670)

☎ 01457 874093 & 870336

Based in an old mill building next to the Huddersfield canal, the museum explores the history of the Saddleworth area. Wool weaving is the traditional industry, displayed in the 18th century Weaver's Cottage and the Victoria Mill Gallery. The textile machinery is run regularly by arrangement. The Art Gallery has regular exhibitions.

Times: Open all year, Nov-late Mar, daily 1-4; late Mar-Oct, Mon-Sat 10-5, Sun 12-5.

Fee: £1.25 (concessions 65p) Family ticket £3.15.

(charged) (stairlift, ramps, braille & large print guides, wheelchair) toilets for disabled shop (ex guide dogs)

WIGAN

Wigan Pier

Trencherfield Mill WN3 4EF (Follow brown & white tourist signs from motorways)

☎ 01942 323666 📠 01942 701927

Part museum, part theatre, Wigan Pier is a mixture of entertainment and education. The professional actors of the Wigan Pier Theatre Company perform plays, Victorian music hall shows and their infamous schoolroom. Opie's Museum of Memories ensures a memorable day for all ages, based on the domestic lifestyle collection of the social historian Robert Opie.

Times: Open all year, Mon-Thu 10-5; Sat & Sun 11-5. (Closed 25 & 26 Dec & 1 Jan & Fri (ex Good Fri).

Fee: £6.95 (concessions £5.25). Family ticket (2 adults & 3 ch) £19.50.

licensed toilets for disabled shop (ex guide dogs)

EVENTS & FESTIVALS

February
Children's Festival, Winchester

June
29 Jun-1 July Hat Fair (oldest street theatre fair in England), Winchester
tbc Bishop's Waltham Festival
tbc Butser Festival of Flight, Portsmouth
tbc Southampton Balloon & Flower Festival, Southampton
tbc Southsea Spectacular, Southsea Common

July
20-22 Netley Marsh Steam Engine Rally, Netley Marsh, Southampton
28 July Music in the Air, Middle Wallop Airfield, Middle Wallop

August
3-5 Portsmouth & Southsea Show, Southsea Common
25-26 Kite Festival, Southsea Common

September
8 Romsey Show, Romsey
14-23 Southampton International Boat Show, Mayflower Park
16 Great South Run 10-mile international event

November
7th Winchester Grand Firework Display

Top: Lyndhurst

Hampshire

Hampshire is mainly rural with a gentle landscape and coastal cities - Portsmouth and Southampton that enjoy a proud maritime history.

Portsmouth has been an important naval base since the 12th century, and Southampton has long been associated with the romance of the ocean liner. Both cities were badly bombed in World War II, though areas of interest remain for the visitor

A more attractive destination is the charming town of Lyndhurst at the heart of the glorious New Forest. Recently celebrating its 900th anniversary, the Forest is a huge expanse of woodland, heath and hills set aside as a royal hunting ground by William the Conqueror in 1079, and spreads across some 93,000 acres. Now millions visit every year. 'Forest' can seem a bit of a misnomer as large areas are quite open and covered only by heather and gorse. In 1992 it was given the protection of National Park status. Wildlife flourishes in this huge expanse, and walkers can see red, fallow, roe and muntjac deer, as well as badgers, adders, and the well-known ponies. Lyndhurst itself was home to Alice Hargreaves, (née Liddell) who was the inspiration for Alice in Lewis Carroll's world-famous books. She is buried in the graveyard of St Michael and All Angels Church.

Hampshire also has many small and picturesque villages. Alresford is home to the Watercress Line, Silchester has nearby Roman remains including an amphitheatre, and Old Basing has the delightful River Loddon and the remains of Basing House.

ALDERSHOT

Airborne Forces Museum

Browning Barracks, Queens Av GU11 2BU (from motorway take A325 to Aldershot then take next left)

☎ 01252 349619 ▯ 01252 349203

Times: Open all year, daily 10-4.30 (last admission 3.45pm) (Closed Xmas).

P ♿ Wheelchair ramps shop (ex guide dogs) *Details not confirmed for 2001*

Aldershot Military Museum

Evelyn Woods Rd, Queens Av GU11 2LG (follow brown signs to museum)

☎ 01252 314598 ▯ 01252 342942

e-mail: musmim@hants.gov.uk

A look behind the scenes at the daily life of soldiers and civilians as Aldershot and Farnborough grew up around the military camps to become the home of the British Army.

Times: Open Mar-Oct, daily 10-5; Nov-Feb, daily 10-4.30.

Fee: £2 (ch/pen/UB40 £1) P ♿ shop

ALRESFORD

Watercress Line

The Railway Station SO24 9JG (stations at Alton & Alresford signposted off A31)

☎ 01962 733810 ▯ 01962 735448

e-mail: watercressline@compuserve.com

The Watercress Line runs through ten miles of rolling scenic countryside between Alton and Alresford. All four stations are `dressed' in period style, and there's a locomotive yard and picnic area at Ropley.

Times: Open wknds throughout the year except for Nov & Jan, also some wkdays over Xmas, Easter, school half term holidays and Jun-Aug. Alresford station shop & buffet open daily ex 25 Dec.

Fee: Unlimited travel for the day, £8 (ch £5, pen £6). Family ticket £20. P (charged) ✕ licensed ♿ (ramp access to trains) toilets for disabled shop (at Alresford, Alton & Ropley staions)

AMPFIELD

The Sir Harold Hillier Gardens & Arboretum

Jermyns Ln SO51 OQA (3m NE of Romsey, signposted off A3090 & B3057)

☎ 01794 368787 ▯ 01794 368027

Established in 1953, this 180-acre public garden comprises the greatest collection of hardy trees and shrubs in the world. A garden for all seasons with stunning range of seasonal colour and interest and featuring eleven national plant collections. Champion trees, the Gurkha Memorial Garden and the largest Winter Garden in Europe.

Times: Open all year, Apr-Oct wkdays 10.30-6, wknds & BHs 9.30-6. Nov-Mar daily 10.30-5 or dusk if earlier (closed Xmas).

Fee: Apr-Oct: £4.25 (ch 5-16 £1, pen £3.75). Nov-Mar: £3.25 (ch 5-16 £1, pen £2.75). Under 5's free.

P ✕ licensed ♿ (all ability path) toilets for disabled garden centre (ex guide dogs)

ANDOVER

Finkley Down Farm Park

SP11 6NF (signposted from A303 & A343)

☎ 01264 352195 ▯ 01264 363172

A wide range of farm animals and poultry can be seen here, including some rare breeds. The pets corner has tame, hand-reared animals that can be stroked and petted. There are also a Countryside Museum, housed in a barn, Romany caravans and rural bygones to see, an adventure playground and a large picnic area.

Times: Open 19 March-29 Oct, daily 10-6. Last admission 5pm.

Fee: £4 (ch 2-14 £3, pen £3.50). Family ticket £13.

P ♿ toilets for disabled shop (ex guide dogs)

ASHURST

Longdown Dairy Farm

Longdown SO40 4UH (off A35 between Lyndhurst & Southampton)

☎ 023 8029 3326 ▯ 023 8029 3376

e-mail: bookings@longdowndairyfarm

A wonderful opportunity to get close to lots of friendly farm animals - piglets, ducklings, goats, cows, and many more. You can touch and feed many of the residents, watch the afternoon milking from the viewing gallery and learn about modern farming methods.

Times: Open Etr-Oct, daily.

Fee: £4.30 (ch 2-14 £3, pen £3.50). Saver ticket £14 (2 adults + 2 children) £9.75 (1 adult + 2 children).

P ♿ toilets for disabled shop (kennels provided)

BASINGSTOKE

Milestones - Hampshire's Living History Museum

Leisure Park RG21 6YR (M3 junct 6, clockwise around ringroad to Town Centre West roundabout, follow Leisure Park signs)

☎ 01256 477766 ▯ 01962 869836

e-mail: musmjb@hants.gov.uk

When open, Milestones will bring Hampshire's recent past to life through stunning period street scenes and exciting interactive areas, all under one roof. Nationally important collections of transport, technology and everyday life are presented in an entertaining way. Staff in period costumes, mannequins, sounds and smells will bring the streets to life.

Times: Open 25 Nov 2000. Mon-Fri 10-5 (Mon pre-booked groups only), wknds 10-6. (Xmas closure dates to be confirmed).

Fee: £5.95 (ch 5-16 £2.95, pen & students £4.75). Family £14.90. Prices for disabled & unemployed to be decided.

P ✕ ♿ (induction loops & audio trials) toilets for disabled shop (ex guide dogs)

See advert on p99.

BEAULIEU

BEAULIEU : NATIONAL MOTOR MUSEUM

SO42 7ZN (M27 Westbound J2, A326, B3054, then follow tourist signs)

☎ 01590 612345 🖷 01590 612624

e-mail: info@beaulieu.co.uk

This 16th-century house is worth seeing just for its lovely setting, but it has become most famous as the home of the National Motor Museum, one of the world's largest collections of vehicles and motoring memorabilia. Other attractions are a high-level monorail through the grounds, veteran bus rides and a replica of a 1930s country garage.

Times: Open all year - Palace House & Gardens, National Motor Museum, Beaulieu Abbey & Exhibition of Monastic Life, May-Sep 10-6; Oct-Apr 10-5. (Closed 25 Dec)

Fee: £9.25 (ch £6.50, pen £8). Family £29.50.

P ☕ ♿ (ramp access to most areas) toilets for disabled shop ✗ (ex on a lead)

BISHOP'S WALTHAM

BISHOP'S WALTHAM PALACE

SO32 1DH (on A333)

☎ 01489 892460

Bishop's Waltham Palace was once among the greatest stately homes of the medieval period. Although mostly destroyed in the Civil War, remains are still impressive.

Times: Open Apr-Oct, daily 10-6 (Oct 10-5).

Fee: £2 (ch 5-15 £1, under 5's free). P ♿ ✗ (in certain areas) #

BOLDRE

SPINNERS

School Ln SO41 5QE (off A337, between Brockenhurst & Lymington)

☎ 01590 673347

The garden has been entirely created by the owners since 1960. It has azaleas, rhododendrons, camellias and magnolias, interspersed with primulas, and blue poppies. The nursery is famed for its rare trees, shrubs and plants.

Times: Open Apr-14 Sep daily 10-5. Other times on application. Nursery and part of garden open all year, but garden and nursery both closed on Sun & Mon. **Fee:** £1.50 (accompanied ch under 6 free). P garden centre ✗ (ex guide dogs)

BREAMORE

BREAMORE HOUSE & COUNTRYSIDE

SP6 2DF (on A338, between Salisbury & Fordingbridge)

☎ 01725 512468 🖷 01725 512858

e-mail: breamore@estate.fsnet.co.uk

The handsome manor house was completed in around 1583 and has a fine collection of paintings, china and tapestries. The museum has good examples of steam engines, and uses reconstructed workshops and other displays to show how people lived and worked a century or so ago. There is also a children's playground.

Times: Open Apr, Tue, Wed, Sun & Etr, May-Jul & Sep, Tue-Thu & Sat, Sun & all BH, Aug, daily 2-5.30 (Countryside Museum 1pm).

Fee: Combined tickets £5 (ch £3.50). Party.

P ☕ ♿ (ramps, parking by house) toilets for disabled shop ✗ (ex guide dogs)

BUCKLER'S HARD

BUCKLER'S HARD VILLAGE & MARITIME MUSEUM

SO42 7XB (M27 Westbound J2, A326, B3054 then follow tourist signs)

☎ 01590 616203 🖷 01590 612624

Wooden warships, including some of Nelson's fleet, were built here, using New Forest oak, and the wide main street was used for rolling great logs to the 'hard' where the ships were built. The 18th-century homes of a shipwright and labourer, and a master shipbuilder's office can be seen.

Times: Open all year, Etr-Spring BH 10-6; Spring BH-Aug 10-9; Sep-Etr 10-4.30. (Closed 25 Dec).

Fee: £4 (ch £2, pen £3). When paying £3 car park charge prices reduced: £2 (ch £1, pen £1.50)

P (charged) ☕ ✕ licensed ♿ shop

BURGHCLERE

SANDHAM MEMORIAL CHAPEL

RG20 9JT (4m S Newbury off A34)

☎ 01635 278394 🖷 01635 278394

Stanley Spencer, one of the most original artists of his generation, painted the murals covering the walls of the Chapel between 1927 and 1932. Celebrating the daily routine of the common soldier during the Great War, they present a symbolic narrative which Spencer described as 'a mixture of real and spiritual fact'.

Times: Open Apr-Oct, Wed-Sun, 11.30-5 & BH Mon. Nov & Mar, Sat & Sun 11.30-4. Dec-Feb by appointment only.

Fee: £2.50 (ch £1.25).

P ♿ (Braille guide) ✗ (ex on leads in grounds)

CHAWTON

Jane Austen's House

GU34 1SD (1m SW of Alton, in centre of village)
☎ 01420 83262 📠 01420 83262

Jane Austen lived and wrote here from 1809 to 1817. Restored to look as it would have done in the early 1800s, with items such as the author's donkey cart and writing table to be seen.

Times: Open daily Mar-1 Jan, also Feb half term. Jan & Feb wknds only. (Closed 25 & 26 Dec).
Fee: £3 (ch 8-18, 50p, pen & students £2.50). Party.
P (300yds) ♿ (wheelchair ramp) toilets for disabled shop (ex guide dogs & service dogs)

EXBURY

Exbury Gardens

Exbury Estate Office SO45 1AZ (3m from Beaulieu, off B3054)
☎ 023 8089 1203 📠 023 8089 9940

A 200-acre landscaped woodland garden on the East bank of the Beaulieu River, with one of the finest collections of rhododendrons, azaleas, camellias and magnolias in the world - as well as many rare and beautiful shrubs and trees. A labyrinth of tracks and paths enable you to explore the beautiful gardens and walks.

Times: Open daily 26 Feb-5 Nov 10-5.30 or dusk if earlier.
Fee: 26th Feb-mid Mar £3.50 (ch 10-15 £2.50, OAP £3). Mid Mar-mid Jun £5 (ch £4, OAP £4.50. Mid Jun-5 Nov £3.50 (ch £2.50, OAP £3) OAP £4 Tues-Thur. Under 10's free.
P ♿ (wheelchair access, impaired mobility routes within gardens) toilets for disabled shop garden centre

GOSPORT

Royal Navy Submarine Museum & HMS Alliance

Haslar Jetty Rd PO12 2AS (M27 junct 11, follow signs for Submarine Museum)
☎ 023 9252 9217 & 9251 0354
📠 023 9251 1349
e-mail: rnsubs@submarinemuseum.demon.co.uk

The great attraction of this museum is the chance to see inside a submarine, and there are guided tours of *HMS Alliance*, as well as displays exploring the development of submarines. Two periscopes from *HMS Conqueror* can be seen in the reconstruction of a nuclear submarine control room, giving panoramic views of Portsmouth Harbour. A new gallery shows the development of submarine weapons from the tiny torpedo to the huge polaris nuclear missile.

Times: Open all year, Apr-Oct 10-5.30; Nov-Mar 10-4.30. (Closed 24 Dec-1 Jan). Allow 3 hrs for visit. Last tour 1 hour before closing.
Fee: £3.50 (ch & pen £2.50). Family ticket (2 adults & 4 ch) £10. Party 12+. Discounted entry scheme "Follow the Drum", in association with Southern Military Museums.
P ♿ (information in Braille) toilets for disabled shop

HARTLEY WINTNEY

West Green House Gardens

West Green RG27 8JB (off A30, at Phoenix Green take sign to West Green, along Thackhams Lane. House last left)
☎ 01252 844611 📠 01252 844611

The gardens surrounding this Queen Anne house date back 300 years and have been closed for the past three years for major repairs and replanting. When restoration is complete there will be ten acres of garden and pleasure grounds - four walled gardens, a lake, follies, green theatre, nymphaeum, mixed border and potager.

Times: Open May-Aug, Weds-Sun 11am-4pm. **Fee:** £3 (ch 7 free).
P ♿ (most areas accessible) toilets for disabled (ex guide dogs)

HAVANT

Staunton Country Park

Middle Park Way PO9 5HB (off B2149, between Havant & Horndean)
☎ 023 9245 3405 📠 023 9249 8156
e-mail: ccgsrc@hants.gov.uk

This colourful Victorian park offers a wonderful range of attractions for all age groups. Meet and feed the animals at the Ornamental Farm where there is a broad range of animals from llama and shirehorses to pigs and pigmy goats. Explore the Victorian tropical glasshouses with exotic flowers from around the world, including the giant Amazonian waterlily.

Times: Open 10-5 (4pm winter)
Fee: £3.60 (ch £2.60, pen £3.20). Family £10.50.
P ♿ (wheelchair for visitors) toilets for disabled shop (dogs in parkland only)

HIGHCLERE

Highclere Castle & Gardens

RG20 9RN (4.5m S of Newbury, off A34)
☎ 01635 253210 📠 01635 255315
e-mail: theoffice@highclerecastle.co.uk

This splendid early Victorian mansion stands in beautiful parkland. It has sumptuous interiors and numerous Old Master pictures. Also shown are early finds by the 5th Earl of Carnarvon, one of the discoverers of Tutankhamun's tomb.

Times: Open Jul-2 Sept, Mon-Fri & Sun 11-5 (last admission 4pm). Sat 11-3.30 (last admission 2.30pm).
Fee: £6.50 (ch £3, pen £5). Grounds & gardens only £3 (ch £1.50). Party 20+. P licensed ♿ (wheelchair available) toilets for disabled shop (ex guide dogs)

HINTON AMPNER

Hinton Ampner

So24 0LA (off A272, 1m W of Bramdean)
☎ 01962 771305 📠 01962 771305

Set in superb Hampshire countryside, this delightful garden combines formality of design with informality of planting. Full of scent and colour, the walks open up into unexpected vistas. The house, restored after a fire

in 1960, displays a fine collection of Regency furniture and Italian paintings.
Times: Open Garden: 19 & 26 Mar then Apr-Sep, Sat, Sun, BH Mon, Tue & Wed 1.30-5.30. Last admission 5pm. House: 4 Apr-end Jul & Sep, Tue & Wed only. Tue, Wed, Sat & Sun in Aug 1.30-5.30.
Fee: House and Garden £4.50, garden only £3.50. Party.
(Braille guides, special parking) toilets for disabled

HURST CASTLE

Hurst Castle
(on Pebble Spit S of Keyhaven)
☎ 01590 642344

Built by Henry VIII, Hurst Castle was the pride of Tudor England's coastal defences. Crouched menacingly on a shingle spit, the castle has a fascinating history, including involvement in the smuggling trade in the 17th and 18th centuries.
Times: Open Apr-Oct, daily 10-5.30.
Fee: £2.50 (ch £1.50 & concessions £2). (in certain areas)

LIPHOOK

Bohunt Manor
GU30 7DL (on old A3)
☎ 01428 722208

Bohunt includes woodland gardens with a lakeside walk, a water garden, roses, tulips and herbaceous borders, and a collection of ornamental ducks, black and white swans, and geese. Several unusual trees and shrubs include a handkerchief tree and a Judas tree. The property has been given to the Worldwide Fund for Nature.
Times: Open all year, daily, until 5pm. **Fee:** £1.50 (ch free, pen £1).

Hollycombe Steam Collection
Iron Hill, Midhurst Rd GU30 7LP (1.5m SE)
☎ 01428 724900 01428 723682
e-mail: hooker-chris@hotmail.com

A comprehensive collection of working steam-power, including a large Edwardian fairground, three railways, including one with spectacular views of the South Downs, traction engine hauled rides, steam agricultural machinery, pets corner, sawmill and even a paddle steamer engine.
Times: Open 2 Apr-22 Oct, Sun & BH's; 23 Jul -28 Aug, daily 12-5. Rides open from 1.
Fee: £6.50 (ch & pen £5). Saver ticket (2 adults & 2 ch) £20. Party 15+.
shop (guide dogs on request)

LYMINGTON

Braxton Gardens
Braxton Courtyard, Lymore Ln SO41 0TX (leave A337 at Everton onto B3058 then turn left into Lymore Ln, Braxton Courtyard on left)
☎ 01590 642008

Beautiful gardens set around attractive Victorian farm buildings. A courtyard with raised lily pool leads into a walled garden which during the summer overflows with

aromatic plants. Above the shop in a converted granary is the Tennyson Room (available for private hire).
Times: Open daily, Apr-Oct, 9-5, 10-5 Sun. Shorter opening hours in winter. **Fee:** Free. shop garden centre (ex guide dogs)

LYNDHURST

New Forest Museum & Visitor Centre
Main Car Park, High St SO43 7NY (leave M27 at Cadnam & follow A337 to Lyndhurst. Museum signposted)
☎ 023 8028 3914 023 8028 4236
e-mail: nfmuseum@lineone.net

The story of the New Forest - history, traditions, character and wildlife, told through an audio-visual show and exhibition displays. With life-size models of Forest characters, and the famous New Forest embroidery.
Times: Open all year, daily from 10am (Closed 25 Dec)
Fee: £2.75 (ch £1.75 pen £2.25) Family ticket £7.50. Party 10+.
toilets for disabled shop

MARWELL

Marwell Zoological Park
Colden Common SO21 1JH (M3 junct 11 or M27 Junct 5. Zoo located on B2177)
☎ 01962 777407 01962 777511
e-mail: marwell@marwell.org.uk

Devoted to the conservation and breeding of rare wild animals, Marwell has a worldwide reputation. There is

contd.

an encounter village where animals can be approached and stroked by children. Covering 100 acres of parkland, the collection includes over 1000 animals, and some of the species here no longer exist in the wild. There is also a gift shop and many attractions for younger children, including a children's farmyard, Tropical World, Penguin World and road trains.

Times: Open all year, daily (ex 25 Dec), 10-6 (in summer), 10-4 (in winter). Last admission 1 hour before closing.
Fee: £8.80 (ch 3-14 £6.30, pen £7.80). Family ticket £28.
licensed (tours for visually impaired/disabled groups by arrangement) toilets for disabled shop (inc guide dogs)

MIDDLE WALLOP

Museum of Army Flying

SO20 8DY (on A343, between Andover & Salisbury)
01980 674421 01264 781694
e-mail: pb@flyingmuseum.org.uk

One of the country's finest historical collections of military kites, gliders, aeroplanes and helicopters. Imaginative dioramas and displays trace the development of Army flying from before the First World War to more recent conflicts in Ireland, the Falklands and the Gulf. Sit at the controls of a real Scout helicopter and test your skills on the helicopter flight simulator, plus children's interactive science and education centre.
Times: Open all year, daily 10-4.30. Closed week prior to Xmas. Evening visits by special arrangement.
Fee: £4.50 (ch £3, OAP/student £3.50) Family £12.50. Party 10+.
licensed (lifts to upper levels) toilets for disabled shop (ex guide dogs or in grounds)

MINSTEAD

Furzey Gardens

SO43 7GL (1m S of junct A31/M3 Cadnam off A31 or A337 near Lyndhurst)
023 8081 2464 & 8081 2297
023 8081 2297

A large thatched gallery is the venue for refreshments and displays of local arts and crafts, and the eight acres of peaceful glades which surround it include winter and summer heathers, rare flowering trees and shrubs and a mass of spring bulbs. There is a 16th-century cottage, lake, and the nursery, run by the Minstead Training Project for Young People with Learning Disabilities, sells a wide range of produce.
Times: Open daily 10-5 (or dusk if earlier). (Closed Xmas).
Fee: Mar-Oct: £3 (ch £1.50, OAP £2.50) Family £8. Nov-Feb: £1.50 (ch 50p, OAP £1) Family £3. Party 10+.
(gardens accessible for wheelchair visitors with assistance) shop garden centre (guide dogs)

MOTTISFONT

Mottisfont Abbey Garden

SO51 0LP (4.5m NW Romsey, 1m W of A3057)
01794 340757 01794 341492

In a picturesque setting by the River Test, Mottisfont Abbey is an 18th-century house adapted from a 12th-century priory. The north front shows its medieval church origins quite clearly, and the garden has splendid old trees and a walled garden planted with the national collection of old-fashioned roses. The estate includes Mottisfont village, farmland and woods.
Times: Open Garden & Grounds: 18 Mar-1 Nov, Sat-Wed 12-6 (or dusk if earlier). 10-25 June special opening daily from 11-8.30. Last admission to grounds 1hr before closing. House: 1-5 (last admission 4.30). Derek Hill Picture Collection: Sun-Tue 1-5.
Fee: £5 (ch £2.50) Family ticket £12.50.
licensed (Braille guide,wheelchair available,volunteer driven buggy) toilets for disabled shop garden centre

NETLEY

Netley Abbey

(4m SE of Southampton, facing Southampton Water)
023 80453076

A romantic ruin, set among green lawns and trees, this 13th-century Cistercian abbey was founded by Peter des Roches, tutor to Henry III. Nearby is the 19th-century, Gothic Netley Castle.
Times: Open any reasonable time. **Fee:** Free.

NEW MILTON

Sammy Miller Motorcycle Museum

Bashley Cross Rd BH25 5SZ (signposted off A35)
01425 620777 01425 619696
e-mail: info@sammymiller.co.uk

With machines dating back to 1900, some are the only surviving examples of their type. The Racing collection features world record-breaking bikes and their history, including the first bike to lap a Grand Prix Course at over 100 miles per hour. Special events include Triumph Day, Velocette & Brough Day.
Times: Open all year, daily 10-4.30. **Fee:** £3.50 (ch £1.50)
toilets for disabled shop

OLD BASING

Basing House

Redbridge Ln RG24 7HB (signed from Basingstoke Ring Road)

☎ 01256 467294 ▯ 01256 326283

The largest house of Tudor England, almost entirely destroyed by Parliament during a two-year siege ending in 1645. Built on the site of a Norman castle in 1530, the ruins include a 300ft long tunnel. There is a re-creation of a garden of 1600 and exhibitions showing the history of the house. A fine 16th-century tithe barn stands nearby.

Times: Open Apr-Sep, Wed-Sun & BH 2-6.

Fee: £1.50 (ch & pen 70p). Registered disabled free.

P ♿ (disabled parking by prior arangement) toilets for disabled shop

OWER

Paultons Park

SO51 6AL (exit junc 2 M27, near junc A31 & A36)

☎ 023 8081 4455 & 8081 4442

▯ 023 8081 3025

Paultons Park offers a great day out for all the family with over forty different attractions, including Rio Grande Railway, bumper boats, 6-lane astroglide and raging river ride log flume. Attractions for younger children include Kid's Kingdom, Tiny Tots Town, Rabbit Ride and Ladybird ride. A beautiful parkland setting with extensive 'Capability' Brown gardens and aviaries for exotic birds, lake and hedge maze.

Times: Open 11 Mar-29 Oct, daily 10-6, earlier closing at certain times of year - daily info on hotline. Nov-Dec, wknds only until Xmas.

Fee: £9.50 (ch under 14 & pen £8.50). Children under 1m tall enter for free. Range of Family Supersavers.

P ☕ ✕ ♿ (wheelchair hire - some rides unsuitable) toilets for disabled shop ✗ (ex guide dogs)

PETERSFIELD

Bear Museum

38 Dragon St GU31 4JJ (100yds from bottom of the High Street, signed)

☎ 01730 265108

e-mail: bears@dial.pipex.com

This was the world's first Teddy Bear Museum, and children are allowed to cuddle and play with some of the exhibits. A variety of bears are displayed in the Victorian-style nursery while downstairs is the 'Teddy Bear's Picnic' where children are encouraged to sing along to the famous song.

Times: Open Tue-Sat 10-4.30. **Fee:** Free entry. Contributions welcomed. P (200yds) shop ✗ (ex guide dogs)

PORTCHESTER

Portchester Castle

PO16 9QW (off A27)

☎ 023 9237 8291

Built on the site of a Roman fort, the castle has witnessed many famous events of English history. From here Henry V embarked for France and the Battle of Agincourt; here Henry VIII courted Anne Boleyn, and later still the castle was 'home' to prisoners during the Napoleonic wars. The castle has the most complete Roman walls in Europe; remains of the church and other medieval buildings can also be seen.

Times: Open all year, Apr-Oct, daily 10-6 (Oct 10-5); Nov-Mar, daily 10-4. Closed 24-26 Dec & 1 Jan.

Fee: £2.70 (ch 5-15 £1.40, under 5's free).

P ♿ shop ✗ (in certain areas) #

PORTSMOUTH & SOUTHSEA

Charles Dickens' Birthplace Museum

393 Old Commercial Rd PO1 4QL (accessible from M27, first left at first roundabout)

☎ 023 9282 7261 ▯ 023 9287 5276

e-mail: cspendlove@portsmouthcc.gov.uk

A small terraced house built in 1805 – the birthplace and early home of the famous novelist, born in 1812. On display are items pertaining to Dickens' work, portraits of the Dickens' family, and the couch on which he died. Dickens readings are given in the exhibition room on the first Sunday of each month.

Times: Open Mar-Sep, daily 10-5.30 (last admission 5pm). Also 27 Nov-22 Dec 10-5 (last admission 4.30pm).

Fee: £2 (ch & student £1.20, accompanied ch 13 free, pen £1.50p). Family ticket £5.20.

P (150mtrs) shop ✗ (ex guide & helper dogs)

City Museum & Records Office

Museum Rd PO1 2LJ (M27/M275 into Portsmouth, follow museum symbol signs)

☎ 023 9282 7261 ▯ 023 9287 5276

e-mail: cspendlove@portsmouthcc.gov.uk

Dedicated to local history and decorative and fine art, 'The Story of Portsmouth' displays room settings showing life here from the 17th century to the 1950s. The 'Portsmouth at Play' exhibition features leisure pursuits from the Victorian period to the 1970s.

Times: Open all year, Apr-Sep daily 10-5.30; Oct-Mar daily 10-5. Closed 24-26 Dec and Record Office closed on public holidays.

Fee: Free.

P ☕ ♿ (induction loops, lift & wheelchair available) toilets for disabled shop ✗ (ex guide & helper dogs)

D-Day Museum & Overlord Embroidery

Clarence Esplanade PO5 3NT (M27/M275 into Portsmouth follow D-Day Museum signposts)

☎ 023 9282 7261 ▯ 023 9287 5276

e-mail: cspendlove@portsmouthcc.gov.uk

Portsmouth's D-Day Museum tells the dramatic story of the Allied landings in Normandy in 1944. Centrepiece is the magnificent 'Overlord Embroidery', 34 individual panels and 83 metres in length. Experience the world's largest ever seaborne invasion, and step back in time to scenes of wartime Britain. Military equipment, vehicles, landing craft and personal memories complete this special story.

Times: Open all year, Apr-Sep daily 10-5.30. Oct-Mar, 10-5.30.

Fee: £4.75 (ch £2.85, pen £3.60). Family ticket £12.35.

P (charged) ☕ ♿ (induction loops,sound aids for blind,wheelchairs available) toilets for disabled shop ✗ (ex guide & helper dogs)

Eastney Beam Engine House

Henderson Rd, Eastney PO4 9JF (accessible from A3, A27 & A2030, 1st left at Branbury Park traffic lights)
☎ 023 9282 7261 023 9287 5276
e-mail: cspendlove@portsmouthcc.gov.uk

Eastney Beam Engine House main attraction is a magnificent pair of James Watt Beam Engines still housed in their original High-Victorian engine house opened in 1887. One of these engines is in steam when the museum is open. A variety of other pumping engines, many in running order are also on display.

Times: Open all year, last (whole) weekend of every month Apr-Sep 1-5.30, Nov-Mar 1-5 (last admission 30 minutes before closing).

Fee: £2 (ch & student £1.20, accompanied ch under 13 free & pen £1.50). Family ticket £5.20. P (adjacent or 300m)

Flagship Portsmouth

HM Naval Base PO1 3LJ (follow brown historic ships sign from M27/M275)
☎ 023 9287 0999 023 9229 5252
e-mail: enquiries@flagship.org.uk

Flagship Portsmouth is home to the world's greatest historic ships: *Mary Rose*, *HMS Victory*, *HMS Warrior* and the Royal Naval Museum. Action Stations is an attraction demonstrating life aboard a modern naval frigate.

Times: Open all year, Apr-Oct, daily 10-5.30; Nov-Mar, daily 10-5. (Closed 25 Dec).

Fee: Combined ticket: £12.50 (ch £9.25 & pen £11); HMS Victory: £6.50 (ch £4.75 & pen £5.75); Mary Rose or HMS Warrior: £6 (ch £4.50 & pen £5.25).

P (charged) toilets for disabled shop (ex on leads)

Natural History Museum & Butterfly House

Cumberland House, Eastern Pde PO4 9RF
☎ 023 9282 7261 023 9282 5276

Focussing on the natural history and geology of the area, with wildlife dioramas including a riverbank scene with fresh water aquarium. During the summer British and European butterflies fly free in the Butterfly House.

Times: Open daily, Apr-Sep 10-5.30.

Fee: £2 (ch £1.40, accompanied ch under 13 free & pen £1.60). Family ticket £5.40; Oct-Mar £1.50 (ch 90p & pen £1.10) Family ticket £3.90 P (200mtrs) shop (guide & helper dogs)

The Royal Marines Museum

PO4 9PX (signposted from seafront)
☎ 023 9281 9385 023 9283 8420
e-mail: info@royalmarinesmuseum.co.uk

Telling the story of the 330-year history of the Marines through dramatic displays, exciting films and videos, state of the art interactives and even a live snake and scorpion! There's also a world famous medal collection, portraits and silverware.

Times: Open all year, Spring BH-Aug daily 10-5; Sep-May daily 10-4.30. (Closed 3 days Xmas)

Fee: £4 (ch £2.25, pen £3) Family ticket £12.

P licensed toilets for disabled shop (ex guide dogs or in grounds)

Southsea Castle

Clarence Esplanade PO5 3PA (accessible from M27, follow castle signposts)
☎ 023 9282 7261 023 9287 5276
e-mail: c spendlove@portsmouthcc.gov.uk

Part of Henry VIII's national coastal defences, this fort was built in 1544. In the "Time Tunnel" experience, the ghost of the castle's first master gunner guides you through the dramatic scenes from the castle's eventful history. Audio-visual presentation, underground passages, Tudor military history displays, artillery, and panoramic views of the Solent and Isle of Wight.

Times: Open all year, Apr-Sep, daily 10-5.30.

Fee: £2 (ch & students £1.20, ch accompanied 13 free, pen £1.50). Family ticket £5.20.

P (charged) (wheelchair available) shop (ex guide & helper dogs)

Spitbank Fort

(Ferries depart from HM Naval Base Portsmouth, Portsmouth Hard & Gosport Ferry Pontdon)
☎ 01329 664286 07977 066560

Built in the 1860s as part of the coastal defences against the French, this massive granite and iron fortress stands a mile out to sea, with magnificent views across the Solent. The interior is a maze of passages connecting over 50 rooms on two levels.

Times: Open May-Sep, Tue-Sun. (Weather permitting).

Fee: £6.50 (ch £5) includes ferry charge. Boat ride takes approx 20 mins, visitors should allow 2hr to view. Ferries depart HM Naval Base Portsmouth. P

RINGWOOD

Moors Valley Country Park

Horton Rd, Ashley Heath BH24 2ET (1.5m from Ashley Heath roundabout on A31 near Three Legged Cross)
☎ 01425 470721 01425 471656
e-mail: mvalley@eastdorsetdc.gov.uk

Fifteen hundred acres of forest, woodland, heathland, lakes, river and meadows provide a home for a wide variety of plants and animals, and there's a Visitor Centre, Adventure Playground, picnic area, Moors Valley Railway, and Tree Top Trail.

Times: Open all year (ex 25 Dec), 8-dusk. Visitor centre open 9.30-4.30 (later in summer).

Fee: No admission charge but parking up to £4 per day.

P (charged) (visitor centre & most of park accessible) toilets for disabled shop (ex in park on lead)

ROCKBOURNE

ROMAN VILLA

SP6 3PG (from Salisbury, take A354 to Blandford, follow signs from Coombe Bissett)

☎ 01725 518541

Times: Open Apr-Oct, Mon-Fri noon-6, Sat, Sun & BH 10.30-6; Jul & Aug daily 10.30-6. Last admission 5.30pm.

(ramps in/out of museum) toilets for disabled shop

Details not confirmed for 2001

ROMSEY

BROADLANDS

SO51 9ZD (main entrance on A3090 Romsey by-pass)

☎ 01794 505010 01794 505040

e-mail: admin@broardlands.net

Famous as the home of the late Lord Mountbatten, Broadlands is now home to his grandson Lord Romsey. An elegant Palladian mansion in a beautiful landscaped setting on the banks of the River Test, Broadlands was also the country residence of Lord Palmerston, the great Victorian statesman.

Times: Open daily, 12 Jun-1 Sep, 12-5.30. Last admission 4pm.

Fee: £5.50 (ch 12-16 £3.80, pen/stu/disabled £4.70). Party 15+.

toilets for disabled shop (ex guide dogs)

SELBORNE

GILBERT WHITE'S HOUSE & THE OATES MUSEUM

The Wakes, High St GU34 3JH (on village High St)

☎ 01420 511275 01420 511040

Charming 18th-century house, home of famous naturalist, the Rev. Gilbert White, author of *The Natural History and Antiquities of Selborne*. There are also exhibitions on two famous members of the Oates family - Captain Oates who accompanied Scott to the South Pole, and Frank Oates, a Victorian explorer. Special events include an Unusual Plants Fair in June.

Times: Open daily 1 Jan-24 Dec, 11-5.

Fee: £4 (ch £1, pen £3.50).

P (200yds) shop (es guide dogs)

SHERBORNE ST JOHN

THE VYNE

RG24 9HL (4m N of Basingstoke, off A340, signposted)

☎ 01256 881337 01256 881720

Much of the exterior of the house is 16th-century, with several major alterations and additions, including the earliest classical portico to be added to an English country house. The chapel has original 16th-century stained glass, and the Oak Gallery has superb linenfold panelling. The house is set in a pleasant garden with a lake.

Times: Open House Apr-29 Oct daily except Mon & Fri 1-5. Grounds open wknds in Feb & Mar, 11-4; 1 Apr-29 Oct daily except Mon & Fri, 11-6. Open Good Fri & BH Mons.

Fee: House & Grounds £5. Family ticket £12.50. Grounds only £3 (ch half price for each ticket). Party

licensed (Braille guide) shop (ex guide & hearing dogs)

SILCHESTER

CALLEVA MUSEUM

Bramley Rd RG7 2LU (between Basingstoke & Reading. Reached from A340)

Little remains of the Roman town of Calleva Atrebatum except the 1.5 miles of city wall, still an impressive sight, and the ampitheatre. This small museum shows what life may have been like in a Roman town, while the main artefacts from the site can be seen in the Silchester Gallery at Reading Museum.

Times: Open daily 9am-sunset. Closed 25 Dec.

Fee: Free.

P

SOUTHAMPTON

MUSEUM OF ARCHAEOLOGY

God's House Tower, Winkle St SO14 2NY (near the waterfront close to Queen's Park and the Town Quay)

☎ 023 806 35904 & 808 32768

023 803 39601

e-mail: historic.sites@southampton.gov.uk

The museum housed in an early fortified building, dating from the 1400s and taking its name from the nearby medieval hospital. Exhibits on the Roman, Saxon and medieval towns of Southampton are displayed.

Times: Open Tue-Fri 10-12 & 1-5; Sat 10-12 & 1-4; Sun 2-5. Also open BH Mon. **Fee:** Free.

P (400 yds) (designated areas only, parking charges) shop (ex guide dogs)

SOUTHAMPTON CITY ART GALLERY

Civic Centre, Commercial Rd SO14 7LP (situated on the Watts Park side of the Civic Centre, a short walk from the station)

☎ 023 8063 2601 023 8083 2153

e-mail: artgallery@southampton.gov.uk

Times: Open all year, Tue, Wed & Fri 10-5, Thu 10-5, Sat 10-5, Sun 1-4. (Closed 25-27 & 31 Dec).

P (250yds) toilets for disabled shop *Details not confirmed for 2001*

Southampton Hall of Aviation

Albert Rd South SO1 1FR

☎ 023 8063 5830

Times: Open all year, Tue-Sat 10-5, Sun 12-5. Also BH Mon & School Holidays. (Closed Xmas).

P (150 yds) (roadside parking on meter) ♿ (lift to all levels) toilets for disabled shop *Details not confirmed for 2001*

Southampton Maritime Museum

The Wool House, Town Quay SO14 2AR (on the waterfront, near to the Town Quay)

☎ 023 8022 3941 & 8063 5904

023 8033 9601

e-mail: historic.sites@southampton.gov.uk

The Wool House was built in the 14th century as a warehouse for wool, and now houses a maritime museum, with models and displays telling the history of the Victorian and modern port of Southampton. There are exhibitions of the "Titanic", "The Queen Mary" and an interactive area for children.

Times: Open all year, Tue-Fri 10-12 & 1-5, Sat 10-12 & 1-4, Sun 2-5. Also open BH Mon. **Fee:** Free.

P (400 yds) (metered parking adjacent) ♿ shop (ex guide dogs)

Tudor House Museum

St Michael's Square, Bugle St SO14 2AD (follow signs for Old Town & Waterfront, Tudor House is 500 yards up the road from the Wool House)

☎ 023 8033 2513 & 8063 5904

023 8033 9601

e-mail: historic.sites@southampton.gov.uk

This fine half-timbered house, built at the end of the 15th century and therefore older than its name suggests, is now a museum. Exhibitions include a Tudor Hall and displays on Georgian and Victorian social and domestic life in Southampton as well as temporary exhibitions. The unique Tudor garden with knot garden, fountain and 16th-century herbs and flowers is not to be missed.

Times: Open Tue-Fri 10-5 (closed between 12-1), Sat 10-4 (closed between 12-1), Sun 2-5. Open BH Mon.

Fee: Free.

P (20 yards) (metered & disabled parking opposite) ♿ toilets for disabled shop (ex guide dogs)

STRATFIELD SAYE

Stratfield Saye House

RG7 2BZ (off A33 between Reading & Basingstoke)

☎ 01256 882882 01256 882882

Times: Open Sat & Sun in May and BH Mon; Daily ex Fri Jun-Aug; Sat & Sun in Sep. Groups by prior booking during week.

P ✕ licensed ♿ toilets for disabled shop (ex in grounds) *Details not confirmed for 2001*

Wellington Country Park

RG7 1SP

☎ 0118 932 6444 0118 932 6445

(For full entry see Riseley, Berkshire)

TITCHFIELD

Titchfield Abbey

(0.5m N off A27)

☎ 023 9252 7667

Also known as 'Palace House', in Tudor times this was the seat of the Earl of Southampton, built on the site of the abbey founded in 1232. He incorporated the gatehouse and the nave of the church into his house.

Times: Open Apr-Sep, daily 10-6; Oct, daily 10-5; Nov-Mar, daily 10-4.

Fee: Free. P ♿ #

WEYHILL

The Hawk Conservancy

SP11 8DY (3m W of Andover, signposted from A303)

☎ 01264 772252 01264 773772

e-mail: info@hawk-conservancy.org

This is the largest centre in the south for birds of prey from all over the world including eagles, hawks, falcons, owls, vultures and kites. Exciting birds of prey demonstrations are held daily at noon, 2pm, and 3.30pm, including the 'Valley of the Eagles' at 2pm. Different birds are flown at these times and visitors may have the opportunity to hold a bird and adults can fly a Harris hawk.

Times: Open mid Feb-last Sun in Oct, daily from 10.30 (last admission 4pm).

Fee: £5.75 (ch £3.25, pen £5.25). Family ticket £16.50.

P ♿ (Wheelchair area in flying grounds) toilets for disabled shop

WINCHESTER

Guildhall Gallery

The Broadway SO23 9LJ

☎ 01962 848296 & 848289 01962 848299

Times: Open during exhibitions, Tue-Sat 10-5, Sun & Mon 2-5. (Closed Mon, Oct-Mar). Subject to alteration.

P (100yds) ✕ licensed ♿ toilets for disabled shop *Details not confirmed for 2001*

Gurkha Museum

Peninsula Barracks, Romsey Rd SO23 8TS (off B3040)

☎ 01962 842832 01962 877597

This museum tells the fascinating story of the Gurkha's involvement with the British Army. Travel from Nepal to the North-West Frontier and beyond, with the help of life-sized dioramas, interactive exhibits and sound displays.

Times: Open all year, BH Mon, Tue-Sat 10-5, Sun 12-4. Telephone for Xmas opening times. (Closed 25-26 Dec, 1 Jan and Tue following BH Mon) **Fee:** £1.50 (pen 75p). Party 15+.

P ♿ (lift & stair lift) toilets for disabled shop

Hospital of St Cross

St Cross SO23 9SD (1.5m S of city, on A3335)

☎ 01962 851375 01962 878221

Founded in 1132 for the benefit of 13 poor men, and still functioning as an almshouse. Throughout the Middle Ages the hospital handed out the Dole - bread

and beer - to travellers, and this is still done. The Church of St Cross, Brethrens Hall and medieval kitchen, and the walled Master's Garden are all worthy of note.
Times: Open all year, Apr-Oct, Mon-Sat 9.30-5; Nov-Mar 10.30-3.30. (Closed Sun, Good Fri & 25 Dec).
Fee: £2 (ch 50p, students & pen £1.25).
P (200 yds) (2 hrs) (A resident Brother can act as guide and assistant) toilets for disabled shop (ex guide dogs)

The King's Royal Hussars Regimental Museum

Peninsula Barracks, Romsey Rd SO23 8TS
01962 828539 01962 828538
e-mail: beresford@krhmuseum.freeserve.co.uk

The Royal Hussars were formed by the amalgamation of two regiments raised at the time of the Jacobite Rebellion in 1715. The museum was formed by the amalgamation of the Royal Hussars and the 14th/20th King's Hussars. This museum tells their story.
Times: Open 5 Jan-18 Dec, Tue-Fri 10-4, Sat, Sun & BH's 12-4.
Fee: Free.
P (lift to first floor) toilets for disabled shop

Royal Hampshire Regiment Museum & Memorial Garden

Serle's House, Southgate St SO23 9EG
01962 863658 01962 888302
Times: Open all year(ex 2 weeks Xmas & New Year), Mon-Fri 10-12.30 & 2-4; Apr-Oct wknds & BH noon-4.
P (800mtrs) shop (ex guide dogs) *Details not confirmed for 2001*

The Great Hall

Castel Av SO23 8PJ
01962 846476 01962 841326

The only surviving part of Winchester Castle, once home to the Domesday Book, this 13th-century hall was the centre of court and government life. The round table, closely associated with the legendary King Arthur, has hung here for over 600 years. A visitor centre and the Winch Castle exhibition add to the displays to be seen.
Times: Open all year, Mar-Oct daily 10-5; Nov-Feb, daily 10-5, weekends 10-4. Closed Xmas. **Fee:** Donations welcome.
P (200yds) toilets for disabled shop garden centre (ex guide dogs)

Winchester Cathedral

SO23 9LS (in city centre - follow city heritage signs)
01962 857200 & 866854 01962 857201

The longest medieval church in Europe, founded in 1079 on a site where Christian worship had already been offered for over 400 years. Among its treasures are the 12th-century illuminated Winchester Bible, the font, medieval wall paintings and Triforium Gallery Museum.
Times: Open all year, daily 8.30-6.30. Subject to services and special events. **Fee:** £3 (ch 50p, concessions £2.50)
P licensed (chair lift to east end of Cathedral, touch & hearing model) toilets for disabled shop (except guide dogs)

Winchester City Mill

Bridge St SO23 8EJ (by the city bridge between King Alfred's statue & Chesil St)
01962 870057 01962 870057
e-mail: swigen@smtp.ntrust.org.uk

Built over the fastflowing River Itchen in 1744, the mill has a delightful small island garden and an impressive millrace.
Times: Open Apr-Oct, Wed-Sun & BH Mons 11-4.45; Mar wknds only. Last admission 15 mins before closing.
Fee: Free. P (200 yds) shop

Winchester City Museum

The Square SO23 9ES
01962 848269 01962 848299
Times: Open all year, Mon-Sat 10-5, Sun 2-5 (Closed Mon Oct-Mar, Good Fri, Xmas & 1 Jan).
shop *Details not confirmed for 2001*

Winchester College

College St SO23 9NA (S of Cathedral Close)
01962 621209 01962 621215
e-mail: icds@bursary.wincoll.ac.uk

Founded in 1382, Winchester College is one of the oldest schools in England. The college has greatly expanded over the years but the original buildings remain intact. The chapel and (during term time) the cloisters and Fromond's Chantry are open to the public. Also open is the War Cloister, which contains memorials to Wykhamists killed in World War I.
Times: Open for unbooked guided tours Jun-Aug Mon-Sat (ex Sun am) 10, 11, 12, 2.15 & 3.15. Sep-May Mon-Sat 11, 12, 2.15 & 3.15) (Sun 2.15 & 3.15 only) (Booked tour parties of 10+ all year).
Fee: Booked tours £2.50 (pen & students 18 £2), unbooked tours £1.50 (pen & students £2)
P (250 yards) (Most streets have permit parking) toilets for disabled shop

Herefordshire

Herefordshire is split in two by the River Wye which meanders through the county on its way to the Severn and the sea. The entire county is largely rural, with Hereford, Leominster and Ross-on-Wye the only towns or cities of any size.

The countryside and ancient villages of Herefordshire are probably the county's major asset, and visitors can take advantage of a number of trails which will guide them through much of interest. These are set out on leaflets available from Tourist Information Centres. Those especially interested in villages should try the Black and White Village Trail, which takes the motorist on a 35 mile drive around timber-framed villages in the northwest of the county from Leominster to Weobley, (established in the 7th century and known as a centre of witchcraft in the 18th), Kinnersley Castle, Eardisley (where the Church of St Mary Magdalene boasts a early 12th-century carved font), Great Oak, Kington (one of the five market towns of Herefordshire), Pembridge, and others.

Other trails include the Mortimer Trail; - a 30 mile walk through unspoilt countryside between Ludlow and Kington - the Hop Trail; - which goes from Bromyard to Ledbury through surrounding fields which display the varying stages of hop growing - and the Hidden Highway, which begins at Ross-on-Wye and ends in Chester, taking in much of the area's dramatic countryside and secret places on the way.

EVENTS & FESTIVALS

May
14-15 Ross-on-Wye Natural Health & Ecology Festival, Larruperz Centre, Ross-on-Wye
25 May-3 Jun Hay-on-Wye Festival of Literature
tbc Bromyard Spring Festival
tbc Hereford Marathon
tbc Hereford May Fair

June
1-10 Leominster Festival
22-24 Music Festival, Dore Abbey, Abbeydore
28 Jun-8 Jul Ledbury Poetry Festival

July
tbc Madley Festival

August
tbc The Hereford Show, The Bullinghope Fields, Hereford (off A49)
tbc Ross-on-Wye International Festival
tbc Three Choirs Fringe Festival
tbc Eardisland Annual Duck Races

September
21-23 Bromyard Folk Festival

October
tbc Big Apple Weekend, Much Marcle, nr Ledbury
19 Oct-17 Nov Herefordshire Photography Festival

Top: Abbey Dore

ASHTON

Berrington Hall

Berrington HR6 0DW (3m N of Leominster, on A49)
☎ 01568 615721 ▯ 01568 613263
e-mail: benington@smtp.ntrust.org.uk

An elegant neo-classical house of the late 18th century, designed by Henry Holland and set in a park landscape by `Capability' Brown. There is a restored bedroom suite, a nursery, a Victorian laundry and a tiled Georgian dairy.

Times: Open Apr-Oct, Sat-Wed & Good Fri 1.30-5.30 (4.30pm in Oct). Last admission 30min before closing. Garden open 12.30-6 (5pm in Oct). Park walk open Jul-Oct, same times as house.
Fee: £4.20 (ch £2.10) Family ticket £10. Garden only £2.
P ✕ licensed ♿ (by arrangement, Braille guide, 2 wheelchairs) toilets for disabled shop ✗ (ex guide dogs) ✿

BROCKHAMPTON

Lower Brockhampton

WR6 5UH (2m E of Bromyard on A44)
☎ 01885 488099 & 482077 ▯ 01885 482151

A late 14th-century moated manor house, with an attractive half-timbered 15th-century gatehouse, a rare example of this type of structure, and the ruins of a 12th-century chapel. It is part of a larger National Trust property covering over 1700 acres of Herefordshire countryside with various walks including a Sculpture Trail.

Times: Open: Medieval hall, Parlour, Minstrel gallery, Information room, gatehouse & chapel 29 Mar-Sep, Wed-Sun & BH Mon 10-5. Oct, Wed-Sun 10-4.
Fee: £2.50 (ch £1.25).
P ☕ ♿ (special parking for disabled) toilets for disabled ✗ ✿

CROFT

Croft Castle

HR6 9PW (off B4362)
☎ 01568 780246 ▯ 01568 780462
e-mail: croft@smtp.ntrust.org.uk

Home of the Croft family since Domesday (with a break of 170 years from 1750); walls and towers date from the 14th and 15th centuries; the interior is mainly 18th century. There is a splendid avenue of 350-year-old Spanish chestnuts, and an Iron Age Fort (Croft Ambrey) may be reached by footpath.

Times: Open Etr Sat & Sun; Apr Sat, Sun & BH Mon 1.30-4.30; Oct-1 Nov Sat & Sun 1.30-4.30; May-Sep, Wed-Sun & BH Mon 1.30-5.30. Last admission to house half hour before closing. Parkland open all year. (Closed Good Fri).
Fee: House & grounds £3.80. Family ticket £9.50. Grounds only, £2 per car.
P (charged) ☕ ♿ (parking available, braille guide) ✗ (ex in parkland) ✿

GOODRICH

Goodrich Castle

HR9 6HY (5m S of Ross-on-Wye, off A40)
☎ 01600 890538

Goodrich Castle dominates an ancient crossing of the River Wye. Its huge towers, graceful arches and chapel are well worth the visit, and there is a maze of rooms, passages and a gloomy dungeon to be explored. It was besieged in the Civil War, and the locally made canon used to bombard it, and nicknamed 'Roaring Meg', is on display in Hereford Cathedral.

Times: Open all year, Apr-Sep, daily 10-6 (Oct 10-5); Nov-Mar 10-4. Closed 24-26 Dec & 1 Jan.
Fee: £3.20 (ch 5-15 £1.60, under 5's free)
P ✗ #

HEREFORD

Churchill House Museum & Hatton Art Gallery

3 Venn's Ln HR1 1DE
☎ 01432 267409 & 260693 ▯ 01432 342492

The museum is laid out in a Regency house with fine grounds, and has 18th and early 19th-century rooms, Victorian nursery, kitchen and parlour, displays of costume and furniture, and a gallery devoted to works by the local artist Brian Hatton.

Times: Open 2-5 Apr-Sep, Wed-Sun, inc BH Mons.
P ♿ (access guide & tape,braille guides & plans) shop ✗ *Details not confirmed for 2001*

Cider Museum & King Offa Distillery

21 Ryelands St HR4 OLW (off A438 Hereford to Brecon road)
☎ 01432 354207 ▯ 01432 371641

Explore the fascinating history of cider making - old cidermaking equipment, the cooper's workshop and Vat house with hydraulic presses and bottling machinery.

Times: Open all year, Apr-Oct, daily 10-5.30; Nov-Dec, daily 11-3. Jan-Mar, Tue-Sun 11-3. Pre-booked groups at anytime.
Fee: £2.40 (concessions £1.90). Party 15+.
P ☕ ♿ shop ✗ (ex guide dogs)

Hereford Cathedral

Broad St HR1 2NG (A49 to Hereford, signed from city inner ring roads)
☎ 01432 374202 ▯ 01432 374220
e-mail: office@herefordcathedral.co.uk

The first bishop was appointed to the See of Hereford in 676AD. The cathedral is mainly Norman with a 13th-century Lady Chapel. Hereford's two outstanding treasures are exhibited together in the museum building at the West front. The Mappa Mundi - drawn in 1289, and the famous Chained Library - containing over 1400 chained books and 227 manuscripts dating from the 8th century.

Times: Cathedral open daily for visitors 9.30-5; Mappa Mundi & Chained Library Exhibition Mon-Sat 11-4.15 (last admission), Sun 12-3.15.

contd.

Fee: Cathedral admission free (donation invited). Mappa Mundi & Chained Library Exhibition £4 (concessions £3). Family £10. Party 10+.
P (0.25m) ♿ (touch facility for blind & partially sighted) toilets for disabled shop (ex guide dogs)

OLD HOUSE

High Town HR1 2AA (located in the centre of the High Town)
☎ 01432 260694

This good example of a Jacobean house was built in around 1621, and was once in a row of similar houses. The hall, kitchens, and a bedroom with a four-poster bed can be seen along with a number of wall paintings.
Times: Open Mon 10-4.45, Tue-Thu 9.15-4.45, Fri 9.15-4.
Fee: Free.
P ♿ shop (ex guide dogs)

KINGTON

HERGEST CROFT GARDENS

HR5 3EG (0.25m W off A44)
☎ 01544 230160 📠 01544 230160
e-mail: banks@hergest.kc3.co.uk

From spring bulbs to autumn colour, this is a garden for all seasons. A fine collection of trees and shrubs surrounds the Edwardian house. There's an old fashioned kitchen garden with spring and summer borders, and Park Wood, a hidden valley with splendid rhododendrons.
Times: Open Apr-Oct, 1.30-6.00.
Fee: £3.50 (ch under 16 free). Party 20+
P ♿ (portable ramp available) toilets for disabled shop garden centre

LEDBURY

EASTNOR CASTLE

Eastnor HR8 1RL (the castle is 2.5m E of Ledbury on the A438 Tewkesbury road)
☎ 01531 633160 📠 01531 631776
e-mail: eastnorcastle@btinternet.com

A magnificent Georgian castle in a lovely setting, with a deer park, arboretum and lake. Inside are tapestries, fine art and armour, and the Italianate and Gothic interiors have been beautifully restored. There's an adventure playground, nature trails and lakeside walks.

Times: Open Etr-end Sep Sun & Bh Mon, Jul & Aug Sun-Fri 11-5 last admission 4.30pm.
Fee: Castle & grounds £4.75 (ch £2.50) Family £12. Grounds £2.75 (ch £1.50).
P ✕ ♿ shop garden centre

SWAINSHILL

THE WEIR GARDENS

HR4 8BS (5m W of Hereford, on A438)
☎ 01981 590509 (info line)
e-mail: sevinfo@smtp.ntrust.org.uk

A delightful riverside garden which is at its best in spring when there are lovely displays of naturalised bulbs set in woodland and grassland walks. Cliff garden walks can be taken here, with fine views of the River Wye and the Welsh hills.
Times: Open 14 Feb-Oct, Wed-Sun & BH Mon 11-6.
Fee: £2.
P

Hertfordshire

Southeastern county of England, close to London, making its county town of Hertford and the towns of Hemel Hempstead, Watford and Harpenden a haven for commuters to the capital.

St Albans, less than 19 miles (30km) from London, has retained its distinctive character, along with many historic remains. The Roman city of Verulamiun is situated in a nearby park, and excavations have revealed an amphitheatre, a temple, parts of the city walls and the foundations of houses. Some spectacular mosaic pavements are displayed in the Verulamiun Museum.

The abbey church at St Albans is built on the site where St Alban, the first British Christian martyr, was executed in the 4th century. The abbey was founded in 793, and contains his shrine, made of Purbeck marble. Lost for years, it was discovered in the 19th century, broken in peices, and restored by Sir Giles Gilbert Scott. Rebuilt by the Normans, the abbey contains some wonderful medieval wall paintings.

Nicholas Breakspear was born in St Albans, the son of an abbey tenant. In 1154 he took the name Adrian IV, and became the first, and so far only, English pope.

Another famous historic son of Hertfordshire was Sir Francis Bacon, Elizabethan scholar and Lord High Chancellor, who some believe was the real author of Shakespeare's plays. He was born at Gorhambury House near Hemel Hempstead in 1561.

In the market town of Hitchin lavender is grown and distilled in the time honoured way. The practice was introduced from Naples in the 16th century.

EVENTS & FESTIVALS

May
28 Luton Carnival
28 May-2 Jun Enjoy Your City Week, St Albans
Knebworth House
tbc Herts County Show, Redbourn

June
tbc Hertford Carnival
23-24 Festival of Gardening, Hatfield House

July
11-21 St Albans Organ Festival, cathedral and various venues
tbc Fireworks & Laser Concert, Knebworth House

August
28 St Albans Carnival

September
1-2 Discover St Albans Festival
8 Hoddeson Carnival
27-30 St Albans Beer Festival, Alban Arena

October
21 Apple Day Fair & Market, St Albans

November
3 Firework display, Verulamium Park, St Albans

Top: Grand Union Canal, Berkhampstead

AYOT ST LAWRENCE

SHAW'S CORNER
AL6 9BX (at SW end of village)
☎ 01438 820307
e-mail: tsc.gen@smtp.ntrust.org.uk

George Bernard Shaw lived here from 1906 until his death in 1950. He gave the house to the National Trust in 1946, and the contents are much as they were in his time. Among the displays are his hats, including a soft homburg he wore for 60 years, his exercise machine, fountain pen, spectacles and several pictures.

Times: Open Apr-29 Oct, Wed-Sun & BH Mon 1-5. Last admission 4.30pm. (Closed Good Fri)
Fee: £3.50. Family ticket £8.75
(braille guide to house, scented plants, items to touch) (ex on lead in car park)

BERKHAMSTED

BERKHAMSTED CASTLE
HP4 1HF
☎ 01536 402840

Roads and a railway have cut into the castle site, but its huge banks and ditches remain impressive. The original motte-and-bailey was built after the Norman Conquest, and there is a later stone keep, owned by the Black Prince, eldest son of King Edward III, where King John of France was imprisoned.

Times: Open all year, daily 10-4. Keykeeper.
Fee: Free.

HATFIELD

HATFIELD HOUSE
AL9 5NQ (2m from jct 4 A1(M) on A1000, 7m from M25 jct 23)
☎ 01707 262823 01707 275719

Robert Cecil built this great Jacobean mansion in 1607-11, replacing the palace where Elizabeth I spent much of her childhood. There are portraits of the queen, and historic possessions such as her silk stockings. The great park and gardens include a parterre planted with yews and roses, a scented garden and a knot garden. Hatfield is still the home of the Cecils, who once had a private waiting room at the nearby railway station.

Times: Open 24 Mar-23 Sep. (Closed Good Fri). House: Tue-Thur, 12-4, wknds 1-4.30. (Closed Mon ex BH 11-4.30). Gardens: daily 11-6 (ex Mon)
Fee: House Park & Gardens £6.40 (ch £3.20). Park only £2 (ch £1). Party 20+.
licensed toilets for disabled shop garden centre (ex guide dogs & in park)

KNEBWORTH

KNEBWORTH HOUSE, GARDENS & COUNTRY PARK
SG3 6PY (direct access from junct 7 A1(M) at Stevenage)
☎ 01438 812661 01438 811908
e-mail: info@kebworthhouse.com

The original Tudor manor was transformed in 1843 by the spectacular high Gothic decoration of Victorian novelist Sir Edward Bulwer Lytton. The formal gardens, laid out by Lutyens in 1908, include a Jekyll herb garden, a maze, recently restored walled garden and wilderness walks. The 250-acre park includes a miniature railway, an adventure playground, and a deer park.

Times: Telephone for details
Fee: £6 (ch & pen £5.50); Park, Playground & Gardens only: £5. Family ticket £17.50. Party 20+.
(with prior notice visitors can be driven to front door) toilets for disabled shop (2 shops) garden centre (ex guide dogs & in park)

LETCHWORTH

MUSEUM & ART GALLERY
Broadway SG6 3PF (Museum is situated next door to the Public Library, in the Town Centre, near the Broadway Cinema)
☎ 01462 685647 01462 481879
e-mail: letchworth.museum@nhdc.gov.uk

Opened in 1914 to house the collections of the Letchworth Naturalists' Society, this local museum has exhibits on local wildlife, geology, arts and crafts, and archaeology. Also a museum shop and a regular programme of workshops.

Times: Open all year Mon-Sat 10-5. (Closed most BHs).
Fee: Free.
P (100 yds) (special provisions on request) shop (ex guide dogs)

LONDON COLNEY

De Havilland Aircraft Heritage

Salisbury Hall AL2 1EX (signposted from junct 22 of M25)
01727 822051 & 826400 01727 826400

The oldest aircraft museum in Britain, opened in 1959 to preserve the de Havilland Mosquito prototype on the site of its conception. The collection includes photographs, memorabilia and aero-engine displays, as well as aircraft: Mosquitoes, Venoms, a Tiger Moth, a Dove and a Horsa among others.
Times: Open Mar-Oct, Sun & BH Mons 10.30-5.30, Tue, Thu & Sat 2-5.30.
Fee: £4 (ch & pen £2) Family ticket £10.
P (wheelchairs available) toilets for disabled shop (not accessible for disabled) (ex on lead & under control)

ST ALBANS

Clock Tower

Market Place
01727 853301

This early 15th-century curfew tower, which faces the High Street, provides fine views over the city (especially of the abbey) and the surrounding countryside. This is one of the only two medieval curfew towers in the country. It has a bell which strikes on the hour and is older than the tower itself.
Times: Open Good Fri-mid Sep, Sat, Sun & BH 10.30-5.
Fee: 30p (ch 5-11 15p, accompanied ch under 5 free)
P (400yds) shop

Gardens of The Rose (Royal National Rose Society)

Chiswell Green AL2 3NR (2m S off B4630 Watford Rd in Chiswell Green Ln)
01727 850461 01727 850360
e-mail: mail@rnrs.org.uk

The gardens of the Royal National Rose Society, which include the International Trial Ground for new roses. The gardens contain over 30,000 plants in 1,650 different varieties. These include old-fashioned roses, modern roses and the roses of the future. The National Miniature Rose Show takes place during July.

Times: Open 27 May-24 Sep, Mon-Sat 9-5 (Sun & BH Mon 10-6).
Fee: Summer season: £4 (ch £5-15 £1.50, pen & UB40 £3.50) Party 20+.
P (ramps where necessary) toilets for disabled shop

Gorhambury

AL3 6AH (entry via lodge gates on A414)
☎ 01727 855000 📠 01727 843675

This house was built by Sir Robert Taylor between 1774 and 1784 to house an extensive picture collection of 17th-century portraits of the Grimston and Bacon families and their contemporaries. Also of note is the 16th-century enamelled glass collection and an early English pile carpet.

Times: Open May-Sep, Thu 2-5.
Fee: £6 (ch £3, pen £4). Party.
P shop

Museum of St Albans

Hatfield Rd AL1 3RR (situated in City Centre on A1057 Hatfield road)
☎ 01727 819340 📠 01727 837472

Exhibits include the Salaman collection of craft tools, and reconstructed workshops. The history of St Albans is traced from the departure of the Romans up to the present day.

Times: Open all year, daily 10-5, Sun 2-5. Closed 25 & 26 Dec.
Fee: Free.
P ♿ toilets for disabled shop (ex guide dogs)

Roman Theatre of Verulamium

St Michaels AL3 6AH (off A4147)
☎ 01727 835035 📠 01727 843675

The theatre was discovered in 1847 and excavated in 1935. It is unique in England. First constructed around AD160, it is semi-circular in shape, 180ft across and could hold 1,600 spectators.

Times: Open all year, daily 10-5 (4 in winter). Closed 25-26 Dec. New years day by appointment only.
Fee: £1.50 (ch 50p, students & OAPs £1). Ch under 5yrs free.
P ♿ shop

St Albans Cathedral

Sumpter Yard AL1 1BY (in the centre of St Albans)
☎ 01727 860780 📠 01727 850944
e-mail: admin@stalbanscathedal.org.uk

An imposing Norman abbey church built on the site of the execution of St Alban, Britain's first martyr (c250AD). The cathedral is constructed from recycled Roman brick taken from nearby Verulamium.

Times: Open daily, 9-5.45
Fee: Free.
P (200mtrs) ✕ licensed ♿ (touch & hearing centre, braille guides) toilets for disabled shop (ex guide dogs)

Verulamium Museum

St Michaels AL3 4SW (follow signs for St Albans, museum signposted)
☎ 01727 751810 📠 01727 859919
e-mail: acoles@stalbons.gov.uk

Verulamium was one of the largest and most important Roman towns in Britain - by the lst century AD it was declared a `municipium', giving its inhabitants the rights of Roman citizenship, the only British city granted this honour. A mosaic and underfloor heating system can be seen, and the museum has wall paintings, jewellery, pottery and other domestic items. On the second weekend of every month legionaries occupy the galleries and describe the tactics and equipment of the Roman Imperial Army and the life of a legionary.

Times: Open all year weekdays 10-5.30, Sun 2-5.30.
Fee: £3 (ch, pen & students £1.70). Family ticket £7.50. Subject to change.
P (charged) ♿ (ramp access to main entrance) toilets for disabled shop (ex guide dogs)

TRING

The Walter Rothschild Zoological Museum

Akeman St HP23 6AP (signposted from A41)
☎ 020 7942 6171 📠 020 7942 6150

An unusual museum, founded in the 1890s by Lionel Walter, 2nd Baron Rothschild, scientist, eccentric and natural history enthusiast. Now part of the Natural History Museum, it houses more than 4000 specimens from whales to fleas, and humming birds to tigers.

Times: Open all year, Mon-Sat 10-5, Sun 2-5. (Closed 24-26 Dec).
Fee: £3.50 (concessions £2, Ch 16 and under & pen free).
P ♿ (ramps provided to shop & cafe) toilets for disabled shop (ex guide dogs)

WARE

Scott's Grotto

Scott's Rd SG12 9JQ (off A119)
☎ 01920 464131

Scott's Grotto, built in the 1760s by the Quaker poet John Scott, has been described by English Heritage as `one of the finest in England'. Recently restored by the Ware Society, it consists of underground passages and chambers decorated with flints, shells, minerals and stones, and extends 67ft into the side of the hill. Please wear flat shoes and bring a torch.

Times: Open early Apr-end Sep, Sat & BH Mon 2-4.30. Other times by appointment only.
Fee: Free.
P (on street)

Kent

Often called the 'garden of England', Kent is renowned for its fruit production in the agricultural area of the Weald, and its hop growing for the brewing industry. Hops were picked by itinerant workers, many from London, who moved in for the season.

For many years, Londoners have flocked to the seaside resorts of the Isle of Thanet, Margate, Broadstairs and Ramsgate. Of these, Broadstairs retains a quiet charm, and is probably best known as Charles Dickens' resort of choice, where he lived overlooking the bay, in a rather forbidding residence since known as Bleak House. More popular yet with visitors from all over the world is the ancient city of Canterbury, the metropolis of the Anglican church since Augustine's mission to England in 597, and site of the magnificent cathedral.

The Channel Tunnel and the Channel ports of Dover, Folkestone and Ramsgate ensure good transport links into the county. The administrative centre is Maidstone, and other main towns are Chatham, home of the historic Royal Naval Dockyard; Rochester with its lovely cathedral; and the elegant spa town of Royal Tunbridge Wells.

Kent is blessed with some fine castles, houses and gardens. Chief among these are Leeds Castle, east of Maidstone; Hever Castle, birthplace of Anne Boleyn; Knole, southeast of Sevenoaks, England's largest house with 365 rooms; Churchill's house, Chartwell, near Westerham; Penshurst Place, a 14th-century house with a splendid hall and long gallery; and the inspirational Sissinghurst Garden created by Vita Sackville-West.

THE ROMNEY, HYTHE & DYMCHURCH LIGHT RAILWAY

EVENTS & FESTIVALS

May
20 May-2 Jun Ramsgate Spring Festival, various venues (mixed arts event)
28 Sellindge Steam Festival, Ashford
tbc Finchcocks Spring Garden Fair, Goudhurst, Cranbrook
tbc Kent Garden Show, Kent & County Showground
tbc Tonbridge Carnival

June
tbc Broadstairs Dickens Festival

July
12-14 Kent County Show, Maidstone
25-29 July Scandals at the Spa Georgian Festival, The Pantiles, Tunbridge Wells

August
27 Sedan Chair Race, The Pantiles, Tunbridge Wells
tbc Broadstairs & St Peters Carnival
tbc Broadstairs Folk Week
tbc Margate Summer Carnival

October
tbc Celebrity Connections, Broadstairs

December
27-30 Winter Street Festival, Tunbridge Wells

Top: Whitstable Harbour

AYLESFORD

Aylesford Priory

The Friars ME20 7BX (M20 J6 then signed)
☎ 01622 717272 Fax 01622 715575
e-mail: friarsevents@hotmail.com

Built in the 13th and 14th centuries, the Priory has been restored and is now a house of prayer, guesthouse, conference centre and a place of pilgrimage and retreat. It has fine cloisters, and displays sculpture and ceramics by modern artists.

Times: Open all year, daily 9-dusk. Gift & book shop May-Sep, 10-5; Oct-Apr, 10-4 (Sun 11am). Guided tours of the priory by arrangement.
Fee: Donations. £2 for annual fund-raising day.
(wheelchairs available, ramps) toilets for disabled shop (ex guide & hearing dogs)

BEKESBOURNE

Howletts Wild Animal Park

CT4 5EL (off A2, 3m S of Canterbury, follow brown tourist signs)
☎ 01227 721286 Fax 01227 721853
e-mail: philiph@howletts.net

Howletts is one of John Aspinall's wild animal parks and has the world's largest breeding gorilla colony in captivity. It also has tigers, small cats, free-running deer and antelope, snow leopards, bison, honey badgers, African elephants, and many endangered species of monkey.

Times: Open all year, daily 10-5, (3.30pm in winter). Closed 25 Dec.
Fee: £9.80 (ch 4-14 & pen £7.80) family ticket £28
licensed toilets for disabled shop

BELTRING

Hop Farm & Country Park

TN12 6PY (on A228 at Paddock Wood)
☎ 01622 872068 Fax 01622 872630

The largest group of Victorian oast houses and galleried barns in the country, with features including the Hop Story Exhibition, Shire Horse Centre and pottery workshop.

Times: Open all year from 10am (Closed 25-26 & 31 Dec)
Fee: £5.80 (ch 5-15 & pen £3.80). Family ticket £16 (2 adults & 2 ch) under 4's free.
licensed toilets for disabled shop

BIDDENDEN

Biddenden Vineyards

Little Whatmans TN27 8DH (0.5m S off A262, between Biddenden & Tenterden)
☎ 01580 291726 Fax 01580 291933

The present vineyard was established in 1969 and now covers 22 acres. Visitors are welcome to stroll around the vineyard and to taste wines, ciders and apple juice available at the shop.

Times: Open all year, Shop: Mon-Fri 10-5, Sat 10-5, Sun &BH 11-5. Closed noon 24 Dec-2 Jan & Sun in Jan & Feb.
Fee: Non-guided groups and individuals free. Pre-booked guided tours (minimum 15 adults) £2.85 (ch 10-18 £1, ch under 12 free).
shop

BOROUGH GREEN

Great Comp Garden

TN15 8QS (2m E off B2016)
☎ 01732 882669 & 886154

A beautiful seven-acre garden created since 1957 by Mr and Mrs R Cameron for low maintenance and year-round interest. There is a plantsmans' collection of trees, shrubs, heathers and herbaceous plants in a setting of fine lawns and grass paths. The 17th-century house is not open. Chamber music, classical concerts and other events are organised by the Great Comp Society.

Times: Open Apr-Oct, daily 11-6.
Fee: £3.50 (ch £1). Annual ticket £10 (pen £7).
toilets for disabled garden centre (ex guide dogs)

BRASTED

Emmetts Garden

Ide Hill TN14 6AY (1m S of A25, Sundridge-Ide Hill road)
☎ 01732 868381 (Chartwell office) Fax 01732 868193
e-mail: kchxxx@smpt.ntrust.org.uk

Emmetts is a charming hillside shrub garden, with bluebells, azaleas and rhododendrons in spring and fine autumn colours. It has magnificent views over Bough Beech Reservoir and the Weald. Emmetts Blues Concert in August.

Times: Open Apr & May, Wed-Sun; Jun-Oct, Wed & wknds 11-5.30 (last admission 4.30pm). Special arrangement for pre-booked parties at other times.
Fee: £3.20 (ch £1.60). Family ticket £7.50.
(buggy service from car park to garden) toilets for disabled shop

BROADSTAIRS

Bleak House Dickens Maritime & Smuggling

Fort Rd CT10 1EY (off Eastern Esplanade, near Viking Bay)
☎ 01843 862224

The house was a favourite seaside residence of Charles Dickens, and he wrote the greater part of *David Copperfield* and other works here, and drafted the idea for *Bleak House*. There are also exhibitions of relics salvaged from the Goodwin Sands, and Kent's only smuggling museum.

Times: Open mid Feb-mid Dec, daily; Jan-mid Feb wknds only.
Fee: £3 (ch under 12 £2, pen £2.50, students £2.20).
(100 yds) (provisions made for blind) shop

Dickens House Museum

Victoria Pde CT10 1QS (on the seafront)
☎ 01843 862853

The house was immortalised by Charles Dickens in *David Copperfield* as the home of the hero's aunt, Betsy Trotwood. Dickens' letters and possessions are shown, with local and Dickensian prints, costumes and general

Victoriana. The Broadstairs Dickens Festival takes place in June.

Times: Open Apr-mid Oct, daily 2-5.

Fee: £1.50 (ch 50p).

P (400yds) (play & display) shop (ex guide dogs)

CANTERBURY

Canterbury Heritage Museum

Stour St CT1 2RA (in the Medieval Poor Priest's Hospital, just off Saint Margaret's St)

☎ 01227 452747 01227 455047

Times: Open all year, Mon-Sat 10.30-5 & Sun (Jun-Oct) 1.30-5 (last admission 4pm). (Closed Good Fri & Xmas period).

P shop *Details not confirmed for 2001*

Canterbury Roman Museum

Butchery Ln, Longmarket CT1 2RA

☎ 01227 785575 01227 455047

Times: Open all year, Mon-Sat 10-5 & Sun (Jun-Oct) 1.30-5. Last admission 4pm. (Closed Good Fri & Xmas period).

P (500mtrs) (lift) toilets for disabled shop *Details not confirmed for 2001*

Canterbury Royal Museum, Art Gallery & Buffs Regimental Museum

High St CT1 2RA

☎ 01227 452747 01227 455047

Times: Open all year, Mon-Sat 10-5. (Closed Good Fri and Xmas period).

P shop *Details not confirmed for 2001*

Canterbury Tales Visitor Attraction

Saint Margaret's St CT1 2TG (In heart of city centre, follow finger sign-posting)

☎ 01227 479227 01227 765584

e-mail: thecanterburytaleshotmail.com

Step back in time to join Chaucer's famous band of pilgrims on their journey to the shrine of St Thomas Becket in Canterbury Cathedral. Hear their tales of love, greed, chivalry and intrigue and experience life in the 14th century, complete with authentic sights, sounds and smells.

Times: Open all year, Mar-Jun & Sep-Oct daily 9.30-5.30; Jul-Aug daily 9-5.30, Nov-Feb, Sun-Fri 10-4.30, Sat 9.30-5.30.

Fee: £5.50 (concessions £4.60). Family ticket £17.50.

P (200 mtrs) (notice required for wheelchairs) toilets for disabled shop (except guide dogs)

Canterbury West Gate Museum

Saint Peter's St (at the end of the main street beside the river, the entrance is under the main arch)

☎ 01227 452747 01227 455047

Times: Open all year (ex Good Fri & Xmas period), Mon-Sat; 11-12.30 & 1.30-3.30. Last admission 15 mins before closure

P (100 yds) shop *Details not confirmed for 2001*

Druidstone Wildlife Park

Honey Hill, Blean CT2 9JR (3m NW on A290)

☎ 01227 765168 01227 768860

Enjoy the company of the animals and birds in a relaxing country setting. Experience a taste of the South American plains with the rhea, mara and peccary. Make friends with the animals in the farmyard, meet the parrots, walk through the gardens which are home to the owls and wallaby, or along the woodland trail.

Times: Open Etr-Oct daily 10-5.30; Nov Fri-Wed 10-4.30.

Fee: £3.50 (ch £2.50 & concessions £3). Family ticket £10.

P toilets for disabled shop (ex guide dogs)

St Augustine's Abbey

Longport CT1 1TF (off A28)

☎ 01227 767345

The abbey, founded by St Augustine in 598, when he brought Christianity from Rome to England, is one of the oldest monastic sites in the country. Its long and fascinating history can be traced in the ruins.

Times: Open all year, Apr-Oct, daily 10-6 (Oct 10-5); Nov-Mar, daily 10-4. Closed 24-26 Dec & 1 Jan.

Fee: £2.50 (ch 5-15 £1.30, under 5's free).

P shop #

CHARTWELL

Chartwell

TN16 1PS (2m S of Westerham, off B2026)

☎ 01732 866368 (info line) & 868381

01732 868193

e-mail: kchxxx@smpt.ntrust.org.uk

The former home of Sir Winston Churchill is filled with reminders of the great statesman, from his hats and uniforms to gifts presented by Stalin and Roosevelt. There are paintings of Churchill and other works by notable artists, and also many paintings by Churchill himself.

Times: Open Apr-29 Oct, house, garden & studio, Wed-Sun & BH Mon 11-5. Open BH Mons & Tue in Jul/Aug. Last admission 4.15pm.

Fee: House, Garden & studio £5.50 (ch £2.75). Gardens and studio only £2.75 (ch £1.30). Family ticket £13.75.

P ✕ licensed (2 steps to lift, grounds partially accessible, parking) toilets for disabled shop (ex garden)

CHATHAM

FORT AMHERST

Dock Rd ME4 4UB (adjacent to the A231 dock road, 0.5m from Chatham Dockyard)

☎ 01634 847747 📠 01634 847747

Times: Open daily 10.30-last entry 4pm

P ☕ ♿ (wheelchair provided, road access up to fort) toilets for disabled shop 🐕 (ex guide dogs) *Details not confirmed for 2001*

WORLD NAVAL BASE

The Historic Dockyard ME4 4TZ (short distance from M25. Signposted as 'Historic Dockyard' from junct 1, 3 & 4 of M2)

☎ 01634 823800 📠 01634 823801

e-mail: info@worldnavalbase.org.uk

The World Naval Base celebrates over 400 years of naval history in one 80-acre site. Exhibits include Battle Ships with WWII destroyer *HMS Cavalier* and the spy sub *Ocelot;* Lifeboat with a display of 15 full size boats, archive film and artifacts; and Wooden Walls which looks at the life of a carpenter's apprentice in the 18th century.

Times: Open Apr-Oct, daily 10-5; Feb, Mar & Nov, Wed, Sat & Sun 10-4.

Fee: £8.50 (ch 5-16 £5.50, student & pen £6.30). Family ticket (2 adults & 4 ch) £22.50.

P ☕ ✕ licensed ♿ (wheelchair available, Braille guides) toilets for disabled shop

CHIDDINGSTONE

CHIDDINGSTONE CASTLE

TN8 7AD (off B2027, at Bough Beech)

☎ 01892 870347

Times: Open Apr-May, Oct, Easter & Public Holidays, Jun-Sep, Wed-Fri & Sun. Weekdays 2-5.30; Sun & BH 11.30-5.30.

P ☕ ♿ shop 🐕 (ex guide dogs or lead) *Details not confirmed for 2001*

DEAL

DEAL CASTLE

Victoria Rd CT14 7BA (SW of Deal town centre)

☎ 01304 372762

This huge, austere structure, shaped like a Tudor rose, was an important part of the coastal defences built by Henry VIII. Its unrelenting walls are rounded to deflect cannon shot and inside, the dark passages tell the reality of garrison life.

Times: Open all year, Apr-Oct, daily 10-6 (Oct 10-5); Nov-Mar, Wed-Sun 10-4. Closed 24-26 Dec & 1 Jan.

Fee: £3 (ch 5-15 £1.50 under 5's free). Personal stereo tour included in admission price.

♿ shop #

WALMER CASTLE

Walmer, Kingsdown Rd CT14 7LJ (1m S on coast, off A258)

☎ 01304 364288

Of similar design to Deal Castle, Walmer was also part of the defences of Tudor England. It is the official residence of the Lord Warden of the Cinque Ports (Dover, Sandwich, Hythe, Romney and Hastings were the original five) an honorary post now held by Queen Elizabeth the Queen Mother.

Times: Open all year, Apr-Oct, daily 10-6 (Oct 10-5); Nov-Mar, Wed-Sun 10-4. Closed 24-26 Dec, 1 Jan & when Lord Warden in residence Jan & Feb.

Fee: £4.50 (ch 5-15 £2.30, under 5's free). Personal stereo tour included in admission price, also available for the partially sighted, those with learning difficulties.

P ♿ shop 🐕 (in certain areas) #

DOVER

CRABBLE CORN MILL

Lower Rd, River CT17 0UY (follow signs to River from A258)

☎ 01304 823292 📠 01304 826040

e-mail: mill@invmed.demon.co.uk

Times: Open all year, Etr-Jun & Sep, Sat & Sun 11-5; Jul-Aug, Wed-Sun 11-5; Winter Sun 11-5.

P ☕ ✕ licensed ♿ shop 🐕 *Details not confirmed for 2001*

DOVER CASTLE & SECRET WARTIME TUNNELS

CT16 1HU

☎ 01304 211067

A giant among England's castles, set high on the famous white cliffs, Dover Castle traces its history back to the Iron Age, and many relics of its different periods remain. The underground tunnel system, nicknamed Hellfire Corner, was originally built in medieval times.

Times: Open all year, Apr-Sep, daily 10-6 (Oct 10-5); Nov-Mar, daily 10-4. Closed 24-26 Dec & 1 Jan.

Fee: £6.90 (ch 5-15m £3.50, under 5's free).

P ✕ ♿ shop 🐕 (in certain areas) #

OLD TOWN GAOL

Dover Town Hall, Biggin St CT16 1DL (Follow brown tourist signs from Dover town centre)

☎ 01304 201200 📠 01304 201200

High-tech animation, audio-visual techniques and `talking heads' take visitors back to Victorian England to experience the horrors of life behind bars, listening, as they walk through the reconstructed courtroom, exercise yard, washroom and cells, to the stories of the felons and their jailers. You can even try the prisoners' beds or find out what it's like to be locked in a 6ft x 4ft cell!

Times: Open all year, Tue-Sat 10-4.30, Sun 2-4.30. (Closed Mon & Tue, Oct-May). Telephone 01304 202723 for further information.

Fee: £3.50 (ch & pen £2.10).

(charged) shop (ex guide dogs)

Roman Painted House

New St CT17 9AJ

☎ 01304 203279

Visit five rooms of a Roman hotel built 1800 years ago, famous for its unique, well-preserved Bacchic frescos. The Roman underfloor heating system and part of a late-Roman defensive wall are also on view. There are extensive displays on Roman Dover, and special events are held throughout the year.

Times: Open Apr-Sep, Tue-Sun 10-5, also BH Mon & Mon Jul & Aug.

Fee: £2 (ch & pen 80p)

(touch table, glass panels on gallery for wheelchairs) shop

The White Cliffs Experience

Market Square CT16 1PB (signposting on entering town centre from A2 and M20/A20, follow signs)

☎ 01304 214566 & 210101 01304 212057

e-mail: tourism@doveruk.com

This award-winning attraction provides an entertaining and exciting encounter with life in Roman Britain and during World War II. The new Dover Bronze Age Boat Gallery contains what is believed to be the world's oldest seagoing boat.

Times: Open daily, Apr-Oct 10-5. Closed 1hr after last admissions. Nov-mid Feb open to pre-booked groups only. Closed mid Dec-mid Jan.

Fee: £5.95 (ch 4-14 £4.15, pen & students £4.80) Family ticket £18.95.

(150 yds) (lifts, ramped access, wheelchair & seat sticks) toilets for disabled shop (ex guide dogs/hearing dogs)

DUNGENESS

Dungeness Power Stations' Visitor Centre

TN29 9PP (Follow A259 to New Romney, right turn signposted B2075 to Lydd, power station signposted)

☎ 01797 321815 01797 321844

The `A' and `B' power stations at Dungeness make an extraordinary sight in a landscape of shingle, fishing boats and owner-built houses. There is a high-tech information centre, with `hands-on' interactive videos and many other displays and models including an environmental exhibition which depicts Dungeness from the Ice Age through to today.

Times: Open Mar-Oct, daily, 10-4. Regular Tours of A & B power stations available. No children under 5 allowed on tour. Nov-Feb by appointment only.

Fee: Free.

(information centre only/shortened tour by appointment) toilets for disabled shop (ex guide dogs)

DYMCHURCH

Martello Tower

(access from High St not seafront)

One of the many artillery towers built around the coast, which formed part of a chain of strongholds intended to resist an invasion by Napoleon. It is fully restored, with an original 24-pounder gun on the roof.

Times: Telephone 01304 211067 for opening details.

Fee: £1 (ch 50p, concessions 80p)

EDENBRIDGE

See Hever

EYNSFORD

Eynsford Castle

(off A225)

The walls of this Norman castle, still 30ft high, come as a surprise in the pretty little village. Its founder, William de Eynsford, ended his days as a monk.

Times: Open all year, Mar-Sep, daily 10-6; Oct-Feb, daily 10-4.

Fee: Free.

Lullingstone Castle

DA4 0JA (1m SW of Eynsford via A225)

☎ 01322 862114 01322 862115

The house was altered extensively in Queen Anne's time, and has fine state rooms and beautiful grounds. The 15th-century gate tower was one of the first gatehouses in England to be made entirely of bricks, and there is a church with family monuments.

Times: Open, House May-Aug, Sat, Sun & BH 2-6. Parties by arrangement.

Fee: House & Gardens £4 (ch £1.50 & pen £3).

shop

Lullingstone Roman Villa
DA4 0JA (half mile SW off A225)
☎ 01322 863467

The excavation of this Roman villa in 1939 uncovered one of the most exciting archaeological finds of that century. These are the most remarkable villa remains in Britain, including wonderful mosaic floors, wall paintings and one of the earliest Christian chapels.
Times: Open all year, Apr-Oct, daily 10-6 (Oct 10-5); Nov-Mar, daily 10-4. Closed 24-26 Dec & 1 Jan.
Fee: £2.50 (ch 5-15 £1.30, under 5's free). Personal stereo tour included in admission price.
P ✗ #

FAVERSHAM
Fleur de Lis Heritage Centre
13 Preston St ME13 8NS (3 minutes drive from M2 junction 6)
☎ 01795 534542
e-mail: faversham@btinternet.com

A thousand years of history and architecture in Faversham are shown in award-winning displays, an audio-visual programme, and a working vintage telephone exchange in this 16th-century building. There is a Tourist Information Centre and a bookshop. In July, the Faversham Open House Scheme is held, and over 20 historic properties in Faversham are opened to the public.
Times: Open all year, Mon-Sat, 10-4; Sun 10-1.
P (200 yds) ♿ shop

FOLKESTONE
Russian Submarine
South Quay, Folkestone Harbour CT20 1QH (adjacent to Hoverspeed Seacat Terminal)
☎ 01303 240400
e-mail: info@sovietsub.co.uk

The fascinating history of U475 (known as The Black Widow) is shrouded in secrecy. Only the select few, the Chiefs of Staff of the former Soviet Navy, know the full history. Was it part of their plan for the U475 to patrol the waters off Cuba after the successful deployment of missiles on the island in 1963? A mysterious and sometimes chilling day out.
Times: Open all year, Mon-Fri 10-dusk, wknds 10-7. Closed 25 Dec.
Fee: £3.50 (ch £2, concessions £3). Family ticket £9. Party.
P (charged) shop ✗ (inc guide dogs)

FORDWICH
Town Hall
The Square (off A28)
☎ 01227 710756 🖷 01227 713773

The timber-framed Tudor town hall and courtroom is thought to be the oldest and smallest in Britain. It overlooks the River Stour, peaceful now but hectic in the Middle Ages, because Fordwich was the port for Canterbury. The old town jail can also be visited.
Times: Open Etr, Jun-Sep, Sun 2-4 & Wed in Aug 2-4.
Fee: 60p (ch 15p).
P

GILLINGHAM
Royal Engineers Museum
Prince Arthur Rd ME4 4UG (follow brown signs from Gillingham & Chatham town centres)
☎ 01634 406397 🖷 01634 822371
e-mail: remuseum.rhqre@gtnet.gov.uk

The museum covers the diverse and sometimes surprising work of the Royal Engineers. Learn about the first military divers, photographers, aviators and surveyors; see memorabilia relating to General Gordon and Field Marshal Lord Kitchener, Wellington's battle map from Waterloo and a Harrier jump-jet.
Times: Open all year, Mon-Thu 10-5, Sat-Sun & BH Mon 11.30-5. (Closed Good Fri, 25-26 Dec & 1 Jan). Friday by appointment only.
Fee: £3.50 (ch, pen & UB40s £2). Family ticket £9. Guided tour £5. Party 15+.
P ♿ (help available if required, chair lift to upper level) toilets for disabled shop ✗ (ex guide dogs)

GOUDHURST
Finchcocks
TN17 1HH (off A262)
☎ 01580 211702 🖷 01580 211007
Times: Open Etr-Sep, Sun & BH Mon 2-6; Aug, Wed, Wed, Thu & Sun only 2-6. Private groups on other days by appointment Apr-Oct.
P ☕ ✕ licensed ♿ shop garden centre ✗ (ex guide dogs) *Details not confirmed for 2001*

HAWKINGE
Kent Battle of Britain Museum
Aerodrome Rd CT18 7AG (Hawkinge off A260, 1m along Aerodrome road)
☎ 01303 893140

Once a Battle of Britain Station, today it houses the largest collection of relics and related memorabilia of British and German aircraft involved in the fighting. Also shown full-size replicas of the Hurricane, Spitfire and Me109 used in Battle of Britain films. The year 2000 was the 60th anniversary of the Battle of Britain and a new memorial has been dedicated.
Times: Open Etr-Sep, daily 10-5; Oct, daily 11-4. Closed Nov-Etr. Last admission 1 hour before closing.
Fee: £3 (ch £1.50, pen £2.50). Group 20+.
P ♿ shop ✗ (ex guide dogs)

HEVER
Hever Castle & Gardens
TN8 7NG (M25 J5 or 6, 3m SE of Edenbridge, off B2026)
☎ 01732 865224 🖷 01732 866796
e-mail: mail@hevercastle.co.uk

This enchanting, double-moated, 13th-century castle was the childhood home of Anne Boleyn. Restored by the American millionaire William Waldorf Astor at the beginning of the 20th century, it shows superb Edwardian craftsmanship. Astor also transformed the grounds, creating a lake, a spectacular Italian garden filled with antique sculptures; and a maze. Recent additions to the gardens include a 110 metre herbaceous border and a 'splashing' water maze on the Sixteen Acre Island.

Times: Open 1 Mar-Nov, daily. Castle 12-6, Gardens 11-6. Last admission 5pm. (Closes 4pm Mar & Nov).

Fee: Castle & Gardens £7.80 (ch 5-14 £4.20, pen £6.60). Family ticket £19.80. Gardens only £6.10 (ch 5-14 £4, pen £5.20). Family ticket £16.20. Party 15+.

licensed (wheelchairs available, book in advance) toilets for disabled shop garden centre (ex on leads in grounds)

 HYTHE

ROMNEY, HYTHE & DYMCHURCH RAILWAY

TN28 8PL (off M20 junct 11, off A259 signed New Romney)

☎ 01797 362353 & 363256 01797 363591

e-mail: 106104.245@compuserve.com

The world's smallest public railway has its headquarters here. The concept of two enthusiasts coincided with Southern Railway's plans for expansion, and so the thirteen-and-a-half mile stretch of 15 inch gauge railway came into being, running from Hythe through New Romney and Dymchurch to Dungeness Lighthouse.

Times: Open daily Etr-Sep, also wknds in Mar & Oct. For times apply to: The Manager, RH & DR., New Romney, Kent.

Fee: Charged according to journey.

(charged) (stairlift to Toy & Model Museum) toilets for disabled shop (Dymchurch & Dungeness high season only)

IGHTHAM

IGHTHAM MOTE

TN15 0NT (2.5m S off A227, 6m E of Sevenoaks)

☎ 01732 810378 & 811145 (info line)

01732 811029

e-mail: kimxxx@smtp.ntrust.org.uk

This beautiful moated manor house is a splendid example of medieval architecture. Extensively remodelled through the centuries, notable features

contd.

include the drawing room with its Jacobean fireplace and frieze, Palladian window and hand-painted Chinese wallpaper.
Times: Open Apr-Nov, daily ex Tue & Sat, 11-5.30. Pre-booked parties wkday am only. Open Good Fri. Last admission 4.30pm.
Fee: £5 (ch £2.50). Family ticket £12.50.
(wheelchairs available,special parking ask at ticket office) toilets for disabled shop

LAMBERHURST

Bayham Abbey

TN3 8DE (off B2169, 2m W in East Sussex)
01892 890381

Set in the wooded Teise valley, these ruins date back to the 13th century and include parts of the old church, cloisters and gatehouse.
Times: Open Apr-Sep, daily 10-6 (Oct 10-5). Nov-Mar, wknds 10-4. Closed 24-26 Dec & 1 Jan
Fee: £2.10 (ch 5-15 £1.10 under 5's free).

Scotney Castle Garden

TN3 8JN (1m S, of Lamberhurst on A21)
01892 891081 01892 890110

The beautiful gardens at Scotney were planned in the 19th century around the remains of the old, moated Scotney Castle. There is something to see at every time of year, with spring flowers followed by rhododendrons, azaleas and a mass of roses, and then superb autumn colours.
Times: Open Garden: Apr-29 Oct. Old Castle open May-10 Sep Wed-Fri 11-6, Sat & Sun 2-6 or sunset if earlier. BH Sun & Mon 12-6. Additional opening 4-26 Mar, Sat & Sun 12-4. (Closed Good Fri). Last admission 1hr before closing.
Fee: £4.20 (ch £2.10). Family ticket £10.50.
(wheelchair available) toilets for disabled shop (ex guide & hearing dogs)

LEEDS

For **Leeds Castle** see **Maidstone**

LYDD

RSPB Nature Reserve

Boulderwall Farm, Dungeness Rd TN29 9PN (off Lydd to Dungeness road, 1m SE of Lydd)
01797 320588 01797 321962

This coastal reserve comprises 2106 acres of shingle beach and flooded pits. An excellent place to watch breeding terns, gulls and other water birds. Wheatears, great crested and little grebes also nest here, and outside the breeding season there are large flocks of teals, shovelers, and goldeneyes, goosanders, smews and both Slavonian and red-necked grebes.
Times: Open daily 9am-9pm (or sunset if earlier). Visitor Centre daily 10-5 Mar-Oct, 10-4 Nov-feb. (Closed 25 & 26 Dec).
Fee: £3 (ch £1, concessions £2). Family ticket £6.
(access by car to some hides) toilets for disabled shop (ex guide dogs)

LYMPNE

Port Lympne Wild Animal Park, Mansion & Garden

CT21 4PD (off M20 junct 11, follow brown tourist signs)
01303 264647 01303 264944
e-mail: philiph@howletts.net

John Aspinall's 300-acre wild animal park houses hundreds of rare animals: Indian elephants, rhinos, wolves, bison, black and snow leopards, Siberian and Indian tigers, gorillas and monkeys. The mansion designed by Sir Herbert Baker is surrounded by 15 acres of spectacular gardens. Inside, the most notable features include the recently restored Rex Whistler Tent Room, Moroccan Patio and hexagonal library where the Treaty of Paris was signed after World War I.
Times: Open all year, daily fr 10am, last admission 5pm summer, 3.30pm winter. (Closed 25 Dec).
Fee: £9.80 (ch 4-14 & pen £7.80). Family ticket £28.
licensed (very limited access for disabled) toilets for disabled shop

MAIDSTONE

Leeds Castle

ME17 1PL (4m E of Maidstone at junct 8 of M20/A20)
01622 765400 01622 735616
e-mail: enquires@leeds-castle.co.uk

Set on two islands in the centre of a lake, Leeds Castle has been called the 'loveliest castle in the world', and was home to six medieval Queens of England, as well as being Henry VII's Royal Palace. Among the treasures inside are many paintings, tapestries and furnishings.
Times: Open all year daily, Mar-Oct 10-5 (Castle 11-5.30). Nov-Feb 10-3 (Castle 10.15-3.30).
Fee: Castle, Park & Gardens £9.50 (ch 5-15 £6, students & pen £7.50); Park & gardens £7.50 (ch 5-15 £4.50, students & pen £6). Family ticket £26, Park & gardens only £21. Party 15+.
licensed (Braille information, induction loops & wheelchair, lift) toilets for disabled shop garden centre (ex guide dogs)

Maidstone Museum & Art Gallery

St Faith's St ME14 1LH (close to County Hall)

☎ 01622 754497 🖷 01622 602193

Times: Open all year, Mon-Sat 10-5.15, Sun 11-4 & BH Mon 11-4. (Closed 25-26 Dec).

P (100 yds) ☕ ♿ shop *Details not confirmed for 2001*

Museum of Kent Life

Lock Ln, Sandling ME14 3AU (From A229, follow signs for Aylesford. From M20 junct 6 onto A229 Maidstone road)

☎ 01622 763936 🖷 01622 662024

e-mail: enquires@museum-kentlife.co.uk

Kent's award-winning open air museum is home to an outstanding collection of historic buildings which house exhibitions on life in Kent over the last 100 years. An early 20th-century village hall and reconstruction of cottages from the 17th & 20th-centuries are more recent buildings to be viewed.

Times: Open Mar-end Oct, daily 10-5.30.

Fee: £4.50 (concessions £3). Family ticket £13.

P ☕ ✕ licensed ♿ (wheelchairs available, ramps) toilets for disabled shop

Tyrwhitt Drake Museum of Carriages

The Archbishop's Stables, Mill St ME15 6YE (close to River Medway & Archbishops Palace)

☎ 01622 754497 🖷 01622 682451

Times: Open all year, Apr-Oct daily 10.30-5.30; Nov-Mar noon-4.30. Last admission 4pm. (Closed 25-26 Dec).

P (100 yds) ♿ shop *Details not confirmed for 2001*

MINSTER-IN-THANET

Minster Abbey

CT12 4HF

☎ 01843 821254

One of the first nunneries in England was built on this site in the 7th century. Rebuilt in later centuries, it is still a religious community, run by Benedictine nuns. The ruins of the old abbey and the cloisters are open to the public. One wing dates back to 1027, and there is a 12th-century carving of Christ.

Times: Open all year, May-Sep, Mon-Fri 11-12 & 2.30-4, Sat 11-12; Oct-Apr, Mon-Sat 11-12.

Fee: Free.

P ♿ toilets for disabled shop (ex guide dogs)

PENSHURST

Penshurst Place & Gardens

TN11 8DG (from M25 junct 5 take A21 Hastings road then exit at Hildenborough, then follow signs)

☎ 01892 870307 🖷 01892 870866

e-mail: enquires@penshurstplace.com

Built between 1340 and 1345, the original house is perfectly preserved. Enlarged by successive owners during the 15th, 16th and 17th centuries, the great variety of architectural styles creates a dramatic backdrop for the extensive collections of English, French and Italian furniture, tapestries and paintings. The chestnut-beamed Baron's Hall is the oldest and finest in the country, and the house is set in magnificent formal gardens.

Times: Open: House April-Oct daily. Gardens, Grounds & venture playground open 10.30-6 and also wknds from 4 Mar.

Fee: House & Grounds £6 (ch 5-16 £4, pen & students £5.50) Family (2 adults & 2 ch) £14. Grounds only £4.50 (ch 5-16 £3.50, pen & students £4) amily (2 adults & 2 ch) £13. Party 20+. Garden season ticket £22.

P ✕ licensed ♿ (ramp into Barons Hall, Braille room guides) toilets for disabled shop garden centre (ex guide dogs)

RAMSGATE

Maritime Museum

Clock House, Pier Yard, Royal Harbour CT11 8LS (follow Harbour signs)

☎ 01843 587765 🖷 01843 582359

e-mail: museum@ekmt.fsnet.co.uk

The Maritime Museum Ramsgate is housed in the early 19th-century Clock House, and contains four galleries depicting various aspects of the maritime heritage of the East Kent area. The adjacent restored dry dock and floating exhibits from the museum's historic ship collection include the steam tug *Cervia* and the Dunkirk little ship motor yacht *Sundowner.*

contd.

Times: Open Mar-Sep daily 10am-5pm. Oct-Mar 5 days a week 9.30am-4.30pm.
Fee: Combined ticket for museum & steam tug £1.50. (ch & pen 75p). Family £4.
P (charged) ♿ (restricted) shop

RECULVER

Reculver Towers & Roman Fort

CT6 6SU (3m E of Herne Bay)
☎ 01227 740676

Regulbium was one of the forts built during the 3rd century AD by the Romans to defend the Saxon Shore. It suffered some damage in the 18th century when erosion of the cliff on which it stands caused part of its walls to collapse. The towers are the remains of a Norman church, built on the site of a 7th-century Anglo-Saxon church.
Times: Open any reasonable time.
Fee: Free.
P ♿

RICHBOROUGH

Richborough Castle

CT13 9JW (one and a half miles N of Sandwich off A257)
☎ 01304 612013

Now landlocked in the Kent countryside, Richborough Castle once stood on the coast, the bridgehead from which the Romans launched their invasion of Britain in AD43. The foundations of the great monumental archway can still be seen, and the remains of the massive wall and defensive ditches vividly convey the power of the ancient Roman empire.
Times: Open Apr-Oct, daily 10-6 (Oct 10-5); Nov-Mar, 10-4 Wed-Sun.
Fee: £2.50 (ch 5-15 £1.30, under 5's free).
P ♿ (in certain areas)

ROCHESTER

Charles Dickens Centre

Eastgate House, High St ME1 1EW
☎ 01634 844176 01634 827980

A fine late Tudor building with an early 20th-century extension, which houses a series of displays relating to the life and works of Charles Dickens. In the garden is Dicken's Swiss chalet study from Gads Hill Place. Eastgate House appeared as Westgate House in *Pickwick Papers* and The Nun's House in *Edwin Drood*.
Times: Open all year, daily 10-5.30. (Closed Xmas). Last admission 4.45pm.
Fee: £3.60 (ch & students £2.50, pen £2.60). Family ticket £9.70. Party 20+.
P (250 yds) shop

Guildhall Museum

High St ME1 1PY
☎ 01634 848717 01634 832919

Housed in two adjacent buildings, one dating from 1687 and the other from 1909. The collections are arranged chronologically from Prehistory to the Victorian and Edwardian periods. They cover local history and archaeology, fine and decorative art. There is a gallery devoted to the prison hulks of the River Medway.
Times: Open all year, daily 10-5.30. Last admissions 4.45 (Closed Xmas).
Fee: Donations box.
P (250 yds) ♿ shop (ex guide & hearing dogs)

Rochester Castle

ME1 1SX (by Rochester Bridge, A2, junc 1 M2, junc 2 M25)
☎ 01634 402276

This great Norman castle is one of the largest and best-preserved in England, with walls 100 feet high and 12 feet thick. Inside, the splendid great hall with its gallery is a 'must' and a climb to the battlements is rewarded with superb views.
Times: Open all year, Apr-Sep, daily 10-6; Oct, daily 10-5; Nov-Mar, daily 10-4. (Closed 24-26 Dec & 1 Jan).
Fee: Telephone for details of admission charges.
shop

ROLVENDEN

C M Booth Collection of Historic Vehicles

Falstaff Antiques, 63 High St TN17 4LP (on A28)
☎ 01580 241234

Not just vehicles, but various other items of interest connected with transport. There is a unique collection of three-wheel Morgan cars, dating from 1913, and the only known Humber tri-car of 1904, as well as a 1929 Morris van, a 1936 Bampton caravan, motorcycles and bicycles. There is also a toy and model car display.
Times: Open all year, Mon-Sat 10-6. (Closed 25-26 Dec).
Fee: £1.50 (ch 75p)
P (roadside) shop

SEVENOAKS

Knole

TN15 0RP (S end of Sevenoaks, E of A225)
☎ 01732 462100 & 450608 (info line)
01732 465528
e-mail: kkhxxx@smtp.ntrust.org.uk

In the 15th century Thomas Bourchier, Archbishop of Canterbury, transformed Knole from a simple medieval manor house into a palace. A century later Henry VIII extended it to even grander proportions. In the middle of the 16th century Elizabeth I gave it to Thomas Sackville and the Sackvilles kept the house for ten generations.
Times: Open 27 Mar-Oct, Wed-Sat 12-4 (last admission 3.30pm); Sun, BH Mon & Good Fri 11-5 (last admission 4.30pm), Garden 1st Wed in month, May-Sep 11-4. Last admission 3.30.
Fee: £5 (ch £2.50). Garden £1 (ch 50p). Deer Park free to pedestrians. Family ticket £12.50. Parking £2.50 per car.
P (charged) ♿ toilets for disabled shop (ex in park on lead)

SISSINGHURST

Sissinghurst Castle Garden

TN17 2AB (1m E of village)

☎ 01580 715330 📠 01580 713911

The Tudor mansion of Sissinghurst Castle was bought in a neglected state in 1930 by Sir Harold Nicolson and his wife, the writer Vita Sackville-West. They set about restoring house and gardens and the gardens now rank among the most attractive and popular in England.

Times: Open: Gardens Apr-15 Oct, Tue-Fri 1-6.30; Sat, Sun & Good Fri 10-5.30 (last admission 30mins before close. Closed Mon incl BH Mon). Due to limited capacity timed tickets are in operation so visitors may have to wait for admission, also the garden may be closed when its capacity has been reached. Garden is least crowded in Apr, Sep & Oct.

P ✕ licensed ♿ (Admission restricted to 2 wheelchairs at any one time) toilets for disabled shop (ex guide dogs) *Details not confirmed for 2001*

SITTINGBOURNE

Dolphin Sailing Barge Museum

Crown Quay Ln ME10 3SN (N on A2, signed)

☎ 01795 423215

The museum presents the history of the Thames spritsail sailing barge, many of which were built along the banks of Milton Creek. Tools of the trade, photographs and associated artefacts can be seen at the barge yard along with the sailing barge *Cambria.* Privately owned barges are repaired - there's a forge, shipwright's shop and sail loft.

Times: Open Etr-Oct, Sun & BHs 11-5. Other times by arrangement.

Fee: £1.50 (concession £1).

P ♿ toilets for disabled shop

SMALLHYTHE

Smallhythe Place

TN30 7NG (2m S of Tenterden, on E side of the Rye Road on B2082)

☎ 01580 762334 📠 01580 762334

Once a Tudor harbour master's house, this half-timbered, 16th-century building was Dame Ellen Terry's last home, and is now a museum of Ellen Terry memorabilia. The barn is now a theatre and is open most days courtesy of the Barn Theatre Society.

Times: Open Apr-Oct, Sat-Wed 1.30-6 or dusk if earlier, also Good Fri. Last admission 30 mins before closing. The Barn Theatre may be closed some days at short notice.

Fee: £3 (ch £1.50). Family ticket £7.50.

P (ex guide dogs)

SWINGFIELD MINNIS

The Butterfly Centre

McFarlanes Garden Centre CT15 7HX (on A260 by junction with Elham-Lydden road)

☎ 01303 844244

Times: Open Apr-1 Oct, daily 10-5. Closed Easter Sunday.

P ♿ shop garden centre (ex guide dogs) *Details not confirmed for 2001*

TUNBRIDGE WELLS

A Day at the Wells

The Corn Exchange, The Pantiles TN2 5QJ

☎ 01892 546545 📠 01892 513857

The legacy of the Georgians surrounds the visitor to Royal Tunbridge Wells and 'A Day at the Wells' is a journey to discover the essence of life in this most English of Georgian towns. Experience the sights, sounds and smells of a summer's day on the Pantiles in the 1740s.

Times: Open daily, Apr-Oct 10-5, Nov-Mar 10-4. Closed 25 Dec.

Fee: £4.95 (ch & pen/student £3.95).

P (charged) ♿ (specially designed flat route) toilets for disabled shop (ex guide dogs)

Groombridge Place Gardens & Enchanted Forest

TN3 9QG

☎ 01892 863999 & 861444 📠 01892 863996

(For full entry see Groombridge, East Sussex)

Tunbridge Wells Museum and Art Gallery

Civic Centre, Mount Pleasant TN1 1JN (adjacent to Town Hall, off A264)

☎ 01892 554171 & 526121 📠 01892 534227

The museum displays local history, along with Tunbridge ware, archaeology, toys and dolls, and

contd.

domestic and agricultural bygones. The art gallery has regularly changing art and craft exhibitions and touring displays from British and European museums.
Times: Open all year, daily 9.30-5. (Closed Sun, BH's & Etr Sat).
Fee: Free.
P (200 yds) ♿ shop (ex guide dogs)

UPNOR

UPNOR CASTLE

ME2 4XG (on unclass road off A228)
☎ 01634 718742

This attractive turreted castle stands on the banks of the River Medway, with a backdrop of wooded hills. It saw action in the 17th century in the Civil War, and in more recent times was used as a gunpowder store.
Times: Open Apr-Sep, daily 10-6.
Fee: Telephone for details of admission fees.
P ♿ (in certain areas) #

WESTERHAM

QUEBEC HOUSE

TN16 1TD (at E end of village on N side of A25 facing Junct with B2026 Edenbridge Road.)
☎ 01892 890651 01892 890110

Westerham was the birthplace of General Wolfe, who spent his childhood in this multi-gabled, square brick house, now renamed Quebec House. The house probably dates from the 16th century and was extended and altered in the 17th century. It contains a Wolfe museum and an exhibition on Wolfe and the Quebec campaign.
Times: Open 2 Apr-31 Oct, Tue & Sun only 2-6 (last admission 5.30pm). Parties by written arrangement.
Fee: £2.50 (ch £1.25).
P (150m) ♿ toilets for disabled

SQUERRYES COURT MANOR HOUSE & GARDENS

TN16 1SJ (0.5m W of town centre, signed off A25)
☎ 01959 562345 & 563118 01959 565949

This beautiful manor house, built in 1681, has been the home of the Wardes since 1731. It contains a fine collection of pictures, furniture, porcelain and tapestries. The lovely garden was landscaped in the 18th century and has a lake, restored formal garden, and woodland walks.
Times: Open Apr-Sep, Wed, Sat & Sun, also BH Mon. Garden noon-5.30, House 1.30-5.30. (last entry 5pm).
Fee: House & grounds £4.20 (ch 14 £2.50 & pen £3.80). Grounds £2.50 (ch 14 £1.50 & pen £2.20)
P ✕ licensed ♿ (telephone in advance) toilets for disabled shop (ex on leads in grounds)

WEST MALLING

ST LEONARD'S TOWER

(on unclass road W of A228)

The fine early Norman tower, dating from the 11th century, is all that remains of a castle or fortified manor house built by Gundulf, Bishop of Rochester.
Times: Open any reasonable time for exterior viewing. Contact West Malling Parish Council for interior viewing - 01732 870872.
Fee: Free.
♿ #

Lancashire

Lancashire was at the centre of the British cotton industry in the 19th century, which lead to the urbanisation of great tracts of the area. The cotton boom came and went, but the industrial profile remains.

These days Preston is the county's administrative headquarters, and is part of the Central Lancashire New Town, along with Fulwood, Bamber Bridge, Leyland and Chorley. The former county town, Lancaster, boasts a castle incorporating Roman building and one of the younger English universities dating from 1964. Other towns, built up to accommodate the mill-workers with back-to-back terraced houses, are Burnley, Blackburn, Rochdale and Accrington.

Lancashire's resorts, Blackpool, Southport and Morecambe Bay, were developed to meet the leisure needs of the cotton mill town workers. Blackpool is the biggest and brashest, celebrated for its tower, miles of promenade, and the coloured light 'illuminations'. Amusements are taken very seriously here, day and night, though sadly the beach has suffered some pollution in recent times.

To get out of town, you can head for the Pennines, the 'backbone of England', a series of hills stretching from the Peak District National Park to the Scottish borders. To the north of the county is the Forest of Bowland, which despite its name is fairly open country, high up with magnificent views.

EVENTS & FESTIVALS

March
11 Boosey & Hawkes Brass Band Championships, Blackpool

April
13-16 Easter Maritime Festival, Lancaster
23 Lancashire Food Festival, Accrington

May
13 Beaverbrooks Fun Run, Blackpool

July
14-15 Summer Breeze
21-22 Perapatetic Promenaders, Morecambe
28-29 Streetbands Festival, Morcambe Arena Festival Site (provisional)

August
4-5 Morecambe Festival of Light & Water
19 Morecambe Carnival
28 Lancaster Georgian Festival Fair
31 Aug-4 Nov Blackpool Illuminations

September
21-25 Lancaster Jazz Festival

November
4 Fireworks Spectacular (over historic Lancaster)

Top: Lancaster Canal

BLACKPOOL

Blackpool Zoo Park

East Park Dr FY3 8PP (signed off M55 junct 4)

☎ 01253 765027 📠 01253 798884

Times: Open all year daily, summer 10-6; winter 10-5 or dusk. (Closed 25 Dec).

P ☕ ✕ licensed ♿ (wheelchairs, braille factsheets, sensory experiences) toilets for disabled shop 🐕 *Details not confirmed for 2001*

CHARNOCK RICHARD

Camelot Theme Park

PR7 5LP (from M6 junct 27/28, or M61 junct 8)

☎ 01257 453044 📠 01257 452320

Based on the legend of King Arthur, this theme park offers jousting tournaments and the Sooty Show, as well as a wide variety of stomach-churning rides, including the Tower of Terror, and an indoor entertainment centre.

Times: Open Apr-Oct. Telephone for further details.

Fee: £8.99 (ch over 1 metre £8.99, under 1metre free, pen/disabled £6.99)

P ☕ ♿ (disabled car parking) toilets for disabled shop 🐕 (ex guide dogs)

CHORLEY

Astley Hall Museum & Art Gallery

Astley Park PR7 1NP (2m W of Chorley off A581 Southport road)

☎ 01257 515555 📠 01257 515556

e-mail: astleyhall@lineone.net

A charming Tudor/Stuart building set in beautiful parkland, this lovely Hall retains a comfortable 'lived-in' atmosphere. There are pictures and pottery to see, as well as fine furniture and rare plasterwork ceilings.

Times: Open Apr-Oct, Tue-Sun 12-5; Nov-Mar Sat-Sun 12-4.

Fee: £2.90 (concessions £1.90). Family ticket £7. Party 10+.

P (200 yds) ♿ (video of upper floors, print/braille guide, CD audio guide) shop 🐕 (ex guide dogs)

CLITHEROE

Clitheroe Castle Museum

Castle Gate, Castle St BB7 1BA (follow Clitheroe signs from A59 by-pass. Museum located in town centre).

☎ 01200 424635

The museum has a good collection of carboniferous fossils, and items of local interest. Displays include local history and the industrial archaeology of the Ribble Valley, while special features include the restored Hacking ferry boat, printer's and clogger's shops and Edwardian kitchen. The area is renowned for its early 17th-century witches, and the museum has a small display on witchcraft.

Times: Mar-Etr, Sat-Wed; Etr-Oct, daily inc BH; Nov, Dec & Feb, wkends & school half terms.

Fee: £1.50 (ch 25p, pen 65p). Family ticket £3.20

P (500yds) (disabled only parking at establishment) ♿ shop 🐕 (ex guide dogs)

LANCASTER

City Museum (also 15 Castle Hill)

Market Sq LA1 1HT

☎ 01524 64637 📠 01524 841692

Times: Open all year, Mon-Sat 10-5, (Closed 25 Dec-1Jan). 15 Castle Hill, Etr-Sep, daily 2-5.

P (5 mins walk) ♿ (ramp to entrance/ground floor, stairlifts)) shop 🐕 (ex guide dogs) *Details not confirmed for 2001*

Lancaster Maritime Museum

St George's Quay LA1 1RB (close to M6, junct 33 & 34. From A6 follow signs to Lancaster town centre)

☎ 01524 64637 📠 01524 841692

Graceful Ionic columns adorn the front of the Custom House, built in 1764. Inside, the histories of the 18th-century transatlantic maritime trade of Lancaster, the Lancaster Canal and the fishing industry of Morecambe Bay are well illustrated.

Times: Open all year, daily, Etr-Oct 11am-5pm; Nov-Etr 12.30-4pm.

Fee: £2 (concessions £1).

P ☕ ♿ (ramped access, lift to all floors, ground floor entry) toilets for disabled shop 🐕 (ex guide dogs)

Shire Hall

Lancaster Castle, Castle Pde LA1 1YJ (follow brown tourist signs)

☎ 01524 64998 📠 01524 847914

e-mail: lynette.morrisey@dpshg.lancscc.gov.uk

Founded on the site of three Roman forts, Lancaster Castle dominates Castle Hill, above the River Lune. The Norman keep was built in about 1170 and King John added a curtain wall and Hadrian's Tower. The Shire Hall, noted for its Gothic revival design, contains a splendid display of heraldry. The Crown Court was notorious as having handed out the greatest number of death sentences of any court in the land.

Times: Open 18 Mar-17 Dec, daily 10.30 (1st tour)-4 (last tour). Court sittings permitting -it is advisable to telephone before visiting except in August or at weekends.

Fee: £4 (ch, pen & students £2.50). Part tour when Court in session £2.50 (ch & pen & students £1.50).
P (100m) (voucher system) shop (ex guide dogs) 

LEIGHTON HALL

LEIGHTON HALL

LA5 9ST (off M6 at junct 35 onto A6 & follow signs)
☎ 01524 734474 📠 01524 720357
e-mail: leightonhall@yahoo.co.uk

Early Gillow furniture is displayed among other treasures in the fine interior of this neo-Gothic mansion. Outside a large collection of birds of prey can be seen, and flying displays are given each afternoon. There are also fine gardens, a maze and a woodland walk.
Times: Open May-Sep, Sun, Tue-Fri & BH Mon from 2pm. For Aug only open from 11.30. (Last admission 4.30pm).
Fee: £4 (ch 5-16 £2.70, pen £3.50). Family ticket £12.
P shop garden centre (ex guide dogs & in park)

LEYLAND

BRITISH COMMERCIAL VEHICLE MUSEUM

King St PR5 1LE (0.75m from junct 28 M6)
☎ 01772 451011 📠 01772 623404

A unique line-up of historic commercial vehicles and buses spanning a century of truck and bus building. There are more than 50 exhibits on permanent display.
Times: Open 2 Apr-Sep, Sun, Tue & BH (Oct Sun only).
Fee: £4 (ch & pen £2). Family ticket (2 adults & 3 children) £10
P (ramps to decked viewing area) toilets for disabled shop (ex guide dogs)

LYTHAM ST ANNES

TOY & TEDDY BEAR MUSEUM

373 Clifton Dr North FY8 2PA (350 yds from St Annes town centre, on A584 towards Blackpool)
☎ 01253 713705

The Toy and Teddy Bear Museum has a collection of old toys arranged in five large rooms and the Toytown Arcade. Charming displays include: Teddy Bears' Picnic and Bears at the Seaside. Other attractions include a Mini Motor Museum, a collection of more than 200 dolls, 35 dolls' houses, toy trains, working layouts, Dinky cars, aeroplanes, meccano, books and games.
Times: Open Whitsun-Oct, daily 1-5 (closed Mon & Tue). Winter open for groups & schools daily by appointment only.
Fee: £2.95 (ch & pen £2.25)
P shop

MARTIN MERE

WWT MARTIN MERE

L40 0TA (signposted from M61, M58 &M6, 6m from Ormskirk, off A59)
☎ 01704 895181 📠 01704 892343
e-mail: eileen.beesley@wwt.org.uk

One of Britain's most important wetland sites, where you can get really close to a variety of ducks, geese and swans from all over the world as well as two flocks of flamingos. Thousands of wildfowl, including Pink-Footed geese, Bewick's and Whooper swans, winter

here. Other features include a children's adventure playground, exhibition gallery, craft area and an educational centre.
Times: Open all year, daily 9.30-5.30 (4pm in winter). (Closed 25 Dec).
Fee: £5 (ch £3, pen £4). Family ticket £13.
P (wheelchair loan, Braille trail, heated hide) toilets for disabled shop garden centre (ex guide dogs)

MORECAMBE

FRONTIERLAND - FAMILY PARK

The Promenade LA4 4DG (from M6 take junct 34 northbound and junct 35 southbound)
☎ 01524 410024 📠 01524 831399

Located on the Central Promenade at Morecombe, Frontierland offers a compact selection of family rides and indoor amusements. Admission to the park is free - you just pay for the rides.
Times: Open 8 Apr-3 Sep, days & times vary, telephone for details.
Fee: Admission free. Ride tickets from £1.
P (charged) toilets for disabled shop

PADIHAM

GAWTHORPE HALL

BB12 8UA (off A671)
☎ 01282 771004 📠 01282 770178

An early 17th-century manor house, built around Britain's most southerly pele tower, restored in 1850. A collection of portraits from the National Portrait Gallery

contd.

and the Kay Shuttleworth Collections of costume, embroidery and lace are on show in the expanded exhibition areas.

Times: Open Apr-Oct, Garden: daily 10-6. Hall: Tue-Thu, Sat & Sun 1-5. Also open BH Mon & Good Friday. (Last admission 4.30pm).

Fee: House: £3 (concessions £1.50). Family ticket £8. Garden free. Party 15+.

toilets for disabled shop

PRESTON

Harris Museum & Art Gallery

Market Square PR1 2PP (in town centre)

☎ 01772 258248 01772 886764

e-mail: harris@pbch.demon.co.uk

An impressive Greek Revival building containing extensive collections of fine and decorative art including a gallery of Clothes and Fashion. The Story of Preston covers the town's history and the lively exhibition programmes of contemporary art and social history are accompanied by events and activities throughout the year.

Times: Open all year, Mon-Sat 10-5. (Closed Sun & BHs).

Fee: Free.

P (5 mins walk) (orange badge disabled parking only) (Wheelchair available. Chair lift mezzanine galleries) toilets for disabled shop (ex guide/assistance dogs)

ROSSENDALE

Whitaker Park & Rossendale Museum

Whitaker Park, Haslingden Rd, Rawtenstall BB4 6RE (off A681, 0.25m W of Rawtenstall centre)

☎ 01706 217777 & 226509 01706 250037

Former mill owner's house, built in 1840 and set in the delightful Whitaker Park. Displays include fine and decorative arts, a Victorian drawing room, natural history, costume, local and social history.

Times: Open Mon-Fri, 1-5; Sat 10-5 (Apr-Oct), 10-4 (Nov-Mar); Sun noon-5 (Apr-Oct), noon-4 (Nov-Mar). BH's 1-5. Closed 25-26 Dec, 1 Jan & afternoon 24 Dec)

Fee: Free.

(large print guides, audio guides) toilets for disabled (ex guide dogs)

RUFFORD

Rufford Old Hall

L40 1SG (off A59, 7m North of Ormskirk)

☎ 01704 821254 01704 821254

There is a story that William Shakespeare performed here for the owner Sir Thomas Hesketh in the magnificent Great Hall. Built in 1530, it was the Hesketh family seat for the next 250 years. The Carolean Wing, altered in 1821, features fine collections of 16th and 17th-century oak furniture, arms, armour and tapestries.

Times: Open Apr-1 Nov, Sat-Wed, (but open 1st Thu in June & 1st 4 Thu in Aug). Hall 1-5 (Last admission 4.30pm); Garden & shop 12-5.30.

Fee: £3.80 (ch £1.90). Family ticket £9.50. Garden only £2.

(braille guide, wheelchairs, adapted cutlery etc) shop (ex in grounds)

SAMLESBURY

Samlesbury Hall

Preston New Rd PR5 0UP (fr M6 Junct31/A677 for 3m)

☎ 01254 812010 & 812229 01254 812174

A well restored half-timbered manor house, built during the 14th and 15th centuries, and set in 5 acres of beautiful grounds. Sales of antiques and collector's items, craft shows and temporary exhibitions are held all year round.

Times: Open all year ex last wk Dec & 1st 2 wks Jan, Tue-Sun 11-4.30.

Fee: £2.50 (ch 4-16 £1).

licensed toilets for disabled (ex guide dogs)

SILVERDALE

RSPB Nature Reserve

Myers Farm LA5 0SW (M6 junct 35, then N on A6 for several miles, follow brown tourist signs to reserve)

☎ 01524 701601 01524 701601

A large reed swamp with meres with willow and alder scrub in a valley with woodland on its limestone slopes. The reserve covers 321 acres, and is home to one of Britain's largest concentration of bitterns, together with bearded tits, reed, sedge and grasshopper warblers, shovelers, pochards, tufted ducks and marsh harriers. Black terns and ospreys regularly pass through in spring and greenshanks and various sandpipers in the autumn. Wintering wildfowl include large flocks of mallards, teals, wigeons, and shovelers.

Times: Open daily 9am-9pm (or sunset if earlier). Visitor Centre daily 10-5. (closed Xmas Day).

Fee: £4 (ch £1, concessions £2.50) Family £8.

(chair lift to 1st floor, ramp access to 4 hides) toilets for disabled shop (ex guide dogs)

TURTON BOTTOMS

Turton Tower

BL7 0HG (on B6391, off A666 or A676)

☎ 01204 852203 01204 853759

Times: Open May-Sep, Mon-Thu 10-12 & 1-5. Wknds 1-5; Mar, Apr & Oct Sat-Wed, 1-4; Nov & Feb, Sun 1-4. Other times by prior arrangement.

toilets for disabled shop (ex in grounds) *Details not confirmed for 2001*

WHALLEY

Whalley Abbey

BB7 9SS

☎ 01254 828400 01254 828401

The ruins of a 14th-century Cistercian abbey, set in the delightful gardens of the Blackburn Diocesan Retreat and Conference House, a 17th-century manor house with gardens reaching down to the River Calder. The remains include two gateways, a chapter house and the abbot's lodgings and kitchen.

Times: Grounds open all year; coffee shop, shop & exhibition area, Jan-Dec daily 11-5. (Closed Xmas & New Year).

Fee: £1.50 (ch 25p, pen £1).

licensed (chair lifts, ramps) toilets for disabled shop (ex guide dogs)

Leicestershire

Leicestershire is divided between the large country estates of its eastern side and the industrial towns of the East Midlands to its west.

Coal mining was an important part of the county's industrial development in the 19th and early 20th centuries, and this is reflected in its heritage, including a reclaimed mine near Coalville, now divided between a nature reserve and Snibston Discovery Park.

Agricultural areas focus around the pleasant market towns of Market Harborough and Market Bosworth. The latter was the site of the Battle of Bosworth Field, the final engagement of the War of the Roses in 1485, where Richard III, the Yorkist king was defeated and killed by Henry of Richmond, who was crowned Henry VII.

The administrative centre is the city of Leicester, and other major towns are Loughborough, which includes bell-founding among its many industries, and Melton Mowbray, home of Stilton cheese and a particularly English item, the pork pie.

Around Melton Mowbray is serious fox-hunting country for the Belvoir, Cottesmore and Quorn hunts. Northeast of Melton Mowbray is the lovely Vale of Belvoir, beneath which are large deposits of coal.

Charnwood Forest, with fewer trees than one would expect, provides a wild and rugged landscape conveniently situated for escape from the city. It lies to the northwest of Leicester extending to Loughborough and Coalville, with some interruptions.

EVENTS & FESTIVALS

February
tbc Comedy Festival, Leicester

March
tbc Festival of Jewish Arts & Music, Leicester
tbc Leicester Jazz Festival

April
tbc Leicester Short Film Festival

May
6-7 Leicestershire County Show, Loughborough
20 May-9 Jun Leicester Early Music Festival
28 Melton Show, Melton Mowbray

June
tbc International Music Festival, Leicester

July
tbc Belgrave Mela, Leicester
tbc Mardi Gras, Leicester

August
tbc Abbey Park Festival, Leicester
tbc Caribbean Carnival, Leicester
tbc Castle Park Festival, Leicester

October
tbc Diwali Celebrations, Leicester
tbc Literature Festival, Leicester

November
tbc Bonfire & Fireworks, Leicester

Top: Beacon Hill

ASHBY-DE-LA-ZOUCH

Ashby-de-la-Zouch Castle

☎ 01530 413343

The most striking feature of these impressive ruins is the splendid 15th-century Hastings Tower, named after Edward, Lord Hastings who also built the chapel. During the Civil War, the castle was slighted by Cromwell, and the remains include the tower, walls, underground passage and large kitchen. A torch is recommended for exploring the passage.

Times: Open Apr-Sep, daily 10-6; Oct, daily 10-5; Nov-Mar, daily 10-4. (Closed 24-26 Dec & 1 Jan).

Fee: £2.60 (ch £1.30, concessions £2).

BELVOIR

Belvoir Castle

NG32 1PD (between A52 & A607)

☎ 01476 870262 01476 870443

Although Belvoir Castle has been the home of the Dukes of Rutland for many centuries, the turrets, battlements, towers and pinnacles of the house are a 19th-century fantasy. Amongst the many treasures to be seen inside are paintings by Van Dyck, Murillo, Holbein and other famous artists. Also here is the museum of the Queens Royal Lancers.

Times: Open Apr-Oct, Tue-Thu, Sat-Sun & BH Mon 11-5.

Fee: £5 (ch £3 pen £4).

licensed (permitted to be driven/drive right up to castle entrance) toilets for disabled shop (ex guide dogs)

CASTLE DONINGTON

Donington Grand Prix Collection

Donington Park DE74 2RP (adjacent to Racing Circuit, 2m from M1 junct 23a/24 & M42/A42)

☎ 01332 811027 01332 812829

e-mail: donington@zoom.co.uk

Featuring the biggest collection of Grand Prix Racing cars in the world, Donington has over 130 exhibits in five halls depicting motorsport history from the 1900s up to today. Cars on display include McLaren F1s, Ferraris, and BRMs, as well as those driven by Senna, Mansell and Hill.

Times: Open daily 10-5 (last admission 4pm). Open later on race days. (Closed over Xmas period - telephone to confirm opening times over this period).

Fee: £7 (ch 6-16 £2.50 pen & students £5). Family ticket (2 adults & 3 ch) £14. Party.

licensed shop (ex guide dogs)

COALVILLE

Snibston Discovery Park

Ashby Rd LE67 3LN (4.5m from M1 junct 22/2m or from A42/M42 junct 13 on A511 on the West side of Coalville)

☎ 01530 510851 & 813256 01530 813301

e-mail: snibston@leics.gov.uk

At Leicestershire's all-weather science and industry museum, visitors can try to solve over 50 hands-on experiments, or explore our rich heritage in the Transport, Extractive, Engineering and Textile and Fashion Galleries. Ex-miners give tours of Snibston's colliery buildings, and kids can let off steam in the outdoor science and water playgrounds.

Times: Open all year, May-Aug daily 10-6; Sep-Apr daily 1-4. (Closed 25-26 Dec).

Fee: £4.75 (ch £2.95, concessions £3.25). Family ticket £13.50. Party.

(Braille labels, touch tables, parking available) toilets for disabled shop (ex guide dogs)

DONINGTON-LE-HEATH

Donington-le-Heath Manor House

Manor Rd LE67 2FW (S of Coalville)

☎ 01530 831259 01530 831259

e-mail: museum@leics.gov.uk

This is a rare example of a medieval manor house, tracing its history back to about 1280. It has now been restored as a period house, with fine oak furnishings. The surrounding grounds include period gardens, and the adjoining stone barn houses a tea shop.

Times: Open all year: Etr-Sep, 11-5; Oct-Etr, 11-3. **Fee:** Free.

shop (ex guide dogs)

KIRBY MUXLOE

Kirby Muxloe Castle

Oakcroft St LE9 9MD (off B5380)

☎ 0116 238 6886

When Lord Hastings drew up designs for his castle in the late 15th century, he first had to obtain `licence to crenellate', but his moated, fortified manor was never completed, as he was executed only a few years after the work was begun. It stands as a ruin in his memory.

Times: Open Apr-Oct, wknds & BH's 12-5.

Fee: £1.95 (ch 5-15 £1 under 5's free)

LEICESTER

Abbey Pumping Station

Corporation Rd, Abbey Ln LE4 5PX (off A6, 1m N from city centre)

☎ 0116 299 5111 0116 299 5125

Built as a sewage pumping station in 1891, this fascinating museum features some of the largest steam beam engines in the country, and an exhibition on the history and technology of toilets, water and hygiene. There are also a steam shovel and a railway.

Times: Open Apr-Oct, Mon-Sat 10-5, Sun 2-5; Nov-Mar, Mon-Sat 10-4.30, Sun 2-4.30 (Closed 24-26 & 31 Dec & 1 Jan). Subject to change.

Fee: Free.

(loan of wheelchairs) toilets for disabled shop (ex guide dogs)

Belgrave Hall & Gardens

Church Rd, off Thurcaston Rd, Belgrave LE4 5PE (off Belgrave/Loughborough road, 1m from city centre)

☎ 0116 266 6590 0116 261 3063

A delightful three-storey Queen Anne house dating from 1709 with beautiful period and botanic gardens. Authentic room settings contrast Georgian elegance with Victorian cosiness and include the kitchen, drawing room, music room and nursery.

Times: Open all year, Apr-Oct, Mon-Sat 10-5, Sun 2-5; Nov-Mar, Mon-Sat 10-4.30, Sun 2-4.30. Closed 24-26 Dec/New Year. Opening times subject to change, ring Hall for details.
Fee: Free. P ♿ (loan of wheelchair) toilets for disabled shop

JEWRY WALL MUSEUM & SITE

St Nicholas Circle LE1 4LB (opposite The Holiday Inn)
☎ 0116 247 3021 📠 0116 251 2257

Behind the massive fragment of the Roman Jewry wall and a Roman Baths site of the 2nd century AD is the Museum of Leicestershire Archaeology, which covers finds from the earliest times to the Middle Ages.
Times: Open Apr-Oct, Mon-Sat 10-5, Sun 2-5; Nov-Mar, Mon-Sat 10-4.30, Sun 2-4.30 (Closed 31 Dec & 1 Jan). Subject to change.
Fee: Admission free, however a charge is made for some events. Donations welcome.
P (300yds) (limited on-street parking) ♿ toilets for disabled shop (ex guide dogs)

LEICESTERSHIRE MUSEUM & ART GALLERY

53 New Walk LE1 7EA
☎ 0116 255 4100 📠 0116 247 3005

This major regional venue houses local and national collections. There's an internationally famous collection of German Expressionism and other displays include the Rutland Dinosaur and thousands of butterflies.
Times: Open all year, Apr-Oct, Mon-Sat 10-5, Sun 2-5. Nov-Mar, Mon-Sat 10-4.30, Sun 2-4.30. Closed 24-26 Dec/New Year. **Fee:** Free.
P ♿ (wheelchair for loan) toilets for disabled shop (ex guide dog)

NEWARKE HOUSES

The Newarke LE2 7BY
☎ 0116 247 3222 📠 0116 247 0403

This museum follows Leicestershire's social history from the 15th century to the present, showing everyday life and social change throughout the county. A reconstructed street scene gives a glimpse of Victorian life and the fascinating story of Daniel Lambert, the famous 52-stone gaoler of the 18th century, is also told.
Times: Telephone Newarke Houses Museum on 0116 247 3222 for details of opening hours. **Fee:** Free. P (200 yds) shop

THE RECORD OFFICE FOR LEICESTERSHIRE, LEICESTER & RUTLAND

Long St, Wigston Magna LE18 2AH (Old A50, S of Leicester City)
☎ 0116 257 1080 📠 0116 257 1120
e-mail: museums@leics.gov.uk

Housed in a converted 19th-century school in Wigston, the Record Office holds photographs, electoral registers and archive film, files of local newspapers, history tapes and sound recordings, all of which can be studied.
Times: Open all year, Mon, Tue & Thu 9.15-5, Wed 9.15-7.30, Fri 9.15-4.45, Sat 9.15-12.15. (Closed Sun & BH wknds Sat-Tue).
Fee: Free. P ♿ toilets for disabled

UNIVERSITY OF LEICESTER HAROLD MARTIN BOTANIC GARDEN

Beaumont Hall, Stoughton Dr South, Oadby LE2 2NA (3m SE A6, entrance at 'The Knoll', Glebe Rd, Oadby)
☎ 0116 271 7725

The grounds of four houses, now used as student residences and not open to the public, make up this 16-acre garden. A great variety of plants in different settings provide a delightful place to walk, including rock, water and sunken gardens, trees, borders, heathers and glasshouses.
Times: Open all year, Mon-Fri 10-4. (Closed BHs & other university closure periods). Sat, Sun & BHs, Apr-Sep 10-4.
Fee: Free. P ♿

WYGSTON'S HOUSE MUSEUM OF COSTUME

12 Applegate, St Nicholas Circle LE1 5LD
☎ 0116 247 3056 📠 0116 262 0964
Times: Open Apr-Oct, Mon-Sat 10-5, Sun 2-5; Nov-Mar, Mon-Sat, 10-4.30, Sun 2-4.30 (Closed Good Fri & 25-26 & 31 Dec & 1 Jan).
P (150 yds) ♿ shop *Details not confirmed for 2001*

LOUGHBOROUGH

GREAT CENTRAL RAILWAY

Great Central Rd LE11 1RW (signposted from A6)
☎ 01509 230726 📠 01509 239791
e-mail: booking-office@gcrailway.co.uk

This private steam railway runs over eight miles from Loughborough Central to Leicester North, with all trains calling at Quorn & Woodhouse and Rothley. The locomotive depot and museum are at Loughborough Central. A buffet car runs on most trains.
Times: Open Sat, Sun & BH Mon & midweek Jun-Sep.
Fee: Runabout (all day unlimited travel) £8.50 (ch & pen £5.75). Family ticket £18.50.
P ✕ licensed ♿ (Disabled coach available on most trains, check beforehand) toilets for disabled shop

MARKET BOSWORTH

BATTLEFIELD STEAM RAILWAY LINE

Shackerstone Station, Shackerstone, Nuneaton CV13 6NW (from A444/A447 take B585 to Market Bosworth and follow signs for Congerstone/Shackerstone)
☎ 01827 880754

Together with a regular railway service (mainly steam) from Shackerstone to Shenton, there is an extensive railway museum featuring a collection of rolling stock and many other relics from the age of steam.
Times: Open all year, Station & Museum, Sat & Sun, 10.30-5.30. Passenger steam train service operates Etr-Oct, Sat, Sun & BH Mon. Diesel trains operate Jun-Sep, Wed & Sat only.
Fee: Shackerstone station: £1 (ch 5-15 free). Return train fare £5 (ch £2.50). Family ticket £14.
P ✕ ♿ toilets for disabled shop

Bosworth Battlefield Visitor Centre & Country Park

Ambion Hill, Sutton Cheney CV13 0AD (follow brown tourist signs from A447, A444 & A5)

☎ 01455 290429 📠 01455 292841

The Battle of Bosworth Field was fought in 1485 between the armies of Richard III and the future Henry VII. Special medieval attractions are held in the summer months.

Times: Open all year - Country Park & Battle trails all year during daylight hours. Visitor Centre Apr-Oct, Mon-Sat 11-5. Sun & BH, 11-6. Parties all year by arrangement.

Fee: Visitor Centre £2.80 (concessions £1.80). Family ticket £7.40. Special charges apply on event days. Subject to review.

P (charged) wheelchair hire,trail accessible with help,tactile exhibits toilets for disabled shop

MOIRA

Heart of the National Forest Visitor Centre

Enterprise Glade, Bath Ln DE12 6BD (on B5003)

☎ 01283 216633 📠 01283 210321

The Visitor Centre is a 12-acre site, which uses exhibitions and events to tell the story of the National Forest. There is also a restaurant, a plant centre, craft units, and a fantastic play park.

Times: Open daily, summer 10-6, winter 10-5. Closed 25-26 Dec &1 Jan.

Fee: £2.95 (ch 3-15 £1.95, pen & concessions £2). Ch under 3 yrs free. Family ticket £8. Seasonal party tickets available.

P licensed (multi access walks & trails accessible to wheelchairs) toilets for disabled shop garden centre (ex guide dogs)

OADBY

Farmworld

Stoughton Farm Park, Gartree Rd LE2 2FB (signposted from A6 & A47)

☎ 0116 271 0355 📠 0116 271 3211

Times: Open all year, daily 10-5.

P (specifically designed viewing gallery) toilets for disabled shop (ex guide dogs) *Details not confirmed for 2001*

SWINFORD

Stanford Hall

LE17 6DH (7.5m NE of Rugby, 1.5m from Swinford)

☎ 01788 860250 📠 01788 860870

A beautiful William and Mary house, built in 1697 by Sir Roger Cave, ancestor of the present owner. The house contains antique furniture, paintings (including the Stuart Collection) and family costumes.

Times: Open Etr Sat-end Sep, Sat, Sun, BH Mon & Tue following 2.30-5.30; noon on BH & Event Days (House 2.30). Last admission 5pm.

Fee: House & Grounds £4 (ch £2); Grounds only £2.30 (ch £1); Motorcycle Museum £1 (ch 35p). Party 20+.

P (museum also accessible) toilets for disabled shop (ex guide dogs & in park)

TWYCROSS

Twycross Zoo Park

CV9 3PX (1.5m NW off A444)

☎ 01827 880250 📠 01827 880700

Set up during the 1960s, Twycross specialises in primates, and has collections of gibbons, gorillas, orang-utangs and chimpanzees, as well as tiny tamarins, spider monkeys and howler monkeys. There are also various other animals such as lions, tigers, elephants and giraffes, and a pets' corner for younger children. Other attractions include a Penguin Pool with underwater viewing and a Children's Adventure Playground.

Times: Open all year, daily 10-6 (4pm in winter). (Closed 25 Dec).

Fee: £6 (ch £4, pen £4.50)

P toilets for disabled shop (ex guide dogs)

Lincolnshire

Lincolnshire is an east coast county with an agricultural economy, attractive seaside resorts, some lovely countryside, and quintessentially English market towns.

Much of the fenland around the Wash has been drained of its marshes and reclaimed as highly productive farmland. Further north, the coastline, with its sandy beaches, has been developed to accommodate the holiday industry, with caravans, campsites and the usual seaside paraphernalia. The main resorts are Skegness, Mablethorpe, Cleethorpes and Ingoldmells. Inland, the chalky margin of the Lincolnshire Wolds offers an undulating landscape of hills and valleys, designated as an Area of Outstanding Natural Beauty.

Lincoln, the county town, is dominated from its hilltop position by the magnificent cathedral. Most of interest in the city is in the uphill area, Steep Hill, ascending from the River Witham; the Bailgate spanned by the Newport Arch, and the Minster Yard with its medieval and Georgian architecture.

Boston, on the banks of the River Witham, was England's second biggest seaport in the 13th and 14th centuries, when the wool trade was at its height. The town is distinguished by the Boston Stump, the 272-ft (83m) tower on the church of St Boltoph, which can be seen for miles around.

There are market towns all over the county still holding weekly markets, including Barton-upon-Humber, Boston, Bourne, Brigg, Crowland, Gainsborough, Grantham, Great Grimsby, Holbeach, Horncastle, Long Sutton, Louth, Market Rasen, Scunthorpe, Sleaford, Spalding (the centre of the flower industry), and the elegant Edwardian spa resort of Woodhall Spa.

EVENTS & FESTIVALS

January
6 Haxey Hood Game, Haxey, North Lincolnshire (700-year-old game)

May
4-6 Beer Festival, Cleethorpes
5 Spalding Flower Festival & Springfields Country Fair (provisionally)
28 Folk Festival, Cleethorpes

June
30 Jun-1 Jul Royal Air Force Waddington International Air Show, RAF Waddington

July
tbc Heckington Show, Estate Showground, Heckington
tbc International Dance & Music Festival, Belton House, Park & Gardens, Belton

August
tbc Lincolnshire Steam & Vintage Rally, Lincolnshire Showground, Grange-de-Lings, Lincoln

September
tbc World Ploughing, Lincolnshire Showground, Grange-de-Lings, Lincoln

Top: Surfleet on the River Glen

ALFORD

Manor House Museum

West St LN13 9DJ (on the A1104, in centre of town)
☎ 01507 463073

This thatched 17th-century manor house is now a folk museum with local history displays: a chemist's shop, shoemaker's shop, school room, wash house and garden, photographic display, veterinary display and a nursery and maid's bedroom.

Times: Open Etr-Sep daily, Mon-Sat 10-5, Sun 1-4.30.
Fee: £1.50 (accompanied ch 50p) shop (ex guide dogs)

BELTON

Belton House Park & Gardens

NG32 2LS (3m NE Grantham on A607)
☎ 01476 566116 01476 579071
e-mail: ebahah@smtp.ntrust.org.uk

The ground floor of the house has a succession of state rooms, with the Marble Hall as its centrepiece. Splendid furnishings and decorations throughout the house include tapestries and hangings, family portraits, porcelain and fine furniture.

Times: Open Apr-29 Oct, Wed-Sun & BH Mon (Closed Good Fri). House open 1-5.30 (last admission 5pm). Grounds open 11-5.30.
Fee: £5.30 (ch £2.60). Family ticket £13.20.
licensed (braille guide, hearing scheme) toilets for disabled shop (ex in grounds)

CLEETHORPES

Pleasure Island Theme Park

Kings Rd DN35 0PL (From A46, follow signs to Cleethorpes, then brown tourist signs)
☎ 01472 211511 01472 211087
e-mail: pleasure-island@compuserve.com

Pleasure Island is packed with over seventy rides and attractions, including the new tower ride, the Hyper Blaster.

Times: Open from 16 Apr-Oct, daily.
Fee: £9 (ch under 4 free, pen £5). Family ticket £30.
toilets for disabled shop

CONINGSBY

Battle of Britain Memorial Flight Visitor Centre

LN4 4SY (on A153)
☎ 01526 344041 01526 342330

View the aircraft of the Battle of Britain Memorial Flight, comprising the only flying Lancaster in Europe, five Spitfires, two Hurricanes, a Dakota and two Chipmunks. Because of operational commitments, specific aircraft may not be available. Ring before planning a visit.

Times: Open all year, Mon-Fri, conducted tours 10-3.30. (Closed 2 wks Xmas). (Phone prior to visiting to check security situation)
Fee: £3.50 (ch £1.50, pen £2, under 6's free).
(electric wheelchairs not allowed in hangers) shop

EPWORTH

Old Rectory

1 Rectory St DN9 1HX (on A161, 3m S of M180 junct 2)
☎ 01427 872268
e-mail: epworth@oldrectory63.freeserve.co.uk

John and Charles Wesley were brought up in this handsome rectory, built in 1709. Maintained by the World Methodist Council as 'The Home of the Wesleys' rather than as a museum, the house displays items which belonged to John and Charles Wesley and their parents Samuel and Susanna.

Times: Open daily Mar-Oct, Mon-Sat 10-12 & 2-4, Sun 2-4 (only in Mar, Apr & Oct) May-Sep Mon-Sat 10-4.30. Sun 2-4.30. Other times by prior arrangement.
Fee: £2.50 (ch & student £1, OAP £2) Family £6.
shop (ex guide dogs)

GAINSBOROUGH

Old Hall

Parnell St DN21 2NB
☎ 01427 612669 01427 612779
e-mail: cumminsh@lincolnshire.gov.uk

A complete medieval manor house dating back to 1460-80 and containing a remarkable Great Hall and original kitchen with a variety of room settings. Richard III, Henry VIII, the Mayflower Pilgrims and John Wesley all visited the Old Hall.

Times: Open all year, Mon-Sat 10-5; Etr-Oct, Sun 2-5.30. Closed 25-26 Dec, 1 Jan & Good Fri. **Fee:** £2.50 (ch £1, 60+ £1.50)
(100 yds) (unrestricted parking 100yds from Hall) (audio tour, induction loop, wheelchair for visitors use) shop (ex guide dogs)

GRANTHAM

See Belvoir, Leicestershire

GRIMSBY

National Fishing Heritage Centre

Alexandra Dock DN31 1UZ (follow signs off M180)
☎ 01472 323345 01472 323555

Sign on as a crew member for a journey of discovery, and experience the harsh reality of life on board a deep sea trawler built inside the Centre. Through interactive games and displays, your challenge is to navigate the icy waters of the Arctic in search of the catch.

Times: Open all year, Sat-Thu, telephone for opening times. (Closed 25-26 Dec & 1 Jan).
Fee: £4.95 (concessions £3.85). Family ticket £16.50. Prices subject to change.
(easy access route) toilets for disabled shop

GRIMSTHORPE

Grimsthorpe Castle

PE10 0NB (on A151, 8m E of Colsterworth rbt on A1)
☎ 01778 591205 01778 591259
e-mail: ray@grimsthorpe.co.uk

Seat of the Willoughby de Eresby family since 1516, the castle has a medieval tower and a Tudor quadrangular house with a Baroque north front by Vanbrugh. There

are eight state rooms and two picture galleries, and an important collection of furniture, pictures and tapestries.
Times: Open 22 Apr- Sep, Sun, Thu & BH's. Daily in Aug ex Fri & Sat. Park & Gardens 11-6, Castle 1-6 (last admission 4.30pm).
Fee: Park & Gardens £3 (ch £1.50, concessions £2). Combined ticket £6.50 with castle (ch £3.25, concessions £4.75). Party.
licensed toilets for disabled shop

HECKINGTON

The Pearoom

Station Yard NG34 9JJ (4m E of Sleaford, off A17)
☎ 01529 460765 01529 460948

The Pearoom has a craft shop, galleries and workshops for ten resident craft workers. Their products include pottery, textiles and calligraphy; and also there is a weaver-feltmaker. An active programme of craft exhibitions runs throughout the year accompanied by a programme of weekend course activities.
Times: Open all year, Mon-Sat & BHs 10-5, Sun 12-5.
Fee: Free. toilets for disabled shop (ex guide dogs)

LINCOLN

Museum of Lincolnshire Life

Burton Rd LN1 3LY (100mtrs walk from Castle)
☎ 01522 528448 01522 521264
e-mail: finchj@lincolnshire.gov.uk

A large and varied social history museum, where two centuries of Lincolnshire life are illustrated by displays of domestic implements, industrial machinery, agricultural tools and a collection of horse-drawn vehicles. The Royal Lincolnshire Regiment museum reopens after a major heritage lottery funded redevelopment.
Times: Open all year, May-Sep, daily 10-5.30; Oct-Apr, Mon-Sat 10-5.30, Sun 2-5.30. **Fee:** £2 (ch 60p).
(wheelchair available, parking space) toilets for disabled shop

Usher Gallery

Lindum Rd LN2 1NN (in city centre, signed)
☎ 01522 527980 01522 560165
e-mail: woodr@lincolnshire.gov.uk

Built as the result of a bequest by Lincoln jeweller James Ward Usher, the Gallery houses his magnificent collection of watches, porcelain and miniatures, as well as topographical works, watercolours by Peter de Wint, Tennyson memorabilia and coins.

Times: Open all year, Mon-Sat 10-5.30, Sun 2.30-5. (Closed Good Fri, Xmas & 1 Jan). **Fee:** £2 (ch & students 50p).
(150yds) (large print exhibition guides) toilets for disabled shop (ex guide dogs)

LONG SUTTON

See Spalding

SCUNTHORPE

Normanby Hall Country Park

Normanby DN15 9HU (4m N of Scunthorpe off B1430)
☎ 01724 720588 01724 721248

A whole host of activities and attractions are offered in the 300 acres of grounds, including riding, nature trails and a farming museum. Inside the Regency mansion the fine rooms include a restored and working Victorian kitchen garden.
Times: Open, Park all year, daily 9am-dusk. Walled garden: daily 11-5 (4pm winter). Hall & Farming Museum: Apr-Sep daily 1-5.
Fee: 27 Mar-1 Oct £2.90 (concessions £1.90) Family ticket £8. 2 Oct-26 Mar £2 per car.
(charged) licensed (audio tour & sensory bed in walled garden) toilets for disabled shop ex guide dogs & in park on lead

SKEGNESS

Church Farm Museum

Church Rd South PE25 2HF (follow brown Museum signs on entering Skegness)
☎ 01754 766658 01754 766658
e-mail: willsf@lincolnshire.gov.uk

A farmhouse and outbuildings, restored to show the way of life on a Lincolnshire farm at the end of the 19th century, with farm implements and machinery plus household equipment on display. Craftsmen give demonstrations on summer weekends.
Times: Open Apr-Oct, daily 10.30-5.30 **Fee:** £1 (ch 50p).
(wheelchair available) toilets for disabled shop (ex guide dogs)

Skegness Natureland Seal Sanctuary

North Pde PE25 1DB (north end of seafront)
☎ 01754 764345 01754 764345
e-mail: natureland@fsbdial.co.uk

Natureland houses seals, penguins, tropical birds, aquarium, reptiles, pets' corner, and free-flight tropical butterflies (May-Oct). Well known for rescuing, rearing and returning to the wild, abandoned seal pups. The hospital unit has a viewing area, and a seascape seal pool (with underwater viewing).
Times: Open all year, daily at 10am. Closing times vary according to season. (Closed 25-26 Dec & 1 Jan).
Fee: £4.10 (ch £2.70, pen £3.30). Family ticket £12.20.
(100 yds) toilets for disabled shop

SPALDING

Butterfly & Falconry Park

Long Sutton PE12 9LE (off A17 at Long Sutton)
☎ 01406 363833 & 363209 📠 01406 363182

The Park contains one of Britain's largest walk-through tropical houses, in which hundreds of butterflies and birds from all over the world fly freely. 15 acres of butterfly and bee gardens, wildflower meadows, nature trail and farm animals. Daily birds of prey displays, an iguana den and an ant room.

Times: Open end Mar-end Oct, daily 10-5. (Sep & Oct 10-4).
Fee: £4.80 (ch 3-16 £3.20, pen £4.50). Family ticket £15-£17. Party rates on application.
licensed (wheelchairs available) toilets for disabled shop (ex guide dogs)

Spalding Tropical Forest

Glenside North, Pinchbeck PE11 3SD (signposted)
☎ 01775 710822 📠 01775 710882
e-mail: mike@rosecottagewgc.co.uk

Spalding Tropical Forest is the largest of its kind in the British Isles. There are four zones: oriental, temperate, tropical and dry topics. Cascading waterfalls and lush, colourful tropical plants.

Times: Open daily summer 10-5.30, winter 10-4. Closed 25-Dec-2 Jan.
Fee: £2.45 (ch5-16 £1.40, pen £1.99). Family ticket £6 (2 adults 2 ch) then £1 for each extra child.
(disabled parking close to establishment) toilets for disabled shop garden centre

Springfields Gardens

Camelgate PE12 6ET (1m E on A151)
☎ 01775 724843 & 713253 📠 01755 711209
e-mail: brianwillonghby@springfields.net

The 25-acre gardens provide an amazing spectacle in the spring when thousands of bulbs are blooming among the lawns and lakes. Special events for 2001 : Flower Festival and Parade in May.

Times: Open 10 Mar-7 May, daily 10-6 (last admission 5pm)
Fee: £3.50 (accompanied ch free, pen £3). Prices vary for special events.
licensed (free wheelchair hire) toilets for disabled shop garden centre (guide dogs)

STAMFORD

Burghley House

PE9 3JY (1.5m off A1 at Stamford)
☎ 01780 752451 📠 01780 480125
e-mail: burghley@dial.pipex.com

This great Elizabethan palace, built by William Cecil, has all the hallmarks of that ostentatious period. The vast house is three storeys high and the roof is a riot of pinnacles, cupolas and paired chimneys in classic Tudor style. However, the interior was restyled in the 17th century, and the state rooms are now Baroque, with silver fireplaces, elaborate plasterwork and painted ceilings. These were painted by Antonio Verrio, whose Heaven Room is quite awe-inspiring.

Times: Open Apr-8 Oct, daily, 11-4.30. (Closed 2 Sep).
Fee: £6.50 (ch 5-12 £3.20 or free with every paying adult, pen £6.10) Party 20+
licensed (chairlift access to restaurant and staterooms) toilets for disabled shop (guide dogs)

Stamford Museum

Broad St PE9 1PJ (from A1 follow town centre signs)
☎ 01780 766317 📠 01780 480363

Times: Open all year, Apr-Sep, Mon-Sat 10-5, Sun 2-5; Oct-Mar Mon-Sat 10-5.
(200 yds) (on street parking is limited waiting) shop (ex guide dogs) *Details not confirmed for 2001*

Stamford Shakespeare Company

Rutland Open Air Theatre, Tolethorpe Hall, Little Casterton PE9 4BH (off A6121, follow heritage signs to Tolethorpe Hall)
☎ 01780 54381 📠 01780 481954

Times: Open daily 10-4, May-Sep. Rutland Open Air Theatre performances 1 Jun-29 Aug.
toilets for disabled shop *Details not confirmed for 2001*

TATTERSHALL

Tattershall Castle

LN4 4LR (S of A153)
☎ 01526 342543
e-mail: etcxxx@smtp.ntrust.org.uk

This large fortified house was built in 1440 by Ralph Cromwell, Treasurer of England, and has a keep 100ft high. On each of the four storeys is a fine heraldic chimneypiece: these were sold at one point, but were rescued from export in 1911.

Times: Open 15 Apr-2 Jul, Sat-Wed, 10.30-5.30; 15 Jul-31 Oct Sat-Wed; 4 Nov-17 Dec Sat & Sun only 12-4pm.
Fee: £3 (ch £1.50). Family ticket £7.50. toilets for disabled shop

WOOLSTHORPE

Woolsthorpe Manor

23 Newton Way NG33 5NR (7m S of Grantham)
☎ 01476 860338
e-mail: ewmxxx@smtp.ntrust.org.uk

A fine stone-built, 17th-century farmhouse which was the birthplace of the scientist and philosopher Sir Isaac Newton. He also lived at the house from 1665-67 during the Plague. An early edition of his *Principia Mathematica* (1687) is in the house.

Times: Open Apr-Oct, Wed-Sun & BH Mon 1-5.30. (closed Good Fri).
Fee: £3.20 (ch £1.60). Family ticket £8.

London

The capital of England and the United Kingdom, London is the largest city in Europe with a population of nearly seven million people.

Londinium was established in 43 AD, at the lowest crossing point of the River Thames. In the second century the city walls were built, but London soon grew beyond them to merge with Westminster and, by the 11th century, was the main city in England and the home of William the Conqueror.

London continued to flourish until the plague of 1665 and the Great Fire of London in 1666. Much of the city was rebuilt at this time under the direction of Sir Christopher Wren. During WWII the Blitz did immense damage to the city, razing whole streets and destroying domestic and public buildings alike. Post-war architecture introduced modern structures of concrete and glass. Ancient sights include the Tower of London, built by William the Conqueror on a Roman site; the 15th-century Guildhall; and the Monument, designed by Wren to commemorate the Great Fire. Most of the public buildings are 18th-century or Victorian.

London's role as a port has declined, with most activity now outside the metropolitan area. The East End docks have been redeveloped to provide housing, offices, factories and the Docklands Railway. London is a major financial centre, and the focus of the national media, including film and publishing.

London has been a cosmopolitan city for centuries, and much of the excitement of the city's life is derived from its cultural diversity. The foods, dress, languages, art and music of every continent can be experienced on its streets.

EVENTS & FESTIVALS

January
1 New Year's Day Parade
4-14 International Boat Show, Earls Court

March
17 Head of the River Race

April
22 London Marathon

May
17-26 Hampstead & Highgate Festival
22-25 Chelsea Flower Show

June
2-3 Biggin Hill Air Fair
3 London to Brighton Classic Car Run
4-22 Spitalfields Festival
7-16 Hampton Court Palace Music Festival
26 Jun-19 Jul City of London Festival
tbc Beating the Retreat

July
6-15 Greenwich & Docklands International Festival

August
27 Notting Hill Carnival

October
21 Trafalgar Day Parade

November
10 Lord Mayor's Show, City of London

Top: Law courts building

LONDON

W1

Apsley House, The Wellington Museum

Hyde Park Corner WIV 9FA (Underground - Hyde Park Corner, exit 1)

☎ 020 7499 5676 020 7493 6576

e-mail: e.appleby@vam.ac.uk

Number One, London, is the popular name for one of the Capital's finest private residences, 19th-century home of the first Duke of Wellington. Built in the 1770s, its rich interiors have been returned to their former glory, and house the Duke's magnificent collection of paintings, silver, porcelain, sculpture and furniture.

Times: Open Tue-Sun 11-5. (Closed Mon ex BH Mon, Good Fri, May Day BH, 24-26 Dec & 1 Jan). Last admission 4.30pm.

Fee: £4.50 (ch under 18 & pen free, disabled & UB40 £3). Includes the use of a soundguide.

P (NCP 10mins walk) lift,soundguides for visually impaired/learning disabilities shop (ex guide dogs)

EC2

Bank of England Museum

Threadneedle St EC2R 8AH (museum housed in Bank of London, entrance in Bartholomew Lane)

☎ 020 7601 5545 020 7601 5808

e-mail: museum@bankofengland.co.uk

Located in the heart of The City, this museum traces the history of the Bank from its foundation in 1694, and includes a collection of gold bars, old and new. New interactive programme.

Times: Open all year, Mon-Fri 10-5. (Closed wknds & BH's). Open on the day of the Lord Major's Show.

Fee: Free.

P (10 mins walk) (advance notice helpful) toilets for disabled shop

SW1

Banqueting House at Whitehall Palace

Whitehall SW1A 2ER (Underground - Westminster, Charing Cross or Embankment)

☎ 020 7930 4179 020 7930 8268

Designed by Inigo Jones, this is the only surviving building of the vast Whitehall Palace, destroyed by fire 300 years ago. The Palace has seen many significant royal events, including the execution of Charles I in 1649. The Banqueting House's Rubens ceiling paintings are stunning examples of the larger works of the Flemish Master and its classical Palladian style set the fashion for much of London's later architecture.

Times: Open all year, Mon-Sat 10-5. (Closed Good Fri, 24 Dec-1 Jan & BH's). Liable to close at short notice for Government functions.

Fee: £3.60 (ch 16 £2.30 (under 5 free) students & pen £2.80).

P (no parking in Whitehall) toilets for disabled shop (ex guide dogs)

E2

Bethnal Green Museum of Childhood

Cambridge Heath Rd E2 9PA (Underground - Bethnal Green)

☎ 020 8980 2415 020 8983 5225

e-mail: k.bines@vam.ac.uk

The National Museum of Childhood houses a multitude of childhood delights. Toys, dolls and dolls' houses, model soldiers, puppets, games, model theatres, children's costume and nursery antiques are all included in its well planned displays. There are Saturday workshops and Sunday soft play sessions for children, and activities in the holidays.

Times: Open all year, Mon-Thu & Sat-Sun 10-5.50 (Closed Fri, 25 Dec & 1 Jan).

Fee: Free.

toilets for disabled shop

WC1

British Museum

Great Russell St WC1B 3DG (Underground - Russell Sq, Tottenham Court Rd, Holborn)

☎ 020 7636 1555 020 7323 8616

e-mail: info@british-museum.ac.uk

Behind its imposing Neo-Classical façade the British Museum displays the rich and varied treasures which make it one of the great museums of the world. Founded in 1753, displays cover the works of humanity from pre-historic to modern times. The galleries are the responsibility of ten departments, which include Egyptian, Greek and Roman, Japanese, Medieval and later, Prints and Drawings, and Ethnography. Among the treasures to be seen are the Egyptian mummies, the sculptures from the Parthenon, the Anglo-Saxon treasure from the Sutton Hoo ship burial and the Vindolanda Tablets from Hadrian's Wall. There is a regular programme of gallery talks, guided tours and lectures, and young visitors can enjoy special children's trails.

Times: Open all year, Mon-Sat 10-5, Sun 12-6 (Closed Good Fri, 24-26 Dec & 1 Jan).

Fee: Free.

P (5 mins walk) licensed (parking by arrangement; tours for visual/hearing impaired) toilets for disabled shop (ex guide/companion dogs)

W1

Broadcasting House Tour & Exhibition

Broadcasting House W1A 1AA (Underground - Oxford Circus, Great Portland St)

☎ 0870 6030304

A day in the life of Broadcasting House - explore the corporation's heritage through a series of interactive displays which allow visitors to try out a range of broadcasting activities including the chance to 'Present the Weather' 'Direct Eastenders', 'Commentate on a Sports Event' and 'Create a Radio Play'.

Times: Open all year, daily 9.30-5.30 (last tour commences). Closed 25 Dec.

P toilets for disabled shop *Details not confirmed for 2001*

SW1
Buckingham Palace
Buckingham Palace Rd SW1 1AA (Underground - Victoria, Green Park)
☎ 020 7839 1377 🖷 020 7930 9625
e-mail: information@royalcollection.org.uk

The official London residence of Her Majesty The Queen, whose personal standard flies when Her Majesty is in residence. Each August and September the State Rooms are open to visitors. These principle rooms now include the Ballroom, the largest room in the Palace. The rooms occupy the main west front overlooking the garden and are all opulently decorated with the finest pictures and works of art from the Royal Collection.

Times: Open 6 Aug- 1 Oct 9.30-4.30 (provisional dates)
Fee: £10.50 (ch under 17 £5, pen £8) Family ticket (2 adults & 2 ch) £25.50. Tickets bought in advance £10.50, no concessions.
P (200yds) (very limited, driving not recommended) ♿ (except gardens, pre booking essential) toilets for disabled shop ✗ (ex guide dogs)

WC2
Cabaret Mechanical Theatre
33/34 The Market, Covent Garden WC2E 8RE (Underground - Covent Garden)
☎ 020 7379 7961 🖷 020 7497 5445
e-mail: barecat@cabaret.co.uk

Times: Open all year, Mon-Sat 10-6.30, Sun 11-6.30, school holiday open until 7pm. (Closed 25 & 26 Dec & 1 Jan).
shop ✗ *Details not confirmed for 2001*

SW1
Cabinet War Rooms
Clive Steps, King Charles St SW1A 2AQ (Underground - Westminster or St James Park)
☎ 020 7930 6961 🖷 020 7839 5897
e-mail: cwr@iwm.org.uk

The underground emergency accommodation used to protect the Prime Minister, Winston Churchill, his War Cabinet and the Chiefs of Staff during WWII provides a fascinating insight into those tense days and nights. Among the 21 rooms are the Cabinet Room, the Map Room (where information about operations on all fronts was collected) and the Prime Minister's room, all carefully preserved since the end of the war. There is a changing exhibition of war documents.

Times: Open all year, daily 9.30-6. (10-6 Oct-Mar) last admission 5.15 (Closed 24-26 Dec).
Fee: £5 (ch under 16 free, students & pen £3.60). Party 10+.
P (10 mins walk) ♿ toilets for disabled shop ✗

SW3
Carlyle's House
24 Cheyne Row SW3 5HL (Underground - Sloane Square)
☎ 020 7352 7087

'The Sage of Chelsea' - distinguished essayist and writer of historical works, Thomas Carlyle - lived in this 18th-century town house from 1834 until his death in 1881. His soundproofed study and the kitchen, where such literary notables as Tennyson, Thackeray and Browning were entertained have been preserved exactly as the Carlyles knew them.

Times: Open Apr-Oct, Wed-Sun & BH Mons 11-5. Last admission 4.30. (Closed Good Fri)
Fee: £3.50 (ch £1.75).
P (street metered) ✗

SW3
Chelsea Physic Garden
66 Royal Hospital Rd, (entrance in Swan Walk) SW3 4HS (Underground - Sloane Square)
☎ 020 7352 5646 🖷 020 7376 3910

Begun in 1673 for the study of plants used by the Society of Apothecaries. This garden is one of Europe's oldest botanic gardens and is the only one to retain the title 'Physic' after the old name for the healing arts. The garden is still used for botanical and medicinal research, and offers displays of many fascinating plants in lovely surroundings.

Times: Open Apr-Oct, Wed 12-5, Sun 2-6. Additional opening during Chelsea Flower Show week, 22-26 May & Chelsea Festival week Jun, 19-23. Groups at other times by appointment.
Fee: £4 (ch 5-15, students & unemployed £2).
P (0.5m) (west end of Battersea Park) ♿ (disabled parking) toilets for disabled shop garden centre ✗ (ex guide dogs)

W4
Chiswick House
Burlington Ln, Chiswick W4 2RD (Underground - Gunnersbury)
☎ 020 8995 0508

Built by Lord Burlington in the 1720s, Chiswick House is inspired by the architecture of ancient Rome. The interior has a fine collection of art and the Italianate gardens delight visitors with their statues, temples, urns and obelisks.

Times: Open all year, Apr-Sep, daily 10-6 (Oct 10-5); Nov-Mar, Wed-Sun 10-4. Closed 24-26 Dec & 1-18 Jan.
Fee: £2.50 (ch 5-15 £1.30, umder5's free). Personal stereo tour included in admission, also available for the partially sighted, those with learning difficulties, and in French & German)
P ♿ shop ✗ (in certain areas) #

W8

Commonwealth Institute

Kensington High St W8 6NQ (Underground - High Street Kensington)

☎ 020 7603 4535 020 7602 7374

e-mail: info@commonwealth.org.uk

Times: Commonwealth Institute is being redeveloped please ring 020 7603 4535 for details.

P (500yds) ♿ (lift from car park, intercom at Holland Park gate) toilets for disabled shop *Details not confirmed for 2001*

WC2

Courtauld Gallery

Somerset House, Strand WC2R 0RN (Underground - Temple, Embankment)

☎ 020 7848 2526 020 7848 2589

e-mail: galleryinfo@courtauld.ac.uk

The Galleries contain the superb collection of paintings begun by Samuel Courtauld in the 1920s and 1930s and presented to the University of London in memory of his wife. This is the most important collection of Impressionist and post-Impressionist works in Britain and includes paintings by Monet, Renoir, Degas, Cézanne, Van Gogh and Gauguin. There are also works by Michelangelo, Rubens, Goya, and other notable Masters, as well as early Italian paintings.

Times: Open Mon-Sat 10-6, Sun & BH's 12-6.

Fee: £4 (concessions £3).

P (NCP Drury Lane) ♿ (parking arranged, lift) toilets for disabled shop (ex guide dogs)

SE17

Cuming Museum

155-157 Walworth Rd SE17 1RS (Underground - Elephant & Castle, North line exit follow signs for the shopping centre)

☎ 020 7701 1342 020 7703 7415

Times: Open all year, Tue-Sat 10-5. (Closed BH's & Sat of BH wknd).

P (20 yds) (on street pay & display meters) shop (ex guide dogs) *Details not confirmed for 2001*

SE10

Cutty Sark Clipper Ship

King William Walk, Greenwich SE10 9HT (situated in dry dock beside Greenwich Pier)

☎ 020 8858 3445 & 020 8858 2698 020 8853 3589

e-mail: info@cuttysark.org.uk

The fastest tea clipper ever, built in 1869, she once sailed 363 miles in a single day. Preserved in dry dock since 1957, her graceful lines dominate the riverside at Greenwich. Exhibitions and a video presentation the story of the ship, and restoration work can be seen.

Times: Open all year, daily 10-5 (Closed 24-26 Dec). Last ticket 30 mins before closing.

Fee: £3.50 (concessions £2.50). Family ticket £8.50. Party 10+ 20% reduction.

P car park 500 metres (100 yds metered) ♿ shop

SE1

Design Museum

Butler's Wharf, 28 Shad Thames SE1 2YD (Underground - London Bridge & Tower Hill)

☎ 020 7403 6933 020 7378 6540

The Design Museum is the first dedicated to the study of 20th-century design. Housed within a converted 1950s warehouse, the Museum's highly acclaimed programme of exhibitions strives to capture the excitement of design evolution, ingenuity and inspiration.

Times: Open all year: wkdays 11.30-6; wkends 10.30-6. (last entry 5.30) closed 25-26 Dec only.

Fee: £5.50 (concessions £4) Family £15.

P (3 mins walk) (NCP car park is chargeable) licensed ♿ (ramped entrance, wheelchair & lift, Audio guides.) toilets for disabled shop (ex guide dogs)

WC1

The Dickens House Museum

48 Doughty St WC1N 2LF (Underground - Russell Square or Chancery Lane)

☎ 020 7405 2127 020 7831 5175

e-mail: dhmuseum@rmplc.co.uk

Charles Dickens lived in Doughty Street in his twenties and it was here he worked on his first full-length novel, *The Pickwick Papers*, and later *Oliver Twist* and *Nicholas Nickelby*. Pages of the original manuscripts are on display, together with valuable first editions, his marriage licence and many other personal mementoes.

Times: Open all year, Mon-Sat 10-5.

Fee: £4 (ch under 16 £2, concession £3). Family ticket £9.

P (in street) (metered, 2 hrs max) ♿ shop

EC4

Dr Johnson's House

17 Gough Square EC4A 3DE (Underground - Temple, Blackfriars, Chancery Lane)

☎ 020 7353 3745 020 7353 3745

e-mail: curator@drjh.dircon.co.uk

The celebrated literary figure, Dr Samuel Johnson, lived here between 1748 and 1759. He wrote his English Dictionary here, and a facsimile first edition is on display at the house. The dictionary took eight and a half years to complete and contained 40,000 words. Johnson then undertook the formidable task of editing the complete works of Shakespeare. The house is a handsome example of early 18th-century architecture, and includes a collection of prints, letters and other Johnson memorabilia.

Times: Open all year, May-Sep, daily 11-5.30; Oct-Apr 11-5. (Closed Sun, BH's, Good Fri & 24 Dec).

Fee: £3 (ch £1, under 10 free, students & pen £2). Party.

P (500 yards) (limited meters) (Large print info sheets) shop

SE21
DULWICH PICTURE GALLERY
Gallery Rd, Dulwich SE21 7AD (off South Circular A205 follow signs to Dulwich village)
☎ 020 8693 5254 🖷 020 8299 8700

Now reopened after recent refurbishment, this is the oldest public picture gallery in England, housing a magnificent collection of Old Masters, including works by Poussin, Claude, Rubens, Murillo, Van Dyck, Rembrandt, Watteau and Gainsborough.
Times: Dulwich Picture is closed for refurbishment until 25 May 2000. Open all year, Tue-Fri 10-5, wkends & BH Mon 11-5. (Closed Mon). Guided tours Sat & Sun 3pm.
Fee: £3 (pen, students £1.50, UB40, disabled & ch free). Guided tours £5 per person.
P ✕ licensed ♿ (wheelchair available) toilets for disabled shop 🐕 (ex guide dogs)

SE9
ELTHAM PALACE HOUSE & GARDENS
Court Yard SE9 5QE
☎ 020 8294 2548

Stephen and Virginia Courtauld's stunning country house in 1930s art-deco style, incorporating a medieval Great Hall. One of its most charming features is the old bridge, spanning the moat.
Times: Open all year, Apr-Sep, Wed-Fri & Sun 10-6 (Oct 10-5); Nov-Mar, Wed-Fri & Sun 10-4. Also open BH's. Closed 24-26 Dec & 1 Jan.
Fee: House & Gardens: £5.90 (ch 5-15 £3); Gardens only:£3.50 (ch 5-15 £1.80, under 5's free)

NW3
FENTON HOUSE
Windmill Hill NW3 6RT (Underground - Hampstead)
☎ 020 7435 3471 🖷 020 7435 3471
e-mail: tfehse@smtp.ntrust.org.uk

A William and Mary mansion built about 1693 and set in a walled garden, Fenton House is now owned by the National Trust. It contains a display of furniture and some notable pieces of Oriental and European porcelain as well as the Benton Fletcher collection of early keyboard instruments, including a harpsichord once played by Handel.
Times: Open Apr-Oct, Sat-Sun & BH Mon 11-5pm, Wed-Fri 2-5pm. Last admission 30mins before closing.
Fee: £4.20. Family ticket £10.50.
♿ 🐕

SE1
FLORENCE NIGHTINGALE MUSEUM
Gassiot House, 2 Lambeth Palace Rd SE1 7EW (Underground - Westminster, Waterloo. On the site of St Thomas' Hospital)
☎ 020 7620 0374 🖷 020 7928 1760
e-mail: curator@florence-nightingale.co.uk

Florence Nightingale needs no introduction, but this museum shows clearly that she was more than *'The Lady with the Lamp'*. Beautifully designed, the museum creates a personal setting in which are displayed some of Florence's possessions, a lamp from the Crimean War, and nursing artefacts.
Times: Open all year, Mon-Fri 10-5; wkends & BH's 11.30-4.30. (last admission 1hr before closing). (Closed Xmas, 1 Jan, Good Fri & Etr Sun).
Fee: £4.80 (concessions £3.60) Family ticket (2 adults & 2 ch) £10.
P (charged) ♿ toilets for disabled shop 🐕 (ex guide dogs)

NW3
FREUD MUSEUM
20 Maresfield Gardens, Hampstead NW3 5SX (Underground - Finchley Road)
☎ 020 7435 2002 & 7435 5167
🖷 020 7431 5452
e-mail: freud@gn.apc.org
Times: Open all year, Wed-Sun 12-5 (Closed BH's, telephone for Xmas Holiday times).
P ♿ (personal tours can be arranged if booked in advance) shop 🐕
Details not confirmed for 2001

E2
GEFFRYE MUSEUM
Kingsland Rd E2 8EA (Underground - Old Street or Liverpool Street)
☎ 020 7739 9893 🖷 020 7729 5647
e-mail: info@geffrye-museum.org.uk

The only museum in the UK to specialise in the domestic interiors and furniture of the urban middle classes. Displays span the 400 years from 1600 to the present day, forming a sequence of period rooms which capture the nature of English interior style. The museum is set in elegant, 18th-century buildings, surrounded by delightful gardens including an award-winning walled herb garden and a series of historical gardens which highlight changes in urban middle-class gardens from the 17th to 20th centuries.
Times: Open all year, Tue-Sat 10-5, Sun & BH Mons 12-5 (Closed Mon, Good Friday, Xmas & New year).
Fee: Free. Prices for special lectures on request.
P (150yds) (meter parking) ✕ ♿ (wheelchair available) toilets for disabled shop 🐕 (ex guide dogs)

WC2
GILBERT COLLECTION
Somerset House, Strand WC2R 1LN (Underground - Temple, Covent Garden)
☎ 020 7240 9400 🖷 020 7240 4060
e-mail: info@gilbert-collection.org.uk

An oustanding collection of decorative arts and an important bequest to the nation. The Gilbert Collection is the gift of Sir Arthur Gilbert and is on permanent display at Somerset House. This new museum includes European silver, gold snuff boxes and Italian mosaics, the displays will also include furniture, clocks and potrait miniatures.
Times: Open Mon-Sat 10-6, Sun & BH Mon's noon-6pm. Last admission 5.15pm.

contd.

Fee: £4 (pen £2, under 18, uk students, unemployed free). Joint ticket with Courtauld Gallery £7 (pen £5).
P (400 metres) toilets for disabled shop (ex guide dogs)

SE1
Golden Hinde Educational Museum

St Mary Overie Dock, Cathedral St SE1 9DE (On the Thames path between Southwark Cathedral and the new Globe Theatre)
☎ 020 7403 0123 020 7407 5908
e-mail: info@goldenhide.co.uk

A full size replica of Sir Francis Drake's famous 16th century galleon. Just like the original, this *Golden Hinde* has circumnavigated the globe. You can explore the five decks, and costumed crew add to the atmosphere. Special events include Living History re-enactments. There are holiday workshops for children and the ship is also available for private hire.
Times: Open all year, Summer daily 10-6, Winter daily 10-5. Visitors are advised to check opening times as they may vary due to closures for functions.
Fee: £2.50 (ch 4-13 £1.75, under 4's free, concessions £2.10)
P (on street parking) shop (ex guide dogs)

EC2
The Guildhall

Gresham Steet EC2V 5AE (Underground - Bank, St Paul's)
☎ 020 7606 3030 020 7260 1119
Times: Open all year, May-Sep, daily 10-5; Oct-Apr, Mon-Sat 10-5. (Closed Xmas, New Year, Good Fri, Etr Mon & infrequently for Civic occasions).
shop *Details not confirmed for 2001*

N6
Highgate Cemetery

Swains Ln N6 6PJ (Underground - Archway, see directions posted at exit)
☎ 020 8340 1834

Highgate Cemetery is the most impressive of a series of large, formally arranged and landscaped cemeteries which were established around the perimeter of London in the mid-19th century. There's a wealth of fine sculpture and architecture amongst the tombstones, monuments and mausoleums as well as the graves of such notables as the Rossetti family, George Eliot, Michael Faraday and Karl Marx.
Times: Open all year. Eastern Cemetery: daily 10 (11 wknds)-5 (4 in winter). Western Cemetery by guided tour only: Sat & Sun 11-4 (3 in winter); midweek tours 12, 2 & 4 (12, 2 & 3 in winter). No weekday tours in Dec, Jan & Feb. Special tours by arrangement. (Closed 25-26 Dec & during funerals).
Fee: East cemetery £1. Tour of West cemetery £3 (ch 8-16 £1, no ch under 8 on tours). Donations encouraged to assist restoration. Camera permits for private use £2 (no video or flash).
P shop

SE1
HMS Belfast

Morgans Ln, Tooley St SE1 2JH (Underground - London Bridge/Tower Hill/Monument. Rail: London Bridge)
☎ 020 7940 6300 020 7403 0719

Europe's last surviving big gun, armoured warship from WWII, *HMS Belfast* was launched in 1938 and served in the North Atlantic and Arctic with the Home Fleet. She led the Allied naval bombardment of German positions on D-Day, and was saved for the nation in 1971. A tour of the ship will take you from the Captain's Bridge through nine decks to the massive Boiler and Engine Rooms. You can visit the cramped Messdecks, Officers' Cabins, Galley, Sick Bay, Dentist and Laundry.
Times: Open all year, daily. Mar-Oct 10-6, last admission 5.15; Nov-28 Feb 10-5, last admission 4.15. (Closed 24-26 Dec).
Fee: £5 (ch under 16 free, students & pen £3.80). Party.
P (150yds) (wheelchair lift for access on board) toilets for disabled shop (ex guide dogs)

W4
Hogarth House

Hogarth Ln, Great West Rd W4 2QN (50yds W of Hogarth roundabout on Great West Road)
☎ 020 8994 6757 020 8583 4595

This 18th-century house was the country home of artist William Hogarth (1697-1764) during the last 15 years of his life. The house contains displays on the artist's life, and many of his satirical engravings.
Times: Open Apr-Oct, Tue-Fri 1-5, Sat-Sun 1-6; Nov-Mar, Tue-Fri 1-4, Sat-Sun 1-5. (Closed Mon, Jan, 25-26 Dec, Good Fri).
Fee: Free.
P (25 & 50yds) (spaces marked in Axis Centre car park) toilets for disabled shop (ex guide dogs)

SE23
The Horniman Museum & Gardens

London Rd, Forest Hill SE23 3PQ (situated on A205)
☎ 020 8699 2339 (rec info) 020 8699 1872
020 8291 5506
e-mail: marketing@horniman.ac.uko.uk

Founder Frederick Horniman, a tea merchant, gave the museum to the people of London in 1901. The collection covers Natural History - including Vanishing Birds; African Worlds; and The Music Room, which is currently undergoing redevelopment. There are 16 acres of gardens, and the museum hosts a variety of workshops and activities.
Times: Open all year, Mon-Sat 10.30-5.30, Sun 2-5.30 (Closed 24-26 Dec). Gardens close at sunset.
Fee: Free.
P (opposite museum) (chair lift to parts of upper floor) toilets for disabled shop (closed until 2001) (ex guide dogs or in gardens)

SW1

Houses of Parliament

Westminster SW1A 0AA (Underground - Westminster)
☎ 020 7219 4272 020 7219 5839
e-mail: poi@parliament.uk

From the time of Edward the Confessor until Henry VIII moved to Whitehall Palace in 1529, the site of the present-day Houses of Parliament was the main residence of the monarch, hence the term the 'Palace of Westminster'. The building stands at 940ft long, covers eight acres and includes 1100 apartments. There are over two miles of passages.

Times: Telephone well in advance for information on how to go about arranging permits for a tour of the building, or to listen to debates from the Strangers Gallery. Tours must be arranged through a Member of Parliament. **Fee:** Free.
P (250yds) ♿ (by arrangement) toilets for disabled shop

SE1

Imperial War Museum

Lambeth Rd SE1 6HZ (Underground - Lambeth North, Elephant & Castle or Waterloo)
☎ 020 7416 5000 020 7416 5374

Founded in 1917, this museum illustrates and records all aspects of the two World Wars and other military operations involving Britain and the Commonwealth since 1914. There are always special exhibitions and the programme of events includes film shows and lectures. The museum has a wealth of military reference material, but some reference departments are open to the public by appointment only.

Times: Open all year, daily 10-6. (Closed 24-26 Dec).
Fee: £5.50 (ch free, concessions £4.50). Free admission after 4.30 daily. P (on street 100 mtr) (metered Mon-Fri) ♿ (disabled parking sometimes available, wheelchair access) toilets for disabled shop (ex guide dogs)

NW1

The Jewish Museum

Raymond Burton House, 129-131 Albert St, Camden Town NW1 7NB (Underground - Camden Town, 3 mins walk from station)
☎ 020 7284 1997 020 7267 9008
e-mail: admin@jmus.org.uk

The Jewish Museum opens a window onto the history and religious life of the Jewish community in Britain and beyond. The elegant Victorian building in Camden Town includes a History Gallery, and a Ceremonial Art Gallery illustrates Jewish religious life with an outstanding collection of rare and beautiful objects.

Times: Open Sun-Thu, 10-4. Closed Jewish Festivals & public holidays.
Fee: £3 (ch, students, disabled & UB40 £1.50) Family ticket £7.50.
P (outside museum) (pay & display parking) ♿ (induction loop in lecture room linked to audio-visual unit) toilets for disabled shop (ex guide dogs)

N3

The Jewish Museum

The Sternberg Centre, 80 East End Rd, Finchley N3 2SY (Underground - Finchley Central, 10 mins walk via Station Rd & Manor View)
☎ 020 8349 1143 020 8343 2162
e-mail: jml.finchley@btinternet.com

The Jewish Museum traces the story of Jewish immigration and settlement in London, including a reconstruction of an East End tailoring workshop. It also has a Holocaust Education Gallery with an exhibition on Leon Greenman - British Citizen and Auschwitz survivor.

Times: Open all year, Sun 10.30-4.30, Mon-Thu 10.30-5. Closed Jewish festivals, public holidays & 24 Dec-4 Jan. Also closed Sun in Aug & BH wkends.
Fee: £2 (concessions £1, ch free)
P (50m) (on street parking) ♿ toilets for disabled shop

NW3

Keats House

Keats Grove, Hampstead NW3 2RR (Underground - Hampstead, about 15mins walk from station)
☎ 020 7435 2062 020 7431 9293
e-mail: keatshouse@corpoflondon.gov.uk

The poet John Keats lived in this house from 1818-1820 and wrote some of his most famous poems, including *'Ode to a Nightingale'* here. His fiancee, Fanny Brawne, lived next door, and they often walked together on nearby Hampstead Heath. The house contains many of his personal items including inkstand, engagement ring, paintings, jewellery and manuscripts.

Times: Open 23 Apr-10 Dec, Tue-Sat 12-5. Tue-Sat between 10-12 guided tours, schools & visits by appointment take place. Wed between 5-8 a programme of tours & lectures are available. Sun & BH'S 12-5.
Fee: £3 (under 16's free, concessions £1.50) Party 10+. Garden free.
P (500yds) (residents parking in operation) ♿ shop (ex guide dogs)

W8

Kensington Palace State Apartments & Royal Ceremonial Dress Collection

Kensington Gardens W8 4PX (Underground - High Street Kensington or Notting Hill Gate)
☎ 020 7937 9561 020 7376 0198

Highlights of a visit to Kensington include the recently restored Kings Apartments with a fine collection of Old

contd.

Masters; Tintoretto and Van Dyke amongst them. The Royal Ceremonial Dress Collection includes a selection of HM The Queen's dresses, representations of tailor's and dressmaker's workshops, and Queen Mary's Wedding Dress.

Times: Open 10-4, from Mar-Winter season daily 10-5, Open Wed-Sun 10-4 during Winter.
Fee: £8.50 (ch £6.10, concessions £6.70) Family ticket £26.10. Prices subject to change.
P (500yds) ☕ ♿ (cafeteria has wheelchair access ramp) toilets for disabled shop 🐕 (ex guide dogs) 🎟

NW3
Kenwood
Hampstead Ln NW3 7JR (Underground - Hampstead)
☎ 020 8348 1286 📠 020 8348 7325

Forming part of Hampstead Heath, the wooded grounds of Kenwood were laid out in the 18th century by the first Earl of Mansfield. House, contents and grounds were bequeathed to the nation in the 1920s by Lord Iveagh. The house contains a notable collection of paintings, and musical evenings and other events are held in its grounds in summer.
Times: Open all year, Apr-Oct, daily 10-6 (Sun 10-8 in Aug); Oct, daily 10-5; Nov-Mar, daily 10-4. (Closed 24-25 Dec & 1 Jan).
Fee: House & gardens free. Donations welcome. Fee payable for exhibitions.
P ☕ ✕ licensed ♿ toilets for disabled shop 🐕 (ex grounds) #

W14
Leighton House Museum & Art Gallery
12 Holland Park Rd W14 8LZ (Underground - High Street Kensington)
☎ 020 7602 3316 📠 020 7371 2467

An opulent and exotic example of high Victorian taste, Leighton House was built for the President of the Royal Academy, Frederic Lord Leighton. The main body of the house was built in 1866 but the fabulous Arab Hall, an arresting `Arabian Nights' creation, was not completed until 13 years later.
Times: Open all year, daily 11-5.30. Garden open Apr-Sep 11-5. (Closed Tue). Open Spring & Summer BH's.
Fee: Free.
🐕

W8
Linley Sambourne House
18 Stafford Ter W8 7BH (Underground - High Street Kensington)
☎ 020 7937 0663 📠 020 7995 4895

The home of Linley Sambourne (1844-1910), chief political cartoonist at *Punch* magazine, has had its magnificent artistic interior preserved, almost unchanged, since the late 19th century. Also displayed are many of Sambourne's own drawings and photographs.
Times: Open Mar-Oct, Wed 10-4, Sun 2-5. Guided tours Sun only, 2.15, 3.15 & 4.15. At other times by appointment only.
Fee: £3.50 (ch under 16 £2, pen £2.50).
P (metered parking) shop 🐕

SE1
London Aquarium
County Hall, Riverside Building, Westminster Bridge Rd SE1 7PB (Underground-Waterloo & Westminster. On south bank next to Westminster Bridge)
☎ 020 7967 8000 📠 020 7967 8029
e-mail: info@londonaquarium.co.uk

One of Europe's largest displays of global aquatic life. Explore the waters of the world and witness breathtakingly beautiful and dramatic underwater scenes, featuring thousands of living specimens from rivers, oceans and seas across our planet.
Times: Open all year, daily 10-6. Last admission 1hr before closing. Closed 25 Dec.
Fee: £8.50 (ch 3-14 £5, pen & students £6.50, ch under 3yrs free). Family ticket £24.
P (600m) ♿ (free entry for wheelchair users, wheelchairs available) toilets for disabled 🐕 (ex guide & hearing dogs) 🎟

N1
The London Canal Museum
12/13 New Wharf Rd N1 9RT
(Underground - Kings Cross)
☎ 020 7713 0836
e-mail: martins@dircon.co.uk
Times: Open all year, Tue-Sun & BH Mon 10-4.30 (last admission 4). Closed 24-26 & 31 Dec.
P (250yds) (metered parking Mon-Fri before 6pm) ♿ shop 🐕 (ex guide dogs) *Details not confirmed for 2001* 🎟

SE1
London Dungeon
28-34 Tooley St SE1 2SZ (Underground - London Bridge)
☎ 0900 1600 066 📠 020 7378 1529

A modest entrance off a street near London Bridge station will lead you through a series of vaults where the seamy side of life in past centuries is re-created. Not recommended for the faint-hearted. Entry includes the `Jack the Ripper' show, which presents a 15 minute tour through Victorian Whitechapel and `Great Fire of London'.

Times: Open all year, daily, Apr-Sep 10-5.30; Oct-Mar 10.30-5. Late night opening in the Summer. Telephone for exact times.
Fee: £9.95 (ch 14 & pen £6.50, students £8.50).
P (NCP 200yds) ☕ ♿ toilets for disabled shop (ex guide dogs)

NW1
London Planetarium

Marylebone Rd NW1 5LR (Underground - Baker Street)
☎ 020 7935 6861 📠 020 7465 0862
e-mail: firstname.lastname@madame-tussauds.com

A visit to the Planetarium consists of two interactive Space Zone areas plus a half hour star show under the famous green dome. Visitors go on an intergalactic journey of discovery that is both educational and entertaining. Not recommended for under 5s.
Times: Open daily (ex 25 Dec), star shows from 12.20, every 40 mins (10.20am wknds & holidays).
Fee: £6.30 (ch 16 £4.20, pen £4.85).
P (200 mtrs) ♿ (induction loop) toilets for disabled shop (ex guide dogs)

WC2
London Transport Museum

The Piazza, Covent Garden WC2E 7BB (Underground - Covent Garden, Leicester Sq)
☎ 020 7379 6344 & 020 7565 7299 📠 020 7565 7250
e-mail: contact@ltmuseum.co.uk

Covent Garden's original Victorian flower market is home to this excellent museum which explores the colourful story of London and its famous transport system from 1800 to the present day. There are buses, trams, tube trains, and posters, as well as touch-screen displays, videos and working models to bring the story to life.
Times: Open all year, daily 10-6, Fridays 11-6. Last admission 5.15pm. (Closed 24-26 Dec).
Fee: £5.50 (concessions £2.95, under 5 free). Family ticket £13.95. Family season ticket £24.95) Party.
P (5 mins walk) (parking meters) ☕ ♿ (lift & ramps) toilets for disabled shop (ex guide dogs)

NW1
London Zoo

Regents Park NW1 4RY (Underground - Camden Town or Regents Park)
☎ 020 7722 3333 📠 020 7586 5743
e-mail: marketing@zsl.org

London Zoo is home to over 12,000 animals, insects, reptiles and fish. First opened in 1828, the Zoo can claim the world's first aquarium, insect and reptile house. Daily events such as Animals in Action, feeding times and Animal Encounters give an insight into animal behaviour. Exhibits include the Aquarium, Reptile House, and the Moonlight World where day and night are reversed. The 'Web of Life' exhibition

introduces the amazing range of life forms found in Earth's major habitats, through live animal exhibits and interactive displays.
Times: Open all year, daily from 10am. (Closed 25 Dec).
Fee: £9 (ch 4-14 £7, concessions £8).
P (charged) ☕ ♿ (wheelchairs & booster scooter available) toilets for disabled shop

NW8
Lord's Tour & M.C.C. Museum

Lord's Ground NW8 8QN (Underground - St John's Wood)
☎ 020 7432 1033 📠 020 7266 3825
e-mail: tours@mcc.org.uk

Established in 1787, Lord's is the home of the MCC and cricket. Guided tours take you behind the scenes, and highlights include the Long Room and the MCC Museum, where the Ashes and a large collection of paintings and memorabilia are displayed. The Museum is open on match days for spectators.
Times: Open all year, Oct-Mar tours at 12 & 2pm. Apr-Sep 10am, 12 & 2pm (restrictions on some match days). Telephone for details & bookings.
Fee: Guided tour £6 (ch, students & pen £4.40). Family ticket (2 adults & 2 ch) £18. Party 25+. Museum only £2 (concessions £1) plus ground admission (match days only).
P ✕ licensed ♿ (by arrangment) toilets for disabled shop (ex guide dogs)

NW1
Madame Tussaud's
Marylebone Rd NW1 5LR (Underground - Baker Street)
☎ 020 7935 6861 🖷 020 7465 0862
e-mail: firstname.lastname@madame-tussauds.com

Madame Tussaud's world-famous waxwork collection was founded in Paris in 1770. It moved to England in 1802 and found a permanent home in London's Marylebone Road in 1884. Mingle with the famous and infamous, meeting such diverse characters as Nicolas Cage, Cassius Clay, the Queen and Marilyn Monroe all in one afternoon. The Spirit of London takes you back in time through 400 years of London's history.

Times: Open all year 10-5.30 (9.30am wknds, 9am summer). (Closed 25 Dec).
Fee: £10.95 (ch under 16 £7, pen £8).
P (200 mtrs) ♿ (All parts accessible except Spirit of London ride) toilets for disabled shop (ex guide dogs)

SW1
Mall Galleries
The Mall SW1Y 5BD (Underground - Charing Cross)
☎ 020 7930 6844 🖷 020 7839 7830
Times: Open all year, daily 10-5.
P (50 yds) (no parking at the Mall) ♿ (chairlift to galleries)
Details not confirmed for 2001

EC4
Middle Temple Hall
The Temple EC4Y 9AT (Underground - Temple, Blackfriars)
☎ 020 7427 4800 🖷 020 7427 4801
Times: Open all year, Mon-Fri 10-12 & 3-4 (Closed BH & legal vacations).
♿ *Details not confirmed for 2001*

EC3
The Monument
Monument St EC3R 8AH (Underground - Monument)
☎ 020 7626 2717 🖷 020 7403 4477

Designed by Wren and Hooke and erected in 1671-7, the Monument commemorates the Great Fire of 1666 which is reputed to have started in nearby Pudding Lane. The fire destroyed nearly 90 churches and about 13,000 houses. This fluted Doric column stands 202ft high (Pudding Lane is exactly 202ft from its base) and you can climb the 311 steps to a platform at the summit, and receive a certificate as proof of your athletic abilities.

Times: Open Mon-Sun, 10-6. Last admission 5.40pm.
Fee: £1.50 (ch 16 50p).

SE18
Museum of Artillery in the Rotunda
Repository Rd, Woolwich SE18 4BH
☎ 020 8781 3127 🖷 020 8316 5402
e-mail: info@firepower.org.uk

The guns, muskets, rifles and edged weapons that form the collections in this museum are contained in the rotunda designed by John Nash. The collection tells the story of the gun from the 13th-century to the present day. May 2001 is the date a new museum, at the historic Arsenal site, is due to open. In addition to the current display, the museum will house the Royal Artillery's unique collection of uniforms, photographs, books and manuscripts.

Times: Open all year, Mon-Fri 1-4.
Fee: Free. P ♿ shop (ex guide dogs)

SE1
Museum of Garden History
Lambeth Palace Rd SE1 7LB (Underground - Waterloo)
☎ 020 7401 8865 🖷 020 7401 8869
e-mail: curator@museumgardenhistory.freeserve.co.uk

Adjacent to the south gateway of Lambeth Palace is the former church of St Mary-at-Lambeth, now the Museum of Garden History. There is a permanent exhibition on the history of gardens and a collection of ancient tools. The shop sells souvenirs, gifts and seeds from the plant collection. Admiral Bligh of the *Bounty* is buried in the garden.

Times: Open 1st Sun in Mar-2nd Sun in Dec. Mon-Fri & Sun 10.30-5. (Closed Sat).
Fee: Free.
P (100yds) (metered) ♿ (ramps, main cafeteria area not accessible) shop (ex guide dogs)

EC2
Museum of London
150 London Wall EC2Y 5HN (Underground - St Paul's, Barbican)
☎ 020 7814 5500 🖷 020 7600 1058
e-mail: info@museumoflondon.org.uk

Dedicated to the story of London and its people, the Museum of London exists to inspire a passion for London in all who visit it. As well as the permanent collection, the Museum has a varied exhibition programme with three major temporary exhibitions and six topical displays each year. There are also smaller exhibitions in the newly-developed foyer gallery. A wide programme of lectures and activities are provided.

Times: Open all year, Mon-Sat 10-5.50, Sun 12-5.50 (closed 24-26 Dec & 1 Jan).
Fee: £5 (concessions £3, under 16 free). An annual ticket, 1 year from date of purchase.
P (NCP 600yds) ♿ (wheelchairs available, lifts & induction loops, parking) toilets for disabled shop (ex guide dogs)

EC1

Museum of The Order of St John

St John's Gate, St John's Ln EC1M 4DA (Underground - Farringdon, Barbican)

☎ 020 7253 6644 🖹 020 7336 0587

One of the most obscure and fascinating museums in London, St John's Gate displays treasures that once belonged to the Knights Hospitaller, the crusading knights who are now better known as first aiders. Maltese silver, Italian furniture, paintings, coins and pharmacy jars are among the objects on view. Guided tours are available.

Times: Open all year, Mon-Sat 10-5, Sat 10-4 (Closed Etr, Xmas wk & BH wknds). Guided tours 11 & 2.30 Tue, Fri & Sat.

Fee: Museum free. For tours of St John's Gate & Grand Priors Church a donation of £4 (pen £3).

P (meters/ NCP 300yds) ♿ toilets for disabled shop (ex guide dogs)

WC2

Museums of the Royal College of Surgeons

35-43 Lincoln's Inn Fields WC2A 3PN (Underground - Holborn)

☎ 020 7869 6560 🖹 020 7869 6564
e-mail: museums@rcseng.ac.uk

Two museums are housed here - the Hunterian Museum contains the anatomical and pathological specimens collected by John Hunter FRS (1728-1793), a renowned surgeon and teacher of anatomy, and displays relating to the work of Sir Joseph Lister, pioneer of antiseptic surgery. The Odontological Museum contains an extensive collection of human and animal skulls and teeth as well as dental instruments.

Times: Open Mon-Fri 10-5. Closed wkends, BHs & Xmas/New Year.

Fee: Free.

P (25 metres) (pay & display 8-6pm) ♿ (prior notice required) shop (ex guide dogs)

SW3

National Army Museum

Royal Hospital Rd, Chelsea SW3 4HT (Underground - Sloane Square)

☎ 020 7730 0717 🖹 020 7823 6573
e-mail: info@national-army-museum.ac.uk

The museum offers a unique insight into the lives of Britain's soldiers, with displays including weapons, paintings, equipment, models, medals, and uniforms.

Times: Open all year, daily 10-5.30. (Closed Good Fri, May Day, 24-26 Dec & 1 Jan).

Fee: Free.

P ♿ (wheelchair lift to access lower ground floor) toilets for disabled shop (ex guide dogs)

WC2

National Gallery

Trafalgar Square WC2N 5DN (Underground - Charing Cross, Leicester Square, Embankment & Piccadilly. Rail: Charing Cross)

☎ 020 7747 2885 🖹 020 7747 2423
e-mail: information@ng-london.org.uk

All the great periods of Western European painting from 1260-1900 are represented here, although most of the national collection of British works is housed at the Tate. The gallery's particular treasures include Velazquez's *Toilet of Venus,* Leonardo da Vinci's cartoon *(the Virgin and Child with Saints Anne and John the Baptist)*, Rembrandt's *Belshazzar's Feast*, Van Gogh's *Sunflowers*, and Titian's *Bacchus and Ariadne.* The British paintings include Gainsborough's *Mr and Mrs Andrews* and Constable's *Haywain.*

Times: Open all year, daily 10-6, (Wed until 9pm). Special major charging exhibitions open normal gallery times. Closed Good Fri, 24-26 Dec & 1 Jan.

Fee: Free.

P (100yds) ✕ licensed ♿ (wheelchairs available, induction loop, lifts, special tours toilets for disabled shop (ex guide dogs)

SE10

National Maritime Museum

Romney Rd SE10 9NF (central Greenwich)

☎ 020 8858 4422 & 8312 6565 info line
🖹 020 8312 6632

Times: Open all year, daily 10-5. (Closed 24-26 Dec & 1 Jan)

P (50 yds) (parking in Greenwich limited) ✕ licensed ♿ (wheelchairs, advisory service for hearing/sight impaired) toilets for disabled shop *Details not confirmed for 2001*

WC2

National Portrait Gallery

2 St Martin's Place WC2H 0HE (Underground - Charing Cross, Leicester Square)

☎ 020 7306 0055 🖹 020 7306 0058

Times: Open all year 10-6, Sat 10-6 & Sun 12-6. (Closed Good Fri, May Day, 24-26 Dec & 1 Jan).

P (200yds) ♿ (direct access, stair climber, touch tours) toilets for disabled shop *Details not confirmed for 2001*

SW7

The Natural History Museum

Cromwell Rd SW7 5BD (Underground - South Kensington)

☎ 020 7942 5000 🖹 020 7942 5536
e-mail: marketing@nhm.ac.uk

This vast and elaborate Romanesque-style building, with its terracotta facing showing relief mouldings of animals, birds and fishes, covers an area of four acres. A multitude of fascinating galleries cover every aspect of natural history. A major permanent exhibition on dinosaurs includes new skeletons, recreated robotic models, and displays on how dinosaurs lived, why they became extinct, and how they were dug up and studied by scientists.

contd.

Times: Open all year, Mon-Sat 10-5.50, Sun 11-5.50 (last admission 5.30)
Fee: £7.50 (ch under 17 & pen free, concessions £4.50).
(metered 180yds) limited parking,public transport advised licensed (ex top floor & one gallery, wheelchairs available) toilets for disabled shop (4 giftshops) (ex guide dogs)

SE10
Old Royal Observatory
Greenwich Park, Greenwich SE10 9NF (off A2)
020 8858 4422 & 8312 6565 recording
020 8312 6632
Times: Open all year, daily 10-5 (Closed 24-26 Dec & 1 Jan)
toilets for disabled shop *Details not confirmed for 2001*

WC1
Petrie Museum of Egyptian Archaeology
Malet Place, Univerity College London WC1E 6BT (on first floor of the D M S Watson building, in Malet Place, off Torrington Place)
0171 504 2884 **0171 504 2886**
e-mail: petrie.museum@ucl.ac.uk

One of the largest and most inspiring collections of Egyptian archaeology anywhere in the world. The displays illustrate life in the Nile Valley from prehistory, through the era of the Pharoahs to Roman and Islamic timsa. Especially noted for its collection of the personal items that illustrate life and death in Ancient Egypt, including the world's earliest surviving dress (c 2800BC).
Times: Open all year, Tue-Fri 1-5, Sat 10-1. Closed for 1 wk at Xmas/Etr.
Fee: Free.
shop (ex guide dogs)

W1
Pollock's Toy Museum
1 Scala St W1P 1LT (Underground - Goodge Street)
020 7636 3452
e-mail: toymuseum@hotmail.com

Teddy bears, wax and china dolls, dolls' houses, board games, toy theatres, tin toys, mechanical and optical toys, folk toys and nursery furniture, are among the attractions to be seen in this appealing museum. Items from all over the world and from all periods are displayed in two small, interconnecting houses with winding staircases and charming little rooms. Toy theatre performances available for groups.
Times: Open all year, Mon-Sat 10-5. (Closed Sun & Xmas).
Fee: £3 (ch 3-18 £1.50)
(100 yds) (Central London restrictions) shop 

SW1
The Queen's Gallery
Buckingham Palace, Buckingham Palace Rd SW1A 1AA (Underground - Victoria)
020 7839 1377 **020 7930 9625**
e-mail: infomation@royalcollection.org.uk

The Queen's Gallery at Buckingham Palace was first opened to the public in 1962 to display paintings, drawings, furniture and other works of art in the Royal Collection.
Times: Closed for major refurbishment, due to re-open 2002, the year of The Queen's Golden Jubilee.
(200yds) shop (ex guide dogs)

SE10
The Queens House
Romney Rd SE10 9NF (central Greenwich)
020 8858 4422 & 8312 6565 info line
020 8312 6632
Times: Open from 1 Dec - 24 Sep.
(50 yds) (parking in Greenwich limited in 2000) licensed (Blind kit/stairclimber/wheelchairs) toilets for disabled shop *Details not confirmed for 2001*

SE3
Rangers House
Chesterfield Walk SE10 8QY
020 8853 0035

This beautiful villa, built around 1700 on the edge of Greenwich Park, houses two important collections: one of Jacobean and Stuart portraits, the second of musical instruments. The house has a busy programme of chamber concerts, poetry readings, holiday projects and workshops.
Times: Open all year, Apr-Sep, daily 10-6 (Oct 10-5); Nov-Mar, Wed-Sun 10-4. (Closed 24-25 Dec & 1 Jan). Ranger's House may close late autumn 2000 - winter 2001 for refurbishment.
Please telephone before travel.
Fee: £2.80 (ch 5-15 £2.10, under 5's free). Personal stereo tour included in admission.
toilets for disabled (in certain areas)

W1
Rock Circus
London Pavilion, Piccadilly Circus W1V 9LA (Underground - Piccadilly Circus)
020 7734 7203 **020 7734 8023**

Rock Circus gives you an insider's tour of the world of rock and pop. Figures include Madonna on a video shoot, Bob Marley in the recording studio and experience the feeling of appearing on stage at Wembley Stadium.

Times: Open all year, Mar-Sep, Sun-Mon & Wed-Thu 10-8, Tue 11-8, Fri & Sat 10-9; Oct-Feb, Sun-Mon & Wed-Thu 10-6, Tue 11-6, Fri & Sat 10-7.

P (200yds) (lift to all floors with member of staff) toilets for disabled shop *Details not confirmed for 2001*

W1

Royal Academy Of Arts

Burlington House, Piccadilly W1V 0DS (Underground - Piccadilly Circus)

☎ 020 7300 8000 & 0171 439 4996/7 020 7300 8001

Times: Open all year, daily 10-6. (Closed 25 Dec & Good Fri).

licensed toilets for disabled shop *Details not confirmed for 2001*

NW9

Royal Air Force Museum

Grahame Park Way, Hendon NW9 5LL (Underground - Colindale)

☎ 020 8205 2266 & 020 8200 1763 020 8205 8044

e-mail: keith.blumire@rafmuseum.org.uk

Seventy full-size original aeroplanes and other exhibits, all under cover, tell the story of flight through the ages. Extensive galleries show the political and historical impact of flight - including the 'Battle of Britain Experience'. There's a Tornado flight simulator, guided tours, and the 'touch and try' Jet Provost.

Times: Open daily 10-6. (Closed 24-26 & 31 Dec-1 Jan).

Fee: £7 (pen £5.50, ch & concessions £4.50). Family ticket (2 adults & 2 ch) £18.50. Party 20+.

P licensed (lifts, ramps & wheelchairs available) toilets for disabled shop (ex guide dogs)

SW1

The Royal Mews

Buckingham Palace, Buckingham Palace Rd SW1W 0QH (Underground - Victoria)

☎ 020 7799 2331 (info line)

020 7930 9625

Designed by John Nash and completed in 1825, the Royal Mews houses the State Coaches. These include the Gold State Coach, made in 1762, with panels painted by the Florentine artist Cipriani. As one of the finest working stables in existence, the Royal Mews provides a unique opportunity for you to see a working department of the Royal Household.

Times: Open Oct-Jul, Mon-Thu, 12-4; Aug-Sep, Mon-Thu, 10.30-4.30.

Fee: £4.30 (ch 5-17 £2.10, under5's free, pen £3.30) Family ticket (2 adults & 2 ch) £10.70.

P (200yds) toilets for disabled shop (ex guide dogs)

SE10

Royal Naval College

Greenwich SE10 9NN

☎ 020 8858 2256 020 8858 7854

Times: Open all year (Painted Hall and Chapel only), daily 12-5 (last admission 4.30).

P (200m) (all local streets: yellow line roads) (can be given access if prior notice given) shop *Details not confirmed for 2001*

SW7

Science Museum

Exhibition Rd, South Kensington SW7 2DD (Underground - South Kensington)

☎ 020 7942 4000 020 7942 4421

e-mail: sciencemuseum@nmsi.ac.uk

Ideal for children (and often adults too), the displays feature many working models with knobs to press, handles to turn and buttons to push to various different effects: exhibits are set in motion, light up, rotate and make noises. The collections cover science, technology, engineering and industry through the ages; there are galleries dealing with printing, chemistry, nuclear physics, navigation, photography, electricity, communications and medicine. The new Wellcome Wing includes an IMAX cinema, 6 new galleries and a restaurant.

Times: Open all year, daily 10-6. (Closed 24-26 Dec).

Fee: £6.50 (concessions £3.50, under 16's free).

toilets for disabled shop (ex guide dogs)

SE1

Shakespeare's Globe Exhibition

New Globe Walk, Bankside SE1 9DT (Underground - London Bridge, walk along Bankside. Mansion House, walk across Southwark Bridge)

☎ 020 7902 1500 020 7902 1515

Guides help to bring England's theatrical heritage to life at the 'unparalleled and astonishing' recreation of this famous theatre. Discover what an Elizabethan audience would have been like, find out about the rivalry between the bankside theatres, the bear baiting and the stews, hear about the penny stinkards and find out what a bodger is.

Times: Open all year; Sep-May, daily 10-5 (ex 24-25 Dec). May-Sep (theatre season), opening times restricted, phone for details.

P (10 mins walk) licensed toilets for disabled shop (ex guide dogs) *Details not confirmed for 2001*

WC2

Sir John Soane's Museum

13 Lincoln's Inn Fields WC2A 3BP (Underground - Holborn)

☎ 020 7405 2107 020 7831 3957

Sir John Soane was responsible for some of the most splendid architecture in London, and his house, built in 1812, contains his collections of antiquities, sculpture, paintings, drawings and books. Amongst his treasures are the *Rake's Progess* and *Election* series of paintings by Hogarth.

contd.

Times: Open all year, Tue-Sat 10-5. Also first Tue of month 6-9pm. (Closed BH). Lecture tour Sat 2.30 (limited no of tickets sold from 2pm)
Fee: Free.
P (200yds) (metered parking) ♿ (wheelchair available, phone for details of accessibility) shop (ex guide dogs)

SE5
South London Gallery
65 Peckham Rd SE5 8UH
☎ **020 7703 6120 7703 9799-taped info**
020 7252 4730
e-mail: mail@southlondonart.com

The gallery presents a programme of up to eight exhibitions a year of cutting-edge contemporary art, and has established itself as South East London's premier venue for contemporary visual arts. The Gallery also aims to bring contemporary art of the highest standards to audiences in South London and to assist in the regeneration of the area by attracting audiences from across Britain and abroad.
Times: Open only when exhibitions are in progress, Tue-Fri 11-6, Thu 11-7, wknds 2-6 (Closed Mon).
Fee: Free.
P (50yds)

E9
Sutton House
2 & 4 Homerton High St E9 6JQ (Hackney Central train station)
☎ **020 8986 2264**
e-mail: tshtan@smtp.ntrust.org.uk

In London's East End, the building is a rare example of a Tudor red-brick house. Built in 1535 by Sir Rufe Sadleir, Principal Secretary of State for Henry VIII, the house has 18th-century alterations and later additions.
Times: Open 7 Feb-Nov, Wed, Sun & BH Mon 11.30-5.30. Last admission 5pm. (Closed Good Friday).
Fee: £2.10. Family ticket £4.80.
P (on street parking) (meters) ♿ (induction loop braille guide) toilets for disabled shop

SW1
Tate Britain
Millbank SW1P 4RG (Underground - Pimlico)
☎ **020 7887 8000 & rec info 020 7887 8008**
e-mail: information@tate.org.uk

In 1892 Sir Henry Tate, sugar magnate and prominent collector of contemporary British painting and sculpture, offered to finance the building of a new and permanent home for his growing collection of British Art. Officially opened to the public in 1897, a number of extensions to the building have followed, the most recent being the Clore Gallery in 1987 which houses the Turner Bequest. A series of new developments will transform the gallery for the new millennium, with a new gallery for British art at the current site, and modern international art at the converted Bankside Power Station in Southwark.
Times: Open daily 10-5.50. (Closed 24-26 Dec).
Fee: Free. Donations welcomed.
P licensed ♿ (wheelchairs on request, parking by prior arrangement). toilets for disabled shop (ex guide & hearing dogs)

SE1
Tate Modern
Bankside SE1 9TG
☎ **020 7887 8008 (info) & 020 7887 8888**
020 7401 5052
e-mail: information@tate.org.uk

Tate Modern is now Britain's major public artspace, exhibiting works from the 20th century in four themed groups: Landscape, Matter, Environment; Still Life, Object, Real Life; Nude, Action, Body; and History, Memory, Society. Some of world's best-known modern artworks are on display here.
Times: Open all year, Sun-Thu 10-6, Fri & Sat 10am-10pm. (Closed 24-26 Dec).
Fee: Free.
P (limited) licensed ♿ (parking available) toilets for disabled shop (ex guide dogs)

SE18
Thames Barrier Visitors Centre
Unity Way SE18 5NJ
☎ **020 8305 4188** **020 8855 2146**
e-mail: jane.finch@environment-agency.gov.uk

Spanning a third of a mile, the Thames Barrier is the world's largest movable flood barrier. The visitors' centre and exhibition on the South Bank explains the flood threat and the construction of this £535 million project, now valued at £1 billion. Each month a test closure of all ten gates, lasting over 2 hours, is carried out and the annual full day closure of all ten gates takes place in the autumn.
Times: Open all year, telephone for opening times. (Closed Xmas - telephone for details).
Fee: £3.40 (ch & pen £2). Car park £1. Coach park Free. Family ticket £7.50. Party.
P (charged) ♿ (lift from river pier approach) toilets for disabled shop

WC2
Theatre Museum
Russell St, Covent Gardent WC2E 7PA (Underground - Covent Garden, Leicester Sq)
☎ **020 7943 4700** **020 7943 4777**
e-mail: tmmailing@theatremuseum.vam.ac.uk

Major developments, events and personalities from the performing arts, including stage models, costumes, prints, drawings, posters, puppets, props and a variety of other theatre memorabilia. There are guided tours, demonstrations on the art of stage make-up, and you can dress up in costumes from National Theatre companies. Groups are advised to book in advance.

Times: Open all year, Tue-Sun 10-7. (closed 25 Dec & other public hols)
Fee: £4.50 (concessions £2.50, ch under 16 free)
P (meters, NCP 250yds) toilets for disabled shop (ex guide dogs)

SE1
The Tower Bridge Experience
SE1 2UP (Underground - Tower Hill or London Bridge)
020 7378 1928 020 7357 7935
e-mail: enquires@towerbridge.org.uk

One of the capital's most famous landmarks, its glass-covered walkways stand 142ft above the Thames, affording panoramic views of the river. Much of the original machinery for working the bridge can be seen in the engine rooms. The exhibition, The Tower Bridge Experience, uses state-of-the-art effects to present the story of the bridge in a dramatic and exciting fashion.
Times: Open all year, Apr-Oct, 10-6.30; Nov-Mar 9.30-6 (last ticket sold 75 mins before closing). (Closed 24-25 Dec, 17 Jan).
Fee: £6.25 (ch 5+, Pen, Student £4.25) Family ticket £18.50. Party 10+.
P (100yds) toilets for disabled shop

EC3
Tower of London
Tower Hill EC3N 4AB (Underground - Tower Hill)
020 7709 0765

Perhaps the most famous castle in the world, the Tower of London has played a central part in British history. The White Tower, built by William the Conqueror as a show of strength to the people of London, remains one of the most outstanding examples of Norman military architecture in Europe. For hundreds of years the Tower was used, among other things, as the State Prison. It was here that Henry VIII had two of his wives executed, here that Lady Jane Grey died and here that Sir Walter Raleigh was imprisoned. The Yeoman Warders, or `Beefeaters' play an important role in the protection of the Tower - home of the Crown Jewels - and are informative and entertaining. Look out for the ravens, whose continued residence is said to ensure that the Kingdom does not fail. The Crowns and Diamonds exhibition features a number of crowns never displayed to the public before and more than 12,000 rough and polished diamonds.
Times: Open all year, Mar-Oct, Mon-Sat 9-6, Sun 10-6 (last admission 5pm); Nov-Feb, Tue-Sat 9-5, Sun 10-5 (last admission 4pm). (Closed 24-26 Dec & 1 Jan).
Fee: £11 (ch £7.30, concessions £8.30) Family ticket £33.
P (100yds) (NCP Lower Thames St) (access guide can be obtained in advance call 0171 488 5694) toilets for disabled shop (x4) (ex guide dogs)

SW7
Victoria & Albert Museum
Cromwell Rd, South Kensington SW7 2RL
(Underground - South Kensington)
020 7942 2000 020 7942 2266

The world's finest museum of the decorative arts, with collections spanning 2000 years, and comprising sculpture, furniture, fashion and textiles, paintings, silver, glass, ceramics, jewellery, books, prints, and photographs from Britain and all over the world. Highlights include the national collection of watercolours; the Dress Court showing fashion from 1500 to the present day; a superb Asian collection; the Jewellery Gallery including the Russian Crown Jewels; and the 20th Century Gallery, devoted to comtemporary art and design. Special exhibitions for 2001 are: Imperfect Beauty: the making of fashion images (28 Sept 2000-March 2001; Brand New (19 Oct 2000-14 Jan

contd.

2001); The Victorians (5 April 2000-29 July 2001) and Vivienne Westwood (18 Oct 2001-6 Jan 2002)

Times: Open all year, Mon-Sun 10-5.45. (Closed 24-26 Dec). Tel for BH openings. British Galleries closed for redevelopment. Wed late view 6.30-9.30.

Fee: £5 (pen, ES40, disabled with carer, students & under 18 free).

P (500yds) licensed (braille guide, tour tape. for further info, please phone) toilets for disabled shop (ex guide dogs)

SE1
Vinopolis, City of Wine

1 Bank End SE1 9BU (Underground-London Bridge. Borough High Street West exit, R into Stoney St, then L into Park St)

☎ 0870 241 4040 020 7403 7093

e-mail: sales@vinopolis.co.uk

Vinopolis is a journey through the world of wine that covers two and a half acres. Included in this interactive tour are the Vinopolis Art Gallery and 5 wine tastings.

Times: Open all year, Tue-Fri 10-5.30 (last admission 3.30pm); Sat-Mon from 10 (last admisssion 6pm). Closed 25 Dec & 1 Jan.

Fee: £11.50 (ch 5-15 £5, pen £10.50) including entry, personal audioguide, five wine tastings (adults only) plus entry into art gallery.

P (5-10 min walk) (NCP parking) licensed (lifts & ramps) toilets for disabled shop (ex guide dogs)

W1
Wallace Collection

Hertford House, Manchester Square W1M 6BN (Underground - Bond Street, Baker Street)

☎ 020 7935 0687 020 7224 2155

e-mail: admin@wallcoll.demon.co.uk

Times: Open all year, Mon-Sat 10-5, Sun 2-5. Apr-Sep, Sun 11-5 (Closed Good Fri, May Day, 24-26 Dec & 1 Jan).

P (NCP & meters) (ramp wheelchair available upon request) shop *Details not confirmed for 2001*

EC1
Wesley's Chapel, House & Museum Of Methodism

49 City Rd EC1Y 1AU (Underground - Old Street- exit number 4)

☎ 020 7253 2262 020 7608 3825

Wesley's Chapel has been the Mother Church of World Methodism since its construction in 1778. The crypt houses a museum which traces the development of Methodism from the 18th century to the present day. Wesley's house - built by him in 1779 - was his home when not touring and preaching. Special events are held on May 24 (the anniversary of Wesley's conversion), and November 1st (the anniversary of the Chapel's opening).

Times: Open all year, Mon-Sat & BH 10-4 (Closed BH's, 25 & 26 Dec). Main service 11am Sun followed by an opportunity to tour the museum and house.

Fee: House & museum £4 (ch, students, UB40's & pen £2) Party 20+ 10% discount.

P (lift to the crypt of the chapel) toilets for disabled shop (ex guide dogs)

SW1
Westminster Abbey

Broad Sanctuary SW1P 3PA (Underground - Westminster, St James's Park)

☎ 020 7222 5152 020 7233 2072

e-mail: press@westminster-abbey.org

At the heart of English history for nearly a thousand years, the Abbey has been the setting for every coronation since 1066. The Abbey is a 'Royal Peculiar' and unlike other churches is under the jurisdiction of a Dean and Chapter subject only to the Sovereign. The beautiful Gothic nave is the tallest in Britain and the Chapter House is one of the largest in England. Many famous people are buried here, including Kings and Queens of England, and in Poets' Corner are memorials to poets from Chaucer to the present time.

Times: Open all year. Abbey: Mon-Fri 9.30-4.45, Sat 9-2.45. Last admission 60 mins before closing. Cloister daily 8-6. No tourist visiting on Sundays, however visitors are welcome at services. The Abbey may at short notice be closed for special services & other events.

Fee: £5 (ch 11-15 £2, under11's free, pen & students £3). Family ticket (2 adults & 2 ch) £10.

(areas accessible induction loop) shop (ex guide dogs)

SW1
Westminster Cathedral

Victoria St SW1P 1QW (300 yards from Victoria Station)

☎ 020 7798 9055 020 7798 9090

e-mail: bpalmer@westminstercathedral.org.uk

Westminster Cathedral is a fascinating example of Victorian architecture. Designed in the Early Christian Byzantine style by John Francis Bentley, its strongly oriental appearance makes it very distinctive. The foundation stone was laid in 1895 but the interior was never completed. The Campanile Bell Tower is 273ft high and has a four-sided viewing gallery with magnificent views over London. The lift is open daily 9am-5pm Mar-Nov but shut Mon-Wed from Dec-Feb.

Times: Open all year, daily 7am-7pm.

Fee: Free.

P (0.25m) (2hr metered parking) (all parts accessible except side chapels) shop

SW1
Westminster Hall

Westminster SW1A 0AA (Underground - Westminster Hall)

☎ 020 7219 4272

The great Westminster Hall, where Charles I was tried in 1649, has survived virtually intact since it was remodelled at the end of the 14th century. It escaped the fire in 1834 which destroyed much of the medieval Palace of Westminster, and the magnificent hammerbeam roof is the earliest surviving example of its kind.

Times: Westminster Hall can only be viewed by those on a tour of the Houses of Parliament, which must be arranged by an MP or Peer.

Fee: Free although guides require payment if employed.

toilets for disabled shop

SW13

The Wetland Centre

Queen Elizabeth Walk SW13 9WT

☎ 020 8409 4400 🖹 020 8409 4401

e-mail: info@wetlandcentre.org.uk

Twenty-five minutes from the heart of London, the Wetland Centre is unique in being the first created wetland habitat on such a huge scale (105 acres) to have been developed in any capital city in the world. Built on the site of the former Barn Elms reservoirs and waterworks, the site has a Discovery Centre, an observatory, an audio-visual theatre, an art gallery, and a restaurant.

Times: Open - Summer, daily 9.30-6 (last admission 5); Winter, daily 9.30-5 (last admission 4).

Fee: £6.50 (ch £4 & pen £5.25). Family ticket £17. Groups 10+

P (charged) toilets for disabled shop (ex guide dogs)

E17

William Morris Gallery

Lloyd Park, Forest Rd E17 4PP (Underground - Walthamstow Central)

☎ 020 8527 3782 🖹 020 8527 7070

Victorian artist, craftsman, poet and free thinker William Morris lived here from 1848 to 1856, and the house has been devoted to his life and work. Displays include fabrics, stained glass, wallpaper and furniture, as well as Pre-Raphaelite paintings, sculpture by Rodin, ceramics and a collection of pictures by Frank Brangwyn, who worked briefly for Morris.

Times: Open all year, Tue-Sat and 1st Sun in each month 10-1 & 2-5. (Closed Mon & BH's). Telephone for Xmas/New Year opening times.

Fee: Free.

P shop

SW19

Wimbledon Lawn Tennis Museum

All England Lawn Tennis & Croquet Club, Church Rd SW19 5AE (Underground - Southfields, 15 mins walk to museum)

☎ 020 8946 6131 🖹 020 8944 6497

Trophies, pictures, displays and memorabilia trace the development of the game over the last century. See the world famous Centre Court, and the Championships' trophies, as well as film and video footage of great players in action from the 1920s to the present day.

Times: Open daily all year, 10.30-5. (Closed Fri-Sun before the Championships, middle Sun of Championships, Mon immediately following the Championships, 24-26 Dec & 1 Jan).

Fee: £5 (concessions £4). Party 15+.

P (lift) toilets for disabled shop (ex guide dogs)

SE1

Winston Churchill's Britain at War Experience

64/66 Tooley St SE1 2TF

☎ 020 7403 3171 🖹 020 7403 5104

e-mail: britainatwar@dial.pipex.com

How did it feel to be a British citizen during WWII? Journey back in time and take the lift to the London Underground and shelter from the air raids. Crouch in an Anderson Shelter and hear enemy aircraft overhead. The special effects recreate the sights, sounds and smells of the London Blitz.

Times: Open all year, Apr-Sep 10-5.30pm; Oct-Mar 10-4.30. (Closed 24-26 Dec)

Fee: £5.95 (ch 16 £2.95, student, pen & UB40 £3.95). Family ticket £14.

P (100mtrs) shop (ex guide dogs)

BEXLEY

Hall Place

Bourne Rd DA5 1PQ (near jct of A2 & A233)
☎ 01322 526574 01322 522921

Times: Open all year, House: Mon-Sat 10-5, Sun & BHs 2-6 (summer); Mon-Sat 10-4.15 (winter). Gardens: Mon-Fri 7.30-dusk, Sat & Sun 9-dusk.

licensed toilets for disabled shop (ex guide/hearing dogs) *Details not confirmed for 2001*

BRENTFORD

Kew Bridge Steam Museum

Green Dragon Ln TW8 0EN (Underground - Kew Gardens, district line then 391 bus. Museum 100yds from the N side of Kew Bridge)
☎ 020 8568 4757 020 8569 9978

This Victorian pumping station has steam engines and six beam engines, of which five are working and one is the largest in the world. A forge, diesel house, waterwheel and old workshops can also be seen along with London's only steam narrow-gauge railway which operates on the second and last weekend of each month (Mar-Nov). The Water for Life Gallery tells the story of London's water supply from Pre-Roman times.

Times: Open all year, daily 11-5. In steam wknds & BHs. (Closed Good Fri & Xmas wk).

Fee: Weekdays: £3 (ch 5-15 £1, OAP/students £2) Family ticket £7. Weekends: £4 (ch £2, OAP/students £3) Family ticket £10.50.

(tours for partially sighted by arrangement) toilets for disabled shop

Musical Museum

368 High St TW8 0BD (Underground - Gunnersbury)
☎ 020 8560 8108

This museum will take you back to a bygone age to hear and see a marvellous working collection of automatic musical instruments from small music boxes to a mighty Wurlitzer theatre organ. Working demonstrations.

Times: Open Apr-Oct, Sat & Sun 2-5. Also Jul-Aug, Wed 2-4. (Tour 1hr 30mins).

Fee: £3.20 (ch & pen £2.50). Family ticket £10.

(200 yds) shop (guide dogs)

CHESSINGTON

Chessington World of Adventures

KT9 2NE (M25 junc 9/10, on A243)
☎ 01372 727227 0870 444 7777
01372 725050

At Chessington World of Adventures there's something different around every corner, from spine-tingling rides and fun-filled family attractions to crazy entertainers and rare and endangered animals all set in magnificently themed areas. The Samurai ride includes a 360 triple rotation from over 60 feet. Join Dennis the Menace, Gnasher and all the favourite characters in Beanoland.

Times: Open 25 Apr-29 Oct, daily. Late opening until 9pm during July & August.

Fee: £19.50 (ch 4-13 £15.50). Family ticket £59.

licensed (some rides not accessible, disabled guide available) toilets for disabled shop (ex guide dogs)

CHISLEHURST

Chislehurst Caves

Old Hill BR7 5NB (off A222)
☎ 020 8467 3264 020 8295 0407
e-mail: thecaves@cwcom.net

Miles of mysterious caverns and passages hewn out of the chalk over some 4,000 years can be explored with experienced guides to tell the history and legends of the caves.

Times: Open all year, daily during school hols (incl half terms). All other times Wed-Sun, 10-4. Closed Xmas.

Fee: £3 (ch & pen £1.50); longer tours: Sun & BH's only £5 (ch & pen £2.50).

(ramps) toilets for disabled shop (ex guide dogs)

CRAYFORD

World of Silk

Bourne Rd DA1 4BP (on A223, signposted from A2 Black Price Interchange. 10mins from M25 junct 2)
☎ 01322 559401 01322 556420
e-mail: retail@davidevans.co.uk

Established in 1843 on the banks of the River Cray, David Evans is the last of the old London silk printers. Pre-book a guided tour of the printshop and museum and learn about the traditional methods of printing silk.

Times: Open all year, Mon-Sat 9.30-5. (Closed Sun & BH).

Fee: Museum only: £2 (pen & student £1.50). Guided Tour of Craft Centre & Mill by appointment £3 (pen & student £2.50). Family ticket £8.

toilets for disabled shop (ex guide dogs) 

DOWNE

Down House - Home of Charles Darwin

Luxted Rd BR6 7JT (Off A233, signposted)
☎ 01689 859119

The home of Charles Darwin for forty years. The drawing room and Old Study are furnished as they were when he was working on his famous book *On the Origin of Species by means of Natural Selection*. The

Museum includes memorabilia from his voyage on HMS *Beagle*. The garden is also maintained, including the famous Sand Walk or thinking path, along which he took his daily walk.

Times: Open all year, Apr-Sep, Wed-Sun 10-6 (last admission 5.30)(Oct); Nov-Mar, Wed-Sun 10-4. Also BH Mon. (Closed 24 Dec-7 Feb).

Fee: £5.50 (ch 5-15 £2.80, under 5's free). Visits must be booked in advance.

shop

ENFIELD

Forty Hall Museum

Forty Hill EN2 9HA (M25 junct 25 onto A10, turn right into Bullsmoor Lane)

020 8363 8196 & 020 8363 4046 020 8367 9098

Built in 1629 for Sir Nicholas Raynton, Lord Mayor of London, and altered in the 18th century. The house has fine plaster ceilings and collections of furniture, paintings, ceramics and glass, as well as local history displays and temporary exhibitions.

Times: Open all year, Thu-Sun 11-5 & BH's.

Fee: Free.

(Disabled parking in main carpark & 3 near house) toilets for disabled shop (ex guide dogs)

ESHER

Claremont Landscape Garden

Portsmouth Rd KT10 9JG (E of A307)

01372 467806 01372 464394

e-mail: sclgen@smtp.ntrost.org.uk

Laid out by Vanbrugh and Bridgeman before 1720, extended and naturalised by Kent, this is the earliest surviving example of an English landscaped garden. Its 50 acres include a lake with an island pavilion, a grotto and a turf amphitheatre. Telephone 01372 451596 for details of events.

Times: Open all year Apr-end of Oct daily, Nov-end Dec & Jan-end Mar daily (ex Mon). Apr-Oct Mon-Fri 10-6, Sat-Sun & BH Mon 10-7 (closed all day 11 & 12 Jul closes 2pm 13-16 Jul); Nov-Mar 10-5 or sunset if earlier. Closed 25 Dec and 1 Jan. House open Feb-Nov, 1st wknd of month 2-3 (ex 1st Sat in Jul)

Fee: £3.20 (ch £1.60). Family ticket £8.

(wheelchairs available, Braille guide) toilets for disabled shop (ex on leads, Nov-Mar only)

HAM

Ham House

TW10 7RS (W of A307, between Kingston & Richmond)

020 8940 1950 020 8332 6903

This lovely house was built in 1610 and redecorated by the Duke and Duchess of Lauderdale in the 1670s. There are secret servants' passages and stories of a ghostly Duchess. Special events include Spring Plant Fair, garden and ghost tours, childrens activities in school holidays and summer proms concert.

Times: Open gardens: all year, Sat-Wed 10.30-6 or dusk if earlier. (Closed 25-26 Dec & 1 Jan). House: 1 Apr-29 Oct, Sat-Wed 1-5. Last admission 4.30.

Fee: House £5 (ch £2.50). Family ticket £12.50. Garden only £1.50 (ch 75p). Family £3.75. Groups 15+

(500 yds) (Braille guide, wheelchairs & stairclimber, lift access) toilets for disabled shop (ex guide/hearing dogs)

HAMPTON COURT

Hampton Court Palace

KT8 9AU (on A308, close to A3, M3 & M25 exits. Train from Waterloo - Hampton Court, 2mins walk from station)

020 8781 9500 & 8781 9501

020 8781 5362

With over 500 years of royal history Hampton Court

contd.

Palace has something to offer everyone, from the magnificent State Apartments to the domestic reality of the Tudor Kitchens. Costumed guides and audio tours bring the palace to life and provide an insight into how life in the palace would have been in the time of Henry VIII and William III.

Times: Open all year, mid Mar-Oct, Mon 10.15-6, Tue-Sun 9.30-6 (4.30pm Nov-mid Mar). (Closed 24-26 Dec).

Fee: £10 (ch 5-16 £6.60, pen, students £7.60). Family £29.90.

P (charged) licensed (lifts, buggies for gardens, wheelchairs, wardens to assist) toilets for disabled shop (4 shops on site) (ex in gardens)

ISLEWORTH

Syon House

TW8 8JF (Approach via A310 Twickenham road into Park Rd)

☎ 020 8560 0881 020 8568 0936

Set in 200 acres of parkland, Syon House is the London home of the Duke of Northumberland, whose family have lived here since the late 16th century. During the second half of the 18th century the first Duke of Northumberland engaged Robert Adam to remodel the interior and 'Capability' Brown to landscape the grounds. Adam was also responsible for the furniture and decorations, and the result is particularly spectacular in the superbly coloured Ante-Room and Long Gallery.

Times: Open 15 Mar-Oct, Wed-Thu, Sun & BH 11-5 (last ticket 4.15pm).

Fee: Combined ticket for house and gardens £6 (concessions £4.50). Family ticket £15.

P toilets for disabled shop garden centre

Syon Park

TW8 8JF (A310 Twickenham road into Park Rd)

☎ 020 8560 0881 020 8568 0936

Contained within the 40 acres that make up Syon Park Gardens is one of the inspirations for the Crystal Palace at the Great Exhibition of 1851: a vast crescent of metal and glass, the first construction of its kind in the world and known as the Great Conservatory. Although the horticultural reputation of Syon Park goes back to the 16th century, its beauty today is thanks to the master of landscape design, 'Capability' Brown.

Times: Open all year, daily 10-5.30 or dusk if earlier. (Closed 25 & 26 Dec).

Fee: £3 (concessions £2.50). Combined ticket for house & gardens £6 (concessions £4.50). Family ticket £7.

P toilets for disabled shop garden centre

KEW

Kew Gardens (Royal Botanic Gardens)

TW9 3AB (Underground - Kew Gdns)

☎ 020 8940 1171 020 8332 5197

e-mail: info@kew.org

The world-famous gardens at Kew began with George III's mother, Princess Augusta, in 1759. The 19th-century botanist, Sir Joseph Banks, and head gardener, William Aiton (later curator), were largely responsible for laying the foundations of the great collection of plants, shrubs and trees which exist here today. The elegant Palm House is an early example of a glass and wrought iron building, completed in 1848. But the most famous landmark at Kew is the Chinese Pagoda, standing 163ft high.

Times: Open all year, Gardens daily 9.30-between 4 & 6.30pm on weekdays, between 4-7.30pm Suns & BH's, depending on the time of sunset.(Closed 25 Dec & 1 Jan)

Fee: £5 (concessions £3.50, ch 5-16 £2.50). Family ticket (2 adults & 4 ch) £13.

P (charged) licensed (16 seat bus tour: enquiries ring 020 8332 5623) toilets for disabled shop (ex guide dogs)

Kew Palace

Royal Botanic Gardens TW9 3AB (Underground - Kew Bridge)

☎ 020 8781 9540

A favourite country residence during the reign of the first three Hanoverian Kings, Kew was the site of several royal houses. A fairly modest red-brick building, built in the Dutch style with gables, Kew Palace was built in 1631 and used for nearly a century until 1818 when Queen Charlotte died. Family paintings and personal relics, furniture and tapestries are on display, and a charming 17th-century garden has been recreated.

Times: Closed for refurbishment.

Public Record Office Museum

Ruskin Av TW9 4DU (Underground - Kew Gardens)

☎ 020 8876 3444 020 8392 5266

e-mail: events@pro.gov.uk

Times: Please telephone for details.

P shop *Details not confirmed for 2001*

Queen Charlotte's Cottage

Royal Botanic Gardens TW9 3AB (Underground - Kew Bridge)

☎ 020 8332 5189

Typical of the fashionable rustic style popular with the gentry in the 18th century, the cottage was built for George III and Queen Charlotte as a home for their menagerie of exotic pets, as well as a picnic spot and summer house.

Times: Open weekends only between May & Sep.

Fee: Free. shop

OSTERLEY

Osterley Park House

TW7 4RB (Underground - Osterley)

☎ 020 8560 7714 020 8568 7714

e-mail: tsogen@smtp.ntrust.org.uk

This Elizabethan mansion has been transformed into an 18th-century villa, its elegant interior decoration designed in neo-classical style by Robert Adam. The State Apartments include a Gobelin tapestry ante-room and a dressing-room decorated in the Etruscan style.

Times: Open all year: Park & pleasure grounds, daily 9-7.30 or sunset if earlier. House: Apr-1 Nov, Wed-Sun 2-5, BH Sun & Mon 1-5. Last admission 4.30. (Closed Good Fri & 25-26 Dec). **Fee:** £4.20. Family ticket £10.50. (charged) toilets for disabled shop (ex on lead in park)

RICHMOND

RICHMOND PARK

Holly Lodge, Richmond Park TW10 5HS (Underground - Richmond)

☎ 020 8948 3209 020 8332 2730

With its herds of deer, abundant wild life and centuries-old oaks, Richmond Park is a favourite haunt for visitors and naturalists. There is a formal garden at Pembroke Lodge, and the Isabella Plantation shows a wealth of exotic shrubs and wild flowers. Model sail boats are allowed on Adam's Pond, where the deer drink, and the 18-acre Pen Ponds have been specially made for angling (permit required).

TWICKENHAM

MARBLE HILL HOUSE

Richmond Rd TW1 2NL

☎ 020 8892 5115

An example of the English Palladian school of architecture, Marble Hill House was built in the 18th century for a mistress of George II. The perfectly proportioned Thames-side villa, contains a notable collection of paintings and furniture, as well as the Lazenby Chinoiserie Bequest.

Times: Open all year, daily, Apr-Sep 10-6 (Oct, 10-5); Nov-Mar, Wed-Sun 10-4. (Closed 24-25 Dec & 1-18 Jan).
Fee: £3.30 (ch 5-15 £1.70, under 5's free)
licensed toilets for disabled shop (ex in grounds)

MUSEUM OF RUGBY & TWICKENHAM STADIUM TOURS

Rugby Football Union, Rugby Rd TW1 1DZ (M3 into London, A316 follow signs to museum)

☎ 020 8892 8877 020 8892 2817
e-mail: museum@rfu.com

Located beneath the East Stand of the Twickenham Stadium, home of the England team and headquarters of the Rugby Football Union, the museum uses interactive displays, period set pieces and video footage to bring the history of the game to life. The tour includes a visit to the England dressing room, and magnificent views of the stadium from the top of the north stand.

Times: Museum: open Tue-Sat 10-5, Sun 2-5. Last admission 4.30pm. Tours: 10.30am, noon, 1.30pm, & 3pm; Sun 3pm. No tours on match days. Museum open on match days for ticket holders only. Ground closed Mon (ex BH), 24-26 Dec, Good Fri & the Sunday after a match.
Fee: Museum: £3 (ch, pen, student £2). Twickenham Stadium Tour: £3 (ch, pen, students £2). Joint ticket for Museum and Tour £5 (ch, pen, students £3). Family ticket £15.
licensed (special tours and lifts to all floors) toilets for disabled shop (ex guide dogs)

Orleans House Gallery

Riverside TW1 3DJ (off A305, along Orleans Rd to Riverside)

☎ 020 8892 0221 🖷 020 8744 0501

e-mail: jane.dalton@virgin.net

Times: Open all year, Tue-Sat 1-5.30 (4.30pm Oct-Mar), Sun & BH 2-5.30 (Oct-Mar 2-4.30). (Closed 24-25 Dec). Woodland Gardens daily, 9-dusk.

P ♿ (handling objects & large print labels for some exhibitions) toilets for disabled shop (ex guide dogs) *Details not confirmed for 2001*

WEMBLEY

Wembley Stadium Tours

Wembley Stadium HA9 0WS (Underground - Wembley Park, Wembley Stadium)

☎ 020 8795 8090 🖷 020 8903 5733

e-mail: info@wnsl.co.uk

A fascinating tour of this world famous stadium, including behind-the-scenes areas such as the event control rooms, TV studio, cinema, hospital, England changing room and the player's tunnel. You can walk up the famous steps to receive the cup to the roar of the crowd and sit in the Royal Box. The tour also includes a vast display of Wembley memorabilia dating back to 1923.

Times: Open all year, daily summer 10-4, winter 10-3 (Closed on event days & 25-26 Dec). The Stadium is scheduled to be re-developed from Sep 2000. Please telephone for opening details.

Fee: £7.95 (ch & pen £5.50, students £5.95). Party 20+.

P ♿ (limited tour by arrangement) toilets for disabled shop (ex guide dogs)

Merseyside

Northwestern metropolitan county on the River Mersey, with Liverpool as its administrative centre, Merseyside incorporates the towns of Bootle, Birkenhead, St Helens, Wallasey, and Southport.

The fortunes of the area have declined since the 19th century when Liverpool was England's second greatest port, and the area has been dogged by urban deprivation and unemployment. The area is now on the upturn, due in part to the indomitable Scouse spirit.

When the port of Chester silted up in medieval times, Liverpool took up the slack. The first dock was built in 1715 and the port came to prominence with the slave trade. Following abolition, the port grew to a seven-mile stretch of docks, busy with freight cargoes of cotton, tobacco and sugar and the huge wave of emigration from Europe to the New World in the 19th and early 20th centuries. In its turn, immigration brought an influx of people to Merseyside to join its expanding population, including many from Ireland fleeing the potato famine of 1845.

In the second half of the 20th century, accessible air travel brought to an end the era of the ocean-going liners. At the same time, trade with Europe was picked up by the southeastern ports. Merseyside waned and its population dwindled.

Liverpool's shipping heritage is part of its attraction today, in the museums and galleries of the redeveloped Albert Dock, and in the impressive architecture reflecting the city's civic pride. Look out for the Royal Liver Building and the Cunard Building on the waterfront, and the architecture around St George's Hall, Dale Street, Water Street and William Brown Street.

EVENTS & FESTIVALS

February
Chinese New Year

April
5-7 Grand National Meeting, Aintree Racecourse

May
20 Liverpool Princes Women's 10k Run
25-26 The Liverpool Show, Wavertree Playground

June
15-18 Mersey River Festival
tbc Hope Street Festival

July
1 Liverpool-Chester-Liverpool Bike Ride
tbc Middlesbrough Mela, Albert Park
St Helens Show, Sherdley Park

August
16-18 Southport Flower Show
22-28 International Beatles Week & Convention

September
9 Liverpool Corporate Cup Run
tbc The Southport Airshow

November
5 City of Liverpool River Mersey Fireworks Display

Top: The Liver Building overlooking the Mersey

BIRKENHEAD

Birkenhead Priory

Priory St CH41 5JH
☎ 0151 666 1249

Founded in 1150, the Priory provided accommodation for the Prior and 16 Benedictine monks. Most of the buildings were neglected after the Dissolution, but not all are ruined. An interpretive centre traces the history and development of the site. St Mary's, the first parish church of Birkenhead, was opened in 1821 adjacent to the Priory: only the tower now stands.

Times: Open all year, Sat & Sun 1-5 (in summer), 12-4 (in winter) & Tue-Sun 1-5 (school holidays), 12-4 (Oct & Feb half term). Telephone to confirm.

P ♿ toilets for disabled shop (ex guide dogs)

HMS Plymouth & HMS Onyx

East Float, Dock Rd L41 1DJ (end of M53 all docks turn off follow tourist signs.)
☎ 0151 650 1573 🖷 0151 650 1473

Times: Open all year, Sep-Mar daily 10-4, Apr-Aug daily 10-5. (Closed 24-26 Dec).

P shop *Details not confirmed for 2001*

Williamson Art Gallery & Museum

Slatey Rd CH43 4UE
☎ 0151 652 4177 🖷 0151 670 0253
e-mail: wag@museum-service.freeserve.co.uk

English watercolours and works by the Liverpool school are an outstanding feature of the gallery. There is a large collection of pictures by P Wilson Steer, and also on view are sculpture, ceramics, glass, silver and furniture. The museum is linked to the gallery, and has displays on the history of the town and its port. Birkenhead was a hamlet before the 19th century, but grew large and rich through ship-building and the docks. Also on view are the Baxter Motor Collection, cars and motorbikes in a period garage setting.

Times: Open all year, Tue-Sun & BHs 1-5, (Closed Xmas & Good Fri).

P ♿ toilets for disabled shop

LIVERPOOL

The Beatles Story

Britannia Pavilion, Albert Dock L3 4AA
☎ 0151 709 1963 🖷 0151 708 0039

Relive the story of the four lads from Liverpool who took the world by storm and changed the face of popular music for ever.

Times: Open Apr-Oct daily 10-6, Nov-Mar daily 10-5 (last admission always 1hr before close).

Fee: £6.95 (concessions £4.95). Family ticket £17.

P ♿ toilets for disabled shop (ex guide dogs)

Croxteth Hall & Country Park

Muirhead Av East L12 0HB (5m NE of city centre, near junct 4 M57)
☎ 0151 228 5311 🖷 0151 228 2817

Times: Open, all facilities daily 11-5 in season (phone for details); Some facilities remain open through winter, hours on request.

P ♿ (permit parking next to the Hall) toilets for disabled shop (ex in park & grounds) *Details not confirmed for 2001*

HM Customs & Excise National Museum

Merseyside Maritime Museum, Albert Dock L3 4AQ
☎ 0151 478 4499 🖷 0151 478 4590

Times: Open all year, daily 10-5. Last admission 4. (Closed 23-26 Dec & 1 Jan)

P licensed ♿ (restricted wheelchair access, no access to basement) toilets for disabled shop (ex guide dogs) *Details not confirmed for 2001*

Liverpool Football Club Visitors Centre Tour

Anfield Rd L4 0TH
☎ 0151 260 6677 🖷 0151 264 0149

See all the first team kit set out for a match day, listen to a recorded 'team talk' from Gerard Houllier, and then touch the famous 'This is Anfield' sign to the sound of 45,000 cheering fans - a marvellous experience for any Liverpool fan!

Times: Open: Museum daily 10-5 last admission 4pm. (Closed 25-26 Dec). Match days 9am until last admission- 1hr before kick off. Museum & Tour - tours are run subject to daily demand. Advance booking is essential to avoid disappointment.

Fee: Museum only £5 (ch under 6 & pen £3) Family £13. Museum & Tour £8.50 (ch under 16 & pen £5.50) Family £23.

P ♿ (lifts to all areas for wheelchairs) toilets for disabled shop (ex guide dogs)

Liverpool Libraries & Information Services

William Brown St L3 8EW
☎ 0151 233 5829 🖷 0151 233 5886
e-mail: refham.central.library@liverpool.gov.uk

The Picton, Hornby and Brown buildings, situated in the Victorian grandeur of William Brown Street, house Liverpool's collection of over one million books, forming one of Britain's largest and oldest public libraries. The Liverpool Record Office is one of the country's largest and most significant County Record offices.

Times: Open all year, Mon-Thu 9-7.30 (Fri 9-5 & Sat 10-4) Closed BHs.

Fee: Free.

P (50 yds) (pay & display parking only) ♿ (lift, text magnification, reading machine) toilets for disabled (ex guide dogs)

Merseyside Maritime Museum

Albert Dock L3 4AA

☎ 0151 478 4499 📠 0151 478 4590

Times: Open all year, daily 10-5 (Closed 23-26 Dec & 1 Jan).

P ☕ ♿ (lifts, wheelchairs, ramps, ex pilot boat & basement) toilets for disabled shop (ex guide dogs) *Details not confirmed for 2001*

Metropolitan Cathedral of Christ the King

Mount Pleasant L3 5TQ (5 mins walk from either Liverpool Lime Street or Liverpool Central Railway Station)

☎ 0151 709 9222 📠 0151 708 7274

e-mail: met.cathedral@cwcom.net

A modern Roman Catholic cathedral which provides a focal point on the Liverpool skyline. The imposing structure of curving concrete ribs and stained glass was designed by Sir Frederick Gibberd and consecrated in 1967.

Times: Open daily 8-6 (Sun 5pm in winter).

Fee: Free.

P ♿ (lift, loop system, no access to Crypt) toilets for disabled shop (ex guide dogs)

Museum of Liverpool Life

Pier Head L3 4AA (follow signs for Albert Dock, museum is on Pier Head side)

☎ 0151 478 4080 📠 0151 478 4090

Times: Open all year, daily 10-5. (Closed 23-26 Dec & 1 Jan).

P (charged) ♿ (wheelchairs available) toilets for disabled shop (ex guide dogs) *Details not confirmed for 2001*

National Wildflower Centre

Court Hey Park L16 3NA (M62 junct 5, take B5080 to rdbt. Exit into Roby Rd, entrance 0.5 mile on left)

☎ 0151 737 1819 📠 0151 737 1820

e-mail: info@nwc.org.uk

Set in a public park on the outskirts of Liverpool, the National Wildflower Centre is inside a large building based around four courtyards. It promotes the creation of wildflower habitats around the country and provides educational materials, wildflower seeds and interactive facilities.

Times: Open Etr Sat-Oct, Wed-Sun 11-5; Nov-Good Fri, Thu-Sun 10.30-4. Telephone for confirmation as times may vary.

Fee: £3 (ch 5-16, pen, students & unemployed £1.50). Family ticket (2 adults & 2 ch) £7.50.

P ☕ ♿ toilets for disabled shop garden centre (ex guide dogs & in park)

Tate Liverpool

Albert Dock L3 4BB (within walking distance of Liverpool Lime Street train station)

☎ 0151 702 7400 & 0151 702 7402 📠 0151 702 7401

e-mail: liverpoolinfo@tate.org.uk

A converted Victorian warehouse with stunning views across the River Mersey, Tate Liverpool displays the

best of the National Collection of 20th-Century Art. A changing programme of exhibitions draws on works from public and private collections across the world.

Times: Open Tue-Sun 10-5.30. (Closed Mon ex BH Mon, 24-26 Dec, 1 Jan & Good Fri).

Fee: Free.

P ☕ ♿ (wheelchairs available, leaflets in braille, hearing loop) toilets for disabled shop

Walker Art Gallery

William Brown St L3 8EL (follow brown and white signs)

☎ 0151 478 4199 🖷 0151 478 4199

e-mail: public@nmgm.epp2.demon.co.uk

Times: Open all year, Mon-Sat 10-5, Sun 12-5. (Closed 23-26 Dec & 1 Jan).

P (charged) ☕ ♿ (prior notice appreciated, wheelchair on request) toilets for disabled shop (ex guide dogs) *Details not confirmed for 2001*

PRESCOT

Knowsley Safari Park

L34 4AN (M62 junct 6 onto M57 junct 2. Follow 'safari park' signs)

☎ 0151 430 9009 🖷 0151 426 3677

e-mail: safari.park@knowsley.com

A five-mile drive through the reserves enables visitors to see lions, tigers, elephants, rhinos, monkeys and many other animals in spacious, natural surroundings. Also a children's amusement park, reptile house, pets' corner plus sealion shows. Other attractions include an amusement park and a miniature railway.

Times: Open, Game reserves Mar-Oct. Other attractions Mar-Oct, daily 10-4. Winter Nov-Feb, wknds, 11-3.

Fee: £7 (ch & pen £5).

P ☕ ♿ toilets for disabled shop (kennels provided)

Prescot Museum

34 Church St L34 3LA (situated on corner of High St (A57) & Church St. Follow the brown tourism signs)

☎ 0151 430 7787 🖷 0151 430 7219

Permanent exhibitions reflecting the clock and watch-making industry of the area; with a special changing exhibition area. There is a programme of events and holiday activities.

Times: Open all year, Tue-Sat 10-5, Sun 2-5 (also BH Mon 10-1 & 2-5). (Closed 24-26 Dec, 1 Jan & Good Fri).

Fee: Free.

P (100 yrds) ♿ (ramp to ground floor) shop (ex guide dogs)

SOUTHPORT

Atkinson Art Gallery

Lord St PR8 1DH (located in centre of Lord Street, next to the Town Hall)

☎ 01704 533133 ext 2110 🖷 0151 934 2110

The gallery specialises in 19th-and 20th-century oil paintings, watercolours, drawings and prints, as well as 20th-century sculpture.

Times: Open all year, Mon-Wed & Fri 10-5, Thu & Sat 10-1. (Closed 25-26 Dec & 1 Jan).

Fee: Free.

P (pay & display) ♿ shop

The British Lawnmower Museum

106-114 Shakespeare St PR8 5AJ (From M6, follow signs to Town Centre, then brown signs to museum)

☎ 01704 501336 🖷 01704 500564

e-mail: info@lawnmowerworld.co.uk

The museum houses a private collection of over 200 rare exhibits of garden machinery of special interest. In addition to grass cutting and garden machinery dating from 1830, there is also the largest collection of vintage toy lawnmowers and games in the world. A tribute to the garden machine industry over the last 200 years.

Times: Open daily, 9-5.30, except Sunday & BH Mondays.

Fee: £1 (ch 50p). Guided tour £4.

P (50yds) shop

Southport Zoo & Conservation Trust

Princes Park PR8 1RX (from outskirts of Southport follow brown tourist signs, situated next to Pleasurland Town Centre)

☎ 01704 538102 & 548894 🖷 01704 538102

e-mail: info@southportzoo.F9.co.uk

Among the animals here are lions, snow leopards, lynx, chimpanzees, parrots, penguins and llamas. An extension houses a pets' corner barn, a giant tortoise house, primate house, porcupines and a baby chimpanzee house. There is also a reptile house with an aquarium. During the summer there are snake handling sessions with talks. There is an education centre for schools who have booked in advance. Mums free of charge (if accompanying children 2-13) on Mother's Day, ditto for Father's Day.

Times: Open all year (ex 25 Dec) 10-6 in summer, 10-4 in winter,

Fee: £3.80 (ch £2.80, pen £3.20). Party 20+

P (100 yds) (metered) ☕ ♿ (wide pathways, wide doorways) toilets for disabled shop

SPEKE

Speke Hall

The Walk L24 1XD (follow signs for Liverpool Airport)

☎ 0151 427 7231 🖷 0151 427 9860

A remarkable timber-framed manor house set in tranquil gardens and grounds. The house has a Tudor Great Hall, Stuart plasterwork, and William Morris wallpapers. Outside are varied grounds, including a rose garden, bluebell woods, and woodland walks. Special events include Open Air Shakespeare.

Times: House open: Apr-Oct, daily (ex Mon but open BH Mon) 1-5.30; Nov-mid Dec, Sat & Sun 1-4.30. Garden open daily (ex Mon & closed 24-26 Dec, 31 Dec, 1 Jan & Good Fri).

P ☕ ♿ (Wheelchairs & Electric car) toilets for disabled shop *Details not confirmed for 2001*

Norfolk

A fertile agricultural county in the east of the country, sparsely populated with plenty of fresh air and wide open spaces.

Norfolk is the northern bit of East Anglia, en route to nowhere, and too far from London to be colonised. Its coastline encompasses fenland round the Wash, the wonderfully unspoilt seaside towns of the north coast, and two of the country's most important nature reserves at Blakeney Point and the Cley marshes. Common features of the countryside are windmills, and attractive houses built of Norfolk flint with Dutch gables, a relic of the area's historical trade links with the Low Countries.

The Norfolk Broads are the county's main tourist attraction. The 'broads' are waterways set in marshy fenland, which came about from extensive peat cutting and subsequent flooding in the 13th and 14th centuries. Reed cutting for local thatching helped to keep the waterways clear. The Broads now has National Park status, to help protect the important wetland site from the demands of tourism and agriculture. The best way to see the Broads is to hire a boat, and there is plenty of opportunity for this at boatyards in Wroxham and Hoveton.

The county town is the city of Norwich, the largest in East Anglia, with a fine cathedral, a huge market place and an attractive medieval centre. Norwich came to prominence in the 17th century as a centre for the textile industry. Today it is most famously associated with Coleman's, the mustard company.

EVENTS & FESTIVALS

April
Primrose Weeks, Fairhaven Gardens, Norwich

May
tbc King's Lynn May Garland Procession, town centre, King's Lynn
tbc Norwich Bike Ride (50/100-mile ride around Norfolk)

June
27-28 Royal Norfolk Show, Royal Norfolk Showground
tbc Long Stratton Carnival
tbc Wymondham Carnival

July
7-8 Morris & Folk Festival, Sheringham
tbc Harleston Carnival
tbc Worstead Festival

August
5-12 Mundesley Festival
11-17 Cromer Carnival Week (Carnival on Wednesday 15)
27 Aylsham Show

September/October
Norfolk & Norwich Festival (music and the arts)

Top: Hickling Broad in the Norfolk Broads

BACONSTHORPE

Baconsthorpe Castle

NR25 6LN (0.75m N off unclass road)

The 'castle' was really a moated and semi-fortified house, built by the Heydon family in the 15th century. Gatehouses, curtain walls and towers still remain.

Times: Open all year, daily 10-4.

Fee: Free.

BANHAM

Banham Zoo

The Grove NR16 2HE (on B1113)

01953 887771 & 887773   01953 887445

Times: Open all year, daily from 10am. (Closed 25-26 Dec).

licensed (3 wheelchairs for hire) toilets for disabled shop *Details not confirmed for 2001*

BLICKLING

Blickling Hall

NR11 6NF (on B1354, 1.5m NW of Aylsham, signposted off A140 Norwich to Cromer road)

01263 738030   01263 731660

e-mail: abgusr@smtp.ntrust.org.uk

Flanked by dark yew hedges and topped by pinnacles, the warm red brick front of Blickling is a memorable sight. The grounds include woodland and a lake, a formal parterre, and a dry moat filled with roses, camellias and other plants.

Times: Open: 8 Apr-29 Oct, Wed-Sun 1-4.30. Garden open same days as Hall 10.30-5.30 (Tue-Sun in Aug).

Fee: £6.50 (ch £3.25).

licensed (wheelchairs & batricars, Braille guide, lift, parking) toilets for disabled shop garden centre (ex guide dogs)

BRESSINGHAM

Bressingham Steam Museum & Gardens

IP22 2AB (on A1066 2.5 miles W of Diss)

01379 687382 & 687386   01379 688085

Times: Open - Steam Museum & Dell Garden - Apr-Oct, daily 10.30-5.30. Telephone to confirm details.

licensed (wheelchair can be taken onto Nursery Line Railway) toilets for disabled shop garden centre *Details not confirmed for 2001*

BURGH CASTLE

Berney Arms Windmill

NR30 1SB

01493 700605

Access is by boat from Great Yarmouth or by rail to Berney Arms station: the road is unsuitable for cars. The seven-storey landmark was built in the 19th century to grind clinker for cement and then to help drain the marshes.

Times: Open Apr-Oct, daily 9-1 & 2-5.

Fee: £1.60 (ch 80p, concessions £1.20).

The Castle

NR31 9PZ (off A143)

Burgh Castle was built in the third century AD by the Romans, as one of a chain of forts along the Saxon Shore - the coast where Saxon invaders landed. Sections of the massive walls still stand.

Times: Open any reasonable time.

Fee: Free.

CAISTER-ON-SEA

Roman Town

The name Caister has Roman origins, and this was in fact a Roman naval base. The remains include the south gateway, a town wall built of flint with brick courses and part of what may have been a seamen's hostel.

Times: Open any reasonable time.

Fee: Free.

CASTLE ACRE

Castle Acre Priory & Castle

Stocks Green PE32 2XD

01760 755394

The priory was built for the Cluniac order in the Norman period. After the Dissolution under Henry VIII, the priory fell into ruin, but its extensive remains are dominated by the glorious, arcaded west front of the priory church, a reminder of past splendour. The chapel and 15th-century gatehouse also remain, and there are impressive ruins of a great castle which also stood nearby.

Times: Open all year, Apr-Sep, daily 10-6 (Oct 10-5); Nov-Mar, Wed-Sun 10-4. Closed 24-26 Dec & 1 Jan.

Fee: £3.20 (ch 5-15 £1.60, under 5's free). Personal stereo tour included in admission.

shop (in certain areas)

CASTLE RISING

Castle Rising Castle

PE31 6AH (off A149)

01553 631330

The fine Norman keep was built around 1140 by Henry Albini to celebrate his marriage to the widow of Henry I. The walls still stand to their full height, towering above the 12 acres of impressive man-made earthworks.

Times: Open all year, Apr-Sep, daily 10-6; Oct, daily 10-5; Nov-Mar, Wed-Sun 10-4. (Closed 24-26 Dec & 1 Jan).

Fee: £2.95 (concessions available).

(exterior only) toilets for disabled shop

CROMER

Cromer Museum

East Cottages, Tucker St NR27 9HB

01263 513543   01263 511651

Times: Open all year, Mon-Sat 10-5, Sun 2-5. Closed Mon 1-2. (Closed Good Fri, Xmas period & 1 Jan).

(200yds) shop *Details not confirmed for 2001*

Henry Blogg Museum
No 2 Boathouse, The Promenade NR27 9HE (located at the bottom of East Gangway)
☎ 01263 511294 📠 01263 513018
e-mail: rfmuirhead@csma-netlink.co.uk

A lifeboat has been stationed at the Cromer since 1804, and the museum in No 2 Boathouse at the bottom of The Gangway covers local lifeboat history and the RNLI in general. The main exhibit is the WWII Watson Class lifeboat "H F Bailey", the boat Henry Blogg coxed. In ten years he helped to save over 500 lives.
Times: Open Etr-Oct daily 10-4. Or by appointment with the Curator.
Fee: Donations welcome.
P (pay & display in town) ♿ shop

FAKENHAM
See also Thursford Green

Pensthorpe Waterfowl Park & Nature Reserve
Pensthorpe NR21 0LN (signed off A1067 Norwich to Fakenham road)
☎ 01328 851465 📠 01328 855905

Covering 200 acres of beautiful Norfolk countryside, with five lakes which are home to the largest collection of waterfowl and waders in Europe. Spacious walk-through enclosures and a network of hard-surfaced pathways ensures close contact with birds at the water's edge.
Times: Open all year, daily 10-5 mid Mar-end of year.
Fee: £4.80 (ch £2.25, pen £4.20)
P ✕ licensed ♿ (network of hard surfaced pathways ensures access to shore) toilets for disabled shop (ex guide dogs)

FELBRIGG
Felbrigg Hall
NR11 8PR (off B1436)
☎ 01263 837444
📠 afgusr@smtp.ntrust.org.uk

Felbrigg is a 17th-century house built on the site of an existing medieval hall. It contains a superb collection of 18th-century furniture and pictures and an outstanding library. A 550-acre wood shelters the house from the North Sea.
Times: Open: House 1 Apr-31 Oct, Sat-Wed 1-5. BH Sun & Mon 11-5. Garden opens 11-5.30. Park walks daily dawn-dusk (closed Xmas day)
Fee: House & garden £5.70 (ch £2.80). Family ticket £14.20. Garden only £2.20. Party.
P ✕ licensed ♿ (battery operated vehicle for garden, braille guide) toilets for disabled shop (ex park)

FILBY
Thrigby Hall Wildlife Gardens
NR29 3DR (on unclass road off A1064)
☎ 01493 369477 📠 01493 368256
e-mail: thrigby@globalnet.co.uk

The 250-year-old park of Thrigby Hall is now the home of animals and birds from Asia, and the lake has ornamental wildfowl. There are tropical bird houses, a unique blue willow pattern garden and tree walk and a summer house as old as the park. The enormous jungled Swamp Hall has special features such as underwater viewing of large crocodiles.
Times: Open all year, daily from 10.
Fee: £5.50 (ch 4-14 £3.90, pen £4.90).
P ♿ (wheelchairs available) toilets for disabled shop (ex guide dogs)

FLEGGBURGH
The Village
Burgh St. Margaret NR29 3AF (7m from Great Yarmouth, on A1064 between Acle and Caister-on-Sea)
☎ 01493 369770 📠 01493 369318

The Village Experience is set in over 35 acres of Norfolk countryside. Working steam traditional fairground rides, a steam-hauled trailer ride and two live shows including the Compton-Christie organ. Other attractions include vehicles, motorcycles, a 2ft narrow gauge railway, animals, fairground, adventure play area, indoor soft play area, Victorian gallopers and traditional crafts.
Times: Open 16 Apr-29 Oct, daily 10-5. Other times not confirmed. Saturday is grounds only day (admission reduced accordingly)
Fee: £5.95 (ch £3.95 pen £5.45). Grounds only Sat £2.75.
P ✕ licensed ♿ toilets for disabled shop (ex guide dogs)

GREAT BIRCHAM
Bircham Windmill
PE31 6SJ (0.5m W off unclassified Snettisham road).
☎ 01485 578393

This windmill is one of the last remaining in Norfolk. Sails turn on windy days, and the adjacent tea room serves home-made cakes, light lunches and cream teas. There is also a bakery museum and cycle hire.
Times: Open daily during school hols and bank holiday wknds. 28 Mar-Sep, Wed-Sun.
Fee: £2.50 (ch £1, pen £2.25, student £1.50)
P ♿ toilets for disabled shop

GREAT YARMOUTH
Elizabethan House Museum
4 South Quay NR30 2QH
☎ 01493 855746
Times: Open 6-19 Apr, Mon-Fri 10-5, Sun 2-5 (closed Good Fri); 24 May-25 Sep, Sun-Fri 10-5.
P (100yds) ♿ shop *Details not confirmed for 2001*

Maritime Museum For East Anglia
Marine Pde NR30 2EN
☎ 01493 842267
Times: Open Etr fortnight, Mon-Fri 10-5, Sun 2-5 (closed Good Fri); Sun before Whitsun-end Sep, Sun-Fri 10-5. Under review.
P shop *Details not confirmed for 2001*

Merrivale Model Village

Wellington Pier Gardens, Marine Pde NR30 3JG
☎ 01493 842097

Set in attractive landscaped gardens, this comprehensive miniature village is built on a scale of 1:12. The layout includes a two and a half inch gauge model railway, radio-controlled boats, and over 200 models set in an acre of landscaped gardens. There are additional amusements and remote-controlled cars and boats.

Times: Open Etr 9.30-6, Jun-Oct 9.30-10.
Fee: £3 (ch 3-14 £1.50, pen £2.50).
P (opposite) shop (ex on leads)

Old Merchant's House

Row 111, Greyfriar's Cloister NR30 2RQ (follow signs to dock and south quay)
☎ 01493 857900

Two 17th-century Row Houses, a type of building unique to Great Yarmouth, contain original fixtures and display items salvaged from the bombing raids of the Second World War. Nearby are the remains of a Franciscan friary, with a rare vaulted cloister, accidentally discovered during bomb-damage repairs.

Times: Open Apr-Sep 10-6. Oct 10-5.
Fee: £1.85 (ch 5-15 90p, under 5's free)

Tolhouse Museum

Tolhouse St NR30 2SH
☎ 01493 858900 01493 745459

Times: Open 6-19 Apr, Mon-Fri 10-5, Sun 2-5 (closed Good Fri); 24 May-25 Sep, Sun-Fri 10-5. Under review.
P (100yds) (lift to ground & 2nd floor) shop *Details not confirmed for 2001*

GRESSENHALL

Norfolk Rural Life Museum & Union Farm

Beech House NR20 4DR (A47, B1110 through East Dereham towards Holt, onto B1146 to Fakenham, museum is 1.5m on right)
☎ 01362 860563 01362 860385

Times: Open 5 Apr-1 Nov, Mon-Sat 10-5, Sun 12-5.30. Also BH Mons 10-5.
P (sound guide & wheelchair loan) toilets for disabled shop *Details not confirmed for 2001*

GRIMES GRAVES

Grimes Graves

Lynford IP26 5DE (7m NW of Thetford off A134)
☎ 01842 810656

Grimes Graves is the largest known group of Neolithic flint mines in Britain. It consists of a network of hundreds of pits, the oldest dating from about 3000BC. Vertical shafts lead through the flint seams to galleries. Visitors can descend 10 metres (30 feet) into an excavated shaft and there are regular demonstrations of the craft of flint-knapping.

Times: Open all year, Apr-Sep, daily 10-6 (Oct 10-5); Nov-Mar, Wed-Sun 10-4. Closed 1-2pm. Last visit to pit 20 minutes before closing).
Fee: £2 (ch 5-15 £1 under 5's free). A torch is useful.
P (exhibition area, grounds only; access track rough) shop (in certain areas)

HEACHAM

Norfolk Lavender

Caley Mill PE31 7JE (on A149 at junct with B1454)
☎ 01485 570384 01485 571176
e-mail: admin@norfolk-lavender.co.uk

This is the largest lavender-growing and distilling operation in Britain. Different coloured lavenders are grown in strips and harvested in July and August. There are also rose and herb gardens and a fragrant Plant Centre, and guided tours of the distillery and gardens.

Times: Open all year, daily 10-5. (Closed 25-26 Dec & 1 Jan).
Fee: Admission to grounds Free. Guided tours £1.50 (May-Sep). Trip to Lavender Field £3.95, mid Jun-mid Aug.
P (wheelchairs for loan) toilets for disabled shop garden centre

HOLKHAM

Holkham Hall & Bygones Museum

NR23 1AB (off A149, 2m W of Wells-next-the-Sea)
☎ 01328 710227 01328 711707

This classic Palladian mansion was built between 1734 and 1764 by Thomas Coke, 1st Earl of Leicester, and is home to his descendants. It has a magnificent alabaster entrance hall and the sumptuous state rooms house Greek and Roman statues, fine furniture and paintings by Rubens, Van Dyck, Gainsborough and others. The Bygones Museum, housed in the stable block, has over 5,000 items on display - from gramophones to fire engines.

Times: Open 28 May-30 Sep Sun-Thu, 1-5. May, Spring & Summer BHs Sun & Mon 11.30-5.
Fee: Hall £4 (ch £2). Bygones £4 (ch £2). Combined ticket Hall & Bygones: £6 (ch £3)
P licensed (wheelchair ramps at all entrances) toilets for disabled shop garden centre ex guide dogs & on lead inpark

HORSEY

Horsey Windpump

NR29 4EF (2.5m NE of Potter Heigham)
☎ 01493 393904

The windpump mill was built 200 years ago to drain the area, and then rebuilt in 1912 by Dan England, a noted Norfolk millwright. It has been restored since being struck by lightning in 1943, and overlooks Horsey Mere and marshes, noted for their wild birds and insects.

Times: Open Apr-Oct, daily 11-5. (Closed Good Fri).
Fee: £1.30
P (charged) shop

HORSHAM ST FAITH

City of Norwich Aviation Museum

Old Norwich Rd NR10 3JF (follow brown tourist signs from A140 Norwich to Cromer Road)

☎ 01603 893080

e-mail: derek.waters@virgin.net

Administered by enthusiastic volunteers, the museum offers many displays relating to the aeronautical history of Norfolk. Several types of aircraft are on display, including a Vulcan bomber. A feature is the RAF 100 Group Memorial Museum Collection. A major addition to the history of RAF Bomber Command.

Times: Open all year, Apr-Oct daily 10-5, Tues-Sat. Sun 12-5. Nov-Mar, Wed & Sat 10-4. Sun 12-4.

Fee: £2.50 (ch & concessions £1.50, pen £2) Family ticket (2 adults & 2 ch) £7.

P ♿ (assistance available) shop (ex guide dogs)

HOUGHTON

Houghton Hall

PE31 6UE (1.25m off A148)

☎ 01485 528569 01485 528167

Times: Open Etr Sun-last Sun Sep, Thu, Sun & BH's 12-5.30. House open Etr Sun-last Sun Sep, Thu, Thu & BH's2-5.30. Last admission 5pm.

P ♿ toilets for disabled shop *Details not confirmed for 2001*

KING'S LYNN

African Violet Centre

Terrington St Clement PE34 4PL (4m W of Kings Lynn, on A17)

☎ 01553 828374 01553 828376

A mecca for African violet and garden plant lovers. A winner of many Chelsea Gold Medals, visitors can explore in all weathers.

Times: Open daily Mon-Sat 9-5, Sun 10-5. (Closed Xmas & New Year).

Fee: Free.

P ♿ (ramps to reach tea room & outside sales areas) toilets for disabled shop garden centre (ex guide dogs)

King's Lynn Arts Centre

27-29 Kings St (located just off Tuesday Market Place in Kings Street, next to Globe Hotel)

☎ 01553 765565 01553 764864 01553 770591

e-mail: marketing.section@dialpipex.com

Although it has been used for many purposes, the theatrical associations of this 15th-century Guildhall are strongest: Shakespeare himself is said to have performed here. The annual King's Lynn Festival takes place towards the end of July.

Times: Open Mon-Fri 10-2. Closed show days, Sun & B Hols.

Fee: Free.

P ✕ ♿ (hearing loop, ramp) toilets for disabled

Lynn Museum

Market St PE30 1NL

☎ 01553 775001 01553 775001

Times: Open all year, Tue-Sat, 10-5.

P (500yds) ♿ shop *Details not confirmed for 2001*

LITTLE WALSINGHAM

Walsingham Abbey Grounds & Shirehall Museum

NR22 6BP (take B1105 from Fakenham)

☎ 01328 820259 01328 820098

e-mail: walsingham.museum@farmling.com

In the grounds of the Abbey are the ruins of the original Augustinian priory built in the 1100s. The priory was built over the shrine of Our Lady of Walsingham which had been established in 1061. Shirehall Museum consists of an original Georgian Courthouse, displays on the history of Walsingham and local artifacts.

Times: Open Apr-late Oct, daily 10-4.30; Oct-Dec, wkends only 10-4; late Jan-late Feb, daily 10-4. Other times through Estate office Mon-Fri 9-5.

Fee: not confirmed

P (100 yds) ♿ toilets for disabled shop garden centre

NORTH CREAKE

Creake Abbey

NR21 9LF (1m N off B1355)

Church ruin with crossing and eastern arm belonging to a house of Augustinian canons founded in 1206.

Times: Open any reasonable time.

Fee: Free.

#

NORWICH

Bridewell Museum

Bridewell Alley NR2 1AQ

☎ 01603 667228 📠 01603 765651

Times: Open Apr-Sep, Tue-Sat, 10-5.

P shop *Details not confirmed for 2001*

Guildhall

Guildhall Hill NR2 1NF

☎ 01603 666071 📠 01603 765389

Times: Open all year 6 days a week.

P (200yds) toilets for disabled *Details not confirmed for 2001*

Norwich Castle Museum

Castle Meadow NR1 3JU

☎ 01603 223624 📠 01603 765651

Times: Open all year, Mon-Sat 10-5, Sun 2-5. (Closed Good Fri, Xmas period & New Year).

P (200mtrs) (lift to first floor, special parking by prior arrangement) toilets for disabled shop *Details not confirmed for 2001*

Norwich Cathedral

The Close NR1 4DH (A47, A11 to city centre, inner ring rd to Barrack St rdbt, take rd towards city centre to Tombland)

☎ 01603 764385 & 767617 (weekends)

📠 01603 766032

e-mail: vis&profficer@cathedral.org.uk

Originally a Benedictine foundation, the cathedral possesses the largest monastic cloisters in England and is of great architectural and artistic interest. Of particular note are the Saxon bishop's throne, nave bosses depicting Biblical scenes, and the 14th-century Despenser reredos.

Times: Open daily, 7.30-7 (6pm mid Sep-mid May).

Fee: Free.

P (440yds) (parking at Cathedral for services only) licensed (parking on site, touch & hearing centre) toilets for disabled shop (ex guide dogs)

Royal Norfolk Regimental Museum

Shirehall, Market Av NR1 3JQ (adjacent to Norwich Castle Museum)

☎ 01603 493649 📠 01603 765651

Museum displays deal with the social as well as military history of the county regiment from 1685, including the daily life of a soldier. Audio-visual displays and graphics complement the collection and there's a programme of temporary exhibitions.

Times: Open all year, Mon-Sat 10-5, Sun 2-5. (Closed Good Fri, Xmas period & 1 Jan).

Fee: £1.80 (ch 90p, concessions £1.30). Joint ticket with Castle Museum available.

P (400yds) (stair lift available, ring for details) shop (ex guide dogs)

Sainsbury Centre for Visual Arts

University of East Anglia NR4 7TJ

☎ 01603 456060 & 593199 📠 01603 259401

e-mail: scva@uea.ac.uk

The collection of Sir Robert and Lady Sainsbury was given to the University in 1973. European art of the 19th and 20th centuries is on display together with ethnographical art. You can see African tribal sculpture and Oceanic works along with North American and Pre-Colombian art.

Times: Open Tue-Sun 11-5. (Closed Mon & University closure at Xmas).

Fee: Collection & exhibition £2 (concessions £1).

P licensed (parking at main entrance, wheelchair available on loan) toilets for disabled shop (guide dogs by arrangement)

St Peter Hungate Church Museum

Princes St (near Elm Hill) NR3 1AE

☎ 01603 667231 📠 01603 765651

Times: Open Apr-Oct Mon-Sat 10-5.

P shop *Details not confirmed for 2001*

OXBOROUGH

Oxburgh Hall

PE33 9PS

☎ 01366 328258 📠 01366 328066

e-mail: aohusr@smtp.ntrust.org.uk

The outstanding feature of this 15th-century moated building is the 80ft high Tudor gatehouse which has remained unaltered throughout the centuries. Henry VII lodged in the King's Room in 1487. A parterre garden of French design stands outside the moat, and rare needlework by Mary Queen of Scots and Bess of Hardwick is on display.

Times: Open House: 1-26 Apr & 1-29 Oct daily Sat-Sun & Tue-Wed (also open BH Mon); 29 Apr-31 Jul & 1-30 Sep daily, Sat-Wed. Aug open daily 1-5 (11-5 BH Mon).Garden: 4-26 Mar wknds, 11-4; 1 Apr-31 Jul & 1 Sep-29 Oct daily Sat-Wed; Aug open daily, 11-5.30.

Fee: House & Garden £5.30 (ch £2.60). Garden & Estate £2.60 (ch £1.30). Family & party 15+ discounted tickets are available.

P licensed (braille guide & wheelchairs available) toilets for disabled shop

REEDHAM

Pettitts Animal Adventure Park

NR13 3UA (off A47 at Acle)

☎ 01493 700094 & 701403 📠 01493 700933

Three parks in one, aimed at the younger child. Rides include railways, roller coasters and water rides; the adventure play area has a golf course, ball pond and tearooms; and entertainment is provided by clowns, puppets and live musicians. Among the animals that can be seen are small horses, wallabies, birds of prey, goats, chickens and ducks.

Times: Open Etr Sun-Oct, daily 10-5.30. (Closed Sat).

Fee: £6.50 (ch £6.25 & pen £6). Disabled & helpers £4. Party.

P (ramps to all areas) toilets for disabled shop

ST OLAVES

St Olaves Priory

(5.5m SW of Great Yarmouth on A143)

The fine brick undercroft in the cloister is one of the most notable features of the ruin of this small 13th-century Augustinian priory.

Times: Open any reasonable time.

Fee: Free.

SANDRINGHAM

Sandringham House, Grounds, Museum & Country Park

PE35 6EN (off A148)

01553 772675 01485 541571

The private country retreat of Her Majesty The Queen, this neo-Jacobean house was built in 1870 for King Edward VII. The main rooms used by the Royal Family when in residence are all open to the public. Sixty acres of glorious grounds surround the House and offer beauty and colour throughout the season. Sandringham Museum contains fascinating displays of Royal memorabilia.

Times: Open Apr-8 Oct, daily (House closed good Fri, 18 Jul-3 Aug inc; Museum & Grounds closed 18 Jul-3 Aug inc). House 11-4.45. Museum 11-5. Grounds 10.30-5.

Fee: House, Museum & Grounds: £5.50 (ch £3.50, pen £4.50). Family ticket £14.50. Grounds & Museum £4.50 (ch £3, pen £4). Family ticket £12.

licensed (wheelchair loan, free transport in grounds, braille guide) toilets for disabled shop (ex guide dogs)

SAXTHORPE

Mannington Gardens & Countryside

Mannington Hall NR11 7BB (signposted from Corpusty/Saxthorpe on B1149 Norwich-Holt road. Follow brown signs)

01263 584175 01263 761214

The moated manor house, built in 1460 and still a family home, forms a centre-piece for the pretty gardens which surround it. Enjoy the roses, the chief feature of the gardens, and lovely countryside walks.

Times: Open: Gardens Jun-Aug, Wed-Fri 11-5; also Sun noon-30 Apr-1 Oct. Walks open every day from 9am. Hall open by prior appointment only.

Fee: Garden £3 (accompanied ch 16 free, students & pen £2.50). Walks free (car park for walkers £1).

(boardwalk across meadow, wheelchair ramps) toilets for disabled shop garden centre (ex guide dogs)

SHERINGHAM

North Norfolk Railway

Sheringham Station, Station Approach NR26 8RA

01263 822045 01263 823794

A steam railway with trains operating on most days (Apr-Sep), with extra days as the season progresses and a daily service in the summer. On Sundays, lunch is served on the train. At Weybourne Station there is a collection of steam locomotives and rolling stock, some of which are undergoing or awaiting restoration. There is also a museum of railway memorabilia.

Times: Open Apr-Sep; daily during summer season; Dec (Santa specials). Telephone for details of other running days.

Fee: Return £6.50 (ch £3.50, pen £5.50). Family ticket £17.50.

(adjacent) (ramps to trains) shop

SNETTISHAM

Park Farm

PE31 7NQ (signposted on A149)

01485 542425 01485 543503

You can see farming in action here with lambing in the spring, sheep shearing in May and deer calving in June and July. Sheep, goats, lambs, rabbits, turkeys, ducks, chickens, ponies, piglets etc can be seen in the paddocks, and the sheep centre has over 40 different breeds. Other attractions include a large adventure playground, horse and pony rides, 2.5 miles of farm trails, visitor centre and craft workshops, including pottery studio and leather worker.

Times: Open all year, Spring, Summer & Autumn, daily 10-5; Winter, Fri-Mon, 10-dusk. Closed Xmas day.

Fee: £3.95 (ch £2.95, pen £3.50). Family ticket £13.50.

(gravel paths, ramps where needed) toilets for disabled shop (ex on farm trails)

SOUTH WALSHAM

FAIRHAVEN GARDEN TRUST

School Rd NR13 6DZ (9m NE of Norwich on B1140)

01603 270449 01603 270449

e-mail: fairhavengardens@norfolkbroads.com

These delightful woodland and water gardens offer a combination of cultivated and wild flowers. In spring there are masses of primroses and bluebells, with azaleas and rhododendrons in several areas. Candelabra primulas and some unusual plants grow near the waterways, and in summer the wild flowers provide a habitat for butterflies, bees and dragonflies.

Times: Open daily 10-5, extended opening until 9pm Wed & Thu, May-Aug. (Closed 25 Dec).

Fee: £3 (ch £1, under 5 free, pen £2.70). Season tickets £10. Family season ticket £25.

(ramp, grab rail) toilets for disabled shop garden centre (on leads)

THETFORD

ANCIENT HOUSE MUSEUM

White Hart St IP24 1AA (in town centre)

01842 752599

Times: Open all year, Mon-Sat, 10-5 (Closed Mon 12.30-1); Jun-Aug also Sun 2-5. (Closed Good Fri, Xmas period & New Year's Day).

(20yds) shop *Details not confirmed for 2001*

THETFORD PRIORY

(on W side of Thetford near station)

Extensive remains of the Cluniac monastery founded in 1103 include the 14th-century gatehouse and complete ground plan of the cloisters.

Times: Open any reasonable time.

Fee: Free.

WARREN LODGE

(2m NW, on B1107)

The remains of a two-storey hunting lodge, built in 15th-century of flint with stone dressings.

Times: Open any reasonable time.

Fee: Free.

THURSFORD GREEN

THURSFORD COLLECTION

NR21 0AS (1m off A148)

01328 878477 01328 878415

This exciting collection specialises in organs, with a Wurlitzer cinema organ, fairground organs, barrel organs and street organs among its treasures. There are live musical shows every day. The collection also includes showmen's engines, ploughing engines and farm machinery. There is a children's play area and a breathtaking 'Venetian gondola' switchback ride.

Times: Open Apr-Oct, daily noon-5.

Fee: £4.70 (ch 4-14 £2.20, pen £4.40, ch under 4 free, students £3.95). Party 15+.

toilets for disabled shop (x3) (ex guide dogs) 

TITCHWELL

RSPB NATURE RESERVE

PE31 8BB (6m E of Hunstanton on A149, signposted entrance)

01485 210779 01485 210779

A firm path takes you to three hides and on to the beach where a platform overlooking the sea is suitable for wheelchairs. A colony of avocets nest on the enclosed marsh with gadwalls, tufted ducks, shovelers and black-headed gulls. During the season many migrants visit the marsh including wigeon, black-tailed godwits, curlews and sandpipers.

Times: Open at all times. Visitor Centre daily 10-5 (4pm Nov-Mar)

Fee: Free.

(charged) (ramps to hides, wheelchair bays in hides) toilets for disabled shop (ex guide & dogs on footpaths)

WEETING

WEETING CASTLE

IP27 0RQ (2m N of Brandon off B1106)

This ruined 11th-century fortified manor house stands in a moated enclosure. There are interesting but slight remains of a three-storey cross-wing.

Times: Open any reasonable time.

Fee: Free.

WELLS-NEXT-THE-SEA

WELLS & WALSINGHAM LIGHT RAILWAY

NR23 1QB (A149 Cromer road)

01328 710631

The railway covers the four miles between Wells and Walsingham, and is the longest ten and a quarter inch gauge track in the world. The line passes through some very attractive countryside, particularly noted for its wild flowers and butterflies. This is the home of the unique Garratt Steam Locomotive specially built for this line.

Times: Open daily Etr-31 Oct.

Fee: £5.50 return (ch £4 return).

shop

WELNEY

WWT Welney

Hundred Foot Bank PE14 9TN (off A1101, N of Ely)
☎ 01353 860711 📠 01353 860711
e-mail: welney@wwt.org.uk

This important wetland site on the Ouse Washes is famous for its spectacle of wild ducks, geese and swans which spend the winter here. Impressive observation facilities, including hides, towers and an observatory, offer outstanding views of the huge numbers of wildfowl. Floodlit evening swan feeds take place between November and February. There are two hides for wheelchair users.

Times: Open all year, daily 10-5. (Closed 25 Dec).
Fee: £3.50 (ch £2). Family ticket £9. Party 15+.
♿ (wheelchair access to major parts of reserve) toilets for disabled shop

WEST RUNTON

Norfolk Shire Horse Centre

West Runton Stables NR27 9QH (off A149)
☎ 01263 837339 📠 01263 837132
e-mail:
bakewell@norfolkshirehorse.fsnet.co.uk

The Shire Horse Centre has a collection of draught horses and some breeds of mountain and moorland ponies. There are also exhibits of horse-drawn machinery, waggons and carts, and harnessing and working demonstrations are given twice every day. Other attractions include a children's farm, a photographic display of draught horses past and present, talks and a video show. There is a riding school on the premises as well.

Times: Open 9 Apr-Oct, Sun-Fri; also Sats Jul-Aug & BHs.
Fee: £4.75 (ch £2.75, pen £3.75).
licensed ♿ toilets for disabled shop (ex on lead)

WEYBOURNE

The Muckleburgh Collection

Weybourne Military Camp NR25 7EG (on A149, coast road, 3m W of Sheringham)
☎ 01263 588210 & 588608 📠 01263 588425
e-mail: jenny@muckleburgh.demon.co.uk

The largest privately-owned military collection of its kind in the country, which incorporates the Museum of the Suffolk and Norfolk Yeomanry. Exhibits include restored and working tanks, armoured cars, trucks and artillery of WWII, and equipment and weapons from the Falklands and the Gulf War. Live tank demonstrations are run daily (except Saturdays) during school holidays.

Times: Open 13 Feb-29 Oct, daily 10-5.
Fee: £4 (ch £2.50 & pen £3.50). Family ticket £11.50.
licensed ♿ (ramped access, wheelchairs available) toilets for disabled shop (ex guide dogs)

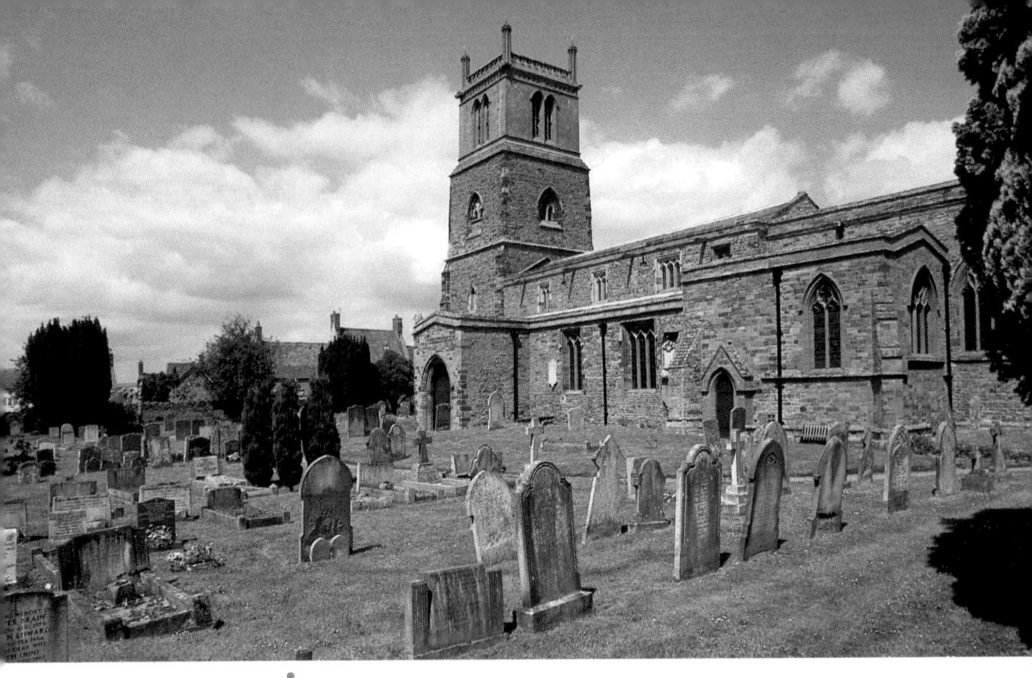

Northamptonshire

Northamptonshire is a mainly rural county of gentle beauty, with farmland, forest and great country estates. Rivers, canals and watermeadows are all part of the tranquil scene, providing a haven for wildlife.

EVENTS & FESTIVALS

May
14 Moulton village Festival
tbc British Waterways Annual Boat Show (date & venue to be confirmed)

July
7-8 Hollowell Steam & Heavy Horse Show, Hollowell nr Northampton
tbc Northampton Town Show, Abington Park, Northampton

August
17-19 Northampton Hot Air Balloon Festival, Northampton Racecourse, Northampton

Northamptonshire is ideal country for touring, walking and exploring lovely villages of stone and thatch, and visiting some particularly impressive churches. Among the most interesting of these are the Saxon churches at Brixworth and Earls Barton.

In the main square of the pretty village of Geddington stands one of the three surviving Eleanor Crosses. Edward I, grief-stricken with the death of his queen, erected a series of these crosses to mark the resting place of his wife's body, each night, on its journey south from Leicestershire to London. Another such cross can be seen on the southern outskirts of Northampton at Hardingstone. In recent times, Althorp, home of the Spencer family and last resting place of Diana Princess of Wales, has put the county firmly on the tourist map, in quite a similar way.

Northampton is the county town, and along with Kettering, has long been associated with the production of footwear. Kettering was the second largest town until it was overtaken by the rapid development of Corby as a major centre of the steel industry. With the decline of the steel industry, Corby, as an enterprise zone, has fought back to provide a home for a variety of modern industries.

Top: Church of St Mary Magdalen, Ecton

CANONS ASHBY

Canons Ashby House

NN11 3SD (easy access from either M40, junct 11 or M1, junct 16)

☎ 01327 860044 📠 01327 860168

e-mail: ecaxxx@smtp.ntrust.org.uk

Home of the Dryden family since the 16th century, this is an exceptional small manor house, with Elizabethan wall paintings and Jacobean plasterwork. It has restored gardens, a small park and a church - part of the original 13th-century Augustinian priory.

Times: Open Apr-Oct, Sat-Wed & BH Mon (closed Good Fri) 1-5.30 or dusk if earlier. Last admission 5pm.

Fee: £4 (ch £2). Family ticket £10.

(hearing scheme taped guide wheelchair available) toilets for disabled shop (ex on lead in home paddock)

DEENE

Deene Park

NN17 3EW (0.5m off A43, between Kettering & Stamford)

☎ 01780 450278 & 450223 📠 01780 450282

A mainly 16th-century house of great architectural importance, and home of the Brudenell family since 1514 (including the 7th Earl of Cardigan who led the Charge of the Light Brigade). There's a large lake and park, and extensive gardens with old-fashioned roses, rare trees and shrubs. Phone for details of antiques fairs and garden openings.

Times: Open 2-5 BH's (Sun & Mon) Etr, May, Spring & Aug; Jun-Aug, Sun. Party 20+ by prior arrangement with House Keeper.

Fee: House & Gardens: £5 (ch 10-14 £2.50). Gardens only: £3 (ch £1.50). Children under 10 free admission with accompanying adult.

(ramps to cafeteria and gardens) toilets for disabled (ex guide dogs in garden only)

Kirby Hall

NN17 5EN (on unclass road off A43, 4m NE of Corby)

☎ 01536 203230

A beautiful Elizabethan manor house boasting an unusual richness and variety of architectural detail in the Renaissance style. The extensive gardens were among the finest in England at their peak during the 17th century.

Times: Open all year, Apr-Sep, daily 10-6 (Oct 10-5); Nov-Mar, daily 10-4. Closed 24-26 Dec & 1 Jan.

Fee: £2.70 (ch 5-15 £1.40, under 5's free). Personal stereo tours included in admission.

shop (in certain areas)

DESBOROUGH

Shire Falconry Centre

West Lodge Rural Centre, West Lodge, Pipewell Rd NN14 2SH

☎ 01536 760666

Times: Open all year, daily 10-5 (Nov-Feb weekends only)

toilets for disabled shop *Details not confirmed for 2001*

HOLDENBY

Holdenby House, Gardens & Falconry Centre

NN6 8DJ (7m NW of Northampton, off A5199 or A428)

☎ 01604 770074 📠 01604 770962

Just across the fields from Althorp, this former palace and prison of Charles I provides a stately backdrop to a beautiful garden and host of attractions. Falconry, 17th-century farmstead and children's amusements.

Times: Open; Gardens & Falconry Centre 2 Apr-end Sep, Sun1-5. Jul & Aug open daily 1-5 (ex Sat). House open 24 Apr, 29 May & 28 Aug. Contact for details of additional Falconry Centre opening days.

Fee: Gardens & Falconry Centre £3 (ch £1.75, pen £2.50). House, Gardens & Falconry Centre £5 (ch £3, pen £4.50).

(gravel paths with ramps) toilets for disabled shop (on leads)

KETTERING

Alfred East Gallery

Sheep St NN16 OAN (A43/A6, located in town centre)

☎ 01536 534274 📠 01536 534370

The Gallery has a new permanent exhibition space showing work by Sir Alfred East, Thomas Cooper Gotch and other local artists, as well as selections from the Gallery's contemporary collection, including Sir Howard Hodgkin and John Bevan. Two further display spaces are dedicated to monthly changing sales exhibitions of art, craft and photography.

Times: Open all year, Mon-Sat 9.30-5 (ex Wed closed until 10am & closed BHs)

Fee: Free.

(300yds) shop (ex guide dogs)

LYVEDEN NEW BIELD

Lyveden New Bield

PE8 5AT (4m SW Oundle via A427)

☎ 01832 205358

e-mail: elnxxx@smtp.ntrust.org.uk

The 'New Bield', or 'new building', is an unfinished shell of a garden lodge dating from around 1600. It was designed by Sir Thomas Thresham to symbolise the Passion. The shape is a Greek cross, on which a frieze shows the cross, crown of thorns and other 'emblems of the Passion'. Even the building's dimensions are symbolic.

Times: Open Wed-Sun, 9-5.

Fee: £2 (ch £1).

(0.5 m along track) (ex on leads)

NASSINGTON

Prebendal Manor House

PE8 6QG

☎ 01780 782575

e-mail: info@prebendal-manor.demon.co.uk

Dating from the early 13th century, this is the oldest manor in Northamptonshire. There's a 15th-century dovecote and tithe barn museum, and the largest re-created medieval garden in Europe, boasting fishponds, herbers, arbours, turf seats, trellised herbers, medieval vegetable garden and vineyard.

Times: Open May-Jun & Sep Sun & Wed 1-5.30; Jul & Aug Sun, Wed & Thu 1-5.30. BH Mon (Closed Xmas)

Fee: House & garden £4 (ch £1.20) Party 20+; Garden only £3.

(ramps) shop (guide dogs)

NORTHAMPTON

Central Museum & Art Gallery

Guildhall Rd NN1 1DP (situated in the town centre)

☎ 01604 238548 01604 238720

Reflecting Northampton's proud standing as Britain's boot and shoe capital, the museum houses a collection of boots and shoes which is considered one of the finest in the world. Other displays include the History of Northampton, Decorative Arts, the Art Gallery, and special temporary exhibitions.

Times: Open all year, Mon-Sat 10-5, Sun 2-5.

Fee: Free.

(200 yds) (wheelchairs available, large print catalogues) toilets for disabled shop (ex guide/assistance dogs)

ROCKINGHAM

Rockingham Castle

LE16 8TH (2m N of Corby, off A6003)

☎ 01536 770240 01536 771692

e-mail: michaeltebbutt@lineone.net

Set on a hill overlooking five counties, the castle was built by William the Conqueror. The site of the original keep is now a rose garden, but the outline of the curtain wall remains as do the foundations of the Norman hall, and the twin towers of the gatehouse. A royal residence for 450 years, the castle was granted to Edward Watson in the 16th century, and the Watson family have lived there ever since.

Times: Open Apr-Sep, Thu, Sun, BH Mon & following Tue (also Tues in Aug) 1-5. Grounds open at 11.30 am on Sun & BH Mon.

Fee: £4.40 (ch £2.90 & pen £3.90). Family ticket £12. Party. Grounds only £2.90.

(may alight at entrance, ramped) shop

RUSHTON

Triangular Lodge

NN14 1RP

☎ 01536 710761

Almost every detail of the lodge built by Sir Thomas Tresham in 1593 has a meaning. The building was designed as an expression of his staunch Roman Catholic faith; intriguing symbols of the Trinity and the Mass abound.

Times: Open Apr-Sep, daily 10-6; Oct, daily 10-5.

Fee: £1.50 (ch 80p, concessions £1.10).

STOKE BRUERNE

Canal Museum

NN12 7SE (A508, 4m S of Junct 15 of M1)

☎ 01604 862229 01604 864199

e-mail: britishwaterways@sosb.globalnet.co.uk

Housed on three floors of an old cornmill, the colourful collection vividly portrays the many aspects of inland waterways from their origins to the present day, complementing the flight of locks and long canal tunnel outside.

Times: Open Etr-Oct daily, 10-5; Nov-Etr Tue-Sun, 10-4. Closed 25-26 Dec. Last admission 30 mins before closing time.

Fee: £3 (ch, pen & student £2). Family ticket (2 adults & 2 ch) £7.

(charged) toilets for disabled shop (ex guide dogs)

SULGRAVE

Sulgrave Manor

Manor Rd OX17 2SD (off B4525)

☎ 01295 760205 01295 768056

Home to George Washington's ancestors until 1656 when his great grandfather, John, emigrated to Virginia. Inside the house there are many relics of George Washington. Though much of the house is a 20th-century restoration, original parts include the porch (with a carving of the original American flag), a screens passage, the great hall and the great Chamber.

Times: Open Apr-Oct, Mon-Fri (ex Wed) 2-5.30, Sat, Sun & BH 10.30-1 & 2-5.30; Mar, Nov & Dec, Sat & Sun only 10.30-1 & 2-4.30; Other times by appointment. (Closed 25-26 Dec & Jan).

Fee: £4 (ch £2). Party 12+. Special event days £4.50 (ch £2.25). Family ticket £12. Party 12+.

licensed (induction loop available in shop or ticket office) toilets for disabled shop garden centre (ex guide & outside on leads)

Northumberland

Northumberland is a county of wide open spaces taking in the Northumberland National Park to the northwest, with miles of moorland around Hadrian's Wall rising to the Cheviot Hills on the Scottish border, and incorporating great swathes of Forestry Commission planted conifers.

The Pennine Way walking trail runs through the park from Hadrian's Wall to The Cheviot, the National Park's highest peak at 2,674 feet/815 metres, and crosses the border into Scotland. Towards the east, the park changes character in the gentle valleys of the rivers Coquet, Redesdale and North Tyne.

Hadrian's Wall, the Roman's astonishing feat of engineering and an enduring legacy, runs for 73 miles across northern England, and there are several well preserved forts, including Housestead's, one of the most popular sites on the wall.

The long, low lying coastline of Northumberland, designated an Area of Outstanding Natural Beauty, is dotted with a series of magnificent castles, Warworth, Alnick, Bamburgh, plus the remains of the 12th-century castle at Berwick-upon-Tweed and the impressive Elizabethan ramparts. Berwick is England's northernmost town, held alternately by the Scottish and English over centuries of bitter struggle.

The county town is Morpeth, which is the administrative centre, though this is disputed to some extent by Alnwick, the seat of the Duke of Northumberland. The attractive market town of Hexham warrants some exploration, with its Abbey, Moot Hall and other medieval remains, and also makes a good base for visiting Hadrian's Wall.

EVENTS & FESTIVALS

May
1 Riding the Bounds, Berwick-upon-Tweed
28 Northumberland County Show, Corbridge

June
2 Allendale Fair
24-30 Alnwick Fair (provisional)
tbc Ovingham Goose Fair, Goose Fair Cross, Ovingham

July
Amble Sea Fair(usually 1st weekend in July)
29 Alnwick Castle Tournament
tbc Rothbury Traditional Music Festival

August
4 Powburn Show & Sheepdog Trials
4-10 Alnwick International Music Festival (provisional)

September
1 Alnwick District Horticultural Show
1-2 Military Tattoo, Berwick-upon-Tweed (provisional)

October
tbc Northumberland Traditional Music Festival

November
3 Northumbrian Gathering

Top: Hadrian's Wall

ALNWICK

Alnwick Castle
NE66 1NQ (off A1)
☎ 01665 510777 & 511100 24hr info
01665 510876
e-mail: enquiries@alnwickcastle.com

Alnwick Castle is the main seat of the Duke of Northumberland whose family have lived here since 1309. The stern, medieval exterior belies the treasure house within, furnished in Renaissance style, with paintings by Titian, Van Dyck and Canaletto, and an exquisite collection of Meissen china. The Regiment Museum of Royal Northumberland Fusiliers is housed in the Abbot's Tower of the Castle. Recently refurbished towers include museums of local archaeology and the Percy Tenantry volunteers.
Times: Open 15 Apr-27 Oct, daily 11-5. Last admission 4.15.
Fee: £6.25 (ch £3.50, concessions £5.25). Family ticket £15. Party 14+.
P ♿ (Castle lift for those able to walk a little) toilets for disabled shop (ex guide dogs)

BAMBURGH

Bamburgh Castle
NE69 7DF (A1 Belford by-pass, East on B1342 to Bamburgh)
☎ 01668 214515 & 214208 01668 214060

Rising dramatically from a rocky outcrop, Bamburgh Castle is a huge, square Norman castle. Last restored in the 19th century, it has an impressive hall and an armoury with a large collection of armour from the Tower of London. Guide services are available.
Times: Open Apr-Oct, daily 11-5 (last admission 4.30pm). Other times by prior arrangement.
Fee: £4 (ch £1.50 & pen £3). Party 15+.
P (charged) ♿ shop (ex guide dogs)

Grace Darling Museum
Radcliffe Rd NE69 7AE (Follow A1, turn off at Bamburgh & follow signposts to Northumbria Coastal route, museum on right)
☎ 01668 214465

Pictures, documents and other reminders of the heroine are on display, including the boat in which Grace Darling and her father, keeper of Longstone Lighthouse, Farne Islands, rescued nine survivors from the wrecked *'SS Forfarshire'* in 1838.
Times: Open Etr-Oct, daily 10-5 (Sun 12-5).
Fee: Free.
P (400yds) ♿ (ramps on request) shop (ex guide dogs)

BARDON MILL

Vindolanda (Chesterholm)
Vindolanda Trust NE47 7JN (signposted from A69 or B6318)
☎ 01434 344277 01434 344060
e-mail: vindolandatrust@btinternet.com

Vindolanda was a Roman fort and frontier town. It was started well before Hadrian's Wall, and became a base for 500 soldiers. The civilian settlement lay just west of the fort and has been excavated. The excellent museum in the country house of Chesterholm nearby has displays and reconstructions. There are also formal gardens, and an open-air museum with Roman Temple, shop, house and Northumbrian croft.
Times: Open daily from 10am, all facilities mid Feb-mid Nov.
Fee: £3.80 (ch £2.80, student & pen £3.20, free admission for disabled). Saver ticket for joint admission to sister site - The Roman Army Museum £5.60 (ch £4.10, pen £4.70) Party.
P ♿ toilets for disabled shop (ex guide dogs)

BELSAY

Belsay Hall, Castle and Gardens
NE20 0DX (on A696)
☎ 01661 881636

Belsay Castle, with its splendid turrets and battlements, dates from 1370 and was the home of the Middleton family, until they built the Jacobean manor house beside it, and then the magnificent Grecian-style Hall. There are also wonderful gardens.
Times: Open all year, daily Apr-Sep 10-6 (Oct 10-5); Nov-Mar, daily 10-4. Closed 24-26 Dec & 1 Jan.
Fee: £3.80 (ch 5-15 £1.90, under 5's free).
P ♿ toilets for disabled shop (in certain areas)

BERWICK-UPON-TWEED

Berwick Barracks, Museum & Art Gallery
TD15 1DF (on the Parade, off Church St, Berwick town centre)
☎ 01289 304493

Enclosed by its Elizabethan ramparts, Berwick is an outstanding example of a fortified town, and the barracks have changed little since 1721. The museum covers 200 years of military and regimental history, and the Art Gallery houses the important Burrell collection.
Times: Open all year, Apr-Oct daily 10-6 (Oct 10-5); Nov-Mar Wed-Sun 10-4. Closed 1-2pm & 24-26 Dec & 1 Jan.
Fee: £2.60 (ch 5-15 £1.30, under 5's free).
P ♿ shop

Paxton House
TD15 1SZ (3m from A1 Berwick-upon-Tweed bypass on B6461 Kelso road)
☎ 01289 386291 01289 386660
e-mail: info@paxtonh

Built in 1758 for the Laird of Wedderburn, the house is a fine example of neo-Palladian architecture. Much of the house is furnished by Chippendale and there is a large picture gallery. The house is set in 80 acres beside the River Tweed, and the grounds include an adventure playground.
Times: Open daily from Apr-Oct, House & gallery 11-5 (last tour of house 4.15pm). Grounds 10-sunset.
Fee: House & Grounds: £5 (ch £2.50, adult concessions £4.50) Family ticket £14. Grounds only: £2.50 (ch £1, adult concessions £2) Family ticket £6.
P ♿ (lifts to main areas of house, parking close to reception) toilets for disabled shop (ex guide/on lead in grounds)

CAMBO

Wallington House Walled Garden & Grounds

NE61 4AR (6m NW of Belsay)

☎ 01670 774283

The house is set in a great moorland estate of over 12,000 acres. It features delicate plasterwork, 'Capability' Brown gardens and William Bell Scott murals. In the 19th century Ruskin and other writers and artists came here as guests. Special events include open air concerts and theatre productions.

Times: Open: House Apr-Sep, daily (ex Tue) 1-5.30, Oct daily (ex Tue) 1-4.30. Last admission half hour before closing. Walled garden Apr-Oct, daily 10-7 or dusk; Nov-Mar, 10-4 or dusk if earlier. Grounds open all year.

Fee: House, walled garden & grounds: £5.40, family ticket £13.50. Walled gardens & grounds only: £3.90. Party.

P ✕ ♿ (Vessa Ventura scooter, braille guide) toilets for disabled shop garden centre (ex on lead in grounds)

CARRAWBROUGH

Roman Wall (Mithraic Temple)

(on B6318)

This fascinating Mithraic temple was uncovered by a farmer in 1949. Its three altars to the war god, Mithras date from the third century AD, and are now in the Museum of Antiquities in Newcastle, but there are copies on site.

Times: Open any reasonable time.

Fee: Free.

P #

CHILLINGHAM

Chillingham Castle

NE66 5NJ (signposted from A1 & A697)

☎ 01668 215359 & 215390 01668 215463

Times: Open Etr wknd & May-Sep, daily (ex closed Tue in May, Jun & Sep) 12-5 (Last admission 5.30pm). Other times by prior arrangement.

P ✕ licensed ♿ shop *Details not confirmed for 2001*

Chillingham Wild Cattle Park

NE66 5NP (off B6348, follow brown tourist signs off A1 and A697)

☎ 01668 215250 01668 215250

The park, a registred charity, at Chillingham boasts an extraordinary survival: a herd of wild white cattle descended from animals trapped in the park when the wall was built in the 13th century; they are the sole surviving pure-bred examples of their breed in the world. Binoculars are recommended for a close view. Visitors are accompanied into the park by the Warden.

Times: Open Apr-Oct, daily 10-12 & 2-5, Sun 2-5. (Closed Tue).

Fee: £3 (ch £1 & pen £2.50).

P shop

CORBRIDGE

Corbridge Roman Station

NE45 5NT (0.5m NW on minor road - signposted)

☎ 01434 632349

The remains of Roman `Corstopitum', built around AD210, include granaries, portico columns and the probable site of legionary headquarters.

Times: Open all year, Apr-Sep, daily 10-6 (or dusk if earlier in Oct); Nov-Mar, Wed-Sun 10-4 (or dusk if earlier, closed 1-2pm). Closed 24-26 Dec & 1 Jan.

Fee: £2.80 (ch 5-15 £1.40, under 5's free).

P ♿ (in certain areas) #

EMBLETON

DUNSTANBURGH CASTLE

Craster NE66 2RD (1.5m E on footpaths from Craster or Embleton)

☎ **01665 576231**

The skeletal ruins of the huge castle, partly built by John of Gaunt, stand on cliffs 100ft above the North Sea. Already a ruin by Tudor times, its setting has inspired many paintings, including three by Turner.

Times: Open all year, Apr-Sep, daily 10-6 (Oct 10-5) 10-4; Nov-Mar, Wed-Sun 10-4 (or dusk if earlier). Closed 24-26 Dec & 1 Jan.

Fee: £1.80 (ch 5-15 80p, under 5's free)

P (charged) #

FORD

LADY WATERFORD HALL

TD15 2QA (situated approx 1.5m E of A697)

☎ **01890 820338** ℻ **01890 820384**

Times: Open Mar-Nov, daily 10.30-12.30 & 1.30-5.30. Open by appointment in winter.

P ♿ shop *Details not confirmed for 2001*

HOLY ISLAND (LINDISFARNE)

LINDISFARNE CASTLE

TD15 2SH (8m S Berwick from A1 on Holy Island)

☎ **01289 389244**

The 16th-century castle was restored by Sir Edwin Lutyens in 1903 for the owner of *Country Life* magazine. The austere outside walls belie the Edwardian comfort within, and there is a little garden designed by Gertrude Jekyll.

Times: Open Apr-Oct, daily (closed Fri ex Good Fri) as Lindisfarne is a tidal island, the Castle will open 4.5hrs which will always include 12-3 and then either earlier opening or later closing as the tide allows. Other times by arrangement with the administrator, please phone for details.

Fee: £4. Family ticket £10.

P (1m in village)

LINDISFARNE PRIORY

TD15 2RX (Can only be reached at low tide across a causeway. Tide tables posted at each end of the causeway)

☎ **01289 389200**

St Aidan and monks from Iona founded the first monastery on the island in the 7th century, and from here preached the gospel to much of Northern England, also producing the illuminated Lindisfarne Gospels, now in the British Library. The priory ruins date from the 11th century and the island can be reached by a causeway at low tide (tide tables are displayed), or phone the custodian for details.

Times: Open all year, Apr-Sep, daily 10-6 (Oct 10-5); Nov-Mar, daily 10-4 (or dusk if earlier). Subject to tides. Closed 24-26 Dec & 1 Jan.

Fee: £2.80 (ch 5-15 £1.40, under 5's free)

shop (in certain areas) #

HOUSESTEADS

HOUSESTEADS ROMAN FORT

Bardon Mills NE47 6NN (2.5m NE of Bardon Mill on B6318)

☎ **01434 344363**

Housesteads was the Roman fort of *Vercovicium*. It has a spectacular site on Hadrian's Wall, and is also one of the best preserved Roman forts. It covers five acres, including the only known Roman hospital in Britain, and a 24-seater latrine with a flushing tank.

Times: Open all year, Apr-Sep, daily 10-6 (Oct 10-5); Nov-Mar, daily 10-4. Closed 24-26 Dec & 1 Jan.

Fee: £2.80 (ch 5-15 £1.40, under 5's free).

P (0.25m from fort) shop #

LONGFRAMLINGTON

BRINKBURN PRIORY

NE65 8AR (off B6344)

☎ **01665 570628**

The priory was founded in 1135 for Augustinian canons, and stands on a bend of the River Coquet. After the Dissolution of the Monasteries it fell into disrepair, but was restored in 1858.

Times: Open Apr-Oct, daily 10-6, (Oct 10-5).

Fee: £1.60 (ch 5-15 80p, under 5's free).

P (in certain areas) #

MORPETH

MORPETH CHANTRY BAGPIPE MUSEUM

Bridge St NE61 1PJ (off A1)

☎ **01670 519466** ℻ **01670 511326**

This unusual museum specialises in the history and development of Northumbrian small pipes and their music. They are set in the context of bagpipes from around the world, from India to Inverness.

Times: Open all year, Mon-Sat 10-5. (Closed 25-26 Dec, 1 Jan & Etr Mon).

Fee: £1.50 (concessions 80p). Family ticket £3.50.

P (100 metres) ♿ (induction loop, not suitable for wheelchairs) shop

NORHAM

CASTLE

TD15 2JY

☎ **01289 382329**

One of the strongest Border fortresses, this castle has a fine Norman keep and overlooks the River Tweed.

Times: Open Apr-Oct, 10-6 (Oct 10-5).

Fee: £1.80 (ch 5-15 90p, under 5's free)

P ♿ #

PRUDHOE

Prudhoe Castle

NE42 6NA (on minor road off A695)
☎ 01661 833459

Standing on the River Tyne, this medieval castle was the stronghold of the d'Umfravelles and Percys. The keep stands in the inner bailey and a notable gatehouse guards the outer bailey. Access is to the Pele Yard only.
Times: Open Apr-Oct, daily 10-6 (Oct 10-5).
Fee: £1.80 (ch 5-15 90p, under 5's free).
shop (in certain areas)

ROTHBURY

Cragside House, Garden & Estate

(1m N of Rothbury, off A697 & B6341)
☎ 01669 620333 & 620150

This splendid Victorian masterpiece was designed by the architect Richard Norman Shaw. The huge drawing room has a curved glass roof and 10-ton marble-lined inglenook. This was the first house to be lit by electricity generated by water-power. The grounds were planted with seven million trees, streams were diverted and lakes created.
Times: Open, Grounds: Apr-29 Oct, daily ex Mon 10.30-7; Weekends & 1-17 Dec, Wed-Sun, 11-4. House: daily (ex Mon, open BH Mon's) 1-5.30, last admission 4.30pm. Gardens Apr-Oct, daily ex Mon 10.30-7 (last admission 5pm). Weekends & selected days in Nov & Dec.
Fee: House, Garden & Grounds & Visitor Centre £6.50 Garden, Grounds & Visitor Centre only £4. Family ticket for House, Garden & Estate £16. Family ticket for Garden & Estate £10. Party.
licensed (fishing pier braille guide) toilets for disabled shop (ex in grounds on lead)

WALWICK

Chesters Roman Fort & Museum

Chollerford NE46 4EP (0.5m W of Chollerford on B6318)
☎ 01434 681379

One of the Roman forts on Hadrian's Wall is now in the park of Chesters, an 18th-century mansion. The fort named *Cilurnum* housed 500 soldiers and covered nearly 6 acres. Excavations have shown that it was destroyed and rebuilt three times. Evidence of an aqueduct and substantial remains of a bath house show that the standard of living was high.
Times: Open all year, Apr-Sep, daily 9.30-6; Oct, daily 10-5 or dusk; Nov-Mar, daily 10-4 (or dusk if earlier). Closed 24-26 Dec & 1 Jan.
Fee: £2.80 (ch 5-15 £1.40, under 5's free.
shop (in certain areas)

WARKWORTH

Warkworth Castle

NE66 OUJ
☎ 01665 711423

The castle dominates Warkworth from its site on the bands of the River Coquet. It makes a splendid ruin, with its keep and curtain wall. Once home of the turbulent Percy family, one of whose members, Sir Henry Percy (Harry Hotspur) was immortalised by Shakespeare in *Henry IV*. Nearby is the 14th-century bridge over the river, now only open to pedestrians.
Times: Open all year, Apr-Oct, daily 10-6 (Oct 10-5); Nov-Mar, daily 10-4 (or dusk if earlier, closed 1-2pm). Closed 24-26 Dec & 1 Jan.
Fee: £2.40 (ch 5-15 £1.20, under 5's free)
(in certain areas)

Warkworth Hermitage

☎ 01665 711423

Upstream from Warkworth Castle is the Hermitage, a refuge dug into the rockface by a 14th-century hermit. It consists of a chapel and two living chambers. Nearby is Coquet island, which was also the home of hermit monks.
Times: Open Apr-Sep, daily 10-6, (Oct 10-5); Nov-Mar, daily 10-4> Closed 24-26 Dec & 1 Jan.
Fee: £1.60 (ch 5-15 £1.60, under 5's free)

Nottinghamshire

The inland county of Nottinghamshire in eastern England is strongly associated with the legend of Robin Hood, though Robin's territory, the former royal hunting ground of Sherwood Forest, has been somewhat tamed since his outlaw days.

EVENTS & FESTIVALS

May
Nottingham County Show, Newark & Nottingham Showground, Winthorpe

July
Annual Robin Hood Festival, Sherwood Forest Country Park & Visitor Centre, Edwinstowe

The county is divided between the old coalfields north of the Nottingham, the commuter belt of the Wolds to the south, and the area of most interest, that of Sherwood Forest and the great country estates known as the 'Dukeries'. One of these, Clumber Park is now owned by the National Trust.

The traditional industry of Nottinghamshire, alongside agriculture, was coal mining, though this has declined in recent years. It is also an oil producing area, and during World War 11 produced the only oil out of reach of the U-Boats.

D H Lawrence was a Nottinghamshire man, the son of a miner and former schoolteacher. He grew up in poverty, and his book *Sons and Lovers* reflects the experiences of his early years. There is a D H Lawrence commemorative walk from his home at Eastwood to Old Brinsley Colliery.

Other towns of note are the river port and market town of Newark, which hosts a major antiques fair six times a year, and Southwell, known for its medieval minster with its exquisite carving depicting the foliage of Sherwood Forest.

Top: Sherwood Forest

EASTWOOD

Durban House Heritage Centre

Mansfield Rd NG16 3DZ (signed on A610)
☎ 01773 717353 🖷 01773 713509

Tread in the footsteps of D H Lawrence and go on a fascinating journey through the development of his hometown - Eastwood - exploring the landscape, people and their influence on the writer in an exciting interactive exhibition.

Times: Open all year, Apr-Oct, daily 10-5; Nov-Mar, daily 10-4. Closed 24 Dec-1 Jan.

Fee: £2 (concessions £1.20)

(lift to exhibition) toilets for disabled shop (ex guide dogs)

EDWINSTOWE

Sherwood Forest Country Park & Visitor Centre

NG21 9HN (on B6034 N of village between A6075 and A616)
☎ 01623 823202 & 824490 🖷 01623 823202
e-mail: marilynlouden@nottscc.gov.uk

At the heart of the Robin Hood legend is Sherwood Forest. Today it is a country park and visitor centre with 450 acres of ancient oaks and shimmering silver birches. Waymarked pathways guide you through the forest. A year round programme of events includes the spectacular Robin Hood Festival.

Times: Country Park: open daily dawn to dusk. Visitor Centre: open daily 10.30-5 (4.30pm Nov-Mar) **Fee:** Free.

(charged) toilets for disabled shop (ex guide dogs)

See advert on p185.

FARNSFIELD

White Post Modern Farm Centre

NG22 8HL (12m N of Nottingham on A614)
☎ 01623 882977 & 882026 🖷 01623 883499
e-mail: tim@whitepostfarmcentre.co.uk

This award-winning working farm gives an introduction to a variety of modern farming methods. It explains how farms work, and llamas, deer, pigs, cows, snails, quails, snakes and fish can be seen. There's lots to see indoors, including the owl houses, incubator room, mousetown and a reptile house.

Times: Open all year, Mon-Fri 10-5. Wknds & BH's 10-6.

Fee: £4.95 (ch 3-16 £3.95, under 3 free, pen & people with special needs £3.95). Party 10+.

(sign language, free hire wheelchairs, book if more than 6) toilets for disabled shop (ex guide dogs)

HAUGHTON

World of Robin Hood

Haughton Farm DN22 8DZ (on B6387 just outside Walesby, signposted off A1)
☎ 01623 860210 🖷 01623 836003
e-mail: worldofrobinhood@talk21.com

Medieval history is brought to life in an adventure of sound and vision, taking the visitor back through time to the 12th century complete with sights, sounds and smells. Journey through the Crusades fought by King Richard I, to the life and times of Robin Hood, which includes a visit to a medieval market place - complete with waifs and wandering chickens.

Times: Open 10.30-4. Telephone for winter opening times.

Fee: £4.95 (ch & pen £3.95, under 5's free) Family ticket (2 adults & 2 ch) £15.

licensed toilets for disabled shop (outside areas only)

NEWARK-ON-TRENT

Millgate Museum of Social & Folk Life

48 Millgate NG24 4TS
☎ 01636 655730 🖷 01636 655735
e-mail: museums@newark-sherwooddc.gov.uk

Fascinating exhibitions - recreated streets, shops and houses in period settings. The museum displays illustrate the working and domestic life of local people, from Victorian times to 1950. The mezzanine gallery is home to a number of temporary exhibitions showing the work of local artists, designers and photographers.

Times: Open all year, Mon-Fri 10-5, Sat & Sun & BH 1-5. Last admission 4.30 (Closed 25 & 26 Dec).

Fee: Free.

(250yds) toilets for disabled shop (ex aid dogs)

Newark Air Museum

The Airfield, Winthorpe NG24 2NY (easy access from A1, A46, A17 & Newark relief road, follow tourism signs)
☎ 01636 707170 🖷 01636 707170
e-mail: newarkair@lineone.net

A diverse collection of transport, training and reconnaisance aircraft, jet fighters, bombers and helicopters, now numbering more than fifty. An Undercover Aircraft Display Hall and an Engine Hall make the museum an all-weather attraction. Everything is displayed around a WWII airfield.

Times: Open all year, Mar-Sep, Mon-Fri 10-5, Sat & Sun 10-6; Oct-Feb, daily 10-4. (Closed 24-26 Dec). Other times by appointment.

toilets for disabled shop

Vina Cooke Museum of Dolls & Bygone Childhood

The Old Rectory, Cromwell NG23 6JE (5m N of Newark off A1)

☎ 01636 821364

All kinds of childhood memorabilia are displayed in this 17th-century house: prams, toys, dolls' houses, costumes and a large collection of Victorian and Edwardian dolls including Vina Cooke hand-made character dolls.

Times: Open all year, Tue-Thu 10.30-12 & 2-5. Sat, Sun & BH Mon 10.30-5. Mon, Fri & other times open by appointment.

Fee: £2.50 (ch £1.50, pen £2). P ♿ shop

NEWSTEAD

Newstead Abbey

Newstead Abbey Park NG15 8GE (off A60, between Nottingham & Mansfield)

☎ 01623 455900 🖷 01623 455904

This beautiful house is best known as the home of poet Lord Byron. Visitors can see Byron's own rooms, mementoes of the poet and other splendidly decorated rooms. The grounds of over 300 acres include waterfalls, ponds, water gardens and Japanese gardens. Special events include outdoor theatre and opera, Christmas events and Ghost Tours.

Times: Open: Grounds all year, daily 9-dusk (ex last Fri in Nov); House Apr-Sep, daily 12-5. Last admission 4pm

Fee: House & Grounds £4 (ch £1.50, concessions £2) Family ticket (2 adults & 3 ch) £10. Grounds only £2 (ch & concessions £1.50) Family ticket £6. Subject to change.

P ☕ ✕ licensed ♿ (audio tour for visually impaired, mobility car for loan) toilets for disabled shop 🐕 (ex guide dogs or in garden)

NOTTINGHAM

Brewhouse Yard Museum

Castle Boulevard NG7 1FB

☎ 0115 915 3600 & 0115 915 3640 🖷 0115 915 3601

Housed in 17th-century cottages, the museum depicts everyday life in Nottingham over the past 300 years. Locally made or used objects are shown in a mixture of period rooms, re-created shops and displays. Caves behind the houses are also part of the museum.

Times: Open all year 10-4.30. (Closed Fridays Nov-Mar & 25-26 Dec).

Fee: Free Mon-Fri but donations appreciated. Weekends & BH's £1.50 (concessions 80p). Family ticket £3.80.

P (100yds) ♿ toilets for disabled shop 🐕

Castle Museum

NG1 6EL

☎ 0115 915 3700 🖷 0115 915 3653

This 17th-century building is both museum and art gallery, with major temporary exhibitions as well as the permanent collections. There is a 'Story of Nottingham' exhibition, and the new 'Meet you at the Lions' exhibition, which celebrates the diversity of people living in Nottingham today. Guided tour of the underground passages most afternoons.

Times: Open all year, daily 10-5. (ex Fri Nov-Feb 12-5) Grounds 8-dusk. (Closed 25 & 26 Dec).

Fee: Mon-Fri free, wknds & BH's £2 (ch & concessions £1). Family ticket £5.

P (400yds) ☕ ♿ (chair lift, mobility car available) toilets for disabled shop 🐕

The Caves of Nottingham

Drury Walk, Broadmarsh Centre NG1 7LS (within Broadmarsh Shopping Centre, on the first floor)

☎ 0115 924 1424 🖷 0115 924 1430

e-mail: info@cavesofnottingham.co.uk

A unique 750-year-old cave system situated beneath a modern day shopping centre. A digital audio tour guides you through the only remaining underground medieval tannery in England, beer cellars, an air raid shelter and the remains of Drury Hill, one of the oldest streets in Nottingham.

Times: Open daily 10-5, Sun 11-5 (last admission 4.15pm, Sun 4pm). (Closed 24-26 Dec, 1 Jan & Etr Sun).

Fee: £3.25 (concessions £2.25). Family ticket £9.50.

P (charged) ♿ (non-accessible to wheelchairs,induction loop,textual guide) shop 🐕 (ex guide dogs) 💳

The Galleries of Justice

The Shire Hall, High Pavement, Lace Market NG1 1HN (follow signs to City Centre, then brown & white tourist signs to Lace Market & Galleries of Justice)

☎ 0115 952 0555 🖷 0115 952 0557

e-mail: inf@galleriesof justice.org.uk

There are two 19th-century prisons, complete with cells and bath house, a transportation gallery, and exercise yard. Costumed interpreters help bring the scene to life. Visitors can attend a modern crime scene and assess evidence through the use of forensic science and state-of-the-art computers. Exhibition on Civil Law demonstrates how the law affects our daily life.

Times: Open Tue-Sun & BH Mon's 10-5. Last admission one hour before closing. (Closed 24-26 Dec & 1 Jan).

Fee: £7.95 (ch £4.95, concesssions £5.95). Family ticket (2 adults & 3 ch) £23.95, (1 adult & 3 ch) £15.95, (2 pen & 3 ch) £19.95. Ticket vaild for one visit to three exhibitions for 12 months from date of purchase.

P (5 mins walk) ✕ licensed ♿ (braille control lifts, induction loop, large print lables) toilets for disabled shop 🐕 (ex guide dogs) 💳

The Lace Centre

Severns Building, Castle Rd NG1 6AA (follow signs for the Castle, situated opposite the Robin Hood statue on Castle road)

☎ 0115 941 3539 📠 0115 941 3539

Exquisite Nottingham lace fills this small building, with panels also hanging from the beamed ceiling. There are weekly demonstrations of lace-making on Thursday afternoons from Easter to October.

Times: Open all year, Jan-Mar, daily 10-4; Apr-Nov, 10-5. Every Sun 11am-4pm. (Closed Xmas & New Year)

Fee: Free.

P (100yds) (metered street parking) ♿ shop 💳

Museum of Costume & Textiles

43-51 Castle Gate NG1 6AF (Close to City Centre, near the Robin Hood statue & Nottingham Castle Museum & Art Gallery)

☎ 0115 915 3500 📠 0115 915 3653

Costume from 1730 to 1960 is displayed in appropriate room settings. Other rooms contain embroidery, dress accessories, the Lord Middleton collection and map tapestries. Knitted, woven and printed textiles are also on show, together with embroidery from Europe and Asia.

Times: Open all year, Wed-Sun & BHs 10-4.

Fee: Free.

P (200yds) ♿ shop 🐕

Museum of Nottingham Lace

3-5 High Pavement, The Lace Market NG1 1HF (Follow signs for Lace Market Parking in the city centre)

☎ 0115 989 7365 📠 0115 989 7301

e-mail: info@nottinghamlace.org

The atmospheric lace market is the setting for this fascinating museum which traces the history of machine lace from its earliest beginnings to its height in the Victorian era. Working machines are on display most days of the week, and audio tours are available.

Times: Open daily 10-5, machine demonstrations 11-3.30. (Closed 25-26 Dec & New Year's Day). Last admission 4pm.

Fee: £2.95 (ch 5-16 £1.95, concessions £2.50) Party 12+. Lace Market Audio Tour £1.95 (deposit required for equipment)

P (100yds) ☕ ♿ (counters at lower level, lift, audio & written tour) shop 🐕 (ex guide dogs) 💳

Natural History Museum

Wollaton Hall, Wollaton NG8 2AE (3m W, off A52 & A6514)

☎ 0115 915 3911 📠 0115 915 3932

Standing in a large deer park, this imposing Elizabethan mansion houses a wide variety of displays, including birds, mammals, fossils and minerals.

Times: Open all year, daily 11-5 (Closed Fri Nov-Mar & 25-26 Dec).

Fee: Weekdays free, wknds & BH £1.50 (concessions 80p) Family £3.80. P (charged) ♿ toilets for disabled shop 🐕

Nottingham Industrial Museum

Courtyard Buildings, Wollaton Park NG8 2AE (3m W of City Centre, off A609 Ilkeston Rd)
☎ 0115 915 3910 📠 0115 915 3941

Nottingham's industrial history is on display in this 18th-century stable block. Lace, hosiery, pharmaceuticals (Nottingham was the home of the founder of Boots the Chemists), tobacco and much else are among the exhibits. There is a beam engine and other steam engines, regularly in steam.

Times: Open Apr-Sep, daily 11-5; Oct-Mar only open on steaming days, contact for details.
Fee: Mon-Fri free. Sat, Sun & BH's £1.50 (ch 80p).
P (charged) ♿ (hand & powered wheelchairs available) toilets for disabled shop (ex guide dogs)

Tales of Robin Hood

30-38 Maid Marian Way NG1 6GF
☎ 0115 948 3284 📠 0115 950 1536
e-mail: robinhoodcentre@mail.com

Special effects and adventure cars transport the visitor back to medieval Nottingham and Sherwood Forest, legendary home of Robin Hood. There is commentary in seven languages via portable CD players. Medieval banquets take place.

Times: Open all year, daily 10-6 (last admission 4.30pm). (Closed 25-26 Dec).
Fee: £4.95 (ch £3.95, pen & students £4.25) Family ticket (2 adults & 2 ch) £15.75, (2 adults & 3 ch) £18.75. Party.
P (NCP 200 yds) ♿ (specially adapted 'car') toilets for disabled shop (ex guide dogs)

OLLERTON

Rufford Abbey and Country Park

NG22 9DF (2m S of Ollerton, adjacent to A614)
☎ 01623 822944 📠 01623 825919
e-mail: marilyn.louden@nottscc.gov.uk

At the heart of the wooded country park stand the remains of a 12th-century Cistercian Abbey, housing an exhibition on the life of a monk at Rufford. Many species of wildlife can be seen on the lake, and there are lovely formal gardens, with sculptures and Britain's first centre for studio ceramics. Special event for 2001 : Annual Earth Fire Ceramics Fair (23-24 June).

Times: Open all year 10.30-5.30 (closes 4pm Jan & feb). For further details of opening times telephone establishment. **Fee:** Free.
P (charged) ✕ licensed ♿ (lift to craft centre gallery, free parking, wheelchair loan) toilets for disabled shop garden centre (ex park)

RAMPTON

Sundown Kiddies Adventureland

(Sundown Pets Garden), Treswell Rd DN22 0HX (3m off A57 at Dunham crossroads)
☎ 01777 248274 📠 01777 248967

The children's story book theme park – a land where wonderful stories spring magically to life. There's Santa's All Year Sleigh Ride, the Mouses' Tales Walkthrough, Musical Pet Shop and Witches' Cauldron. Other attractions include; The Smugglers Cove with boatride, Shotgun City, Rocky Mountain Railroad and Indoor Jungle (Height Restriction).

Times: Open all year, daily from 10am, earlier in winter. (Closed 25-26 Dec & weekdays in Jan & 1st week in Feb)
Fee: £4.75 (ch under 2 free).
P ♿ (ramps to rides, assistance to rides) toilets for disabled shop (ex guide dogs)

SUTTON-CUM-LOUND

Wetlands Waterfowl Reserve & Exotic Bird Park

Off Loundlow Rd DN22 8SB (Signposted on A638)
☎ 01777 818099

The Reserve is a 32-acre site for both wild and exotic waterfowl. Visitors can see a collection of birds of prey, parrots, geese, ducks, and wigeon among others. There are also many small mammals and farm and wild animals, including llamas, wallabies and emus.

Times: Open all year, daily 10-5.30 (or dusk whichever is earlier). (Closed 25 Dec). **Fee:** £2 (ch & pen £1.25).
P ♿ (wheelchair available) shop (ex guide dogs)

WORKSOP

Clumber Park

The Estate Office, Clumber Park S80 3AZ (4.5m SE of Worksop, signposted from A1)
☎ 01909 476653 📠 01909 500721

An impressive, landscaped park, laid out by 'Capability' Brown. An outstanding feature is the lake running through the park, a haven for wildfowl, covering an area of 80 acres. The park is a mixture of woodland, open grass and heathland.

Times: Open all year, daily during daylight hours. Walled Garden, Victorian Apiary, Fig House, Vineries & Garden Tools exhibition Apr-Sep Wed & Thu, Sat, Sun & BH Mon 10.30-5.30. Conservation centre open throughout summer contact Warden, Estate Office. Chapel: Apr-Sep, daily 10.30-5.30 (until 6 Sat & Sun); Oct-Jan 2001 daily 10.30-4.
Fee: Pedestrians free; cars, motorbikes & caravanettes £3, mini-coaches and cars with caravans £4.30, coaches: midweek: free, weekends & BH £7.
P (charged) ✕ licensed ♿ (powered self-drive vehicle available if booked) toilets for disabled shop garden centre

Oxfordshire

The city of Oxford, situated on the River Thames (known locally as the Isis), is renowned for its ancient buildings and 'dreaming spires'. It is home to Britain's oldest university, established during the 12th century, with a collegiate system dating from the 13th.

Other well-known towns include Banbury, though the Banbury Cross of nursery rhyme fame was destroyed in 1602 by the Puritans, to be replaced in 1858. Henley-on-Thames is home to the Royal Regatta, an amateur rowing competition of world renown and a highlight of the social calendar. Witney is a blanket-making town, using two important local resources, wool, and power from the River Windrush.

The Cotswold Hills extend over the border from Gloucestershire into the east of Oxfordshire, dotted with pretty towns and villages built of mellow Cotswold stone hewn from the hillsides. These settlements prospered from the sheep who grazed the hills, producing wool for the flourishing medieval wool trade. Great churches are a feature of the area, an enduring symbol of medieval wool wealth.

To the southeast of the county are the Chiltern Hills, chalk downlands excellent for walking. The Chilterns range from the Berkshire Downs to the East Anglian Ridge, passing through Oxfordshire and reaching their highest point at Coombe Hill, near Wendover in Buckinghamshire, at 852 ft (260m).

Southwest of Oxford is the Vale of the White Horse, a prehistoric figure, 374 ft (114m) long, carved into the chalk, some 18 miles (29km) from the city.

EVENTS & FESTIVALS

March
tbc Oxford & Cambridge Women's Boat Race
tbc Poohsticks World Championships, Little Wittenham

May
1 6am Morning Choir, singing from Magdalen Tower, Oxford
12 Oxfordshire Visual Arts Festival
tbc Henley Rugby Club, International Sevens
tbc Lord Mayor's Parade, Oxford

July
4-8 Henley Royal Regatta
11-15 Henley Festival
29 Asian Music Festival, Henley-on-Thames
23 Swan Upping, Sunbury-Abingdon (provisional)

August
16-18 English Sheepdog Trials, Edgcott

September
8 Henley Show
20 Thame & Oxfordshire County Agricultural Show
tbc Florence Park Open Day
tbc St Giles Fair, Oxford

October
7 Ploughing Match, Dunsden
tbc Abingdon Fair

Top: Clifton Hampton on the River Thames

BANBURY

Banbury Museum

8 Horsefair OX16 0AA
☎ 01295 259855 📠 01295 270556

Times: Open all year, Oct-Mar, Tue-Sat 10-4.30; Apr-Sep, Mon-Sat 10-5.
P (behind museum) ☕ ♿ (induction loop) toilets for disabled shop 🐕 *Details not confirmed for 2001*

BROUGHTON

Broughton Castle

OX15 5EB (2m W of Banbury Cross on B4035)
☎ 01295 276070 & 01869 337126
📠 01869 337126 & 01295 276070

Originally owned by William of Wykeham, and later by the first Lord Saye and Sele, the castle is an early 14th- and mid 16th-century house with a moat and gatehouse. Period furniture, paintings and Civil War relics are displayed.
Times: Open Etr & 19 May-12 Sep, Wed & Sun (also Thu in Jul & Aug) & BH Sun & Mon 2-5.
Fee: £4 (ch 5-15 £2, pen & students £3.50). Party 20+.
P ☕ ♿ shop 🐕 (ex in grounds on leads)

BURFORD

Cotswold Wildlife Park

OX18 4JW (2m S of Burford on the A361)
☎ 01993 823006 📠 01993 823807

This 180-acre landscaped zoological park, surrounds a listed Gothic-style manor house. There is a varied collection of animals from all over the world, many of which are endangered species such as Asiatic Leopards, White Rhinos and Red Pandas. There's an adventure playground, a children's farmyard, and train rides during the summer.
Times: Open all year, daily (ex 25 Dec) from 10am, last admission 5pm Mar-Sep, 4pm Oct, 3.30pm Nov-Feb.
Fee: £6 (ch 3-16 & pen £4). Party 20+
P ☕ ✕ licensed ♿ (parking, free hire of wheelchairs) toilets for disabled shop

BUSCOT

Buscot Park

SN7 8BU (off A417)
☎ 01367 240786 📠 01367 241794
e-mail: estbuscot@aol.com

A highlight of this 18th-century house is the Faringdon Collection which includes work by Reynolds, Gainsborough, Rembrandt, Murillo, several of the Pre-Raphaelites, and some 20th-century artists. The charming formal water gardens were laid out by Harold Peto in the early 20th century. There is also an attractively planted kitchen garden, with unusual concentric walls.

Times: House & grounds Apr-29 Sep (incl Good Fri, Etr Sat & Sun) Wed-Fri 2-6. Also every 2nd & 4th wknd in each month 2-6 (last admission to house 5.30pm). Grounds as House but also Mon & Tue 2-6 (ex BH Mon)
Fee: House & Gardens £4.40 Grounds only £3.30.
P ☕ 🐕

DEDDINGTON

Deddington Castle

OX5 4TE (S of B4031 on E side of Deddington)

The large earthworks of the outer and inner baileys can be seen; the remains of 12th-century castle buildings have been excavated, but they are not now visible.
Times: Open any reasonable time. **Fee:** Free. #

DIDCOT

Didcot Railway Centre

OX11 7NJ (on A4130 at Didcot Parkway Station)
☎ 01235 817200 📠 01235 510621
e-mail: didrlyc@globalnet.co.uk

Based around the original GWR engine shed, the Centre is home to the biggest collection anywhere of Great Western Railway steam locomotives, carriages and wagons. A typical GWR station has been re-created and a section of Brunel's original broad gauge track relaid.
Times: Open all year: 13 Apr-Sep, daily 10-5; Nov-Feb, 10-4. Steam days first & last Sun of each month from Mar, BH's & Wed Jul-Aug.
Fee: £4-£8 depending on event (ch £3-£7.50, over 60's £3.50-£6.50).
P (100yds) ☕ ✕ ♿ (advance notice recommended) toilets for disabled shop

GREAT COXWELL

Great Coxwell Barn

(2m SW of Faringdon between A420 & B4019)
☎ 01793 762209
e-mail: tbcjaw@smtp.ntrust.org.uk

William Morris said that the barn was 'as noble as a cathedral'. It is a 13th-century stone-built tithe barn, 152ft long and 44ft wide, with a beautifully crafted framework of timbers supporting the lofty stone roof. The barn was built for the Cistercians.
Times: Open all reasonable times. For details please contact Estate Office. **Fee:** 50p P 🐕 (ex on leads)

HENLEY-ON-THAMES

Greys Court

Rotherfield Greys RG9 4PG (3m W)
☎ 01491 628529
e-mail: tgrgen@smtp.ntrust.org.uk

This appealing house has evolved over hundreds of years. The present gabled building has a pre-medieval kitchen but dates mainly from the 16th century. Additions were made in the 18th century and there are some fine decorations and furniture. Also of great interest is the wheelhouse with its huge wheel, once turned by a donkey to bring water up from the well.

Times: Open: House (part of ground floor only) Apr-Sep, Mon, Wed & Fri 2-6. (Closed Good Fri). Garden daily except Thu & Sun 2-6. Last admission 5.30pm. (Closed Good Fri).

Fee: House & Garden £4.60. Family ticket £11.50. Garden only £3.20 Family ticket £8. (ex on lead in car park)

River & Rowing Museum

Mill Meadows RG9 1BF (off A4130, signposted to Mill Meadows)

01491 415600 01491 415601

e-mail: museum@rrm.co.uk

The award-winning River and Rowing Museum is the only museum in the world with galleries dedicated to rowing and the 'Quest for Speed', from the Greek Trireme to Modern Olympic rowing boats; the River Thames from source to sea with its rich history and varied wildlife; and the riverside town of Henley featuring the Royal Regatta.

Times: Open Mon-Fri 10-5 (Oct-Etr), 10-6 (Etr-Sep) & wkends 10.30-5/6. Closed 24-25 Dec & 31 Dec & 1 Jan.

Fee: £4.95 (concessions £3.75). Family ticket from £13.25. Party 10+. licensed toilets for disabled shop

LONG WITTENHAM

Pendon Museum

OX14 4QD (follow brown signs from A4130 Didcot-Wallingford or A415 Abingdon-Wallingford road)

01865 407365

This charming exhibition shows highly detailed and historically accurate model railway and village scenes transporting the visitor back into 1930s country landscapes. Skilled modellers can often be seen at work on the exhibits.

Times: Open Sat & Sun 2-5, BH wknds 11-5 also Wed in Jun, Jul & Aug 2-5. Open daily 27 May-4 Jun 11-5 & 30 May-4 Jun 2-5.(Closed Dec). **Fee:** £3 (ch £2, pen £2.50, ch 6 free).

(phone in advance) toilets for disabled shop

MAPLEDURHAM

Mapledurham House & Watermill

RG4 7TR (off A4074, follow tourist signs)

0118 972 3350 0118 972 4016

e-mail: mtrust1997@aol.com

The small community at Mapledurham includes the house, a watermill and a church. The fine Elizabethan mansion, surrounded by quiet parkland which runs down to the River Thames, was built by the Blount family in the 16th century. The estate has literary connections with the poet Alexander Pope, with Galsworthy's *Forsyte Saga* and Kenneth Graham's *Wind in the Willows*.

Times: Open Etr-Sep, Sat, Sun & BH's 2-5.30 Picnic area 2-5.30. Last admission 5pm. Group visits midweek by arrangement.

Fee: Combined house, watermill & grounds £6 (ch £3). House & grounds £4 (ch £2). Watermill & grounds £3 (ch £1.50).

shop (ex park area)

Mapledurham Watermill

RG4 7TR (off A4074)

0118 972 3350 0118 972 4016

e-mail: mtrust1997@aol.com

Close to Mapledurham House stands the last working corn and grist mill on the Thames, still using traditional wooden machinery and producing flour for local bakers and shops. The watermill's products can be purchased in the shop. When Mapledurham house is open the mill can be reached by river launch.

contd.

Times: Open Easter-Sep, Sat, Sun & BHs 2-5.30. Picnic area 2-5.30. Last admission 5. Groups midweek by arrangement.
Fee: Watermill & grounds £3 (ch £1.50)
shop (ex in country park)

MINSTER LOVELL

Minster Lovell Hall & Dovecot

(adjacent to church, 3m W of Witney off A40)
☎ 01993 775315

Home of the ill-fated Lovell family, the ruins of the 15th-century house are steeped in history and legend. One of the main features of the estate is the medieval dovecote.
Times: Open any reasonable time. **Fee:** Free. (ex Dovecot)

NORTH LEIGH

North Leigh Roman Villa

Excavations show that the villa was occupied from the second to fourth centuries AD. A tessellated pavement and a 2-3ft high wall span, are on show.
Times: Open, grounds all year. No access to mosaic. Pedestrian access only from the main road - 600 yds. **Fee:** Free.

OXFORD

Ashmolean Museum of Art & Archaeology

Beaumont St OX1 2PH (opposite The Randolph Hotel)
☎ 01865 278000 01865 278018

The oldest museum in the country, opened in 1683, the Ashmolean contains Oxford University's priceless collections. Many important historical art pieces and artefacts are on display, including work from the Renaissance, Greece, Rome and the East.
Times: Open all year, Tue-Sat 10-5, Sun 2-5. (Closed Etr & during St.Giles Fair in early Sep, Xmas & 1 Jan).
Fee: Free. Guided tours by arrangement.
P (100-200metres) (pay & display) (entry ramp from Beaumont St) toilets for disabled shop

Harcourt Arboretum

Nuneham Courtenay OX44 9PX (400 yds S of Nuneham Courtenay on A4074)
☎ 01865 343501 01865 341828

The gardens consist of 75 acres of mixed woodland, meadow, rhododendron walks and fine specimen trees.
Times: Open May-Oct, daily 10-5; Nov-Apr, Mon-Fri 10-4.30. Closed 22 Dec-4 Jan & Good Fri-Etr Mon. **Fee:** Free. (ex guide dogs)

Museum of Oxford

St Aldate's OX1 1DZ
☎ 01865 252761 01865 252254
Times: Open all year, Tue-Fri 10-4, Sat 10-5 & Sun 12-4. (Closed 25-26 Dec, Good Fri & Etr Sun). shop *Details not confirmed for 2001*

Museum of the History of Science

Old Ashmolean Building, Broad St OX1 3AZ
☎ 01865 277280 01865 277288
e-mail: museum@mhs.ox.ac.uk

The first purpose built museum in Britain, containing the world's finest collection of early scientific instruments used in astronomy, navigation, surveying, physics and chemistry.
Times: Closed for major building work and gallery refurbishment. Will open Oct 2000. Contact for opening dates & times. **Fee:** Free.
P (300 metres) (limited street parking, meters) toilets for disabled shop (ex guide dogs)

The Oxford Story Exhibition

6 Broad St OX1 3AJ (city centre, follow signs)
☎ 01865 728822 01865 791716
e-mail: oxford@story47.fsnet.co.uk

Captivate the essence of Oxford University's fascinating 900-year history as you travel through the exhibitions recreated scenes. Learn about the University's early beginnings, the facts behind its record breaking discoveries and come face to face with some of the famous people who have studied there.
Times: Open all year, Apr-Oct daily 9.30-5, Jul-Aug 9-5.30 & Nov-Mar daily 10-4.30 (weekends 5pm).
Fee: £5.70 (concessions £4.70). Family ticket £17.50.
P (300 metres) (Park & Ride all round city) (advisable to phone in advance) toilets for disabled shop (ex guide dogs)

University of Oxford Botanic Garden

High St OX1 4AZ
☎ 01865 286690 01865 286690
e-mail: postmaster@botanic-garden.ox.ac.uk

Founded in 1621, these botanic gardens are the oldest in the country. There is a collection of over 8000 species of plants from all over the world.
Times: Open all year, daily 10-4 (9-4.30 Oct-Mar), Greenhouses, daily 2-4. Last admission 4.15. (Closed Good Fri & 25 Dec).
Fee: Apr-Aug £2. otherwise free. Accompanied ch under 12 free.
P (0.5 mile) toilets for disabled (ex guide dogs)

ROUSHAM

Rousham House

OX6 3QX (1m E of A4260. 0.5m S of B4030)
☎ 01869 347110

This attractive mansion was built by Sir Robert Dormer in 1635. During the Civil War it was a Royalist garrison. The house contains over 150 portraits and other pictures, and also much fine contemporary furniture. The gardens are a masterpiece by William Kent, and are his only work to survive unspoiled.

Times: Open all year, garden only, daily 10-4.30. House, Apr-Sep, Wed, Sun & BH Mon 2-4.30 (last entry).

Fee: House £3, Garden £3. Groups by arrangement. No children under 15.

RYCOTE

Rycote Chapel

OX9 2PE (off B4013)

This small private chapel was founded in 1449 by Richard Quatremayne. It has its original font, and a particularly fine 17th-century interior. The chapel was visited by both Elizabeth I and Charles I.

Times: Open Apr-Sep, Fri-Sun & BH's 2-6.

Fee: £1.60 (ch 5-15 80p, under 5's free) (if assisted)

STONOR

Stonor House & Park

RG9 6HF (on B480)
☎ 01491 638587 01491 638587
e-mail: lisa@stonorpark.co.uk

The house dates back to 1190 but features a Tudor façade. It has a medieval Catholic chapel which is still in use today, and shows some of the earliest domestic architecture in Oxfordshire. Its treasures include rare furniture, paintings, sculptures and tapestries from Britain, Europe and America. The house is set in beautiful gardens commanding views of the surrounding deer park.

Times: Open Apr-Sep, Sun 2-5.30; Jul & Aug, Wed 2-5.30; BH Mons, Sat 27 May, 24 Jun & 26 Aug only 2-5.30. Parties by appointment.

Fee: £4.50 (ch 14 accompanied free). Gardens only £2.50. Party 12+ shop (ex in grounds on lead)

UFFINGTON

Castle, White Horse & Dragon Hill

(S of B4507)

The 'castle' is an Iron Age fort on the ancient Ridgeway Path. It covers about eight acres and has only one gateway. On the hill below the fort is the White Horse, a 375ft prehistoric figure carved in the chalky hillside and thought to be about 2000 years old.

Times: Open - accessible any reasonable time. **Fee:** Free.

WITNEY

Cogges Manor Farm Museum

Church Ln, Cogges OX8 6LA (0.5m SE off A4022)
☎ 01993 772602 01993 703056

The museum includes the Manor, dairy and walled garden, and has breeds of animals typical of the Victorian period. The first floor of the manor contains period rooms.

Times: Open Apr-Oct, Tue-Fri & BH Mon 10.30-5.30, Sat & Sun 12-5.30. Early closing Oct. (Closed Good Fri).

Fee: £4 (ch £2, pen, students & UB40 £2.50). Family ticket (2 adults + 2 children) £11.

(wheelchair available) toilets for disabled shop 

WOODSTOCK

Blenheim Palace

OX20 1PX (M40 junct 9, follow signs to Blenheim, on A44 8m N of Oxford)
☎ 01993 811091 & 811325 (information line)
01993 813527

The Royal Manor of Woodstock and the sum of £240,000 to build the Palace were given to the Duke of Marlborough by Queen Anne as a reward for his victory over the French at Blenheim in 1704. The Palace is set in a 2100-acre park landscaped by 'Capability' Brown who created a lake spanned by a 390-foot bridge. Sir Winston Churchill was born in the Palace in 1874 and is buried nearby.

Times: Open: Palace & Gardens mid Mar-Oct, daily 10.30-5.30 (last admission 4.45pm). Park all year.

Fee: £9 (pen, 16-17 year olds & students £7). Family ticket £22.50. Group rates. licensed (ramps, disabled parking) toilets for disabled shop (ex in park on leads)

Oxfordshire Museum

Fletcher's House OX20 1SN (A44 Stratford-upon-Avon road from Oxford)
☎ 01993 811456 01993 813239
e-mail: oxon.museum@oxfordshire.go.uk

Permanently displayed in Fletcher's House is an exhibition of the story of Oxfordshire and its people, from early times to the present day. The house, which is an elegant townhouse with pleasant gardens, also has temporary exhibitions.

Times: Open all year, Jan-Apr & Oct-Dec, Tue-Fri 10-4, Sat 10-5, Sun 2-5; May-Sep Tue-Sat, 10-5, Sun 2-5. (Closed Good Fri & 25-26 Dec). Galleries are closed on Mon

Fee: £1 (concessions 50p under 18's free). Credit cards can only be used if combined admissions exceeds £10. shop

Rutland

A mere twenty miles across, the county of Rutland was reinstated in 1997 due to public demand from Rutlanders who had fiercely maintained their identity through twenty years as part of Leicestershire. The county motto is "Multum in Parvo", which is Latin for 'much in little'.

Oakham is the only town of any size in the county, and as Rutland only has a population of around 35,000 it's not hard to imagine what kind of size that is! Those who don't live there inhabit one of the fifty or so villages, or the other two towns, Uppingham and Stamford.

Many of these villages have their own little oddities which are so tantalising to students of eccentric England. For example, Wing has a strange ancient turf maze, the story of the fools who tried to fence a cuckoo in, and the Wise Woman of Wing.

Some famous connections with Rutland are John Clare, the 18th-century pastoral poet; the Gunpowder Plotters (who are said to have met at Stoke Dry); Thomas Barker, a pioneer of modern weather forecasting, and more recently the TV production of George Eliot's '*Middlemarch*', which was filmed at Stamford.

Apart from its small attractions, Rutland also has a large one. Rutland Water is, at 5,000 acres, the largest man-made reservoir in Europe. As well as a mass of wildlife and water pursuits such as windsurfing and sailing, Rutland Water has its own church, Normanton Church, which sits on an outcrop that juts out onto the Water itself.

Top: Normanton Church at Rutland Water

LYDDINGTON

Bede House

Blue Coat Ln
☎ 01572 822438

Built in the late 15th century as the episcopal residence of the Bishops of Lincoln, Bede House was the administrative centre of their vast diocese. Later it became an almshouse. Beautiful wooden ceilings, painted glass and a grand fireplace bear witness to its former life as a palace.

Times: Open Apr-Sep, daily 10-6 (Oct 10-5).
Fee: £2.60 (ch 5-15 £1.30, under 5's free).
♿ 🐕 #

OAKHAM

Oakham Castle

off Market Place (off Market place in the town centre)
☎ 01572 723654 📠 01572 757576

An exceptionally fine Norman Great Hall of a 12th-century fortified manor house. Earthworks, walls and remains of an earlier motte can be seen along with medieval sculptures and unique presentation horseshoes forfeited by peers of the realm and royalty to the Lord of the Manor. Licensed for Civil Marriages. Please enquire for details of the Oakham Festival.

Times: Open all year. Grounds daily 10-5.30 (4pm late Oct-late Mar). Great Hall Tue-Sat & BH Mon 10-1 & 2-5.30, Sun 2-5.30 (4pm late Oct-late Mar).Closed Mon, Good Fri & Xmas. Hours are subject to change).
Fee: Free.
P (400 yds) (disabled parking only by notification) ♿ shop 🐕 (ex guide dogs)

Rutland County Museum

Catmos St LE15 6HW (on A6003, S of town centre)
☎ 01572 723654 📠 01572 757576

The Museum of Rutland Life has displays of farming equipment, machinery and wagons, rural tradesmen's tools, domestic collections and local archaeology, all housed in a splendid late 18th-century cavalry riding school. There is a special gallery on the Volunteer Soldier in Leicestershire and Rutland.

Times: Open all year, Mon-Sat 10-5. Sun 2-5 (Apr-Oct, 2-4 Nov-Mar). (Closed Good Fri & Xmas)
Fee: Free.
P (adjacent) ☕ ♿ (induction loop in cafe & meeting room) toilets for disabled shop 🐕 (ex guide dogs)

Shropshire

Shropshire is a mainly agricultural county in the west of England, on the Welsh border. Home to beautiful rivers and lakes, as well as spectacular walking opportunities, the county is sparsely populated and has some fine market towns.

Britain's longest river, the Severn, flows from northwest to southeast, and other natural features are the 'Shropshire Lakes' at Ellesmere in the northwest, and the Clee Hills in the south, between Ludlow and Kidderminster, rising to 1,800 ft (610m). Brown Clee is the highest coalfield in Britain. The two ridges, Wenlock Edge and the Long Mynd, running either side of Church Stretton, are much favoured by walkers. This lovely part of the country was immortalised in A E Houseman's nostalgic collection of verses, *A Shropshire Lad*, published in 1896.

The two largest centres of population in a generally sparsely populated county are Shrewsbury, the county town, situated on a hilly site in a loop of the River Severn, and Telford New Town, named after the famous engineer, Thomas Telford. In the 5th century, Shrewsbury was the capital of the kingdom of Powys, with the name Pengwern (later part of Mercia). A rich legacy of half-timbered Tudor buildings and red brick Georgian buildings remains, along with the castle, which has Norman origins.

There are some fine market towns, well worth a visit. Chief among these are Ludlow, capital of the Marches, and widely held to be one of the most beautiful of British towns, with its intricately decorated black and white buildings; Bishop's Castle, retaining much of its medieval character, and the dramatically located hilltop town of Bridgnorth.

EVENTS & FESTIVALS

May
6-7 Shropshire Game Fair, Chetwynd Park, Newport
18-19 West Midland Agricultural Show, Shrewsbury
28 Fun Day in the Quarry, Shrewsbury

June
16 Shrewsbury Carnival
20-25 Much Wenlock Festival
29 Jun-6 Jul International Music Festival, Shrewsbury
23 Jun-8 Jul Ludlow Festival in the ruins of Ludlow Castle
tbc International Kite & Boomerang Festival, Shrewsbury

July
7-8 Bishops Castle Real Ale Festival

August
4 Oswestry Show, Oswestry
10-11 Shrewsbury Flower Festival
25-26 Bridgnorth Folk Festival
26-27 County of Salop Steam Rally
tbc Shrewsbury Real Ale Festival

December
6 Dec-5 Jan Music Hall Pantomime, Shrewsbury

Top: Telford, the River Severn

ACTON BURNELL

Acton Burnell Castle

SY5 7PE (on unclass road 8m S of Shrewsbury)

Now ruined, this fortified manor house was built in the late 13th century by Robert Burnell, the Chancellor of the time.

Times: Open at all reasonable times.

Fee: Free.

♿ ⌗

ACTON SCOTT

Acton Scott Historic Working Farm

Wenlock Lodge SY6 6QN (follow tourist signs off A49)

☎ 01694 781306 & 781307 📠 01694 781569

Times: Open 28 Mar-29 Oct, Tue-Sun 10-5; BH Mon 10-5.

P ☕ ♿ (Braille guide, wheelchairs available) toilets for disabled shop 🐕 (ex guide dogs) *Details not confirmed for 2001*

ATCHAM

Attingham Park

SY4 4TP (4m SE of Shrewsbury on B4380)

☎ 01743 708123 📠 01743 708175

e-mail: matsec@smtp.ntrust.org.uk

Though Attingham was constructed around an earlier building, most of what one sees today dates from the 18th and early 19th centuries. This even applies to the garden, where the planting remains very much as advised by Humphry Repton in 1797-8. The picture gallery was designed by Nash, who made early use of curved cast iron and glass for the ceiling.

Times: House open mid Mar-Oct, Fri-Tue 1.30-5, BH Mon 11-5. Deer park & grounds daily Mar-Oct 9am-8pm, Nov-Feb 9am-5pm.

P ☕ ♿ (2 electric self drive buggies) toilets for disabled shop 🐕 (ex guide & hearing dogs) ❀ *Details not confirmed for 2001*

BENTHALL

Benthall Hall

TF12 5RX (on B4375)

☎ 01952 882159

The exact date of the house is not known, but it seems to have been started in the 1530s and then altered in the 1580s. It is an attractive sandstone building with mullioned windows, fine oak panelling and a splendid carved staircase.

Times: Open Apr-Sep, Wed, Sun & BH Mon 1.30-5.30. Last admission 5pm. Other days by appointment only.

P ♿ 🐕 ❀ *Details not confirmed for 2001*

BOSCOBEL

Boscobel House and The Royal Oak

Brewood ST19 9AR (on unclass road between A41 and A5)

☎ 01902 850244

The house was built around 1600 by John Giffard, a Roman Catholic, and includes a number of secret hiding places. One of them was used by King Charles II after his defeat at the Battle of Worcester in 1651.

Times: Open all year, Apr-Sep, daily 10-6 (Oct 10-5); Nov-Mar, Wed-Sun 10-4, last admission 30 minutes before closing. Closed 24-26 Dec & all Jan.

Fee: £4.30 (ch 5-15 £2.20, under 5's free).

P ☕ ♿ shop 🐕 ⌗

Whiteladies Priory (St Leonards Priory)

Only the ruins are left of this Augustinian nunnery, which dates from 1158 and was destroyed in the Civil War. After the Battle of Worcester Charles II hid here and in the nearby woods before going on to Boscobel House.

Times: Open any reasonable time.

Fee: Free.

⌗

BUILDWAS

Buildwas Abbey

TF8 7BW (on S bank of River Severn on B4378)

☎ 01952 433274

The beautiful, ruined, Cistercian abbey was founded in 1135, and stands in a picturesque setting. The church with its stout round pillars is roofless but otherwise almost complete.

Times: Open Apr-Sep, daily 10-6; Oct, daily 10-5.

Fee: £1.95 (ch £1, concessions £1.50)

♿ ⌗

BURFORD

Burford House Gardens

WR15 8HQ (off A456)

☎ 01584 810777 📠 01584 810673

e-mail: treasures@burford.co.uk

Times: Open all year 10-5. Dusk if earlier.

P ☕ ✕ licensed ♿ (ramp into gardens, sloping paths) toilets for disabled shop garden centre 🐕 (ex in Plant Centre) *Details not confirmed for 2001*

COSFORD

Royal Air Force Museum

TF11 8UP (on A41, 1m S of Jct 3 on M54)

☎ 01902 376200 📠 01902 376211

Times: Open all year daily, 10-6 (last admission 4pm). Closed 24-26 Dec & 1 Jan).

P ✕ ♿ (limited amount of wheelchairs on request) toilets for disabled shop 🐕 *Details not confirmed for 2001*

CRAVEN ARMS

Shropshire Hills Discovery Centre

Ludlow Rd (on A49)

☎ 01743 252593 📠 01743 252277

e-mail: shiraz.kamaran@shropshire-cc.gov.uk

This brand new attraction explores the history, nature and geography of the Shropshire Hills, through a series of interactive displays and simulations. These include Landscape of Contrasts, Ancient Landscape, a simulated Balloon Flight, and Land of Inspiration. There is also a shop, restaurant and visitors' information centre.

contd.

Times: Open daily from 10am. (Closed mid Dec-mid Jan).
Fee: £4.75 (ch £2.75 & pen £3.75). Family ticket £12.25. Groups 20+
toilets for disabled shop (ex assistance dogs)

HAUGHMOND ABBEY

Haughmond Abbey

Upton Magna SY4 4RW (off B5062)
01743 709661

The ruined abbey was founded for Augustinian canons around 1135, and partly converted into a house during the Dissolution. The chapter house has a fine Norman doorway, and the abbot's lodging and the kitchens are well preserved.
Times: Open Apr-Oct, daily 10-6 (5pm Oct)
Fee: £1.95 (ch 5-15 £1, under 5's free).

HODNET

Hodnet Hall Gardens

TF9 3NN
01630 685202 01630 685853

Sixty acres of landscaped gardens offer tranquillity among pools, lush plants and trees. Big game trophies adorn the 17th-century tearooms, and plants are usually for sale in the kitchen gardens. The house, rebuilt in Victorian-Elizabethan style, is not open.
Times: Open Apr-Sep, Tue-Sun & BH Mon 12-5.
Fee: £3.25 (ch £1.20, pen £2.75). Party.
(1 wheelchair available) toilets for disabled shop garden centre

IRONBRIDGE

Ironbridge Gorge Museums

TF8 7AW (M54 junct 4, signposted)
01952 433522, 432166 or 0800 590258
01952 432204
e-mail: info@ironbridge.org.uk

Ironbridge is the site of the world's first iron bridge, it was cast and built here in 1779, to span a narrow gorge over the River Severn. Now Ironbridge is the site of a remarkable series of museums relating the story of the bridge, recreating life in Victorian times and featuring ceramics and social history displays.
Times: Open all year, 10-5. Some small sites closed Nov-Mar. Telephone or write for exact winter details.
Fee: £10 (ch & student £6, pen £9). Family £30. Passport to all sites, until all have been visited. It is therefore possible to return to Ironbridge on different days to ensure the whole atmosphere of the museums are captured.
licensed (wheelchairs,potters wheel,braille guide,lifts,hearing loop) toilets for disabled shop (ex Blists Hill & guide dogs)

LILLESHALL

Lilleshall Abbey

TF10 9HW (1.5m SW off A518 on unclass road)

In the beautiful grounds of Lilleshall Hall, ruined Lilleshall Abbey was founded shortly before the middle of the 12th century and from the high west front visitors can look down the entire 228ft length of the abbey church.
Times: Open Apr-Oct, any reasonable time. (Closed Nov-Mar).
Fee: Free.

LUDLOW

Ludlow Castle

Castle Square SY8 1AY
01584 873355

Ludlow Castle dates from about 1086. In 1473, Edward IV sent the Prince of Wales and his brother - later to become the Princes in the Tower - to live here and Ludlow Castle became a seat of government. John Milton's *Comus* was first performed at Ludlow Castle in 1634; now contemporary performances of Shakespeare's plays, together with concerts, are put on in the castle grounds during the Ludlow Festival (2 weeks, end June-early July).
Times: Open Jan Sat-Sun 10-4; Feb-Apr daily 10-4; May-Jul daily 10-5; Aug daily 10-7; Sep daily 10-5; Oct-Dec daily 10-4 (last admission 30 minutes before closing).
Fee: £3 (ch under 6 free, ch 6+ £1.50, pen £2.50). Family ticket £8.50.
(100 yds) toilets for disabled shop

LYDBURY NORTH

Walcot Hall

SY7 8AZ (3 miles E of Bishops Castle, on B4385, beside the Powls Arms)
020 7581 2782 020 7589 0195
e-mail: robin@explorationplc.com

Built by Sir William Chambers for Lord Clive of India. The Georgian House possesses a free-standing and recently restored Ballroom, stableyard with matching clock towers and extensive walled garden, in addition to its ice house, meat-safe and dovecote. There is an Arboretum, noted for its rhododendrons and azaleas, specimen trees, pools and a lake.
Times: Open BH & last Sun-Mon in May. Other times, by appointment.
Fee: £2.50 (ch under 15 free)
(lift to 1st floor) toilets for disabled

MORETON CORBET

Castle

A small 13th-century keep and the ruins of an impressive Elizabethan house are all that remain: the house was destroyed in the Civil War.
Times: Open all reasonable times.
Fee: Free.

MUCH WENLOCK

Much Wenlock Priory

TA3 6HS
01952 727466

The original priory, founded here as a convent in the 7th century, was destroyed by the Danes but was rebuilt and the ruins date from the 11th century and later periods.

Times: Open all year, Apr-Oct, daily 10-6 (Oct 10-5); Nov-Mar, Wed-Sun 10-4. Closed 24-26 Dec & 1 Jan.

Fee: £2.70 (ch £1.40, under 5's free). Personal stereo tour included in price, also available for the partially sighted, those with learning difficulties and in French & German.

P #

OSWESTRY

Old Oswestry Hill Fort

(1m N, accessible from unclass road off A483)

This Iron Age hill-fort covers 68 acres, has five ramparts and an elaborate western portal. Part of the prehistoric Wat's Dyke abuts the site.

Times: Open any reasonable time.

Fee: Free.

#

QUATT

Dudmaston

WV15 6QN (4m SE of Bridgnorth on A442)

☎ 01746 780866 📠 01746 780744

e-mail: mouefe@smtp.ntrust.org.uk

The 17th-century flower paintings which belonged to Francis Darby of Coalbrookdale are exhibited in this house of the same period, with modern works, botanical art and fine furniture. The house stands in an extensive parkland garden and there are dingle and lakeside walks.

Times: Open Apr-Sep, Teu, Wed & Sun & BH Mons, 2-5.30. Garden noon-6. Closed Good Fri.

P ♿ (Braille guides, taped tours) toilets for disabled shop (ex in grounds) *Details not confirmed for 2001*

SHREWSBURY

Shrewsbury Castle and Shropshire Regimental Museum

The Castle, Castle St SY1 2AT (located in town centre, adjacent to railway station)

☎ 01743 358516 📠 01743 354811

e-mail: museums@shrewbury-atcham.gov.uk

The museum of The King's Shropshire Light Infantry and The Shropshire Yeomanry is housed in the main surviving building of Shrewsbury Castle which once dominated the town. The grounds contain the medieval 'motte' and the romantic 'Laura's Tower'.

Times: Open Tue-Sat 10-4.30, also Sun from Etr-1 Oct & BH Mon. Castle grounds open Mon also. Closed Dec/Jan. Telephone for winter opening times.

Fee: £2 (£1 concessions). All local residents, ch under 18 or in full time education free.

P (3 mins NCP) (on street parking by voucher only) ♿ (please ask staff for assistance) toilets for disabled shop (ex guide dogs)

Shrewsbury Quest

193 Abbey Foregate SY2 6AH (opposite Shrewsbury Abbey)

☎ 01743 243324 📠 01743 244342

An opportunity to experience the sights, sounds and smells of medieval England. The Quest is based on 12th-century England in general and monastic life in particular. It provides a full 'hands-on' experience for visitors, who are encouraged to create their own illuminated manuscript, try their hand at medieval cloister games and interact with the historical characters in this 12th-century world.

Times: Open Apr-Oct 10-5 (last admission); Nov-Mar 10-4 (last admission). Closed 25-26 Dec & 1 Jan.

Fee: £4.50 (ch £2.95, concessions £3.80). Family £13.40.

P (charged) ✕ licensed ♿ (Braille maps, lift) toilets for disabled shop (ex assistance dogs)

STOKESAY

Stokesay Castle

SY7 9AH (1m S of Craven Arms off A49)

☎ 01588 672544

Well-preserved and little altered, this 13th-century manor house has a romantic setting. It has a fine timber-framed Jacobean gatehouse, a great hall and a solar with 17th-century panelling.

Times: Open all year, Apr-Sep, daily 10-6 (Oct 10-5); Nov-mid Mar, Wed-Sun 10-4, closed 1-2pm Nov-Mar.

Fee: £3.50 (ch 5-15 £1.80, under 5's free). Personal stereo tour included in admission price.

P ♿ (tape tour for visually handicapped, ramp for wheelchairs) toilets for disabled

WESTON-UNDER-REDCASTLE

Hawkstone Historic Park & Follies

SY4 5UY (3m from Hodnet off A53)

☎ 01939 200611 📠 01939 200311

e-mail: info@hawkstone.co.uk

Times: Open Apr-2 Jul, Wed-Sun & BHs from 10.30am (10pm wknd), last admission 4pm. 3 Jul-3 Sep, every day, last admission 5pm. 4 Sep-29 Oct, Wed-Sun, last admission 4pm. 6 Jan-Mar, wknds from 10am, last admission 3.30pm

P ✕ licensed ♿ (no access to follies due to terrain) toilets for disabled shop *Details not confirmed for 2001*

WROXETER

Roman Town

SY5 6PH (5m E of Shrewsbury, 1m S of A5)

☎ 01743 761330

These excavated remains of the Roman town of Virconium probably date from AD140 - 150. The fourth largest city in Roman Britain with impressive remains of the 2nd century municipal baths. There is an interesting museum with educational facilities.

Times: Open all year, Apr-Oct, daily 10-6 (Oct 10-5); Nov-Mar, Wed-Sun 10-4 (closed 1-2pm). Closed 24-26 Dec & 1 Jan.

Fee: £3.20 (ch 5-15 £1.60, under 5's free). Personal stereo tour included in admission.

P ♿ shop

Somerset

Somerset is rich with history and legend, as well as having some beautiful coastline and countryside. The name of the county comes from the Saxon, and literally translated means 'Land of the Summer People.'

One of the county's most famous landmarks is Glastonbury Tor, which once gave refuge to the ancient Britons. Legend has it that Joseph of Arimathea came to Glastonbury in a bid to convert the English. It is also the place where King Arthur and Gwynevere are said to be buried. Those interested in Arthurian legend should also visit South Cadbury, an Iron Age hill fort reputed to be the site of Camelot.

At the other end of the county lies the timeless, rugged beauty of Exmoor, most of which is now a National Park. R. D. Blackmore's novel *Lorna Doone* is set here. There is also a mystery on Exmoor. No one knows when the Tarr Steps were built across the Barle, but they may be prehistoric.

The seaside resorts of Minehead, Burnham-on-Sea and Weston-super-Mare are great places to enjoy a family holiday. Dunster is further inland and walking through it is a little like taking a time machine through 900 years of history. The town is overshadowed by the Norman splendour of Dunster Castle, owned by the National Trust.

In the heart of Somerset lies Wells, the smallest city in England, whose cathedral is decorated with stone figures. The city also boasts Vicar's Close, often described as the most complete medieval street in Europe.

EVENTS & FESTIVALS

April
tbc Taunton Marathon

May
5-6 Bath Annual Spring Flower Show, Royal Avenue
18 May-3 June Bath International Music Festival
25 May-10 Jun Bath Fringe Festival
30 May-2 Jun The Royal Bath & West Show, Shepton Mallet

June
tbc Glastonbury Festival of Contemporary Performing Arts, Worthy Farm, Pilton

July
7 Glastonbury Pilgrimage (Glastonbury Abbey, Abbey Gatehouse, Magdalene Street)
27 Jul-4 Aug Glastonbury International Dance Festival (various venues)

August
1-2 Flower Show, Taunton

September
tbc Wellington Carnival

October
20 Taunton Carnival

November
tbc Bridgwater Guy Fawkes Carnival, Bridgwater

Top: Stogursey Castle gatehouse

AXBRIDGE

King John's Hunting Lodge

The Square BS26 2AP
☎ 01934 732012

Nothing to do with King John or with hunting, this jettied and timber-framed house was built around 1500. It gives a good indication of the wealth of the merchants of that time and is now a museum of local history, with old photographs, paintings and items such as the town stocks and constables' staves.

Times: Open Etr-Sep, daily 2-5.
Fee: Free.

BARRINGTON

Barrington Court Garden

TA19 0NQ (5m NE of Ilminster on B3168)
☎ 01460 241938
e-mail: wbagen@smtp.ntrust.org.uk

The house dates from the 17th century, but the gardens were created in the 1920s, with the help (through the post) of Gertrude Jekyll. They are laid out in 'rooms' and there is a large walled kitchen garden supplying fresh fruit and vegetables to the restaurant.

Times: Open Mar & Oct: Fri, Sat & Sun 11-4.30; Apr- 29 Jun & Sep: daily ex Fri 11-5.30; Jul & Aug daily 11-5.30.
Fee: £4.20 (ch £2.10). Family £10.50. Parties.
licensed (batricars available, braille guides)

BATH

American Museum

Claverton Manor BA2 7BD (2.5m SE)
☎ 01225 460503 01225 480726
e-mail: amibbath@aol.com

Claverton Manor is two miles south east of Bath, in a beautiful setting above the River Avon. The house was built in 1820 by Sir Jeffrey Wyatville, and is now a museum of American decorative arts. The gardens are well worth seeing, and include an American arboretum and a replica of George Washington's garden at Mount Vernon. The Folk Art Gallery and the New Gallery are among the many exhibits in the grounds along with seasonal exhibitions.

Times: Open 25 Mar-29 Oct, Tue-Sun 2-5. Gardens 1-6. BH Sun & Mon 11-5.
Fee: £5.50 (ch £3, pen £5).
toilets for disabled shop (on leads only) 

Bath Abbey

BA1 1LY (centre of Bath, next to Pump Rooms)
☎ 01225 422462 01225 429990
e-mail: office@bathabbey.org

The 15th-century abbey church was built on the site of the Saxon abbey where King Edgar was crowned in 973. The church is Perpendicular style with Norman arches and superb fan-vaulting. The famous West Front carvings represent the founder-bishop's dream of angels ascending and descending from heaven.

Times: Open all year, Apr-Oct Mon-Sat 9-6; Nov-Mar 9-4.30. Sun all year 1-2.30 & 4.30-5.30.
Fee: Free.
P (limited street parking) toilets for disabled shop

Bath Postal Museum

8 Broad St BA1 5LJ
☎ 01225 460333 01225 460333

Discover how 18th-century Bath influenced and developed the Postal System, including the story of the Penny Post. The first letter sent with a stamp was sent from this very building. Visitors can explore the history of written communication from Egyptian clay tables thousands of years ago, to the first Airmail flight from Bath to London in 1912. See the Victorian Post Office and then visit the tea room and shop.

Times: Open all year, Mon-Sat 11-5, Sun 2-5. Parties by appointment. (Closed 25-26 Dec & 1 Jan).
Fee: £2.90 (ch £1.20, ch 7 free, pen, UB40 & students £1.95). Party 10+.
P (200yds) toilets for disabled shop

The Book Museum

Manvers St BA1 1JW
☎ 01225 466000 01225 482122

The Museum includes an exhibition of first and early editions of authors who lived in Bath, such as Jane Austen and Charles Dickens.

Times: Open all year, Mon-Fri 9-1 & 2-5.30, Sat 9.30-1. (Closed 25 Dec & BH).
Fee: £2 (ch £1).
P (NCP) shop

The Building of Bath Museum

Countess of Huntingdons Chapel, The Vineyards, The Paragon BA1 5NA (M4 junct 18, A46 towards Bath city centre. Take A4, 2nd exit at mini rdbt. Along road on right)
☎ 01225 333895 01225 445473

Times: Open 15 Feb-1 Dec, Tue-Sun & BH's 10.30-5.
P (500m) shop (ex guide dogs) *Details not confirmed for 2001*

Holburne Museum of Art

Great Pulteney St BA2 4DB (follow signs to Bristol via A4 or A431)
☎ 01225 466669 01225 333121

This elegant building shows 17th and 18th-century collections of fine and decorative art, notably silver, porcelain, glass, furniture and Old Master paintings. There is an annual programme of events and lively lectures.

Times: Open mid Feb-mid Dec, Mon-Sat & BHs 11-5, Sun 2.30-5.30 (Closed Mon Nov-Etr).
Fee: £3.50 (ch £1.50, UB40 & student £2, other concessions £3). Family ticket £7.
(lift to all floors) toilets for disabled shop (ex guide dogs)

Museum of Bath at Work

Julian Rd BA1 2RH
☎ 01225 318348 📠 01225 318348
e-mail: stuart@bihc.freeserve.co.uk

The centre houses the Bowler collection, and the entire stock-in-trade of various Victorian craftsmen. Also here is 'The Story of Bath Stone', with a replica of a mine face before mechanisation, and a Bath cabinet-maker's workshop. Horstmann Car Gallery is a new feature, plus a computerised information point of Bath's heritage at work.

Times: Open all year, Etr-1 Nov, daily 10-5; Nov-Etr, wknds 10-5. (Closed 25-26 Dec).
Fee: £3.50 (ch, pen & students £2.50). Family ticket £10.
P (0.25 mile) shop

Museum of Costume

Bennett St BA1 2QH
☎ 01225 477785 📠 01225 477743
e-mail: costume.bookings.gov.uk

The Museum of Costume is a prestigious collection of fashionable dress covering the period from the late 16th century to the present day. It is housed in Bath's famous 18th-century Assembly Rooms designed by John Wood the Younger in 1771. Entrance to the Assembly Rooms is free. Special event: Fashion in the Fifties (early Dec 2000 to early Nov 2001) a special exhibition of clothes from the modern collection.

Times: Open all year, daily 10-5 (Closed 25 & 26 Dec). Last admission 30 mins before closing.
Fee: £4 (ch £2.90). Family ticket £11. Combined ticket with Roman Baths, £8.90 (ch £5.30)
P (5 mins walk) (park & ride recommended) ♿ (audio guides available) toilets for disabled shop (ex guide books)

No 1 Royal Crescent

BA1 2LR
☎ 01225 428126 📠 01225 481850
e-mail: admin@bobm.freeserve.co.uk

Bath is very much a Georgian city, but most of its houses have naturally altered over the years to suit changing tastes and lifestyles. Built in 1768 by John Wood the Elder, No 1 Royal Crescent has been restored to look as it would have done some 200 years ago.

Times: Open 15 Feb-29 Oct Tue-Sun 10.30-5; 31 Oct-26 Nov Tue-Sun 10.30-4. Open BH Mon & Bath Festival Mon 22 May. (Closed Good Fri). Last admission 30 mins before closing.
Fee: £4 (concessions £3.50). Family ticket £10. Party 10+.
P (5 mins walk) (street parking with card £1 per hour) shop (ex guide dogs)

Roman Baths & Pump Room

Abbey Church Yard BA1 1LZ
☎ 01225 477785 📠 01225 477743
e-mail: romanbaths.bookings.gov.uk

The remains of the Roman baths give a vivid impression of life nearly 2000 years ago. Built next to Britain's only hot spring, the baths served the sick and the pilgrims visiting the adjacent Temple of Sulis Minerva. Above the Temple Courtyard, the Pump Room became a popular meeting place in the 18th century. No visit is complete without a taste of the famous hot spa water.

Times: Open all year, Apr-Jul & Sep, daily 9-6; Aug daily 9-9.30; Oct-Mar, daily 9.30-5. (Closed 25 & 26 Dec). Last admission 30 mins before closing.
Fee: £6.90 (ch £4). Family ticket £17.50. Combined ticket with Museum of Costume £8.90 (ch £5.30). Disabled visitors free admission to ground floor areas.
P (5 mins walk) (park & ride recommended) ✕ licensed ♿ (sign language & audio tours) toilets for disabled shop (ex guide dogs)

Royal Photographic Society

The Octagon, Milsom St BA1 1DN
☎ 01225 462841 📠 01225 448688
e-mail: rps@rps.org

Built in 1796 as a chapel, The Octagon now houses the world's oldest photographic society. Its galleries host an exciting and varied programme of exhibitions featuring names such as Heather Angel, David Bailey, and Linda McCartney. Our interactive Museum of Photography traces the development of the art from 1827 to the present day.

contd.

Times: Open all year, daily 9.30-5.30, last admission 4.45pm. (Closed 25-26 Dec).
Fee: £4 (ch, pen, students & UB40 £2, ch 7 & disabled free). Family ticket £8. Party 12+.
P (5 mins walk) licensed (chair lift to all floors) toilets for disabled shop (ex guide dogs)

SALLY LUNN'S REFRESHMENT HOUSE & MUSEUM

4 North Pde Passage BA1 1NX (Centre of Bath, follow signs, next to Bath Abbey)
☎ 01225 461634 & 811311 (office)
01225 447090
e-mail: corsham@aol.com

This Tudor building is Bath's oldest house and was a popular 17th-century meeting place. The traditional 'Sally Lunn' is similar to a brioche, and it is popularly believed to carry the name of its first maker who came to Bath in 1680. The bun is still served in the restaurant, and the original oven, Georgian cooking range and a collection of baking utensils are displayed in the museum.
Times: Open all year, Museum - Mon-Fri 10-6, Sat 10-6, Sun 11-6. (Closed 25-26 Dec & 1 Jan).
Fee: 30p (concessions free)
P (cards required for street parking) licensed (braille menu for the blind) shop (ex guide dogs)

CASTLE CARY

HADSPEN GARDEN & NURSERY

Hadspen House BA7 7NG (2m SE off A371)
☎ 01749 813707 01749 813707

Situated within a 17th-century curved wall, this five acre garden has borders planted with roses and herbaceous plants, many of which have been developed here. Plants grown in the garden are available in the adjoining nursery.
Times: Open Mar-1 Oct, Thu-Sun & BHs 10-5.
Fee: £3 (ch 50p). Free admission for wheelchair users.
P toilets for disabled garden centre (ex guide dogs)

CHARD

FORDE ABBEY

TA20 4LU (4m S of Chard, follow brown tourist signs)
☎ 01460 221290 01460 220296

This 12th-century Cistercian monastery was converted into a private dwelling in the mid-17th century by Cromwell's attorney general. In the house there are good pictures and furniture and an outstanding set of Mortlake tapestries. The large grounds include a kitchen garden, rock garden and bog garden as well as herbaceous borders and many outstanding trees.
Times: Gardens, open all year, daily 10-4.30. Abbey & gardens Apr-Oct Tue-Thu, Sun & BH 1-4.30.
Fee: Gardens £4 (ch free, pen £3.80). House & Gardens £5.20 (ch free, pen £5).
P (wheelchair can be borrowed) toilets for disabled shop garden centre (ex garden)

CLEVEDON

CLEVEDON COURT

Tickenham Rd BS21 6QU (off B3130 1.5m E of Clevedon)
☎ 01275 872257

Clevedon Court is a remarkably complete manor house of around 1320AD. Additions have been made in each century, so it has a pleasing variety of styles, with an 18th-century terraced garden.
Times: Open 2 Apr-28 Sep, Wed-Thu, Sun & BH Mon 2-5.
Fee: £4 (ch £2). Party 20+ by arrangement.
P (ground floor accessible via 4 steps)

CRANMORE

EAST SOMERSET RAILWAY

Cranmore Railway Station BA4 4QP (on A361 between Frome & Shepton Mallet)
☎ 01749 880417 01749 880764
Times: Open daily Mar-24 Dec from 10am. For days when steam trains are operating phone 01749 880417.
P licensed (ramp from road to platform) toilets for disabled shop *Details not confirmed for 2001*

CRICKET ST THOMAS

THE WILDLIFE PARK AT CRICKET ST THOMAS

TA20 4DB (3m E of Chard on A30, follow brown & white signs).
☎ 01460 30111 01460 30817

The Wildlife Park has over 600 animals and birds from around the world, many at risk from extinction. The walk-through Lemur World is a sanctuary for three different species of lemur, providing a natural habitat for breeding. Other attractions include leopards, daily falconry displays, animal feeding, and a safari train, all set in over 1,000 acres of countryside.
Times: Open all year, daily from 10, last admission 4. (Closed 25 Dec).
Fee: £4.95 (ch 4-14 £3.75 & pen £4, under 3's free). Family ticket £16.
P licensed toilets for disabled shop (ex guide dogs)

DUNSTER

DUNSTER CASTLE

TA24 6SL (3m SE of Minehead, approach from A39)
☎ 01643 821314 01643 823000
e-mail: wdugen@smtp.ntrust.org.uk

The castle's picturesque appearance is largely due to 19th-century work, but older features can also be seen, the superb 17th-century oak staircase for example. Sub-tropical plants flourish in the 28-acre park and the terraced gardens are noted for exotica such as a giant lemon tree, yuccas, mimosa and palms.
Times: Open: Castle - Apr-27 Sep Sat-Wed 11-5; 30 Sep-1 Nov 11-4. Garden & Park - Apr-29 Sep daily 10-5; Jan-Mar & 30 Sep-Dec, daily 11-4. (Closed 25-29 Dec).
Fee: Castle, Garden & Park £5.50 (ch under 16 £3). Family ticket £14. Garden & park only £3 (ch under 16 £1.30). Family ticket £7.30.
P (Braille guide, Batricar for grounds) toilets for disabled shop

EAST HUNTSPILL

Secret World-Badger & Wildlife Reserve Centre

New Rd TA9 3PZ (Signposted from A38, 1m S of Highbridge)

☎ 01278 783250 01278 793109

This wildlife rescue centre enables visitors to see foxes, badgers, owls and other animals in natural surroundings. The 17th-century farmhouse is now a tearoom, serving meals throughout the day. There are farm demonstrations and talks as well.

Times: Open Mar-Nov, daily 10-6. Nov-Dec, daily 10-5. Feb- Mar, daily 10-5.

Fee: £4.95 (ch £3.50, pen £4.50). Family £15.50. Party.

toilets for disabled shop garden centre

EAST LAMBROOK

East Lambrook Manor Garden

TA13 5HH (signed off A303, at South Petherton roundabout)

☎ 01460 240328 01460 242344

e-mail: elambrook@aol.com

It was the late Margery Fish who created the concept of 'cottage gardening' in the 1930s, and her wonderful Grade I listed gardens are known to garden lovers throughout the world. The gardens are now under extensive restoration and house the National Collection of Geraniums, a specialist plant nursery, a tea shop and art gallery.

Times: Open all year Mon-Sat 10-5.

Fee: £2.50 (ch 50p & pen £2). Party.

shop garden centre (ex guide dogs)

FARLEIGH HUNGERFORD

Farleigh Hungerford Castle

BA3 6RS (3.5m W of Trowbridge on A366)

☎ 01225 754026

The ruined 14th-century castle has a chapel containing wall paintings, stained glass and the fine tomb of Sir Thomas Hungerford who built the castle. His powerful family and the castle are linked with various grim tales.

Times: Open all year, Apr-Oct, daily 10-6 (Oct 10-5); Nov-Mar, daily 10-4 (closed 1-2pm). Closed 24-26 Dec & 1 Jan.

Fee: £2.30 (ch 5-15 £1.20, under 5's free)

GLASTONBURY

Glastonbury Abbey

Abbey Gatehouse, Magdalene St BA6 9EL (on A361 between Frome & Taunton)

☎ 01458 832267 01458 832267

e-mail: glastonbury.abbey@dial.pipex.com

Few places in Britain are as rich in myth and legend as Glastonbury. Tradition maintains that the impressive ruins mark the birth place of Christianity in Britain. Joseph of Arimathea is said to have founded a chapel here in AD61, planting his staff in the ground where it flowered both at Christmas and Easter. Later, it is said, King Arthur and Guinevere were buried here, and the abbey has been a place of pilgrimage since the Middle Ages. The present abbey ruins date mostly from the 12th and 13th centuries, but it fell into decay after the Dissolution. The display area contains artefacts and a model of the Abbey as it might have been in 1539.

Times: Open all year, daily, Jun-Aug 9-6; Sep-May 9.30-6pm or dusk, whichever is the earliest. Dec-Feb open at 10am. (Closed 25 Dec).

Fee: £3 (ch 5-15 £1, pen & students £2.50). Family ticket £6.50.

(charged) (all areas except Lady Chapel, audio tape, deaf loop) toilets for disabled shop (only on leads)

KINGSDON

Lytes Cary Manor

TA11 7HU (off A303)

☎ 01985 843600

Much of the present house was built in the 16th century although the oldest part, the chapel, dates from 1343. The Great Hall was a 15th-century addition. Unfortunately the gardens did not survive, but the present formal gardens are being restocked with plants that were commonly grown at the time of building.

Times: Open Apr-30 Oct, Mon, Wed & Sat 2-6 or dusk if earlier. Also Fri in Jun, Jul & Aug.

Fee: £4 (ch £2)

(braille guide. scented plants)

MONKSILVER

Combe Sydenham Country Park

TA4 4JG

☎ 01984 656284 01984 656273

Times: Open Apr-Sep. Country Park: daily 9-5. Other attractions open by guided tour, Spring BH-Sep, Mon, Thu & Fri at 2pm.

(charged) (ex in park) *Details not confirmed for 2001*

MONTACUTE

Montacute House

TA15 6XP (off A3088)

☎ 01935 823289 01935 823289

e-mail: wmogen@smtp.ntrust.org.uk

Set amidst formal gardens, Montacute House was built by Sir Edward Phelips. He was a successful lawyer, and became Speaker of the House of Commons in 1604. Inside there are decorated ceilings, ornate fireplaces,

contd.

heraldic glass and fine wood panelling. The Long Gallery displays a permanent collection of Tudor and Jacobean portraits from the National Portrait Gallery in London.

Times: Open, Garden & Park: Apr-30 Oct daily (ex Tue) 11.30-5.30. Nov-Mar Wed-Sun 11.30-4. House: Apr-30 Oct, daily (ex Tue) 12-5.30.
Fee: House, Garden & Park £5.50 (ch £2.80) Family ticket £13.70. Garden & Park Apr-30 Oct £3.10 (ch £1.30), Nov-Mar £1.50. Party 15+.
P ✕ licensed ♿ (Braille guide) toilets for disabled shop garden centre (ex park)

MUCHELNEY

MUCHELNEY ABBEY

TA10 0DQ
☎ 01458 250664

Encircled by marshes, Muchelney seemed a suitably remote spot in the 8th century for a Benedictine Abbey. The ruins that remain date from the 15th and 16th centuries, however, and there is also a 14th-century priest's house nearby. Exhibitions include Stuart furnishings and examples of the work of modern potter, John Leach.

Times: Open Apr-Sep, daily 10-6 (5pm Oct).
Fee: £1.70 (ch 5-15 90p, under 5's free)
P ♿ #

NETHER STOWEY

COLERIDGE COTTAGE

TA5 1NQ (off A39)
☎ 01278 732662

It was in this small cottage that Coleridge was most inspired as a poet and here that he wrote *The Ancient Mariner*. The Coleridge family moved to Nether Stowey in 1796 and became friendly with the Wordsworths who lived nearby.

Times: Open 2 Apr-1 Oct, Tue-Thu & Sun 2-5.
Fee: £2.60. (ch £1).
P

NUNNEY

NUNNEY CASTLE

(3.5m SW of Frome, off A361)

Built in 1373, and supposedly modelled on France's Bastille, this crenellated manor house has one of the deepest moats in England. It was ruined by Parliamentarian forces in the Civil War.

Times: Open any reasonable time.
Fee: Free.
♿ #

RODE

RODE BIRD GARDENS

BA3 6QW (off A36 between Bath & Warminster)
☎ 01373 830326 01373 831288

Rode Bird Gardens consist of 17 acres of grounds, planted with trees, shrubs, and flower gardens, in a pretty and little-visited village. The bird collection consists of around 1200 birds of 200 different species, and there is also a clematis collection, an ornamental lake, a Pets' Corner, a children's play area, and an information centre. Children must be accompanied by an adult.

Times: Open all year daily (ex 25 Dec); Summer 10-6 (last admission 5pm); Winter 10-dusk (last admission 1hr before closing time).
Fee: £5.70 (ch under 15 £3.20, pen £5). Family ticket £17. Train ticket £1.30 (ch & pen £1.10).
P ♿ (special route, wheelchairs for hire) toilets for disabled shop (ex guide dogs)

SPARKFORD

HAYNES MOTOR MUSEUM

BA22 7LH (from A303 follow A359 road towards Castle Cary, the museum is clearly signposted)
☎ 01963 440804 01963 441004
e-mail: marc@haynesmotormuseum.co.uk

Spectacular collection of historic cars, motorcycles and motoring memorabilia. Vehicles range from a 1903 Oldsmobile to sports cars of the 50s and 60s and modern day classics. Also at the Museum is a 70 seat video cinema, the Hall of Motorsports, a millennium hall and a picnic area and children's adventure playground.

Times: Open all year, Mar-Oct , daily 9.30-5.30; Nov-Feb, 10-4.30. Etr-summer hols open to 6.30pm. (Closed 25 Dec & 1 Jan).
Fee: £4.95 (ch 5 £2.95, concessions £3.95)
P ♿ (ramps & loan wheelchairs available) toilets for disabled shop (ex guide dogs & in grounds)

STOKE ST GREGORY

WILLOW & WETLANDS VISITOR CENTRE

Meare Green Court TA3 6HY (between North Curry & Stoke St Gregory)
☎ 01823 490249 01823 490814
e-mail: phcoate@globalnet.co.k

The centre is owned and run by Somerset Basketmakers and willow growers P H Coate & Son. The environmental exhibition gives a fascinating insight into the Somerset Levels and Moors. Guided tours are available.

Times: Open all year, Mon-Fri 9-5 (guided tours 10-4), Sat (no tours) 9-5. Closed Sun.
Fee: Free.
P ♿ shop

STOKE-SUB-HAMDON

STOKE-SUB-HAMDON PRIORY

North St TA4 6QP (between A303 & A3088)
☎ 01985 843600

This 15th-century house is built of Ham Hill stone and was once the home of the priests of the chantry belonging to the now vanished Beauchamp Manor. The 14th-and 15th-century farm buildings and the screens passage of the chantry remain.

Times: Open 27 Mar-31 Oct, daily 10-6 or dusk if earlier. Great Hall only open to visitors.
Fee: Free.
P

STREET

The Shoe Museum

C & J Clark Ltd, High St BA16 0YA
☎ 01458 842169 📠 01458 443196
e-mail: jean.brook@clarks.com

The museum is in the oldest part of the shoe factory set up by Cyrus and James Clark in 1825. It contains shoes from Roman times to the present, buckles, engravings, fashion plates, machinery, hand tools and advertising material.

Times: Open all year.
Fee: Free.
(charged) toilets for disabled shop

TAUNTON

Hestercombe Gardens

Cheddon Fitzpaine TA2 8LG (3m N, off A361 near Cheddon Fitzpaine).
☎ 01823 413923 📠 01823 413727
e-mail: info@hestercombegardens.com

There are three period gardens to enjoy at Hestercombe: the 40-acre Georgian pleasure grounds with woodland walks, temples, Witch House and Great Cascade; the Victorian terrace with its newly restored fountain; and the Edwardian gardens, where the work of Gertrude Jekyll and architect Edwin Lutyens are shown off to full effect.

Times: Open every day, 10-6 (last admission 5).
Fee: £3.60 (ch5-15 £1).
toilets for disabled shop garden centre (Apr-Oct) (ex on lead)

TINTINHULL

Tintinhull House Garden

BA22 9PZ (0.5m S off A303)
☎ 01935 822545
e-mail: wtifxs@smtp.ntrust.org.uk

An attractive, mainly 17th-century farmhouse with a Queen Anne façade, it stands in four acres of beautiful formal gardens and orchard. The gardens were largely created by Mrs Reiss, who gave the property to the National Trust in 1953.

Times: Open Apr-Sep, Wed-Sun & BH Mons 12-6.
Fee: £3.80 (ch £1.80)

WASHFORD

Cleeve Abbey

TA23 0PS (0.25m S of A39)
☎ 01984 640377

The now ruined Cistercian abbey was founded at the end of the 12th century. Little remains of the church, but the gatehouse, dormitory and refectory are in good condition, with traceried windows, a fine timbered roof and wall paintings to be seen.

Times: Open all year, Apr-Sep, daily 10-6 (5pm Oct); Nov-Mar, daily 10-4 (closed 1-2pm). Closed 24-26 Dec & 1 Jan.
Fee: £2.60 (ch 5-15 £1.30, under 5's free).
shop (in certain areas)

Tropiquaria

TA23 0JX (on A39, between Williton and Minehead)
☎ 01984 640688 📠 01984 640688
e-mail: tropical@globalnet.co.uk

Housed in a 1930s BBC transmitting station, the main hall has been converted into an indoor jungle with a 15-foot waterfall, tropical plants and free-flying birds. (Snakes, lizards, iguanas, spiders, toads and terrapins are caged!) Downstairs is the submarine crypt with local and tropical marine life. Other features include landscaped gardens, the Shadowstring Puppet Theatre, and 'Wireless in the West' museum.

Times: Open Apr-Sep, daily 10-5; Oct, daily 11-5, Nov & Feb-Mar wknds & school hols 11-5. (Closed Dec & Jan).
Fee: £4.50 (ch £3, pen £4).
shop

WELLS

The Bishop's Palace

Henderson Rooms BA5 2PD (next to cathedral off the Market Sq)
☎ 01749 678691 📠 01749 678691

Close to the cathedral is the moated bishop's palace. The early part of the palace, the bishop's chapel and the ruins of the banqueting hall date from the 13th century and the undercroft remains virtually unchanged from this time. There are several state rooms and a long gallery which houses portraits of former Bishops. Events include a Living History re-enactment.

contd.

Times: Open Apr-Oct, Tue-Fri & BH's; daily in Aug 10.30-6 Sun 2-6. Gates close at exactly 6pm.
Fee: £3 (ch 12 accompanied free, UB40's £1.50, pen £2, disabled £1.50) . Party 10+.
P licensed (free use of electric wheelchair)

WESTON-SUPER-MARE

The Helicopter Museum

The Heliport, Locking Moor Rd BS22 8PL (outskirts of town on A371)
☎ 01934 635227 01934 822400
e-mail: helimuseum@hotmail.com

The world's largest rotary-wing collection and the only helicopter museum in Britain. More than 50 helicopters and autogyros are on display - including examples from France, Germany, Poland, Russia and the United States, from 1935 to the present day - with displays of models, engines and other components explaining the history and development of the rotocraft. Special events include `Open Cockpit Days', when visitors can learn more about how the helicopter works.
Times: Open all year, Nov-Mar Wed-Sun 10-4. Apr-Oct daily 10-6. (closed 24-26 Dec & 1 Jan)
Fee: £3.75 (ch under 5 free, ch 5-16 £2.75, pen £3.25). Family ticket £11. Party 10+.
P toilets for disabled shop

Time Machine

Burlington St BS23 1PR
☎ 01934 621028 01934 612526
e-mail: peterjones@n-somerset.org.uk

This museum, housed in the former workshops of the Edwardian Gaslight Company, has displays on the seaside holiday, an old chemist's shop, a dairy, and Victorian pavement mosaics. Adjoining the museum is Clara's Cottage, a Westonian home of the 1900s with period kitchen, parlour, bedroom and back yard. One of the rooms has an additional display of Peggy Nisbet dolls. Other displays include wildlife gallery, Mendip minerals, mining and local archaeology.
Times: Open all year: Mar-Sept daily 10-5, Nov-Dec 10-4 & BH Mon. (Closed 25-26 Dec & 1 Jan).
Fee: £3 (ch £1.50, pen £2). Family ticket (2 adults & 3 ch or 1 adult & 4 ch) £7.50. These tickets permit unlimited free return visits for rest of financial year.
P (800 yds) (some disabled parking outside museum) toilets for disabled shop garden centre (ex guide dogs)

WOOKEY HOLE

Wookey Hole Caves & Papermill

BA5 1BB (M5 junct 22 follow signs via A38 & A371, from Bath A39 to Wells then 2m to Wookey Hole)
☎ 01749 672243 01749 677749
e-mail: witch@wookeyhole.demon.co.uk

A half-mile guided tour leads visitors through this amazing complex of caves, with stalagmites, stalactites and other interesting geological features. There is also a Victorian papermill, with handmade papermaking and an old penny pier with mirror maze and penny arcade.
Times: Open all year, Mar-Oct 10-5; Nov-Feb 10.30-4.30. (Closed 17-25 Dec).
Fee: £7.20 (ch £4.20)
P licensed (Papermill only) toilets for disabled shop (ex guide dogs)

YEOVILTON

Fleet Air Arm Museum

Royal Naval Air Station BA22 8HT (on B3151)
☎ 01935 840565 01935 842630
e-mail: info@fleetairarm.com

A collection of over 50 historic aircraft are on display here. Special exhibitions using modern audio visual aids and displays put the exhibits in their original context. In addition, you can walk through Concorde 002, the British prototype. The Ultimate Aircraft Carrier Experience offers all the sights, sounds, smells and action of a real aircraft carrier.
Times: Open all year, daily (ex 24-26 Dec) 10-5.30 (4.30pm Nov-Mar).
Fee: phone for price details.
P licensed (wheelchairs available) toilets for disabled shop (ex guide dogs)

Staffordshire

For many, the main attractions of Staffordshire are the rollercoaster entertainment of Alton Towers or the precision craftsmanship of the world-famous potteries of Stoke-on-Trent. Yet the county also has some beautiful countryside and historic sites.

Part of the Peak District National Park forms the top right-hand corner of the county, and contains landscape ideal for hiking or pony trekking, as well as more adventurous pastimes such as rock climbing or hang-gliding.

Toward the south lies Cannock Chase, 30,000 acres of forest and heathland that was once a royal hunting preserve, and where a large herd of fallow deer still run free. The Chase is also home to cemeteries of fallen servicemen, including 5,000 Germans who died in Britain during two World Wars.

The Vale of Trent is known for its gentle beauty, and provides a welcome contrast to the craggy splendour of the moorland. Miles of rural canals (more than any other county) are also a welcoming sight.

Staffordshire has many historic attractions, including Lichfield's three-spired cathedral which contains the 7th-century Gospels of St Chad. The town was also the birthplace of Dr Samuel Johnson, who was born in a bookshop, and each year there are celebrations to commemorate the man who gave us the first Dictionary of the English Language.

Burton-upon-Trent is the 'Brewing Capital of England', and the Bass Museum Visitors Centre will surely provide a certain something that will banish the thirst.

EVENTS & FESTIVALS

January/February
28 Jan or 4 Feb Tough Guy 2001, Old Perton (assault course event)

April
23 St George's Day Court, Guildhall, Bore St, Lichfield. Ancient Manorial Court where high constables report on their work

June
tbc Lichfield Folk Festival (various venues)
tbc Midland Counties Show, Uttoxeter Racecourse, Wood Lane, Uttoxeter

July
15-17 Lichfield International Arts Festival (various venues)
tbc World Toe Wrestling Championships, Ye Olde Royal Oak, Wetton

September
10 Abbots Bromley Horn Dance (throughout village)

Top: Sir Henry Doulton, Burslem

ALTON

Alton Towers

ST10 4DB (signposted from M1 junct 23A, M6 junct 15, M1 junct 28 or M6 junct 16)

☎ 0990 204060 🖷 01538 704097

Alton Towers offers rides, shows and attractions guaranteed to suit every member of the family. There are enchanting children's areas and the theme park has more thrill rides than any other in Europe. The Alton Towers Hotel displays a wonderful array of artefacts and memorabilia from a bygone age. On top of all this, there are 200 acres of landscaped gardens and the majestic ruins of the Towers themselves.

Times: Open Apr-29 Oct, daily 9.30-5,6 or 7.

Fee: Jul-Aug, wknds & sch hols £19.95 (ch £15.95, under 4's free). All other times £14.95 (ch £11.95).

P ☕ ✕ licensed ♿ (disabled guest guide books) toilets for disabled shop 🐕 (ex guide dogs) 💳

BIDDULPH

Biddulph Grange Garden

Grange Rd ST8 7SD (off A527, 0.5m N of Biddulph)

☎ 01782 517999 🖷 01782 510624

This exciting and rare survival of a high Victorian garden has undergone extensive restoration. Conceived by James Bateman, the fifteen acres are divided into a number of smaller gardens which were designed to house specimens from his extensive plant collection.

Times: Open mid Mar-Oct, Wed-Fri 12-6. Sat-Sun & BH Mon 11-6 (last admission 5.30 or dusk if earlier); early Nov-mid Dec, Sat-Sun 12-4 or dusk.

P ☕ shop 🐕 ✿ *Details not confirmed for 2001*

BURTON-UPON-TRENT

The Bass Museum

PO Box 220, Horninglow St DE14 1YQ (from N junct 28 M1, A38, A511; from S junct 24 A564, A38)

☎ 01283 511000 🖷 01283 513509

e-mail: enquires@bass-museum.com

This museum is housed in the original Engineers Dept and Joiners shop, and was opened in 1977, the bi-centenary of the founding of the Bass brewery. Visitors can explore the history of brewing through a wide range of visual and interactive displays, and also visit the majestic Bass Shire horse team. The Bass Museum also plays host to conferences, exhibitions and a variety of entertainment.

Times: Open all year, Mon-Fri 10-5, Sat & Sun 11-5. Last admission 4pm. (Closed 25-26 Dec & 1 Jan).

Fee: £4.50 (ch £2, pen £3). Family ticket £12.50. Brewery tours by arrangement only, at extra charge (inc free glass of beer/lager/soft drink)

P ✕ licensed ♿ (lift to all floors) toilets for disabled shop 🐕 (ex guide dogs) 💳

CHEDDLETON

Cheddleton Flint Mill

Beside Caldon Canal, Leek Rd ST13 7HL (3m S of Leek on A520)

☎ 01782 502907

Two water mills complete with wheels are preserved here, and both are in running order. The 17th-century south mill was used to grind corn, while the north mill was built to grind flint for the pottery industry. The restored buildings have displays on aspects of the pottery industry. Exhibits include examples of motive power, such as a Robey steam engine, and of transport, such as the restored 70ft horse-drawn narrow boat *'Vienna'*.

Times: Open all year, Sat & Sun 2-5, Mon-Fri 10-5.

Fee: Donations.

P ♿

HIMLEY

Himley Hall & Park

DY3 4DF (off A449, on B4176)

☎ 01902 324093 & 326665 🖷 01902 894163

The extensive parkland offers a range of attractions, including a nine-hole golf course and coarse fishing. The hall is open to the public when exhibitions are taking place. Permanent orienteering course, a charge is made for the maps. Guided tours at the hall available by prior arrangement. Hall available for private hire.

Times: Open Apr-Sep, 2-5. Closed Mon ex BH. Park open all year.

Fee: Free.

P (charged) ☕ ♿ toilets for disabled 🐕 (ex guide dogs & in park)

LICHFIELD

Erasmus Darwin Centre

Beacon St WS13 7AD (signposted Lichfield Cathedral. Access by foot through the cathedral close)

☎ 01543 306260 🖷 01543 306109

e-mail: erasmus.d@virgin.net

The Centre is dedicated to Erasmus Darwin, Charles Darwin's grandfather, a talented doctor, inventor, philosopher and poet, who resided in Lichfield for more than 20 years. It is contained in a beautiful 18th-century house complete with a delightful period garden. Period rooms, audio-visual and interactive displays re-create the story of Erasmus' life, ideas and inventions.

Times: Open Tue-Sat 10-4.30, Sun noon-4.30, BH Mons 10-4.30. Last admission 3.45.

Fee: £2 (concessions £1.50). Family ticket £5. Subject to change.

P (200mtrs) toilets for disabled shop garden centre (ex guide dogs)

Lichfield Cathedral

WS13 7LD (signposted from all major roads and within city)

01543 306240 01543 306109

e-mail: lich.cath@virgin.net

Times: Open daily 7.45-6.

P (200mtrs) licensed (Touch & hearing centre for blind) toilets for disabled shop (ex guide dogs) *Details not confirmed for 2001*

Lichfield Heritage Centre

Market Square WS13 6LG

01543 256611 01543 414749

Fine silver in the Treasury and lively presentations on the Civil War are featured here. The displays tell the story of the city and feature photographs and memorabilia. The City's ancient charters and archives can be seen in the Muniment room.

Times: Open all year, daily 10-5. Last admission 4.14pm. (Closed Xmas & New Year)

Fee: £2 (ch, students & pen £1.50. Family ticket £6. (Joint ticket with Samuel Johnson Birthplace Museum £3.20, concessions £1). Viewing platform £1 (80p concessions) School parties by arrangement. Prices are under review.

P (200yds) (lift) toilets for disabled shop (ex guide dogs)

Samuel Johnson Birthplace Museum

Breadmarket St WS13 6LG

01543 264972 01543 258441

e-mail: curator@lichfield.gov.uk

A statue of Dr Johnson sits at one end of Market Square facing his birthplace on the corner of Breadmarket Street. The house, where Samuel's father had a bookshop, is now a museum containing many of Johnson's personal relics. His favourite armchair and walking stick are among the collection.

Times: Open daily 10.30-4.30. (Closed Xmas, New Year & Sun Nov-Jan).

Fee: £2 (ch & pen £1.10). Joint ticket with Lichfield Heritage Centre £3.20 (ch & pen £2.20). Family ticket £5.40.

P (500yds) shop

MOSELEY

Moseley Old Hall

V10 7HY (4m N of Wolverhampton, off A460)
01902 782808 01902 782808
e-mail: mmodxl@smtp.ntrust.org.uk

Charles II sheltered in Moseley Old Hall after the Battle of Worcester in 1651. There are numerous pictures and other reminders of the king. The house itself is an Elizabethan timber-framed building which was encased in brick in the 19th century. The small garden has a nut walk, period herbs and plants, and a formal knot garden.

Times: Open 20 Mar-19 Dec; Mar-May Wed, Sat-Sun, BH Mon and Tues 1.30-5.30 (BH 11-5). June-Oct Wed & Sat-Sun, BH Mon and Tue; also Tue in July & Aug 1.30-5.30 (BH Mon 11-5); Nov & Dec: Sun 1.30-4.30 (guided tour only, last tour at 4pm).

licensed (braille & large print, 1 wheelchair) toilets for disabled shop (ex guide dogs) *Details not confirmed for 2001*

SHUGBOROUGH

Shugborough Estate

ST17 OXB (6m E of Stafford off A513, signposted from M6 junct 13)
01889 881388 01889 881323
e-mail: promotions@staffordshire.gov.uk

Set on the edge of Cannock Chase, Shugborough is the magnificent 900-acre seat of the Earls of Lichfield. The 18th-century mansion house contains fine collections of ceramics, silver, paintings and French furniture. Part of the house is still lived in by the Lichfield family. Visitors can enjoy the Grade I listed historic garden and a unique collection of neo-classical monuments. Other attractions include the museum and the original servants quarters, the laundry, kitchens, brewhouse and coachhouses which have all been restored and are fully operational. Shugborough Park Farm is a Georgian farmstead that has an agricultural museum, working corn mill and rare breeds centre.

Times: Open 25 Mar-1 Oct, daily (ex Mon, but open BH Mon) 11-5. Sun only during Oct. Site open all year to pre-booked parties.
Fee: Site admission £2 per vehicle. Mansion £4 (concession £3); County Museum £4 (concession £3); Park Farm £4 (concession £3). Family Voyager (all 3 sites) £18. National Trust Members free.

(charged) licensed (step climber for wheelchairs, 2 Batricars) toilets for disabled shop (ex guide dogs & in parkland)

STAFFORD

Shire Hall Gallery

Market Square ST16 2LD (M6 exit 13 or 14, follow signs to Town Centre)
01785 278345 01785 278327
e-mail: shirehallgallery@staffordshire.gov.uk

A fine gallery housed in the 18th-century Shire Hall - one of Staffordshire's most magnificent buildings. It holds exhibitions of contemporary arts, contains historic courtrooms and a Crafts Council selected craft shop.

Times: Open all year, Mon & Fri 9.30-6, Tue-Thu 9.30-5, Sat 10-5. Closed BH. **Fee:** Free.

(200yds) (minicom telephone & hearing loop) toilets for disabled shop (ex guide dogs)

STOKE-ON-TRENT

Ceramica

Burslem Old Town Hall, Market Place, Burslem ST6 4AR
01782 832001 01782 832001
e-mail: ceramica@6trust.force9.co.uk

Times: Open daily 10-5 (Sun 10-4).

(charged) toilets for disabled shop (ex guide dogs) *Details not confirmed for 2001*

Etruria Industrial Museum

Lower Bedford St, Etruria ST4 7AF (M6 junct 16, A500 onto Stoke Rd (A5006))
01782 233144 01782 233145

Times: Open all year, Wed-Sun 10-4. (Closed Xmas & New Year).

toilets for disabled shop (ex guide dogs) *Details not confirmed for 2001*

Gladstone Pottery Museum

Uttoxeter Rd, Longton ST3 1PQ (on A50, signposted from A500 link with M6)
01782 319232 01782 598640
e-mail: gladstone@stoke.gov.uk

The last complete Victorian pottery factory from the days of bottle kilns. Tour the factory and see the pottery making skills of the craftsmen and craftswomen. The Museum shop stocks a wide range of gifts with craftspeople in mind. With its cobbled yard and giant bottle kilns, Gladstone perfectly captures the City's atmospheric past. Meet the head clerk of 1910 who will talk about life in the factory at that time. There is also a cinema and a 'family-sized' potters' wheel.

Times: Open all year, daily 10-5 (last admission 4pm). Limited opening Xmas & New Year.
Fee: £3.95 (ch £2.50, students & pen £2.95). Family ticket £10.

licensed special potters wheel for wheelchair users to experiment on toilets for disabled shop (ex guide dogs)

Royal Doulton Visitor Centre

Nile St, Burslem ST6 2AJ (M6 junct 15 from S or 16 from N. Join A500 leaving at exit for Tunstall A527, follow tourist signs)
01782 292434 01782 292424
e-mail: visitor@royal-doulton.com

The Centre houses over 1,500 Royal Doulton figures including many rare models. The Sir Henry Doulton Gallery restaurant combines magnificent treasures from the varied Royal Doulton past. Factory tours can be booked from Monday to Friday.

Times: Open all year, Mon-Sat 9.30-5, Sun 10.30-4.30. Factory tours by advance booking Mon-Fri 10.30-2 (1.30 Fri). (Closed Xmas week). No tours during factory holidays.

Fee: Visitor Centre only £3 (concessions £2.25); Factory Tour & Visitor Centre £6.50 (concessions £5). Parties 12+

(Visitor Centre fully accessible) toilets for disabled shop (ex guide dogs)

Spode

Church St ST4 1BX (M6 junct 15, then A500 to Stoke. Turn left at Stoke roundabout, follow brown tourist signs)

01782 744011 01782 744012

e-mail: visitorcentre@spode.co.uk

Spode is the oldest English pottery company still on its original site. Here Josiah Spode first perfected the formula for fine bone china. The Spode site houses a restaurant, factory shop outlets, and a visitors centre with exhibits on the history and heritage of the ceramics industry. Factory tours are available, pre-booking essential.

Times: Visitor Centre, Museum, Factory Shops & licenced restaurant. Mon-Sat 9-5, Sun 10-4. Factory Tours by prior appointment weekdays only, not available during factory closures-ring for details.

Fee: Visitor Centre & Museum £2.75 (ch over 5 & concessions £2.25). Standard factory tours £4.75 (ch over 12 & concessions £3.75). Connoisseur factory tour £7 & £6. Tours by appointment only.

(charged) licensed (limited access for the disabled) toilets for disabled shop (ex guide dogs)

The Potteries Museum & Art Gallery

Bethesda St, Hanley ST1 3DE

01782 232323 01782 232500

e-mail: museums@stoke.gov.uk

Times: Open all year, Mon-Sat 10-5, Sun 2-5. (Closed Xmas-New Year).

(500mtrs) (lift, induction loop, 2 wheelchairs available) toilets for disabled shop (ex guide/helping dogs) *Details not confirmed for 2001*

Wedgwood Visitor Centre

Barlaston ST12 9ES (5m S)

01782 204141 & 204218 01782 204402

Times: Open all year, Mon-Fri 9-5, Sat & Sun 10-5; (Closed Xmas & 1 Jan).

licensed toilets for disabled shop *Details not confirmed for 2001*

TAMWORTH

Drayton Manor Theme Park & Zoo

B78 3TW (M42, junct 9, follow Brown tourist board signs on A4091)

01827 287979 01827 288916

A family theme park set in 250 acres of parkland and lakes with over 100 rides and attractions for all age groups, includes 'Apocalypse' – the world's first stand up tower drop, 'Shockwave' – Europe's only stand up rollercoaster, and 'Stormforce 10' – the biggest and wettest water ride ever! Also Children's Corner, Dinosaurland, Zoo, farm and museum.

Times: Park & Zoo open Etr-30 Oct, daily 10.30-6. Park (rides) 10.30-5, 6 or 7 (depending on season).

Fee: Admission & rides wristband: £14 (ch under 14 £10, ch under 900mm free, pen £6). Wheelchair and helper £6 each.

licensed toilets for disabled shop garden centre (ex in park)

Tamworth Castle

The Holloway B79 7NA (from M42 junct 10 & M6 junct 12, access via A5)

01827 709626 01827 709630

Tamworth is a dramatic Norman motte and bailey castle set in an attractive town centre park with floral terraces. 15 authentically furnished rooms are open to the public, including the Great Hall, the Dungeon, and

contd.

the Haunted Bedroom. There are also 'Living Images' of Baron Marmion, the Black Lady ghost, and a Victorian prisoner. "The Tamworth Story" exhibition tells the history of the town.

Times: Open all year, Mon-Sat 10-5.30; Sun 2-5.30. Last admission 4.30. Telephone to confirm.

Fee: £4.20 (ch £2.10). Family £11.60. Prices subject to change

P (100yds & 400yds) ♿ (one wheelchair for use inside the castle) shop (ex guide dogs & hearing dogs)

WALL

Wall Roman Site

Watling St WS15 0AW (off A5)

☎ 01543 480768

Wall was originally the Roman fort of Letocetum, standing at the crossroads of Watling Street and Rykneild Street. It was an important military base from about AD50. Excavations have revealed the most complete bath house ever found in Britain.

Times: Open Apr-Sep, daily 10-6 (Oct 10-5)

Fee: £2.30 (ch 5-15 £1.20, under 5's free).

WESTON PARK

Weston Park

TF11 8LE (7m W of M6 junct 12; 3m N of M54 junct 3)

☎ 01952 852100 01952 850430

e-mail: weston-park@freeserve.com

Built in 1671, this fine mansion stands in elegant gardens and a vast park designed by 'Capability' Brown. Three lakes, a miniature railway, and a woodland adventure playground are to be found in the grounds, and in the house itself there is a notable collection of pictures, furniture and tapestries.

Times: Open Etr, May-Jun, wknds & BH's (Closed 7 May); 24 Jun-3 Sep, daily (Closed 15 Jul, 12, & 18-21 Aug); 4-17 Sep wknds only.

Fee: Park & Gardens £4 (ch £2.50, pen £3). House, Park & Gardens £5.50 (ch £3.50, pen £4.50).

P ♿ (disabled route) toilets for disabled shop

WHITTINGTON

Staffordshire Regiment Museum, Whittington Barracks

WS14 9PY (on A51 between Lichfield/Tamworth)

☎ 0121 311 3240/3229 0121 311 3205

Located next to Whittington Barracks, the museum tells the story of the soldiers of the Staffordshire Regiment and its predecessors. Exhibits include vehicles, uniforms, weapons, medals and memorabilia relating to three hundred years of regimental history, including distinguished service in the First and Second World Wars and the Gulf War.

Times: Open all year, Tue-Fri 10-4.30 (last admission 4); also Apr-Oct wknds and BH 1-4.30. (Closed Xmas-New Year). Parties at other times by arrangement.

Fee: £1.50 (concessions £1). Regimental Association Members & Serving Soldiers free.

P ♿ (ramps) toilets for disabled shop (outside only ex guide dogs)

WILLOUGHBRIDGE

The Dorothy Clive Garden

TF9 4EU (on A51 between Nantwich & Stone)

☎ 01630 647237 01630 647902

This 200-year-old gravel quarry has been converted into a delightful woodland garden. The quarry is at the top of a small hill and the garden has fine views of the countryside and adjoining counties. There is a variety of rare trees and shrubs. The garden provides colour and interest throughout the seasons from spring to glowing autumn tints.

Times: Open Apr-Oct, daily 10-5.30.

Fee: £3 (ch up to 11 yrs free, ch 11-16 £1, pen £2.50). Party 20+.

P ♿ (wheelchairs for use, special route) toilets for disabled (ex on leads)

Suffolk

Britain's most easterly county has plenty to offer to visitors, aside from the enviable fact that it has the driest regional climate in England.

Suffolk was once part of the kingdom of East Anglia. Back then the kingdom was protected by almost impenetrable boundaries; sea to the north and east, the undrained Fens to the west, and a barrier of oak forest to the south. However, these natural defences didn't stop invasion from Romans, Angles, Vikings, and Saxons, all of whom have left their mark on the area. In later years Icelandic fisherfolk settled in the coastal towns, and Flemish weavers helped the wool towns boom and also took part in the brewing industry.

Lavenham has some marvellous medieval timber houses as well as a church with a massive tower. John Constable, world-famous painter of '*The Haywain*', went to school here and was born in nearby East Bergholt. Thomas Gainsborough was another artistic son of Suffolk, born in Sudbury, where a statue of him stands in the village square. Sudbury also features as 'Eatanswill' in Dickens' *The Pickwick Papers*.

Known collectively as the Sunrise Coast, the resorts of Lowestoft, Kessingland and Southwold have won awards for the cleanliness and safety of their sandy beaches. Lowestoft is Britain's most easterly town and sits between sandy beaches on one side and beautiful broadland on the other. Sparrow's Nest Park is located just below the lighthouse and the town also features a maritime museum, a War Memorial Museum and the Royal Naval Patrol Museum.

EVENTS & FESTIVALS

May

26-27 Mildenhall Air Fete, US Airforce, Mildenhall

30-31 Suffolk Show, Suffolk Showground, Bucklesham Road, Ipswich

tbc Bury St Edmunds Festival, arts festival (various venues)

tbc South Suffolk Show, Point-to-Point Course, Ampton Park, Ingham

June

8-22 Aldeburgh Festival of Music & the Arts, Snape Maltings Concert Hall, Snape

30 Jun-1 Jul Maritime Ipswich, Ipswich Wet Dock, Ipswich

tbc Long Melford Country Fair, Melford Hall Park, Long Melford

August

26-27 Eye Show, Eye Show Ground, Eye

Top: Moot Hall, Aldeburgh

BUNGAY

Otter Trust

Earsham NR35 2AF (off A143)

☎ 01986 893470 🖷 01986 892461

The Otter Trust's main aim is to breed this endangered species in captivity in sufficient numbers so that it can re-introduce young otters into the wild wherever suitable habitat remains. This re-introduction programme has been running since 1983. The Otter Trust covers 23 acres on the banks of the River Waveney. As well as otter pens, there are three lakes with a large collection of European waterfowl.

Times: Open Apr (or Good Fri if earlier)-Oct, daily 10.30-6.

Fee: £4.50 (ch over 3 £2.50, pen £4). Disabled person in wheelchair free.

P ☕ ♿ toilets for disabled shop ✱ (ex guide dogs)

BURY ST EDMUNDS

Abbey Visitor Centre

Abbey Precinct, Abbey Gardens IP33 1RS

☎ 01284 763110

Housed in lower section of abbey tower. Casette tours of nearby ruins available.

Times: Open Etr Sat-Oct, daily 10-5.

Fee: Free.

P (200yds) ♿ shop ✱

Manor House Museum

Honey Hill IP33 1HF (Edge of Town Centre, follow signs to Police Station, opposite is museum car park)

☎ 01284 757072 🖷 01284 757079

The Georgian mansion specialises in costumes, textiles, horology and fine and decorative art from the 17th to the 20th centuries. There is a temporary exhibition gallery as well as workshops in textiles and horology - a new feature is an interactive horological room and feely pictures and boxes.

Times: Open all year Sun-Wed 12-5. Other times by arrangement.

Fee: £2.50 (concessions £1.50).

P (charged) ☕ ✕ licensed ♿ (Special tours can be arranged for disabled groups) toilets for disabled shop ✱ (ex guide dogs)

Moyse's Hall Museum

Cornhill IP33 1DX (in town centre)

☎ 01284 757488 🖷 01284 757079

Moyse's Hall is a 12th-century Norman house built of flint and stone which now serves as a local history museum, and among the fascinating exhibits are memorabilia of the notorious William Corder "Murder in the Red Barn".

Times: Open all year Mon-Sat 10-5, Sun 2-5. (Closed 25-26 Dec & Good Fri). Museum may be closed for four months in 2001 for redevelopment.

Fee: £1.70 (concessions £1.20).

P (200yds) ♿ shop ✱ (ex guide dogs)

CAVENDISH

The Sue Ryder Foundation Museum

Sue Ryder Home & Headquarters CO10 8AY (on A1092 Long Melford to Clare road)

☎ 01787 280252 🖷 01787 280548

Times: Open all year, daily 10-5.30. (Closed 25 Dec).

P ✕ ♿ toilets for disabled shop ✱ *Details not confirmed for 2001*

EASTON

Easton Farm Park

IP13 0EQ (signed from A12 at Wickam Market, and from A1120)

☎ 01728 746475 🖷 01728 747861

e-mail: easton@eastonfarmpark.co.uk

A Victorian model farm setting situated in the Deben River Valley. There are lots of breeds of farm animals, including Suffolk Punch horses. A purpose built dairy centre enables visitors to watch the cows being milked every afternoon, and there is the original Victorian Dairy which houses a collection of dairy bygones. Pets paddocks allow children to feed and touch the smaller animals. 150 years of farming and food production are displayed in the 'foodchains' exhibition.

Times: Open 19 Mar-30 Sep, daily 10.30-6. Closed Mon ex BHs and Mon in Jul-Aug.

Fee: £4.50 (ch under 3 free, ch 3-16 £3, pen £4). Party 20+

P ☕ ♿ (special parking) toilets for disabled shop

EUSTON

Euston Hall

IP24 2QP (on A1088, 3m S of Thetford)

☎ 01842 766366 🖷 01842 766764

Home of the Duke and Duchess of Grafton, this 18th-century house is notable for its fine collection of pictures, by Stubbs, Lely, Van Dyck and other Masters. The grounds were laid out by John Evelyn, William Kent and `Capability' Brown, and include a 17th-century church in the style of Wren.

Times: Open 1 Jun-28 Sep, Thu only & Suns 25 Jun & 3 Sep 2.30-5.

Fee: £3 (ch 50p, pen £2.50).

P ☕ ♿ shop ✱ (guide dogs by permission)

FLIXTON

East Anglia's Aviation Heritage Centre

Buckeroo Way, The Street NR35 1NZ (off A143, take B1062, 2m W of Bungay)
☎ 01986 896644
e-mail: nsam.flixton@virgin.net

Situated in the Waveney Valley, the museum has over 24 historic aircraft. There is also a Bloodhound surface-to-air missile, the 446th Bomb Group Museum, RAF Bomber Command Museum, the Royal Observer Corps Museum, RAF Air-Sea Rescue and Coastal Command and a souvenir shop. Among the displays are Decoy Sites and Wartime Deception, and Fallen Eagles - Wartime Luftwaffe Crashes.

Times: Open Apr-Oct Sun-Thu 10-5 (last admission 4); Nov-Mar 10-4 (last admission 3) Tue, Wed, Sun. New year closed 2 weeks either side.

Fee: Free.

P ♿ (ramps) toilets for disabled shop (ex guide dogs)

FRAMLINGHAM

Framlingham Castle

IP13 9BP (on B1116)
☎ 01728 724189

Built by Hugh Bigod between 1177 and 1215, the castle has fine curtain walls, 13 towers and an array of Tudor chimneys. In the 17th century the castle was bequeathed to Pembroke College, Cambridge, which built almshouses inside the walls.

Times: Open all year, Apr-Oct, daily 10-6 (5pm in Oct); Nov-Mar, daily 10-4. Closed 24-26 Dec & 1 Jan.

Fee: £3.20 (ch 5-15 £1.60, under 5's free). Personal stereo tour included in admission.

P ♿ shop #

HORRINGER

Ickworth House, Park & Gardens

The Rotunda IP29 5QE (2.5m S of Bury St Edmunds in the village of Horringer on A143)
☎ 01284 735270 📠 01284 735175

The eccentric Earl of Bristol created this equally eccentric house, begun in 1795, to display his collection of European art. The Georgian Silver Collection is considered the finest in private hands. 'Capability' Brown designed the parkland, and also featured are a deer enclosure, waymarked walks and an adventure playground.

Times: Open: House 1 Mar-29 Oct, Tue, Wed, Fri, wkends & BH Mons 1-5 (4.30 in Oct); Garden open daily 18 Mar-29 Oct 10-5. 30 Oct-Mar 10-4 wkdays; Park daily 7am-7pm.

Fee: House, Garden & Park £5.50 (ch £2.40); Garden & park £2.40 (ch 80p). Party 12+.

P ✕ licensed ♿ (braille guide batricars stairlift to shop & restaurant) toilets for disabled shop garden centre (ex in park)

IPSWICH

Christchurch Mansion

Soane St IP4 2BE (South side of Christchurch Park)
☎ 01473 253246 & 213761 📠 01473 210328

The house was built in 1548 on the site of an Augustinian priory. Set in a beautiful park, it displays period rooms and an art gallery which has changing exhibitions. The Suffolk Artists' Gallery has a collection of Constables and Gainsboroughs.

Times: Open all year, Tue-Sat 10-5 (dusk in winter), Sun 2.30-4.30 (dusk in winter). (Closed Good Fri & 24-26 Dec & 1-2 Jan). Open BH Mon.

P ♿ (tape guide for partially sighted) shop *Details not confirmed for 2001*

Ipswich Museum

High St IP1 3QH (Follow tourist signs to Crown St carpark. Museum 3 mins walk from here)
☎ 01473 433550 📠 01473 433558
e-mail: museum.service@ipswich.gov.uk

The Museum has sections on Victorian Natural History, Suffolk wildlife, Suffolk geology, Roman Suffolk, Anglo-Saxon Ipswich and Peoples of the World. There is also one of the best bird collections in the country.

Times: Open all year, Tue-Sat 10-5. (Closed Sun, BH's, 24-26 Dec & 1 Jan).

Fee: Free.

P (3 min walk) ♿ (step crawler to first floor) shop (ex guide dogs)

LAVENHAM

Lavenham Guildhall

Market Place CO10 9QZ
☎ 01787 247646
e-mail: almjtg@smtp.ntrust.org.uk

Although it has been much restored, there are still many of the original Tudor features left in this picturesque timber-framed building. The hall and its small museum are a testament to the time when East Anglia had a flourishing woollen industry. There is a walled garden with a 19th-century lock-up and mortuary.

Times: Open Mar-Nov, wkends 11-4. 1-20 Apr, Thu-Sun 11-5 (Closed Good Fri). 22 Apr-5 Nov, daily 11-5.

Fee: £3 (accompanied ch free). Party.

P (adjacent) shop

LEISTON

Leiston Abbey

(1m N off B1069)

For hundreds of years this 14th-century abbey was used as a farm and its church became a barn. A Georgian house, now used as a retreat house, was built into its fabric and remains of the choir, the church transepts and parts of the cloisters still stand.

Times: Open any reasonable time.

Fee: Free.

P ♿ #

Long Shop Museum

Main St IP16 4ES

☎ 01728 832189 01728 832189

Discover the Magic of Steam through a visit to the world famous traction engine manufacturers. Trace the history of the factory and Richard Garrett engineering. See the traction engines and road rollers in the very place that they were built. Soak up the atmosphere of the Long Shop, built in 1852 as one of the first production line engineering halls in the world. An award-winning museum with three exhibition halls full of items from the glorious age of steam.

Times: Open 1 Apr-31 Oct, Mon-Sat 10-5, Sun 11-5.

Fee: £3 (ch 75p, under 5's free, concessions £2.50)

toilets for disabled shop (ex guide dogs)

LINDSEY

St James's Chapel

Rose Green

Built mainly in the 13th century, this small thatched, flint-and-stone chapel incorporates some earlier work.

Times: Open all year.

Fee: Free.

LONG MELFORD

Kentwell Hall

CO10 9BA (signposted off A134)

☎ 01787 310207 01787 379318

Kentwell Hall is a moated red brick Tudor manor with gardens, woodland walks and a rare breeds farm. The house and grounds are open to the public at certain times of the year, and recreations of Tudor and 1940s life take place at weekends.

Times: Open: Gardens & Farm, Sun during Mar. House, Gardens & Farm: Apr-11 Jun, Sun only; Also 16-28 Apr, 30 May-2 Jun & 12 Jul-24 Sep daily. 27 Sep-29 Oct, Sun only. open 23-27 Oct daily. Historical re-creations on selected wknds & BH through the year.

Fee: Inclusive ticket £5.50 (ch £3.30, pen £4.75). Garden & Farm only £3.50 (ch £2.25, pen £3). Special prices apply for Re-Creations.

(wheelchair ramp & 2 wheelchairs for loan) toilets for disabled shop (ex guide dogs)

Melford Hall

CO10 9AA (off A134, 3m N of Sudbury)

☎ 01787 880286

Queen Elizabeth I was a guest at this turreted, brick-built Tudor house in 1578. It features an 18th-century drawing room, a Regency library and a Victorian bedroom. There is also a large collection of Chinese porcelain, and a display on Beatrix Potter, who was related to the owners and often stayed here. The garden has a Tudor pavilion, which may have been built as a guardhouse.

Times: Open Apr & Oct wknds & BH; May-Sep, daily Wed-Sun (open BH Mon) 2-5.30.

Fee: £4.30

(stairlift) toilets for disabled (ex in park)

LOWESTOFT

East Anglia Transport Museum

Chapel Rd, Carlton Colville NR33 8BL (3m SW of Lowestoft, on B1384. Follow brown signs from A12 & A146)

☎ 01502 518459 01502 518459

A particular attraction of this museum is the reconstructed 1930s street scene which is used as a setting for working vehicles: visitors can ride by tram, trolley bus and narrow gauge railway. Other motor, steam and electrical vehicles are exhibited. There is also a woodland picnic area served by trams.

Times: Open Good Fri & Etr Sat 2-4, Etr Sun-Etr Mon 11-5.30. May-Sep, Sun & BH's 11-5.30; Jun-Sep, Wed & Sat 2-5 (last entry 1 hour before closing).

Fee: £4.50 (ch 5-15 & pen £3). Price includes rides. Party.

toilets for disabled shop

Maritime Museum

Sparrow Nest Gardens, Whapload Rd NR32 1XG (on A12, 100 metres N of Lowestoft Lighthouse, turn right down Ravine)

☎ 01502 561963 & 511260

Models of ancient and modern fishing and commercial boats, fishing gear and shipwrights' tools are among the exhibits. Exhibition of the evolution of lifeboats, a replica of the aft cabin of a steam drifter. There is also an art gallery.

Times: Open 21 Apr-8 Oct, daily, 10-5.

Fee: 75p (ch, students 25p, pen 50p)

shop (ex guide & small dogs)

Pleasurewood Hills Family Theme Park

Leisure Way, Corton NR32 5DZ (off A12 at Lowestoft)

☎ 01502 586000 (Admin) & 508200 (info)

01502 567393

e-mail: info@pleasurewoodhills.co.uk

Pleasurewood Hills has over 40 rides to choose from, including the Cannonball Express Rollercoaster, the Tidal Waters and Log Flume. The popular Sea Lion and Parrot show is ideal for all the family, while the chair lift offers a bird's eye view of the park. A range of shops includes a restaurant and bar.

Times: Open 16 Apr-1 May; wknds 6-14 May. 20 May-10 Sep & 21-29 Oct, daily; wknds in Sep & Oct.
Fee: Prices Under Review. Telephone 01502 586000 for admission prices.
licensed all shows accessible. Most ride operators are able to assist toilets for disabled shop (ex guide dogs)

NEWMARKET

National Horseracing Museum and Tours

99 High St CB8 8JL
01638 667333 01638 665600
e-mail: nhrm@fsnet.co.uk

A chance to meet the horses and stable staff at close quarters, watch the horses on the historic gallops and see them in the equine swimming pool. Retired jockeys will answer questions and let you ride the horse simulator at up to 40mph. Another attraction lets you record your own racing commentary.
Times: Open 11 Apr-29 Oct, Tue-Sat (also BH Mons & Mon in Jul & Aug) 10-5.
Fee: £3.50 (ch £1.50, pen £2.50). Party 20+. Equine tours Tue-Sat when museum is open.
(300yds) licensed (ramps) toilets for disabled shop (ex guide dogs)

ORFORD

Orford Castle

IP12 2ND (on B1084)
01394 450472

Built by Henry II circa 1165, the castle's magnificent keep survives almost intact with three immense towers reaching to 90 feet. Inside there are many rooms to explore.
Times: Open all year, Apr-Sep, daily 10-6; (Oct 10-5); Nov-Mar, Wed-Sun, 10-1 & 2-4. Closed 24-26 Dec & 1 Jan.
Fee: £2.60 (ch 5-15 £1.30, under 5's free).

SAXMUNDHAM

Bruisyard Winery, Vineyard & Herb Centre

Church Rd, Bruisyard IP17 2EF (4m W of Saxmundham bypass (A12))
01728 638281 01728 638442
e-mail: 106236.463@compuserve.com

This picturesque, 10-acre vineyard produces the award-winning Bruisyard St Peter English wine. There is also a herb garden, water garden, a wooded picnic area, and a children's play area. English wine, herbs, crafts and souvenirs are for sale.
Times: Open Feb-Xmas, daily 10.30-5.
Fee: £3.50 (ch £2, pen £3)
licensed shop garden centre (herds) (ex in vineyard)

SAXTEAD GREEN

Saxtead Green Post Mill

The Mill House IP13 9QQ (2.5m NW of Framlingham on A1120)

☎ 01728 685789

Dating from 1854, this is one of the finest examples of a traditional Suffolk post-mill. Machinery and millstones are in perfect order.

Times: Open Apr-Oct, Mon-Sat 10-6 (Oct 10-5). Closed 1-2pm.

Fee: £2.10 (ch 5-15 £1.60, under 5's free).

(exterior only)

STOWMARKET

Museum of East Anglian Life

IP14 1DL (located in centre of Stowmarket opposite Asda Supermarket & is signposted from A14 & B1115)

☎ 01449 612229 01449 672307

This 70-acre, all-weather museum is set in an attractive river-valley site. There are reconstructed buildings, including a water mill, a smithy and also a wind pump, and the Boby Building houses craft workshops. There are displays on Victorian domestic life, gypsies, farming and industry. These include working steam traction engines, the only surviving pair of Burrell ploughing engines of 1879, and a working Suffolk Punch horse.

Times: Open 2 Apr-29 Oct.

Fee: £4.25 (ch 4-16 £2.75, concession £3.75) Family ticket £13.75. Party 10+.

P (adjacent) (wheelchairs available, special parking facilities) toilets for disabled shop

SUDBURY

Gainsborough's House

46 Gainsborough St CO10 2EU

☎ 01787 372958 01787 376991

e-mail: mail@gainsborough.org

The birthplace of Thomas Gainsborough RA (1727-88). The Georgian-fronted town house, with an attractive walled garden, displays more of the artist's work than any other gallery, together with 18th-century furniture and memorabilia. There's a varied programme of exhibitions throughout the year including fine art, craft, photography, printmaking and sculpture.

Times: Open all year - House Tue-Sat 10-5, Sun & BH Mons 2-5; (4pm Nov-Mar). (closed Good Fri & Xmas-New Year).

Fee: £3 (ch, students & disabled £1.50 pen £2.50). Party rates available.

P (300 yds) (no parking in Gainsborough Street) toilets for disabled shop (ex guide dogs)

SUFFOLK WILDLIFE PARK

Suffolk Wildlife Park

Kessingland NR33 7SL (on A12)

☎ 01502 740291 01502 741104

Times: Open all year, daily from 10am. (Closed 25-26 Dec).

P (wheelchairs available for hire) toilets for disabled shop

Details not confirmed for 2001

WESTLETON

RSPB Nature Reserve Minsmere

IP17 3BY (signposted from A12 & Westleton)

☎ 01728 648281 01728 648770

e-mail: minsmere@interramp.co.uk

One of the RSPB's most popular sites. It is famous for its nesting avocets, marsh harriers and bitterns. Ideal for families and birdwatchers alike, there are countryside walks of varying lengths and eight hides. The Visitor Centre provides information about the reserve, as well as a shop and tearoom. Education programmes for school groups are also available.

Times: Open Wed-Mon 9am-9pm (or sunset if earlier). Visitor centre, shop & tearoom Mar-Oct 9-5, Nov-Feb 9-4.

Fee: £5 (ch £1.50, concessions £3). Family ticket £10. RSPB members free.

P (ramps to hides, viewing areas in hides) toilets for disabled shop (ex guide dogs)

WEST STOW

West Stow Anglo Saxon Village

West Stow Country Park, Icklingham Rd IP28 6HG (off A1101, follow brown tourist signs)

☎ 01284 728718 01284 728277

e-mail: weststow@burybo.stedsbc.gov.uk

The village is a reconstruction of a pagan Anglo Saxon settlement dated 420-650 AD. Seven buildings have been reconstructed on the site of the excavated settlement. There is a Visitors' Centre and a children's play area. A new Anglo-Saxon Centre houses the original objects found on the site.

Times: Open all year, daily 10-5. Last entry 4pm

Fee: £4.50 (ch £3.50). Family ticket £13.

P (ramps) toilets for disabled shop (ex guide dogs)

WOODBRIDGE

Woodbridge Tide Mill

Tide Mill Way

☎ 01473 626618

The machinery of this 18th-century mill has been completely restored. There are photographs and working models on display. Situated in a busy quayside, this unique building looks over towards the historic site of the Sutton Hoo Ship Burial. Every effort is made to run the machinery for a short time whenever the mill is open and the tides are suitable.

Times: Open Etr, then daily May-Sep. Apr, Oct wknds only. 11-5

P (400 yds) (no parking or turning in Tide Mill Way) shop (ex guide dogs)

Surrey

Surrey is profoundly affected by its proximity to London, and much of the county has been developed to accommodate affluent commuters to the capital. Despite this, it has the reputation of being Britain's most wooded county, and it has some lovely countryside.

Particularly attractive are the areas around Haslemere and Shere. High points are the North Downs west of Guildford rising to a peak at Box Hill near Dorking, and Leith Hill which is 970 ft (294m) tall, making it the highest point in the southeast of England.

There are a number of attractions located within the area bounded by the M25 motorway. These include Sandown Park and Epsom racecourses, and the south's two huge theme parks, Thorpe Park and Chessington World of Adventures, where you can enjoy all the thrills and spills of white knuckle rides and a variety of themed areas to appeal to all age groups.

Kingston-upon-Thames is the county's administrative headquarters. Other main towns are Woking, Dorking and Guildford. The latter has a modern cathedral, consecrated in 1961, and the keep of the Norman Castle. The castle was frequented by King John, who signed the Magna Carta at Runnymede, a meadow on the south bank of the Thames, in 1215. The castle at Farnham is still in one piece, it dates from 1160 and was occupied until 1927. Farnham is a pleasant town with some graceful Georgian buildings, particularly in Castle Street.

EVENTS & FESTIVALS

March
5-27 Guildford International Music Festival

May
27 Surrey County Show, Stoke Park, Guildford

July
tbc Guildford Live Music Festival
tbc Guildford Summer Spectacular

August
5 Cranleigh Show, Showground, Cranleigh

October
tbc Guildford Book Festival

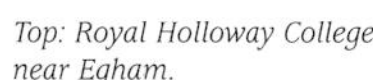

Top: Royal Holloway College near Egham.

ASH VALE

Army Medical Services Museum

Keogh Barracks GU12 5RQ (off M3 junct 4 on A331 to Mytchett then follow tourist signs)

☎ 01252 340212 01252 340224

e-mail: museum@keogh72.freeserve.co.uk

The museum traces the history of Army medicine, nursing and dentistry from 1660 until the present day. Displays including uniforms and medals are complemented by medical equipment and ambulances. There is also a small veterinary display.

Times: Open all year, Mon-Fri 10-3.30, Fri 9-3. (Closed Xmas, New Year & BH). Wknds & BH by appointment only.

Fee: Free.

toilets for disabled shop (large shop selling souvenirs) (ex guide dogs)

CHARLWOOD

Gatwick Zoo

Russ Hill RH6 0EG (signed off the A23 near Horley, Airport & Crawley)

☎ 01293 862312 01293 862550

The zoo covers almost 12 acres and has hundreds of birds and mammals. The monkey island has spider and squirrel monkeys, and other animals and birds can be seen in large, naturalised settings. A play area for children up to 12 years old has been added.

Times: Open all year, Mar-Oct, daily 10-6 (earlier by appointment for schools). Nov-Mar, 10-4 or dusk if earlier. (Closed 25-26 Dec). No butterflies during winter.

Fee: £5.45 (ch 3-14 £4.45, pen £4.95 ex Sun & BH). Family ticket (2 adults & 2 ch) £17.50. Admission price includes Butterfly House.

toilets for disabled shop (ex guide dogs)

CHERTSEY

Thorpe Park

Staines Rd KT16 8PN (off M25 junct 11 or 13 then A320)

☎ 01932 569393 01932 566367

Set in 500 acres of park, Thorpe Park is possibly the UK's wettest family theme park. The newest ride is Tidal Wave, Europe's highest water ride. Other attractions include X:No Way Out, the world's first 'backward' ride, Logger's Leap, and Thunder River. Forthcoming events include the Moonlight Mardi Gras in summer, and the park's largest ever firework display in late October.

Times: Open 5 Apr-29 Oct, call 0870 444 4466 for opening times. Last admission 1hr before closing.

Fee: £18.50 (concessions £11-£14.50, ch under 1m tall, free)

licensed toilets for disabled shop (ex guide dogs)

CRAWLEY

See Charlwood

EAST CLANDON

Hatchlands

GU4 7RT (E off A246)

☎ 01483 222482 01483 223176

Robert Adam's first commission was to decorate the interior of this 18th-century house. A collection including instruments played by Chopin, Mahler and Elgar is housed here. The garden, by Gertrude Jekyll, has been restored and new walks opened in the Repton park. Concerts are held in the house and gardens. Please contact Regional Box Office for details (01372) 451596.

Times: Open House & Gardens 2 Apr-Oct, daily, Tues-Thur & Sun, 2-5.50 (also open BH & Fri in Aug). Park Walks open Apr-Oct, daily, 11-6.

Fee: £4.40 (ch £2.20). Joint ticket with Clandon Park £6.40. Grounds and Park walks £1.80. Family ticket £11. Party Tues-Thur only.

licensed (wheelchair available & special parking) toilets for disabled shop (ex guide dogs)

FARNHAM

Birdworld & Underwaterworld

Holt Pound GU10 4LD (3m S on A325)

☎ 01420 22140 01420 23715

e-mail: bookings@birdworld.co.uk

Birdworld is the largest bird collection in the country and includes toucans, pelicans, flamingoes, ostriches and many others. Underwater World is a tropical aquarium with brilliant lighting that shows off collections of marine and freshwater fish, as well as the swampy depths of the alligator exhibit. Visitors can also visit some beautiful gardens, the Jenny Wren farm and the Heron Theatre.

Times: Open all year, daily from 19 Feb-29 Oct & 9 Dec-7 Jan (ex 25 & 26 Dec) from 9.30. 30 Oct-9 Dec & 8 Jan-16 Feb wkends only.

Fee: £7.95 (ch 3-14 £4.75, pen £6.50) Family ticket (2 adults & 2 ch) £22.95.

(wheelchairs available) toilets for disabled shop (ex guide dogs)

Farnham Castle Keep

Castle Hill GU6 0AG (half mile N on A287)

☎ 01252 713393

Built by an 11th-century bishop of Winchester, the castle made a convenient resting place on the journey to London. His tower, standing on a mound, was later encircled by high walls.

Times: Open Apr-Oct, daily 10-6 (Oct 10-5.

Fee: £2 (ch 5-15 £1, under 5's free).

GREAT BOOKHAM

Polesden Lacey

RH5 6BD (2m S off A246 from village of Bookham)

☎ 01372 452048 01372 452023

e-mail: spldjd@smtp.n.trust.org.uk

King George VI and Queen Elizabeth (the Queen Mother) spent part of their honeymoon here, and photographs of other notable guests can be seen. The house is handsomely furnished and full of charm, and it is set in spacious grounds. There is also a summer festival, where concerts and plays are performed. Please phone 01372 451596 for details of special events.

Times: Open all year. Grounds, Garden & Landscape walks: daily 10-6. House: 29 Mar-29 Oct, Wed-Sun 1-5. Also BH Mon 11-5 (last admission 30mins before closing)

Fee: Ground, Garden & Landscape walks: £3 (Family ticket £7.50); House: £3 extra (Family £7.50 extra). Ch under 17 half price, ch under 5's free. Party 15+.

licensed (braille guide & disabled parking by arrangement) toilets for disabled shop (ex guide dogs or grounds)

GUILDFORD

Dapdune Wharf

Wharf Rd GU1 4RR (off Woodbridge Road to rear of Surrey County Cricket Ground)

01483 561389 01483 531667

The Wey is one of the earliest historic waterways in Britain dating from 1653. A series of exhibitions, models and displays tells the story of the Waterway, the people who lived and worked on it and the barges built there. A restored Wey barge, the 'Reliance', can be explored.

Times: Open 1 Apr-31 Oct, Thu, wknds & BHs 11-5. River bus service 11-5 (conditions permitting)

Fee: £2.50 (ch £1.25). Family ticket £6

(braille guide) toilets for disabled (ex on lead)

Guildford Castle

GU1 3TU

01483 444718 01483 444444

e-mail: dandol@guildford.gov.uk

The three-storey ruined castle keep dates from the 12th century and gives fine views; the castle ditch has been transformed into a colourful garden. Concerts and open-air theatre performances are sometimes given in summer.

Times: Open: Grounds daily 8-dusk (Closed 25 Dec); Keep Apr-Sep 10.30-6.

Fee: 85p (ch 40p).

P (50yds)

Guildford House Gallery

155 High St GU1 3AJ (N side of High St, opposite Sainsbury's)

01483 444740 01483 444742

e-mail: guildfordhouse@remote.guildford.gov.uk

An impressive building in its own right, Guildford House dates from 1660 and has been Guildford's art gallery since 1959. A changing selection from the Borough's Art Collection is on display, including pastel portraits by John Russell, topographical paintings and contemporary craftwork, as well as temporary exhibitions.

Times: Open Tue-Sat 10-4.45.

Fee: Free.

P (100yds) shop

Loseley Park

GU3 1HS (2m SW of Guildford, off A3 onto B3000)

01483 304440 & 505501 01483 302036

e-mail: enquires@loseley.park.com

Sir William More built this house over four hundred years ago with stone from the ruins of Waverley Abbey, and the house is a fine example of Elizabethan architecture, set in magnificent parkland. The Walled Gardens include a Herb Garden, which illustrates the culinary, medicinal, dyeing, cosmetic uses of herbs and an award-winning rose garden.

Times: Walled Garden open 1 May-30 Sep, Wed-Sat & BH 11-5. House open 29 May-Aug, Wed-Sat & BH 2-5 (last tour 4pm). House & Garden open Jun-Aug, Sun only.

Fee: House & Gardens £5 (ch £3, ch under 3 free, concessions £4). Gardens only £2.50 (ch £1.50, concessions £2). Party. Garden summer ticket £15, admits ticket holder & guest from May-Sep.

(wheelchair available, parking outside house) toilets for disabled shop (ex guide dogs)

HASCOMBE

Winkworth Arboretum

Hascombe Rd GU8 4AD (2m NW on B2130, follow brown tourist signs from Godalming)

01483 208477

e-mail: swagen@smtp.ntrust.org.uk

This lovely woodland covers a hillside of nearly 100 acres, with fine views over the North Downs. The best times to visit are April and May, for the azaleas, bluebells and other flowers, and October for the autumn colours.

Times: Open all year, daily during daylight hours. (could close when weather is bad)

Fee: £3 (ch £1.50). Family ticket £7.50, additional family member £1.50.

toilets for disabled shop (Apr-Sep, Wed-Sun 11-5.30 & BH Mon) (ex on leads)

OUTWOOD

Old Mill

Outwood Common RH1 5PW (turn S off A25 at Bletchingley, between The Prince Albert & The White Hart, mill is in 3m)

01342 843458 & 843644 01342 843458

e-mail: sheila@outwoodwindmill.co.uk

This award-winning example of a post-mill dates from 1665 and is the oldest working windmill in England and one of the best preserved in existence. Standing 400ft above sea level, it is surrounded by common land and National Trust property. Ducks, goats and geese wander freely in the grounds, and there is a small museum of bygones.

Times: Open Etr Sun-last Sun in Oct, Sun & BH Mons only 2-6. Other days & evening tours by arrangement.

Fee: £2 (ch £1).

P (10yds) toilets for disabled shop

PAINSHILL PARK

Painshill Landscape Garden

KT11 1JE (W of Cobham, on A245)

☎ 01932 868113 📠 01932 868001

Painshill covers 158 acres and was created by the Hon. Charles Hamilton between 1738 and 1773. Visitors can walk through a series of delightful scenes. There are also a huge lake, shrubberies, massive waterwheel, Gothic temple, ruined abbey, Turkish tent and a crystal grotto.

Times: Open Apr-Oct, Tue-Sun & BH, 10.30-4.30. (gates close 6pm). Nov-Mar, Tue-Thu, wknds & BH 11-4 (gates close 4pm). Closed 25-26 Dec.

Fee: £3.80 (ch 5-16 £1.50, concessions £3.30). Pre-booked adult groups 10+.

P ☕ ♿ (wheelchairs & buggies available - prebooked) toilets for disabled shop (ex guide dogs)

REIGATE

Reigate Priory Museum

Bell St RH2 7RL (off A217)

☎ 01737 222550

Times: Open Wed & Sat 2-4.30 in term time.

P (50yds) ♿ ("Hands On" facilities) shop *Details not confirmed for 2001*

TILFORD

Rural Life Centre

Reeds Rd GU10 2DL (off A287, 3m S of Farnham, sign posted)

☎ 01252 792300 & 795571 📠 01252 795571

e-mail: rural.life@orgonet.co.uk

The Old Kiln houses a collection of farm implements and machinery, and examples of the craft and trades allied to farming may be seen. The larger exhibits are displayed in the pleasant garden and woodland surroundings which cover some ten acres. In the old farm buildings are a smithy and a wheelwright's shop, hand tools and other artefacts.

Times: Open Apr-Sep, Wed-Sun & BH 11-6.

Fee: £4 (ch £2 & pen £3). Family ticket (2 adults & 2 ch) £10.

P ☕ ♿ (3 wheelchairs for use) toilets for disabled shop

WEST CLANDON

Clandon Park

GU4 7RQ (on A247)

☎ 01483 222482 📠 01483 223479

An 18th-century house displaying a collection of Meissen Italian comedy figures and the Gubbay collection of porcelain, furniture and needlework. This is also home to The Queens Royal Surrey regimental museum. There is a garden with parterre, grotto and Maori House. Concerts are held in the Marble Hall, please contact Regional Box Office for details - 01372 451596.

Times: Open House: 2 Apr-31 Oct, Tue, Wed, Thu, Sun & Good Fri, Etr Sat & BH Mons, 11.30-4.30. Last admission 4pm. Garden open daily 9-dusk. Museum open as House, 12-5. Garden open all year daily, 9 until dusk.

Fee: House & Garden £4.40 (ch £2.20). Family ticket £11. Combined ticket with Hatchlands £6.40. Group tickets available Tue-Thu.

P ☕ ✕ licensed ♿ (wheelchairs, braille guide & disabled parking) toilets for disabled shop (ex guide dogs)

WEYBRIDGE

Brooklands Museum

Brooklands Rd KT13 0QN (exit M25 at junct 10/11, museum off B374)

☎ 01932 857381 📠 01932 855465

Times: Open Tue-Sun & BHs 10-5 (4pm in winter). Closed Good Friday & 23-31 Dec.

P ☕ ♿ toilets for disabled shop *Details not confirmed for 2001*

WISLEY

RHS Garden Wisley

GU23 6QB (on A3, close to M25 junct 10)

☎ 01483 224234 📠 01483 211750

Covering over 240 acres, Wisley is the flagship of the Royal Horticultural Society demonstrating the very best in gardening practices. The gardens have a wide variety of trees, shrubs and plants, many of which are unusual in Britain. Whatever the season the garden serves as a working encyclopedia for gardeners of all levels.

Times: Open all year, Mon-Fri 10-6 or dusk (4.30pm Jan, Nov & Dec), opens 9am Sat. Sun members only 9-6 (4.30 Nov-Jan). (Closed 25 Dec). Glasshouses close at 4.15 or sunset Mon-Fri.

Fee: £5 (ch 6-16 £2). Affiliated society garden entry card £3.50. Party 10+. Companion for wheelchair user or visually impaired visitor free.

P ☕ ✕ licensed ♿ (free wheelchairs) toilets for disabled shop garden centre (ex guide dogs)

East Sussex

Natural features of East Sussex include Beachy Head, the highest headland on the South Coast at 590 feet (180m), and the South Downs, the great chalky ridge that once connected England and the Continent, which stretches from Beachy Head into Hampshire.

The heathlands of Ashdown Forest are Winnie the Pooh country, including the bridge where Poohsticks was first played and a monument to A A Milne on Gill's Lap, the Enchanted Place of the much loved Pooh Bear stories.

The coastline is almost entirely built up, and major resorts are Brighton, Hastings and Eastbourne, with Newhaven as the cross channel port. Eastbourne enjoys the reputation of being one of Britain's sunniest seaside destinations, consistently at the top of the sunshine league tables. It is the most respectable of 19th-century resorts with a shingle beach and a fine Victorian pier. Hastings has a fading grandeur, but the Old Town is the most interesting quarter, which can be reached by the West Hill Cliff funicular railway.

Lewes, the county town, is set either side of the River Ouse, where it cuts through the South Downs and provides some dramatic vistas. Attractive streets and lanes known as 'twittens' are overlooked by the Norman castle.

There are castles in abundance in East Sussex: Hastings, Herstmonceux, Pevensey and Bodiam. The town of Battle, six miles (10km) from Hastings, is the site of the famous Battle of Hastings, where the Normans led by William I, defeated Wessex, led by Harold II, on 14 October 1066.

EVENTS & FESTIVALS

May
5-27 Brighton International Festival, various venues
13 MG Regency Run (London to Brighton run)
27-28 Battle Medieval Fair
tbc East Sussex Young Farmers Country Fayre, Laughton

June
3 London to Brighton Classic Car Run

July
5-7 Hastings Beer & Music Festival, Hastings (provisional)
22 Brighton Lions Carnival
tbc Battle Abbey Classic Car Show & Country Fayre, High Street, Battle

August
4-5 Rye Medieval Festival (provisional)

September
1-15 Rye Festival (provisional)

October
6-14 or 13-21 Hastings Week

November
4th London to Brighton Veteran Car Run (provisional)

Top: Seven Sisters, Seaford

ALFRISTON

Alfriston Clergy House

The Tye BN26 5TL (4m NE of Seaford, E of B2108, next to church in village)

☎ 01323 870001 01323 871318

e-mail: ksdxxx@smtp.ntrust.org.uk

Step back into the Middle Ages with a visit to this 14th-century thatched Wealden Hall House. Trace the history of this magnificent building - the first to be acquired by the National Trust in 1896 - and discover why the chalk floor is soaked in sour milk! Explore the colourful cottage garden, and savour the idyllic setting beside Alfriston's famous parish church, with stunning views across the meandering River Cuckmere.

Times: Open Apr-Oct Sat-Mon, daily (ex Tue & Fri), 10-5. Last entrance 4.30 or sunset if earlier).

Fee: £2.50.(ch £1.25). Family ticket £6.25.

P ((0.25 mile) (braille guide) shop (ex guide dogs)

Drusillas Park

BN26 5QS (off A27)

☎ 01323 870234 & 870656 01323 870846

e-mail: info@drusilla.co.uk

Masses of hands-on activities for children, and a wide variety of animals in cleverly designed natural environments, including a walk-through Bat Enclosure, Penguin Pool, Meerkat Dome, and Bug World. Plus keeper walks, Animal encounters and the Discovery Centre. Playland features the Toddler Indoor Village and Stables, a waterwheel, and lots of climbing, sliding and jumping fun.

Times: Open all year, daily 10-5 (winter 10-4). Closed 24-26 Dec.

Fee: £7.60 (ch 3-12 £6.50, pen/concessions £6). Ch under 3 free. Party 15+.

P licensed (rear carriage & sensory trails) toilets for disabled shop (ex guide dogs)

BATTLE

Battle & District Historical Society Museum (opposite Abbey Green car park)

Memorial Hall, High St TN33 0AQ

☎ 01424 775955

e-mail: ann@battlehill.freeserve.co.uk

The focal point of this museum is a diorama of the Battle of Hastings and a reproduction of the Bayeux Tapestry. There are also local history exhibits. A Summer Arts Festival is held, and the Battle Festival takes place in June/July. Special displays are arranged throughout the season.

Times: Open Apr-Sep, daily 10.30-4.30 (Sun 2-5).

Fee: £1 (ch 20p, ch accompanied free).

P (20yds) (stair lift & toilet due to be installed) shop (ex guide dogs)

Buckleys Yesterday's World

89-90 High St TN33 0AQ (A2100, next to Battle Abbey)

☎ 01424 775378 01424 775174

e-mail: info@yesterdaysworld.demon.co.uk

Here are over 30 shop and room displays with thousands of exhibits dating from Victorian times to the 1950s. There is a moving and speaking life-size figure of Queen Victoria, a Penny Arcade, Miniature Golf Course, Childrens Play Village, Toddlers Activity Area, and Nostalgic Video Show. Due to the main buildings' historic nature and location on top of a hill, disabled access is very limited.

Times: Open all year, daily 10-6 (last admission 5pm) (Oct to Mar times subject to change). Closed 25-26 Dec & 1 Jan.

Fee: £4.50 (ch 4-15 £2.99, pen £3.99, disabled £2.20). Family ticket £13.95. Parties of 15+.

P (100yds) (50p per day) toilets for disabled shop

1066 Battle of Hastings Abbey & Battlefield

High St TN33 0AD (leave A21 onto A2100, Abbey at end of Battle High St)

☎ 01424 773792

Built by William the Conqueror, to atone for the terrible slaughter of the Battle of Hastings in 1066, the Abbey's high altar stood on the spot where Harold fell, and is still marked by a memorial stone. The mile-long Battlefield Walk takes you round the full perimeter of the battlefield itself.

Times: Open all year, Apr-Sep, daily 10-6 (Oct 10-5); Nov-Mar, daily 10-4 . Closed 24-26 Dec & 1 Jan.

Fee: £4 (ch 5-15 £2, under 5's free). (Personal stereo tour available at an additional charge).

P (charged) shop (allowed in certain areas) #

BODIAM

Bodiam Castle

TN32 5UA (2m E of A21 Hurst Green)

☎ 01580 830436 01580 830398

e-mail: kboxxx@smtp.ntrust.org.uk

With its tall round drum towers at each corner, Bodiam is something of a fairytale castle. It was built in 1386 by

Sir Edward Dalnygrigge, for comfort and defence. The walls measure some 6ft 6in thick, and the great gatehouse was defended by gun loops and three portcullises.
Times: Open 19 Feb-Oct, daily 10-6 or dusk if earlier; Nov-mid Feb, Sat & Sun 10-4 or dusk. (Closed 24-26 Dec). Last admission 1 hour before closing.
Fee: £3.60 (ch £1.80). Family ticket £9. Car £1.50.
P (charged) (Braille guides, special parking on request) toilets for disabled shop (ex in grounds on a lead)

BRIGHTON

Booth Museum of Natural History

194 Dyke Rd BN1 5AA (from A27 Brighton by pass, 1.5m NW of town centre, opposite Dyke Rd Park)
☎ 01273 292777 01273 292778
e-mail: boothmus@pavilion.co.uk

The museum was built in 1874 to house the bird collection of Edward Thomas Booth (1840-1890). His collection is still on display, but the museum has expanded considerably since Booth's day and now includes thousands of butterfly and insect specimens, geology galleries with fossils, rocks and local dinosaur bones and a magnificent collection of animal skeletons, largely collected by F W Lucas (1842-1932), a Brighton solicitor.
Times: Open all year, Mon-Sat (ex Thu) 10-5, Sun 2-5. (Closed Good Fri, Xmas & 1 Jan).
Fee: Free.
P (road opposite) (two hour limit) shop (ex guide dogs)

Museum & Art Gallery

Church St BN1 1UE (in centre of Brighton within the Pavilion Estate)
☎ 01273 290900 01273 292841

Undergoing major restoration until autumn 2001 with phased gallery closures. The museum will remain open throughout with a phased programme of gallery redisplay. Telephone for details.
Times: Open all year, Mon, Tue, Thu, Fri, & Sat 10-5. Sun 2-5. (Closed Wed, Good Fri, 24, 25 & 26 Dec & 1 Jan).
Fee: Free.
P (5 mins walk) (Church St NCP & on Street) lift,tactile exhibits,induction loops,ramps & automatic door toilets for disabled shop (ex guide dogs)

Preston Manor

Preston Drove BN1 6SD (off A23)
☎ 01273 290900 & 292770 01273 292771

This charming Edwardian manor house is beautifully furnished with notable collections of silver, furniture and paintings and presents a unique opportunity to see an Edwardian home both 'upstairs' and 'downstairs'. The servants' quarters can also be seen, featuring kitchen, butler's pantry and boot hall. The house is set in beautiful gardens, which include a pet cemetery and the 13th-century parish church of St Peter.
Times: Open all year, Tue-Sat 10-5, Sun 2-5, Mon 1-5 (BH Mons 10-5). (Closed Good Fri & 25-26 Dec).
Fee: £3.20 (ch 5-15 £2, pen, students & UB40 £2.70). Family ticket £5.20-£8.40. Party 20+. Joint ticket with Royal Pavilion £7.
P shop (ex guide dogs)

Royal Pavilion

BN1 1EE (Centre of Brighton, at the Old Steine)
☎ 01273 290900 01273 292871

Justifiably termed 'the most extraordinary palace in Europe', this former seaside residence of King George IV with its myriad domes and minarets and opulent interiors is a building no visitor to Brighton should miss. It is set in stunning Regency gardens and group tours are available by arrangement.
Times: Open all year, Jun-Sep, daily 10-6; Oct-May, daily 10-5. (Closed 25-26 Dec).
Fee: £4.90 (ch £3, concessions £3.55) Family ticket £7.85-£12.70. Joint ticket with Preston Manor £7 Groups 20+.
P (5 mins walk) (NCP & on street) (tours for the blind by arrangement, wheelchairs) toilets for disabled shop (ex guide dogs)

Sea Life Centre

Marine Pde BN2 1TB
☎ 01273 604234 & 604233 (rec info)
01273 681840

Experience spectacular marine displays, set in the world's oldest functioning aquarium. Take a look at over 100 species in their natural habitat, including seahorses, sharks and rays. Over forty exhibits include Adventures at 20,000 Leagues complete with NASA-designed walkthrough observation tunnel. Features also include a Captain Pugwash quiz trail, a soft play area, a cafe and a giftshop.
Times: Open all year, daily (ex 25 Dec), 10-5. Last admission 4. (Open later on wknds in summer & school holidays)
Fee: £5.95 (ch 4-14 £3.95, students & UB40 £3.95, under 4 free, free entry to the blind). Party 10+. Subject to change.
P (200 yds) toilets for disabled shop (ex guide dogs)

BURWASH

Bateman's

TN19 7DS (0.5m SW off A265)
☎ 01435 882302 01435 882811

Rudyard Kipling lived for over 34 years in this 17th-century manor house, and it remains much the same as it did during his lifetime. His 1928 Rolls Royce Phantom is on display, and the watermill at the bottom of the garden grinds corn into flour on a Saturday afternoon.
Times: Open Apr-1 Nov, Sat-Wed 11-5.30, also open Good Fri, (last admission 4.30pm). House closes at 5pm.
Fee: £5 (ch £2.50). Family ticket £12.50. Party 15+.
P licensed (braille guide available) toilets for disabled shop (dog creche in car park)

EASTBOURNE

"How We Lived Then" Museum of Shops & Social History

20 Cornfield Ter BN21 4NS (just off the seafront, half way between the town centre & main theatres)

☎ 01323 737143

Over the last 40 years, Jan and Graham Upton have collected over 100,000 items which are now displayed on four floors of authentic old shops and room-settings, transporting visitors back to the age of their grandparents. Other displays, such as seaside souvenirs, wartime rationing and Royal mementoes, help to capture 100 years of social history.

Times: Open daily all year, 10-5.30 (last entry 5pm). Winter times subject to change, telephone establishment.

Fee: £3 (ch 5-15 £2, under 5's free, pen £2.50). Party 10+.

P (outside & st nearby ♿ shop

Redoubt Fortress and Museum

Royal Pde BN22 7AQ

☎ 01323 410300 📠 01323 732240

This huge fortification was built in 1804 in case of invasion by Napoleon, and has places for 11 guns. It is now the home of the Sussex Combined Services Museum (The Royal Sussex Regiment and the Queen's Royal Irish Hussars) and the National Collection of the British Model Soldier Society. There are over 50,000 exhibits covering 300 years of conflict on land, sea and air.

Times: Open Etr-5 Nov, 9.30-5.30.

P (200yds) shop *Details not confirmed for 2001*

Wish Tower Puppet Museum

Martello Tower No 73, King Edward Pde BN21 4BU (on seafront, W of pier)

☎ 01323 417776 📠 01323 644440 or 728319

e-mail: puppet.workshop@virgin.net

The Wish Tower Puppet Museum hosts a unique display of puppets from all over the world. From early shadow puppets of Asia, through over 300 years of Punch and Judy in England to television and film puppets of today. Puppet shows take place during the summer.

Times: Open May-Nov, daily 9.30-5.30.

P (100m) shop (inc guide dogs) *Details not confirmed for 2001*

FIRLE

Firle Place

BN8 6LP (off A27, Eastbourne to Brighton road)

☎ 01273 858335 & 858188 📠 01273 858188

Times: Open Jun-Sep, Sun, Wed & Thu; also Etr, Spring, May & Aug BH Sun & Mon 2-4.30. Party 25+.

P ✕ licensed ♿ toilets for disabled shop (ex in garden) *Details not confirmed for 2001*

GLYNDE

Glynde Place

Lewes BN8 6SX (off A27 between Lewes & Eastbourne)

☎ 01273 858224 📠 01273 858224

Times: Open Jun & Sep, Wed & Sun 2-5, Jul & Aug Wed, Thu & Sun, also BH's & Suns in May. Garden open Suns in Apr.

P *Details not confirmed for 2001*

GROOMBRIDGE

Groombridge Place Gardens & Enchanted Forest

TN3 9QG (off A264 4m SW of Tunbridge Wells on B2100)

☎ 01892 863999 & 861444 📠 01892 863996

Surrounded by acres of breathtaking parkland, Groombridge Place has an intriguing history stretching back to medieval times. The beautiful formal gardens are flanked by a medieval moat, with a classical 17th-century manor as a backdrop. Hidden from view, high above the gardens and vineyard, secret mysterious gardens to challenge and delight are found in The Enchanted Forest.

Times: Open Apr-Oct daily 9-6.(to be confirmed).

P ✕ licensed ♿ (Enchanted Forest not accessible) toilets for disabled shop garden centre (ex guide dogs)

HAILSHAM

Michelham Priory

Upper Dicker BN27 3QS (off A22 & A27, 2m W of Hailsham)

☎ 01323 844224 📠 01323 844030

e-mail: adminmich@sussexpast.co.uk

Set on a moated island surrounded by gardens, Michelham Priory is one of the most beautiful historic houses in Sussex. Founded in 1229 for Augustinian canons, the Priory is approached through a 14th-century gatehouse spanning the longest medieval moat in the country. Most of the original priory was demolished during the Dissolution, but the remains were incorporated into a Tudor farm that became a country house. Outside, the gardens are enhanced by a

working watermill, physic garden, smithy, rope museum and the dramatic Elizabethan Great Barn.
Times: Open mid Mar-end Oct, Wed-Sun (daily in Jul, Aug & BH Mons). Mar & Oct 10.30-4, Apr, Jul & Sep 10.30-5, Aug 10.30-5.30.
Fee: £4.40 (ch 5-15 £2.30, pen & student £3.80, disabled/carer £2.20). Family ticket (2 adults & 2 ch) £11.40. Party 20+.
licensed (wheelchairs & braille guide available) toilets for disabled shop (ex guide dogs & in car park)

HALLAND

Bentley Wildfowl & Motor Museum

BN8 5AF (7m NE of Lewes, signposted on A22/A26/B2192)
☎ 01825 840573 01825 841322
e-mail: barrysutherland@pavilion.co.uk

Hundreds of swans, geese and ducks from all over the world can be seen on lakes and ponds along with flamingoes and peacocks. There is a fine array of Veteran, Edwardian and Vintage vehicles, and the house has splendid antiques and wildfowl paintings. The gardens specialise in old fashioned roses. Other attractions include woodland walks, a nature trail, Education Centre, adventure playground and a miniature train.
Times: Open 20 Mar-Oct, daily 10.30-4.30 (5pm Jul & Aug), House open from noon, 1 Apr-31 Oct. Nov, Feb & part of Mar, wknds only. Estate closed Dec & Jan. House closed all winter.
Fee: Summer £4.80 (ch 4-15 £3, pen & students £3.80). Family ticket (2 adults & 4 ch) £14.50. Winter £3.80. Special rates for disabled.
(wheelchairs available) toilets for disabled shop (guide dogs ex in bird reserve

HASTINGS

Hastings Embroidery

White Rock Theatre, White Rock TN34 1JX (situated on A259 seafront road opposite the pier)
☎ 01424 781010 01424 781170
e-mail: whiterocktheatre@hastings.gov.uk

Eighty-one events in British history from 1066 to 1966 depicted in 27 panels and 74 metres in length, Hastings embroidery was sewn by the Royal School of Needlework, using threads, cords, metals, lace, jewels and appropriate cloths.
Times: Open Mon-Sun 11-4 (last entry 3.30). Closed during March & subject to closure for selected events.
Fee: £2 (concessions £1).
(charged) toilets for disabled shop (ex guide dogs)

Old Town Hall Museum of Local History

Old Town Hall, High St TN34 3EW
☎ 01424 781166 01424 781165
e-mail: curator-breathemail.net

Situated in the heart of Hastings Old Town, the museum was originally a Georgian Town Hall built in 1823. Refurbished displays tell the story of Hastings Old Town as a walk back in time, with features including a Cinque Ports ship, and interactive displays.

Times: Open Apr-Sep, daily 10-5. Oct-Mar, daily 11-4.
Fee: Free.
P (150yds) (parking metres in operation) (lift, evac chair, low-level displays, audio tour) toilets for disabled shop (ex guide dogs)

Smugglers Adventure

St Clements Caves, West Hill TN34 3HY
☎ 01424 422964 01424 721483
e-mail: smugglers@tnet.co.uk

A Smuggler's Adventure is a themed experience housed in a labyrinth of caverns and passages deep below the West Hill. Visitors first tour a comprehensive exhibition and museum, followed by a video theatre, before embarking on the Adventure Walk - a trip through several acres of caves with life-size tableaux, push-button automated models and dramatic scenic effects depicting life in the days of 18th-century smuggling.
Times: Open all year daily, Etr-Sep 10-5.30; Oct-Etr 11-4.30. (Closed 25-26 Dec).
Fee: £4.95 (ch £3.25, pen & students £3.90). Family ticket £13.95.
P (500yds) shop

1066 Story in Hastings Castle

Castle Hill Rd, West Hill TN34 3RG
☎ 01424 781111 01424 781186

The ruins of the Norman castle stand on the cliffs, close to the site of William the Conqueror's first motte-and-bailey castle in England. It was excavated in 1825 and 1968, and old dungeons were discovered in 1894. An

contd.

unusual approach to the castle can be made via the West Hill Cliff Railway.
Times: Open Mar-Sep 10-5 (5.30 school holidays). Oct-Feb 11-3.30 (Closed 24-26 Dec).
Fee: £3 (ch £2, pen & students £2.50). Family ticket £9.
P (seafront) ♿ shop 🐕

HERSTMONCEUX

The Truggery

Coopers Croft BN27 1QL (from A22 at Hailsham, Boship roundabout, take A271 in direction of Bexhill for 4m)
☎ 01323 832314 📠 01323 832314
e-mail: sarah@truggery.fsnet.co.uk

The art of Sussex trug making can be seen through all the work processes including preparing timber, use of the draw knife and assembly of the trug.
Times: Open May-Sep 10-5. Closed all day Sun, Mon ex BHs & Sat pm. Oct-Apr opening times may vary.
Fee: Free.
P shop

HOVE

British Engineerium-Museum of Steam & Mechanical Antiquities

off Nevill Rd BN3 7QA
☎ 01273 559583 📠 01273 566403
e-mail: engineerium@mistral.co.uk

This restored Victorian water pumping station has an original working beam engine of 1876, and a French Corliss horizontal engine which won first prize at the Paris International Exhibition of 1889. There are also traction engines, fire engines, and many other full-size and model engines. Boilers are fired up and in steam on certain days.
Times: Open all year, daily 10-4. In steam first Sun in month & Sun & Mon of BH's. Telephone for details of days closed prior to Xmas.
Fee: £4 (ch, students & pen £3, ch under 5 free). Family ticket £12.
P ♿ shop 🐕 (ex guide dogs)

LEWES

Anne of Cleves House Museum

52 Southover High St BN7 1JA (S of Lewes Town Centre off A27/A26/A275)
☎ 01273 474610 📠 01273 486990
e-mail: castle@sussexpast.co.uk

This 16th-century town house was given to Anne of Cleves by her ex-husband, Henry VIII as part of her divorce settlement, though she never lived in the house. It is now devoted to Sussex arts and crafts, agricultural, industrial and domestic life, with a notable collection of Sussex ironwork including early gun-founding material. Artefacts include Lewes memorabilia and "finds" from nearby Lewes Priory.
Times: Open early Jan-mid Feb, Tue, Thu & Sat, 10-5; mid Feb-early Nov daily 10-5 (Sun 12-5); early Nov-mid Dec, Tue & Sat 10-5 (Sun 12-5)
Fee: £2.50 (ch 5-15 £1.20, pen & student £2.30). Family ticket (2 adults & 2 ch) £6.70.
P (25yds) (on street-2 hr restriction) shop 🐕 (ex guide dogs)

Lewes Castle & Barbican House Museum

Barbican House, 169 High St BN7 1YE (off the High Street)
☎ 01273 486290 📠 01273 486990
e-mail: castle@sussexpast.co.uk

High above the medieval streets stands Lewes Castle, begun soon after 1066 by William de Warenne as his stronghold in Sussex and added to over the next 300 years, culminating in the magnificent Barbican. Thomas Read Kemp and his family owned and updated the ruins during Georgian times. Barbican House's Georgian façade conceals a much older timber house which is the home of the Museum of Sussex Archaeology.
Times: Open daily, Mon-Sat 10-5.30, Sun & BH 11-5.30. Castle closes at dusk in winter (Closed 25-26 Dec).
Fee: £3.70 (ch £1.90, pen/student £3.20). Family ticket £10.50. Combined ticket with Anne of Cleves House £5 (ch £2.60, pen/student £4). Family ticket £12.80.
P 200yds (on street parking) (touch screen) shop 🐕 (ex guide dogs & hearing dogs)

NEWHAVEN

Paradise Family Leisure Park

Avis Rd BN9 0DH (signposted off A26 & A259)
☎ 01273 512123 📠 01273 616000 or 616005
e-mail: paradise@fastnet.co.uk

With themed areas illustrating different habitats from around the world, this fine botanical garden makes for a surprising and delightful day out. Thousands of shrubs and trees are the backdrop for waterfalls, fountains and lakes teeming with fish. There are also exhibits on the Planet Earth, and the history of Sussex.
Times: Summer - park & shops, Wed-Fri 9-8, Sat-Tue 9-6; attractions 9.30-5.15. Winter - park & shops, 9-5; attractions 10-4.30.
Fee: £4.50 (ch £3.99). Family ticket £15.99.
P ☕ ✕ licensed ♿ (all areas level or ramped) toilets for disabled shop garden centre 🐕 (ex guide dogs)

NORTHIAM

Great Dixter

TN31 6PH (off A28, signposted)
☎ 01797 252878 📠 01797 252879
e-mail: greatdixter@compuserve.com

Birthplace and home of Christopher Lloyd, gardening writer, Great Dixter was built in 1460 and boasts one of the largest timber-framed buildings in the country. Lutyens was employed to restore both the house and gardens in 1910. The gardens are now a combination of meadows, ponds, topiary and notably the Long Border and Exotic Garden.
Times: Open Apr-29 Oct, Tue-Sun & BH Mon, 2-5.30(last admission 5); Gardens only open from 11am on Sun & Mon BH wknds only.
Fee: House & Gardens £6 (ch £1.50). Gardens only £4.50 (ch £1). Party 25+.
P ♿ (one wheelchair available free of charge) toilets for disabled shop garden centre 🐕 (ex guide dogs)

PEVENSEY

Pevensey Castle

BN24 5LE (off A259)
☎ 01323 762604

Witness to seventeen centuries of conflict, from its origins as a Roman fortress to its use as a coastal base during the Second World War, this powerful castle has never been taken by force.

Times: Open all year, Apr-Oct, daily 10-6 (Oct 10-5); Nov-Mar, Wed-Sun 10-4 (closed 1-2pm). Closed 24-26 Dec & 1 Jan.
Fee: 2.50 (ch 5-15 £1.30, under 5's free).
(charged) (in certain areas)

RYE

Lamb House

West St TN31 7ES (in West St facing W end og Church)
☎ 01892 890651 01892 890110

This 18th-century house was the home of novelist Henry James from 1898 until his death in 1916, and was later occupied by the writer, E F Benson. Some of James' personal posessions can be seen. There is also a charming walled garden.

Times: Open Apr-28 Oct; Wed & Sat 2-6, (last admission 5.30pm).
Fee: £2.50 (ch £1.25).
P (200m)

Rye Castle Museum

3 East St TN31 7JY
☎ 01797 226728

Part of the museum is housed in a stone tower built as a fortification in 1249. The museum's collection of ironwork, medieval pots and smuggling items are on display here, while the East Street site contains the rest of the collection, including pottery made in Rye, military uniforms, fashions, an 18th-century fire engine, toys, cinque port regalia and information on Rye's history.

Times: Open Nov-Mar wknds only 10.30-4; Apr-Oct Thu-Mon 10.30-5.30. (last entry 5pm).
Fee: Entrance to both sites: £3 (ch 7-16 £1.50, concessions £2). Family ticket £6. Single entry only: £2 (ch 7-16) £1, concessions £1.50). Family ticket £4. Party 8+
P (30yds) (street limited to 1hr) toilets for disabled shop

SHEFFIELD PARK

Sheffield Park Garden

TN22 3QX (5m E of Haywards Heath off A275)
☎ 01825 790231 01825 791264
e-mail: kshxxx@smtp.ntrust.org.uk

Sheffield Park was originally landscaped by `Capability' Brown, in about 1775 to create a beautiful park with four lakes and cascades. Further extensive planting was done at the beginning of the 20th century, to give emphasis to autumn colour among the trees. In May and June masses of azaleas and rhododendrons bloom and later there are magnificent waterlilies on the lakes. Autumn brings stunning colours from the many rare trees and shrubs. Special events throughout the season.

Times: Open Jan-Feb Sat-Sun 10.30-4; Mar-Oct Tue-Sun (open BH Mons) 10.30-6; Nov-Dec Tue-Sun 10.30-4 (Last admission 1 hour before closing).
Fee: £4.50 (ch £2.25, under 5's free). Family ticket £11.25.
(powered self drive cars & wheelchairs available) toilets for disabled shop (ex guide/hearing dogs)

SHEFFIELD PARK STATION

Bluebell Railway

Sheffield Park Station TN22 3QL (4.5m E of Haywards Heath, off A275)
☎ 01825 723777, 722370 & 722008 01825 724139 or 724084

Times: Open all year, Sat & Sun, daily May-Sep & during school holidays. Santa Specials run Dec. For timetable and information regarding trains contact above.
licensed (contact for details) toilets for disabled shop
Details not confirmed for 2001

West Sussex

West Sussex is a county of weald and downland, once dominated by the forest that stretched through The Weald from Kent into Hampshire. The oaks of the forest were used to smelt the local iron ore, and though the forest is now somewhat diminished, the country remains green and lush.

The county town of Chichester, the only city in Sussex, is a gem in its own right. South of the city is the headland of Selsey. Selsey was originally an island and is still almost encircled by water, it offers a number of beaches of different character, including the Witterings and Pagham Harbour which is notable for its birdlife. Pre-Norman Selsey, with its cathedral, was lost to the sea long ago.

Further east, the county's main seaside resorts are Bognor Regis, Littlehampton and Worthing. Bognor Regis was one of the first bathing resorts in the late 18th century, and Queen Victoria was particularly fond of the place.

Outside Worthing, at Highdown Hill, there is a Bronze Age settlement beneath an Iron Age hill fort, where the Saxons later buried their own dead.

The main towns are Horsham, Haywards Heath, and Crawley. The third of these is the only new town south of London, and is close to Gatwick Airport. Despite its new town status it has several buildings dating back to the 15th century. Arundel is a particularly handsome town, at a crossing point on the River Arun, dominated by the sprawling, much restored castle and the Roman Catholic Cathedral.

EVENTS & FESTIVALS

April
16 British & World Marbles Championships, Greyhound pub, Tinsley Green, Crawley

May
27-28 Spring Carnival, Crawley

June
7-9 South of England Agricultural Show, Ardingly, Haywards Heath
13-14 Corpus Christi Carpet of Flowers & Floral Festival, Arundel
16-17 Parham Steam Rally, Pulborough
29 Jun-1 July Crawley Folk Festival, Crawley

July
19-22 Southern Cathedrals Festival, combined choirs of Chichester, Salisbury & Winchester cathedrals
22 Bognor Birdman, The Esplanade & Seafront, Bognor Regis

August
24 Aug-2 Sep Arundel Festival
tbc Littlehampton Regatta

September
8 Findon Great Sheep Fair, Nepcote Green, Findon

October
7 South of England Autumn Show, Haywards Heath

Top: The Causeway, Horsham

ARDINGLY

Wakehurst Place Garden

RH17 6TN (1.5m NW, on B2028)

☎ 01444 894066 01444 894069

Woodland and lakes linked by a pretty watercourse make this large garden a beautiful place to walk, and it also has an amazing variety of interesting trees and shrubs, a Winter Garden, and a Rock Walk. It is administered and maintained by the Royal Botanic Gardens at Kew.

Times: Open all year, Nov-Jan 10-4; Feb & Oct 10-5; Mar 10-6; Apr-Sep 10-7. (Closed 25 Dec & 1 Jan). Last admission 30 mins before closing. Mansion closes one hour before garden.

Fee: Telephone for details. Parties 10+.

licensed (wheelchair available) toilets for disabled shop garden centre (ex guide dogs)

ARUNDEL

Arundel Castle

BN18 9AB (on A27 between Chichester & Worthing)

☎ 01903 882173 01903 884581

e-mail: arundelcastle@compuserve.com

This great castle, home of the Dukes of Norfolk, dates from the Norman Conquest. Containing a very fine collection of furniture and paintings, it is still a family home reflecting the changes of nearly a thousand years.

Times: Open Apr-last Fri in Oct, Sun-Fri 12-5. Last admission 4pm (Closed Sat & Good Fri).

Fee: £7 (ch 5-15 £4.50, pen £6). Family ticket £19. Party 20+

toilets for disabled shop (ex guide dogs)

WWT Arundel

Mill Rd BN18 9PB (signposted from A27 & A29)

☎ 01903 883355 01903 884834

e-mail: enquiries@wwt.org.ukk

Times: Open all year, daily. Summer 9.30-5.30; Winter 9.30-4.30. Last admission Summer 5pm; Winter 4pm. (Closed 25 Dec).

licensed (level paths, free wheelchair loan) toilets for disabled shop *Details not confirmed for 2001*

ASHINGTON

Holly Gate Cactus Garden

Billingshurst Rd RH20 3BB (B2133)

☎ 01903 892930

e-mail: hollygate@tmh.globalnet.co.uk

A mecca for the cactus enthusiast, with more than 30,000 succulent and cactus plants, including many rare types. They come from both arid and tropical parts of the world, and are housed in over 10,000 sq ft of greenhouses.

Times: Open all year, daily 9-5. (Closed 25-26 Dec).

Fee: £1.50 (ch & pen £1). Party 20+.

shop garden centre

BIGNOR

Bignor Roman Villa & Museum

RH20 1PH (between A29 & A285)

☎ 01798 869259 01798 869259

Rediscovered in 1811, this Roman house was built on a grand scale. It is one of the largest known, and has spectacular mosaics. The heating system can also be seen, and various finds from excavations are on show. The longest mosaic in Britain (82ft) is on display here in its original position.

Times: Open Mar-May & Oct 10-5 (Closed Mon ex BHs). Jun-Sep daily 10-6.

Fee: £3.50 (ch 16 £1.50, pen £2.50). Party 10+. Guided tours by arrangement.

shop (ex guide dogs)

BRAMBER

Bramber Castle

BN4 3FB (on W side of village off A283)

A former home of the Dukes of Norfolk, this ruined Norman stronghold lies on a ridge of the South Downs and gives wonderful views.

Times: Open any reasonable time.

Fee: Free.

CHICHESTER

Chichester Cathedral

West St PO19 1PX

☎ 01243 782595 01243 536190

The beauty of the 900-year-old cathedral, site of the shrine of St Richard, is enhanced by many art treasures, ancient and modern.

Times: Open Etr-mid Sep daily 7.30-7; mid Sep-Etr 7.30-5. Visiting restricted during services and concerts.

Fee: Free.

(within city walls) (touch & hearing centre, loop system) toilets for disabled shop (ex guide dogs)

Mechanical Music & Doll Collection

Church Rd, Portfield PO19 4HN (1m E, signposted off A27)

☎ 01243 372646 01243 370299

A unique opportunity to see and hear barrel organs, polyphons, musical boxes, fair organs etc - all fully restored and playing for your pleasure. A magical musical tour to fascinate and entertain all ages. The doll collection contains fine examples of Victorian china and wax dolls, also felt and velvet dolls of the 1920s.

Times: Open Jun-Sep, Wed 1-4; Group bookings anytime in the year by prior arrangment.

Fee: £2.50 (ch £1.25).

shop (ex guide dogs)

Pallant House Gallery
9 North Pallant PO19 1TJ
☎ 01243 774557 01243 536038
e-mail: pallant@pallant.co.uk

The gallery is housed in a restored Queen Anne townhouse. The rooms contain fine furniture, and there is a Victorian kitchen. Permanent collections on display include the Modern British Art of the Hussey and Kearley bequests; the Geoffrey Freeman collection of Bow porcelain.

Times: Open all year, Tue-Sat 10-5, Sun & BHs 12.30-5.
Fee: £4 (ch & W Sussex students free, other students & unemployed £2.50, concessions £3).
P (100 yds) shop (ex guide dogs)

EAST GRINSTEAD

Standen
RH19 4NE (2m S of East Grinstead, signposted from B2110)
☎ 01342 323029 01342 316424

Standen is a showpiece of the 19th-century Arts and Crafts movement. It was designed by Philip Webb for the Beale family, and was always meant to be decorated with William Morris wallpapers and fabrics. The interior has been carefully preserved. Webb also designed some of the furniture and details. There is a beautiful hillside garden. For events please contact the Regional Box Office 01372 451596.

Times: House open 29 Mar-5 Nov, Wed-Sun (open BH Mon) 12.30-4.30. Garden: open same dates as house 11.30-6, plus 10 Nov-17 Dec 1-4.
Fee: House & garden £5. Garden only £3. Children half price. Family ticket £12.50Joint ticket which includes same day entry to Nymans garden £7, available Wed-Fri. Groups Wed-Fri only.
P licensed (braille guide) shop (ex guide dogs/Woodland Walk)

FISHBOURNE

Fishbourne Roman Palace
Salthill Rd PO19 3QR (N of A259 in Fishbourne)
☎ 01243 785859 01243 539266
e-mail: adminfish@sussexpast.co.uk

This is the largest known Roman residence in Britain. It was occupied from the 1st to the 3rd centuries AD, and has mosaic floors and painted walls; 25 of these mosaic floors can still be seen in varying states of completeness, including others rescued from elsewhere in the area. Outside, part of the garden has been replanted to its original 1st-century plan. The museum gives an account of the history of the palace, and shows a full-size reconstruction of a Roman dining room.

Times: Open all year, daily early Feb-mid Dec. Feb, Nov-Dec 10-4; Mar-Jul & Sep-Oct 10-5; Aug 10-6. Winter wkends 10-4.
Fee: £4.40 (ch £2.30, pen & students £3.70, redistered disabled £3.50). Family ticket (2 adults & 2 ch)£11.50. Group.
P (self guiding tapes & tactile objects for the blind) toilets for disabled shop garden centre (ex guide dogs)

FONTWELL

Denmans Garden
BN18 0SU (5m E of Chichester on A27)
☎ 01243 542808 01243 544064
Times: Open Mar-Oct daily 9-5.
P shop garden centre (ex guide dogs) *Details not confirmed for 2001*

GOODWOOD

Goodwood House
PO18 0PX (3m NE of Chichester)
☎ 01243 755000 01243 755005
e-mail: enquires@googwood.co.uk

Ancestral home of the Dukes of Richmond for 300 years. Following refurbishment the State Apartments have taken on new life, including the restored tapestry drawing room. Goodwood was the country home of the scandalous and glamorous Lennox sisters, immortalised in the BBC TV production of Aristocrats. Unrivalled as an English ancestral collection, the paintings include works by Van Dyck, Reynolds, Stubbs and Canaletto.

Times: Open 2 Apr-25 Sep, Sun & Mon & 6 Aug-7 Sep, Sun-Thur 1-5. (Closed 9 Apr, 14-15 May, Jun & 30 Jul, 1-3 Aug &17 Sep).
Fee: £6 (ch & disabled £3). Groups 20+.
P (ramp at front of house, disabled parking area) toilets for disabled shop

HANDCROSS

Nymans Garden
RH17 6EB (on B2114)
☎ 01444 400321 & 400777 01444 400253

Set in the Sussex Weald, Nymans has flowering shrubs and roses, a flower garden in the old walled orchard, and a secret sunken garden. There are some fine and rare trees. Summer events are held in the garden. For details please call regional box office (01372) 451596.

Times: Open Garden: Mar-29 Oct, daily Wed, Thur & wkends, (also open BH Mon) 11-6 or sunset if earlier. Nov-Mar, Wkends, 11-4, restricted according to ground conditions. Closed 25-26 & 30-31 Dec. Phone for more information. House open 29 Mar-29 Oct 12-4.
Fee: £5. Family ticket £12.50, joint ticket which includes same day entry to Standen £7 available Wed-Fri. Reduced admission at winter wknds: £2.50 (ch £1.50) Family £6.50.
P (wheelchair route, wheelchair available, braille guide) toilets for disabled shop (ex guide dogs & hearing dogs)

HAYWARDS HEATH

Borde Hill Garden
Balcombe Rd RH16 1XP (1.5m N of Hayward Heath on Balcombe Road)
☎ 01444 450326 01444 440427
e-mail: info@bordehill.co.uk

Borde Hill set in 200 acres of spectacular Sussex parkland boasts fine displays of rhododendrons, camellias, magnolias and azaleas during the spring. Extensive planting with a new rose and herbaceous garden for the summer. Attractions include coarse fishing, childrens' trout fishing and an adventure playground.

Times: Open all year, 10-6 (or dusk if earlier).

Fee: £4.50 (ch 3-15 £1.75). Family ticket £11. Group 20+.

licensed (wheelchairs available) toilets for disabled shop garden centre (on leads)

LOWER BEEDING

LEONARDSLEE GARDENS

RH13 6PP (4m SW from Handcross, at junct of B2110/A281)

☎ 01403 891212 01403 891305

This Grade I listed garden is set in a peaceful valley with walks around seven beautiful lakes. It is a paradise in spring, with banks of rhododendrons and azaleas along paths lined with bluebells. Wallabies live in parts of the valley, deer in the parks and wildfowl on the lakes. Enjoy the Rock Garden, the fascinating Bonsai, and the new 'Behind the Doll's House' exhibition.

Times: Open Apr-Oct, daily 9.30-6 (May 9.30-8).

Fee: Apr & Jun-Oct £4, May (Mon-Fri) £5, (wknds & BH) £6 (ch £2.50 anytime).

licensed (No wheelchair access. Other disablities are catered for) shop garden centre (inc guide dogs)

PETWORTH

PETWORTH HOUSE & PARK

GU28 0AE (in centre of Petworth, A272/A283)

☎ 01798 342207 & 343929 01798 342963

Petworth was rebuilt by the Duke of Somerset in the 17th century, and all that remains of the 13th-century building is the chapel. The state rooms and galleries contain one of the finest art collections in England, including works by Turner, Gainsborough, Rembrandt and Van Dyck.

Times: Open House & Servants Quarters: Apr-1 Nov, Sat-Wed (open Good Fri & every Fri in Jul & Aug). House 1-5.30, last admission 4.30. Park open daily 8-sunset (ex 25-27 Jun). Extra rooms shown on weekdays but not BH. Pleasure Ground & Car Park: 18-19 & 25-26 Mar, 12-4. Apr-1 Nov, 12-6 (11am in Jul, Aug & BH's).

Fee: £6 (ch £3). Family ticket £15. Party 15+. Pleasure Ground £1.50 (ch free).

(charged) licensed (wheelchairs available, braille guide) toilets for disabled shop (ex guide dogs)

PULBOROUGH

PARHAM HOUSE & GARDENS

Parham Park RH20 4HS (3m SE off A283, between Pulborough & Storrington)

☎ 01903 744888 (info line) 742021

01903 746557

e-mail: parham@dial.pipex.com

Surrounded by a deer park, finc gardens and 18th-century Pleasure Grounds in a beautiful downland setting, this Elizabethan family home contains an important collection of paintings, furniture, carpets and rare needlework. A brick and turf maze has been created in the grounds - designed with children in mind, it is called 'Veronica's Maze'.

Times: Open 4 Apr-31 Oct, Wed, Thu, Sun & BH. Gardens 12-6; House 2-6 (last entry 5). Guided tours on Wed & Thu mornings and Tue & Fri afternoons by special arrangement.

Fee: House & Gardens £5.25 (ch 5-15 £1, pen £4.50). Family ticket £11. Gardens £3.25 (ch 50p). Party.

(wheelchairs available by arrangement/tape tour) shop garden centre (ex guide dogs & in grounds)

RSPB NATURE RESERVE

Uppertons Barn Visitor Centre, Wiggonholt RH20 2EL (signposted on A283, 2m SE of Pulborough & 2m NW of Storrington)

☎ 01798 875851 01798 873816

Set in the scenic Arun Valley and easily reached via the visitor centre at Wiggonholt, this is an excellent reserve for year-round family visits. A nature trail winds through hedgerow-lined lanes to viewing hides overlooking water-meadows. Breeding summer birds include nightingales and warblers, ducks and wading birds, and nightjars and hobbies on nearby heathland. Unusual wading birds and hedgerow birds regularly pass through on spring and autumn migration.

Times: Open daily, 9-9, (or sunset if earlier). Visitor centre daily, 10-5. Reserve closed 25 Dec, visitor centre closed 25-26 Dec.

Fee: £3.50 (ch 5-16 £1, concessions £2.50) Family (2 adults & 4 ch) £7.

(ramps at some hides/batricar bookable/easy gradient trail) toilets for disabled shop (ex guide dogs)

SINGLETON

WEALD & DOWNLAND OPEN AIR MUSEUM

PO18 0EU (6m N of Chichester on A286)

☎ 01243 811348 01243 811475

e-mail: wealddown@mistral.co.uk

A showcase of English architectural heritage, where historic buildings have been rescued from destruction and rebuilt in a parkland setting. Vividly demonstrating the evolution of building techniques and use of local materials, these fascinating buildings bring to life the homes, farms and rural industries of the past 500 years.

Times: Open all year, Mar-Oct, daily 10.30-6 (last admission 5); Nov-Feb, Wed, Sat & Sun 10.30-4, also 26 Dec-1 Jan daily & Feb half term, 10.30-4.

Fee: £6 (ch & students £3, pen £5.50). Family ticket (2 adults & 3 ch) £15. Party.

toilets for disabled shop (ex on leads)

SOUTH HARTING

Uppark

GU31 5QR (1.5m S on B2146)
☎ 01730 825415 825857 01730 825873
e-mail: sopgen@smtp.ntrust.org.uk

On 30th August 1989 this late 17th-century house was partially destroyed by fire. The attic and the first floor were completely gutted, but virtually all of the 18th-century contents were saved. Following an ambitious restoration project, Uppark has been restored to its state `the day before the fire'.

Times: Open 2 Apr-31 Oct, Sun-Thu. House 1-5. Car park, woodland walk, garden & Exhibition 11.30-5.30. Last admission to house 4pm. Timed tickets will be in operation on BH Sun & Mon & Sun in Jul & Aug.

Fee: House, garden & exhibition £5.50. Family ticket £13.75.

(ramps, lift, stair to exhibition) toilets for disabled shop (ex woodland walk & car park)

TANGMERE

Tangmere Military Aviation Museum Trust

PO20 6ES (off A27, 3m E of Chichester)
☎ 01243 775223 01243 789490

Based at an airfield which played an important role during the World Wars, this museum spans 80 years of military aviation. There are photographs, documents, aircraft and aircraft parts on display along with a Hurricane replica, Spitfire replica and cockpit simulator. A hangar houses a Supermarine Swift and the record-breaking aircraft Meteor and Hunter.

Times: Open Mar-Oct, daily 10-5.30; Feb & Nov, daily 10-4.30.

Fee: £3 (ch £1.50 & pen £2.50).

(wheelchairs available) toilets for disabled shop (ex guide dogs)

WEST DEAN

West Dean Gardens

Estate Office PO18 0QZ (on A286, 6m N of Chichester)
☎ 01243 818210 & 811301 01243 811342
e-mail: westdean@pavilion.co.uk

Award winning historic garden of 35 acres in a tranquil downland setting. Noted for its 300ft long Harold Peto pergola, mixed and herbaceous borders, rustic summerhouses, water garden and specimen trees. Walled kitchen garden with magnificent collection of 13 Victorian glasshouses. The Visitors Centre provides a high level of facilities with a beautiful prospect of the River Lavant and West Dean Park.

Times: Open Mar, Apr & Oct, daily 11-5; May-Sep 10.30-5. Last ticket 4.30pm.

Fee: £4 (ch £2, pen £3.50). Party+.

licensed (reserved parking) toilets for disabled shop (ex guide dogs)

Tyne & Wear

Tyne & Wear is a metropolitan county, created by local government reorganisation in 1974. It includes the towns of Newcastle-upon-Tyne, Gateshead, South Shields and Sunderland. It is cut through by the two rivers the Tyne and the Wear, and includes a section of Hadrian's Wall.

The area grew prosperous on coal and shipbuilding, and buildings of Victorian grandeur reflect its heyday. George Stephenson established an ironworks here in 1826, and the first engine on the Stockton and Darlington railway was made in Newcastle. Industrial decline has hit hard, but the Geordie spirit survives and brings immense vitality to the place.

Newcastle's 'new castle' is believed to date from the 11th century, though the present keep dates from the 12th. Other ancient buildings include the 14th-century cathedral, and the 17th-century Guildhall. Contemporary constructions include the Metro, which links Newcastle to Gateshead (along with several bridges), and the Metro Centre in Gateshead, Britain's largest shopping centre. The most famous of the bridges are High Level Bridge, a road and rail bridge, built by Robert Stephenson in 1849, and the Tyne Bridge dating from 1929.

Jarrow, five miles east of Newcastle, is remembered for the Jarrow Crusade of 1936, when 200 men marched to London to bring attention to the plight of unemployed shipbuilders. The town was also the home of monk-scholar, the Venerable Bede, whose 8th-century work, *Historia Ecclesiastica Gentis Anglorum*, was the first important history written about the English. He was buried at Jarrow, and his bones remained there until the 11th century when they were moved to Durham.

EVENTS & FESTIVALS

April
7-8 Gateshead Spring Flower Show, Gateshead Central Nursery

July
13-15 International Jazz Festival, Park Hotel, Tynemouth
tbc Gateshead Summer Flower Show, Gateshead Central Nursery
tbc North of England Motorshow, Links, Whitley Bay
tbc Sunderland International Air Show, Promenade, Seaburn, Sunderland

August
tbc Newcastle Mela (free Asian festival), Exhibition Park, Newcastle-upon-Tyne

October
tbc Junior Great North Run, Gateshead International Stadium, Gateshead
tbc Great North Run (Newcastle-upon-Tyne to South Shields)

November
tbc Newcastle Comedy Festival (various venues), Newcastle-upon-Tyne

Top: New Tyne Road Bridge

JARROW

Bedes World & St Paul's Church

Church Bank NE32 3DY (off A185 near south end of Tyne tunnel)
☎ 0191 489 2106 📠 0191 428 2361
e-mail: visitor.info@bedesworld.co.uk

The Venerable Bede was one of early Britain's greatest scholars, and was the author of the *"Historia Ecclesiastica Gentis Anglorum"*, the definitive history of the early medieval period. As well as exhibits detailing Bede's monastic life and work, the museum demonstrates Anglo-Saxon farming and living history re-enactments.

Times: Open all year, Apr-Oct, Tue-Sat & BH Mons 10-5.30, Sun noon-5.30; Nov-Mar, Tue-Sat 10-4.30 & Sun 12-4.30; Xmas-New Year opening times vary. Church open Mon-Sat 10-4 & Sun 2.30-4, unless service being held.

Fee: £3 (ch & concessions £1.50). Family ticket £7.20. UB40 family ticket £4. Prices will increase in 2000 due to new museum opening.

P ☕ ♿ (electric wheelchair on request) toilets for disabled shop 🐕 (ex guide dogs) 💳

NEWCASTLE UPON TYNE

Hancock Museum

Barras Bridge NE2 4PT
☎ 0191 222 7418 📠 0191 222 6753
e-mail: hancock.museum@ncl.ac.uk

The museum houses geological exhibits and John Hancock's magnificent collection of birds. Land of the Pharaohs explores life and death in Ancient Eygpt. The Earth galleries explore the cosmic and geological processes that have shaped the earth, and investigate the history of life on our planet.

Times: Open all year, Mon-Sat, 10-5, Sun 2-5. Closed 25 & 26 Dec & 1 Jan.

Fee: £2.25 (concessions £1.50). Family ticket (2 adults & 2 ch) £6.50. Prices vary with special exhibitions, call 0191 222 7418 for details.

P ☕ ♿ (stair lift,audio/braille guide, staff trained in sign lang) toilets for disabled shop 🐕 (ex guide dogs) 💳

Museum of Antiquities

The University NE1 7RU (on campus of Newcastle University)
☎ 0191 222 7849 📠 0191 222 8561
e-mail: m.o.antiquities@ncl.ac.uk

Artefacts from north east England from prehistoric times to AD 1600 are on display here. The principal museum for Hadrian's Wall, this collection includes models of the wall, life-size Roman soldiers and a recently refurbished reconstruction of the Temple of Mithras.

Times: Open all year, daily (ex Sun), 10-5 (Closed Good Fri, 24-26 Dec & 1 Jan).

Fee: Free.

P (400yds) ♿ (Large print guide) shop 🐕 (ex guide dogs) 💳

ROWLANDS GILL

Gibside

NE16 6BG (6m SW of Gateshead, on B6314)
☎ 01207 542255

The important early 18th-century landscaped park contains a chapel - an outstanding example of Palladian architecture, built to a design by James Paine as the mausoleum for members of the Bowes family. It stands at one end of the Great Walk of Turkey oaks, looking towards the column of British Liberty.

Times: Open: Grounds all year (ex Mon), 11-5. Open BH Mon(Mar-Oct 10-6, Nov-Feb 10-sunset). Last admission 4.30, or 1hr before sunset. Chapel: Apr-Oct as grounds 10-5, otherwise by prior arrangment.

Fee: £3. Family ticket £8. Party.

P ☕ ♿ (braille guide, wheelchair) shop 🐕 (ex on leads) ✿ 💳

SOUTH SHIELDS

Arbeia Roman Fort & Museum

Baring St NE33 2BB (5 mins walk from South Shields Town Centre)
☎ 0191 456 1369 454 4093
📠 0191 427 6862

In South Shields town are the extensive remains of Arbeia, a 2nd-century Roman fort. It was the supply base for the Roman army's campaign against Scotland. On the site of the west gate is a full-scale simulation of a Roman gateway with interior scenes of life at the fort. Archaeological excavations are in progress throughout the summer.

Times: Open all year, Apr-Sep, Mon-Sat 10-5.30, Sun 1-5; Oct-Mar, Mon-Sat 10-4. Closed 25-26 Dec, 1 Jan & Good Friday.

Fee: Fort & Museum free of charge ex for 'Timequest'Archaeological Interpretation Gallery £1.50 (ch & concessions 80p).

P ♿ (Minicom system) toilets for disabled shop

SUNDERLAND

Museum & Art Gallery

Borough Rd SR1 1PP
☎ 0191 565 0723 📠 0191 565 0713

Times: Open all year, Mon-Fri 10-5, Sat 10-4.30, Sun 2-5.

P (150 yds) ☕ ♿ toilets for disabled shop 🐕 *Details not confirmed for 2001* 💳

TYNEMOUTH

Tynemouth Castle & Priory

NE30 4BZ (near North Pier)
☎ 0191 257 1090

The castle and priory are a testament to the strategic importance of the site and its great religious significance. The soaring arches of the presbytery are an eloquent reminder of the priory's former wealth, and the Percy Chantry is still almost complete.

Times: Open all year, Apr-Oct, daily 10-6 (Oct 10-5); Nov-Mar, Wed-Sun 10-4 (or dusk if earlier, closed 1-2pm). Closed 24-26 Dec & 1 Jan.

Fee: £1.80 (ch 5-15 90p, under 5's free).

♿ shop 🐕 #

WASHINGTON

Washington Old Hall

(follow signs for District 4 Washington New Town)
☎ 0191 416 6879

The home of George Washington's ancestors from 1183 to 1613, the Old Hall was originally an early medieval manor, but was rebuilt in the 17th century. The house has been restored and filled with period furniture. The property was given to the National Trust in 1956. There will be celebrations to mark American Independence Day in July.

Times: Open 2 Apr-31 Oct, Sun-Wed; open Good Fri,11-5. Last admission 4.30.

Fee: £2.80. Family ticket (2 adults & 3 ch) £7. Party.

(braille guide, tactile opportunities in house) toilets for disabled shop

WWT Washington

NE38 8LE (signposted off A195, A1231 & A182)
☎ 0191 416 5454 0191 416 5801

In a parkland setting, on the north bank of the River Wear, WWT Washington is the home of a wonderful collection of exotic wildfowl from all over the world. There is also a heronry where visitors can watch a colony of wild Grey Herons on CCTV. The 100-acre site includes an area for wintering wildfowl which can be observed from hides, and a flock of Chilean Flamingos. Other features include a discovery centre, waterfowl nursery, picture windows and a viewing gallery from which to observe the birds.

Times: Open all year, daily 9.30-5 (summer) or 9.30-4 (winter). Closed 25 Dec.

Fee: £4.75 (ch £2.75). Family ticket (2 adults & 2 ch) £12. Party 10+.

(lowered windows in certain hides, wheelchairs to hire free) toilets for disabled shop (ex guide dogs)

WHITBURN

Souter Lighthouse

(coast road 2m S from South Shields)
☎ 0191 529 3161

This 150ft-high lighthouse was opened by Trinity House in 1871 and contains a bi-optic light, still in its original condition, which was the first reliable electrically powered lighthouse light. The Engine and Battery Rooms are all in working order and are included in the guided tour, along with the light tower, museum cottage and video.

Times: Open Apr-Oct daily ex Fri,(open Good Fri),11-5. Last admission 4.30.

Fee: £2.80. Family ticket £7.

toilets for disabled shop

Warwickshire

The countryside of south Warwickshire, located in the Heart of England, was beloved of William Shakespeare. The bard is forever associated with the town of Stratford-upon-Avon, the place of his birth and death, which now has two theatres built in his honour.

These days, the small market town he knew as home is packed with tourists - the most visited British tourist destination outside London. North of the county, around Coventry, which is itself officially part of the West Midlands, the scene is much more industrial/urban and seems a world away from this mainly rural area.

Warwickshire has some fine towns, including Warwick itself, the county town, which boasts one of the greatest English castles. The castle is medieval, though it was comprehensively restored in the 19th century, and its enormous bulk dominates the town. The centre of Warwick is mainly Georgian, built following a fire in 1694 that destroyed the earlier medieval buildings, though some do remain on the periphery. The county's other great castle is Kenilworth, a Norman fortress built of sandstone standing to the west of Kenilworth town.

Leamington Spa came to prominence when the fashion for 'taking the waters' was at its height in the late 18th and early 19th century. Rugby, however, is best known as the home of one of England's most elevated public schools, immortalised in Thomas Hughes' *Tom Brown's Schooldays*. The school was also the home of the ballgame that bears its name.

EVENTS & FESTIVALS

February
tbc February Frolics, Hatton Country World

March
tbc Spring Craft Fair, Alcester

April
tbc Easter Egg Trail, Baddesley Clinton

May
21-22 Amateur Gardening Spring Show, National Agricultural Centre, Stoneleigh Park

July
2-5 The Royal Show, National Agricultural Centre, Stoneleigh Park
4-15 Warwick & Leamington Festival
27-29 Warwickshire Folk Festival
tbc Newfoundland Dog Trials, Alcester

August
25-27 Town & Country Fair, NAC Stoneleigh
tbc Fireworks & Laser Show, Alcester
tbc Warwickshire & West Midlands Game Fair, Alcester

October
tbc Autumn Craft Fair, Ragley Hall, Alcester

November
tbc Yuletide Craft Fair, Ragley Hall, Alcester

Top: Long Compton

ALCESTER

RAGLEY HALL

B49 5NJ (off A46/A435)
☎ 01789 762090 01789 764791
e-mail: ragley.hall@virginnet.co.uk

Ragley Hall is set in four hundred acres of parkland and gardens. The Great Hall contains some of England's finest Baroque plasterwork designed by James Gibbs. Graham Rust's mural The Temptation can be seen on the south staircase. Ample picnic areas beside the lake, as well as an adventure playground, maze and woodland walks.

Times: Open mid Apr-early Oct, Thu-Sun & BH Mon. Park & Garden open daily, late Jul-early Sep.
Fee: House (including garden & park) £5 (ch £3.50, pen £4.50).
(lift to first floor) toilets for disabled shop (on leads in the park only)

BADDESLEY CLINTON

BADDESLEY CLINTON HALL

B93 0DQ (0.75m W off A4141, 7.5m NW of Warwick)
☎ 01564 783294 01564 782706
e-mail: baddesley@smtp.ntrust.org.uk

A romantically-sited medieval moated house, dating from the 14th century, that has changed very little since 1634. With family portraits, priest holes, chapel, garden, ponds, nature trail and lake walk. An autumn lecture programme is planned.

Times: House open Mar-29 Oct, Wed-Sun & BH Mon (closed Good Fri). Mar-Apr & 1-29 Oct 1.30-5; May-Sep 1.30-5.30. (Last admissions 30 mins before closing). Grounds open 13 Feb-17 Dec, Wed-Sun & BH Mon (open Good Fri). Feb & Nov-17 Dec 12-4.30; Mar-Apr & Oct 12-5; May-Sep 12-5.30.
Fee: £5.20. Family ticket £13. Grounds, restaurant & shop only £2.60.
licensed (wheelchairs available, hearing scheme, braille guides) toilets for disabled shop (ex guide dogs)

CHARLECOTE

CHARLECOTE PARK

CV35 9ER (5m E of Stratford, 1m W of Wellesbourne on B4086)
☎ 01789 470277 01789 470544
e-mail: charlecote@smtp.ntrust.org.uk

Built in the 1550s and later visited by Queen Elizabeth I, Charlecote Park was landscaped by 'Capability' Brown and has a herd of red and fallow deer, reputedly poached by Shakespeare, and a flock of Jacob sheep first introduced in 1756. The principal rooms are decorated in Elizabethan Revival style.

Times: Open 25 Mar-4 Nov, Fri-Tue 12-5.
Fee: £5.40 (ch £2.70). Family ticket £13.50.
licensed (Braille guides & hearing scheme available) toilets for disabled shop

COUGHTON

COUGHTON COURT

B49 5JA (2m N of Alcester on E side of A435)
☎ 01789 762435 01789 765544

During the Civil War this formerly moated and mainly Elizabethan house was attacked by both Parliamentary and Royalist forces. There are exhibitions on the Gunpowder Plot and Children's Clothes. Outdoor concert with fireworks in July.

Times: Open 18 Mar-end Mar & Oct, Sat-Sun. Apr-Sep, Wed-Sun & BH Mon-Tue and all Tues in Jul & Aug. (Closed Good Fri). Oct, Fri & Sat. Open 11.30-5 (BH Mon 11-5).
Fee: £6.40. Family ticket £19.40. Grounds only £4.60. Family ticket £14.40.
licensed (braille guide, wheelchair available) toilets for disabled shop

FARNBOROUGH

FARNBOROUGH HALL

OX17 1DU (6m N of Banbury, 0.5m W of A423)
☎ 01295 690202
e-mail: upton@smtp.ntrust.org.uk

A classical mid 18th-century stone house with notable plasterwork; the entrance hall, staircase and two principal rooms are shown. The grounds contain charming 18th-century temples, a 3/4-mile terrace walk and an obelisk.

Times: House, grounds & terrace walk open Apr-Sep, Wed & Sat, & 30 Apr-1 May 2-6. Terrace walk Thu & Fri only, 2-6. Last admission 5.30pm.
Fee: House, Grounds & Terrace walk £3. Garden & Terrace walk £1.50. Terrace walk only (Thu & Fri) £1.
(ex guide dogs)

GAYDON

HERITAGE MOTOR CENTRE

Banbury Rd CV35 0BJ (Exit M40 at junc 12 and take B4100)
☎ 01926 641188 01926 641555

Times: Open all year, Apr-Oct, daily 10-6; Nov-Mar. daily 10-4.30. (check fo Christmas opening. Closed 24-26, 31 Dec & 1 Jan).
licensed (lifts, wide doors, graded ramps & pathways) toilets for disabled shop (ex guide dogs & hearing dogs) *Details not confirmed for 2001*

KENILWORTH

KENILWORTH CASTLE

CV8 1NE
☎ 01926 852078

Kenilworth is the largest castle ruin in England, its massive walls towering over the countryside. Originally founded in the 11th century, it was already ancient when Queen Elizabeth I visited her favourite, Robert Dudley, Earl of Leicester, here in 1575; he built a new wing for her use.

Times: Open all year, Apr-Sep daily 10-6 (Oct 10-5); Nov-Mar, daily 10-4. Closed 24-26 Dec & 1 Jan.
Fee: £3.50 (ch 5-15 £1.80, under 5's free).
shop

Stoneleigh Abbey
CV8 2LF (Entrance to the abbey is off B4115 close to the junction of A46 and A452)
☎ 01926 858585 📠 01926 850724
e-mail: enquire@stoneleigh.org

Stoneleigh Abbey is one of the finest country house estates in the Midlands and reopens in 2001 after considerable restoration work. The abbey, founded in the reign of Henry II, is now managed by a charitable trust. Visitors will experience a wealth of architectural styles spanning more than 600 years. The magnificent state rooms and chapel, the medieval Gatehouse and the Regency stables are some of the major areas to be admired. Set in 600 acres of parkland.
Times: For opening dates please phone 01926 858585. The abbey has been the subject of a restoration project, since early 1997 and will formally reopen Easter 2001.
Fee: For admission prices please phone 01926 858585.
P ☕ ♿ (State rooms are also accessible) toilets for disabled shop

MIDDLETON

Ash End House Childrens Farm
Middleton Ln, Middleton B78 2BL (signposted from A4091)
☎ 0121 329 3240 📠 0121 329 3240

Ideal for young children this is a small family-owned farm with many friendly animals to feed and stroke, including some rare breeds. Cafe, shop, gift shop, play areas, picnic barns and lots of undercover activities.
Times: Open daily 10-5 or dusk in winter. (Closed 25-28 Dec & 1 Jan).
Fee: £1.80 (ch £3.60 includes animal feed, badge & pony ride)
P ☕ ♿ toilets for disabled shop 🐕 (ex guide dogs) 💳

Middleton Hall
B78 2AE (M42 junct 9, on A4091 midway between Belfry & Drayton Manor, follow brown signs)
☎ 01827 283095 📠 01827 285717

Once the home of two great 17th-century naturalists, Francis Willughby and John Ray, the Hall shows several architectural styles, from c1300 to a Georgian west wing. The grounds include a nature reserve, lake, meadow, orchard and woodland, all Sites of Special Scientific Interest.
Times: Open Apr-30 Sep, Sun 2-5, BH 11-5.
Fee: £2 (ch free, pen £1)
P ☕ ♿ (wheelchairs available) toilets for disabled shop

NUNEATON

Arbury Hall
CV10 7PT (2m SW of Nuneaton, off B4102 Meriden road)
☎ 024 7638 2804 📠 024 7664 1147

The 16th-century Elizabethan house, Gothicised in the 18th century, has been the home of the Newdegate family for over 450 years. It is the finest complete example of Gothic revival architecture in existence, and contains pictures, furniture, and beautiful plasterwork ceilings. The 17th-century stable block, with a central doorway by Wren, houses the tearooms and lovely gardens with lakes and wooded walks.
Times: Open Etr-Sep 2-5.30 (last admission 5pm). Hall & gardens: Sun & Mon of BH weekends only. For other opening days & times, contact the Administrator.
Fee: £4.50 (ch £2.50) gardens only £3. (ch £2.)
P ☕ ♿ shop 🐕 (ex guide dogs & in grounds)

PACKWOOD HOUSE

Packwood House
B94 6AT (on unclass road off A34)
☎ 01564 783294 📠 01564 782706
e-mail: baddesley@smtp.ntrust.org.uk

Dating from the 16th century, Packwood House has been extended and much changed over the years. An important collection of tapestries and textiles is displayed. Equally important are the stunning gardens with renowned herbaceous borders and the almost surreal topiary garden based on the Sermon on the Mount.
Times: Open May-Sep, Wed-Sun & BH Mon 1.30-5.30; end Mar-Apr & Oct, Wed-Sun & BH Mon 12.30-4.30. Garden: May-Sep, Wed-Sun & BH Mon 10-5.30; Mar-Apr & Oct, Wed-Sun & BH Mon 10-4.30.
Fee: £4.60 (ch £2.30). Family ticket £11.50. Garden only £2.30 (ch £1.15).
P ♿ (wheelchairs available) toilets for disabled shop 🐕 (ex guide dogs) 💳

RUGBY

The James Gilbert Rugby Football Museum
5 Saint Matthew's St CV21 3BY
☎ 01788 333888 & 333889 📠 01788 540795
e-mail: museum@james-gilbert.com

An intriguing collection of Rugby football memorabilia is housed in the shop in which Gilbert's have made their world famous Rugby balls since 1842. Visitors can watch a craftsman at work, hand-stitching the footballs. Situated near to Rugby School and its famous playing field.
Times: Open all year, Mon-Sat 9-5. Phone for holiday opening times.
Fee: Free.
P (500 yds) ♿ shop 🐕

RYTON-ON-DUNSMORE

Ryton Organic Gardens
CV8 3LG (5m SE of Coventry signposted off A45, on the road to the village of Wolston)
☎ 024 7630 3517 📠 024 7663 9229
e-mail: enquiry@hdra.org.uk

The gardens are the home of the Henry Doubleday Research Association, Europe's largest organic organisation. The HDRA promotes organic gardening, farming and food, and its gardens cover 10 acres. Guided tours are available.
Times: Open all year 9-5. (Closed Xmas).
Fee: £3 (ch under 16 free).
P ✕ licensed ♿ (wheelchairs available) toilets for disabled shop garden centre 🐕 (ex guide dogs) 💳

SHOTTERY

Anne Hathaway's Cottage

☎ 01789 292100 204016
e-mail: info@shakespeare.org.uk

Before her marriage to William Shakespeare, Anne Hathaway lived in this substantial 12-roomed thatched Tudor farmhouse with her prosperous yeoman family. The house now shows many aspects of domestic life in 16th-century England, and has a lovely traditional cottage garden and Shakespeare tree garden.

Times: Open all year, 20 Mar-19 Oct Mon-Sat 9-5, Sun 9.30-4; 20 Oct-19 Mar Mon-Sat 9.30-4, Sun 10-4. (Closed 23-26 Dec).
Fee: £4.20 (ch £1.70, concessions £3.70). Family ticket £10. Inclusive ticket to all 5 Shakespearian properties £12 (ch £6, concessions £11). Family £29.
P (charged) licensed toilets for disabled shop garden centre

STRATFORD-UPON-AVON

Butterfly Farm

Tramway Walk, Swan's Nest Ln CV37 7LS (south bank of River Avon opposite RSC)
☎ 01789 299288 01789 415878
e-mail:
stratford_butterfly_farm@compuserve.com

Europe's largest live Butterfly and Insect Exhibit. Hundreds of the world's most spectacular and colourful butterflies, in the unique setting of a lush tropical landscape, with splashing waterfalls and fish-filled pools. See also the strange and fascinating Insect City, a bustling metropolis of ants, bees, stick insects, beetles and other remarkable insects. See the dangerous and deadly in Arachnoland!

Times: Open daily 10-6 (winter 10-5.30). Closed 25 Dec.
Fee: £3.75 (ch £2.75, pen & students £3.25). Family (2 adults & 2 ch) £10.75. Party 10+.
P (opposite entrance) (site parking orange badge holders only) toilets for disabled shop

Cox's Yard

Bridgefoot CV37 6YY (opposite Bancroft Gardens)
☎ 01789 404600 01789 404633
e-mail: info@coxsyard.co.uk
Times: Open all year, daily from 9am.
P licensed (lift to all levels, parking on site) toilets for disabled shop *Details not confirmed for 2001*

Hall's Croft

Old Town
☎ 01789 292107 & 204016

A Tudor house with outstanding furniture and paintings where Shakespeare's daughter Susanna, and her husband, Dr John Hall, lived before moving to New Place on the dramatist's death. There is an exhibition on Tudor medicine, and fine walled gardens can also be seen.

Times: Open all year, 20 Mar-19 Oct Mon-Sat 9.30-5; Sun 10-5; 20 Oct-19 Mar, Mon-Sat, 10-4; Sun 10.30-4. (Closed 23-26 Dec).
Fee: £3.50 (ch £1.70 concession £3) Family ticket £8.50.Three In-town Properties ticket: £8.50 (ch £4.20,concession £7.50) Family ticket £20. Five Properties ticket: £12 (ch £6, concession £11) Family ticket £29.
P (100metres) (2hr limit on-street parking) (ramp access for garden & lawns) toilets for disabled shop

New Place / Nash's House

Chapel St CV37 6EP
☎ 01789 292325 & 204016

Only the foundations remain of the house where Shakespeare spent the last five years of his life and died in 1616. The house was destroyed in 1759, but the picturesque garden has been planted as an Elizabethan knot garden. There is a small museum of furniture and local history in the adjacent Nash's House.

Times: Open all year,20 Mar-19 Oct, Mon-Sat, 9.30-5, Sun 10-5; 20 Oct-19 Mar, Mon-Sat, 10-4, Sun 10.30-4. (Closed 23-26 Dec).
Fee: £3.50 (ch £1.70, concessions £3.70) Family ticket £10. Three In-town properties £8.50 (ch £4.20, concessions £7.50) Family ticket £20. Five Properties Ticket £12 (ch £6, concessions £11) Family ticket £29.
P (250yds) toilets for disabled shop

Royal Shakespeare Company Collection

Royal Shakespeare Theatre, Waterside CV37 6BB
☎ 01789 262870 📠 01789 262870

The RSC gallery is housed in the original Victorian building which was part of Charles Flower's Shakespeare Memorial, opened in 1879, comprising Theatre, Paintings and Sculpture Gallery, Library and Reading Room, the latter were not destroyed when the Theatre was burnt down in 1926.

Times: Open all year, Mon-Sat 12-6.30, Sun 12-4.30 (Nov-Mar Sun 11-3.30).(Closed 24 & 25 Dec).Theatre tours usually Mon-Fri (ex matinee days), 1.30 & 5.30, Sun 12, 1, 2 & 3.

Fee: Exhibition £2 (ch, pen & students £1.50). Family ticket £4. Theatre Tours £4 (ch, pen & students £3) - advisable to book in advance.

P (charged) licensed toilets for disabled shop (ex guide dogs)

Shakespeare's Birthplace

Henley St CV37 6QW
☎ 01789 204016 📠 01789 296083
e-mail: info@shakespeare.org.uk

Shakespeare was born in the timber-framed house in 1564. It contains numerous exhibits of the Elizabethan period and Shakespeare memorabilia, and the acclaimed exhibition, Shakespeare; His Life and Background.

Times: Open all year, 20 Mar-19 Oct Mon-Sat 9-5, Sun 9.30-5; 20 Oct-19 Mar Mon-Sat 9.30-4, Sun 10-4. (Closed 23-26 Dec).

Fee: £5.50 (ch £2.50, concession £5) Family ticket £14. Three In-town Properties Ticket £8.50 (ch £4.20, concessions £7.50) Family ticket £20. Five Properties Ticket £12 (ch £6, concessions £11) Family £29.

P (100 yds) (no vehicle access to Henley Street) toilets for disabled shop

The Teddy Bear Museum

19 Greenhill St CV37 6LF (exit 1 off M40, follow signs to Stratford Town Centre)
☎ 01789 293160
e-mail: enquires@teddybearmuseum.uk.com

Hundreds of enchanting teddy bears in a beamed 16th-century house. Famous bears, bears of the famous, rare early bears and much, much more.

Times: Open all year, daily 9.30-6, Jan-Feb 9.30-5. Closed 25 & 26 Dec.

Fee: £2.25 (ch £1). Family ticket £5.95.Party 20+.

P (30yds & 200yds) (access to ground floor shop only) shop (ex guide dogs)

UPTON HOUSE

Upton House

OX15 6HT (on A422, 7m NW of Banbury, 12m SE of Stratford)
☎ 01295 670266 📠 01295 670266
e-mail: upton@smtp.ntrust.org.uk

The house, built of mellow local stone, dates from 1695, but its outstanding collections are the chief attraction. They include paintings by English and Continental Old Masters, Brussels tapestries, Sèvres porcelain, Chelsea figures, 18th-century furniture, and a collection of original artwork used to advertise Shell oil during the 1920s and 30s. Viscount Bearsted, the donor of Upton, was chairman of Shell at one time.

Times: Open Apr-Oct, Sat-Wed & BH Mon 2-6. Last admission 5.30pm (Oct 5pm).

Fee: £5.40. Family ticket £13.50. Garden only £2.70. Party.

P (Braille guide, parking nr house, buggy for lower garden) toilets for disabled shop (ex guide dogs)

WARWICK

Warwick Castle

CV34 4QU (2m from M40 exit 15)
☎ 01926 406600 ▯ 01926 401692
e-mail: customer.information@warwick-castle.com

From the days of William the Conqueror to the reign of Queen Victoria, Warwick Castle has provided a backdrop for many turbulent times. Attractions include the gloomy Dungeon and Torture Chamber, the grand State Rooms, the Great Hall, and a reconstruction of the Royal Weekend Party of 1898, where "Daisy", Countess of Warwick held sway.

Times: Open daily 10-6 (5pm Nov-Mar). Closed 25 Dec.
Fee: £9.75 (ch 4-16 £5.95, pen £7). Family ticket £28. May-Sep £10.95 (ch £6.50, pen £7.85). Family ticket £29.
P (charged) licensed (Free admission to wheelchair bound visitors) toilets for disabled shop (ex assistance dogs)

Warwickshire Yeomanry Museum

The Court House Vaults, Jury St CV34 4EW (situated on the corner of Jury Street & Castle Street)
☎ 01926 492212 ▯ 01926 494837

The vaults of the court house display militaria from the county Yeomanry, dating from 1794 to 1945. It includes regimental silver, paintings, uniforms and weapons. A small room in the cellars is devoted to Warwick Town Museum.

Times: Open Good Fri-Sep, Fri-Sun & BHs 10-1 & 2-4. Other times by prior arrangement.
Fee: Free.
P (300yds) (2hr max in nearby streets) shop

WILMCOTE

Mary Arden's House and the Shakespeare Countryside Museum

(3m NW off A34)
☎ 01789 204016 ▯ 01789 296083

Mary Arden was William Shakespeare's mother, and this picturesque, half-timbered Tudor house was her childhood home. The house is the main historic feature of an extensive complex of farm buildings which house displays of farming and country life, including a remarkable dovecote, kitchen circa 1900, a smithy and cooper's workshop. Daily demonstrations by The Heart of England Falconry. Rare breeds, duck pond and field walk.

Times: Open all year, 20 Mar-19 Oct Mon-Sat 9.30-5, Sun 10-5; 20 Oct-19 Mar, Mon-Sat 10-4, Sun 10.30-4. (Closed 23-26 Dec).
Fee: £5 (ch £2.50, concessions £4.50) Family ticket £12.50. Five Properties Ticket £12 (ch £6, concessions £11) Family ticket £29.
P toilets for disabled shop

West Midlands

At the centre of England, the West Midlands is a metropolitan county with a mainly industrial base. Birmingham is the administrative centre and the other main towns are Coventry, Dudley, Smethick, Walsall, West Bromwich and Wolverhampton.

The area was badly affected by the decline in British manufacturing, but has fought back by diversification into the service sector, with impressive conference and exhibition facilities offered in Birmingham, in the form of the International Convention Centre and National Exhibition Centre, home to many of the country's biggest trade fairs. Industrial heritage museums have blossomed, including the Black Country Museum at Dudley, and Cadbury World, which tells the story of chocolate, and the chocolate factory established at Bournville by the renowned Quaker family.

Birmingham, AKA 'Brum', is Britain's second largest city, its position at the hub of things emphasised by the miles of canals criss-crossing the city and its amazing tangle of flyovers. There are some splendid public buildings, notably the Town Hall and the City Museum and Art Gallery. Modern developments include the infamous 60s-designed Bull Ring shopping centre.

The West Midland's multi-racial population gives a buzz to its cultural life, which offers a feast of arts, products, foods and festivals from around the world. The artistic life of the community is rich, with the world class Birmingham Symphony Orchestra and the Birmingham Royal Ballet in residence, plus a wide range of visual art in a variety of galleries.

EVENTS & FESTIVALS

March
8-11 Crufts Dog Show, NEC Birmingham
8 International Women's Day
17 St Patrick's Day Pageant

May
27 International Street Festival, Coventry

June
2 Godiva on the Street, Coventry
2-10 Godiva Festival, Coventry
10-16 Foleshill Festival, Coventry
24 Jun-1 Jul Hillfields Festival, Coventry
tbc Steam & Vintage Rally, Wolverhampton

July
2-5 Royal Show, Coventry
28 Caribbean Festival, Coventry
tbc Wolverhampton Show
tbc Wolvestock Music Festival

August
4 Donkey Derby, Coventry
19 Kite Festival, Coventry
25-27 Town & Country, Coventry

September
2nd Coventry Shakespeare Car Run

November/December
tbc Festival of Lights, Coventry

Top: Gas Street Canal Basin, Birmingham

BIRMINGHAM

Aston Hall

Trinity Rd, Aston B6 6JD

☎ 0121 200 2700

Built by Sir Thomas Holt, Aston Hall is a fine Jacobean mansion complete with a panelled long gallery, balustraded staircase and magnificent plaster friezes and ceilings. King Charles I spent a night here during the Civil War and the house was damamged by Parliamentary troops. It was also leased to James Watt Junior, the son of the great industrial pioneer.

Times: Open Etr-Oct, daily 2-5.

Fee: Free.

P ☕ ♿ shop 🐕 (ex guide dogs)

Birmingham Botanical Gardens & Glasshouses

Westbourne Rd, Edgbaston B15 3TR (2m W of city centre,follow signs for Edgbaston, then brown tourist signs)

☎ 0121 454 1860 📠 0121 454 7835

e-mail: admin@bham-bot-gdns.demon.co.uk

Originally opened in 1832, the gardens include the Tropical House, which has a 24ft-wide lily pool and lush vegetation. The Orangery features a wide variety of citrus fruits and the Cactus House has a desert scene with its giant agaves and opuntias. Outside, a tour of the gardens includes rhododendrons and azalea borders and a collection of over 200 trees.

Times: Open daily all year, wkdays 9-7 or dusk, Sun 10-8 or dusk whichever is earlier. (Closed 25 Dec).

Fee: £4.30 (concessions £2.40); £4.60 summer Sun (concessions £2.40)

P ☕ ✕ licensed ♿ (3 wheelchairs + 2 electric scooters) toilets for disabled shop garden centre 🐕 (ex guide dogs) 💳

Birmingham Museum & Art Gallery

Chamberlain Sq B3 3DH

☎ 0121 303 2834 📠 0121 303 1394

One of the world's best collections of Pre-Raphaelite paintings can be seen here, including important works by Burne-Jones, a native of Birmingham. Also on display are fine silver, ceramics and glass. The archaeology section has prehistoric Egyptian, Greek and Roman antiquities, and also objects from the Near East, Mexico and Peru.

Times: Open all year Mon-Thu & Sat 10-5, Fri 10.30-5 and Sun 12.30-5.

Fee: Museum & Art Gallery free, admission charged for Gas Hall Exhibitions tel: 0121-303 1966 for details.

P ☕ ✕ licensed ♿ (lift) toilets for disabled shop 🐕 💳

Birmingham Railway Museum

670 Warwick Rd, Tyseley B11 2HL (3m S, A41 Warwick Rd)

☎ 0121 707 4696 📠 0121 765 4645

Times: Open weekends and BH summer, 10-5 and winter 10-4.

P ☕ ✕ ♿ (ramps to platforms) shop 🐕 (ex guide dogs) *Details not confirmed for 2001*

The Jewellery Quarter Discovery Centre

75-79 Vyse St, Hockley B18 6HA

☎ 0121 554 3598 📠 0121 554 9700

Discover the skill of the jeweller's craft and enjoy a unique tour of an original jewellery factory frozen in time. For over eighty years the family firm of Smith and Pepper produced jewellery from the factory. This perfectly preserved 'time capsule' workshop has changed little since the beginning of the century.

Times: Open all year, Mon-Fri 10-4, Sat 11-5. (Closed Sun).

Fee: £2.50 (concessions £2). Family ticket £6.50. Party 10+ booked in advance.

P (pay & display) ☕ ♿ (tours for hearing/visually impaired booked in advance) toilets for disabled shop 🐕 (ex guide dogs)

Sarehole Mill

Cole Bank Rd, Hall Green B13 0BD (off B4146)

☎ 0121 777 6612 📠 0121 236 1766

An 18th-century water mill, restored to working order and containing displays illustrating various aspects of milling, blade-grinding and English rural pursuits. The writer J R R Tolkein lived nearby and found inspiration for his book *'The Hobbit'* here.

Times: Open Apr-Oct, daily, afternoons only.

Fee: Free.

P shop 🐕 (ex guide dogs)

Selly Manor Museum

Maple Rd, Bournville B30 2AE (off A38)

☎ 0121 472 0199 📠 0121 471 4101

e-mail: gillianellis@bvt.org.uk

These two timber-framed manor houses date from the 13th and early 14th centuries, and have been re-erected in the 'garden suburb' of Bournville. There is a herb garden and events are held all year.

Times: Open mid Jan-mid Dec, Tue-Fri & BH 10-5 (Apr-Sep, Sat-Sun 2-5), phone for details.

Fee: £2 (ch 50p, concessions £1.50). Family ticket £4.50.

P ♿ toilets for disabled shop

Soho House
Soho Av, Handsworth B18 5LB
☎ 0121 554 9122

Soho House was the elegant home of industrial pioneer Matthew Boulton between 1766 and 1809. Here, he met with some of the most important thinkers and scientists of his day. The house has been carefully restored and contains many of Boulton's possessions including furniture, clocks, and silverware.
Times: Open all year, Tue-Sat 10-5 & Sun 12-5; also BH Mon.
Fee: £2.50 (concessions £2). Family ticket (2 adults & 3 ch) £6.50. Party 10+
P ☕ ♿ (induction loop) toilets for disabled shop ✘ (ex guide dogs)

BOURNVILLE

Cadbury World
Linden Rd B30 2LD (1m S of A38 Bristol Rd, on A4040 Ring Rd)
☎ 0121 451 4159 & 0121 451 4180
🖷 0121 451 1366
Times: Contact information line 0121 451 4180 for opening times.
P ☕ ✕ ♿ (ex packaging plant) toilets for disabled shop ✘ *Details not confirmed for 2001*

COVENTRY

Coventry Cathedral & Visitor Centre
7 Priory Row CV1 5ES (signposted on all approaches to the city)
☎ 024 7622 7597 🖷 024 7622 7597
e-mail: information@coventrycathedral.org

Coventry's old cathedral was bombed during an air raid of November 1940 which devastated the city. The remains have been carefully preserved. The new cathedral was designed by Sir Basil Spence and consecrated in May 1962. It contains outstanding modern works of art, including a huge tapestry designed by Graham Sutherland, the west screen (a wall of glass engraved by John Hutton with saints and angels), bronzes by Epstein, and the great baptistry window by John Piper.
Times: Open all year, daily, Etr-Sep 9.30-6; Oct-Etr 9.30-4.30. Visitor centre open Oct-Apr 11-3, Apr-Oct 10-4.
Fee: Visitor centre £2 (ch 6 free, ch 6-16, students & pen £1). Party 10+. Cathedral £2 donation. Camera charge £1. Video charge £3.
P (250 yds) ☕ ♿ (lift, touch and hearing centre, paved wheelchair access) toilets for disabled shop ✘

Herbert Art Gallery & Museum
Jordan Well CV1 5QP
☎ 024 7683 2381 & 7683 2565
🖷 024 7683 2410

'Godiva City', tells Coventry's story over 1,000 years, through interactive exhibits, objects, pictures and words. Changing displays of art, craft, social and industrial history.
Times: Open all year, Mon-Sat 10-5.30, Sun 12-5. (Closed 25-27 Dec & 1-2 Jan)
Fee: Free.
P (500yds) ☕ ♿ (disabled parking, automatic doors, tactile/audio displays) toilets for disabled shop ✘ (ex guide/assistance dogs)

Jaguar Daimler Heritage Centre
Browns Ln, Allesley CV5 9DR (on A45, follow signs for Browns Lane Plant)
☎ 024 7640 2121 🖷 024 7620 2777
e-mail: tokeeffe@jaguar.com

A brand new museum that explores the history of Daimler and Jaguar motor vehicles, from the 1897 Daimler Grafton-Paeton to the 1990 Jaguar XJ220.
Times: Open Mon-Fri 9.30-4.30 & last Sun of month 10-4.
Fee: Free.
P ♿ toilets for disabled shop ✘ (ex guide dogs)

Lunt Roman Fort
Coventry Rd, Baginton CV8 3AJ (S side of city, off Stonebridge highway, A45)
☎ 024 7683 2381 & 7683 2565
🖷 024 7683 2410

The turf and timber Roman fort from around the end of the 1st century has been faithfully reconstructed. An Interpretation Centre is housed in the granary.
Times: Open 15 Jul-3 Sep, Thu-Tue 10-5; Spring BH wk daily 10-5; Apr-29 Oct wknds & BH Mons 10-5.
Fee: £1.80 (concessions 80p). Audio tour 80p.
P ♿ (ramp to Granary Interpretation Centre) toilets for disabled shop ✘ (ex guide/assistancedogs)

Museum of British Road Transport
St Agnes Ln, Hales St CV1 1PN (just off junc 1 ring road, Tower Street)
☎ 024 7683 2425 🖷 024 7683 2465
e-mail: museum@mbrt.co.uk

Coventry is the traditional home of the motor industry. The Museum of British Road Transport displays the largest collection of British cars, buses, cycles and motorcycles in the world. Visitors can learn about motoring's early days in 'Memory Lane', how Royalty travelled, and see Thrust 2, the world land speed record story.
Times: Open all year, daily 10-5. (Closed 24-26 Dec).
Fee: Free.
P (adjacent) ☕ ♿ (audio tour, tactile floor & models) toilets for disabled shop ✘ (ex guide dogs)

DUDLEY

Black Country Living Museum
Tipton Rd DY1 4SQ (on A4037, opposite Dudley Guest Hospital)
☎ 0121 557 9643 & 0121 520 8054
🖷 0121 557 4242
e-mail: info@bclm.co.uk

The museum is really a recreation of a Black Country village, complete with cottages, a chapel, chemist, baker and a pub serving real ale. There is also a canal boat dock with a range of narrowboats, and there are daily trips into the Dudley Tunnel. You can go underground in an 1850s mine, and see a replica of the world's first steam engine venture into a pit-pulled cottage (affected by subsidence due to mining). Costumed guides and demonstrations bring the buildings to life.

Times: Open all year, Mar-Oct daily 10-5; Nov-Feb, Wed-Sun 10-4. (Telephone for Christmas closing)

Fee: £7.50 (ch 5-17 £4.50, pen £6.50). Family ticket £20. Party 10+ (rates available on application). Prices subject to change.

(ramps available) toilets for disabled shop (ex guide dogs)

Dudley Zoo & Castle

2 The Broadway DY1 4QB (M5 junct 2 towards Wolverhampton/Dudley. Signposted)

01384 215314 01384 456048

e-mail: marketing@dudleyzoo.org.uk

Set in 40 acres, the castle ruins are an impressive example of feudal splendour, whilst the zoo houses one of the most diverse collections of animals in the country. Home to many endangered species, there is the opportunity to see and learn about animals from every continent.

Times: Open all year, Etr-mid Sep, daily 10-4.30; mid Sep-Etr, daily 10-3.30. (Closed 25 Dec).

Fee: £6.50 (ch 4-15 £4, concessions £4.50). Family ticket (2 adults & 3 ch)£21. Party 15+.

(charged) licensed (land train from gates to castle) toilets for disabled shop

Museum & Art Gallery

St James's Rd DY1 1HU (M5 northbound, exit at junct 2. Take A4123 signposted to Dudley)

01384 815575 01384 815576

The museum houses the Brooke Robinson collection of 17th, 18th and 19th century European painting, furniture, ceramics and enamels. A fine geological gallery, 'The Time Trail' has spectacular displays of fossils from the local Wenlock limestone and coal measures.

Times: Open all year, Mon-Sat 10-4. (Closed BHs).

Fee: Free.

(25mtrs) (Braille & large print text. Tactile objects) shop (ex guide dogs)

KINGSWINFORD

Broadfield House Glass Museum

Barnett Ln DY6 9QA

01384 273011

Times: Open all year, Tue-Fri & Sun 2-5, Sat 10-1 & 2-5. BH's 2-5.

shop *Details not confirmed for 2001*

SOLIHULL

National Motorcycle Museum

Coventry Rd, Bickenhill B92 0EJ (nr junct 6 of M42, off A45 nr NEC)

01675 443311 0121 711 3153

Five exhibition halls showing British motorcycles built during the Golden Age of motorcycling. Spanning 90 years, the immaculately restored machines are the products of around 150 different factories. Over 700 machines are on show, most are owned by the museum, others are from collections or private owners. Restoration work is carried out by enthusiasts, and new motorcycles are acquired from all over the world.

Times: Open all year, daily 10-6. (Closed 24-26 Dec).

Fee: £4.50 (ch 12 & pen £3.25). Party 20+.

licensed toilets for disabled shop (ex guide dogs)

STOURBRIDGE

The Falconry Centre

Hurrans Garden Centre, Kidderminster Rd South, Hagley DY9 0JB (off A456)

01562 700014 01562 700014

The centre houses some 80 birds of prey including owls, hawks and falcons and is also a rehabilitation centre for sick and injured birds of prey. Spectacular flying displays are put on daily from midday. There are picnic areas.

Times: Open all year, daily 10-5. (Closed 25 & 26 Dec).

Fee: £2.50 (ch & pen £1.50, disabled £1). Party 25+.

shop garden centre (ex guide dogs)

WALSALL

Walsall Leather Museum

Littleton St West WS2 8EQ (On Walsall ring-road on North side of town)

☎ **01922 721153** 🖷 **01922 725827**

e-mail: leathermuseum@walsall.gov.uk

Award winning working museum in the saddlery and leathergoods 'capital' of Britain. Watch skilled craftsmen and women at work in this restored Victorian leather factory. Displays tell the story of Walsall's leatherworkers past and present. Large shop stocks range of leathergoods, many at bargain prices. Saddle Room Cafe serves delicious home-cooked cakes and light lunches. Groups very welcome, guided tours available.

Times: Open all year, Tue-Sat 10-5 (Nov-Mar 4pm), Sun noon-5 (Nov-Mar 4pm). Open BH Mon. Closed 24-26 Dec, 1 Jan, Good Fri & Etr Sun.

Fee: Free.

P (10metres) ☕ ♿ (staff with sign language training, hands on activities) toilets for disabled shop 🐕 (ex guide dogs) 💳

WOLVERHAMPTON

Wightwick Manor

WV6 8EE (3m W, beside Mermaid Inn)

☎ **01902 761400** 🖷 **01902 764663**

This house was begun in 1887 and in its style of decoration is one of the finest examples of the achievements of the late 19th-century. All aspects of William Morris's talents are shown in this house - wallpapers, textiles, carpets, tiles, embroidery and even books. The garden reflects late Victorian and Edwardian design.

Times: Open Mar-Dec, Thu, Sat & BH Sun & Mon 2.30-5.30.

P ☕ ♿ shop 🌿 *Details not confirmed for 2001*

WORDSLEY

Stuart Crystal

Red House Glassworks DY8 4AA (1m from Stourbridge on A491 Stourbridge to Wolverhampton Road)

☎ **01384 828282 & 261777** 🖷 **01384 70463**

Times: Open all year, daily. (Closed 25-26 Dec & 1 Jan). Tours:Mon-Thu on the hour 10-4(not 12),Fri 10,11 & 1; Shop open Mon-Sat, 9-5, Sun 10-4; Glass Blowing: Wed-Sat.

P ☕ ♿ (Cone/Museum accessible- factory tours are not) shop 🐕 (ex guide dogs) *Details not confirmed for 2001* 💳

Isle of Wight

Despite its size, - less than 23 miles (39km) across at its widest point - the Isle of Wight offers plenty of scenic variety, and is popular as a holiday destination because of its lovely countryside, pleasant resorts and mild climate.

There's lots to see and do, with an abundance of museums, children's activity parks, and leisure facilities including watersports, riding, cycling, paragliding, golf, and sea and freshwater fishing. Local specialities are freshly caught crab and lobster, which can be enjoyed with a glass of wine from one of the island's five vineyards.

A chalk ridge runs east to west of the island, popular with walkers for the fine views afforded from its vantage points. The interesting coastline takes in the chalky pinnacles of The Needles, some splendid cliffs, and the curious multi-coloured sand at Alum Bay, which can be bought bottled in colourful layers from local souvenir shops. Coastal paths follow the shoreline from Totland to St Lawrence on the south coast, and Yarmouth to Cowes on the north coast.

The east coast has the most developed seaside resorts, with Ryde, Sandown, Shanklin and Ventnor, with their sandy beaches. Newport, the island's capital, is the only inland town and is a good shopping centre.

In addition to its natural features, the island has some fine castles and historic houses. Chief among these are medieval Carisbrooke Castle outside Newport, Osborne House at East Cowes, Brading Roman Villa, and lovely manor houses at Arreton, Barton, Haseley, Nunwell, Appuldurcombe and Morton.

EVENTS & FESTIVALS

May
12-13 Isle of Wight Garden Show

July/August
tbc Cowes Week, sailing event

August
25-28 The Island Steam Show, Havenstreet
tbc Isle of Wight Garlic Festival, Newchurch

Top: Freshwater Bay

ALUM BAY

The Needles Old Battery

West High Down PO39 0JH (0.75m SW)
☎ 01983 754772

This former Palmerston fort, built in 1862, has recently been restored. A tunnel leads to a look-out position with spectacular views of the Needles chalk stacks and lighthouse, and across the bay to Dorset. In the fort are two of the original 12-ton gun barrels. The powder house has an exhibition of the history of the Needles headland.

Times: Open 26 Mar-29 Jun Sun-Thu & Jul-Aug daily 10.30-5. Property closes in bad weather.
Fee: £2.50 (ch £1.25). Family ticket £6.
P (0.75m) shop

The Needles Park

PO39 0JD (signposted, on B3322)
☎ 01983 752401 01983 755260
e-mail: needles@alumbay87.fsnet.co.uk

Overlooking the Needles on the western edge of the Island, the park has attractions for all the family. Visitors can ride the chairlift to the beach, and enjoy views of the Needles Rocks, the Lighthouse and the world-famous coloured sands. Park attractions include the Super X Motion Simulator, Crazy Golf, open-top bus rides and a traditional carousel. The Isle of Wight Sweet Manufactory is the newest attraction.

Times: Open Apr-early Nov, daily 10-5. Hours extended in high season.
Fee: No admission charged for entrance to Park. Supersaver Attraction Discount ticket £5.95 (ch £4.25), or chargeable attractions individually priced.
P (charged) licensed ♿ toilets for disabled shop 

ARRETON

Haseley Manor

PO30 3AN (on Sandown to Newport road)
☎ 01983 865420 01983 867547

This is the oldest and largest manor open to the public on the Island. Parts of the south wing have some of the original building, c1300, but the rest of the house is a mixture of styles. The manor has since been carefully restored and 20 rooms can be viewed. Outside, there is a re-constructed 18th-century farm complete with animals. There is also a children's play area with a tree house, and a small lake with an island castle.

Times: Open Etr-Sep, Mon-Fri 10-5.30. (Closed Sat & Sun).
Fee: £4.95 (ch £3.65, pen £4.10) Family £16.
P licensed ♿ (wheelchair ramps) toilets for disabled shop

BEMBRIDGE

Bembridge Windmill

PO30 4EB (0.5m S of Bembridge on B3395)
☎ 01983 873945

The only windmill on the island to survive, Bembridge mill was built about 1700 and was in use until 1913. The stone-built tower with its wooden cap and machinery have been restored since it was given to the National Trust in 1961.

Times: Open 27 Mar-Jun & Sep-27 Oct, Sun-Fri (Closed Sat ex Etr Sat) & Jul-Aug, daily 10-5. Last admission 4.45.
Fee: £1.50 (ch 75p)
P shop

BLACKGANG

Blackgang Chine Fantasy Park

PO38 2HN (off A3055 Ventnor to Freshwater rd)
☎ 01983 730330 01983 731267
e-mail: vectisventureltd@btinternet.com

Opened as scenic gardens in 1843 covering some 40 acres, the park has imaginative play areas, water gardens, maze and coastal gardens. Set on the steep wooded slopes of the chine are the themed areas Smugglerland, Nurseryland, Dinosaurland, Fantasyland and Frontierland. St Catherine's Quay has an exhibition showing local and maritime history.

Times: Open 3 Apr-29 Oct daily, 10-5.30.Whitsun & high season floodlit every evening (phone for details).
Fee: Combined ticket to chine, sawmill & quay £5.95 (ch 3-13 £4.95, pen £5.50, disabled £3). Family £19.50. Return within 3 days - Free.
P (charged) ♿ (some paths steep) toilets for disabled shop

BRADING

Isle of Wight Waxworks

46 High St PO36 0DQ (on A3055)
☎ 01983 407286 01983 402112
e-mail:
waxworks@bradingisleofwight.fsnet.co.uk

Rub shoulders with famous and infamous characters through 2000 years of the island's colourful fantasies, legends and facts - brought to life in dramatic scenes with sound, light and animation. Visitors can also see the Ancient Rectory mansion (c1066 AD), the Chamber of Horrors, set in the castle dungeons, and adjacent Animal World of Natural History.

Times: Open all year, Summer 10-9; Winter 10-5. Telephone for Dec opening times.
Fee: £4.75 (ch £3.25, under 5 free, pen £4). Family £15 (2 adults, 3 ch) Party 20+. Includes free entry into "Chamber of Horrors" & Animal World of Natural History.
P ♿ (Disabled route planner) shop

Lilliput Antique Doll & Toy Museum

High St PO36 0DJ (A3055 Ryde/Sandown road, in Brading High Street)
☎ 01983 407231

This private museum contains one of the finest collections of antique dolls and toys in Britain. There are over 2000 exhibits, ranging in age from 2000BC to 1945 with examples of almost every seriously collectable doll, many with royal connections. Also dolls' houses, teddy bears and rare and unusual toys.

Times: Open all year, daily, 10-5.
Fee: £1.95 (ch & pen £1, ch under 5 free). Party.
P (200 yds) ♿ (ramps provided on request) shop 

Morton Manor
PO36 0EP (off A3055 in Brading, well signposted)
☎ **01983 406168**

The manor dates back to 1249, but was rebuilt in 1680 with further changes during the Georgian period. The house contains furniture of both the 18th and 19th centuries, but its main attraction lies in the gardens and vineyard. The garden is landscaped into terraces, with ornamental ponds, a sunken garden and a traditional Elizabethan turf maze. Morton Manor has an established vineyard and winery.
Times: Open Apr-Oct, daily 10-5.30 (Closed Sat).
Fee: £4 (ch £1.50, pen £3.50). Party 15+.
P licensed shop garden centre (ex in gardens)

Nunwell House & Gardens
Coach Ln PO36 0JQ (Off Ryde-Sandown Rd, A3055)
☎ **01983 407240**

Set in beautiful gardens, Nunwell is an impressive, lived-in and much loved house where King Charles I spent his last night of freedom. It has fine furniture and interesting collections of family militaria. In summer, concerts are occasionally held in the music room and Shakespeare plays in the garden.
Times: Open House & Gardens: 27-28 May then 2 Jul-5 Sep, Mon-Wed 1-5. Groups welcome when house open & at other times by appointment.
Fee: £4 inc guide book, (concessions).
P shop (ex guide dogs)

CARISBROOKE

Carisbrooke Castle
PO30 1XY (1.25 miles SW of Newport, off B3401)
☎ **01983 522107**

This is the only medieval castle on the island and its most famous resident was King Charles I who was imprisoned here. There are two medieval wells: the one in the keep can be reached by climbing down 71 steps; the one in the courtyard had winding gear traditionally driven by a donkey, and displays of it working are still given.
Times: Open all year, Apr-Sep, daily 10-6; Oct, daily 10-5; Nov-Mar, daily 10-4. (Closed 24-26 Dec & 1 Jan).
Fee: £4.50 (ch £2.30 & concessions £3.40). Family ticket (2 adults & 3 ch) £11.30.
P shop

FRESHWATER

Dimbola Lodge
Terrace Ln, Freshwater Bay PO40 9QE (off A3054)
☎ **01983 756814** 🖷 **01983 755578**
e-mail: administrator@dimbola.co.uk

Home of Julia Margaret Cameron, the pioneer Victorian portrait photographer. The house has the largest permanent collection of Cameron prints on display in the UK, as well as galleries exhibiting work by young, up and coming, and acclaimed modern photographers; and a large display of cameras and accessories.

Times: Open all year 10-5 (Closed 5 days at Xmas).
Fee: £2.50 (ch 16 free)
P toilets for disabled shop

HAVENSTREET

Isle of Wight Steam Railway
The Railway Station PO33 4DS (Situated between Ryde & Newport. Railway well signposted)
☎ **01983 882204** 🖷 **01983 884515**

When the Newport to Ryde railway was closed, Haven Street Station was taken over by a private company, the Isle of Wight Steam Railway. A number of volunteers restored the station, locomotives and rolling stock, and steam trains now run the five miles from Wootton, via Haven Street to Smallbrook Junction where there is a direct interchange with the Ryde-Shanklin electric trains.
Times: Open Mar 23,26,30. Apr 2,6,9,13,16,20-30. May 1-7,& all Wed, Thur, Sat & Sun. Jun-Sep daily. Oct Thur & wkends.
Fee: Return Fares £6.80 (ch 4-15 £4). Family ticket £19.
P (with assistance) toilets for disabled shop

NEWPORT

Roman Villa
Cypress Rd PO30 1EX (S of Newport, signposted 'Roman Villa')
☎ **01983 529720** 🖷 **01983 823841**
Times: Open Etr-Oct, daily 10-4.30. Other times by appointment.
P (100 yds) shop *Details not confirmed for 2001*

NEWTOWN

Old Town Hall

Town Ln PO30 4PA (1m N of A3054 between Yarmouth & Newport)

☎ **01983 531785**

This unusual town hall stands alone, surrounded by grass and a few houses. Newtown was once the island's capital, returning two members to Parliament. It was badly burned in 1377 and never fully recovered. In 1699 the town hall was rebuilt and has been further restored recently. An exhibition depicts the exploits of the anonymous group of National Trust benefactors known as 'Ferguson's Gang'.

Times: Open 27 Mar-end Jun, Sep-25 Oct, Mon Wed & Sun (also open Good Fri & Etr Sat); Jul & Aug Sun-Thu, 2-5. Last admission 4.45pm.

Fee: £1.40 (ch 70p)

P (Braille guide books available)

OSBORNE HOUSE

Osborne House

PO32 6JY (1m SE of East Cowes)

☎ **01983 200022**

Designed by Prince Albert and Thomas Cubitt in the mid 19th century, Osborne was Queen Victoria's favourite home, especially after the death of Prince Albert. She died here in 1901. The interior of the house is largely unchanged since Victorain times, and is a fascinating insight into the private life of the Royal family of that day.

Times: House open Apr-Nov, daily 10-5. Grounds 10-6 (last admission 5); Nov-17 Dec & 31 Jan-Mar Sun, Mon, Wed & Thu 10-2.30

Fee: £6.90 (ch 5-15 £3.50, under 5's free).

P shop

SHANKLIN

Shanklin Chine

12 Pomona Rd PO37 6PF

☎ **01983 866432** Fax **01983 874215**

Shanklin Chine is a natural gorge of great scenic beauty with a spectacular 45ft waterfall. A path winds down through the gorge, overhanging trees, ferns and other flora that cover its steep sides. The Heritage Centre features details of nature trails, rare flora and life in Victorian Shanklin. Features of historic interest include sections of PLUTO (pipeline under the ocean), which carried petrol to the Allied troops in Normandy. There is a memorial to 40 Commando, Royal Marines.

Times: Open 2 Apr-17 May 10-5, 18 May-16 Sep 10-10 (illuminated at night), 17 Sept-28 Oct 10-5, (opening period may be extended depending on weather conditions)

Fee: £2.50 (ch £1, pen & students £1.50, disabled £1). Family ticket £6.50

P (450 yds) shop (ex on lead at all times)

SHORWELL

Yafford Water Mill Farm Park

PO30 3LH (on B3399, Shorwell to Brightstone Road)

☎ **01983 740610 & 741125** Fax **01983 740610**

The mill is situated in attractive surroundings with a large mill pond. The great overshot wheel still turns and all the milling machinery is in working order. An unusual attraction is the millpond, which is home to a seal. The millstream has pools and falls with flowers and trees along its banks. Old farm wagons, agricultural machinery and a narrow gauge railway can also be seen along with rare breeds of sheep, pigs and cattle.

Times: Open all year, daily 10-6 or dusk in winter. (Last admission 5pm).

Fee: £3.70 (ch 4 £2.70, pen £2.50). Party 10+.

P toilets for disabled shop (ex guide dogs)

VENTNOR

Museum of the History of Smuggling

Botanic Gardens PO38 1UL (on A3055, 1m W of Ventnor)

☎ **01983 853677**

Situated underground in extensive vaults, this unique museum shows methods of smuggling used over a 700-year period right up to the present day. There is an adventure playground in the Botanic Gardens.

Times: Open Apr-Sep, daily 10-5.30.

Fee: £2.20 (ch & pen £1.10). Parties by arrangement.

P (charged) licensed shop garden centre

Ventnor Botanic Garden

Undercliff Dr PO38 1UL

☎ 01983 855397 🖷 01983 856154

Times: Open all year - Garden; Temperate House 8 Mar-1 Nov, daily 10-5.30 O8 Nov-Mar 1999, Sun 11-4.

P (charged) ✕ licensed ♿ toilets for disabled shop 🐕 (ex in garden) *Details not confirmed for 2001*

WROXALL

Appuldurcombe House

PO38 3EW (off B3327, 0.5 miles W)

☎ 01983 852484

The manor began life as a priory in 1100, but when it came into the hands of the Worsley family they demolished it and built this Palladian house on the site. Now ruined, it stands in beautiful grounds, landscaped in the 18th century by 'Capability' Brown.

Times: Open May-Sep, daily 10-6; Oct-15 Dec & 14 Feb-Apr, daily 10-4. Last entry 1 hour before closing.

Fee: £2 (ch £1 & concessions £1.50)

P ♿ ⌗

YARMOUTH

Yarmouth Castle

Quay St PO41 0PB (adjacent to car ferry terminal)

☎ 01983 760678

Modern buildings surround this well preserved castle, the last addition to Henry VIII's coastal defences completed in 1547. Fine views of the harbour can be obtained from the gun platform.

Times: Open Apr-Sep, daily 10-6 (Oct 10-5).

Fee: £2.10 (ch 5-15 £1.10, under 5's free)

P (200yds) ♿ 🐕 ⌗

Wiltshire

To many visiting the county, Wiltshire has three attractions: Salisbury, Stonehenge and Longleat. While these are all worthwhile, (indeed Stonehenge could be rightly called one of the wonders of the world) there is still plenty more to be discovered in the county.

After seeing Stonehenge, those interested in prehistoric sites should visit Avebury, where the stones are more approachable. Even though there is a lot of tourist activity in the village, the area remains relatively untouched, mostly given over to farmland and moor. This is also a good area for encountering crop circles.

Stonehenge and the Avebury circles seem to be part of a larger complex which still baffles investigators, and includes nearby features such as Windmill Hill with the remains of an earthwork camp some 5,500 years old; Silbury Hill, a man-made mound of earth which covers 5.5 acres; West Kennet Long Barrow, a burial mound; and possibly the chalk-carved White Horses on surrounding hillsides.

Miss Matilda Talbot left the village of Lacock to the National Trust in the 1940s. Another Talbot, William Henry Fox, produced the first-ever photographic negative here in 1831. The village was also used for the recent BBC production of Jane Austen's *Pride & Predjudice*.

Malmesbury in Northern Wiltshire, is the oldest borough in England and is home to a partially ruined 12th-century abbey, notable for a very impressive porch carving of the Apostles.

EVENTS & FESTIVALS

April
23-24 (Easter Sun & Mon), Easter Bunny Trail, Woodland Park, Westbury
22 Downton Cuckoo Fair, Downton, Salisbury

May
26-29 Chippenham Folk Festival
tbc Salisbury Festival
tbc Steam & Vintage Rally, Castle Combe

June
tbc Dickens Festival, Pickwick, Corsham
7-25 Devizes Festival

July
tbc Festival of Music & Arts/International Jazz Festival, Marlborough
tbc Bradford-on-Avon Town Festival
19-25 Royal International Air Tattoo Tel 01285 713000
22-23 Salisbury Country & Garden Show, Hudson's Field, Salisbury

September
1-3 City of Birmingham Dog Show, Perry Park
23 Pewsey Illuminated Carnival

Top: Avebury

AVEBURY

Avebury Manor

SN8 1RF (from A4 take A4361/B4003)
☎ 01672 539250 📠 01672 539388
e-mail: wavgen@smtp.ntrust.org.uk

Avebury Manor has a monastic origin, and has been much altered since then. The present buildings date from the early 16th century. The flower gardens contain medieval walls, and there are examples of topiary.
Times: Open: House 2 Apr-Oct, Tue-Wed, Sun & BH Mon 2-5.30 (last admission 5pm or dusk if earlier). Garden 2 Apr-Oct daily ex Mon & Thu (open BH Mon). **Fee:** Manor & garden £3.20 (ch £1.50). Garden £2.25 (ch £1). P ♿ shop

Avebury Museum (Alexander Keiller Museum)

☎ 01672 539250 📠 01672 539388
e-mail: wavgen@smtp.ntrust.org.uk

This is one of the most important prehistoric sites in Europe, and was built before Stonehenge. An avenue of great stones leads to the site, which must have been a place of great religious significance. The small museum contains many new exhibits.
Times: Open Apr-Oct, daily 10-6 or dusk if earlier; Nov-Mar, 10-4. (Closed 24-26 Dec & 1 Jan). **Fee:** £1.80 (ch 80p). P ♿ shop

BRADFORD-ON-AVON

Great Chalfield Manor

SN12 8NJ (3m SW of Melksham)
☎ 01225 782239 📠 01225 783379

Built during the Wars of the Roses, the manor is a beautiful moated house which still has its great hall. There is a small 13th-century church.
Times: Open 4 Apr-Oct, Tue-Thu, guided tours only at 12.15, 2.15, 3, 3.45, 4.30. **Fee:** £3.70. P

Tithe Barn

This impressive tithe barn, over 160ft long by 30ft wide, once belonged to Shaftesbury Abbey. The roof is of stone slates, supported by buttresses, massive beams and a network of rafters.
Times: Open all year, daily 10.30-4. (Closed 25 Dec). Keykeeper. **Fee:** Free. P ♿

CALNE

Bowood House & Gardens

SN11 0LZ (off A4 in Derry Hill village)
☎ 01249 812102 📠 01249 821757
e-mail: enquires@bowood-estate.co.uk

Built in 1624, the house was finished by the first Earl of Shelburne, who employed celebrated architects, notably Robert Adam, to complete the work. Adam's library is particularly admired, and also the laboratory where Dr Joseph Priestley discovered oxygen in 1774. The chief glory of Bowood is its 2000-acre expanse; 100 acres are pleasure gardens laid out by 'Capability' Brown and carpeted with daffodils and bluebells in spring.

Times: Open Apr-Oct, daily 11-6, including BH. Rhododendron Gardens (separate entrance off A342) open 6 weeks during mid Apr-early Jun 11-6. **Fee:** House & Grounds £5.70 (ch £3.50 & pen £4.70). Rhododendrons only £3. P ✕ licensed ♿ (parking by arrangement) toilets for disabled shop garden centre (ex guide & hearing dogs)

CORSHAM

Corsham Court

SN13 0BZ (4m W of Chippenham off A4)
☎ 01249 701610 📠 01249 701610

The Elizabethan manor was built in 1582, and then bought by the Methuen family in the 18th century to house their collections of paintings and statues. 'Capability' Brown made additions to the house and laid out the park, and later John Nash made further changes. There is furniture by Chippendale, Adam, Cobb and Johnson inside, as well as the Methuen collection of Old Master paintings. The garden has a Georgian bath house and peacocks.
Times: Open Summer: 20 Mar-Sep daily ex Mon but incl BH's 2-5.30. Winter: Oct-19 Mar open wknds only 2-4.30pm. Last admission 30 minutes before closing. (Closed December). Open throughout year by appointment for groups 15+.
Fee: House & Gardens: £5 (ch £2.50, pen £4.50). Gardens only £2 (ch £1 & pen £1.50). Party 15+ P ♿ shop

HOLT

The Courts

BA14 6RR (3m N of Trowbridge, on B3107)
☎ 01225 782340

Weavers came to The Courts to have their disputes settled until the end of the 18th century. The house is not open, but it makes an attractive backdrop to the gardens - with stone paths, yew hedges and pools with a strange, almost magical atmosphere.

Times: Open 2 Apr-15 Oct, daily (ex Sat) 1.30-5.30. Out of season by appointment.

Fee: £3.10 (ch £1.50). Parties by arrangement.

LACOCK

Lackham Countryside Centre

SN15 2NY (3m S of Chippenham, on A350)
☎ 01249 466800 01249 466818

Various visitor attractions are situated within the 210-hectare estate of the Lackham College. Thatched and refurbished farm buildings accommodate the farm museum and the grounds feature a walled garden, glasshouses, rhododendron glades, riverside and woodland walks, also a farm park. Also grown in this garden was the largest citron (large lemon) which earned a place in the Guinness Book of Records.

Times: Open Etr-Aug, Sun & BH Mon. Last admission 4pm.

Fee: £2 (concessions £2, up to 2 ch under 16 free).

(wheelchair available) toilets for disabled shop

Lacock Abbey

SN15 2LG (3m S of Chippenham, E of A350)
☎ 01249 730227 (abbey) 730459 (museum)

Lacock Abbey is not only historic and beautiful, it was also the venue for a series of innovative photographic experiments by William Henry Fox Talbot. The abbey was founded in the 13th century. At the Dissolution it was sold to William Sherrington, who destroyed the church and turned the nuns' quarters into a grand home. A museum devoted to Fox Talbot (one of Sherrington's descendants) is housed in an old barn.

Times: Museum, Cloisters & Grounds, 26 Feb-29 Oct, daily 11-5.30. Closed Good Fri. Abbey, 1 Apr-29 Oct daily, ex Tue, 1-5.30. Closed Good Fri. Museum open winter wknds, but closed 23/24 Dec-7 Jan.

Fee: Museum, Abbey, Grounds & Cloisters £5.80 (ch £3.20) Family ticket £15.90. Party. Grounds, Cloisters & Museum only £3.70 (ch £2.20) Family ticket £10.60. Abbey & garden only £4.70 (ch £2.60) Family ticket £12.

(taped guides) toilets for disabled shop

LONGLEAT

Longleat

The Estate Office BA12 7NW (Entrance on A362).
☎ 01985 844400 01985 844885
e-mail: longleat@btinternet.com

The late Marquess of Bath was the first peer to open his house to the public on a regular basis. Discover many of the world's most majestic and endangered creatures roaming freely in the park. An exciting Adventure Castle; mazes; safari boats; narrow-gauge railway. The centrepiece is the majestic Elizabethan house, built by Sir John Thynne in 1580 and decorated in the Italian Renaissance style in the late-19th century. It contains a mixture of furnishings and artefacts assembled by the Thynne family through the centuries, and the fully restored Victorian kitchens offer an interesting glimpse of life 'below stairs'. The magnificent grounds were laid out by 'Capability' Brown. Heaven's Gate is particularly spectacular when the rhododendrons are flowering. Longleat is licensed for Civil Weddings. For up to date event details check the website http://www.longleat.co.uk or phone.

Times: Open: 24 Mar-28 Oct (house open until Dec except Xmas Day) daily; house 10-5.30 . Safari park, 10-5, all other attractions 11-5.30. Last admissions may be earlier in Oct. Times may vary therefore it is advisable to phone in advance.

Fee: House: £5 (ch £4, pen £4) Safari Park: £6 (ch £4.50 pen £4.50). Longleat recommends the all inclusive passport ticket offering a great saving on entry to all 12 individual attractions. Please phone for details.

licensed (Informative leaflet available or see website) toilets for disabled shop (free kennels for Safari park)

LUDGERSHALL

Ludgershall Castle

SP11 9QR (7m NW of Andover on A342)

Although a ruin since the 16th century, this was once a royal castle and hunting palace. The visitor can see large earthworks of the Norman motte-and-bailey castle and the flint walls of the later hunting palace. The stump of a medieval cross stands in the village street.

Times: Open all reasonable times. **Fee:** Free.

LYDIARD PARK

Lydiard Park

Lydiard Tregoze SN5 9PA (from M4 exit 16. Follow brown Tourist signs)
☎ 01793 770401 01793 877909

Set in country parkland, Lydiard Park belonged to the St John family (the Bolingbrokes) for 500 years up until 1943. Since then the house has been restored and many of the original furnishings returned together with a family portrait collection dating from Elizabethan to

Victorian times. Exceptional plasterwork, early wallpaper, a rare painted glass window, and a room devoted to the talented 18th-century amateur artist, Lady Diana Spencer (Beauclerk), can also be seen.
Times: Open all year, House: Mon-Fri 10-1 & 2-5, Sat 10-5, Sun 2-5. Winter closing 4pm (Nov-Feb). Park: all year, daily closing at dusk.
Fee: £1.20 (ch 60p). Car parking 60p for 2 hours, £1 for day.
P (charged) ☕ ♿ (telephone 01793 770401 for access information sheet) toilets for disabled shop 🐕 (ex park/guide dogs in house)

MARLBOROUGH

Crofton Beam Engines

Crofton Pumping Station, Crofton SN8 3DW (signposted from A338/A346/B3087 at Burbage)
☎ **01672 870300**

The oldest working beam engine in the world still in its original building and still doing its original job, the Boulton and Watt 1812, is found here. Its companion is a Harvey's of Hayle of 1845. Both are steam driven, from a hand-stoked, coal-fired boiler, and pump water into the summit level of the Kennet and Avon Canal with a lift of 40ft.
Times: Open daily 21 Apr-1 Oct. Steaming weekends 22-24 Apr, 27-29 May, 24-25 Jun, 29-30 Jul, 26-28 Aug, 30 Sep-1 Oct.
Fee: Steaming weekend: £3.50 (ch £1, under 5 free & pen £2.50). Family ticket £7. Non-steaming days £2 (ch 50p, pen £1.50).
P ☕ ♿ (phone warden in advance, sighted guides provided) shop 🐕 (not inside)

MIDDLE WOODFORD

Heale Gardens, Plant Centre & Shop

SP4 6NT (4m N of Salisbury, between A360 & A345)
☎ **01722 782504**

Heale House and its eight acres of beautiful garden lie beside the River Avon. Much of the house is unchanged since King Charles II sheltered here after the Battle of Worcester in 1651. The garden provides a wonderfully varied collection of plants, shrubs, and musk and other roses, growing in the formal setting of clipped hedges.
Times: Open all year, daily 10-5. **Fee:** £3 (ch under 14 accompanied, free). Party 20+. P ♿ shop garden centre

SALISBURY

The Medieval Hall (Secrets of Salisbury)

Cathedral Close SP1 2EY
☎ **01722 412472 & 324731** 📠 **01722 339983**
e-mail: medihall@aol.com
Times: Open Apr-Sep, performances hourly 11-5. Also open throughout year for prebooked groups.
P (150m) ☕ ♿ shop *Details not confirmed for 2001*

Mompesson House

Chorister's Green, Cathedral Close SP1 2EL
☎ **01722 335659** 📠 **01722 335659**
e-mail: wmpkxr@smtp.ntrust.org.uk

With its perfect proportions this Queen Anne house makes an impressive addition to the elegant Cathedral Close. Inside there are stucco ceilings, a carved oak staircase and an important collection of 18th-century glasses, china and outstanding paintings.
Times: Open Apr-Oct, daily (ex Thu & Fri) 12-5.30. **Fee:** £3.40 (ch £1.70). Garden only 80p. Party. P ☕ ♿ shop 🐕 ✿

Old Sarum

Castle Rd SP1 3SD (2m N on A345)
☎ **01722 335398**

Impressive remains of an Iron-Age camp surround what was the original site of Salisbury cathedral and its thriving community. It was abandoned in medieval times, and the bishop and his flock moved to found a new cathedral where the present city stands. However, for many hundreds of years after its desertion, until the Reform Bill of 1832, ten voters continued to return two MPs to parliament at Westminster.
Times: Open all year, Apr-Sep daily 10-6 (7pm Jul & Aug; Oct 10-5); Nov-Mar, daily 10-4. Closed 24-26 Dec & 1 Jan.
Fee: £2 (ch 5-15 £1, under 5's free). P ♿ #

Royal Gloucestershire, Berkshire & Wiltshire Regiment Museum

The Wardrobe, 58 The Close SP1 2EX
☎ **01722 414536**
Times: Open Apr-Oct, daily 10-4.30; Feb, Mar & Nov, Mon-Fri 10-4.30. (Closed Dec & Jan). P ☕ ♿ shop 🐕 *Details not confirmed for 2001*

Salisbury Cathedral

33 The Close SP1 2EJ (S of city centre)
☎ **01722 555120** 📠 **01722 555116**

Built in one phase between 1220 and 1258, the Cathedral is probably Britain's finest piece of medieval architecture. The spire is 123 metres tall, making it the highest in England. The Chapter House displays a frieze depicting scenes from Genesis and Exodus, the finest surviving Magna Carta. The Choir are continuing a tradition that began around 750 years ago, with performances at daily services, they are accompanied by Europe's finest romantic church organ. The surrounding Cathedral Close contains two museums, two small stately homes and acres of lawn.

contd.

Times: Open all year, Jan-May, Sep-Dec, daily 7.15-6.15; Jun-Aug, Mon-Sat 7.15-8.15. **Fee:** £3 (ch £1, pen & students £2). Family £6. P (100yds) (limited spaces) licensed (loop system, interpretive model for blind, wheelchairs) toilets for disabled shop

Salisbury & South Wiltshire Museum

The King's House, 65 The Close SP1 2EN (in Cathedral Close)

01722 332151 01722 325611
e-mail: museum@salisburymuseum.freeserve.co.uk

One of the most outstanding of the beautiful buildings in Cathedral Close. Galleries include Stonehenge, History of Salisbury, the Pitt Rivers collection, and the Wedgwood room, a reconstruction of a pre-NHS surgery, and a costume, lace and embroidery gallery.
Times: Open all year Mon-Sat 10-5; also Suns Jul & Aug, 2-5. (Closed Xmas). **Fee:** £3 (under 5's free, ch 75p, pen, students & UB40s £2). Party. Five-visit saver tickets available.
P (100 metres) (nearby parking charge) parking by prior arrangement,induction loop in lecture hall toilets for disabled shop (ex guide dogs)

STONEHENGE

Stonehenge

SP4 7DE (2m W of Amesbury on junct A303 and A344/A360)

01980 624715

One of the most famous prehistoric monuments in Europe, the henge was started about 5,000 years ago, but redesigned several times during the following 1,500 years. Enormous sarsens, each weighing more than 50 tons, were dragged from the Marlborough Downs, and were then worked into the design we see today - an outer ring of upright stones with lintels, and an inner horseshoe of five pairs of uprights, also with lintels. The axis of the horseshoe points towards the midsummer sunrise.
Times: Open all year, daily, 16 Mar-May & Sep-15 Oct 9.30-6; Jun-Aug, 9-7; 16-23 Oct 9.30-5; 24 Oct-15 Mar 9.30-4. Closed 24-26 Dec. There is an audio tour available in six languages. Last admission no later than 30 minutes before the advertised closing time. Stonehenge will close promptly 20 minutes after the advertised closing time.
Fee: £4 (ch 5-15 £3, under 5's free).
P shop

STOURHEAD

Stourhead House & Garden

The Estate Office BA12 6QH (off B3092)

01747 841152 & 09001 335205 (info line)
e-mail: wstjxt@smtp.ntrust.org.uk

The Palladian house was built in 1720. What makes Stourhead especially memorable is the superb gardens, laid out in 1741. They feature a grotto and a temple to Flora around two springs and a large triangular lake.
Times: Open - House 1 Apr-29 Oct, Sat-Wed 12-5.30 or dusk if earlier. Garden daily all year 9-7 or dusk if earlier (ex 20-23 Jul when garden closes at 5pm). King Alfreds Tower, 1 Apr-29 Oct, Tue-Sun (but open BH Mon), Tue-Fri 2-5.30, wknds 11.30-5.30 or dusk if earlier.
Fee: House or garden Mar-Oct £4.60 (ch £2.60). Family £20. Garden only Nov-Feb £3.60 (ch £1.50) Family ticket £8. Combined House & Garden ticket £8 (ch £3.80) Family ticket £20. Parties 15+ (ex Nov-Feb). King Alfred's Tower £1.50 (ch 70p).
P licensed toilets for disabled shop (ex in gardens Nov-Feb only)

STOURTON

Stourton House Flower Garden

Stourton House BA12 6QF (3m NW of Mere, on A303)

01747 840417

Set in the attractive village of Stourton, the house has more than four acres of beautifully maintained flower gardens. Many grass paths lead through varied and colourful shrubs, trees and plants; and Stourton House also specialises in unusual plants, and dried flowers, many of which are for sale. It also has collections of daffodils, delphiniums and hydrangeas.
Times: Open Apr-end Nov, Wed, Thu, Sun & BH Mon 11-6 (or dusk if earlier). Also open Dec-Mar, wkdays for plant/dried flower sales.
Fee: £2.50 (ch 50p)
P (wheelchairs available) toilets for disabled shop (plants for sale) garden centre (ex by arrangement)

SWINDON

Steam - Museum of the Great Western Railway

Kemble Dr SN2 2AT (from junct 16 of M4 & A420 follow brown signs to 'Outlet Centre')

01793 466646 01793 466484

This brand new museum celebrates the people who built, operated and travelled on the Great Western Railway. Using interactive exhibits, displays, and many original locomotives, one of England's most important historic railways is brought to life.
Times: Open all year, Mon-Sun 10-6, open until 8pm on Thu during summer season. (Closed 25-26 Dec).
Fee: £4.80 (ch & concessions £3) Family ticket £13. (Charge includes admission to the Railway Village museum).
P (100 yds) (disabled parking only at establisment) toilets for disabled shop (ex guide dogs)

TEFFONT MAGNA

Farmer Giles Farmstead

SP3 5QY (11m W of Salisbury, off A303 at Teffont)
☎ 01722 716338 📠 01722 716993
e-mail: tdeane6995@aol.com

Set in 175 acres of Wiltshire downland, this is a real working dairy farm. You can watch the cows being milked, bottle feed lambs and get to know a host of other animals and pets. There is an adventure playground with tractors and a relaxing walk along the picturesque Beech belt, meeting Highland cattle and Shire horses along the way.

Times: Open 18 Mar-5 Nov, daily 10-6, wknds in winters, 10-dusk. Party bookings all year.
Fee: £3.95 (ch £2.85, under 2's free & pen £3.50) Family ticket £13. licensed complete access for disabled & wheelchairs available for use toilets for disabled shop

TISBURY

Old Wardour Castle

SP3 6RR (2m SW)
☎ 01747 870487

Substantial remains of this hexagonal 14th-century castle are still standing, with walls 60ft high. It was twice besieged, and finally ruined during the Civil War. These ruins are considered among the most attractive in England.

Times: Open all year, Apr-Oct, daily 10-6 (Oct 10-5); Nov-Mar daily 10-4, (closed 1-2pm) . Closed 24-26 Dec & 1 Jan.
Fee: £2 (ch 5-15 £1, under 5's free).

WESTBURY

Woodland Park & Heritage Centre

Brokerswood BA13 4EH (turn off A36 at Bell Inn, Standerwick. Follow brown tourist signs)
☎ 01373 822238 & 823880 📠 01373 858474
e-mail: woodland.park@virgin.net

Woodland Park Heritage Centre nature walks lead through 80 acres of woodlands, with a lake and wildfowl. Facilities include a woodland visitor centre, children's adventure playgrounds, indoor soft play area, guided walks and the 0.3m Smokey Oak railway.

Times: Open all year; Park open daily 10-6. Museum open Mon-Fri 10-5 (summer), 12-3 (winter); Sat 2-6, Sun 10-6 (summer); Sun 2-4.30 (winter). Free admission for wheelchair users.
Fee: £2.50 (unaccompanied ch £1.50, accompanied ch 50p,pen £1.95) shop

WESTWOOD

Westwood Manor

BA15 2AF (1.5m SW of Bradford on Avon, off B3109)
☎ 01225 863374

This late 15th-century stone manor house has some particularly fine Jacobean plasterwork. Situated by the parish church, the house was altered in 1610 but still retains its late Gothic and Jacobean windows.

Times: Open Apr-Sep, Sun, Tue & Wed 2-5 **Fee:** £3.70.

WILTON (near Salisbury)

Wilton House

SP2 0BJ (3m W of Salisbury, on A30)
☎ 01722 746720 & 746729(24 hr line)
📠 01722 744447
e-mail: tourism@wiltonhouse.com

Built on the site of a 9th century nunnery founded by King Alfred, the Tudor origins of the house can be seen in the tower now incorporated within the splendid 17th-century house, based on designs by Inigo Jones. Wilton House boasts a world famous art collection with over 230 paintings, 21 acres of landscaped parkland, rose and water gardens, woodland and riverside walks.

Times: Open 10 Apr-29 Oct daily 10.30-5.30. Last admission 4.30.
Fee: £6.75 (ch 5-15 £4, under 5 free, students & pen £5.75). Family ticket £17.50. licensed toilets for disabled shop garden centre (ex guide dogs)

WOODHENGE

Woodhenge

(1.5m N of Amesbury, off A345 just S of Durrington)

A Neolithic ceremonial monument dating from about 2300 BC, consisting of six concentric rings of timber posts, now marked by concrete piles. The long axis of the rings, which are oval, points to the rising sun on Midsummer Day.

Times: Open all reasonable times. **Fee:** Free.

Worcestershire

In Worcestershire, the fertile plains of the Vale of Evesham and the Severn Valley climb to the Malvern Hills in the west, and the Cotswolds in the south. To the north of the county lies the industrialised area of the Black Country, in sharp contrast to the south's rural idyll.

Worcester is the county town, and home to the Worcestershire County Cricket Club, which has what some regard as the most attractive grounds in the country, in a delightful setting with views of Worcester Cathedral. Worcester Racecourse is one of the oldest in the country, in Pitchcroft Park, close to the city, beside the River Severn.

Sir Edward Elgar was a Worcester man, and his statue stands in the High Street of the city, facing the cathedral. The cottage where he was born, in Lower Broadheath just west of Worcester, is now open as a museum. He has also recently been commemorated on the new £20 note.

Southeast of Worcester is the Vale of Evesham, the main fruit-growing area of the country, dotted with orchards and market gardens - a picture in the spring with the blossom in the trees. The main town in this area is Evesham, set in a loop of the River Avon.

The Malverns, Great and Little, set on the slopes of the Malvern Hills, are renowned for their refinement. Great Malvern, terraced on its hillside site, came to prominence as a genteel spa for well-to-do Victorians, rivalling the likes of Bath, Buxton and Cheltenham with its glorious surroundings.

EVENTS & FESTIVALS

May
11-13 Spring Garden Show, Three Counties Showground, Malvern

June
14-16 Three Counties Show, Three Counties Showground, Malvern

July
tbc Worcester Carnival

September
9/10 The Commandery, Worcester's Civil War Centre will be celebrating the 350th anniversary of the Battle of Worcester
29-30 The Malvern Autumn Show, Three Counties Showground, Malvern

October
tbc Worcester Male Voice Choir Concert

December
tbc Victorian Christmas Fayre Royal Worcester Porcelain
2001 is the 250th anniversary of Royal Worcester Porcelain and various celebrations are planned - contact the Royal Worcester Visitor Centre for details Tel 01905 23221.

Top: Malvern Hills Worcestershire Beacon

BEWDLEY

Severn Valley Railway
Comberton Hill
☎ 01299 403816 🖷 01299 400839
(For full entry see Kidderminster)

West Midland Safari & Leisure Park
Spring Grove DY12 1LF (on A456)
☎ 01299 402114 🖷 01299 404519

This 200 acre site incorporates a drive-through safari with Tiger World one of the attractions. Also on view Pets Corner, Reptile House, Hippo Lakes, live shows, Goat Walk, Seal Aquarium and train ride to the Leisure Area with over 25 rides and amusements.

Times: Open Apr-Oct, daily from 10am including BH's.

Fee: £5.75 (ch 4 free). Multi ride wristband £6.75. Junior restricted £5 (restricted rides only). Ride tickets £1 each from machines (various no of tickets per ride).

P ☕ ✕ licensed ♿ (most area accessible slopes/tarmac paths) shop

BROADWAY

Broadway Tower & Animal Park
WR12 7LB (off A44, 1m SE of village)
☎ 01386 852390 🖷 01386 858038
e-mail: broadway-tower@clara.net

The 65ft tower was designed by James Wyatt for the 6th Earl of Coventry, and built in 1799. The unique building now houses exhibitions depicting its colourful past and various uses such as holiday retreat to artist and designer William Morris. The viewing platform is equipped with a telescope, giving wonderful views over 13 counties. Around the Tower is a park with adventure playground, children's farm, BBQs, giant chess and draughts, and animal enclosures.

Times: Open Apr-Oct, daily 10.30-5. Nov-Mar (tower only) wknds weather permitting 11-3 or by prior booking.

Fee: £4 (ch 4-15 £2.30, concessions £3). Family ticket £11.50. Party 15+.

P ☕ ✕ licensed ♿ toilets for disabled shop

BROMSGROVE

Avoncroft Museum of Historic Buildings
Stoke Heath B60 4JR (2m S, off A38)
☎ 01527 831886 & 831363 🖷 01527 876934
e-mail: avoncroft1@compuserve.com

A visit to Avoncroft takes you through nearly 700 years of history. Here you can see 25 buildings rescued from destruction and authentically restored on a 15 acre rural site. There are 15th and 16th-century timber framed buildings, 18th-century agricultural buildings and a cockpit. There are industrial buildings and a working windmill from the 19th century, and from the 20th a fully furnished pre-fab.

Times: Open Jul-Aug daily 10.30-5; Apr-Jun & Sep-Oct 10.30-4.30 (wknds 5.30), (Closed Mon); Mar & Nov 10.30-4, (Closed Mon & Fri). Open BHs.

Fee: £4.60 (ch £2.30, pen £3.70). Family ticket £12.50.

P ☕ ♿ (ramps, wheelchair available) toilets for disabled shop

EVESHAM

The Almonry Heritage Centre
Abbey Gate WR11 4EJ (on A4184, opposite Merstow Green, main North/South route through Evesham)
☎ 01386 446944 🖷 01386 442348
e-mail: almonry@eveshamtc.ndirect.co.uk

The 14th-century stone and timber building was the home of the Almoner of the Benedictine Abbey in Evesham. It now houses exhibitions relating to the

contd.

history of Evesham Abbey, the Battle of Evesham, and the culture and trade of Evesham. Evesham Tourist Information Centre is also located here.

Times: Open all year, Mon-Sat & BHs (ex Xmas & Sun in Nov, Dec & Jan) 10-5, Sun 2-5.

Fee: £2 (ch 16 free, pen & students £1) P (110yds) shop

GREAT WITLEY

WITLEY COURT

WR6 6JT (on A433)

☎ 01299 896636

Spectacular ruins of a once great house. An earlier Jacobean manor house was converted in the 19th-century into a vast Italianate mansion with porticoes by John Nash. The adjoining church by James Gibbs, has a remarkable 18th-century baroque interior. The gardens were equally elaborate and contained immense stone fountains, the largest is the Poseidon Fountain.

Times: Open all year Apr-Sep, daily 10-6, (Oct 10-5); Nov-Mar, Wed-Sun 10-4. Closed 24-26 Dec & 1 Jan.

Fee: £3.50 (ch 5-15 £1.80, under 5's free) P ♿ #

HANBURY

HANBURY HALL

School Rd WR9 7EA (4.5m E of Droitwich, 1m N of B4090 and 1.5m W of B4091)

☎ 01527 821214 📠 01527 821251

e-mail: hanbury@smtp.ntrust.org.uk

This William and Mary style red-brick house, completed in 1701, was built by a prosperous local family. The house contains outstanding painted ceilings and staircase by Thornhill, and the Watney collection of porcelain. The restored 18th-century garden has a parterre, bowling green and working orangery.

Times: Open 2 Apr-29 Oct, Sun-Wed Hall 2-6 & Gardens 12.30-5.30. Last admission 5.30 (dusk if earlier).

Fee: House & Garden £4.60 (ch £2.30). Family ticket £11.50. Garden only £2.90 (ch £1.45). P ♿ (Braille guide) toilets for disabled shop (ex in park)

KIDDERMINSTER

SEVERN VALLEY RAILWAY

Comberton Hill (on A448 clearly signposted)

☎ 01299 403816 📠 01299 400839

The leading standard gauge steam railway, with one of the largest collections of locomotives and rolling stock in the country. Services operate from Kidderminster and Bewdley to Bridgnorth through 16 miles of picturesque scenery along the River Severn. Special steam galas, "Day out with Thomas" Weekends and Santa Specials.

Times: Trains operate wknds throughout year, daily early May to end Sep, plus school holidays & half terms, Santa Specials.

Fee: Subject to Review.(Train fares vary according to journey. Main through ticket £9.60 return, Family ticket £23)

P ♿ toilets for disabled shop (at Kidderminster/Bridgnorth)

See advert on p261.

WORCESTERSHIRE COUNTY MUSEUM

Hartlebury Castle, Hartlebury DY11 7XZ (4m S of Kidderminster clearly signed from A449)

☎ 01299 250416 📠 01299 251890

e-mail: museum@worcestershire.gov.uk

Housed in the north wing of Hartlebury Castle, the County Museum contains a delightful display of crafts and industries. There are unique collections of toys, costume, domestic life, room settings and horse-drawn vehicles as well as a reconstructed forge, schoolroom, wheelwright's and tailor's shop.

Times: Open Feb-Nov, Mon-Thu 10-5, BH's 11-5, Fri & Sun 2-5. (Closed Sat & Good Fri).

Fee: £2.20 (ch & pen £1.10). Family ticket £6.

P ♿ (car parking close to main building) toilets for disabled shop (ex guide dogs & in grounds)

REDDITCH

FORGE MILL NEEDLE MUSEUM & BORDESLEY ABBEY VISITOR CENTRE

Forge Mill, Needle Mill Ln, Riverside B98 8HY (N side of Redditch, off A441)

☎ 01527 62509

e-mail: museum@redditchbc.gov.uk

The Needle Museum tells the fascinating and sometimes gruesome story of how needles are made. Working, water-powered machinery can be seen in an original needle-scouring mill. The Visitor Centre is an archaeological museum showing finds from excavations at the nearby Bordesley Abbey.

Times: Open Etr-Sep, Mon-Fri 11-4.30, Sat-Sun 2-5; Feb-Etr & Oct-Nov, Mon-Thu 11-4 & Sun 2-5. Parties by arrangement.

Fee: £3.50 (ch 50p, pen £2.50). Family ticket £7.50. Reduced admission charge for holders of a Reddicard.

P ♿ toilets for disabled shop (ex guide dogs)

SPETCHLEY

SPETCHLEY PARK GARDENS

Spetchley Park WR5 1RS (3m E of Worcester, off A422)

☎ 01905 345213 or 345224

e-mail: hb@omegaland.net

The 110-acre deer park and the 30-acre gardens surround an early 19th-century mansion (not open), with sweeping lawns, herbaceous borders, a rose lawn and enclosed gardens with low box and yew hedges. There is a large collection of trees (including 17th-century Cedars of Lebanon) and rare shrubs and plants.

Times: Open Apr-Sep, Tue-Fri 11-5, Sun 2-5; BH Mons 11-5. Other days by appointment.

Fee: £3.20 (ch £1.60). Party 25+. P ♿

STONE

Stone House Cottage Gardens

DY10 4BG (2m SE of Kidderminster, on A448)
☎ 01562 69902 ▯ 01562 69960

A beautiful walled garden with towers provides a sheltered area of about one acre for rare shrubs, climbers and interesting herbaceous plants. Adjacent is a nursery with a large selection of unusual plants.
Times: Open Gardens & nursery Mar-18 Oct, Wed-Sat 10-5.30.
Fee: £2 (ch free). P ♿ garden centre

WORCESTER

City Museum & Art Gallery

Foregate St WR1 1DT
☎ 01905 25371 ▯ 01905 616979

The gallery has temporary art exhibitions from both local and national sources. Of particular interest is a complete 19th-century chemists shop. There are collections relating to the Worcestershire Regiment and the Worcestershire Yeomanry Cavalry.
Times: Open all year, Mon, Tue Wed & Fri 9.30-5.30, Sat 9.30-5.(Closed 25-26 Dec & 1 Jan also Good Fri)
Fee: Free. P ♿ (lift (Taylors Lane ent) induction loop Art Gallery) toilets for disabled shop

The Commandery

Sidbury WR1 2HU (M5 junct 7, A44, signposted)
☎ 01905 361821 ▯ 01905 361822

The headquarters of Charles II's army during the Battle of Worcester in 1651. The Commandery is an impressive complex of medieval timber framed buildings. Various exhibitions include 'Civil War',which details the events of England's bloody revolution.
Times: Open all year, Mon-Sat 10-5, Sun 1.30-5. (Closed 25-26 Dec & 1 Jan) **Fee:** £3.70 (concessions £2.60). Family ticket £9.90.
P (100yds) shop (ex guide dogs)

Elgar's Birthplace Museum

Crown East Ln, Lower Broadheath WR2 6RH (3m W, off A44 to Leominster).
☎ 01905 333224 ▯ 01905 333224
Times: Open daily ex Wed, May-Sep 10.30-6. Oct-15 Jan & 16 Feb-Apr 1.30-4.30.
P ♿ shop (ex guide dogs & in gardens) *Details not confirmed for 2001*

Hawford Dovecote

(3m N on A449)
☎ 01684 850051

An unusual square, half-timbered 16th-century dovecote. Access on foot only via the entrance drive to the adjoining house.
Times: Open Apr-1 Nov, daily 9-6 or sunset. (Closed Good Fri). Other times by prior appointment only. P (on street parking)

Museum of Local Life

Friar St WR1 2NA
☎ 01905 722349

This interesting 500-year-old timber-framed house has a squint and an ornate plaster ceiling. It is now a museum of local life and displays show life here over the last 200 years.
Times: Open all year, Mon-Wed & Fri-Sat 10.30-5. Also BH's. (Closed 25-26 Dec & 1 Jan). **Fee:** Free.
P (200yds) ♿ toilets for disabled shop

Museum of Worcester Porcelain

Severn St WR1 2NE
☎ 01905 23221 ▯ 01905 617807
e-mail: museum@royal-worcester.co.uk

The Victorian buildings lead into the heart of a world famous porcelain industry and was founded in 1751. The guided tours and the Museum of Worcester Porcelain take visitors on a design journey through time. Exhibits include room settings, dining scenes and shop fronts in the Georgian, Victorian and 20th century galleries.
Times: Open all year: Mon-Sat 9-5.30, Sun 11-5.
Fee: Museum: £3 (concessions £2.25), family £6.50. Guided factory tour £5. Special all-in-one £8 (concessions £6.75), family £20.
P (charged) ✕ licensed ♿ (ex factory) toilets for disabled shop

Worcester Cathedral

WR1 2LH
☎ 01905 28854 & 21004 ▯ 01905 611139

Worcester Cathedral with its 200-foot tower stands majestically beside the River Severn. The Crypt, built by St Wulstan in 1084, is a classic example of Norman architecture. The 12th-century Chapter House and Cloisters are a reminder of the cathedral's monastic past. King John (who signed the Magna Carta) and Prince Arthur (elder brother of Henry VIII) are buried near the High Altar.
Times: Open all year, daily 7.30-6.
Fee: Donations. (Suggested £2 per adult.)
P (500yds) ♿ (limited access due to nature of building) toilets for disabled shop (ex guide dogs)

East Riding of Yorkshire

From the imposing chalk cliffs at Flamborough, to the rolling green pastures of the Yorkshire Wolds, and the flourishing port of Hull, the East Riding of Yorkshire boasts some of the finest unspoilt countryside in England, and some wonderful places to visit.

EVENTS & FESTIVALS

April
29 Fifth RSPCA Annual Dog Show, Driffield Showground

May
tbc East Riding of Yorkshire Classic Cycle Race, Beverley
tbc Beverley & East Riding Early Music Festival

June
tbc Beverley & East Riding Folk Festival

July
tbc Driffield Agricultural Show, Driffield Showground
tbc Hornsea Music Festival

August
tbc Bridlington Harbour Gala
tbc Driffield Steam & Vintage Rally
tbc International Sea Shanty Festival, Hull

September
tbc Beverley & East Riding Chamber Music Festival
tbc Hull Show

October
tbc Hull Fair, Walton Street Fairground, Hull

November
tbc Hull Literature Festival

Top: Groynes at Spurn Head

Beverley Minster is big enough to be a cathedral. Among its treasures are a 1000-year old sanctuary chair and some wonderfully intricate wooden carvings. The magnificent Percy Tomb is a fine example of 14th-century stonemasonry. Beverley is also home to the Museum of Army Transport.

Driffield is known as the 'Capital of the Wolds', and is home to a livestock auction that attracts farmers from all around. Close by is Sledmere House, an impressive manor house set among parkland designed by Capability Brown.

Coastal areas of the East Riding can be a little daunting. Flamborough Head is a plateau of rolling turf 150ft high and surrounded on three sides by the sea. The Heritage Coast Project puts on a wide range of events which includes lectures, guided walks and nature expeditions. The lighthouse has defied the elements since 1806.

Further down the coast, Spurn Head is an unusual sand and shingle peninsula curving across the mouth of the Humber, formed of deposits washed from the crumbling cliffs of Holderness a few miles to the north. The earliest record of Spurn is from 670 AD, when a monastery was established there. Since then the spit has been broken down and rebuilt by the sea three times.

BEMPTON

RSPB Nature Reserve

YO15 1JD (take cliff road from B1229, Bempton Village)
☎ 01262 851179 & 851533 📠 01262 851533

Part of the spectacular chalk cliffs, this is one of the sites in England to see thousands of nesting seabirds including gannets, puffins, guillemots, razorbills, kittiwakes, fulmars, herring gulls and several pairs of shag. This is the only gannetry on the mainland of England and is growing annually. Many migrants pass off-shore including terns, skuas and shearwaters.

Times: Open for visitor centre daily, Mar-Nov 10-5. Winter wknds only 9.30-4.
Fee: Free.
P (charged) ♿ toilets for disabled shop

BEVERLEY

Guildhall

Register Sq HU17 9AU
☎ 01482 884414 📠 01482 884747
e-mail: museum@sewerby.clara.net

A Guildhall has been on this site since 1500, although parts of the building date back to a private dwelling of 1320. Largely remodelled in the Palladian style in the 1760s, the Courtroom features a magnificent stucco work ceiling, and the Magistrate's Room houses rare 17th-century Civic furniture.

Times: Opens in 2001. Telephone for dates & times.
Fee: Free.
P (100yds) ♿ (ex guide dogs)

Museum of Army Transport

Flemingate HU17 0NG
☎ 01482 860445 📠 01482 872767

The museum tells the story of army transport from horse drawn waggons to the recent Gulf conflict: everything from prototype vehicles to Montgomery's Rolls Royce and the last Blackburn Beverley aircraft. There are also other exhibits to be explored including `Monty's Men and D-Day Dodgers".

Times: Open all year, daily 10-5. (Closed 24-26 Dec).
Fee: £4.50 (ch 5-15, pen & student £3). Family ticket £12 (2 adults & 2 ch). Under 5's free.
P (charged) ♿ (parking next to entrance) toilets for disabled shop (ex guide dogs)

BURTON AGNES

Burton Agnes Hall

Estate Office YO25 0ND (on A166)
☎ 01262 490324 📠 01262 490513

Times: Open Apr-Oct, daily 11-5.
P ♿ (scented garden for the blind) toilets for disabled shop garden centre *Details not confirmed for 2001*

Norman Manor House

This rare survivor from Norman times was replaced by Burton Agnes Hall. Some interesting Norman architectural features can still be seen, but the building was encased in brick at a later period.

Times: Open all year.
Fee: Free.
#

HULL

Maister House

160 High St HU1 1NQ
☎ 01482 324114

The house is a mid 18th-century rebuilding, notable for its splendid stone and wrought-iron staircase, ornate stucco work and finely carved doors. Only the staircase and entrance hall are open.

Times: Open all year, Mon-Fri 10-4 (Closed BH).
P *Details not confirmed for 2001*

Maritime Museum

Queen Victoria Square HU1 3DX (from M62 follow A63 to town centre)
☎ 01482 613902 📠 01482 613710
e-mail: museums@hullcc.demon.co.uk

Hull's maritime history is illustrated here, with displays on whales and whaling, ships and shipping, and other aspects of this Humber port. There is also a Victorian court room which is used for temporary exhibitions. The restored dock area, with its fine Victorian and Georgian buildings, is well worth exploring too.

Times: Open all year, Mon-Sat 10-5 & Sun 1.30-4.30. (Closed 25-2 Jan & Good Fri).
Fee: Free.
P (100yds) ♿ shop (ex guide dogs)

`Streetlife' - Hull Museum of Transport

High St (A63 from M62, follow signs for Old Town)

☎ 01482 613902 📠 01482 613710

This purpose built museum uses a 'hands-on' approach to trace 200 years of transport history. With a vehicle collection of national importance, state of the art animatronic displays and authentic scenarios, you can see Hull's Old Town brought vividly to life. The mail coach ride uses the very latest in computer technology to recreate a Victorian journey by four-in-hand.

Times: Open all year, Mon-Sat 10-5, Sun 1.30-4.30. (Closed 24-25 Dec & Good Fri). (Closed May 2000 for 12 month building programme)

Fee: Free.

P (500m) ♿ toilets for disabled shop (ex guide dogs)

Wilberforce House

23-25 High St HU1 1NE (A63 from M62 or A1079 from York, follow signs for Old Town)

☎ 01482 613902 📠 01482 613710

e-mail: <museum@hullcc.demon.co.uk>

The early 17th-century Merchants house was the birthplace of William Wilberforce, who became a leading campaigner against slavery. There are Jacobean and Georgian rooms and displays on Wilberforce. The house also has secluded gardens. There is a special exhibition The A-Z of Costume, with displays of Hull Museum's extensive costume collection.

Times: Open all year, Mon-Sat 10-5 & Sun 1.30-4.30. (Closed 25-26 Dec, 1 Jan & Good Fri).

Fee: Free.

P (500m) (meters on street) ♿ (large print, video area & audio guides) shop (ex guide dogs)

POCKLINGTON

Burnby Hall Garden & Stewart Collection

The Balk YO42 2QF (off A1079 at turning for Pocklington off B1247)

☎ 01759 302068

The two lakes in this garden have an outstanding collection of 80 varieties of hardy water lilies, designated a National Collection. The lakes stand within seven acres of beautiful gardens including a lovely walled garden, heather beds, a rock garden and a spring and summer bedding area. The museum contains sporting trophies and ethnic material gathered on world-wide travels.

Times: Open 31 Mar-Sep, daily 10-6. (last admission 5pm).

Fee: £2.40 (ch 5-15 £1, pen £1.90). Party 20+.

P ♿ (free wheelchair hire) toilets for disabled shop (ex guide dogs)

SPROATLEY

Burton Constable Hall

HU11 4LN (1.5m N of Sproatley)

☎ 01964 562400 📠 01964 563229

e-mail: burtonconstable@btclick.com

This superb Elizabethan house was built in 1570, but much of the interior was remodelled in the 18th century. There are magnificent reception rooms and a Tudor long gallery with a pendant roof: the contents range from pictures and furniture to a unique collection of 18th-century scientific instruments. Outside are 200 acres of parkland landscaped by `Capability' Brown, with oaks and chestnuts, and a lake with an island.

Times: Open, Hall & grounds Etr Sun-31 Oct, Sat-Thu. Grounds noon-5, Hall 1-5.

Fee: House £4 (ch £1.50, pen £3.70). Family £9.

P ♿ (stair list to first foor) toilets for disabled shop (dogs in ground on leads)

THORNTON

Thornton Abbey

☎ 01469 40357

A magnificent 14th-century gatehouse and the ruins of the church and other buildings survive from the 12th-century Augustinian abbey. The approach is across a long bridge, spanning a dry moat.

Times: Open Apr-Sep, 1st & 3rd Sun of month 12-6; Oct-Mar, 3rd Sun of month 12-4. Grounds open any reasonable time.

Fee: Free.

P ♿ (in certain areas) #

North Yorkshire

England's largest county, North Yorkshire has a stunning natural landscape, encompassing part of the Pennines, the rolling farmlands of the Vale of York, the Cleveland Hills and the North York Moors, plus the Yorkshire Dales National Park, which includes Swaledale and Wensleydale.

The coastline offers its own treasures, from the fishing villages of Staithes and Robin Hood Bay to Scarborough, one time Regency spa and Victorian bathing resort.

York, traditionally the capital of the North of England, was second only to London prior to the Industrial Revolution. It is a city of immense historical significance: capital of the British province under the Romans in AD 71 and a Viking settlement in the 10th century. In the Middle Ages its prosperity depended on the wool trade. The city's earliest surviving building is the Roman Multangular Tower, and the city walls, dating from the 14th century, are among the finest in Europe, including four gates or 'bars'. However, the gothic Minster is York's crowning glory, built between 1220 and 1470.

The Georgian Theatre
BUILT BY
ACTOR-MANAGER
Samuel Butler
1788

Northallerton, rather than York, is the administrative centre of the county. Harrogate, another celebrated North Yorkshire town, is a traditional spa resort renowned for its gentility and excellent tea rooms. Its handsome stone buildings and lovely gardens have earned it the title of Floral Resort of England. To the south of the town, an area of some 200 acres of common land known as The Stray is popular for walking and picnicking.

EVENTS & FESTIVALS

March
10-17 Eskdale Festival of the Arts, Whitby
3-4, 10-11, & 17-18 Harrogate Competitive Festival of Music, Speech & Drama

April
13-20 Harrogate International Youth Music Festival
26-29 Harrogate Spring Flower Show

May
tbc Ripon Spring Bank Festival

June
tbc North Yorkshire County Show, South Otterington

July
6-15 York Early Music Festival
10-12 Great Yorkshire Show, Harrogate
21-22 Thirty-seventh Masham Steam Engine & Fair Organ Rally
28 Cleveland Show, Middlesbrough

August
5 Trans Pennine Vintage Commercial Vehicle Run

September
tbc Nidderdale Show

October
Captain Cook Festival, Whitby

Top: Askrigg

ALDBOROUGH

Roman Town

(0.75m SE of Boroughbridge, on minor road off B6265 within 1m of junction of A1 & A6055)
☎ 01423 322768

The pretty present-day village occupies the site of the northernmost civilian Roman town in Britain. Remains include two mosaic pavements and part of the town walls.

Times: Open Apr-Sep, daily 10-1 & 2-6 (Oct 10-1 & 2-5).
Fee: £1.70 (ch 5-15 90p, under 5's free)

AYSGARTH

National Park Centre

DL8 3TH
☎ 01969 663424
e-mail: aysgarth@ytbtic.co.uk

A visitor centre for the Yorkshire Dales National Park, with maps, guides, walks and local information. Displays explain the history and natural history of the area.

Times: Open Etr, May-Aug, daily 10-5; Sep & Oct, daily 10-4.30. Nov-Apr limited wknd opening.
Fee: Free.
(charged) shop (ex guide dogs)

Yorkshire Carriage Museum

Yore Mill DL8 3SR (1.75m E on unclass rd N of A684.Turn rt at Palmer Flatt Hotel, museum 300yds)
☎ 01969 663399

Times: Open Apr-Oct, daily 9.30-7.30, other times 9.30-dusk. Closed 24 Dec-12 Jan.
(150 yds) shop *Details not confirmed for 2001*

BEDALE

Bedale Hall

DL8 1AA (on A684, 1.5m W of A1 at Leeming Bar)
☎ 01677 422037 01677 422037

Housed in a building of 17th-century origin, with Palladian and Georgian extensions, the centre of this fascinating museum is the Bedale fire engine dated 1742. Old documents, photographs, clothing, toys, craft tools and household utensils give an absorbing picture of the life of ordinary people.

Times: Open Etr-Sep, Mon, Tue & Wed-Fri 2-4, Sat 10-2. Other times by prior arrangement.
Fee: Free.
toilets for disabled shop (ex guide dogs)

BENINGBROUGH

Beningbrough Hall

YO6 1DD (off A19, 8m NW of York. Entrance at Newton Lodge)
☎ 01904 470666 01904 470002

Beningbrough was built around 1716. It houses 100 pictures from the National Portrait Gallery in London. Ornately carved wood panelling is a feature of several of the rooms. The other side of country house life can be seen in the restored Victorian laundry.

Times: Open Apr-Jun & Sep-Oct, Sat-Wed & Good Fri. Also Fris during Jul & Aug daily except Thu. House 12-5. Last admission 4.30pm. Grounds 11am-5.30pm. Last admission 5pm.
licensed (access to Victorian laundry, shop & restaurant) toilets for disabled shop *Details not confirmed for 2001*

BRIMHAM

Brimham Rocks

Summerbridge HG3 4DW (off B6265)
☎ 01423 780688 01423 781020
e-mail: yorkbm@smtp.nttrust.org.uk

A Victorian guidebook describes the rocks as `a place wrecked with grim and hideous forms defying all description and definition'. The rocks have remained a great attraction, and stand on National Trust open moorland at a height of 950ft. An old shooting lodge in the area is now an information point and shop.

Times: Open all year: 8am-dusk. Facilities may be closed in bad weather. Exhibition room mid Mar-mid May wknds, BH & school holidays & late May-early Oct, daily 11-5. Oct school holidays, Sun in Nov & Dec incl 36 Dec New Year's Day & Feb school holidays, 11-dusk weather permitting.
(specially adapted path) toilets for disabled shop *Details not confirmed for 2001*

CASTLE BOLTON

Bolton Castle

DL8 4ET (off A684, 6 miles W of Leyburn)
☎ 01969 623981 01969 623332
e-mail: harry@boltoncastle.co.uk

Medieval Castle completed in 1399, overlooking Wensleydale. Stronghold of the Scrope family. Mary Queen of Scots, was imprisoned here for 6 months. The Castle was besieged and taken by Parliamentary forces in 1645. Tapestries, tableaux, arms & armour, etc, can be seen. Medieval gardens have been developed.

Times: Open Apr-Oct 10-5, Nov-Mar 10-4.
Fee: £4 (ch & pen £3). Family ticket £10.
shop

CASTLE HOWARD

See Malton

CLAPHAM

Yorkshire Dales National Park Centre

LA2 8ED
☎ 015242 51419

Times: Open Apr-Oct, daily 10-5.Limited opening Nov-Mar.
(charged) (Radar key scheme) shop *Details not confirmed for 2001*

COXWOLD

Byland Abbey

YO6 4BD (2m S of A170 between Thirsk & Helmsley, near Coxwold village)
☎ 01347 868614

The abbey was built for the Cistercians in the 12th and 13th centuries and enough remains of the buildings to show how beautiful it most have been. There are well preserved floor tiles, carved stones and other finds.

Times: Open Apr-Sep, daily 10-6 (Oct 10-5). Closed 1-2pm.

Fee: £1.60 (ch 5-15 80p, under 5's free).

toilets for disabled

DANBY

Moors Centre

Lodge Ln YO21 2NB

☎ 01287 660654 01287 660308

e-mail: moorscentre@ytbtic.co.uk

The former shooting lodge provides information on the North York Moors National Park, with an exhibition, video, bookshop and information desk. There are riverside and woodland grounds, with terraced gardens, and a brass-rubbing centre.

Times: Open all year, Apr-Oct, daily 10-5. Nov, Dec & Mar daily 11-4. Jan & Feb wknds only 11-4.

Fee: Free.

(woodland & garden trails, motorised & manual wheelchairs) toilets for disabled shop (ex guide dogs & in grounds)

EASBY

Easby Abbey

(1m SE of Richmond off B6271)

Set beside the River Swale, the Premonstratensian Abbey was founded in 1155 and dedicated to St Agatha. Extensive remains of the monks' domestic buildings can be seen.

Times: Open any reasonable time.

Fee: Free.

ELVINGTON

Yorkshire Air Museum & Allied Air Forces Memorial

Halifax Way YO41 4AU (from York take A1079 then immediate right onto B1228, museum is signposted on right)

☎ 01904 608595 01904 608246

The Yorkshire Air Museum is based on a part of the site of a typical World War II bomber base and its aim is to preserve it as a Memorial to the Allied Air Force air and ground crews who served in World War II. Visitors can see aircraft including one of the last of the RAF's Victor tankers, a Lightning and two Buccaneers.

Times: Open all year, Mon-Fri 10.30-4, Sat & Sun 10.30-5, BH's 10.30-5. In winter times vary, telephone establishment.

Fee: £4 (ch & pen £3).

licensed toilets for disabled shop

FAIRBURN

RSPB Nature Reserve

Fairburn Ings, The Visitor Centre, Newton Ln WF10 2BH (W of A1, N of Ferrybridge)

☎ 01767 680551

One-third of the 618-acre RSPB reserve is open water, and over 260 species of birds have been recorded. A visitor centre provides information, and there is an elevated boardwalk, suitable for disabled visitors.

Times: Access to the reserve from the village at all times. Visitor Centre only open Sat, Sun & BHs 10-5. (Closed 25 & 26 Dec). Car park & walkway at centre open daily 9-6 or dusk.

Fee: Free.

(raised boardwalk for wheelchair) toilets for disabled shop (ex guide dogs)

GRASSINGTON

National Park Centre

Colvend, Hebden Rd BD23 5LB (follow B6265 to Grassington, located in car park on B6265 (Hebden Rd), heading to Pateley Bridge)

☎ 01756 752774 01756 753358

e-mail: grassington@ytbtic.co.uk

The centre is a useful introduction to the Yorkshire Dales National Park. It has a video and a display on 'Wharfedale - Gateway to the Park', and maps, guides and local information are available. There is also a 24-hr public access information service through computer screens and a full tourist information service.

Times: Open Apr-Oct daily, 10-5. Also limited wknds Nov-Mar.

Fee: Free.

(charged) (Radar key scheme) toilets for disabled shop

GUISBOROUGH

Gisborough Priory

(next to parish church)

☎ 01287 633801

The remains of the east end of the 14th-century church make a dramatic sight here. The priory was founded in the 12th century for Augustinian canons.

Times: Open all year Apr-Sep, Tue-Sun 9-5; Oct-Mar, Wed-Sun 9-5. (Closed 24 Dec & 1 Jan).

Fee: 90p (ch 45p, concessions 65p)

HARROGATE

Harlow Carr Botanical Gardens

Crag Ln, Otley Rd HG3 1QB (off B6162,1.5 miles from Harrogate centre)

☎ 01423 565418 01423 530663

The gardens were begun in 1950 on a rough site of pasture and woodland. Today there are 68 impressive acres of ornamental and woodland gardens, including the northern trial grounds. Courses, demonstrations and practical workshops are held in the Study Centre.

Times: Open all year, daily 9.30 until dusk.

Fee: £4 (ch 16 free, pen £3). Party 20+.

licensed (electric wheelchairs available) toilets for disabled shop garden centre (ex guide dogs)

The Royal Pump Room Museum

Crown Place HG1 2RY
☎ 01423 556188 🖷 01423 556130
e-mail: ig23@harrogate.gov.uk

The octagonal Pump Room building houses changing exhibitions from the museum's own collections. This part of the building still houses the original sulphur wells, now below modern street level. The wells are enclosed by glass to contain their pungent smell, but the water can be tasted, by those brave enough, at the original spa counter.

Times: Open all year, Apr-Oct, Mon-Sat 10-5, Sun 2-5, (Nov-Mar close at 4pm). (Closed 25-26 Dec & 1 Jan).
Fee: £2 (ch £1.25, concession £1.50). Family rate £5.50 (2 adults & 2 ch). Party. Combined seasonal tickets available for The Royal Pump Room Museum & Knaresborough Castle & Museum.
P (100yds) (restricted to 3hrs, need parking disk) ♿ toilets for disabled shop (guide dogs only)

HAWES

Dales Countryside Museum Centre

Station Yard DL8 3NT
☎ 01969 667450 & 667494 🖷 01969 667165

Fascinating museum telling the story of the people and landscape of the Yorkshire Dales, past, present and future. Static steam loco and carriages with video and displays. Interactive area.

Times: Open Apr-Oct, daily 10-5. Limited winter opening.
Fee: Admission fee payable for museum. National park centre free.
P (charged) ♿ toilets for disabled shop (ex guide dogs)

HELMSLEY

Duncombe Park

YO62 5EB (1m from town centre, off A170)
☎ 01439 770213 & 771115 🖷 01439 771114
e-mail: sally@duncombepark.com

Times: Open: Apr & Oct Sun-Thu; May-Sep Sun-Fri 10.30-6 (tours every hour).
P ✕ licensed ♿ toilets for disabled shop (ex park) *Details not confirmed for 2001*

Helmsley Castle

YO5 5AB
☎ 01439 770442

The ruined castle dates from the 12th century and stands within enormous earthworks. It was besieged in the Civil War, and destroyed in 1644.

Times: Open all year, Apr-Sep, daily 10-6 (Oct 10-5); Nov-mid Mar, Wed-Sun 10-4 (or dusk if earlier). Closed 1-2pm all year, 24-26 Dec & 1 Jan.
Fee: £2.30 (ch £1.20, under 5's free).
P (charged) (in certain areas) #

KIRBY MISPERTON

Flamingo Land Theme Park & Zoo

The Rectory YO17 6UX (off A169 & A64)
☎ 01653 668287 🖷 01653 668280

Times: Open 28 Mar-26 Sep, as well as weekends and full half term week in Oct.
P ✕ ♿ (parking) toilets for disabled shop *Details not confirmed for 2001*

KIRKHAM

Kirkham Priory

Whitwell-on-the-Hill YO6 7JS (5m SW of Malton on minor road off A64)
☎ 01653 618768

The ruins of this former house of Augustinian canons stand on an entrancing site on the banks of the River Derwent. The remains of the finely sculpted 13th-century gatehouse and lavatorium, where the monks washed in leaded troughs, are memorable.

Times: Open Apr-Sep, daily 10-6, (Oct,10-5).
Fee: £1.60 (ch 5-15 80p, under 5's free) P ♿ #

KNARESBOROUGH

Knaresborough Castle & Museum

Castleyard HG5 8AS
☎ 01423 556188 🖷 01423 556130
e-mail: ig23@harrogate.gov.uk

High above the town, the ruins of this 14th-century castle look down over the gorge of the River Nidd. This imposing fortress was once the hiding place of Thomas Becket's murderers and served as a prison for Richard II. Remains include the keep, the sally-port and the Old Court of Knaresborough.

Times: Open good Fri-Sep, daily 10.30-5. Guided tours available.
Fee: £2 (ch £1.25, concessions £1.50). Family ticket (2 adults & 2 ch) £5.50. Party 10+. Joint & season tickets available for Knaresborough Castle & Museum & The Royal Pump Room Museum.
P (100 metres) (disabled parking in adjacent car park) ♿ toilets for disabled shop (ex guide dogs)

MALHAM

Yorkshire Dales National Park Centre

BD23 4DA

☎ 01729 830363

Times: Open Apr-Oct, daily 10-5. Limited winter opening.

P (charged) ♿ (Radar key scheme for toilet) toilets for disabled shop

Details not confirmed for 2001

MALTON

Castle Howard

YO60 7DA (15m NE of York, off A64)

☎ 01653 648333 648444 📠 01653 648501

e-mail: mec@castlehoward.co.uk

In its dramatic setting of lakes, fountains and extensive gardens, this 18th-century palace was designed by Sir John Vanbrugh. Castle Howard was begun in 1699 for the 3rd Earl of Carlisle, Charles Howard. The interior has a 192ft Long Gallery, as well as a Chapel with magnificent stained glass windows by the 19th-century artist, Edward Burne-Jones. The Castle contains a portrait of Henry VIII by Holbein and works by Rubens, Reynolds and Gainsborough. The grounds include the domed Temple of the Four Winds by Vanbrugh, and the family Mausoleum.

Times: Open 17 Mar-5 Nov, grounds, exhibition wing, plant centre & stable court yard, daily from 10. House 11. Last admissions 4.30pm. Grounds close 6.30.

Fee: £7.50 (ch £4.50, pen £6.75). Grounds only £4.50(ch £2.50).

P ✕ licensed ♿ (chairlift, free adapted transport to house) toilets for disabled shop garden centre (ex in grounds & guide dogs)

Eden Camp Modern History Theme Museum

Eden Camp YO17 6RT (junct of A64 & A169, between York & Scarborough)

☎ 01653 697777 📠 01653 698243

e-mail: admin@edencamp.co.uk

The story of the peoples' war unfolds in this museum devoted to civilian life in World War II. The displays, covering the blackout, rationing, the Blitz, the Homeguard and others, are housed in a former prisoner-of-war camp built in 1942 for German and Italian soldiers. Hut 13, part of a Millennium project, covers the conflicts that Britain has been involved with from 1945 to present day.

Times: Open 2nd Mon in Jan-23 Dec, daily 10-5. Last admission 4pm. Allow at least 3-4hrs for a visit.

Fee: £3.50 (ch & pen £2.50) Party 10+.

P ♿ (taped tours, Braille guides) toilets for disabled shop

Malton Museum

Old Town Hall, Market Place YO17 7LP (leave A64, follow signs for Malton town centre)

☎ 01653 695136

The extensive Roman settlements in the area are represented and illustrated in this museum, including collections from the Roman fort of Derventio. There are also displays of local prehistoric and medieval finds plus changing exhibitions of local interest.

Times: Open Etr Sat-Oct, Mon-Sat 10-4.

Fee: £1.50 (ch, pen & students £1) Family ticket (2 adults & 2 ch) £4.

P (adjacent) (pay & display-2hrs) ♿ shop (ex guide dogs)

MIDDLEHAM

Middleham Castle

DL8 4RJ (2m S of Leyburn on A6108)

☎ 01969 623899

The historic town of Middleham is dominated by the 12th-century keep which saw its great days during the Wars of the Roses. The seat of the Neville family, Earls of Warwick, it was the home for a time of the young King Richard III, then Duke of Gloucester.

Times: Open all year, Apr-Sep, daily 10-6 (Oct 10-5); Nov-Mar, Wed-Sun 10-4 (or dusk if earlier). Closed 1-2pm during winter season & 24-26 Dec & 1 Jan)

Fee: £2.30 (ch 5-15 £1.20, under 5's free).

P ♿ (ex tower) shop

MIDDLESBROUGH

Captain Cook Birthplace Museum

Stewart Park, Marton TS7 6AS (3m S on A172 at Stewart Park, Marton)

☎ 01642 311211 📠 01642 813781

Times: Open all year: Tues-Sun, Summer hrs 10am-5.30pm. Winter hrs 9am-4pm. Last entry 45 mins before closure. Closed Mon except BH, 25-26 Dec & 1 Jan.

P ♿ (lift to all floors, car parking) toilets for disabled shop (ex guide dogs) *Details not confirmed for 2001*

NEWBY HALL & GARDENS

Newby Hall & Gardens

HG4 5AE (4m SE of Ripon & 2m W of A1M, off B6265, between Boroughbridge and Ripon)

☎ 01423 322583 01423 324452

e-mail: info@newbyhall.com

This late 17th-century house had its interior and additions designed by Robert Adam, and contains an important collection of classical sculpture and Gobelin tapestries. Twenty-five acres of award-winning gardens include a miniature railway, an adventure garden for children, and a woodland discovery walk.

Times: Open Apr-Sep, Tue-Sun & BH's; Gardens 11-5.30; House 12-5. Last admission 5pm (gardens), 4.30pm (house),

Fee: House & Garden £6.50, (ch & disabled £4, pen £5.40). Gardens only £4.70 (ch & disabled £3.20, pen £4). Party rates and family tickets on application. Under 4's go free.

licensed (wheelchairs available, maps of wheelchair routes) toilets for disabled shop garden centre (ex guide dogs)

NORTH STAINLEY

Lightwater Valley Theme Park & Village Shopping Village

HG4 3HT (3m N of Ripon on the A6108)

☎ 01765 635321 & 635368 & 635334

01765 635359

e-mail: leisure@lightwatervalley.co.uk

Set in 175 acres of country park and lakeland, Lightwater Valley offers a selection of rides and attractions. Enjoy the white-knuckle thrills of the world's longest roller coaster as well as the Rat and the Wave, or, for the less adventurous, there are the Ladybird, boating lake, and children's visitor farm. Lightwater Village Factory shopping is a complex of factory outlets, and a garden centre, restaurants, coffee shop etc.

Times: Open 15 Apr-1 May, 27 May- 10 Sep, 21-29 Oct daily; 6-21 May, 16 Sep-15 Oct weekends only.

Fee: £12.50 over 1.3 metres, £9.95 under 1.3 metres, free under 1m; senior citizens £5.95. Family ticket (2 adults & 2 ch or 1 adult & 3 ch) £39, additional members £9.75.

licensed (even pathways) toilets for disabled shop (ex guide dogs)

NUNNINGTON

Nunnington Hall

YO6 5UY (4.5m SE of Helmsley)

☎ 01439 748283 01439 748284

This large 16th to 17th-century house has panelled rooms and a magnificent staircase. The Carlisle collection of miniature rooms is on display.

Times: Open Apr-end Oct, Wed-Sun & BH Mon; Jun-Aug, Tue-Sun, 1.30-5pm. (1.30-4.30 Apr & Oct)

toilets for disabled shop *Details not confirmed for 2001*

ORMESBY

Ormesby Hall

TS7 9AS (3m SE of Middlesborough)

☎ 01642 324188 01642 300937

An 18th-century mansion, Ormesby Hall has stables attributed to John Carr of York. Plasterwork, furniture and 18th-century pictures are on view.

Times: Open early Apr-end Oct; Tue, Wed, Thu, Sun 2-5. BH Mons and Good Friday.

toilets for disabled shop *Details not confirmed for 2001*

OSMOTHERLEY

Mount Grace Priory

DL6 3JG (1m NW)

☎ 01609 883494

A ruined 14th-century Carthusian priory, next to a 17th-century house. One of the monks cells has been fully restored to show how what monastic life was like here, and there are also interesting remains of the cloister, church and outer court.

Times: Open all year, Apr-Sep, daily 10-6; Oct, daily 10-5; Nov-Mar, Wed-Sun 10-1 & 2-4. Last admission 30mins before closing. (Closed 24-26 Dec & 1 Jan).

Fee: £2.80 (ch £1.40, concessions £2.10).

shop

PARCEVALL HALL GARDENS

Parcevall Hall Gardens

BD23 6DE (Off B6265 between Grassington and Pateley Bridge)

☎ 01756 720311 01756 720311

e-mail: jomakin@parcevallhallgardens.co.uk

Enjoying a hillside setting east of the main Wharfedale Valley, these beautiful gardens surround a Grade II listed house which is used as the Bradford Diocesan Retreat House (not open to the public).

Times: Open Apr-Oct, daily 10-6. Winter visitors by appointment.

Fee: £2.50 (ch 5-12 50p).

PICKERING

North Yorkshire Moors Railway

Pickering Station YO18 7AJ

☎ 01751 472508 01751 476970

e-mail: admin@nymr.demon.co.uk

Operating through the heart of the North York Moors National Park between Pickering and Grosmont, steam trains cover a distance of 18 miles. The locomotive sheds at Grosmont are open to the public. Events throughout the year include 'Day Out with Thomas' events, Steam Gala, Santa Specials.

Times: Open Apr-5 Nov, daily; Dec, Santa specials and Christmas to New Year running. Further information available from Pickering Station.

Fee: Return: £9.50 (ch £4.80, pen £8). Family ticket (2 adults 3 ch £27, others on request). All-line ticket £9.50 (ch £4.80, pen £8). Party 20+.
P (charged) ☕ ✕ licensed ♿ (ramp for trains) toilets for disabled shop (at Pickering, Goathland & Grosmont) 💳

Pickering Castle
YO6 5AB
☎ 01751 474989

Standing upon its mound high above the town, the 12th-century keep and baileys are among the interesting remains of what was once a favourite royal hunting lodge. An exhibition tells the castle's history.
Times: Open all year, Apr-Oct, daily 10-6 (Oct 10-5); Nov-Mar, Wed-Sun 10-4 (or dusk if earlier).Closed 1-2pm all year. Closed 24-26 Dec & 1 Jan.
Fee: £2.30 (ch 5-15 £1.20 under 5's free).
P ♿ (ex motte) shop ✗ #

REDCAR
RNLI Zetland Museum
5 King St TS10 3AH (on corner of King St and The Promenade)
☎ 01642 485370 & 471813

The museum portrays the lifeboat, maritime, fishing and local history of the area, including its main exhibit *'The Zetland'* - the oldest lifeboat in the world dating from 1802. There is also a replica of a fisherman's cottage c1900 and almost 2000 other exhibits. The museum is housed in an early lifeboat station, now a listed building.
Times: Open May-Sep, Mon-Fri 1-4, Sat & Sun 12-4. Also Etr. Other times by appointment.
Fee: Free.
P (20m) (50p per hour) ♿ (ground floor accessible only) shop

RICHMOND
Green Howards Museum
Trinity Church Square, Market Place DL10 4QN
☎ 01748 822133 📠 01748 826561

This award-winning museum traces the military history of the Green Howards from the late 17th century onwards. The exhibits include uniforms, weapons, medals and a special Victoria Cross exhibition. Regimental and civic plate is displayed, and there is CD ROM and touch screen video of the First World War Western Front and the Green Howards in the Second World War. Audio guide available.
Times: Open Feb, Mon-Fri 10-4.30; Mar, Mon-Fri 10-4.30; mid Apr-Oct, Mon-Sat 9.30-4.30 & Sun 2-4.30; Nov, Mon-Sat 10-4.30.
Fee: £2 (ch 5-16 £1, pen £1.50). Family ticket £5.
P (in market place) (disk parking) ♿ (stairlift for access to all floors) shop ✗

Richmond Castle
DL10 4QW
☎ 01748 822493

Built high upon sheer rocks overlooking the River Swale, the castle dates from 1071. Its splendid keep and curtain walls, with two massive towers, are among the impressive remains. Scollard's Hall, built in 1080, may well be the oldest domestic building surviving in Britain.
Times: Open all year, Apr-Sep, daily 10-6 (Oct 10-5); Nov-Mar, daily 10-4 (or dusk if earlier, closed 1-2pm). Closed 24-26 Dec & 1 Jan.
Fee: £2.60 (ch 5-15 £1.30, under 5's free).
P (800 yds) ♿ shop ✗ #

RIEVAULX

Rievaulx Abbey

YO6 5LB (2.25m W of Helmsley on minor road off B1257)

☎ 01439 798228

The site for this magnificent abbey was given to a small group of Cistercian monks in 1131; building was completed by the end of the century. In its heyday, this was a prosperous foundation, but its fortunes later declined. Surrounded by wooded hills, the site is beautiful, and the remains impressive. From Rievaulx Terrace, at the top of the hill, there is an excellent bird's eye view of the abbey ruins.

Times: Open all year, Apr-Sep, daily 10-6 (Oct 10-5); Jul-Aug, 9.30-7; Nov-Mar, daily 10-4 (or dusk if earlier). Closed 24-26 Dec & 1 Jan.

Fee: £3.40 (ch 5-15 £1.70, under 5's free)

shop

Rievaulx Terrace & Temples

YO6 5LJ (2m NW of Helmsley on B1257)

☎ 01439 798340

This curved terrace, half a mile long, overlooks the abbey, with views of Ryedale and the Hambleton Hills. It has two mock-Greek temples, one built for hunting parties, the other for quiet contemplation. There are also remarkable frescoes by Borgnis, and an exhibition on English landscape design.

Times: Open Apr-end Oct daily 10.30-5 (4 in Oct). May-Sept daily 10.30-6pm. Last admission one hour before closing.

(runaround vehicle available) shop *Details not confirmed for 2001*

RIPLEY

Ripley Castle

HG3 3AY (off A61,Harrogate to Ripon road)

☎ 01423 770152 📠 01423 771745

e-mail: enquires@ripleycastle.co.uk

Ripley Castle has been home to the Ingilby family since 1320, and stands at the heart of an estate with deer park, lake and Victorian walled gardens. The Castle has a rich history and a fine collection of Royalist armour housed in the 1555 tower. There are also walled gardens, tropical hot houses, woodland walks, pleasure grounds and the National Hyacinth collection in spring.

Times: Open Sep-May & Tue, Thu, Sat & Sun 10.30-3; Jun-Aug daily 10.30-3, also BH and school holidays. Groups any day by prior arrangement.

Fee: Castle & Gardens £5 (ch £2.50, pen £4). Gardens only £2.50 (ch £1, pen £2). Party 25+.

licensed toilets for disabled shop garden centre (ex guide dogs)

RIPON

Fountains Abbey & Studley Royal

HG4 3DY (4m W off B6265)

☎ 01765 608888 📠 01765 608889

Founded by Cistercian monks in 1132, Fountains Abbey is the largest monastic ruin in Britain. It was acquired by William Aislabie in 1768, and became the focal point of his landscaped gardens at Studley. Other interesting features include Fountains Hall, built between 1598 and 1611 using the stone from the abbey ruins.

Times: Open all year. daily (except Fri in Nov, Dec & Jan); Apr-Sep, 10-7 (closes at 4pm some days in July & one day in Aug); Oct-Mar 10-5 or duk if earlier. Last admission one hour before closing.

licensed toilets for disabled shop *Details not confirmed for 2001*

Norton Conyers Hall

HG4 5EQ (from Ripon take A61 to Thirsk. At top of hill just outside Ripon, turn sharp left onto Wath Road)

☎ 01765 640333 📠 01765 692772

This late medieval house with Stuart and Georgian additions has belonged to the Grahams since 1624. It was visited by Charles I and James II. Another visitor was Charlotte Brontë a family legend of a mad woman confined in the attics is said to have given her the idea for the mad Mrs Rochester in *Jane Eyre*. Family costumes are on display in one of the bedrooms. Please note that ladies are requested not to wear stiletto-heeled shoes.

Times: Open - House & garden Etr Sun & Mon; BH Sun & Mon;Sun between 7 May-3 Sep. Open daily 3-8 Jul. House open 2-5, garden open 11.30-5. Telephone for further details.

Fee: £3 (ch 10-16, pen, concessions £2.50). Garden entry is free, with donations welcome, although a charge is made at garden charity openings. Parties by arrangement

(ramp at entrance) toilets for disabled shop (ex guide dogs or lead)

SALTBURN-BY-THE-SEA

Saltburn Smugglers Heritage Centre

Old Saltburn, TS12 1HF (adjoining Ship Inn, on A174)

☎ 01287 625252

Set in old fisherman's cottages, this centre skilfully blends costumed characters with authentic sounds and smells. Follow the story of John Andrew "King of Smugglers", who was at the heart of illict local trade 200 years ago.

Times: Open 3 Apr-30 Sep, daily 10-6; Winter, by arrangement only telephone 01642 444318.
Fee: £1.75 (ch £1.25). Family ticket £4.65. Party.
P (200 mtrs) (charged) shop

SCARBOROUGH

SCARBOROUGH CASTLE

Castle Rd YO1 1HY (E of town centre)
☎ 01723 372451

The ruins of Scarborough Castle stand on a narrow headland which was once the site of British and Roman encampments. The curtain wall is thought to have pre-dated the keep, the shell of which, with the later barbican and remains of medieval buildings, are all that remain.
Times: Open all year, Apr-Sep, daily 10-6 (Oct 10-5); Nov-Mar, daily 10-4 (or dusk if earlier). Closed 24-26 Dec & 1 Jan.
Fee: £2.30 (ch 5-15 £1.20, under 5's free).
P (100 yds) ♿ (ex in keep)

SKINNINGROVE

TOM LEONARD MINING MUSEUM

Deepdale TS13 4AP (just off A174 between Middlesbrough and Whitby)
☎ 01287 642877
e-mail: ptuffs@ompinet.co.uk

The museum offers visitors an exciting and authentic underground experience on the site of the old Loftus mine, and a chance to see how the stone was drilled, charged with explosives and fired. Exhibits include a collection of original tools, lamps, safety equipment, old photographs and domestic objects, providing a glimpse of mining life both above and below ground.
Times: Open Apr-Oct, daily 1-5 (last admission 3.45pm). Nov-Mar, schools & parties only. Parties by arrangement.
Fee: £3 (ch £1.50). Pre booked parties 12+.
P shop (ex guide dogs)

SKIPTON

SKIPTON CASTLE

BD23 1AQ (Centre of Skipton at the head of the high street)
☎ 01756 792442 01756 796100
e-mail: info@skiptoncastle.co.uk

Skipton is one of the most complete and well-preserved medieval castles in England. Some of the castle dates from the 1650s when it was rebuilt after being partially damaged following the Civil War. However, the original castle was erected in Norman times, and the gateway with its Norman Arch still exists. The castle became the home of the Clifford family in 1310 and remained so until 1676. Illustrated tour sheets are available in a number of languages.
Times: Open all year, daily from 10am (Sun noon). Last admission 6pm (4pm Oct-Feb). (Closed 25 Dec).
Fee: £4.20 (inc illustrated tour sheet) (ch under 18 £2.10, under 5 free, concessions £3.60). Family ticket £11.50. Party 15+.
P (200m) shop

SUTTON-ON-THE-FOREST

SUTTON PARK

YO61 1DP (on B1363 York to Helmsley Road)
☎ 01347 810249 & 811239 01347 811251
e-mail: suttonpark@fsbdial.co.uk

The early Georgian house contains fine furniture, paintings and porcelain. The grounds have superb, award-winning terraced gardens, a lily pond and a Georgian ice house. There are also delightful woodland walks as well as spaces for caravans.
Times: Open - Gardens 2 Apr-end Sept, daily 11am-5pm. House open 2 Apr-27 Sep, Wed & Sun, also Good Fri, Etr Mon and all BH Mons.
Fee: Gardens only £2 (ch 50p, pen £1.50). House & Gardens £4.50 (ch £2.50, pen £4)
P ♿ (ex guide dogs in garden)

WHITBY

WHITBY ABBEY

YO22 4JT (on clifftop E of Whitby town centre)
☎ 01947 603568

Dominating the skyline above the fishing port of Whitby the haunting ruins of the 13th-century Benedictine abbey are an impressive site. St Hilda built the first abbey on the site in 657.
Times: Open all year, Apr-Sep, daily 10-6; (Oct 10-5); Nov-Mar, daily 10-4 or dusk if earlier. Closed 24-26 Dec & 1 Jan.
Fee: £1.70 (ch 5-15 90p, under 5's free).
P (charged) shop

YORK

THE ARC

St Saviourgate YO1 8NN (City centre, follow pedestrian signposts for Archaeological Resource Centre)
☎ 01904 643211 01904 627097
e-mail: jorvik@jvcyork.demon.co.uk

The ARC is a 'hands-on' experience of archaeology, housed in the beautifully restored medieval church of St Saviour. Be an archaeologist yourself - sift through the remains of centuries - bones, shell, pottery and much more.
Times: Open: School holidays Mon-Sat 11-3.30. Closed mid Dec-early Jan.
Fee: £3.60. Group rates available on request.
P (50yds) ♿ (induction loop) toilets for disabled shop (except guide dogs)

Borthwick Institute of Historical Research

St Anthony's Hall, Peasholme Green YO1 72PW
☎ 01904 642315

Originally built in the second half of the 15th century for the Guild of St Anthony, the hall was later used as an arsenal, a workhouse, a prison and the Bluecoat School from 1705 to 1946. Now part of York University, it houses ecclesiastical archives and exhibitions of documents.

Times: Open all year, Mon-Fri 9.30-12.50 & 2-4.50. Closed Etr & Xmas. **Fee:** Free.
P (max 5mins walk) (public car park)

City Art Gallery

Exhibition Square YO1 7EW
☎ 01904 551861 01904 551866
e-mail: art.gallery@york.gov.uk

Times: Open all year, daily 9.30-4.30. Closed 25-26 Dec.
P (500mtrs) ♿ (chairlift) toilets for disabled shop (ex guide dogs)
Details not confirmed for 2001

Clifford's Tower

Tower St YO1 1SA
☎ 01904 646940

Named for the unfortunate Roger de Clifford, who was hung in chains from the castle, the tower was unused for centuries, as the first castle burned down and its replacement cracked from top to bottom as a result of subsidence. The walk around the old city walls offers the best way of seeing the ancient city.

Times: Open all year, Apr-Sep, daily 10-6; Jul & Aug 9.30-7; (Oct 10-5); Nov-Mar, Wed-Sun 10-4 or dusk if earlier. Closed between 1-2pm and 24-26 Dec & 1 Jan.
Fee: £1.80 (ch 5-15 90p, under 5's free).
P #

Fairfax House

Castlegate YO1 9RN (city centre, close to Jorvik Centre and Cliffords Tower)
☎ 01904 655543 01904 652262
e-mail: moyra@yorkcivictrust.fsnet.co.uk

An outstanding mid 18th-century house with a richly decorated interior, Fairfax House was acquired by the York Civic Trust in 1983 and restored. The house contains fine examples of Georgian furniture, porcelain, paintings and clocks which were donated by Mr Noel Terry, the great grandson of the founder of the York-based confectionery business. There is a special display of a recreated meal dating from 1763 in the dining room and kitchen.

Times: Open 20 Feb-5 Jan, Mon-Sat 11-5, (Fri guided tours only at 11am & 2pm). Sun 1.30-5. Last admission 4.30pm.
Fee: £4 (ch £1.50, pen & student £3.50)
P (50yds) (3hr short stay) ♿ (with assistance, phone before visit) shop

Guildhall

Off Coney St YO1 9QN (5mins walk from the rail station)
☎ 01904 613161 01904 552015

The present Hall dates from 1446 but in 1942 an air raid virtually destroyed the building. The present Guildhall was carefully restored as an exact replica and was re-opened in 1960. There is an interesting arch-braced roof decorated with colourful bosses and supported by 12 solid oak pillars. There are also some beautiful stained-glass windows.

Times: Open all year, May-Oct, Mon-Fri 9-5, Sat 10-5, Sun 2-5; Nov-Apr, Mon-Fri 9-5.(Closed Good Fri, Spring BH, 25-26 Dec & 1 Jan).
Fee: Free.
P (15-20 mins walk) ♿ (electric chair lift/ramps) toilets for disabled (ex guide dogs)

Jorvik Viking Centre

Coppergate YO1 9WT (Situated in the Coppergate shopping area follow the signs to Jorvik Viking centre)
☎ 01904 643211 01904 627097
e-mail: jorvik@jvcyork.demon.co.uk

In 1984 the Jorvik Viking Centre was opened over the site of the original 1970s excavations. The dig has revealed much of the Viking way of life. The Centre displays the archaeological remains - leather, textiles, metal objects and even timber buildings - in a detailed and vivid reconstruction. 'Time-cars' carry visitors through a 'time tunnel' from WWII back to Norman times and then to a full-scale reconstruction of 10th-century Coppergate. Finally the tour passes through a reconstruction of Coppergate during the dig of the 1970s.

Times: Open all year, Apr-Oct daily 9-5.30; Nov-Mar daily 10-4.30 (Closed 25 Dec). Opening times subject to change, please telephone for up to date details.
Fee: £5.65 (ch 5-15 £4.25, under 5 free, student/pen £5. Family £18.
P (400 yds) (limited to 3 hours) ♿ (lift & time car designed to take a wheelchair) toilets for disabled shop

Merchant Adventurers' Hall

Fossgate YO1 9XD
☎ 01904 654818 📠 01904 654818
e-mail: the.clerk@mahall-york.demon.co.uk

The medieval guild hall of the powerful Merchant Adventurers' Company was built 1357/1361 and is one of the finest in Europe. The Great Hall contains early furniture, one piece dating from the 13th century, paintings, silver, and weights and measures.

Times: Open all year, end Mar-early Nov, daily 8.30-5; early Nov-late Mar, Mon-Sat 8.30-3.30. (Closed 10 days Xmas).
P (500yds) ♿ toilets for disabled

National Railway Museum

Leeman Rd YO26 4XJ (Signposted from City Centre)
☎ 01904 621261 📠 01904 611112
e-mail: nrm@nmsi.ac.uk

Among the impressive exhibits are a reconstruction of Stephenson's Rocket; the record-breaking Mallard; a life-size section of the Channel Tunnel; and Royal Palaces on Wheels. The new wing features the Workshop, the Warehouse, and the Working Railway Gallery.

Times: Open all year, Mon-Sun 10-6,(Closed 24-26 Dec).
Fee: £6.50 (ch under 16 free, over 60's free, concessions £4).
P (charged) ✕ licensed ♿ ("Please Touch" evenings) toilets for disabled shop (ex guide dogs & hearing dogs)

St Williams College

5 College St YO1 7JF (adjacent to York Minster at east end)
☎ 01904 557233 📠 01904 557234
e-mail: info@yorkminster.org

St Williams College, a 15th-century timber-framed building, housed chantry priests until 1549. It now contains York Minster's Information and Conference Centre, shop, restaurant and the medieval rooms are open to view when not being used for functions. Craft Fairs most weekends.

Times: Open all year 10-5 for viewing of medieval rooms subject to private bookings - phone for details. Closed 24-26 Dec & Good Fri.
Fee: Medieval Rooms 60p (ch 30p).
P ✕ licensed shop

Treasurer's House

Chapter House St YO1 2JD
☎ 01904 624247 📠 01904 647372

There has been a house on this site since Roman times and in the basement of this elegant 17th-century building is an exhibition of its history. The house was improved during the 18th century with the addition of a fine staircase. Restored between 1897 and 1930, it was left, with its fine furniture, to the National Trust.

Times: Open Apr-Oct, daily except Friday. 10.30-4.30pm.
P (400 yds) ✕ licensed *Details not confirmed for 2001*

York Castle Museum

The Eye of York YO1 IRY (city centre, next to Clifford's Tower)
☎ 01904 653611 📠 01904 671078

Times: Open all year, Apr-Oct Mon-Sat 9.30-5.30, Sun 10-5.30; Nov-Mar, Mon-Sat 9.30-4, Sun 10-4. (Closed 25-26 Dec & 1 Jan).
♿ toilets for disabled shop *Details not confirmed for 2001*

The York Dungeon

12 Clifford St YO1 9RD
☎ 01904 632599 📠 01904 612602
e-mail: yorkdungeon@merlin-entertainments.com

Deep in the heart of historic York, buried beneath its very paving stones, lies the North's most chillingly famous museum of horror. The York Dungeon brings more than 2,000 years of gruesomely authentic history vividly back to life...and death. As you delve into the darkest chapters of our grim and bloody past, recreated in all its dreadful detail remember - everything you experience really happened... A warning - in the dungeon's dark catacombs it always pays to keep your wits about you. The 'exhibits' have an unnerving habit of coming back to life...

Times: Open all year, daily 10.30-5.30 (4.30 Oct-Mar).Closed 25 Dec.
Fee: £6.50 (ch £4.95, students & pen £4.95). Family £19.90.
P (500yds) ♿ (wheelchair ramps, stairlifts) toilets for disabled shop

York Minster

Deangate YO1 7HH
☎ 01904 639347 📠 01904 613049

Times: Open daily, Mon-Sat 7-6 (later in summer), Sun after 1pm.
P (440yds) ♿ (loop system, tactile model, braille guide) toilets for disabled shop *Details not confirmed for 2001*

York Model Railway

Tearoom Square, York Station YO2 2AB (next to York Station)
☎ 01904 630169

Times: Open daily, Mar-Oct 9.30-6, Nov-Feb 10.30-5 (Closed 25-26 Dec).
P (100 yds) ♿ shop *Details not confirmed for 2001* 

Yorkshire Museum

Museum Gardens YO1 7FR (park & ride service from 3 sites near A64/A19/A1079 & A166, also 3 car parks within short walk)

☎ 01904 629745 📠 01904 651221
e-mail: yorkshire.museum@york.gov.uk

Yorkshire Museum is set in 10 acres of botanical gardens in the heart of the historic City of York, and displays some of the finest Roman, Anglo-Saxon, Viking and Medieval treasures ever discovered in Britain. The Middleham jewel, a fine example of English Gothic jewellery, is on display, and in the Roman Gallery, visitors can see a marble head of Constantine the Great. The Anglo-Saxon Gallery houses the delicate silver-gilt Ormside bowl and the Gilling sword.

Times: Open all year, daily 10-5.
Fee: £3.95 (concessions £2.50) Family ticket £11.50.
P (5 mins walk) ♿ (ramps & lift) toilets for disabled shop

The York Story

St Mary's, Castlegate YO1 1RN (city centre, near Jorvik Centre)

☎ 01904 628632

Times: Open all year, Mon-Sat 10-5 (Wed 10.30-5), Sun 1-5. (Closed 25-26 Dec & 1 Jan). Subject to closure due to refurbishment.
P (1 min walk) ♿ shop *Details not confirmed for 2001*

South Yorkshire

South Yorkshire is an industrial area and all the main towns are traditionally steel and coal producing centres. Both of these industries have declined in recent years and have been replaced to some extent by other forms of manufacturing.

Barnsley is the county's administrative centre, located on one Britain's richest coalfields. The town has an entry in the Domesday Book, and was built on land belonging to the priories of Pontefract and Monk Bretton.

Doncaster, originally a Roman station, is set on the River Don. It is known particularly for its racecourse. The best known race on its calender is the celebrated St Leger, which is held in September. In 1875, Charles Dickens watched it from the 18th-century Italianate grandstand at the Town Moor racecourse. The Lincolnshire Handicap is held in March. The town also possesses some fine Georgian architecture, particularly James Paine's house which was built in 1748.

Rotheram, on the outskirts of Sheffield, has a fine 15th-century church, and a bridge with an old chapel over the Don river.

South Yorkshire claims part of the Peak District National park, whose hills and dales provide relief to the millions of city dwellers within its vicinity.

EVENTS & FESTIVALS

January
6 The Ancient Haxey Hood Game, Doncaster

May
28 Sheffield Mayfest, Hillsborough Park
tbc Groove on the Green, funky music festival, Devonshire Green, Sheffield

June
tbc Music in the Sun Festival, Don Valley Grass Bowl

June/July
tbc Sheffield Children's Festival

July
tbc City Centre Carnival, Sheffield
tbc Our City, The World Sheffield's Multicultural Festival, Devonshire Green, Sheffield
tbc South Yorkshire Festival, Wortley Hall, Sheffield

August
tbc The Sheffield Show, Graves Park, Sheffield

October
tbc Sheffield International Documentary Festival
tbc Off the Shelf Literature Festival, Sheffield

Top: Sheffield

BARNSLEY

Monk Bretton Priory

(1m E of Barnsley town centre, off A633)
☎ 01226 204089

The priory was an important Cluniac house, founded in 1135. The considerable remains of the gatehouse, church and other buildings can be seen.

Times: Open all year, Apr-Sep, daily 10-6; Oct, daily 10-5; Nov-Mar, daily 10-4. Keykeeper.

Fee: Free.

CONISBROUGH

Conisbrough Castle

DN12 3HH (NE of town centre off A630)
☎ 01709 863329

The 12th-century keep is one of the country's oldest and best preserved buildings of the period. Surrounded by a curtain wall with round towers, its circular design, with six buttresses, is unique. It features in Sir Walter Scott's *Ivanhoe*.

Times: Open all year, Apr-Sep, Mon-Sat 10-5, Sun 10-6; Oct-Mar, daily 10-4. Last admission 40mins before closing. (Closed 24-26 Dec & 1 Jan).

Fee: £2.80 (ch £1, concessions £1.80). Family ticket £6.75.

CUSWORTH

The Museum of South Yorkshire Life Cusworth H Hall

Cusworth Ln DN5 7TU (3m NW of Doncaster)
☎ 01302 782342 01302 782342
e-mail: margaret@doncaster.gov.uk

Times: Open all year, Mon-Fri 10-5, Sat 11-5 & Sun 1-5. (4pm Dec & Jan). Closed Good Fri, Xmas & 1 Jan.

Fee: Free.

(wheelchair available) toilets for disabled shop (ex guide dogs)

DONCASTER

Brodsworth Hall

Brodsworth DN5 7XJ (between A635 & A638)
☎ 01302 7222598 01302 337165

Brodsworth Hall is a Victorian country house which has survived largely intact. The faded grandeur of the family rooms contrasts with the functional austerity of the servant's wing. There are fine gardens.

Times: Open Apr-Oct, Tue-Sun & BH's; gardens 1-6, (last admission 5pm); Nov-Mar, 11-4, Mar Gardens, tearooms & shops only.

Fee: House and gardens £5.80 (ch 5-15 £2.50, under 5's free).

toilets for disabled shop

Doncaster Museum & Art Gallery

Chequer Rd DN1 2AE (off inner ring road)
☎ 01302 734293 01302 735409
e-mail: museum@doncaster.gov.uk

The wide-ranging collections include fine and decorative art and sculpture. Also ceramics, glass, silver, and displays on history, archaeology and natural history. The historical collection of the Kings Own Yorkshire Light Infantry is housed here. Temporary exhibitions are held.

Times: Open all year, Mon-Sat 10-5, Sun 2-5. (Closed Good Fri, 25-26 Dec & 1 Jan).

Fee: Free.

(lift, hearing loop in lecture room) toilets for disabled shop (ex guide dogs)

Earth Centre

Denaby Main DN12 4EA
☎ 01709 513933 01709 512010
e-mail: info@earthcentre.org.uk

Earth Centre is a unique theme park exploring sustainable development. You are encouraged to consider what actions you can take now to shape a sustainable future. The Centre itself has been built using environmentally sound materials and methods on the regenerated site of two former coalmines.

Times: Open early Apr-early Nov 10-6 (last entry 4pm). During summer holidays 10-8 (last entry 6pm).

licensed toilets for disabled shop (ex guide dogs)

Details not confirmed for 2001

MALTBY

Roche Abbey

S66 8NW (1.5m S off A634)
☎ 01709 812739

The walls of the south and north transepts of this 12th-century Cistercian abbey still stand to their full height, providing a dramatic sight for the visitor. There is also a fine gatehouse.

Times: Open Apr-Sep, daily 10-6 (Oct 10-5).

Fee: £1.60 (ch 5-15 80p, under 5's free)

ROTHERHAM

Clifton Park Museum

Clifton Park, Clifton Ln S65 2AA (Follow directions from inner ring road)
☎ 01709 382121 ext 3635 01709 823631
e-mail: guy.kilminster@rotherham.gov.uk

Housed in a mansion designed by John Carr, the museum is noted for its collection of Rockingham china. Other attractions include the 18th-century rooms, family portraits, the period kitchen, and Victoriana. Regular programme of temporary exhibitions.

Times: Open all year, Mon-Thu & Sat 10-5, Sun 1.30-5 (4.30 Oct-Mar). (Closed Xmas & New Year). Building work during 2001 may limit opening hours. Contact for details.

Fee: Free.

P ♿ toilets for disabled shop ✗ (ex guide dogs)

SHEFFIELD

Bishops House

Meersbrook Park, Norton Lees Ln S8 9BE (2 miles south of Sheffield, on A61 Chesterfield road)

☎ 0114 278 2600

e-mail: info@sheffieldgalleries.org.uk

This 15th and 16th-century yeoman's house has been restored and opened as a museum of local and social history. Several rooms have been furnished and there are displays of life in Tudor and Stuart times. Special educational facilities can be arranged for schools and colleges.

Times: Please telephone for opening details and latest information.

Fee: Free.

P (roadside parking on nearby streets) ♿ shop ✗

City Museum & Mappin Art Gallery

Weston Park S10 2TP (on A57)

☎ 0114 278 2600 📠 0114 275 0957

e-mail: info@sheffieldgalleries.org.uk

The museum houses exhibits on regional geology, natural history and archaeology, especially from the Peak District. There is a splendid display of cutlery and Sheffield plate, for which the city is famous. Educational facilities are available. The Mappin Art Gallery, in a Victorian listed building, organises a programme of temporary exhibitions with emphasis on Contemporary Art and Victorian paintings.

Times: Open all year, Tue-Sat 10-5, Sun 11-5 also BH Mons. (Closed 25 Dec & 1 Jan). Please telephone prior to visit to confirm opening times.

Fee: Free.

P (on street parking only) ☕ ♿ (Inductive loop. Handling sessions for pre-booked groups) toilets for disabled shop ✗

Kelham Island Museum

Alma St S3 8RY (0.5m NW of city centre, take A61 N to West Bar, follow signposts)

☎ 0114 272 2106 📠 0114 275 7847

Times: Open Mon-Thu 10-4, Sun 11-4.45.Closed Fri and Sat. Check opening days/times at Christmas & New Year before travelling.

P ☕ ♿ (wheelchair on request) toilets for disabled shop ✗ *Details not confirmed for 2001*

West Yorkshire

The West Riding has long been industrialised, and not only produced coal but was also home to the traditional wool industry. The tall mill chimneys are characteristic of its industrial heritage, set against the Pennine Hills.

The county includes the towns of Wakefield, Halifax, Huddersfield and Bradford, centres of the wool industry from the 13th century. Huddersfield is known particularly for its fine wool worsted.

Leeds sprawls over its hilly site and includes a great variety of manufacturing and other industries, notably ready-to-wear clothes. It is also home to the celebrated Yorkshire County Cricket Club at Headingley.

Many visitors to the region come in the wake of the extraordinary Brontë family. A motherless family with the curate of Haworth, Patrick Brontë, at its head. The children, Charlotte, Branwell (Patrick), Emily and Anne created a rich fantasy world, feeding their literary imaginations. Their poems and novels evoked the nature of their moorland home, particularly Emily's *Wuthering Heights*, published in December 1847, a year before her death from consumption at the age of 30. The Brontë Society was founded in 1893. In 1926 the American publisher Henry Houston Bonnell bequeathed his collection to the society, who bought the parsonage, the Brontë's former home to accommodate it.

Natural features of the county encompass Ilkley Moor, Haworth Moor, and parts of the Peak District National Park.

EVENTS & FESTIVALS

March
2-17 March (provisional) Bradford Film Festival
24-25 Complementary Medicine Festival, Ilkley
25 Daffodil Week, Haworth

April
16 World Coal Carrying Championship, Ossett

May
12-19 Wharfedale Music Festival, Ilkley

June/July
16 Wetherby Agricultural Show
tbc Bradford Festival & Mela
tbc Cleckheaton Folk Festival

October
20-21 Complementary Medicine Festival, Ilkley
tbc Leeds International Film Festival, Town Hall, Leeds

November
24-25 Scroggling the Holly, Haworth

December
1-2 Masquerade Weekend, Haworth Victorian Christmas Festival
15-16 Torchlight Weekend, Haworth Victorian Christmas 19 Wassail Wednesday

Top: The Corn Exchange, Leeds

BRADFORD

Bolling Hall

Bowling Hall Rd BD4 7LP (1m from city centre off A650)

☎ 01274 723057 01274 726220
e-mail: abickley@legend.co.uk

A classic West Yorkshire manor house, complete with galleried `housebody' (hall), Bolling Hall dates mainly from the 17th century but has medieval and 18th-century sections. It has panelled rooms, plasterwork in original colours, heraldic glass and a rare Chippendale bed.

Times: Open all year, Wed-Fri 11-4, Sat 10-5, Sun 12-5. (Closed Mon ex BH, Good Fri, 25 & 26 Dec).
Fee: Free.
P ♿ shop

Bradford Industrial Museum and Horses at Work

Moorside Rd, Eccleshill BD2 3HP (off A658)

☎ 01274 631756 01274 636362

Moorside Mills is an original spinning mill, now part of a museum that brings vividly to life the story of the Bradford's woollen industry. There is the machinery that once converted raw wool into cloth and the mill yard rings with the sound of iron on stone as shire horses pull trams, haul buses and give rides. Daily demonstrations and changing exhibitions.

Times: Open all year, Tue-Sat 10-5, Sun 12-5. (Closed Mon ex BH)
Fee: Charges made for rides.
P ♿ (induction loop in lecture theatre) toilets for disabled shop

Cartwright Hall Art Gallery

Lister Park BD9 4NS (1m from city centre on A650)

☎ 01274 751212 01274 481045

Built in dramatic Baroque style in 1904, the gallery has permanent collections of 19th and 20th-century British art, contemporary prints, and older works by British and European masters.

Times: Open all year Apr-Sep, Tue-Sat 10-5, Sun 1-5. (Closed Mon ex BH, Good Fri, 25 & 26 Dec).
Fee: Free.
♿ (wheelchair available) toilets for disabled shop

Colour Museum

Perkin House, 1 Providence St BD1 2PW (from city centre follow signs B6144(Haworth) then follow brown tourist signs)

☎ 01274 390955 01274 392888
e-mail: museum@sdc.org.uk

Britain's only Museum of Colour comprises two galleries packed with visitor-operated exhibits demonstrating the effects of light and colour, including optical illusions, and the story of dyeing and textile printing. There is a programme of special exhibitions and events.

Times: Open Jan-late Dec, Tue-Sat, 10-4.
Fee: £1.50 (concessions £1). Family ticket £3.75.
P (300 yds) ♿ (lift from street level) toilets for disabled shop (ex guide dogs)

National Museum of Photography, Film & Television

BD1 1NQ (2 miles from M62, follow signs)

☎ 01274 202030 01274 394540
e-mail: talk.nmpfe@nmsi.ac.uk

The past, present and future of the media explored with interactive displays and dramatic reconstructions - ride on a magic carpet, become a newsreader for the day or try your hand at vision mixing. At the heart of the Museum is IMAX, a cinema screen more than five storeys high.

Times: Open all year, Tue-Sun & BH's 10-6. (Closed Mon).
Fee: Museum free, 2D & 3D IMAX Cinema £5.80 (concessions £4). Groups 20% discount.
P (charged) licensed ♿ (tailored tours, cinema seating & hearing services) toilets for disabled shop (ex guide dogs)

BRAMHAM

Bramham Park

LS23 6ND (on A1 4m S of Wetherby)

☎ 01937 846005 01937 846006

This fine Queen Anne house was built by Robert Benson and is the home of his descendants. The garden has ornamental ponds, cascades, temples and avenues.

Times: Open 2 Feb-Sep, daily 10.30-5.30. (Closed 5-11 Jun).
Fee: Gardens only £2.95 (ch under 16 & pen £1.95, under 5's free). House open by appointment only.
P ♿ toilets for disabled (ex guide dogs & dogs on lead)

GOMERSAL

Red House

Oxford Rd BD19 4JP (on A651)

☎ 01274 335100 01274 335105

A delightful house decorated as the 1830s home of a Yorkshire wool clothier and merchant. The house and family was frequently visited by Charlotte Brontë in the 1830s and featured in her novel *Shirley*. The gardens have been reconstructed in the style of the period and there are exhibitions on the Brontë connection and local history.

Times: Open all year, Mon-Fri 11-5, Sat-Sun 12-5. Telephone for Xmas opening. (Closed Good Fri & 1 Jan).
Fee: Free.
P ♿ (Braille & tape guide available) toilets for disabled shop (ex guide dogs)

HALIFAX

Bankfield Museum

Boothtown Rd, Akroyd Park HX3 6HG

☎ 01422 354823 & 352334 01422 349020

Times: Open all year, Tue-Sat 10-5, Sun 2-5, BH Mon 10-5.(extended closing times at Xmas and New Year, phone for details)
P ♿ shop *Details not confirmed for 2001* 

Calderdale Industrial Museum

Central Works, Square Rd HX1 0QG

01422 358087 01422 349310

Times: Open all year, Tue-Sat 10-5, Sun 2-5 (Closed Mon ex BH's, 25-26 Dec & 1 Jan).

(lift) toilets for disabled shop *Details not confirmed for 2001*

Eureka! The Museum for Children

Discovery Rd HX1 2NE (M62 exit 24 follow brown tourist signs to Halifax centre(A629))

01422 330069 01426 983191

01422 330275

e-mail: info@eureka.org.uk

A 'hands on' museum designed especially for children 12 and under. There are different exhibition areas where visitors can find out how the body and senses work, investigate everyday objects, role-play in the buildings around the Town Square and explore the world of communications. Outside in the Eureka! Park you can exercise on the Health Trail and enter the Hazard Dome, an audio-visual presentation about home safety.

Times: Open all year, daily 10-5 (except 24-26 Dec)

Fee: £5.75 (ch 3-12 £4.75, under 3 free). Saver ticket £18.75.

(charged) (lift,staff trained in sign language,audio guide,workshop) toilets for disabled shop (ex guide dogs) 

Piece Hall

HX1 1RE (Well signposted with brown signs from major routes, close to Halifax rail & bus stations)

01422 358087 01422 349310

Times: Open all year daily 8-6 (Closed 25-26 Dec). Industrial Museum Tue-Sat 10-5, Sun 2-5. Art Gallery Tue-Sun 10-5.

(50 yds) licensed (lifts, shopmobility on site & audio guide available) toilets for disabled shop *Details not confirmed for 2001*

Shibden Hall

Lister's Rd HX3 6XG (2km E of Halifax on A58)

01422 352246 & 321455 01422 348440

Times: Open Mar-Nov, Mon-Sat 10-5, Sun 12-5. Contact for details of winter opening hours.

shop *Details not confirmed for 2001*

HAREWOOD

Harewood House & Bird Garden

LS17 9LQ (junc A61/A659 Leeds/Harrogate Rd)

0113 288 6331 0113 288 6467

Times: Open 9 Mar-Oct, daily Bird Garden from 10am, House from 11am. Grounds & Bird Garden open wknds Nov-Dec.

licensed (electric ramp to front door of house) toilets for disabled shop garden centre (in gardens on lead) *Details not confirmed for 2001*

HAWORTH

Bronte Parsonage Museum

BD22 8DR (leave A629 & A6033 follow signs for Haworth, take Rawdon Rd, pass 2 car parks, next left, then right)

01535 642323 01535 647131

e-mail: bronte@bronte.prestel.co.uk

Haworth Parsonage was the lifelong family home of the Brontës. An intensely close-knit family, the Brontës saw the parsonage as the heart of their world and the moorland setting provided them with inspiration for their writing. The house contains much personal memorabilia, including the furniture Charlotte bought with the proceeds of her literary success, Branwell's portraits of local worthies, Emily's writing desk and Anne's books and drawings.

Times: Open Apr-Sep, daily 10-5.30; Oct-Mar daily 11-5 (final admission 30 min before closing). Closed 24-27 Dec & 8 Jan-3 Feb.

Fee: £4.50 (ch 5-16 £1.40, concessions £3.30). Family ticket £10.

(charged) (Information in large type & braille) shop (ex guide dogs)

Keighley & Worth Valley Railway & Museum

Keighley BD22 8NJ

01535 645214 & 677777 01535 647317

The line was built mainly to serve the valley's mills, and goes through the heart of Brontë country. Beginning at Keighley (also a BR station), it climbs up to Haworth, and terminates at Oxenhope, which has a storage and restoration building. At Haworth there are locomotive workshops and at Ingrow West, an award-winning museum.

Times: All year weekend service, but daily all BH wks & 19 Jun-1 Sep.

Fee: Full line return ticket £6 reduced fares for ch & pen. Family return ticket £16. Day rover (unlimited travel) £8, Family day rover £20. Under 5's free. Party rates.

(charged) (wheelchairs can be accommodated in brake car). toilets for disabled shop

HUDDERSFIELD

Automobilia Transport Museum

The Heritage Centre, Leeds Rd HD1 6QA (on A62 Leeds road, 1/3 mile from Huddesfield town centre)

01484 559086 01484 559092

Over 100 vintage and classic vehicles on display and for sale on two floors. Museum area exhibits also motorcycles, bicycles, radios, enamel signs, petrol pumps, garage equipment and much more automobilia.

Times: Open all year, Mon-Sat 9-5,Sun 11-4. Groups at other times by arrangement.

Fee: £2 (ch 5-15 £1, pen, students & UB40's £1.50). Family ticket £5.

('hands on' for partially sighted) shop

Huddersfield Art Gallery
Princess Alexandra Walk HD1 2SU
☎ 01484 221964 ext 1962 🖷 01484 221952
Times: Open all year, Mon-Fri 10-5, Sat 10-4. (Closed Sun & BH's).
P ♿ toilets for disabled shop (ex guide dogs) *Details not confirmed for 2001*

Tolson Memorial Museum
Ravensknowle Park, Wakefield Rd HD5 8DJ (on A629)
☎ 01484 223830 🖷 01484 223843

Displays on the development of the cloth industry and a collection of horse-drawn vehicles, together with natural history, archaeology, toys and folk exhibits. There is a full programme of events and temporary exhibitions.
Times: Open all year. Mon-Fri 11-5, Sat & Sun noon-5. (Closed Xmas).
Fee: Free.
P ♿ toilets for disabled shop

ILKLEY

Manor House Gallery & Museum
Castle Yard, Church St LS29 9DT (behind Ilkley Parish Church, on A65)
☎ 01943 600066 🖷 01943 817079

An Elizabethan manor house, one of Ilkley's few buildings to pre-date the 19th century, was built on the site of a Roman fort. Part of the Roman wall can be seen, together with Roman relics and displays on archaeology. There is a collection of 17th and 18th-century farmhouse parlour and kitchen furniture, and the art gallery exhibits works by contemporary artists and craftsmen.
Times: Open all year, Wed-Sat 11-5, Sun 1-4. (Closed Good Fri, 25-28 Dec).
Fee: Free.
♿ shop

KEIGHLEY

Cliffe Castle Museum & Gallery
Spring Gardens Ln BD20 6LH (NW of town off A629)
☎ 01535 618230 🖷 01535 610536

French furniture from the Victoria and Albert Museum is displayed, together with collections of local and natural history, ceramics, dolls, geological items and minerals. The grounds of this 19th-century mansion has a play area and an aviary.
Times: Open all year, Tue-Sat 10-5, Sun 12-5. Also open BH Mon. (Closed Good Fri & 25-28 Dec).
Fee: Free.
P ♿ toilets for disabled shop

East Riddlesden Hall
Bradford Rd BD20 4EA (1m NE of Keighley on south side of Bradford Rd)
☎ 01535 607075 🖷 01535 691462

This charming 17th-century Yorkshire manor house is typical of its kind, although the plasterwork and oak panelling are contemporary. A small secluded garden is found in the grounds, which also feature one of the largest medieval tithe barns in the north of England.
Times: Open Apr-early Nov, Tue-Wed, Sat-Sun & Good Friday and BH Mon & Mon in July & Aug; 12-5 (Sat 1-5pm).
P ♿ shop *Details not confirmed for 2001*

LEEDS

City Art Gallery
The Headrow LS1 3AA (city centre, next to town hall and library)
☎ 0113 247 8248 🖷 0113 244 9689

Home to one of the best collections of 20th-century British art outside London, as well as Victorian and late 19th-century pictures, an outstanding collection of English watercolours, a display of modern sculpture and temporary exhibitions focusing on the contemporary.
Times: Open all year, Mon-Sat 10-5, Wed until 8, Sun 1-5.Closed BHs.
Fee: Free.
P licensed ♿ (restricted access to upper floor) toilets for disabled shop (ex guide dogs)

Kirkstall Abbey
Abbey Rd, Kirkstall LS5 3EH (off A65, W of city centre).
☎ 0113 275 5821

The most complete 12th-century Cistercian Abbey in the country stands on the banks of the River Aire. Many of the original buildings can still be seen, including the cloister, church and refrectory. Regular tours take visitors to areas not normally accessible to the public. During the summer the Abbey hosts plays, fairs and musical events.
Times: Open all year, Tue-Sat 10-5, Sun 1-5. Open Bank Hol's. Abbey site open dawn-dusk.
Fee: Free.
P ♿ toilets for disabled shop

Leeds Industrial Museum at Armley Mills
Canal Rd, Armley LS12 2QF (2m W of city centre, off A65)
☎ 0113 263 7861

Once the world's largest woollen mill, Armley Mills evokes memories of the 18th-century woollen industry, showing the progress of wool from the sheep to knitted clothing. The museum has its own 1930s cinema illustrating the history of cinema projection, including the first moving pictures taken in Leeds. There are demonstrations of static engines and steam locomotives, a printing gallery and a journey through the working world of textiles and fashion.
Times: Open all year, Tue-Sat 10-5, Sun 1-5. Last entry 1 hr before closing. (Closed Mon ex BHs).
Fee: £2 (ch 50p pen, students & UB40's £1) Friends & Family ticket (2 adults & 3 ch) £5.
P ♿ (chair-lifts between floors) toilets for disabled shop

Middleton Railway

Moor Rd, Hunslet LS10 2JQ (M621 junct 5 or follow signs from A61)

☎ 0113 271 0320 (ansaphone) 📠 01977 620585

e-mail: info@middletonrailway.org.uk

This was the first railway authorised by an Act of Parliament (in 1758) and the first to succeed with steam locomotives (in 1812). Steam trains run each weekend in season from Tunstall Road roundabout to Middleton Park. There is a programme of special events.

Times: Moor Road Station open for viewing every wknd. Trains run Sat, Sun & BH, 25 Mar-24 Dec.

Fee: Entry to station free. £2 (ch £1) Return train fare. Family ticket £5.

P ♿ (ramped access to all areas) toilets for disabled shop

Royal Armouries Museum

Armouries Dr LS10 1LT (off A61 close to Leeds centre, follow brown tourist signs)

☎ 0113 220 1999 & 0990 106 666 📠 0113 220 1934

e-mail: enquiries@armouries.org.uk

Situated on the canal waterfront in the heart of Leeds, the museum is designed to bring to life the history and development of arms and armour. Outside on the waterfront there is a 1,000 capacity tilt yard for jousting tournaments and the Beating of the Retreat. A craft court has demonstrations by skilled armourers and the training of hunting dogs and horses.

Times: Open daily, from 10.30-5.30. Closes 4.30 midweek in winter. (Closed 24-25 Dec & 1 Jan)

Fee: £4.90 (ch & concession £3.90). Family ticket £14.90.

P (charged) ✕ licensed ♿ toilets for disabled shop

Temple Newsam House & Park

LS15 0AE (off A63)

☎ 0113 264 7321 (House) & 264 5535 (Park) 📠 0113 260 2285

This Tudor and Jacobean mansion boasts extensive collections of decorative arts in their original room settings, including the incomparable Chippendale collection. Set in 1,200 acres of parkland (landscaped by 'Capability' Brown), there's a Rare Breeds Centre, and the gardens have a magnificent display of rhododendrons.

Times: Open all year. House: Tue-Sat 10am-5pm, Sun 1-5pm. 1 Nov-28 Dec & Mar Tues-Sat 10am-4pm Sun 12-5pm. Open Bank Hols. Home Farm 10am-4pm(3pm in winter); Gardens 10-dusk; Estate: daily: dawn-dusk. Closed Jan-Feb re-opens 28 Feb.

Fee: £2 (concessions £1). Accompanied children 50p. Friends & Family ticket (2 adults & 3 ch) £5.

P (charged) ♿ (ramps giving full accesss to parkland,wheelchairs for hire) toilets for disabled shop

Thackray Medical Museum

Beckett St LS9 7LN (next to St James Hospital)

☎ 0113 244 4343 📠 0113 247 0219

e-mail: medical_museum@msn.com

Housed in a large Victorian building, next to the famous St James's Hospital, the Thackray Medical Museum offers a unique hands-on experience. A cow from Gloucester, green mould and smelly toilets - all these things have helped transform our lives. Find out how by walking back in time and exploring the sights, sounds and smells of Victorian slum life.

Times: Open all year, Tue-Sun & BH Mons 10-5.30. Closed 25-26 Dec & 1 Jan.

P (charged) ♿ (wheelchair loan, induction loop) toilets for disabled shop (ex guide dogs) *Details not confirmed for 2001* 

Thwaite Mills Watermill

Thwaite Ln, Stourton LS10 1RP (2m S of city centre, off A61)

☎ 0113 249 6453 📠 0113 246 5561

A guide will take you on a tour of this water-powered mill which sits between the River Aire and the Aire and Calder Navigation. Two great wheels drive a mass of cogs and grinding wheels which crushed stone for putty and paint throughout the 19th century. This was the hub of a tiny island community, and the Georgian mill-owner's house has been restored, to house displays on the mill's history.

Times: Open Tues-Sat 10am-5pm & Sun 1-5pm. 1 Nov-31 Dec and March Tues-Sat 10am-4pm, Sun 12-4pm. Open BH Mon. Closed Jan & Feb.

Fee: £2 (ch 50p, £1 concessions). Family & Friends ticket (2 adults & 3 ch) £5.

P ♿ (wheelchair lifts) toilets for disabled shop

Tropical World

Canal Gardens, Roundhay Park LS8 2ER (3m N of city centre off A58 at Oakwood)

☎ 0113 266 1850

The atmosphere of the tropics is re-created here as visitors walk among exotic trees. A waterfall cascades into a rock-pool and other pools contain terrapins and carp. There are reptiles, insects and more than 30 species of butterfly. There is also a Nocturnal House, a South American Rainforest, and a Desert House.

Times: Open daily, 10-early evening (dusk in winter), special times at Christmas. Closed 25 Dec
Fee: £1 (ch 8-15 50p, ch under 8 free).
P ☕ ♿ toilets for disabled shop 🐕 (ex guide dogs)

LOTHERTON HALL

LOTHERTON HALL

Aberford LS25 3EB (off A1, 0.75m E of junct with B1217)
☎ **0113 281 3259**

Built in Edwardian times, the museum contains furniture, pictures, silver and ceramics from the Gascoigne collection, and works of art on loan from Leeds galleries. Outside, the Edwardian garden, bird garden and deer park are delightful places in which to stroll.

Times: Open Tue-Sat 10-5. Sun 1-5. Bank Hols. Nov-Dec & Mar Tue-Sat 10-4, Sun 12-4.
Fee: Hall, £2 (ch, pen & students £1, unaccompanied ch 50p). Family & Friends ticket (2 adults & 3 ch) £5. Party 15+. Free admission to Bird Garden, Gardens & Parkland. Free admission to house for driver.
P (charged) ☕ ✕ licensed ♿ shop 🐕 (ex in park)

MIDDLESTOWN

NATIONAL COAL MINING MUSEUM FOR ENGLAND

Caphouse Colliery, New Rd WF4 4RH (on A642 between Wakefield & Huddersfield)
☎ **01924 848806** 📠 **01924 840694**
e-mail: info@ncmme.demon.co.uk

A unique opportunity to go 450ft underground down one of Britain's oldest working mine shafts, guided by an ex-miner, where models and machinery depict methods and conditions of mining from the early 1800s to the present day. You are strongly advised to wear sensible footwear and warm clothing.

Times: Open all year, daily 10-5. (Closed 24-26 Dec & 1 Jan).
Fee: £5.75 (ch £4.25, concessions £4.85).
P ☕ ✕ licensed ♿ (nature trail not accessible) toilets for disabled shop

NOSTELL PRIORY

NOSTELL PRIORY

WF4 1QD (6m SE of Wakefield, off A638)
☎ **01924 863892** 📠 **01924 865282**

Built by Paine in the middle of the 18th century, the priory has an additional wing built by Adam in 1766. It contains a notable saloon and tapestry room and displays pictures and Chippendale furniture. Events being held include the Royal British Legion Rally and a Country Fair.

Times: Open 4 Apr-1 Nov. Apr-Jun, Sept & Oct: Sat & Sun 12pm-5pm. 1 July-3 Sept daily except Friday 12-5. Bank Hols 12-5. Not Good Fri. Last admission 4.30pm.
P ☕ ♿ (lift) toilets for disabled shop 🐕 *Details not confirmed for 2001*

OAKWELL HALL

OAKWELL HALL

Nutter Ln, Birstall WF17 9LG (6m SE of Bradford, off M62 junct 26/27, follow brown tourist signs, turn off A652 onto Nutter Lane)
☎ **01924 326240** 📠 **01924 326249**

A moated Elizabethan manor house, furnished as it might have looked in the 1690s. Extensive 110-acre country park with visitor information centre, period gardens, nature trails, arboretum and children's adventure playground.

Times: Open all year, daily (ex Good Fri, 24 Dec-1 Jan).
Fee: £1.20 (ch 50p). Family ticket £2.50.
P ☕ ♿ (herb garden for the blind, large print & braille guide) toilets for disabled shop 🐕 (park only ex guide dogs)

SHIPLEY

Reed Organ & Harmonium Museum

Victoria Hall, Victoria Rd, Saltaire BD18 3LQ
☎ 01274 585601 after 6pm
Times: Open Sun-Thu, 11-4. (Closed 2 wks Xmas).
P (on street) ♿ toilets for disabled *Details not confirmed for 2001*

WAKEFIELD

Wakefield Art Gallery

Wentworth Ter WF1 3QW (N of city centre by Wakefield College and Clayton Hospital)
☎ 01924 305796 📠 01924 305770

Wakefield was home to two of Britain's greatest modern sculptors - Barbara Hepworth and Henry Moore. The art gallery, which has an important collection of 20th-century paintings and sculptures, has a special room devoted to these two local artists. There are frequent temporary exhibitions of both modern and earlier works.

Times: Open all year, Tue-Sat 10.30-4.30, Sun 2-4.30.
Fee: Free.
P (on street) (on street parking restricted to 2hrs) shop (ex guide dogs)

WEST BRETTON

Yorkshire Sculpture Park

WF4 4LG (1 mile from junct 38 on M1)
☎ 01924 830302 📠 01924 830044
e-mail: office@ysp.co.uk

One of Europe's leading sculpture parks, set in over 100 acres of beautiful parkland. There are changing displays from the loan collection by artists including work by Barbara Hepworth, William Tucker, Grenville Davey and Sol Le Witt. In the adjacent 96-acre Bretton Country Park, there is a permanent exhibition of works by Henry Moore.

Times: Open all year 10-6 (summer) 10-4 (winter). (Closed 25-26 & 31 Dec)
Fee: Free.
P (charged) ☕ ♿ (scooters available for disabled) toilets for disabled shop

Guernsey

If it's sunshine, shopping and sea you're interested in, then the island of Guernsey is the ideal location for a break that combines the feeling of being abroad with the familiarity of the English language and British ways of life.

When William conquered England, he didn't need to conquer Guernsey. It was already part of the Duchy of Normandy. The strategic importance of the island has been recognised through the centuries, from the 13th-century Castle Cornet to the fortifications of the German occupying forces during WWII. There are also many ancient structures, some of which are believed to be among the oldest in Europe.

Guernsey enjoys some 2,000 hours of sunshine a year. This makes its 27 beaches great places to spend time. No matter which way the wind is blowing, you'll be sure to find one that's sheltered.

The island is also known for its conservation efforts. Both the National Trust and the home-grown La Société Guernesiaise maintain some beautiful areas, including a wooded valley and a number of fields.

Shopping is a major attraction on Guernsey, not necessarily for what's on sale, although the shops cover a wide variety and some local specialities including Guernsey sweaters and flowers. The real attraction is the low local taxation and lack of VAT, which makes the island a bargain hunter's paradise.

Close to Guernsey are three smaller islands well worth visiting. Sark, Alderney and Aurigny. Sark was the setting for Mervyn Peake's novel, *Mr Pye*. It was also the location for the TV version starring Derek Jacobi.

EVENTS & FESTIVALS

February
tbc Guernsey Eisteddfod Festival

April
tbc Festival of Food & Wine

May
9 Liberation Day Celebrations, St Peter Port

June
tbc Floral Guernsey Festival Week
tbc Floral Guernsey Show

July
tbc Guernsey Square Dance Festival
tbc Harbour Carnival, St Peter Port Harbour
tbc Guernsey International Folk Festival (various venues)
tbc St Peter Port Town Carnival

August
tbc South Show, agricultural show
tbc West Show, agricultural show

September
tbc Guernsey International Air Rally

October
tbc Guernsey Real Ale & Cider Festival

Top: Jerbourg Point, St Martin

FOREST

German Occupation Museum

GY8 0BG (Behind Forest Church near the airport)

☎ 01481 238205

Times: Open Apr-Oct 10-5. Nov-Mar, daily 10-1. Closed Mons.

(ramps & handrails) *Details not confirmed for 2001*

ROCQUAINE BAY

Fort Grey and Shipwreck Museum

GY7 9BY (on coast road at Rocquaine Bay)

☎ 01481 265036 🖷 01481 263279

e-mail: education@museum.guernsey.net

The fort is a Martello tower, built in 1804, as part of the Channel Islands' extensive defences. It is nicknamed the `cup and saucer' because of its appearance, and houses a museum devoted to ships wrecked on the treacherous Hanois reefs nearby.

Times: Open Apr-Oct, 10-5. **Fee:** £2 (pen £1). Joint ticket with Castle Cornet & Guernsey Museum £6 (pen £3). Students & children free.

(opposite fort) shop

ST ANDREW

German Military Underground Hopsital & Ammunition Store

La Vassalerie GY6 8XR

☎ 01481 239100

The largest structure created during the German Occupation of the Channel Islands, a concrete maze of about 75,000 sq ft, which took slave workers three-and-a-half years to complete, at the cost of many lives. The central heating plant, hospital beds and cooking facilities can still be seen.

Times: Open Jul-Aug, daily 10-noon & 2-4.30; May-Jun & Sep, daily 10-noon & 2-4; Apr & Oct, daily 10-12; Mar & Nov, Sun & Thu 2-3.

Fee: £2.50 (ch 60p). shop

ST MARTIN

Sausmarez Manor

Sausmarez Rd GY4 6SG

☎ 01481 235571 🖷 01481 235572

e-mail: peter@lesausmarez.fsnet.co.uk

The style of each room is different, with collections of Oriental, French and English furniture and paintings. Outside the Formal Garden has herbaceous borders, and the Woodland Garden, set around two small lakes, is planted with colourful plants from the subtropics.

Times: Open - House: last BH in May-last Thu in Sep, Mon-Thu, 10.30-11.30 & 2-3. Also Apr-end of May & Oct, Mon-Thu mornings 10.30-11.30.

Fee: House £4.50 (ch £2, pen £4). Woodland Garden £1.50 (accompanied ch 50p, disabled free). Dolls House Collection £1.95 (ch 75p, concessions £1). Family ticket £5. Railway layout £1 (ch & pen 80p). Train rides £1 (ch & pen 80p). Petland £1.50. Family ticket £5.

(free partial access to garden, wheelchair loan) shop (Specialises in dolls houses etc) (ex dogs for blind and deaf)

ST PETER PORT

Castle Cornet

GY1 1UG (0.5m from town centre)

☎ 01481 721657 🖷 01481 715177

e-mail: education@museum.guernsey.net

The history of this magnificent castle spans eight centuries and its buildings now house several museums. Soldiers fire the noonday gun in a daily ceremony. The Maritime Museum charts Guernsey's nautical history and the 'Story of Castle Cornet' with its mystery skeleton.

Times: Open Apr-Oct, daily 10-5.

Fee: £4 (students/pen £2). Joint ticket with Fort Grey & Guernsey Museum £6 (pen £3). Accompanied children under 12, students & educational groups free (100 yds) (2 hr time zone, 10hr within 200 yards) shop (ex guide dogs)

Guernsey Museum & Art Gallery

Candie Gardens GY1 1UG

☎ 01481 726518 🖷 01481 715177

e-mail: education@museum.guernsey.net

The museum tells the story of Guernsey and its people. There is an audio-visual theatre and an art gallery. It is surrounded by beautiful gardens with superb views.

Times: Open all year, daily 10-5 (summer), 10-4 (winter).

Fee: £2.50 (pen £1.25). Joint ticket with Castle Cornet & Fort Grey £6 (pen £3). Students & children free. (outside museum) (2hr & 5hr) toilets for disabled shop (ex guide dogs)

VALE

Rousse Tower

Rousse Tower Headland

☎ 01481 726611 🖷 01481 721246

e-mail: Louise.Cain@gov.gg

One of the original fifteen towers built in 1778-9 in prime defensive positions around the coast. They were designed primarily to prevent the landing of troops on nearby beaches. Musket fire could be directed on invading forces through the loopholes.

Times: Open 9-5. **Fee:** Free. (ex guide dogs)

Jersey

The Channel Islands are renowned for their hospitality, prosperity and beauty, with their fine cliffs, sandy beaches, splendid harbours and impressive marinas.

The mild climate is conducive to enjoyable holidays, and ensures an abundance of flowers, fruit and vegetables. Notably the Channel Island tomato and the deliciously earthy early Jersey Royal potato, a delicacy in its own right with a knob of Jersey butter.

Like Guernsey, Jersey has its own breed of cow, and its own kind of sweater, the jersey, incorporating an anchor into its design under the neckline at the front. Agriculture and fishing are traditional industries. The conger eel is particularly associated with the island, and conger eel soup is a popular local dish.

Jersey is the largest of the Channel Islands, and the most southerly, just 30 miles (48km) from St Malo. The unique combination of the French and British ways of life contributes much to the island's undoubtable charm. The island is infused with Gallic culture, as you can see by the names of the streets and the baguettes in the bakers'. The local language is traditionally a Norman-French Patois, though this is in decline and English is generally spoken. The islands also have their own banknotes, though the currency is sterling.

The financial industry has transformed the lives of islanders, bringing great prosperity to its economy. Banks of all nationalities are in residence on the island, taking advantage of its low-tax base and proximity to the City of London. Checking out the multi-million pound properties of the rich and famous tax exiles is part of the sightseeing itinerary.

EVENTS & FESTIVALS

April
5th-8th Jersey, Jazz Festival (various venues around the island)

May
tbc Jersey International Food Festival (various events around the island)

July
tbc Jersey Garden Festival (various venues around the island)

August
9th Jersey Battle of Flowers (provisional)
10th Jersey Battle of Flowers Moonlight Parade (provisional)

September
tbc International Air Display over St Aubins Bay

October
tbc Jersey Festival of World Music (various venues around the island)
tbc International Choir Festival of Jersey

December
Fête dé Noué (Christmas festival)

Top: Jersey States chamber, St Helier

GOREY

MONT ORGUEIL CASTLE

JE3 6ET (A3 or coast road to Gorey)
☎ 01534 853292 📠 01534 854303
e-mail: marketing@jerseyheritagetrust.org

Standing on a rocky headland, on a site which has been fortified since the Iron Age, this is one of the best-preserved examples in Europe of a medieval concentric castle, and dates from the 12th and 13th centuries.

Times: Open daily throughout the year 9.30-6; Last admission 5pm. Times in winter change (Fri-Mon 10-dusk)

Fee: £3.50 (ch 10-16, pen & students £2.50, ch under 10 free). Three sites for two ticket £6.95 (concessions £4.95).

P (200 yds) (discs required at harbour) shop (ex guide dogs)

GREVE DE LECQ BAY

GREVE DE LECQ BARRACKS

☎ 01534 483193

Originally serving as an outpost of the British Empire, these barracks, built in 1789, were used for civilian housing from the end of WWI to 1972, when they were bought by the National Trust and made into a museum that depicts the life of soldiers who were stationed here in the 19th century.

Times: Open Etr wknd & 2 May-15 Oct, Tue-Sat 11-5 & Sun 2-5. (Closed Mon).

Fee: Free.

P shop (ex guide dogs)

GROUVILLE

LA HOUGUE BIE

JE2 7UA (A6 or A7 to Five Oaks then Prines Tower Rd)
☎ 01534 853823 📠 01534 856472
e-mail: marketing@jerseyheritagetrust.org

This Neolithic burial mound stands 40ft high, and covers a stone-built passage grave which is still intact and may be entered. The passage is 50ft long, and built of huge stones, the mound is made from earth, rubble and limpet shells. On top of the mound are two medieval chapels, one of which has a replica of the Holy Sepulchre in Jerusalem below. Also on the site is an underground bunker built by the Germans as a communications centre.

Times: Open 29 Mar-Oct, daily 10-5.

Fee: £3.50 (ch 10-16 & pen £2.50, ch 10 free). Discount ticket 3 sites for the price of 2 £6.95 (concessions £4.95).

P shop (ex guide dogs)

ST BRELADE

JERSEY LAVENDER FARM

Rue du Pont Marquet JE3 8DS (on B25 from St.Aubin's Bay to Redhouses)
☎ 01534 742933 📠 01534 745613
e-mail: jerseylavender@localdial.com

Here you can see the complete process of production from cultivation through to harvesting and distillation to the bottling, labelling and packaging of the final product. The National Collection of Lavandula is held here, there's a fine herb garden, an extensive collection of dwarf and slow-growing conifers in the Pygmy Pinetum and a collection of 78 varieties of bamboo.

Times: Open 22 May-23 Sep, Mon-Sat 10-5.

Fee: £2.50 (ch 14 free)

P (wheelchair loan, wide doors, grab rails etc) toilets for disabled shop garden centre

ST CLEMENT

SAMARÈS MANOR

JE2 6QW (2m E of St.Helier on St.Clements inner rd)
☎ 01534 870551 📠 01534 768949

Times: Open 3 Apr-16 Oct.

P licensed toilets for disabled shop garden centre (ex guide dogs) *Details not confirmed for 2001*

ST HELIER

ELIZABETH CASTLE

JE2 3WU (access by causeway or amphibious vehicle)
☎ 01534 723971 📠 01534 610338
e-mail: marketing@jerseyheritagetrust.org

The original Elizabethan fortress was extended in the 17th and 18th centuries, and then refortified by the Germans during the Occupation.

Times: Open 29 Mar-Oct, daily 9.30-6. Last admission 5.

Fee: £3.50 (concessions £2.50, ch under 10 free). Three sites for Two ticket £6.95 (concessions £4.95). Pre-booked group 15% discount.

P shop (ex guide dogs)

JERSEY MUSEUM

The Weighbridge JE2 3NF (near bus station on weighbridge)
☎ 01534 633300 📠 01534 633301
e-mail: marketing@jerseyheritagetrust.org

Home to 'The Story of Jersey', Jersey's art gallery, an exhibition gallery which features a changing programme, a lecture theatre, and an audio-visual theatre. Special exhibitions take place throughout the year.

Times: Open all year, daily 10-5. Winter daily 10-4. (Closed 24-26 Dec & 1 Jan).

Fee: £3.50 (ch under 10 free, concessions £2.50). Discount ticket for 3 sites for the price of 2 £6.95 (concessions £4.95).

P (100yds) (paycard at most public parking) licensed (audio loop, audio guide for partially sighted, car park) toilets for disabled shop (ex guide dogs)

MARITIME MUSEUM & OCCUPATION TAPESTRY GALLERY

New North Quay JE2 3ND (alongside Marina, opposite Liberation Square)
☎ 01534 811043 📠 01534 874099
e-mail: marketing@jerseyheritagetrust

This converted 19th-century warehouse houses the tapestry consisting of 12 two-metre panels that tells the story of the occupation of Jersey during World War II. Each of the 12 parishes took responsibility for stitching a panel, making it the largest community arts project ever undertaken on the island. The Maritime Museum celebrates the relationship of islanders and the sea, including an award winning hand-on experience, especially enjoyed by children. .

Times: Open all year, daily 10-5 (winter closing at 4pm).

Fee: £3.80 (pen/student £2.80).Under 10's free.

P (paycards in public car parks) ♿ (braille books, audio guide etc) toilets for disabled shop (ex guide dogs)

ST LAWRENCE

FLYING FLOWERS

Jersey Flower Centre JE3 1GX

☎ 01534 865553 📠 01534 866000

Flying Flowers is the largest mail order floral company in the world. Take a walk around the giant, 22,000 sq ft glasshouses holding 200,000 plants or view the flamingo lake, wildfowl sanctuary, koi carp reserve, exotic birds and wildflower meadowland. Visitor centre incorporating shop, restaurant and children's play area.

Times: Open Apr-Oct, daily 10-5.

Fee: Free.

P ♿ (Wheelchairs available) toilets for disabled shop (ex guide dogs)

GERMAN UNDERGROUND HOSPITAL

Les Charrieres Malorey JE3 1FU

☎ 01534 863442 📠 01534 865970

On 1 July 1940 the Channel Islands were occupied by German forces, and this vast complex dug deep into a hillside is the most evocative reminder of that Occupation. A video presentation, along with a large collection of memorabilia, illustrates the lives of the islanders at war and a further exhibition records their impressions during 1945, the year of liberation.

Times: Open 12 Mar-5 Nov, daily 9.30-5.30 Last admission 4.15. (Closed 9 May & restricted hours 10 Aug & 14 Sep).

Fee: £5.20 (ch £2.60).

P licensed ♿ (ramp to restaurant & lift in Visitor Centre to restaurant) toilets for disabled shop

HAMPTONNE COUNTRY LIFE MUSEUM

La Rue de la Patente JE3 1HS (5m from St.Helier on A1, A10 and follow signs)

☎ 01534 863955 📠 01534 863935

e-mail: marketing@jerseyheritagetrust.org

Here you will find a medieval 17th-century home, furnished in authentic style and surrounded by 19th-century farm buildings. Guided tours every weekday. Perpetual living history interpretation and daily demonstrations.

Times: Open 29 Mar-Oct, daily 10-4.

Fee: £3.50 (ch 10-16 & concessions £2.50, ch under 10 free). Discount ticket 3 sites for the price of 2 available.

P ♿ toilets for disabled shop (ex guide dogs)

ST OUEN

THE CHANNEL ISLANDS MILITARY MUSEUM

Five Mile Rd

☎ 01534 23136 & 483205 📠 01534 485647

Both British and German militaria is on display here, from uniforms and equipment to motorcycles and paperwork. All from the occupation era, displayed in an original and restored German bunker.

Times: Open 17 Apr-Oct, 10-5 (last entry 4.45).

Fee: £2.50 (ch £1).

P ♿ shop (ex guide dogs)

KEMPT TOWER VISITOR CENTRE

Five Mile Rd

☎ 01534 483651 & 483140 📠 01534 485289

The centre has displays on the past, and the wildlife of St Ouen's Bay, including Les Mielles, which is Jersey's miniature national park. Nature walks are held every Thursday (May to September). Check local press for details.

Times: Open BH's & Apr & Oct, Thu & Sun only 2-5; May-Sep, daily (ex Mon) 2-5.

Fee: Free.

P shop

ST PETER

JERSEY MOTOR MUSEUM

St Peter's Village JE3 7AG (Jct off A12 & B41 at St Peters village)

☎ 01534 482966

The museum has a fine collection of motor vehicles from the early 1900s. There are also Allied and German military vehicles of World War II, a Jersey Steam Railway section, aero-engines and other items.

Times: Open end Mar-late Oct, daily 10-5. (Last admission 4.40).

Fee: £2.50 (ch £1.20). Wheelchair users free.

P ♿ (access doors avoid turnstyles) shop (ex guide dogs)

THE LIVING LEGEND

Rue de Petit Aleval JE3 7ET

☎ 01534 485496 📠 01534 485855

Pass through the granite archways into the landscaped gardens and the world of the Jersey Experience where Jersey's exciting past is recreated in a three dimensional spectacle. Learn of the heroes and villains, the folklore and the story of the Island's links with the UK and her struggles with Europe. An adventure playground, street entertainment, the Jersey Craft and Shopping Village, shops and the Jersey Kitchen Restaurant.

Times: Open Apr-Oct, daily 9.30-5.30; Mar & Nov, Mon-Wed & Sat-Sun 10-5.

Fee: £5.35 (ch £3.25, pen £4.95).

P licensed ♿ (wheelchair available) toilets for disabled shop (ex guide dogs)

Le Moulin de Quetivel

St Peters Valley JE3 3EN (on B58 off A11)

☎ 01534 483193

There has been a water mill on this site since 1309. The present granite-built mill was worked until the end of the 19th century, when it fell into disrepair; during the German Occupation it was reactivated for grinding locally grown corn, but after 1945 a fire destroyed the remaining machinery, roof and internal woodwork. In 1971 the National Trust for Jersey began restoration, and the mill is now producing stoneground flour again.

Times: Open May-mid Oct, Tue-Thu 10-4.

Fee: £1.50 (ch 50p). Trust Members free.

P ♿ shop (ex guide dogs)

St Peter's Bunker Museum

St Peters Village JE3 7AF (at junc of A12 & B41)

☎ 01534 483205 🖷 01534 485647

e-mail: damienhorn@cinergy.co.uk

German uniforms, motorcycles, weapons, documents, photographs and other items from the 1940-45 Occupation are displayed in a wartime bunker which accommodated 33 men and could be sealed in case of attack.

Times: Open 17 Apr-Oct, daily 10-5 (last entry 4.45).

Fee: £2.50 (ch £1).

P shop (ex guide dogs)

TRINITY

Durrell Wildlife Conservation Trust

Les Augres Manor JE3 5BP

☎ 01534 860000 🖷 01534 860001

Gerald Durrell's unique sanctuary and breeding centre for many of the world's rarest animals. Visitors can see these remarkable creatures, some so rare that they can only be found here, in modern, spacious enclosures in the gardens of the 16th-century manor house. Major attractions are the magical Aye-Ayes from Madagascar and the world-famous family of Lowland gorillas. There is a comprehensive programme of keeper talks, animal displays and activities.

Times: Open all year, daily 9.30-6 (dusk in winter). (Closed 25 Dec).

Fee: £8 (ch 4-14 £5.50, pen £6.50).

P ✕ licensed ♿ (trail for the blind, auditory loop in pavilion) toilets for disabled shop

Isle of Man

Going to the Isle of Man is, in many ways, like visiting a foreign country. The island is not ruled by the British monarch, and has its own parliament (the Tynwald) which makes laws that apply only to the island.

The Isle of Man is only 33 miles by 13, yet packs in so much. Celtic crosses, ancient Viking burial grounds and medieval castles are all around, and the history of the island is well chronicled by the award-winning Manx Museum. Inside, visitors can explore the National Art Gallery, the Map Gallery with its large-scale relief map of the island, and see a specially-produced film, 'Story of Mann'.

One of the island's main attractions is its railway network, which began in 1873 and still runs a regular service. 19th-century electric and mountain railways are also still in operation. The Snaefell Mountain Railway is the only electric mountain railway in Britain, and starts its journey from Laxey, home of the Laxey Wheel, the world's largest working waterwheel. Douglas also has horse trams, which have been in continuous operation since 1876, except for wartime breaks.

The island is probably best known for its TT (Tourist Trophy) racing, which is staged in May-June each year. The race, originally for cars only, has been run since 1904, and with motorbikes only since 1911. There are other races too. These include the Ramsey Sprint, the Manx Grand Prix, the Manx International Car Rally, and the Kart Racing Grand Prix.

EVENTS & FESTIVALS

June
tbc Mananan International Festival of Music (various venues)

July
25-27 Irish National Sheepdog Trials
tbc Yn Chruinnaght Inter-Celtic Festival (various venues)
tbc Manx Heritage Flower Show (various venues)

August
tbc International Jazz Festival, Villa Marina, Douglas
tbc Mannin Angling Festival (various venues)
tbc Manx Grand Prix Motorcycle Fortnight (various venues)

September
tbc Mananan Opera Festival, Erin Arts Centre, Port Erin
tbc Manx International Car Rally (various venues)

Top: Cashtal yn Ard

BALLAUGH

Curraghs Wild Life Park

(on main rd halfway between Kirk Michael & Ramsey)
☎ 01624 897323 01624 897327
e-mail: curraghswlp@gov.im

This park has been developed adjacent to the reserve area of the Ballaugh Curraghs and a large variety of animals and birds can be seen. A walk through enclosures lets visitors explore wildlife, local habitats along the Curraghs nature trail. The miniature railway runs on Sundays.
Times: Open Etr-Oct, daily 10-6. Last admission 5.15pm. Oct-Etr, Sat & Sun 10-4. **Fee:** £3.60 (ch £1.80, pen £2.40). Party.
(loan of wheelchair & electric wheelchair) toilets for disabled shop (ex guide dogs by arrangement)

CASTLETOWN

Castle Rushen

☎ 01624 648000 01624 648001

On view to the visitor are the state apartments of this 14th-century stronghold. There is also a Norman keep, flanked by towers from its later rebuilding, with a clock given by Elizabeth I in 1597.
Times: Open Apr-Oct, daily 10-5. **Fee:** £4 (ch £2) Family £10.
P (100 yds) shop

Nautical Museum

☎ 01624 648000 01624 648001

The island's colourful relationship with the sea is illustrated here. There is an 18th-century Manx yacht and interesting Cabin Room and Quayle Room. Also displays of net-making equipment.
Times: Open Apr-Oct, daily 10-5. **Fee:** £2.75 (ch £1.50). Family £7.
P (50 yds) shop

Old Grammar School

☎ 01624 648000 01624 648001

Built in the 12th century, the Island's first church, St Mary's, has had a significant role in Manx education. The school dates back to 1570 and evokes memories of Victorian school life.
Times: Open Apr-Oct, daily 10-5. **Fee:** Free. P shop

CREGNEISH

Cregneash Village Folk Museum

(2m from Port Erin/Port St Mary)
☎ 01624 648000 01624 648001

A group of traditional Manx cottages with their gardens and walled enclosures. Inside the cottages furniture and the everyday equipment used by typical Manx crofting communities are displayed. Spinning demonstrations are given on certain days and sometimes a blacksmith can be seen at work. In the field adjoining the turner's shed, Manx Loghtan sheep can often be seen - the rams have a tendency to produce four, or even six, horns.
Times: Open Apr-Oct, daily 10-5. **Fee:** £2.75 (ch £1.50) Family £7.
P shop (ex in grounds)

DOUGLAS

Manx Museum

☎ 01624 648000 01624 648001

The 'Story of Man' begins at Manx Museum, where a specially produced film portrayal of Manx history complements the award-winning gallery displays. This showcase of Manx heritage provides the ideal starting-point to a journey of rich discovery embracing the length and breadth of the island.
Times: Open all year, Mon-Sat 10-5. (Closed Sun, Xmas, New Year, am of Tynwald Day 5 Jul). **Fee:** Free.
P licensed toilets for disabled shop

LAXEY

Great Laxey Wheel & Mines Trail

☎ 01624 648000 01624 648001

Constructed to keep the lead mines free from water, this big wheel, known as the 'Lady Isabella', is an impressive sight at 72.5ft in diameter. It is the largest working wheel in the world.
Times: Open Apr-Oct, daily 10-5. **Fee:** £2.75 (ch £1.50) Family £7.
P shop

PEEL

House of Manannan

(on quayside)
☎ 01624 648000 01624 648001

This is an unforgettable experience with interactive displays, using 'state of the art' technology. A visit here leaves the visitor in awe of Manx heritage and eager to learn more.
Times: Open daily 10-5. (Closed Xmas & New Year). **Fee:** £5 (ch 5-15 £2.50). Family ticket £12.50. Party. P toilets for disabled shop

Peel Castle

(on Patricks Isle, facing Peel Bay)
☎ 01624 648000 01624 648001

The castle was built to protect the cathedral of St German's, perhaps founded by St Patrick, and contains ruins from the 11th century. A phantom black dog, the Moddey Dhoo, is said to haunt the castle.
Times: Open Apr-Oct, daily 10-5. **Fee:** £2.75 (ch £1.50). P shop

RAMSEY

'The Grove' Rural Life Museum

(on W side of Andreas Road)
☎ 01624 648000 01624 648001

A glimpse into the everyday life of a previous era. Inside are many of the original furnishings and personal belongings of the former owners, the Gibb family, displayed among the minutiae of Victorian life.
Times: Open Apr-Oct, daily 10-5. **Fee:** £2.75 (ch £1.50). Family £7.
P licensed shop

Glen Affric

Scotland

EVENTS & FESTIVALS

January
1 Stonehaven Fireballing Festival, Stonehaven, Aberdeenshire
1 Men's & Boy's 'Ba', mass football game, Orkney Isles
25 Burns Night
25 Up Helly A', Lerwick, Shetland February
3 7-11pm Bothy Ballads, Champion of Champions, Elgin, Morayshire

March
8-11 Telemark Festival, Braemar, Aberdeenshire

April
7-8 City of Dundee Flower Show, Dundee
15 Easter Fun Day, Camperdown Park, Dundee

May
19-21 Strichen Festival, Strichen, Aberdeenshire
25 May-3 Jun Dumfries & Galloway Arts Festival
26-27 Angus Show, Haughmuir by Brechin, Angus
26-27 Atholl Gathering & Highland Games, Blair Atholl, Perth & Kinross
28 May-3 Jun Scottish International Children's Festival, Edinburgh
tbc Dundee Jazz Festival, Dundee

June
3 Pipe Band Contest, The Haughs, Turriff, Aberdeenshire
tbc St Magnus Festival, Orkney10th Forfar Highland Games, Angus
3 Thirtieth Anniversary Borders Historic Motoring Extravaganza, Mellerstain House, Borders
7 Lanimer Day, Lanark, South Lanarkshire
23-24 Moffat Classic Car Rally, Dumfries & Galloway

July
1 Jul-11 Aug Arts Carnival, Aberdeen Arts Centre, Aberdeen
4-8 Glasgow International Jazz Festival
7-8 Traditional Boat Festival, Portsoy, Aberdeenshire
7 Annan Riding of the Marches, Dumfries & Galloway
8 Stirling Highland Games, Stirlingshire
tbc Dundee Blues Bonanza
13-15 Stonehaven Folk Festival, Aberdeenshire
25th Stranraer Show, Dumfries & Galloway
27 Langholm Common Riding, Dumfries & Galloway
28 Banchory Agricultural Show, Aberdeenshire

August
1-11 Aberdeen International Youth Festival
2-4 Scottish Sheepdog Trials, Hawick, Borders
3-25 Edinburgh Military Tattoo
3-6 Speyfest, Fochabers, Morayshire
4 Aboyne Highland Games, Aberdeenshire
9 Highland Games, Monaltrie Park, Ballater, Aberdeenshire
12 Perth Highland Games, Perth & Kinross
12 The Border Gathering Day, Gretna Green, Dumfries & Galloway
12-26 Edinburgh International Film Festival (provisional)
18 Sanquar Riding of the Marches, Dumfries & Galloway
18-19 Arbroath Sea Festival, Angus
20 Crieff Highland Gathering, Perth & Kinross
tbc Edinburgh International Festival
25 Summer Flower Show, Duthie Park, Aberdeen
25 Aug-9 Sep Peebles Art Festival, Borders

September
1 Braemar Gathering, Princess Royal & Duke of Fife Memorial Park, Braemar, Aberdeenshire
2 Blairgowrie Highland Games, Perth & Kinross
7-9 Kirriemuir Festival of Traditional Music & Song, Kirriemuir, Angus
7-9 Borders Festival of Jazz & Blues, Hawick, Borders
8-17 Techfest, Aberdeen
15 September, Battle of Britain Airshow, Leuchars, Fife

October
12-20 Aberdeen Alternative Festival
27th-Oct-4th Nov Scottish International Storytelling Festival, Edinburgh (provisional)

November
23rd-24th Dundee Mountain Film Festival, Bonar Hall, Dundee

ABERDEEN CITY

ABERDEEN

ABERDEEN ART GALLERY

Schoolhill AB10 1FQ
☎ 01224 523700 📠 01224 632133
e-mail: info@aagm.co.uk

One of the city's most popular tourist attractions Aberdeen's splendid art gallery houses an important fine art collection with many 19th and 20th century works.

Times: Open all year ex Xmas & New year. Telephone for opening times.
Fee: Free.
P (500yds) toilets for disabled shop (ex guide dogs)

ABERDEEN MARITIME MUSEUM

Shiprow AB11 5BY
☎ 01224 337700
e-mail: info@aagm.co.uk

The museum is in Provost Ross's House, Aberdeen's oldest building (1593). It highlights the city's maritime history, its oil industry, and its shipbuilding.

Times: Open all year ex Xmas & New year. Telephone for details.
Fee: Free.
P 250yds licensed toilets for disabled shop

CRUICKSHANK BOTANIC GARDEN

University of Aberdeen, St Machur Dr AB24 3UU (enter by gate in Chanonry, in Old Aberdeen)
☎ 01224 272704 📠 01224 272703

Times: Open all year, Mon-Fri 9-4.30; also Sat & Sun, May-Sep 2-5.
P (200metres) (residents only in immediate vicinity) *Details not confirmed for 2001*

PROVOST SKENE'S HOUSE

Guestrow, (off Broad St) AB10 1AS
☎ 01224 641086
e-mail: info@aagm.co.uk

Experience the epitome of style and elegance in this 16th-century townhouse, furnished and decorated in the styles of earlier times. See changing fashions in the Costume Gallery, view an important cycle of religious paintings in the gallery, and relax in the cafe.

Times: Open all year ex Xmas & New Year. Telephone for details.
Fee: Free.
P (200yds) (ex guide dogs)

SATROSPHERE ("HANDS-ON" SCIENCE & TECHNOLOGY CENTRE)

19 Justice Mill Ln AB11 6EQ
☎ 01224 213232 📠 01224 211685
e-mail: satrosphere@ssphere.wintermute.co.uk

Times: Open all year, Mon & Wed-Fri 10-4, Sat 10-5, Sun 1.30-5. School holidays Mon-Sat 10-5, Sun 1.30-5. (Closed 25-26 Dec & 1-2 Jan).
P (charged) toilets for disabled shop *Details not confirmed for 2001*

PETERCULTER

DRUM CASTLE

AB31 5EY (3m W off A93)
☎ 01330 811204 📠 01330 811962
e-mail: aclipson@nts-scot.demon.co.uk

The great 13th-century Square Tower is one of the three oldest tower houses in Scotland and has associations with Robert the Bruce. The handsome mansion, added in 1619, houses a collection of family memorabilia. The grounds contain the 100-acre Old Wood of Drum, a natural oak wood and an old rose garden.

Times: Open mid Apr-May & Sep, daily 1.30-5.30; Jun-Aug, daily 11-5.30; wknds in Oct 1.30-5.30. Last admission 4.45. Grounds open all year 9.30-sunset.
Fee: £4.20 (ch & pen £2.80). Family ticket £11.20. Party.
P (wheelchair available) shop (ex guide dogs)

ABERDEENSHIRE

ALFORD

ALFORD VALLEY RAILWAY

AB33 8AD
☎ 019755 62326 & 62811 📠 019755 63182

Narrow-gauge passenger railway in two sections: Alford-Haughton Park and Haughton Park-Murray Park approximately one mile each. Steam on peak weekends. Diesel traction. Exhibitions.

Times: Open Apr, May & Sep wknds 1-5, Jun-Aug daily from 1pm (30 min service). Party bookings also available at other times.
Fee: £2 (ch £1) return fare.
P (ramps at station platforms) toilets for disabled

BALMORAL

BALMORAL CASTLE GROUNDS & EXHIBITION

AB35 5TB (on A93 between Ballater & Braemar)
☎ 013397 42334 & 42335 📠 013397 42271
e-mail: info@balmoral-castle.co.uk

Queen Victoria and Prince Albert first rented Balmoral Castle in 1848, and Prince Albert bought the property four years later. He commissioned William Smith to build a new castle, which was completed by 1856 and is still the Royal Family's Highland residence. Country walks and pony trekking can be enjoyed, and an exhibition of paintings and other works of art can be seen in the castle ballroom, together with a Travel and Carriage exhibition and a wildlife exhibition.

Times: Open 12 Apr-Jul, daily 10-5.

Fee: £4.50 (ch under 16 £1, pen £3.50)

P (150yds) ☕ ♿ (wheelchairs available & free parking enquire at main gate) toilets for disabled shop ✗ (ex guide dogs/in grounds)

BANCHORY

Banchory Museum

Bridge St AB31 5SX

☎ 01771 622906 📠 01771 622884

e-mail: heritage@aberdeenshire.gov.uk

The museum has displays on Scott Skinner (The 'Strathspey King'), natural history, royal commemorative china, local silver artefacts and a variety of local history displays.

Times: Open Etr-May & Oct, wknds & PH's 11-1 & 2-5; Jun-Sep, Mon-Sat 10-1 & 2-5, Sun 2-6. Details subject to change.

Fee: Free.

P (100yds) (limited) ♿ (toilet in staff area, ask attendant) shop ✗ (ex guide dogs)

BANFF

Banff Museum

High St AB45 1AE

☎ 01771 622906 📠 01771 622884

e-mail: heritage@aberdeenshire.gov.uk

Displays of geology, natural history, local history, Banff silver, arms and armour, and displays relating to James Ferguson (18th-century astronomer) and Thomas Edward (19th-century Banff naturalist).

Times: Open Jun-Sep, Mon-Sat 2-5.15. Dates and times to be confirmed.

Fee: Free.

P (200yds) ♿ shop ✗ (ex guide dogs)

Duff House

AB45 3SX (0.5m S, access south of town)

☎ 01261 818181

The house was designed by William Adam for William Duff, later Earl of Fife. The main block was roofed in 1739, but the planned wings were never built. Although it is incomplete, the house is still considered one of Britain's finest Georgian baroque buildings. Duff House is a Country House Gallery of the National Galleries of Scotland.

Times: Telephone for details of opening dates and times.

Fee: Telephone for details of admission charges.

P ✗ ♿ toilets for disabled shop ✗

CORGARFF

Corgarff Castle

(8m W of Strathdon village)

☎ 01975 651460

The 16th-century tower was beseiged in 1571 and is associated with the Jacobite risings of 1715 and 1745. It later became a military barracks. Its last military use was to control the smuggling of whisky between 1827 and 1831.

Times: Open all year, Apr-Sep, daily 9.30-6.30; Oct-Mar, wknds only. (Closed 25-26 Dec).

Fee: £2.50 (ch £1, concessions £1.90).

P shop

CRATHES

Crathes Castle & Gardens

AB31 3QJ (On A93, 3m E of Banchory)

☎ 01330 844525 📠 01330 844797

This impressive 16th-century castle with magnificent interiors has royal associations dating from 1323. There is a large walled garden and a notable collection of unusual plants, including yew hedges dating from 1702. The grounds contain six nature trails, one suitable for disabled visitors, and an adventure playground.

Times: Open: Castle & Visitor Centre Apr-Sep, daily 10.30-5.30; Oct, daily 10.30-4.30 (last admission 45 mins before closing). Other times by appointment only. Garden & grounds open all year, daily 9.30-sunset. Admission to castle by timed ticket arrangement, (entry may be delayed on busy days). Grounds may be closed at short notice on busy days due to parking limitations.

Fee: Castle, Garden & Grounds £4.80 (ch & concessions £3.20). Grounds £2 (ch £1.30). Family ticket £12.80.

P ✗ licensed ♿ (tape for visually impaired) toilets for disabled shop ✗ (ex guide dogs)

FETTERCAIRN

Fasque

AB30 1DN (0.5m N on B974)

☎ 01561 340569 & 340202

📠 01561 340325 & 340569

Fasque has been the home of the Gladstone family since 1829, and W E Gladstone, four times Prime Minister, lived here from 1830 to 1851. There are impressive state rooms and a handsome, sweeping staircase, as well as extensive servants' quarters. The spacious park has red deer and Soay sheep.

Times: Open May-Sep, daily 11-5.30. (Last admission 5pm). Groups at all other times by arrangement.

Fee: £4 (ch £1.50, concessions £3). Party & guided tours by arrangement.

P ☕ ♿ (wheelchairs available) shop ✗

HUNTLY

Brander Museum

The Square AB54 8AD
☎ 01771 622906 ▯ 01771 622884
e-mail: heritage@aberdeenshire.gov.uk

The museum has displays of local and church history, plus the Anderson Bay and the Sudanese campaigns. Exhibits connected with George MacDonald author and playwright can also be seen.
Times: Open all year, Tue-Sat 10-12 & 2-4.
Fee: Free.
P (25yds) shop (ex guide dogs)

Huntly Castle

AB54 4SH
☎ 01466 793191

The original medieval castle was rebuilt a number of times and destroyed, once by Mary, Queen of Scots. It was rebuilt for the last time in 1602, in palatial style, and is now an impressive ruin, noted for its ornate heraldic decorations. It stands in wooded parkland.
Times: Open all year, Apr-Sep, daily 9.30-6.30; Oct-Mar, Mon-Sat 9.30-4.30, Sun 2-4.30. (Closed Thu pm, Fri in winter & 25-26 Dec).
Fee: £2.50 (ch £1, concessions £1.90).
P shop

INVERURIE

Carnegie Museum

Town House, The Square
☎ 01771 622906 ▯ 01771 622884
e-mail: heritage@aberdeenshire.gov.uk

This fine museum contains displays on local history and archaeology, including Pictish stones, Bronze Age material and the great North of Scotland Railway.
Times: Open all year, Mon-Tue & Thu-Fri 2-5, Sat 10-1 & 2-4. (Closed Wed & Sun)
Fee: Free.
P (50yds) shop (ex guide dogs)

KEMNAY

Castle Fraser

AB51 7LD (off A944, 4m N of Dunecht)
☎ 01330 833463
e-mail: aclipson@nts-scot.demon.co.uk

The massive Z-plan castle was built between 1575 and 1636 and is one of the grandest of the Castles of Mar. The interior was remodelled in 1838 and decoration and furnishings of that period survive in some of the rooms. A formal garden inside the old walled garden, estate trails, a children's play area and a programme of concerts are among the attractions.
Times: Open - Castle Etr-May, daily 1.30-5.30 Jun-Aug, daily, 11-5.30; wknds in Oct 1.30-5.30 (last admission 4.45). Garden all year, daily 9.30-6; grounds all year daily 9.30-sunset.
Fee: Castle, Garden & grounds £4.20 (concessions £2.80). Garden & Grounds £2 (concessions £1.30). Family ticket available.
P shop garden centre (ex guide dogs, certain areas)

KILDRUMMY

Kildrummy Castle

AB54 7XT (10m SW of Alford)
☎ 01975 571331

An important part of Scottish history, at least until it was dismantled in 1717, this fortress was the seat of the Earls of Mar. Now it is a ruined, but splendid, example of a 13th-century castle, with four round towers, hall and chapel all discernible. Some parts of the building, including the Great Gatehouse, are from the 15th and 16th centuries.
Times: Open Apr-Sep, daily 9.30-6.30.
Fee: £2 (ch 75p, concessions £1.50).
P toilets for disabled shop

Kildrummy Castle Gardens

AB33 8RA (on A97)
☎ 019755 71277 & 71203 ▯ 019755 71277

With the picturesque ruin as a backdrop, these beautiful gardens include an alpine garden in an ancient quarry and a water garden. There's a small museum and a children's play area.
Times: Open Apr-Oct, daily 10-5.
Fee: £2 (ch free)
P toilets for disabled shop

MARYCULTER

Storybook Glen

AB12 5FT (5m W of Aberdeen on B9077)
☎ 01224 732941 ▯ 01224 732941

This is a children's fantasy land, where favourite nursery rhyme and fairytale characters are brought to life. Grown-ups can enjoy the nostalgia and also the 20 acres of Deeside country, full of flowers, plants, trees and waterfalls.
Times: Open Mar-Oct, daily 10-6; Nov-Feb, Sat & Sun only 11-4.
Fee: £3.70 (ch £1.85, pen £2.80).
P licensed toilets for disabled shop (ex guide dogs)

METHLICK

Haddo House

AB41 7EQ (off B999, 4m N of Pitmedden)
☎ 01651 851440 ▯ 01651 851888
e-mail: aclipson@nts-scot.demon.co.uk

Haddo House is renowned for its association with the Haddo Choral Society and is the venue for international concerts. It is a splendid Palladian-style mansion built in the 1730s to designs by William Adam. Home to the Earls of Aberdeen, the house was refurbished in the 1880s in the 'Adam Revival' style. The adjoining country park offers beautiful woodland walks.

Times: Open - House mid Apr-Sep, daily 1.30-5.30; wknds in Oct 1.30-5.30 (last admission 4.45). Garden daily, Apr-Oct 9.30-6; Nov-Mar 9.30-4. Country park open all year, daily 9.30-sunset. Occasionally some rooms may be closed to public view due to family occupation.

Fee: £4.20 (ch & pen £2.80). Family ticket £11.20. Party.

P ✕ ♿ (lift to first floor of house & wheelchair) toilets for disabled shop ✗ (ex in grounds guide dogs)

MINTLAW

Aberdeenshire Farming Museum

Aden Country Park AB42 5FQ (1m W of Mintlaw on A950)
☎ 01771 622906 ▯ 01771 622884
e-mail: heritage@aberdeenshire.gov.uk

Housed in 19th-century farm buildings, once part of the estate which now makes up the Aden Country Park. Two centuries of farming history and innovation are illustrated, and the story of the estate is also told. The reconstructed farm of Hareshowe shows how a family in the north-east farmed during the 1950s - access by guided tour only.

Times: Open May-Sep, daily 11-4.30; Apr & Oct, wknds only noon-4.30. Last admission 30 mins before closing. Park open all year, Apr-Sept 7-10, winter 7-7. To be confirmed.

Fee: Free.

P ♿ (garden for partially sighted) toilets for disabled shop ✗ (ex guide dogs)

OLD DEER

Deer Abbey

(10m W of Peterhead)
☎ 0131 668 8800

The remains of the Cistercian Abbey, founded in 1218, include the infirmary, Abbot's House and the southern claustral range. The University Library at Cambridge now houses the famous Book of Deer.

Times: Open at all reasonable times.

Fee: Free.

P ✗

OYNE

Archaeolink

Berryhill AB52 6QP (1m off A96 on B9002)
☎ 01464 851500 ▯ 01464 851544

A stunning audio-visual show, a Myths and Legends Gallery and a whole range of interpretation techniques help visitors to explore what it was like to live 6000 years ago. In addition there are landscaped walkways, and outdoor activity areas including an Iron Age farm, Roman marching camp and Stone Age settlement in the 40-acre park.

Times: Open Apr-Oct, daily 10-5.

Fee: £3.90 (ch 5-16 & concessions £2.35, ch under 5 free). Family ticket £11. Party 10+.

P ✕ licensed ♿ toilets for disabled shop ✗ (ex guide dogs)

PETERHEAD

Arbuthnot Museum & Art Gallery

St Peter St AB42 1QD
☎ 01771 622906 ▯ 01771 622884
e-mail: heritage@aberdeenshire.gov.uk

Specialising in local exhibits, particularly those relating to the fishing industry, this museum also displays Arctic and whaling specimens and a British coin collection. The regular programme of exhibitions changes approximately every six weeks.

Times: Open all year, Mon, Tue & Thu-Sat 10.30-1.30 & 2.30-5, Wed 10.30-1. (Closed Sun and PH). Times to be confirmed.

Fee: Free.

P (150 yds) shop ✗ (ex guide dogs)

PITMEDDEN

Pitmedden Garden

AB41 7PA (1m W of Pitmedden on A920)
☎ 01651 842352 ▯ 01651 843188
e-mail: aclipson@nts.scot.demon.co.uk

The fine 17th-century walled garden, with sundials, pavilions and fountains dotted among the parterres, has been authentically restored, and there is a Museum of Farming Life and a woodland walk.

Times: Open - Garden, Museum of Farming Life & Visitor Centre open May-Sep, daily 10-5.30 last admission 5pm.

Fee: Garden, Museum of Farming Life & Visitor Centre £3.70 (ch & concessions £2.50). Family ticket £9.90.Garden & grounds only £1 honesty box. Party.

P ♿ (2 wheelchairs available) toilets for disabled shop

Tolquhon Castle

(2m NE off B999)
☎ 01651 851286

Now roofless, this late 16th-century quadrangular mansion encloses an early 15th-century tower. There is a fine gatehouse and a splendid courtyard.

Times: Open all year, Apr-Sep, daily 9.30-6.30; Oct-Mar, wknds only. (Closed 25-26 Dec).

Fee: £1.80 (ch 75p, concessions £1.30).

P ♿ toilets for disabled shop ✗

RHYNIE

Leith Hall & Garden

Kennethmont AB54 4NQ (on B9002, 1m W of Kennethmont)

☎ 01464 831216 🖷 01464 831594

e-mail: aclipson@nts.scot.demon.co.uk

Home of the Leith family for over 300 years, the house dates back to 1650, and has a number of Jacobite relics and fine examples of needlework. It is surrounded by charming gardens and extensive grounds.

Times: Open - House Good Fri-Etr Mon & May-Sep, daily 1.30-5.30; wknds in Oct 1.30-5.30. (Last admission 45 mins before closing). Gardens and grounds all year 9.30-sunset.

P ☕ ♿ (parking next to hall, scented garden for the blind) toilets for disabled 🐕 (ex guide dogs) 🏛

STONEHAVEN

Dunnottar Castle

AB39 2TL (2m S of Stonehaven on A92)

☎ 01569 762173

This once-impregnable fortress, now a spectacular ruin, was the site of the successful protection of the Scottish Crown Jewels from the might of Cromwell. A must for anyone who takes Scottish history seriously.

Times: Open all year, summer Mon-Sat 9-6, Sun 2-5; winter Mon-Fri 9-sunset. Last entry 30 minutes before closing. Closed 25-26 Dec/New Year.

Fee: £3.50 (ch 5-15 £1)

P 🐕 (ex on lead)

Tolbooth Museum

Old Pier

☎ 01771 622906 🖷 01771 622884

e-mail: heritage@aberdeenshire.gov.uk

Built in the late 16th centrury as a storehouse for the Earls Marischal at Dunnottar Castle, the building was the Kincardineshire County Tollbooth from 1600-1767. Displays feature local history and fishing.

Times: Open Jun-Sep, Mon & Thu-Sat 10-noon & 2-5; Wed & Sun 2-5. (to be confirmed)

Fee: Free.

P (20yds) ♿ shop 🐕 (ex guide dogs)

TURRIFF

Fyvie Castle

Fyvie AB53 8JS (8m SE of Turriff on A947)

☎ 01651 891266 🖷 01651 891107

e-mail: aclipson@nts.scot.demon.co.uk

This superb castle, founded in the 13th century, has five towers, each built in a different century, and is one of the grandest examples of Scottish Baronial. It contains the finest wheel stair in Scotland, and a 17th-century morning room, lavishly furnished in Edwarian style. The collection of portraits is exceptional, and there are also displays of arms and armour and tapestries.

Times: Open 21 Apr-May & Sep daily 1.30-5.30. Jun-Aug daily 11-5.30, wknds Oct 1.30-5.30. (last admission 4.45). Grounds open all year, daily 9.30-sunset.

Fee: £4.20 (ch & pen £2.80). Family ticket £11.20. Party 20+. Grounds honesty box £1.

P ☕ ♿ (small lift, braille sheets) toilets for disabled shop 🐕 (ex guide dogs) 🏛

WESTHILL

Garlogie Mill Power House Museum

Skene AB32 5FQ (Take Alford road from Aberdeen, at end of Garlogie village turn right into mill grounds)

☎ 01771 622906 🖷 01771 622884

e-mail: heritage@aberdeenshire.gov.uk

A restored building housing the power sources for the now-demolished mill. Notable for the presence of the succession of power generating machinery used, in particular the only beam engine of its type left in situ in Scotland.

Times: Open Thu-Mon 12.30-5, May-Sep. (Dates & times to be confirmed)

Fee: Free.

P ♿ toilets for disabled shop 🐕 (ex guide dogs)

ANGUS

ARBROATH

Arbroath Abbey

☎ 01241 878756

The 'Declaration of Arbroath' - declaring Robert the Bruce as king - was signed at the 12th-century abbey on 6 April 1320. The abbot's house is well preserved, and the church remains are also interesting.

Times: Open all year, Apr-Sep, daily 9.30-6.30; Oct-Mar, Mon-Sat 9.30-4.30, Sun 2-4.30. (Closed Thu pm, Fri in winter & 25-26 Dec).

Fee: £2 (ch 75p, concessions £1.50).

P ♿ 🐕 ▮

Arbroath Museum

Signal Tower, Ladyloan DD11 1PU (on A92)

☎ 01241 875598 🖷 01241 439263

e-mail: signal.tower@angus.gov.uk

Fish and Arbroath Smokies, textiles and engineering feature at this local history museum housed in the 1813 shore station of Stevenson's Bell Rock lighthouse.

Times: Open all year, Mon-Sat 10-5; Jul-Aug, Sun 2-5.(Closed 25-26 Dec & 1-2 Jan).

Fee: Free.

P ♿ (induction loop) shop 🐕 (ex guide dogs)

BARRY

Barry Mill

DD7 7RJ (2m W of Carnoustie)

☎ 01241 856761

This restored 18th-century mill works on a demonstration basis. Records show that the site has been used for milling since the 16th century. Displays highlight the important place the mill held in the community. There is a waymarked walk and picnic area.

Times: Open Apr-Sep, daily 11-5; wknds in Oct, 11-5.
Fee: £2 (concessions £1.30) Family £5.30. Party.
P ♿ ramp from car park to mill toilets for disabled (grounds only)

EDZELL

Edzell Castle

(on B966)
☎ 01356 648631

The 16th-century castle has a remarkable walled garden built in 1604 by Sir David Lindsay. Flower-filled recesses in the walls are alternated with heraldic and symbolic sculptures of a sort not seen elsewhere in Scotland. There are ornamental and border gardens and a garden house.

Times: Open all year, Apr-Sep, daily 9.30-6.30; Oct-Mar, Mon-Sat 9.30-4.30, Sun 2-4.30. (Closed Thu pm, Fri in winter & 25-26 Dec).
Fee: £2.50 (ch £1, concessions £1.90).
P ♿ shop

FORFAR

The Meffan Art Gallery & Museum

20 West High St DD8 1BB
☎ 01307 464123 📠 01307 468451
e-mail: the.meffan@angus.gov.uk

This lively, ever-changing contemporary art gallery and museum are full of surprises. Walk down a cobbled street full of shops, ending up at a witch-burning scene! Carved Pictish stones and a diorama of an archaeological dig complete the vibrant displays.

Times: Open all year. (Closed 25-26 Dec & 1-2 Jan).
Fee: Free.
P (150yds) ♿ toilets for disabled shop (ex guide dogs)

GLAMIS

Angus Folk Museum

Kirkwynd Cottages DD8 1RT (off A94, in Glamis)
☎ 01307 840288 📠 01307 840233

A row of stone-roofed, late 18th-century cottages now houses the splendid Angus Folk Collection of domestic equipment and cottage furniture. Across the wynd, an Angus stone steading houses 'The Life on the Land' exhibition.

Times: Open Jul-Aug, daily 10-5; Apr-Jun & Sep, daily 11-5; Oct, wknds 11-5 (last admission 4.30).
Fee: £2.40 (concessions £1.60). Family ticket £6.40.
P ♿ toilets for disabled (ex guide dogs)

Glamis Castle

DD8 1RJ (5m W of Forfar on A94)
☎ 01307 840393 📠 01307 840733
e-mail: glamis@great-houses-scotland.co.uk

Glamis Castle is the family home of the Earls of Strathmore and Kinghorne and has been a royal residence since 1372. It is the childhood home of HM The Queen Mother, the birthplace of HRH The Princess Margaret and the legendary setting of Shakespeare's play 'Macbeth'. Though the Castle is open to visitors it remains the home of the Strathmore family.

Times: Open Apr-Oct, 10.30-5 (Times may change). Last admission 4.45pm.
Fee: Castle & grounds £6 (ch £3, pen & students £4.50). Family ticket £16.50. Grounds only £3 (ch, pen & students £1.50). Group 20+
P ✕ licensed ♿ toilets for disabled shop (ex in grounds)

KIRRIEMUIR

Barrie's Birthplace

9 Brechin Rd DD8 4BX (on A90/A926 6m NW of Forfar)
☎ 01575 572646
e-mail: aclipson@nts.scot.demon.co.uk

The creator of Peter Pan, Sir James Barrie, was born in Kirriemuir in 1860. The upper floors of No 9 Brechin Road are furnished as they may have been when Barrie lived there, and the adjacent house, No 11, houses an exhibition about him. The wash-house outside was his first 'theatre' and gave him the idea for Wendy's house in 'Peter Pan'.

Times: Open Apr-Sep, Mon-Sat 11-5.30 & Sun 1.30-5.30; wknds in Oct 11-5.30, Sun 1.30-5.30. Last admission 5pm.
Fee: £2 (ch & pen £1.30). Family ticket £5.30. Adult party. Child/school party.
P (100yds) ♿ (stairlift, audio programmes) shop (ex guide dogs)

MONTROSE

House of Dun

DD10 9LQ (on A935, 3m W of Montrose)
☎ 01674 810264 📠 01674 810722
e-mail: aclipson@nts.scot.demon.co.uk

This Georgian house, overlooking the Montrose Basin, was built for Lord Dun in 1730 and is noted for the exuberant plasterwork of the interior. Family portraits, fine furniture and porcelain are on display, and royal mementos connected with a daughter of King William IV and the actress Mrs Jordan, who lived here in the 19th century. There is a walled garden and woodland walks.

contd.

Times: Open mid Apr-Jun & Sep, daily 1.30-5.30; Jul-Aug, daily 11-5.30; wknds in Oct 1.30-5.30. (last admission 5). Garden & grounds, all year daily 9.30-sunset.
Fee: £3.70 (ch & concessions £2.50). Family ticket £9.90. Party. Grounds only £1.
(braille sheets, house wheelchair & stair lift) toilets for disabled shop (ex guide dogs)

Montrose Museum & Art Gallery

Panmure Place DD10 8HE (opposite Montrose Academy)
☎ 01674 673232 & 875598 (pm)
e-mail: montrose.museum@angus.gov.uk

Extensive local collections cover the history of Montrose from prehistoric times, the maritime history of the port, the natural history of Angus, and local art.
Times: Open all year, Mon-Sat 10-5. (Closed 25-26 Dec & 1-2 Jan).
Fee: Free.
shop (ex guide dogs)

ARGYLL & BUTE

ARDUAINE

Arduaine Garden

PA34 4XQ (20m S of Oban, on A816)
☎ 01852 200233 01852 200233

An outstanding 18-acre garden on a promontory bounded by Loch Melfort and the Sound of Jura, climatically favoured by the North Atlantic Drift. It is famous for its rhododendrons and azalea species and other rare trees and shrubs.
Times: Open all year, daily 9.30-sunset.
Fee: £2.40 (concessions £1.60). Party.
toilets for disabled (ex guide dogs)

ARROCHAR

Argyll Forest Park

Forest Enterprise, Ardgartan Visitor Centre G83 7AR (on A83 at the foot of "The Rest and Be Thankful")
☎ 01301 702597 01301 702597
e-mail: fekilmun@forestry.gov.uk

This park extends over a large area of hill ground and forest, noted for its rugged beauty. Numerous forest walks and picnic sites allow exploration; the Arboretum walks and the route between Younger Botanic Gardens and Puck's Glen are particularly lovely. Guided walks and other ranger-led activites are planned; also deer watches and 4X4 safaris.
Times: Open all year.
Fee: Free.
shop

AUCHINDRAIN

Auchindrain Township-Open Air Museum

PA32 8XN (5.5m SW of Inveraray)
☎ 01499 500235

Auchindrain is an original West Highland township of great antiquity, and the only communal tenancy township to have survived on its centuries-old site. The buildings are furnished and equipped to present a fascinating glimpse of Highland life in the last century.
Times: Open Apr-Sep, daily 10-5.
Fee: £3 (ch £1.50, pen £2.50). Family ticket £8.
shop

BARCALDINE

Barcaldine Castle

Benderloch PA37 1SA (9m N of Oban on A828 Oban/Fort William road. Take left turn to Tralee in Benderloch)
☎ 01631 720598 01631 720598
e-mail: barcaldine.castle@tesco.net

The 16th-century home of the Campbells of Barcaldine. The last of the seven castles built by Black Duncan to be held in Campbell hands, and associated with the Appin Murder and Glencoe Massacre. Said to be haunted by the Blue Lady, the castle has secret passages and battle dungeon.
Times: Open Etr wk, Whitsun wk and mid Jun-mid Sep, daily 11-5.30.
Fee: £3.25 (ch £1.70, concessions £2.85)
shop

Oban Seal & Marine Centre

PA37 1SE (10m N of Oban on A828)
☎ 01631 720386 01631 720529

Set in one of Scotland's most picturesque locations, Oban Seal and Marine Centre provides dramatic views of native undersea life including stingrays, seals, octopus and catfish. There are daily talks and feeding demonstrations and during the summer young seals can be viewed prior to their release back into the wild. There is a restaurant, gift shop, children's play park and a nature trail.
Times: Open all year, Feb-Nov, daily 9.30-5. (Jul-Aug 6pm); Dec & Jan, Sat & Sun only.
Fee: £6.50 (ch £3.95, pen & students £4.95). Party 10+.
licensed (assistance available for wheelchairs) toilets for disabled shop (ex guide dogs)

BENMORE

Benmore Botanic Garden

PA23 8QU (7m N of Dunoon on A815)
☎ 01369 706261 & 840599 (shop) 01369 706369

From the formal garden, through the hillside woodlands, follow the paths to a stunning viewpoint with a spectacular outlook across the garden and the Holy Loch to the Firth of Clyde and beyond. Amongst many highlights are the stately conifers, the magnificent avenue of Giant Redwoods, and an extensive magnolia collection.
Times: Open Mar-Oct, daily, 9.30-6. Other times by arrangement.
Fee: £3 (ch £1, concessions £2.50). Family £7. Season ticket and group rates available.
licensed toilets for disabled shop garden centre 

CARNASSARIE CASTLE

Carnassarie Castle

PA31 8RQ (2m N of Kilmartin off A816)
☎ 0131 668 8800

Built in the 16th-century by John Carswell, first Protestant Bishop of the Isles, the castle was taken and partly destroyed in Argyll's rebellion of 1685. It consists of a tower house with a courtyard built around.

Times: Open at all reasonable times.
Fee: Free.

GIGHA ISLAND

Achamore Gardens

PA41 7AD
☎ 01583 505267 & 505254 📠 01583 505244
e-mail: william@isle-of-gigha.co.uk

Wonderful woodland gardens of rhododendrons and azaleas, created by Sir James Horlick, who bought the little island of Gigha in 1944. Many of the plants were brought in laundry baskets from his former home in Berkshire. Sub-tropical plants flourish in the rich soil and virtually frost-free climate, and there is a walled garden for some of the finer specimens.

Times: Open all year, daily.
Fee: £2 (ch £1).

INVERARAY

Bell Tower of All Saints' Church

The Avenue PA32 8YX
☎ 01499 302259

The tower was built in the 1920s and stands at 126ft. It has the world's second heaviest ring of ten bells, installed as a Campbell War Memorial in 1931. An exhibition on campanology is mounted inside and there are visiting bell ringers who give recitals, usually once a month. A splendid view rewards those who climb to the roof.

Times: Open mid May-Sep, daily 10-1 & 2-5.
Fee: £2 (ch & pen 75p). Family ticket £4
P (adjacent to tower) shop (ex guide dogs)

Inveraray Castle

PA32 8XE
☎ 01499 302203 📠 01499 302421
e-mail: enquiries@inveraray-castle.com

The third Duke of Argyll engaged Roger Morris to build the present castle in 1743; in the process the old Burgh of Inveraray was demolished and a new town built nearby. The beautiful interior decoration was commissioned by the 5th Duke; the great armoury hall and staterooms are of particular note.

Times: Open Apr to mid Oct. Apr-Jun, Oct & Sep, Mon-Thu & Sat 10-1 & 2-5.45. Sun 1-5.45; Jul & Aug, Mon-Sat 10-5.45, Sun 1-5.45. Last admission 12.30 & 5.
Fee: £4.50 (ch under 16 £2.50, concessions £3.50) Family ticket £12. School parties. Groups 20+.
shop (ex guide dogs)

Inveraray Jail

Church Sq PA32 8TX (on main Campbeltown Road)
☎ 01499 302381 📠 01499 302195

Enter Inveraray Jail and step back in time. See furnished cells and experience prison sounds and smells. Ask the 'prisoner' how to pick oakum. Turn the heavy handle of an original crank machine, take 40 winks in a hammock or listen to Matron's tales of day-to-day prison life. Visit the magnificent 1820 courtroom and hear trials in progress. Imaginative exhibitions including 'Torture, Death and Damnation' and 'In Prison Today'.

Times: Open all year, Nov-Mar, daily 10-5 (last admisssion 4); Apr-Oct, daily 9.30-6 (last admission 5pm). (Closed 25 Dec & 1 Jan). Extended hours in summer.
Fee: £4.75 (ch £2.30, pen £3). Family ticket £12.95. Party 10+.
P (100 yds) (wheelchair ramp at rear) toilets for disabled shop

KILMARTIN

Dunadd Fort

(1m W of Kilmichael Glassary)
☎ 0131 668 8800

Dunadd was one of the ancient capitals of Dalriada from which the Celtic kingdom of Scotland was formed. Near to this prehistoric hill fort (now little more than an isolated hillock) are carvings of a boar and a footprint; these probably marked the spot where early kings were invested with their royal power.

Times: Open & accessible at all reasonable times.
Fee: Free.

LOCHAWE

Cruachan Power Station

Dalmally PA33 1AN (A85 18m East of Oban)
☎ 01866 822618 📠 01866 822509

Times: Open Etr-end of Nov, daily 9.30-5 (last tour 4.15). Jul-Aug 9.30-6 (last tour 5.15)
toilets for disabled shop (ex guide dogs) *Details not confirmed for 2001*

MINARD

Crarae Gardens

PA32 8YA (10m S of Inveraray on the A83)
☎ 01546 886614 & 886388 📠 01546 886388

Times: Open all year, daily, summer 9-6; winter during daylight hours. Visitor centre, Etr-Oct 10-5.
toilets for disabled shop garden centre *Details not confirmed for 2001*

OBAN

Caithness Glass Visitor Centre

The Waterfront, Railway Pier PA34 4LW (centre of Oban on the pier beside the train station)
☎ 01631 563386 📠 01631 563386

Factory shop selling a wide range of perfect and slightly imperfect paperweights and glassware, as well as ceramics, crystal and jewellery.
Times: Open all year, Factory Shop: Mon-Sat 9-5 (open late Jun-Sep). Etr-Nov Sun 11-5; Nov-Mar 10-5 Mon-Sat.
Fee: Free.
P (100yds) ♿ shop (ex guide dogs)

Dunstaffnage Castle

(3m N on peninsula)
☎ 01631 562465

Now ruined, this four-sided stronghold has a gatehouse, two round towers and walls 10ft thick. It was once the prison of Flora MacDonald.
Times: Open all year, Apr-Sep, daily 9.30-6.30; Oct-Mar, Sat-Wed. (Closed 25-26 Dec).
Fee: £2 (ch 75p, concessions £1.50).
P shop

TAYNUILT

Bonawe Iron Furnace

(0.75m NE off B845)
☎ 01866 822432

The furnace is a restored charcoal blast-furnace for iron-smelting and making cast-iron. It was established in 1753 and worked until 1876. The works exploited the Forest of Lorne to provide charcoal for fuel.
Times: Open Apr-Sep, daily 9.30-6.30.
Fee: £2.50 (ch £1, concessions £1.90).
P ♿ toilets for disabled shop

CITY OF EDINBURGH

BALERNO

Malleny Garden

EH14 7AF (off Lanark Rd (A70))
☎ 0131 449 2283

The delightful gardens are set round a 17th-century house (not open). Shrub roses, a woodland garden, and a group of four clipped yews, survivors of a group planted in 1603, are among its notable features. The National Bonsai Collection for Scotland is also at Malleny.
Times: Open Apr-Oct, daily 9.30-7; Nov-Mar, daily 9.30-4. House not open.
Fee: £1 (honesty box)
P ♿ (ex guide dogs)

EDINBURGH

Brass Rubbing Centre

Trinity Apse, Chalmers Close, High St EH1 1SS
☎ 0131 556 4364 📠 0131 557 3364

Housed in the 15th-century remnant of Trinity Apse, the Centre offers the chance to make your own rubbing from a wide range of replica monumental brasses and Pictish stones. Tuition is available.
Times: Open Apr-Sep, Mon-Sat 10-5 (during Edinburgh Festival Sun 12-5).
Fee: Free. Charge for brass rubbing.
P (250mtrs) shop (ex guide dogs)

City Art Centre

2 Market St EH1 1DE
☎ 0131 529 3993 📠 0131 529 3986
e-mail: enquiries@city-art-centre.demon.uk

The City Art Centre houses the city's permanent fine art collection and stages a constantly changing programme of temporary exhibitions from all parts of the world. It has six floors of display galleries (linked by an escalator).
Times: Open Mon-Sat 10-5 (& Sun 12-5 Jul-Aug).
Fee: Free. Admission charged for some exhibitions.
P (500yds) ♿ (induction loop, lifts, braille signage) toilets for disabled shop (ex guide dogs)

Craigmillar Castle

(2.5m SE, off A68)
☎ 0131 661 4445

Mary Queen of Scots retreated to this 14th-century stronghold after the murder of Rizzio, and the plot to murder Darnley, her second husband, was also hatched here. There are 16th-and 17th-century apartments.
Times: Open all year, Apr-Sep, daily 9.30-6.30; Oct-Mar, Mon-Sat 9.30-4.30. Sun 2-4.30. (Closed Thu pm & Fri in winter & 25-26 Dec).
Fee: £2 (ch 75p, concessions £1.50).
P ♿ toilets for disabled shop

Dean Gallery

73 Belford Rd EH4 3DS
☎ 0131 624 6200 📠 0131 343 3250
e-mail: enquiries@natgalscot.ac.uk

Opened in March 1999, the Dean Gallery provides a home for the Eduardo Paolozzi gift of sculpture and graphic art, the Gallery of Modern Art's renowned Dada and Surrealist collections, a major library and archive centre, along with temporary exhibition space for modern and contemporary art.
Times: Open all year, Mon-Sat 10-5, Sun 2-5. (extended opening during Edinburgh Festival).
P ♿ (lift) toilets for disabled shop (ex guide dogs) *Details not confirmed for 2001*

Dynamic Earth

Holyrood Rd EH8 8AS (on the edge of Holyrood Park, opposite the Palace of Holyrood House)

☎ 0131 550 7800 📠 0131 550 7801

A new attraction that takes you on a fantastic journey of discovery back through time to learn why the Earth has changed. Amazing interactive displays let you see, hear, smell and feel the planet as it was in the past, as it is today and how it will be in the future.

Times: Open Apr-Oct, daily 10-6; Nov-Mar, Wed-Sat 10-5. (Closed 24-25 Dec).

Fee: £6.95 (ch £3.95). Family ticket £21.

P (charged) licensed ♿ (audio guides, large print transcripts) toilets for disabled shop (ex guide dogs)

Edinburgh Castle

☎ 0131 225 9846

This historic stronghold stands on the precipitous crag of Castle Rock. One of the oldest parts is the 11th-century chapel of the saintly Queen Margaret, but most of the present castle evolved later, during its stormy history of seiges and wars, and was altered again in Victorian times. The Scottish crown and other royal regalia are displayed in the Crown Room. Also notable is the Scottish National War Memorial.

Times: Open Apr-Sep, daily 9.30-6; Oct-Mar, daily 9.30-5. Last ticket sold 45 mins before closing time. (Closed 25-26 Dec).

Fee: £7 (ch £2, concessions £5).

P (charged) licensed ♿ (free transport to top of Castle Hill lift) toilets for disabled shop

Edinburgh Zoo

Murrayfield EH12 6TS (3m W of Edinburgh City Centre on A8 towards Glasgow)

☎ 0131 334 9171 📠 0131 316 4050

e-mail: marketing@rzss.org.uk

Scotland's largest wildlife attraction, set in 80 acres of leafy hillside parkland, just ten minutes from the city centre. With over 1,000 animals ranging from the tiny poison arrow frog to massive white rhinos, including many threatened species. See the world's largest penguin pool with underwater viewing, and the Darwin Maze, based on the theme of evolution.

Times: Open all year, Apr-Sep, daily 9-6. (Closes 4.30pm Oct-Mar).

Fee: £7 (ch & disabled £4, student £5, pen £4.50).

P (charged) licensed ♿ (wheelchair loan free, 1 helper free - phone in advance) toilets for disabled shop (ex guide dogs)

General Register House

(East end of Princes St) EH1 3YY

☎ 0131 535 1314 📠 0131 535 1360

e-mail: research@nas.gov.uk

The headquarters of the National Archives of Scotland and repository for public and many private records, designed by Robert Adam and founded in 1774. The historical and legal search rooms are available to researchers, and changing exhibitions are held.

Times: Open Mon-Fri 9-4.45. Exhibitions 10-4. (Closed certain PHs & part of Nov).

Fee: No charge for historical searches or exhibitions.

♿ toilets for disabled shop (ex guide dogs)

Georgian House

7 Charlotte Square EH2 4DR (2 mins walk W end of Princes Street)

☎ 0131 226 3318 📠 0131 226 3318

The house is part of Robert Adam's splendid north side of Charlotte Square, the epitome of Edinburgh New Town architecture. The lower floors of No 7 have been restored in the style of the early 1800s, when the house was new. There also videos of life in the New Town, and this house in particular.

Times: Open Apr-Oct, Mon-Sat 10-5, Sun 2-5. Last admission 4.30pm.

Fee: £4.20 (ch & pen £2.80); (includes audio-visual show). Family ticket £11.20. Party.

P (100 yds) (meters. disabled directly outside) ♿ (induction loop for hard of hearing) shop (ex guide dogs)

Gladstone's Land

477b Lawnmarket EH1 2NT (5 mins walk from Princes Street via Mound)

☎ 0131 226 5856 📠 0131 226 4851

Built in 1620, this six-storey tenement, once a merchant's house, still has its arcaded front - a rare feature now. Visitors can also see unusual tempera paintings on the walls and ceilings. It is furnished as a typical 17th-century merchant's home, complete with ground-floor shop front and goods of the period.

Times: Open Apr-Oct, Mon-Sat 10-5, Sun 2-5. Last admission 4.30pm.

Fee: £3 (ch, pen & students £2). Family ticket £8. Party.

P (440yds) (outside for disabled) ♿ (tours for the blind can be arranged) shop (ex guide dogs)

Huntly House Museum

142 Canongate, Royal Mile EH8 8DD

☎ 0131 529 4143 📠 0131 557 3346

This is one of the best-preserved 16th-century buildings in the Old Town. It was built in 1570 and later became the headquarters of the Incorporation of Hammermen. Now a museum of local history, it has collections of

contd.

silver, glassware, pottery, and other items such as street signs.
Times: Open all year, Mon-Sat 10-5. (During Festival period only, Sun 2-5).
Fee: Free.
P (200yds) ♿ shop (ex guide dogs)

John Knox House
The Netherbow, 43-45 High St EH1 1SR (between The Castle and Holyrood House)
☎ 0131 556 9579 📠 0131 557 5224

John Knox the Reformer is said to have died in the house, which was built by the goldsmith to Mary, Queen of Scots. Renovation work has revealed the original floor in the Oak Room, and a magnificent painted ceiling.
Times: Open all year, Mon-Sat 10-5 & Sun in Aug 12-4. (Closed Xmas).
Fee: £2.25 (ch 75p, under 7's free, concessions £1.75).
♿ (House on 3 levels) toilets for disabled shop (ex guidance dogs)

Lauriston Castle
Cramond Rd South, Davidson's Mains EH4 6AG (NW outskirts of Edinburgh, 1m E of Cramond)
☎ 0131 336 2060 📠 0131 557 3346

The castle is a late 16th-century tower house with 19th-century additions but is most notable as a classic example of the Edwardian age. It has a beautifully preserved Edwardian interior and the feel of a country house, and the spacious grounds are very pleasant.
Times: Open all year by guided tour only; Apr-Oct, 11-1 & 2-5; Nov-Mar, wknds 2-4. (Closed Fri).
Fee: £4 (ch £3). Family ticket £8. Grounds only free.
P ♿ shop (ex guide dogs)

Museum of Childhood
42 High St (Royal Mile) EH1 1TG
☎ 0131 529 4142 📠 0131 558 3103

One of the first museums of its kind, it was reopened in 1986 after major expansion and reorganisation. It has a wonderful collection of toys, games and other belongings of children through the ages, to delight visitors both old and young.
Times: Open all year, Mon-Sat, Jun-Sep 10-6; Oct-May 10-5; (also Sun 12-5 in Jul-Aug).
Fee: Free.
P ♿ (3 floors only) toilets for disabled shop (ex guide dogs)

Museum of Scotland
Chambers St EH1 1JF
☎ 0131 247 4422 📠 0131 220 4819

The museum is a striking new landmark in Edinburgh's historic Old Town. It houses more than 10,000 of the nation's most precious artefacts, as well as everyday objects which throw light on life in Scotland through the ages. Admission to the Royal Museum is included in the admission price to the Museum of Scotland.
Times: Open all year - Mon, Wed-Sat 10-5, Tue 10-8 & Sun 12-5.
Fee: £3 (concessions £1.50 & ch free).
P ✕ licensed ♿ toilets for disabled shop (ex guide dogs)

National Gallery of Scotland
The Mound EH2 2EL (off Princes Street)
☎ 0131 624 6200 📠 0131 343 3250
e-mail: enquiries@natgalscot.ac.uk
Times: Open all year, Mon-Sat 10-5, Sun 2-5; (Extended opening hours during the Edinburgh Festival period).
P (150yds) ♿ (ramps & lift) toilets for disabled shop (ex guide dogs) *Details not confirmed for 2001*

Nelson Monument
Calton Hill
☎ 0131 556 2716 📠 0131 557 3346

Designed in 1807 and erected on Calton Hill, the monument dominates the east end of Princes Street. The views from the top are superb, and every day except Sunday the time ball drops at 1pm as the gun at the castle goes off.
Times: Open all year, Apr-Sep, Mon 1-6 & Tue-Sat 10-6; Oct-Mar Mon-Sat 10-3.
Fee: £2
P shop (ex guide dogs)

Newhaven Heritage Museum
24 Pier Place, Newhaven EH6 4LP
☎ 0131 551 4165 📠 0131 557 3346
Times: Open all year, Mon-Sun 12-5. (Closed 25-26 Dec & 1-2 Jan)
P ♿ shop (ex guide dogs) *Details not confirmed for 2001*

Outlook Tower & Camera Obscura
Castlehill, Royal Mile EH1 2LZ (next to Edinburgh castle)
☎ 0131 226 3709 📠 0131 225 4239

A unique view of Edinburgh - as the lights go down a brilliant moving image of the surrounding city appears. The scene changes as a guide operates the camera's system of revolving lenses and mirrors.
Times: Open all year, daily, Apr-Oct 9.30-6; Nov-Mar 10-5. (Closed 25 Dec). Open later Jul-Aug, phone for details.
Fee: £4.25 (ch £2.10, students £3.40, pen £2.70) Family ticket £12.
P (300mtrs) shop (ex guide dogs)

Palace of Holyroodhouse
EH8 8DX (at east end of Royal Mile)
☎ 0131 556 7371 & 0131 556 1096 📠 0131 557 5256

The Palace grew from the guesthouse of the Abbey of the Holyrood, said to have been founded by David I after a miraculous apparition. Mary, Queen of Scots had her court here from 1561 to 1567, and 'Bonnie' Prince Charlie held levees at the Palace during his occupation of Edinburgh. The Palace is still used by the Royal Family, but can be visited when they are not in residence. There are fine 17th-century state rooms, and the picture gallery is notable for its series of Scottish monarchs.

Times: Open - daily, Apr-Oct 9.30-5.15, Nov-Mar 9.30-3.45. (Closed 25-26 Dec and when Queen in residence).
Fee: £6 (ch 16 £3, pen £4.50). Family ticket £13.50.
P (charged) ♿ (first floor by lift, wheelchair available) toilets for disabled shop (ex guide dogs)

PARLIAMENT HOUSE

Supreme Courts, 2-11 Parliament Square EH1 1RQ (behind St Giles Cathedral)
☎ 0131 225 2595 📠 0131 240 6755

Scotland's independent parliament last sat in 1707, in this 17th-century building hidden behind an 1829 façade, now the seat of the Supreme Law Courts of Scotland. The Parliament Hall has a fine hammerbeam roof. A large stained glass window depicts the inaurguration of the Court of Session in 1540.
Times: Open all year, Mon-Fri 10-4.
Fee: Free.
P (400 mtrs) ✕ ♿ toilets for disabled (ex guide dogs)

THE PEOPLE'S STORY

Canongate Tolbooth, 163 Canongate EH8 8BN
☎ 0131 529 4057 📠 0131 557 3439

The museum, housed in the 16th-century tolbooth, tells the story of the ordinary people of Edinburgh from the late 18th century to the present day. Reconstructions include a prison cell, 1930s pub and 1940s kitchen supported by photographs, displays, sounds and smells.
Times: Open, Mon-Sat 10-5. Also, open Sun during Edinburgh Festival 2-5.
Fee: Free.
P (100yds) meters ♿ (first floor accessible by lift) toilets for disabled shop (ex guide dogs)

ROYAL BOTANIC GARDEN EDINBURGH

20A Inverleith Row EH3 5LR (1m N of city centre)
☎ 0131 552 7171 📠 0131 248 2901
e-mail: press@rbge.org.uk

Established in 1670, on an area the size of a tennis court, the Garden is now over 70 acres of beautifully landscaped grounds. Spectacular features include the Rock Garden, the Pringle Chinese Collection. The amazing glasshouse experience features Britain's palm house and the magnificent woodland gardens and arboretum.
Times: Open all year, daily; Apr-Aug, 9.30-7; Mar & Sep, 9.30-6; Feb & Oct, 9.30-5; Nov-Jan, 9.30-4. (Closed 25 Dec & 1 Jan)
Fee: Free. Donations welcome.
P ✕ licensed ♿ (wheelchairs available at east/west gates) toilets for disabled shop garden centre (ex guide dogs)

ROYAL MUSEUM

Chambers St EH1 1JF
☎ 0131 247 4219 (info) 📠 0131 220 4819

This magnificent museum houses extensive international collections covering the Decorative Arts, Natural History, Science, Technology and Working Life, and Geology. A lively programme of events including temporary exhibitions, films, lectures and concerts takes place throughout the year.
Times: Open all year, Mon-Sat 10-5, Sun 12-5 (Tue late opening till 8). (Closed 25 Dec. Phone for times on 26 Dec/1 Jan).
Fee: Free.
P ✕ licensed ♿ (induction loops) toilets for disabled shop (ex guide dogs)

ROYAL OBSERVATORY VISITOR CENTRE

Blackford Hill EH9 3HJ (3m S of City Centre)
☎ 0131 668 8405 📠 0131 668 8429
e-mail: vis@roe.ac.uk

There are excellent views of Edinburgh from the rooftop here, and one of Scotland's largest telescopes. Play with light, lenses, and prisms, and learn about the history of the Observatory, and its current work in Hawaii and Australia. Public observing on Friday evenings (end Oct to Mar, weather permitting) 7.30pm sharp. Temporary exhibitions throughout the year.
Times: Open all year, Mon-Sat 10-5, Sun noon-5. (Closed 22 Dec-2 Jan).
Fee: £3.50 (ch £2.50, concessions £2). Family ticket £8.
P ✕ ♿ (most floors accesible by lift) toilets for disabled shop (ex guide dogs)

THE ROYAL YACHT BRITANNIA

Ocean Dr, Leith EH6 6JJ
☎ 0131 555 5566 📠 0131 555 8835
e-mail: enquiry@try-britannia.co.uk

The 'Britannia' experience begins in the Visitor Centre which provides an insight into life on board for the Royal Family, officers and yachtsmen, before stepping on board to tour the four main decks. Highlights include the state apartments, engine room, the bridge and the Queen's bedroom.
Times: Open all year 10.30-4.30 with extended hours in summer and some restrictions in winter.
Fee: £7.50 (ch 5-17 £3.75, pen £5.75). Family ticket (2adults & 3 ch) £20.
P ♿ (lift to ship, all areas ramped) toilets for disabled shop (ex guide dogs)

SCOTCH WHISKY HERITAGE CENTRE

354 Castlehill, The Royal Mile EH1 2NE
☎ 0131 220 0441 📠 0131 220 6288
e-mail: enquiry@whisky-heritage.co.uk

This fascinating heritage centre reveals the history of the Scottish Whisky industry. The tour has four main areas: The Making of Scotch Whisky, The Distillery, The Blender's Ghost, and Whisky Barrel Ride. The Whisky Bond Bar has over 220 different whiskies available. There is also a bistro and a shop.
Times: Open daily, 10-5.30 (extended in summer). (Closed 25 Dec).
Fee: £5.50 (ch 5-17 £2.75, concessions £3.85). Family ticket £13.50.
P (.25m) ♿ (braille script) toilets for disabled shop (ex guide dogs)

Scottish National Gallery of Modern Art

Belford Rd EH4 3DR (in the West End of Edinburgh)

☎ 0131 624 6200 Fax 0131 343 3250

e-mail: enquiries@natgalscot.ac.uk

Times: Open all year, Mon-Sat 10-5 & Sun 2-5. (Extended opening hours during the Edinburgh Festival).

P ☕ ♿ (ramps & lift) toilets for disabled shop 🚫 (ex guide dogs) *Details not confirmed for 2001*

Scottish National Portrait Gallery

1 Queen St EH2 1JD (parallel to Princes Street, just behind St Andrew Square)

☎ 0131 624 6200 Fax 0131 558 3691

Times: Open all year, daily, Mon-Sat 10-5, Sun 2-5. Extended opening hours during the Edinburgh Festival. (Closed 25-26 Dec & 1 Jan).

P (200yds) ☕ ♿ (ramps & lift) toilets for disabled shop 🚫 (ex guide dogs) *Details not confirmed for 2001*

Scottish United Services Museum

Edinburgh Castle EH1 2NG (in Edinburgh Castle)

☎ 0131 225 7534 Fax 0131 225 3848

e-mail: alc@nms.ac.uk/scw@nms.ac.uk

Times: Open all year, Apr-Oct, Mon-Sat 9.30-6, Sun 11-6; Nov-Mar, Mon-Sat 9.30-5, Sun 12.30-5

P ♿ toilets for disabled shop 🚫 *Details not confirmed for 2001*

West Register House

Charlotte Square EH2 4ET

☎ 0131 535 1314 Fax 0131 535 1360

e-mail: research@nas.gov.uk

The former church of St George (1811) was designed by Robert Reid in Greco-Roman style and is now the modern record branch of the National Archives of Scotland. It houses the exhibition `The Face of the Country', Scottish rural landscape from historic plans, and the Search Room is available to researchers.

Times: Open Mon-Fri 9-4.45. Exhibitions 10-4. (Closed certain PHs & part of Nov).

Fee: No charge for historical searches or exhibitions.

♿ toilets for disabled 🚫 (ex guide dogs)

The Writers' Museum

Lady Stair's House, Lady Stair's Close, Lawnmarket EH1 2PA

☎ 0131 529 4901 Fax 0131 557 3346

e-mail: enquiries@writersmuseum.demon.co.uk

Situated in the historic Lady Stair's House which dates from 1622, the museum houses various objects associated with Robert Burns, Sir Walter Scott and Robert Louis Stevenson. Temporary exhibitions are planned throughout the year.

Times: Open all year, Mon-Sat 10-5. (During Festival period only, Sun 2-5).

Fee: Free.

P (500mtrs) shop 🚫 (ex guide dogs)

GOGAR

Suntrap Garden Oatridge College Horticultural Centre

43 Gogarbank EH12 9BY (between A8 & A71 W of city bypass)

☎ 0131 339 7283 & 01506 854387

Fax 01506 853373

The three-acre garden comprises many gardens within a single garden, including Italian, Rock, Peat and Woodland. Details from the Principal, Oatridge Agricultural College, Ecclesmachan, Broxburn, West Lothian, EH52 6NH.

Times: Open all year: Apr-Sep, daily 9.30-4.30; Oct-Mar, Mon-Fri 9.30-4.30. (Closed 2 wks Xmas & New Year).

Fee: £1 (accompanied ch and NT members free).

P ♿ toilets for disabled

INGLISTON

Scottish Agricultural Museum

EH28 8NB (at East Gate of Royal Highland Showground)

☎ 0131 333 2674 Fax 0131 333 2674

e-mail: aes@nms.ac.uk

Times: Open Apr-Sep, daily 10-5; Oct-Mar, Mon-Fri. Closed Xmas & New Year.

P ☕ ♿ toilets for disabled shop *Details not confirmed for 2001*

SOUTH QUEENSFERRY

Dalmeny House

EH30 9TQ

☎ 0131 331 1888 Fax 0131 331 1788

e-mail: events@dalmeny.co.uk

This is the home of the Earl and the Countess of Rosebery, whose family have lived here for over 300 years. The house, however, dates from 1815 when it was built in Tudor Gothic style. There is fine French furniture, tapestries and porcelain from the Rothschild Mentmore collection. Early Scottish furniture is also shown, with 18th-century portraits, Rosebery racing mementoes and a display of pictures and items associated with Napoleon.

Times: Open July-Aug, Sun, Mon & Tue 2-5.30. Last admission 4.45. Open other times by arrangement for groups.

Fee: £4 (ch 10-16 £2, pen £3.50, students £3). Party 20+.

P ☕ ♿ toilets for disabled 🚫 (ex guide dogs or in grounds)

Hopetoun House

EH30 9SL (2m W of Forth Road Bridge, off A904)

☎ 0131 331 2451 Fax 0131 319 1885

Times: Open 2 Apr-26 Sep, daily, weekends in Oct 10-5.30 (last admission 4.30).

P ☕ ✕ licensed ♿ toilets for disabled shop *Details not confirmed for 2001*

Inchcolm Abbey
Inchcolm Island (1.5m S of Aberdour Access by ferry Apr-Sep)
☎ 01383 823332

Situated on a green island on the Firth of Forth, the Augustinian abbey was founded in about 1123 by Alexander I. The well-preserved remains include a fine 13th-century octagonal chapter house and a 13th-century wall painting.
Times: Open Apr-Sep, daily 9.30-6.30.
Fee: £2.50 (ch £1, concessions £1.90). Additional charge for ferry trip.
♿ toilets for disabled shop

Queensferry Museum
53 High St EH30 9HP
☎ 0131 331 5545 Fax 0131 557 3346
Times: Open all year, Mon & Thu-Sat 10-1, 2.15-5 (Sun noon-5)
P (0.25m) (mini-induction loop) shop (ex guide dogs) *Details not confirmed for 2001*

City of Glasgow

Glasgow

Burrell Collection
Pollok Country Park G43 1AT (2m S of city centre)
☎ 0141 649 7151 Fax 0141 636 0086

Amassed over some 80 years by Sir William Burrell, who presented it to Glasgow in 1944, the collection is now beautifully housed in a specially designed gallery. Among the 8000 items in the collection are Ancient Egyptian alabaster; bronzes and jade; Japanese prints; Turkish pottery; and European medieval art, including metalwork, sculpture, and illuminated manuscripts. There are also medieval doorways and windows, now set in the walls of mellow sandstone, and paintings and sculptures, ranging from the 15th to the early 20th centuries, with work by Cranach, Bellini, Rembrandt, Millet, Degas, Manet, Cezanne and others.
Times: Open all year, Mon-Sat 10-5, Sun 11-5.
Fee: Free.
P (charged) licensed ♿ (wheelchairs available, tape guides for blind) toilets for disabled shop

Cathedral
Castle St G4 0QZ
☎ 0141 552 6891

The most complete medieval cathedral surviving on the Scottish mainland, founded in the 6th century by St Kentigern, better known as Mungo ('dear one'), Glasgow's patron saint, and dates from the 13th and 14th centuries. The Cathedral was threatened at the time of the Reformation, but the city's trade guilds formed an armed guard to ensure that no damage was done.
Times: Open all year, Apr-Sep, Mon-Sat 9.30-6, Sun 2-5; Oct-Mar, Mon-Sat 9.30-4, Sun 2-4. (Closed 25-26 Dec).
Fee: Free.
♿ shop

Gallery of Modern Art
Queen St G1 3AZ
☎ 0141 229 1996 Fax 0141 204 5316

Set in a magnificent, refurbished neo-classical building the gallery houses Glasgow's collection of post modern and contemporary art over four floors, named after the natural elements of Fire, Earth, Water and Air. There are exhibits by Niki De Saint Phalle, Sebastiao Salgado and Eduard Bersudsky; and the work of Scottish artists Peter Howson, John Bellany, Alan Davie, Adrian Wiszniewski and Alison Watt take pride of place.
Times: Open all year, daily 10-5, Fri & Sun 11-5.
Fee: Free.
P (200yds) licensed ♿ toilets for disabled shop

Glasgow Art Gallery & Museum
Kelvingrove G3 8AG (1m W of city centre)
☎ 0141 287 2699 Fax 0141 287 2690

The collection includes works by Giorgione and Rembrandt, and is especially strong on the French Impressionists, Post-Impressionists, and Scottish artists. Other areas show sculpture, porcelain, silver, and a magnificent display of arms and armour. One section is devoted to the 'Glasgow Style', with furniture by Charles Rennie Mackintosh and others.
Times: Open all year, Mon-Thu 10-5; Fri 11-5; Sat 10-5; Sun 11-5.
Fee: Free.
P licensed ♿ toilets for disabled shop

Glasgow Botanic Gardens
730 Great Western Rd G12 0UE (on A82)
☎ 0141 334 2422 Fax 0141 339 6964

Home of the national collections of Dendrobium Orchids, Begonias and tree ferns. The Victorian Kibble Palace has marble statuary secreted among the plant collections. The Gardens consist of an arboretum, herbaceous borders, a herb garden and unusual vegetables.
Times: Open all year. Gardens open daily 7am-dusk. Kibble Palace & main range of glasshouses Mon-Fri 10-4.45 (4.15 in winter), wknds afternoon only.
Fee: Free.
♿ toilets for disabled (ex in grounds)

Glasgow Science Centre
50 Pacific Quay G51 1EA
☎ 0141 420 5000 Fax 0141 420 5001
e-mail: admin@gsc.org.uk

This ground-breaking new venue comprises three landmark buildings that form a stunning complex on the south bank of the River Clyde. Scotland's first IMAX cinema; the 10,500sq mtr Science Mall which houses exhibits including a planetarium, laboratories and a science theatre; and the Glasgow Tower, a remarkable 100mtr high free-standing structure that gives breathtaking views of the city.
Times: Opening Spring 2001, dates & times to be confirmed.
Fee: Charges to be confirmed.
P ♿ toilets for disabled shop

Greenbank Garden

Flenders Rd, Clarkston G76 8RB (off A726 on southern outskirts of the city)
☎ 0141 639 3281

The spacious, walled woodland gardens are attractively laid out in the grounds of an elegant Georgian house, and best seen between April and October. A wide range of flowers and shrubs are grown, with the idea of helping private gardeners to look at possibilities for their own environment. A greenhouse and garden designed for the disabled gardener also displays specialised tools.

Times: Garden open all year, daily 9.30-sunset. (Closed 25-26 Dec & 1-2 Jan). House open Apr-Oct Sun only 2-4. Shop & Tearoom open Apr-Oct, daily 11-5; Nov-Mar, Sat & Sun 2-4.
Fee: £3 (concessions £2). Family ticket £8. Party.
P ♿ (wheelchairs available) toilets for disabled shop (& plant sales) (ex guide dogs)

House for an Art Lover

10 Dumbreck Rd, Bellahouston Park G41 5BW
☎ 0141 353 4770 0141 353 4771
e-mail: info@houseforanartlover.co.uk

Originally designed by Glasgow's most celebrated architect, Charles Rennie Mackintosh, in 1901, this unusual cultural, corporate and academic resource began construction in 1989 and was completed in 1996. Contains art galleries and rooms that can be hired for conferences.

Times: Open Apr-Sep, Sun-Thu 10-4 & Sat 10-3; Oct-Mar, Sat-Sun 10-4, telephone for wkday opening details.
Fee: £3.50 (ch under 10 free, concessions £2.50).
P ♿ toilets for disabled shop (ex guide dogs)

Hunterian Art Gallery

The University of Glasgow G12 8QQ
☎ 0141 330 5431 0141 330 3618
e-mail: j.e.barrie@museum.gla.ac.uk

Times: Open all year. Main gallery Mon-Sat 9.30-5. Mackintosh House Mon-Sat 9.30-12.30 & 1.30-5. Telephone for PH closures.
P (500 yds) (pay & display) ♿ (lift, wheelchair available) toilets for disabled shop (ex guide dogs) *Details not confirmed for 2001*

Hunterian Museum

The University of Glasgow G12 8QQ (2m W of city centre)
☎ 0141 330 4221 0141 330 3617
e-mail: rpurss@museum.gla.ac.uk

Times: Open all year, Mon-Sat 9.30-5. (Closed certain PH's phone for details).
P (100yds) ♿ (access by lift, prior arrangement) toilets for disabled shop *Details not confirmed for 2001*

Hutchesons' Hall

158 Ingram St G1 1EJ
☎ 0141 552 8391 0141 552 7031

This handsome early 19th-century building was designed by David Hamilton and houses a visitor centre and shop. There is a video about Glasgow's merchant city, and the Hall can be booked for functions. Telephone for details of concerts, recitals, etc.

Times: Open from 21 Apr, Mon-Sat 10-5. (Closed PH's & 24 Dec-6 Jan). Hall on view subject to functions in progress.
Fee: Free.
P (on street) (meters)(outside for disabled) ♿ toilets for disabled shop

McLellan Galleries

270 Sauchiehall St G2 3EH
☎ 0141 331 1854 0141 332 9957

Times: Open Mon-Sat 10-5, Sun 11-5 during exhibitions.
P (500mtrs) ♿ (assistance available) toilets for disabled shop
Details not confirmed for 2001

Museum of Transport

Kelvin Hall, 1 Bunhouse Rd G3 8DP (1.5m W of city centre)
☎ 0141 287 2000 0141 287 2692

Times: Open all year, Mon-Sat 10-5, Sun 11-5.
Fee: Free.
P (charged) ✕ licensed ♿ (assistance available) toilets for disabled shop

People's Palace

Glasgow Green G40 1AT (1m SE of city centre)
☎ 0141 554 0223 0141 550 0892

The refurbished People's Palace houses a museum of the work and leisure of the ordinary people of Glasgow, with exhibits ranging from a 2nd-century Roman bowl to mementoes of the Jacobite risings, football games and boxing matches. There are also numerous banners, posters and other material from Glasgow's days of campaigning for wider voting rights, votes for women and recognition of trade unions. There's also the Winter Gardens where visitors can stroll through lush tropical vegetation.

Times: Phone for details of opening times.
Fee: Free.
P ♿ toilets for disabled shop garden centre

Pollok House

Pollok Country Park G43 1AT (2m S of city centre)
☎ 0141 616 6410 0141 649 0823

Given to the city at the same time as the land for Pollok Country Park, the house contains the remarkable Stirling Maxwell collection of Spanish paintings, including works by El Greco, Murillo and Goya. Silver, ceramics and furniture collected by the family over the generations are also on display.

Times: Open Mon-Sat 10-5; Sun 11-5.
Fee: Admission charged Apr-Oct, free entry during winter
P ♿ shop

Provand's Lordship

3 Castle St G4 0RB (1m E of city centre)
☎ 0141 552 8819 0141 552 4744

The oldest house in Glasgow was built in 1471 for the Lord of Provan as a manse for the Cathedral and St Nicholas Hospital. Carefully restored, the house displays

furniture, pictures and stained-glass panels from various periods in the city's history. There is a fine collection of 17th-century Scottish furniture.
Times: Open all year, Mon-Sat 10-5, Sun 11-5.
Fee: Free.
P shop

Rouken Glen Park
Giffnock G46 7UG
☎ 0141 621 3137 0141 621 3125
Times: Open all year, daily.
P licensed (Radar key) toilets for disabled garden centre
Details not confirmed for 2001

St Mungo Religious Life & Art Museum
2 Castle St G4 0RH (1m NE of city centre)
☎ 0141 553 2557 0141 552 4744

This unique museum, explores the universal themes of life and death and the hereafter through beautiful and evocative art objects associated with different religious faiths. Britain's only authentic Zen garden contributes its own unique sense of peace.
Times: Open all year, Mon-Sat 10-5; Sun 11-5.
Fee: Free.
P (charged) (taped information & lift) toilets for disabled shop

Tenement House
145 Buccleuch St, Garnethill G3 6QN (N of Charing Cross)
☎ 0141 333 0183

This shows an unsung but once-typical side of Glasgow life: it is a first-floor flat, built in 1892, with a parlour, bedroom, kitchen and bathroom, furnished with the original recess beds, kitchen range, sink, and coal bunker, among other articles. The home of Agnes Toward from 1911 to 1965, the flat was bought by an actress who preserved it as a 'time capsule'.
Times: Open Mar-Oct, daily 2-5. (Last admission 30 mins before closing); weekday morning visits by educational & other groups (not to exceed 15), by advance booking only.
Fee: £3 (ch & concession £2). Family ticket £8. Party (not exceeding 15).
P (100yds) (v.restricted, recommend parking in town (braille guide) (ex guide dogs)

University of Glasgow Visitor Centre
University Av G12 8QQ
☎ 0141 330 5511 0141 330 5225

The Visitor Centre is spacious and pleasant, with leaflets, publications and video displays explaining how the university works and its history, plus what courses are available and which university events are open to the public. It forms the starting point for guided tours of the university's historic attractions, including the Hunterian Museum, Memorial Chapel, Bute and Randolph Halls, Professors' Square and Lion and Unicorn Staircase.
Times: Open all year, Mon-Sat 9.30-5. Also May-Sep, Sun 2-5. In summer guided tours of the university start from the Visitor Centre at 11am & 2pm on Wed, Fri & Sat, telephone 0141 330 5511.
Fee: Free. Charge made for tour.
P toilets for disabled shop

CLACKMANNANSHIRE

ALLOA

Alloa Tower
Alloa Park FK10 1PP (on A907)
☎ 01259 211701 01259 218744

Beautifully restored, the tower, completed in 1467, is the only remaining part of the ancestral home of the Earls of Mar. The structure retains rare medieval features, notably the complete timber roof structure and groin vaulting. A superb loan collection of portraits and chattels of the Erskine family includes paintings by Raeburn.
Times: Open Apr-Sep & wknds in Oct, daily 1.30-5.30.
Fee: £2.50 (concessions £1.70). Family ticket £6.70. Party.
P toilets for disabled

ALVA

Mill Trail Visitor Centre
Glentana Mill, West Stirling St FK12 5EN (situated on A91 approx 8m E of Stirling)
☎ 01259 769696 01259 763100
Times: Open all year, Jan-Jun 10-5; Jul-Sep 9-6; Oct-Dec 10-5.
P toilets for disabled shop (ex guide dogs) *Details not confirmed for 2001*

DOLLAR

Castle Campbell
FK14 7PP (10m E of Stirling on A91)
☎ 01259 742408

Traditionally known as the 'Castle of Gloom', the 15th- to 17th-century tower stands in the picturesque Ochil Hills and gives wonderful views. It can be reached by a walk through the magnificent Dollar Glen. Care must be taken in or after rain when the path may be dangerous.
Times: Open all year, Apr-Sep, daily 9.30-6.30; Oct-Mar, Mon-Sat 9.30-4.30, Sun 2-4.30. (Closed Thu pm, Fri in winter & 25-26 Dec).
Fee: £2.50 (ch £1, concessions £1.90).
P shop

DUMFRIES & GALLOWAY

ARDWELL

Ardwell House Gardens
DG9 9LY (10m S of Stranraer, on A716)
☎ 01776 860227 01776 860288

Country house gardens and grounds with flowering shrubs and woodland walks. Plants for sale. House not open to the public.
Times: Open Mar-Oct, 10-5. Walled garden & greenhouses close at 5pm.
Fee: £2 (ch & pen £1).
P garden centre

CAERLAVEROCK

CAERLAVEROCK CASTLE

Glencaple DG1 4RU (8m SE of Dumfries, on B725)
☎ 01387 770244

This ancient seat of the Maxwell family is a splendid medieval stronghold dating back to the 13th century. It has high walls and round towers, with machicolations added in the 15th century.

Times: Open all year, Apr-Sep, daily 9.30-6.30; Oct-Mar, Mon-Sat 9.30-4.30, Sun 2-4.30. (Closed 25-26 Dec).
Fee: £2.50 (ch £1, concessions £1.90)
P ✕ ♿ toilets for disabled shop

WWT CAERLAVEROCK

Eastpark Farm DG1 4RS (9m SE of Dumfries, signposted from A75)
☎ 01387 770200 📠 01387 770539

This internationally important wetland is the winter habitat of the entire Svalbard population of Barnacle Geese which spends the winter on the Solway Firth. Observation facilities include twenty hides, three towers and a heated observatory. A wide variety of other wildlife can be seen, notably the rare Natterjack Toad and a family of Barn Owls which can be observed via a CCTV system.

Times: Open daily 10-5. (Closed 25 Dec).
Fee: £3.50 (ch £2.25 & concessions £2.75). Family ticket £9.25. Party 20+.
P ☕ ♿ toilets for disabled shop

CARDONESS CASTLE

CARDONESS CASTLE

DG7 2EH (1m SW of Gatehouse of Fleet off A75)
☎ 01557 814427

A 15th-century stronghold overlooking the Water of Fleet. It was once the home of the McCullochs of Galloway. The architectural details inside the tower are of very high quality.

Times: Open all year, Apr-Sep, daily 9.30-6.30; Oct-Mar, wknds only. (Closed 25-26 Dec).
Fee: £2 (ch 75p, concessions £1.50).
P shop

CASTLE DOUGLAS

THREAVE CASTLE

(3m W on A75)
☎ 0411 223101

Archibald the Grim built this lonely castle in the late 14th century. It stands on an islet in the River Dee, and is four storeys high with round towers guarding the outer wall. The island is reached by boat.

Times: Open Apr-Sep, daily 9.30-6.30.
Fee: £2 (ch 75p, concessions £1.50). Charge includes ferry trip.
P

THREAVE GARDEN & ESTATE

DG7 1RX (1m W of Castle Douglas off A75)
☎ 01556 502575 📠 01556 502683

The best time to visit is in spring when there is a dazzling display of daffodils. The garden is a delight in all seasons, however, and is home to the National Trust for Scotland's School of Practical Gardening.

Times: Open all year - Garden: daily 9.30-sunset. Walled garden & glasshouses: daily 9.30-5. Visitor centre, Shop & Exhibition: Apr-Oct, daily 9.30-5.30. (Last entry 30 minutes before closing).
Fee: £4 (ch & concessions £2.70).Family ticket £10.70.
P ✕ licensed ♿ (wheelchairs available incl. electric wheelchair) toilets for disabled shop garden centre (ex guide dogs)

CREETOWN

CREETOWN GEM ROCK MUSEUM

Chain Rd DG8 7HJ (follow signs from A75)
☎ 01671 820357 & 820554 📠 01671 820554
e-mail: gem.rock@btinternet.com

A world famous collection of gems, crystals, minerals and fossils. Interactive computer displays provide an opportunity to learn more, and audio visual displays explain how minerals are formed.

Times: Open Etr-Sep, daily 9.30-5.30; Oct-Nov & Mar-Etr, daily 10-4; Dec-Feb, wknds 10-4 or by appointment wkdays. (Closed 23 Dec-Jan).
Fee: £2.90 (ch £1.75, concessions £2.40). Family ticket (2 adults & 3 ch) £7.55. Party.
P ☕ ♿ toilets for disabled shop (ex guide dogs)

DRUMCOLTRAN TOWER

DRUMCOLTRAN TOWER

(7m NE of Dalbeattie)
☎ 0131 668 8800

The 16th-century tower house stands three storeys high and has a simple, functional design.

Times: Open at any reasonable time.
Fee: Free.

DUMFRIES

BURNS HOUSE

Burns St DG1 2PS
☎ 01387 255297 📠 01387 265081
e-mail:
postmaster@dumfriesmuseum.demon.co.uk

It was here that Robert Burns spent the last three years of his short life; he died here in 1796. The house retains much of its 18th-century character and contains many fascinating items connected with the poet. There is the chair in which he wrote his last poems, many original letters and manuscripts, and the famous Kilmarnock and Edinburgh editions of his work.

Times: Open all year, Apr-Sep, Mon-Sat 10-5, Sun 2-5; Oct-Mar Tue-Sat 10-1 & 2-5.
Fee: Free.
P (100yds) shop

Burns Mausoleum
St Michael's Churchyard
☎ 01387 255297 📠 01387 265081
e-mail:
postmaster@dumfriesmuseum.demon.co.uk

The mausoleum is in the form of a Greek temple, and contains the tombs of Robert Burns, his wife Jean Armour, and their five sons. A sculptured group shows the Muse of Poetry flinging her cloak over Burns at the plough.
Times: Unrestricted access.
Fee: Free.
P (100yds) ♿ (visitors with mobility difficulties tel 01387 255297)

Dumfries Museum & Camera Obscura
The Observatory DG2 7SW
☎ 01387 253374 📠 01387 265081
e-mail:
postmaster@dumfriesmuseum.demon.co.uk

Situated in and around the 18th-century windmill tower, the museum's collections were started over 150 years ago and exhibitions trace the history of the people and landscape of Dumfries and Galloway. The Camera Obscura is to be found on the top floor of the windmill tower.
Times: Open all year, Apr-Sep Mon-Sat 10-5, Sun, 2-5; Oct-Mar, Tue-Sat 10-1 & 2-5.
Fee: Free except Camera Obscura £1.50 (concessions 75p)
P ♿ (camera obscura not accessible, parking available) toilets for disabled shop

Old Bridge House Museum
Mill Rd DG2 7BE
☎ 01387 256904 📠 01387 265081
e-mail:
postmaster@dumfriesmuseum.demon.co.uk

The Old Bridge House was built in 1660, and is the oldest house in Dumfries. A museum of everyday life in the town, it has an early 20th-century dentist's surgery, a Victorian nursery and kitchens of the 1850s and 1900s.
Times: Open Apr-Sep, Mon-Sat 10-5 & Sun 2-5.
Fee: Free.
P ♿ shop

Robert Burns Centre
Mill Rd DG2 7BE
☎ 01387 264808 📠 01387 265081
e-mail:
postmaster@dumfriesmuseum.demon.co.uk

This award-winning centre explores the connections between Robert Burns and the town of Dumfries. Situated in the town's 18th-century watermill, the centre tells the story of Burns' last years spent in the busy streets and lively atmosphere of Dumfries in the 1790s. In the evening the centre shows feature films in the Film Theatre.
Times: Open all year, Apr-Sep, daily 10-8 (Sun 2-5); Oct-Mar, Tue-Sat 10-1 & 2-5.
Fee: Free ex audio-visual theatre £1.50 (concessions 75p).
P ☕ ♿ (induction loop hearing system in auditorium) toilets for disabled shop

DUNDRENNAN

Dundrennan Abbey
(6.5m SE of Kirkcudbright, on A711)
☎ 01557 500262

The now ruined abbey was founded for the Cistercians. The east end of the church and the chapter house are of exceptional architectural quality. Mary, Queen of Scots is thought to have spent her last night in Scotland here on 15 May 1568, before seeking shelter in England, where she was imprisoned and eventually executed.
Times: Open all year, Apr-Sep, daily 9.30-6.30; Oct-Mar, wknds only. (Closed 25-26 Dec).
Fee: £1.80 (ch 75p, concessions £1.30).
P ♿

GLENLUCE

Glenluce Abbey
(2m NW, off A75)
☎ 01581 300541

The abbey was founded for the Cistercians in 1192 by Roland, Earl of Galloway. The ruins include a vaulted chapter house, and stand in a beautiful setting.
Times: Open all year, Apr-Sep, daily 9.30-6.30; Oct-Mar, wknds only. (Closed 25-26 Dec).
Fee: £1.80 (ch 75p, concessions £1.30).
P ☕ ♿

KIRKCUDBRIGHT

Broughton House & Garden
12 High St DG6 4JX (off A711/A755)
☎ 01557 330437
e-mail: aclipson@nts.scot.demon.co.uk

An 18th-century house where Edward A Hornel, one of the 'Glasgow Boys' group of artists, lived and worked from 1901-1933. It features a collection of his work, an extensive library of local history, including rare editions of Burns' works, and a Japanese-style garden that he created.
Times: Open daily, Apr-Jun & Sep-Oct 1-5.30; Jul & Aug, 11-5.30 (last admission 4.45pm).
Fee: £2.40 (concessions £1.60). Family ticket £6.40. Party.
P (on street) (limited space) (ex guide dogs)

MacLellan's Castle
(on A711)
☎ 01557 331856

This handsome structure has been a ruin since the mid-18th-century. It was once an imposing castellated mansion, elaborately planned with fine architectural detail. Something of its 16th-century grandeur still remains.
Times: Open Apr-Sep, daily 9.30-6.30; (Closed 25-26 Dec).
Fee: £1.80 (ch 75p, concessions £1.30).
P shop

Stewartry Museum
Saint Mary St DG6 4AQ (from A711 through town, pass parish church, museum approx 200mtrs on right)
☎ 01557 331643 📠 01557 330005
e-mail: DavidD@dumgal.gov.uk

A large and varied collection of archaeological, social history and natural history exhibits relating to the Stewartry district.
Times: Open Mar-Oct, Mon-Sat 11-4 (5pm in May, Jun & Sep; 6pm in Jun-Sep also Sun 2-5); Nov-Feb, Mon-Sat 11-4.
Fee: £1.50 (ch free with adult, concessions £1).
P (outside) ♿ shop 🐕

Tolbooth Art Centre
High St DG6 4JL (From A711, through town pass parish church & Stewarty Museum, take 1st right into High St)
☎ 01557 331556 📠 01557 331643
e-mail: DavidD@dumgal.gov.uk

Dating from 1629, the Tolbooth was converted into an art centre and provides an interpretive introduction to the Kirkcudbright artists's colony, which flourished in the town from the 1880's. It also provides studio and exhibition space for contemporary local and visiting artists. There is a programe of exhibitions from March to October.
Times: Open Mar & Oct, Mon-Sat 11-4; May-Jun & Sept, Mon-Sat 10-6; Nov-Feb, Mon-Sat 11-4. Open Sun Jun-Sep 2-5.
Fee: £1.50 (ch free, concessions £1)
P (on street parking) ☕ ♿ (lift) toilets for disabled shop 🐕

MONIAIVE

Maxwelton House Trust
DG3 4DX (A76 from Dumfries to Thornhill, after 2m take B729 to Monavie, 11m along road to Maxwelton House)
☎ 01848 200385
Times: Open last Sun in May-Sep, Sun-Fri 11-5. Etr-May by booking only.
P shop *Details not confirmed for 2001*

NEW ABBEY

New Abbey Corn Mill
(7m S of Dumfries on A710)
☎ 01387 850260

Built in the late 18th century, this water-driven corn mill is still in working order, and regular demonstrations are held.
Times: Open all year, Apr-Sep, daily 9.30-6.30; Oct-Mar, Mon-Sat 9.30-4.30, Sun 2-4.30. (Closed Thu pm & Fri in winter & 25-26 Dec).
Fee: £2.50 (ch £1, concessions £1.90).
P (100yds) shop 🐕

Sweetheart Abbey
DG2 8BU (on A710)
☎ 01387 850397

Lady Devorgilla of Galloway founded Balliol College, Oxford in memory of her husband John Balliol; she also founded this abbey in his memory in 1273. When she died in 1289 she was buried in front of the high altar with the heart of her husband resting on her bosom; hence the name 'Sweetheart Abbey'. The abbey features an unusual precinct wall of enormous boulders.
Times: Open all year, Apr-Sep, daily 9.30-6.30; Oct-Mar, Mon-Sat 9.30-4.30, Sun 2-4.30. (Closed Thu pm & Fri in winter & 25-26 Dec).
Fee: £1.50 (ch 50p, concessions £1.10).
P ♿ (with assistance) 🐕

PALNACKIE

Orchardton Tower
(6m SE of Castle Douglas)
☎ 0131 668 8800

John Cairns built this rare example of a circular tower in the late 15th century.
Times: Open all reasonable times, on application to key keeper. (Closed 25-26 Dec).
Fee: Free.
P 🐕

PORT LOGAN

Logan Botanic Garden
DG9 9ND (on B7065)
☎ 01776 860231 📠 01776 860333

Logan's exceptionally mild climate allows a colourful array of tender plants to thrive out-of-doors. Amongst the many highlights are tree ferns, cabbage palms, unusual shrubs, climbers and tender perennials found within the setting of the walled, water, terrace and woodland gardens.
Times: Open Mar-Oct, daily 9.30-6.
Fee: £3 (ch £1, concessions £2.50). Family ticket £7.
P ✕ licensed ♿ (wheelchairs available for loan) toilets for disabled shop garden centre 🐕 (ex guide dogs)

RUTHWELL

Ruthwell Cross
(off B724)
☎ 0131 668 8800

Now in a specially built apse in the parish church, the carved cross dates from the 7th or 8th centuries. Two faces show scenes from the Life of Christ; the others show scroll work, and parts of an ancient poem in Runic characters. It was broken up in the 18th century, but pieced together by a 19th-century minister.
Times: Open all reasonable times. Key from Key Keeper, Kirkyett Cottage, Ruthwell.
Fee: Free.
P 🐕

Savings Banks Museum
DG1 4NN (off B724, 10m E of Dumfries & 6m W of Annan)
☎ 01387 870640
e-mail: tsbmuseum@btinternet.com

Housed in the building where Savings Banks first began, the museum traces their growth and development from 1810 up to the present day. The museum also traces the life of Dr Henry Duncan, father of savings banks, and restorer of the Ruthwell Cross. Multi-lingual leaflets available.

Times: Open all year, daily (ex Sun & Mon Oct-Etr), 10-1 & 2-5.

Fee: Free.

P ♿ (touch facilities for blind, guide available) (ex guide dogs)

SANQUHAR

Sanquhar Tolbooth Museum

High St DG4 6BN

☎ 01659 250186 📠 01387 265081

e-mail: postmaster@dumfriesmuseum.demon.co.uk

Housed in the town's fine 18th-century tolbooth, the museum tells the story of the mines and miners of the area, its earliest inhabitants, native and Roman, the history and customs of the Royal Burgh of Sanquhar and local traditions.

Times: Open Apr-Sep, Tue-Sat 10-1 & 2-5, Sun 2-5.

Fee: Free.

P shop

STRANRAER

Castle Kennedy Gardens

Stair Estates DG9 8BX (5m E on A75)

☎ 01776 702024 📠 01776 706248

Situated on a peninsula between two lochs, the gardens around the Old Castle were first laid out in the early 18th century. Noted for their rhododendrons and azaleas (at their best May and early Jun) and walled kitchen garden with fine herbaceous borders (best in Aug and Sep). The gardens contain many avenues and walks amid beautiful scenery.

Times: Open Apr-Sep, daily 10-5.

Fee: £3 (ch 15 £1, pen £2). Party 20+.

P ♿ toilets for disabled shop garden centre

THORNHILL

Drumlanrig Castle

DG3 4AQ (4m N of Thornhill off A76)

☎ 01848 330248 📠 01848 331682

e-mail: bre@drumlanrigcastle.org.uk

This unusual pink sandstone castle was built in the late 17th century in Renaissance style. It contains a collection of paintings by Rembrandt, Da Vinci, Holbein, and many others. There is also French furniture, as well as silver and relics of Bonnie Prince Charlie. The old stable block has a craft centre with resident craft workers, and the grounds offer extensive gardens, working forge and woodland walks. For details of special events phone 01848 331555.

Times: Open early May-late Aug, Castle open seven days a week. Guided tours and restricted route may operate at various times, please verify before visiting.

Fee: £6 (ch £2 & pen £4); grounds only £3. Party 20+

P ✕ licensed ♿ (lift for wheelchair users) toilets for disabled shop (ex in park on lead)

TONGLAND

Galloway Hydros Visitor Centre

Tongland Power Station DG6 4LT (on A711 2m N of Kirkcudbright)

☎ 01557 330114

Times: Open May-Sep, Mon-Sat, and Sundays during August.

(only Fish Pass is not accessible) *Details not confirmed for 2001*

WANLOCKHEAD

Museum of Lead Mining

ML12 6UT (on B797 at N end of Mennock Pass).

☎ 01659 74387 01659 74481

e-mail: pd86@dial.pipex.com

Wanlockhead is Scotland's highest village, set in the beautiful Lowther Hills. Visitors can see miners' cottages, the miners' library as well as the 18th-century lead mine, and there is a Gold Panning Centre.

Times: Open Apr-Oct, daily 10-4.30 (last mine tour 4).

Fee: £3.95 (ch £2.50, concessions £2.70). Family ticket £9.80 (2 adults & 3 children)

toilets for disabled shop (ex guide dogs)

WHITHORN

Whithorn-Cradle of Christianity

45-47 George St DG8 8NS (on main street in the centre of town)

☎ 01988 500508

e-mail: butterworth@whithornl.freeserve.co.uk

The Whithorn Dig is the site of the first Christian settlement in Scotland - the Candida Casa of St Ninian. Friendly guides explain the excavation, and there's a museum of Early Christian stones.

Times: Open daily, Apr-Oct 10.30-5.

Fee: £2.70 (ch, pen & UB40's £1.50). Family ticket £7.50. Season ticket. Party.

P (one short staircase with 'stairmatic') toilets for disabled shop

Whithorn Priory

(on A746)

☎ 01988 500508

The first Christian church in Scotland was founded here by St Ninian in 397AD, but the present ruins date from the 12th century. The ruins are sparse but there is a notable Norman door, the Latinus stone of the 5th century and other early Christian monuments.

Times: Open Etr-Oct, daily 10.30-5.

Fee: Admission charged, please telephone for details.

DUNDEE CITY

DUNDEE

Barrack Street Natural History Museum

Barrack St DD1 1PG

☎ 01382 432067 01382 432070

Times: Open all year, Mon 11-5, Tue-Sat 10-5. (Closed 25-26 Dec & 1-3 Jan).

P (NCP 500 yds) shop (ex guide dogs) *Details not confirmed for 2001*

Broughty Castle Museum

Broughty Ferry DD5 2BE (4m E, off A930)

☎ 01382 436916

Times: Open all year, Mon 11-1 & 2-5, Tue-Thu 10-1 & 2-5. (Sun 2-5 Jul-Sep only). (Closed 25-26 Dec & 1-3 Jan).

shop (ex guide dogs) *Details not confirmed for 2001*

Camperdown Country Park

DD2 4TF (A90 to Dundee and turn onto A923 Coupar Angus rd, turn left at 1st rdbt to Camperdown Country Park)

☎ 01382 434296 01382 433211

Times: Open all year - park. Wildlife Centre - daily, Apr-Sep 10-3.45, Oct-Mar 10-2.45.

(ramps) toilets for disabled shop (ex guide dogs) *Details not confirmed for 2001*

Discovery Point & RRS Discovery

Discovery Quay DD1 4XA (in Dundee follow signs for Historic Ships)

☎ 01382 201245 01382 25891

Discovery Point is the home of *RRS Discovery*, Captain Scott's famous Antarctic ship. Spectacular lighting, graphics and special effects re-create key moments in the *Discovery* story. The restored bridge gives a captain's view over the ship and the River Tay. Learn what happened to the ship after the expedition, during the First World War and the Russian Revolution, and also her involvement in the first survey of the migration patterns of whales.

Times: Open all year, Apr-Oct, Mon-Sat 10-5, Sun 11-5; Nov-Mar, Mon-Sat 10-4, Sun 11-4. Last entry 30 mins before closing. (Closed 25 Dec & 1-2 Jan).

Fee: £5.50 (ch £4.15, pen & concessions £4.15). Family ticket (2 adults & 2 ch) £16.50. Party. Joint ticket with Verdant Works.

(charged) (in-house wheelchairs & lifts, parking, ramps onto ship) toilets for disabled shop (ex guide dogs)

HM Frigate Unicorn

Victory Dock DD1 3JA

01382 200900 & 200893 01382 200923

e-mail: mail@frigateunicorn.org

The *Unicorn* is the oldest British-built warship afloat, and Scotland's only example of a wooden warship. Today she houses a museum of life in the Royal Navy during the days of sail, with guns, models and displays.

Times: Open all year, 25 Mar-Oct, daily 10-5.

Fee: £3.50 (concessions £2.50). Family ticket £7.50-£9.50. Groups 10+

shop (no exceptions)

McManus Galleries

Albert Square DD1 1DA (off A85)

01382 432020 01382 432052

Times: Open all year, Mon 11-5, Tue-Sat 10-5. (Closed 25-26 Dec & 1-3 Jan).

(100 yds) (wheelchair available & high arm chairs, audio loop) toilets for disabled shop (ex guide dogs) *Details not confirmed for 2001*

Mills Observatory

Balgay Park, Glamis Rd DD2 2UB

01382 435846 01382 435962

Times: Open all year, Apr-Sep, Tue-Fri 11-5, Sat 2-5; Oct-Mar, Tue-Fri 4-10, Sat 2-5. (Closed 25-26 Dec & 1-3 Jan).

shop (ex guide dogs) *Details not confirmed for 2001*

Verdant Works

West Henderson's Wynd DD2 5BT (follow brown tourist signs)

01382 225282 01382 221612

e-mail: info@dundeeheritage.sol.co.uk

Dating from 1830, this old Jute Mill covers 50,000 sq ft and has been restored as a living museum of Dundee and Tayside's textile history and award winning European Industrial Museum. Phase I explains what jute is, where it comes from and why Dundee became the centre of its production. Working machinery illustrates the production process from raw jute to woven cloth. Phase II deals with the uses of jute and its effects on Dundee's social history.

Times: Open Apr-Oct, Mon-Sat 10-5, Sun 11-5. Nov-Mar, Mon-Sat 10-4, Sun 11-4. Last entry 30 mins before closing. (Closed 25 Dec & 1-2 Jan).

Fee: £5.50 (ch, pen & concessions £4.15). Family ticket (2 adults & 2 ch) £16.50.

(wheelchairs, induction loops) toilets for disabled shop

EAST AYRSHIRE

GALSTON

Loudoun Castle Theme Park

KA4 8PE (signposted from A74(M), from A77 and from A71)

01563 822296 01563 822408

e-mail: loudouncastle@btinternet.com

Castle ruins, woodland and country walks at Scotland's largest theme park, with roller coasters, go karts, log flume and Britain's largest carousel. Many other attractions, including the recently opened 'Drop Zone' a 140ft drop through the trees, and King Rory's Animal Kingdom.

Times: Open Apr-Aug & following days in Sep 3, 9-10, 16-17, 22-25, 29-30 & Oct 1-2, 7-8, 14-22.

Fee: Height: over 1.25m £10, over 0.90m £9, under 0.90m free (pen £5). Family ticket £25 (2 adults & 2 ch).

licensed toilets for disabled shop (ex guide dogs)

KILMARNOCK

Dean Castle Country Park

Dean Rd KA3 1XB

01563 522702 01563 572552

This fine castle has a 14th-century fortified keep and 15th-century palace. Inside there is an outstanding collection of medieval arms and armour, musical instruments and a display of Burns' manuscripts. The castle is set in a beautiful wooded country park with rivers, gardens, woodlands, adventure playground, children's corner and aviaries. A full programme of events takes place from Apr-Sep.

Times: Open: Country Park all year, dawn to dusk. Dean Castle daily noon-5. Visitor centre & Tearoom 11-5(summer), 11-4(winter). Rare Breeds centre 1-5(summer), 1-4(winter).

(disabled garden, car parks, ramps & level paths) toilets for disabled shop (ex guide dogs inside) *Details not confirmed for 2001*

Dick Institute Museum & Art Gallery

Elmbank Ave KA1 3BU

01563 526401 & 555333 01563 573333

Two museum wings exhibiting geology, natural history, engineering, archaeology and local history, and two art galleries with an important permanent collection of paintings and touring art exhibitions.

Times: Open all year, Gallery & Museum: Mon-Tue, Thu-Fri 10-8, Wed & Sat 10-5. (Closed Sun & PH's).

Fee: Free except for special exhibitions when a charge may be made.

(wheelchair available) toilets for disabled shop (ex guide dogs)

EAST DUNBARTONSHIRE

BEARSDEN

ROMAN BATH-HOUSE
Roman Rd G61 2SG
☎ 0131 668 8800

Considered to be the best surviving visible Roman building in Scotland, the bath-house was discovered in 1973 during excavations for a construction site. It was originally built for use by the Roman garrison at Bearsden Fort, which is part of the Antonine Wall defences.
Times: Open all reasonable times.
Fee: Free.

MILNGAVIE

MUGDOCK COUNTRY PARK
Craigallion Rd G62 8EL (N of Glasgow on A81, signed)
☎ 0141 956 6100 0141 956 5624
e-mail: lain@mcp.ndo.co.uk

This country park incorporates the remains of Mugdock and Craigend castles, set in beautiful landscapes as well as an exhibition centre, craft shops, orienteering course and many walks.
Times: Open all year, daily.
Fee: Free.
shop garden centre

EAST LOTHIAN

ABERLADY

MYRETON MOTOR MUSEUM
EH32 0PZ (1.5m from A198, 2m from A1)
☎ 01875 870288

Opened in 1966 in converted farm buildings, Myreton has a large collection of cars, motorcycles, commercial and military vehicles.
Times: Open all year, daily 10-6 (summer); 10-5 (winter). (Closed 25 Dec & 1 Jan).
Fee: £3 (ch 16 £1).
shop (ex guide dogs)

DIRLETON

DIRLETON CASTLE
EH39 5ER (on A198)
☎ 01620 850330

The oldest part of this romantic castle dates from the 13th century. It was besieged by Edward I in 1298, rebuilt and expanded, and then destroyed in 1650. Now the sandstone ruins have a beautiful mellow quality. Within the castle grounds is a garden established in the 16th century, with ancient yews and hedges around a bowling green.
Times: Open all year, Apr-Sep, daily 9.30-6.30; Oct-Mar, Mon-Sat 9.30-4.30, Sun 2-4.30. (Closed 25-26 Dec).
Fee: £2.50 (ch £1, concessions £1.90).
shop

EAST FORTUNE

MUSEUM OF FLIGHT
East Fortune Airfield EH39 5LF (Signposted from A1 near Haddington)
☎ 01620 880308 01620 880355
e-mail: aes@nms.ac.uk

Situated on 63 acres of one of Britain's best preserved wartime airfields, the museum has three hangars, with more than 50 aeroplanes, plus engines, rockets and memorabilia. Items on display include two Spitfires, a Vulcan bomber and Britain's oldest surviving aeroplane, built in 1896 and more recent exhibits include a phantom jet fighter and harrier jump-jet. Special event for 2001 : Festival of Flight (14-15 July).
Times: Open daily, 10.30-5. (Closed 25 & 31 Dec, 1 Jan).
Fee: £3 (ch free, concessions £1.50). Season ticket available.
toilets for disabled shop

EAST LINTON

HAILES CASTLE
(1m SW on unclass rd)
☎ 0131 668 8800

The castle was a fortified manor house of the Gourlays and Hepburns. Bothwell brought Mary, Queen of Scots here when they were fleeing from Borthwick Castle. The substantial ruins include a 16th-century chapel.
Times: Open at all reasonable times.
Fee: Free.

PRESTON MILL & PHANTASSIE DOOCOT
EH40 3DS (signposted from A1)
☎ 01620 860426

This attractive mill, with conical, pantiled roof, is the oldest working water-driven meal mill to survive in Scotland, and was last used commercially in 1957. Nearby is the charming Phantassie Doocot (dovecote), built for 500 birds.
Times: Open Apr-Sep, Mon-Sat 11-1 & 2-5, Sun 1.30-5; Oct, wknds 1.30-4. Last entry 20 mins before closing morning and afternoon.
Fee: £2 (ch & concessions £1.30). Family ticket £5.30. Party.
toilets for disabled shop (ex guide dogs)

INVERESK

INVERESK LODGE GARDEN
EH21 7TE (A6124 S of Musselburgh)
☎ 01721 722502

This charming terraced garden, set in the historic village of Inveresk, specialises in plants, shrubs and roses suitable for growing on small plots. The 17th-century house makes an elegant backdrop.
Times: Open all year, Apr-Oct, Mon-Fri 10-4.30, Sat-Sun 2-5. (Closed Sat Nov-Mar).
Fee: £1 (honesty box).
(ex guide dogs)

NORTH BERWICK

Scottish Seabird Centre

The Harbour EH39 4SS
☎ 01620 890202 📠 01620 890222
e-mail: info@seabird.org

Get close to nature with a visit to Berwick, Scotland's Seabird town. Explore the fascinating world of seabirds using the latest remote controlled technology to view nesting colonies of many different species of seabird, including puffins and gannets.

Times: Open - Summer, daily 10-6; Winter, daily 10-4.
Fee: £4.50 (concessions £3.20). Family ticket (4 persons) £12.50.
P ☕ ✕ ♿ toilets for disabled shop 🐕 (ex guide dogs)

Tantallon Castle

EH39 5PN (3m E, off A198)
☎ 01620 892727

A famous 14th-century stronghold of the Douglases facing towards the lonely Bass Rock from the rocky Firth of Forth shore. Nearby 16th and 17th-century earthworks.

Times: Open all year, Apr-Sep, daily 9.30-6.30; Oct-Mar, Mon-Sat 9.30-4.30, Sun 2-4.30. (Closed Thu pm & Fri in winter & 25-26 Dec).
Fee: £2.50 (ch £1, concessions £1.90).
P shop 🐕

PRESTONPANS

Prestongrange Museum

Prestongrange (on B1348)
☎ 0131 653 2904 📠 01620 828201
e-mail: elms@elothian-museums.demon.co.uk

The oldest documented coal mining site in Britain, with 800 years of history, this museum shows a Cornish Beam Engine and on-site evidence of associated industries such as brickmaking and pottery, plus a 16th-century customs port. Special Events - weekend events for families and children in July/August.

Times: Open end Mar-mid Oct, daily 11-4. Last tour 3pm.
Fee: Free.
P ☕ ♿ toilets for disabled shop 🐕 (ex guide dogs)

FALKIRK

BIRKHILL

The Birkhill Fireclay Mine

(via A706 from Linlithgow, A904 from Grangemouth, coaches via A706)
☎ 01506 825855 📠 01506 828766
e-mail: mine@srps.org.uk

Tour guides will meet you at Birkhill Station and lead you down into the ancient woodland of the beautiful Avon Gorge, and then into the caverns of the Birkhill Fireclay mine. See how the clay was worked, what it was used for and find the 300-million-year-old fossils in the roof of the mine.

Times: Open Apr-22 Oct wknds only; Jul-27 Aug Tue-Sun. BH Mon's, 1 & 29 May.
Fee: Mine & Train £6.50 (ch £3.50, pen £4.80) Family ticket £16.50. Train only £4 (ch £2, pen £3) Family ticket £10. Mine only £3 (ch £1.70, pen £2.20) Family ticket £7.50.
P

BO'NESS

Bo'ness & Kinneil Railway

Bo'ness Station, Union St EH51 9AQ (A904 from all directions, signposted)
☎ 01506 822298 📠 01506 828233
e-mail: railway@srps.org.uk

Historic railway buildings, including the station and train shed, have been relocated from sites all over Scotland. The Scottish Railway Exhibition tells the story of the development of railways and their impact on the people of Scotland. Take a seven mile return trip by steam train to the tranquil country station at Birkhill. Special events throughout the year.

Times: Open Apr-Jun & Sep-Oct, Sat-Sun; Steam trains depart 11 (ex Apr), 12.15, 1.45, 3 & diesel at 4.15. Jul-Aug, Tue-Sun; 23 May-27 Jun, special timetable, ring for details.
Fee: Return fare £4 (ch 5-15 £2, concessions (disabled & pen) £3). Family ticket £10. Ticket for return train fare and tour of Birkhill Fireclay Mine £6.50 (ch £3.50, concessions £4.80), Family ticket £16.50. Scottish Railway Exhibition £1.50 (accompanied ch free, concessions £1), Family ticket £3.
P ☕ ✕ ♿ (ramps to stn, and adapted carriage) toilets for disabled shop

Kinneil Museum & Roman Fortlet

Duchess Anne Cottages, Kinniel Estate EH51 0PR
☎ 01506 778530

The museum is in a converted stable block of Kinneil House. The ground floor has displays on the industrial history of Bo'ness, while the upper floor looks at the history and environment of the Kinneil Estate. The remains of the Roman fortlet can be seen nearby. An audio visual presentation shows 2000 years of history.

Times: Open all year, Mon-Sat 12.30-4.
Fee: Free.
P ♿ shop 🐕 (ex guide dogs)

FALKIRK

Callendar House

Callendar Park FK1 1YR (from W M80 junct 4; from E M9 junct 4/5; A803 to Falkirk, follow signs into Callendar Park)
☎ 01324 503770 📠 01324 503771

Mary, Queen of Scots, Oliver Cromwell, Bonnie Prince Charlie, noble earls and wealthy merchants all feature in the history of Callendar House. Costumed interpreters describe early 19th-century life in the kitchens and the 900-year history of the house is illustrated in the 'Story of Callendar House' exhibition. The house is set in parkland, offering boating and woodland walks. Christmas at Callendar House will

contd.

include spitroasting goose in the kitchen, traditional tree and carols in the main hall.

Times: Open all year, Mon-Sat 10-5. Apr-Sep Sun 2-5.
Fee: £3 (ch & pen £1.50). Family ticket £7.
(ramps & lift) toilets for disabled shop (ex guide dogs)

Rough Castle
(1m E of Bonnybridge)
☎ 0131 668 8800

The impressive earthworks of a large Roman fort on the Antonine Wall can be seen here. The buildings have disappeared, but the mounds and terraces are the sites of barracks, and granary and bath buildings. Running between them is the military road which once linked all the forts on the wall and is still well defined.
Times: Open any reasonable time. **Fee:** Free.

FIFE

ABERDOUR
Aberdour Castle
KY3 0SL
☎ 01383 860519

The earliest surviving part of the castle is the 14th-century keep. There are also later buildings, and the remains of a terraced garden, a bowling green and a fine 16th-century doocot (dovecote).
Times: Open all year, Apr-Sep, daily 9.30-6.30; Oct-Mar, Mon-Sat 9.30-4.30, Sun 2-4.30. (Closed Thu pm, Fri in winter & 25-26 Dec).
Fee: £2 (ch 75p, concessions £1.50).
toilets for disabled shop

ANSTRUTHER
Scottish Fisheries Museum
St Ayles, Harbour Head KY10 3AB
☎ 01333 310628 01333 310628
e-mail:
andrew@fisheriesmuseum.freeserve.co.uk

This National Museum depicts the history of the Scottish fishing industry, with actual boats and many fine models, photographs and paintings. There is also a reconstruction of a fisherman's cottage.
Times: Open all year, Apr-Oct, Mon-Sat 10-5.30, Sun 11-5; Nov-Mar, Mon-Sat 10-4.30, Sun 12-4.30. (Closed 25-26 Dec & 1-2 Jan). Last admission 45 mins before closing.
Fee: £3.50 (concessions £2.50). Family ticket £10. Party 12+.
P (20yds) (charge in summer) (ramps) toilets for disabled shop (ex guide dogs)

BURNTISLAND
Burntisland Edwardian Fair Museum
102 High St KY3 9AS
☎ 01592 412860 01592 412870
Times: Open all year, Mon, Wed, Fri & Sat 10-1 & 2-5; Tue & Thu 10-1 & 2-7pm. Closed public holidays.
P (on street parking) *Details not confirmed for 2001*

CULROSS
Culross Palace, Town House & The Study
West Green House KY12 8JH (off A985, 3m E of Kincardine Bridge)
☎ 01383 880359 01383 882675

A royal burgh, Culross dates from the 16th and 17th centuries and has remained virtually unchanged since. It prospered from the coal and salt trades, and when these declined in the 1700s, Culross stayed as it was. It owes its present appearance to the National Trust for Scotland, which has been gradually restoring it. In the Town House is a visitor centre and exhibition; in the building called The Study can be seen a drawing room with a Norwegian painted ceiling, and The Palace has painted rooms and terraced gardens.
Times: Open - Palace & Town House: Apr-May & Sep, daily 1-5; Jun-Aug, daily 10-5; Oct, wknds 1-5 (last admission to Palace 4pm, Town House 4.30pm). Study: same dates, 1-5. Groups at other times by appointment.
Fee: £4.20 (ch & concession £2.80). Family ticket £11.20. Ticket includes Palace.
toilets for disabled shop (ex guide dogs)

CUPAR
Hill of Tarvit Mansionhouse & Garden
KY15 5PB (2.5m S of Cupar, off A916)
☎ 01334 653127 01334 653127

Built in the first decade of the 20th century, the Mansionhouse is home to a notable collection of paintings, tapestries, furniture and Chinese porcelain. The grounds include formal gardens, and there is a regular programme of concerts and art exhibitions.
Times: Open- House: 21 Apr-Jun & Sep, daily 1.30-5.30; Jul-Aug, daily 11-5.30; Oct, wknds 1.30-5.30 (last admision 4.45). Garden & grounds: Apr-Sep, daily 9.30am-9pm; Oct-Mar, daily 9.30-4.30.
Fee: House & Garden £3.70 (ch & concessions £2.50). Family ticket £9.90. Garden only, honesty box £1. Party.
toilets for disabled shop (ex guide dogs)

Rankeilour Park - The Scottish Deer Centre

Bow-of-Fife KY15 4NQ (3 miles W of Cupar on A91)
☎ 01337 810391 📠 01337 810477

Guided tours take about 30 minutes and allow you to meet and stroke deer. Children can help with bottle-feeding young fawns, (at certain times of year), and there are indoor and outdoor adventure play areas. Other features include regular falconry displays (from Easter to mid September), viewing platform and a tree top walkway.

Times: Open daily, Etr-Oct 10-6, Nov-Etr 10-5.

Fee: £3.95 (ch £2.50, concessions £3.40). Family ticket £11.70. Party 10+.

P ✕ ♿ (special parking bay, loan of wheelchairs) toilets for disabled shop (ex guide dogs)

DUNFERMLINE

Andrew Carnegie Birthplace Museum

Moodie St KY12 7PL (400yds S from Dunfermline Abbey)
☎ 01383 724302 📠 01383 721862

The museum tells the story of the handloom weaver's son, born here in 1835, who created the biggest steel works in the USA and then became a philanthropist on a huge scale. The present-day work of the philanthropic Carnegie Trust is also explained.

Times: Open all year, Apr-Oct, Mon-Sat 11-5, Sun 2-5.

Fee: £2 (ch 16 free, concessions £1).

P ♿ toilets for disabled shop (ex guide dogs)

Dunfermline Abbey

Pittencrieff Park
☎ 01383 739026

The monastery was a powerful Benedictine house, founded by Queen Margaret in the 11th century. The grave of King Robert the Bruce is marked by a modern brass in the choir. The monastery guest house became a royal palace, and was the birthplace of Charles I.

Times: Open all year, Apr-Sep, daily 9.30-6.30: Oct-Mar, Mon-Sat 9.30-4.30, Sun 2-4.30. (Closed Thu pm, Fri in winter & 25-26 Dec).

Fee: £2 (ch 75p, concessions £1.50).

P shop

Dunfermline Heritage Trust

Abbot House, Maygate KY12 7NE (M90 junct 2, signposted)
☎ 01383 733266 📠 01383 624908
e-mail: dht@abbothouse.fsnet.co.uk

This medieval house, now refurbished as a heritage centre for the ancient capital of Scotland, features an award-winning journey through 1000 years of history from the Picts to the present day.

Times: Open daily 10-5. Last entry to upper exhibitions 4.15pm. (Closed 25 Dec & 1 Jan).

Fee: £3 (accompanied ch under 14 free, ch 5-16 £1.25 & concessions £2). Party 20+

P (150yds) (disabled parking at establishment) ♿ (parking on site, videos of inaccesible areas) toilets for disabled shop (ex guide dogs)

Dunfermline Museum & Small Gallery

Viewfield Ter KY12 7HY
☎ 01383 313838 📠 01383 313837

Interesting and varied displays on local history are shown, including domestic articles and damask linen - an important local product.

Times: Open all year, Mon-Fri 1-4. (Closed Sat, Sun & PH's).

Fee: Free.

P (charged) ♿ shop (ex guide dogs)

Pittencrieff House Museum

Pittencrieff Park KY12 8QH
☎ 01383 722935 & 313838 📠 01383 313837

A fine 17th-century mansion house, standing in a park with lawns, greenhouses and gardens. In the house are galleries with displays on the history of the house, park and costume. Temporary art exhibitions are shown in the top gallery. The house and park were given to the town by Andrew Carnegie.

Times: Open daily Apr-Sep 11-5, Oct-Mar 11-4.

Fee: Free.

P ♿ (ramp) toilets for disabled shop (ex guide dogs)

FALKLAND

Falkland Palace & Garden

KY15 7BU (off A912, 11m N of Kirkaldy)
☎ 01337 857397 📠 01337 857980

The hunting palace of the Stuart monarchs, this fine building, with a French-Renaissance style south wing, stands in the shelter of the Lomond Hills. The beautiful Chapel Royal and King's Bedchamber are its most notable features, and it is also home to the oldest royal tennis court in Britain (1539). The garden has a spectacular delphinium border. Recorded sacred music is played hourly in the Chapel. Please telephone for details of concerts, recitals etc.

Times: Open Jun-Aug, Mon-Sat 10-5.30, Sun 1.30-5.30. (last admission to palace 4.30, to garden 5). Apr-May & Sep-Oct, Mon-Sat 11-5.30, Sun 1.30-5.30. Groups at other times by appointment. Town Hall, by appointment only.

Fee: Palace & Garden £4.80 (ch £3.20). Family ticket £12.80. Garden only at reduced rates.

P ♿ shop (ex guide dogs)

KELLIE CASTLE & GARDENS

Kellie Castle & Gardens

KY10 2RF (3m NW of Pittenweem on B9171)
☎ 01333 720271 📠 01333 720326
e-mail: aclipson@nts-scot.demon.co.uk

The oldest part dates from about 1360, but it is for its 16th and 17th-century domestic architecture that Kellie is renowned. It has notable plasterwork and painted

contd.

panelling, and there are also interesting Victorian gardens.

Times: Open - Castle Good Fri-Etr Mon & May-Sep, daily 1.30-5.30; wknds in Oct 1.30-5.30 (last admission 4.45). Gardens & grounds open all year, Apr-Oct, daily 9.30-sunset.

Fee: Castle & gardens £3.70 (ch & concessions £2.50), gardens only £1. Party 20+ .

P (Induction loop for the hard of hearing) shop (ex guide dogs)

KIRKCALDY

Kirkcaldy Museum & Art Gallery

War Memorial Gardens KY1 1YG (next to Kirkaldy train station)

☎ 01592 412860 01592 412870

Times: Open all year, Mon-Sat 10.30-5, Sun 2-5. (Closed local hols).

P toilets for disabled shop (ex guide dogs) *Details not confirmed for 2001*

NORTH QUEENSFERRY

Deep Sea World

KY11 1JR (from N, M90 take exit for Inverkeithing. From S follow signs to Forth Road bridge, first exit left)

☎ 01383 411880 01383 410514

e-mail: deepsea@sol.co.uk

The world's longest underwater tunnel gives you a diver's eye view of an underwater world. Come face to face with Sand Tiger sharks, and watch divers hand feed a wide array of sea life. Visit the Amazon experience with ferocious Piranhas and electric eels and the amazing amphibian display featuring the world's most poisonous frog. The really brave will enjoy the dangerous animals tank.

Times: Open all year, daily, 27 Mar-Jun Mon-Fri 10-6; Jul-Aug, Mon-Fri 10-6.30; Sep-1 Nov, Mon-Fri 10-6; 2 Nov-26 Mar, Mon-Fri 11-5. Weekends, BH & school holidays 10-6.

Fee: £6.25 (ch 3-5 £3.95, concessions £4.50). Family ticket & group discounts available.

P (ramps) toilets for disabled shop (ex guide dogs)

ST ANDREWS

British Golf Museum

Bruce Embankment KY16 9AB (opposite Royal & Ancient Golf Club)

☎ 01334 478880 01334 473306

e-mail: bgm@purplenet.co.uk

A visit to the museum will transport you down a pathway of surprising facts and striking feats from 500 years of golf history. Using diverse displays and exciting exhibits, the museum traces the history of the game, both in Britain and abroad from the middle ages to the present day. There are also displays exploring St Andrews' golfing heritage.

Times: Open all year, Etr-mid Oct daily 9.30-5.30; mid Oct-Etr Thu-Mon 11-3. (closed Tue & Wed).

Fee: £3.75 (ch 15 £1.50, pen & students £2.75). Family ticket £9.50. Group 10+

P (charged) toilets for disabled shop (ex guide dogs)

Castle & Visitor Centre

☎ 01334 477196

This 13th-century stronghold castle was the setting for the murder of Cardinal Beaton in 1546. The new visitor centre incorporates an exciting multi-media exhibition describing the history of the castle and nearby cathedral.

Times: Open all year, Apr-Sep, daily 9.30-6.30; Oct-Mar, Mon-Sat 9.30-4.30, Sun 2-4.30. (Closed 25-26 Dec).

Fee: £2.50 (ch £1, concessions £1.90). Joint ticket with St Andrews Cathedral available.

P toilets for disabled shop

Cathedral (& Museum)

☎ 01334 472563

The cathedral was the largest in Scotland, and is now an extensive ruin. The remains date mainly from the 12th and 13th centuries, and large parts of the precinct walls have survived intact. Close by is St Rule's church, which the cathedral was built to replace. St Rule's probably dates from before the Norman Conquest, and is considered the most interesting Romanesque church in Scotland.

Times: Open all year, Apr-Sep, daily 9.30-6.30; Oct-Mar, Mon-Sat 9.30-4.30, Sun 2-4.30. (Closed 25-26 Dec).

Fee: £2 (ch 75p, concessions £1.50). Joint ticket for St Andrews Castle available.

P shop

HIGHLAND

AVIEMORE

Strathspey Steam Railway

Aviemore Station, Dalfaber Rd PH22 1PY (off B970)

☎ 01479 810725

e-mail: laurence.grant@strathspey-railway.freeserve.co.uk

This steam railway covers the five and a half miles from Boat of Garten to Aviemore. The journey takes about 20 minutes, but allow around an hour for the round trip. Timetables are available from the station and the tourist information centre.

Times: Open end May-Sep, daily; late Mar-Oct, Wed, Thu, Sat-Sun; Sat services & late season diesel railcar.

Fee: £5.40 Basic return; £13.50 Family return.

P toilets for disabled shop

BALMACARA

Balmacara (Lochalsh Woodland Garden)

IV40 8DN (3m E of Kyle of Lochalsh, off A87)

☎ 01599 566325 01599 566359

The Balmacara estate comprises some 5600 acres and seven crofting villages, including Plockton, a conservation area. There are excellent views of Skye, Kintail and Applecross. The main attraction is the Lochalsh Woodland Garden, but the whole area is excellent for walking.

Times: Open all year, daily 9-sunset.
Fee: Woodland garden £1 (honesty box), (concessions 50p)
P

BETTYHILL

Strathnaver Museum

KW14 7SS
☎ 01641 521418

The museum has displays on the Clearances, with a fine collection of Strathnaver Clearances furnishings, domestic and farm implements, and local books. There is also a Clan Mackay room. The museum's setting is a former church, a handsome stone building with a magnificent canopied pulpit dated 1774. The churchyard contains a carved stone known as the Farr Stone, which dates back to the 9th century and is a fine example of Pictish art.
Times: Open Apr-Oct, Mon-Sat 10-1 & 2-5; Nov-Mar restricted opening.
Fee: £1.90 (ch £1.20 & students £1).
P ♿ shop (ex guide dogs)

BOAT OF GARTEN

RSPB Nature Reserve Abernethy Forest

Forest Lodge, Nethybridge PH25 3EF (signposted from B970)
☎ 01479 831694 01479 821069

Home of the Loch Garten Osprey site, this reserve holds one of most important remnants of Scots Pine forest in the Highlands. Within its 30,760 acres are forest bogs, moorland, mountain top, lochs and crofting land. In addition to the regular pair of nesting ospreys, there are breeding Scottish crossbills, capercaillies, black grouse and many others. The ospreys can be viewed through telescopes and there is a live TV link to the nest.
Times: Reserve open at all times. Osprey Centre daily, Apr-Aug 10-6.
Fee: £2.50 (ch 50p, concessions £1.50) Family ticket £5.
P ♿ toilets for disabled shop (ex guide dogs in centre)

CARRBRIDGE

Landmark Highland Heritage & Adventure Park

PH23 3AJ (off A9 between Aviemore & Inverness)
☎ 01479 841613 & 0800 731 3446 01479 841384
e-mail: landmark@compuserve.com

This innovative centre is designed to provide a fun and educational visit for all ages. Microworld is an amazing exhibition, a journey into inner space; a close up look at the incredible microscopic world around us. There is a 65ft forest viewing tower and a working steam-powered sawmill. There are demonstrations of timber sawing and log hauling by a Clydesdale horse throughout the day. Attractions include the new 3-track Watercoaster, a maze and an adventure play area.
Times: Open all year, daily, Apr-mid Jul 10-6; mid Jul-mid Aug 10-7; Sep-Oct 10-5.30; Nov-Mar 10-5.
Fee: Apr £4.85 (ch £3.45); May-Jun £6.65 (ch £4.65); Jul-Oct £6.90 (ch £4.85); Nov-Mar £3.75 (ch £2.65). Family tickets available.
P licensed ♿ toilets for disabled shop

CAWDOR

Cawdor Castle

IV12 5RD (on B9090 off A96)
☎ 01667 404615 01667 404674
e-mail: cawdor.castle@btinternet.com

Home of the Thanes of Cawdor since the 14th century, this lovely castle has a drawbridge, an ancient tower built round a tree, and a freshwater well inside the house. Gardens Weekend takes place in June - guided tours of gardens and Bluebell Walk in Cawdor Big Wood.
Times: Open May-14 Oct, daily 10-5.30. (Last admission 5pm).
Fee: £5.60 (ch 5-15 £3, pen £4.60). Family ticket £16.50. Party 20+. Gardens, grounds & nature trails only £2.90.
P licensed ♿ toilets for disabled shop (ex guide dogs)

CLAVA CAIRNS

Clava Cairns

(6m E of Inverness)
☎ 0131 668 8800

On the south bank of the River Nairn, this group of circular burial cairns is surrounded by three concentric rings of great stones. It dates from around 1600BC, and ranks among Scotland's finest prehistoric monuments.
Times: Open at all reasonable times.
Fee: Free.
P

CROMARTY

Hugh Miller's Cottage

Church St IV11 8XA
☎ 01381 600245

The cottage houses an exhibition on the life and work of Hugh Miller, a stonemason born here in 1802 who became an eminent geologist and writer. It was built by his great-grandfather around 1698, and now has a charming cottage garden.
Times: Open May-Sep, Mon-Sat 11-1 & 2-5, Sun 2-5.
Fee: £2 (ch & concessions £1.30). Family ticket £5.30. Party.
P (5mins) (disabled is directly outside) ♿ (ex guide dogs)

CULLODEN MOOR

Culloden Battlefield

IV2 5ED (5m E of Inverness)
☎ 01463 790607 01463 794294

A cairn recalls this last battle fought on mainland Britain, on 16 April 1746, when 'Bonnie' Prince Charles Edward Stuart's army was routed by the Duke of Cumberland's forces. The battlefield has been restored to its state on the day of the battle, and in summer there are 'living history' enactments. This is a most

contd.

atmospheric evocation of tragic events. Telephone for details of guided tours.

Times: Open - site always. Visitor Centre open Feb-Mar & Nov-30 Dec, daily 10-4. (Closed 25 & 26 Dec, shop closed 1-7 Nov); Apr-Oct, daily 9-6; Audio visual show closed 30 mins before Visitor Centre.

Fee: Admission to visitor centre & museum (includes audio-visual programme & Old Leanach Cottage) £3 (ch, pen & students £2). Family ticket £8. Party.

(wheelchair, induction loop for hard of hearing, raised map). toilets for disabled shop (ex guide dogs)

DRUMNADROCHIT

Official Loch Ness Monster Exhibition Centre

IV3 6TU (on A82)

01456 450573 & 450218 01456 450770

e-mail: brem@loch-ness-scotland.com

A fascinating multi-media presentation lasting 35 minutes. Seven themed areas cover the story from the pre-history of Scotland, through the cultural roots of the legend in Highland folklore, and into the 50-year controversy which surrounds it. Using latest technology in computer animation, lasers and multi-media projection systems.

Times: Open all year; Etr-May 9.30-5.30; Jun-Sep 9.30-6 (9-8.30 Jul & Aug); Winter 10-4. Last admission 1hr before closing.

Fee: £5.95 (ch £3.50, pen & students £4.50, ch under 7 & disabled free). Family ticket £14.95. Group.

licensed (parking) toilets for disabled shop (ex in grounds)

Urquhart Castle

(on A82)

01456 450551

The castle was once Scotland's biggest and overlooks Loch Ness. It dates mainly from the 14th century, when it was built on the site of an earlier fort, and was destroyed before the 1715 Jacobite rebellion.

Times: Open all year, Apr-Sep, daily 9.30-6.30; Oct-Mar, daily 9.30-4.30. Last admission 45mins before closing. (Closed 25-26 Dec).

Fee: £3.80 (ch £1.20, concessions £2.80).

shop

DUNBEATH

Laidhay Croft Museum

KW6 6EH (1m N on A9)

01593 731244

The museum gives visitors a glimpse of a long-vanished way of life. The main building is a thatched Caithness longhouse, with the dwelling quarters, byre and stable all under one roof. It dates back some 200 years, and is furnished as it might have been 100 years ago. A collection of early farm tools and machinery is also shown. Near the house is a thatched winnowing barn with its roof supported on three 'Highland couples', or crucks.

Times: Open Etr-mid Oct, daily 10-6.

Fee: £1 (ch 50p)

toilets for disabled

ELPHIN

Highland & Rare Breeds Farm

IV27 4HH (on A835 in Elphin)

01854 666204 01854 666204

There are highland cattle, traditional 4-horned sheep with coloured fleeces, traditional Scottish ewes and lambs, rare breeds of pigs and goats. Many types of poultry, duck ponds, and a farm walk among the animals. Also on display are farm tools, crofting history, wool crafts and hand-spinning.

Times: Open mid May-Sep, daily 10-5.

Fee: £3.50 (ch £2.50, students & pen £3)

(assistance available) toilets for disabled shop

FORT GEORGE

Fort George

IV1 2TD (11m NE of Inverness)

01667 462777

Built following the Battle of Culloden as a Highland fortress for the army of George II, this is one of the outstanding artillery fortifications in Europe and still an active army barracks.

Times: Open all year, Apr-Sep, daily 9.30-6.30; Oct-Mar, Mon-Sat 9.30-4.30, Sun 2-4.30. Last admission 45mins before closing. (Closed 25-26 Dec).

Fee: Summer: £4 (ch £1.50, concessions £3); Winter: £3.50 (ch £1.20, concessions £2.60).

toilets for disabled shop

Queen's Own Highlanders Regimental Museum Collection

IV2 7TD

01463 224380 01463 224380

Fort George has been a military barracks since it was built in 1748-1769, and was the Depot of the Seaforth Highlanders until 1961. The museum of the Queen's Own Highlanders (Seaforth and Camerons) is sited in the former Lieutenant Governor's house, where uniforms, medals and pictures are displayed.

Times: Open Apr-Sep, Mon-Sat 10-6, Sun 2-6; Oct-Mar, Mon-Fri 10-4. (Closed Good Fri-Etr Mon, Xmas, New Year & BH).

Fee: Free. (Admission charged by Historic Scotland for entry to Fort George).

(stair lift to 1st floor, wheelchair on 1st floor) toilets for disabled shop (ex guide dogs)

FORT WILLIAM

Inverlochy Castle

PH33 6SN (2m NE)

0131 668 8800

The castle was begun in the 13th century and added to later. It is noted in Scottish history for the battle fought nearby in 1645, when Montrose defeated the Campbells.

Times: Open Apr-Sep. Key available from keykeeper.

Fee: Free.

West Highland Museum

Cameron Square PH33 6AJ (follow signs to tourist office, museum is next door)
☎ 01397 702169 📠 01397 701927

The displays illustrate traditional Highland life and history, with numerous Jacobite relics. One of them is the `secret portrait' of 'Bonnie' Prince Charlie, which looks like meaningless daubs of paint but reveals a portrait when reflected in a metal cylinder.

Times: Open all year - Jun-Sep, Mon-Sat 10-5 (also Sun 2-5 Jul-Aug); Oct-May, Mon-Sat 10-4.
Fee: £2 (ch 50p, concessions £1.50)
P (100yds) (charge May-Oct, max. 2hrs stay) ♿ toilets for disabled shop (ex guide dogs)

GAIRLOCH

Gairloch Heritage Museum

Auchtercairn IV21 2BP
☎ 01445 712287
e-mail: jf@ghmr.freeserve.co.uk

A converted farmstead now houses the award-winning museum, which shows the way of life in this typical West Highland parish from early times to the 20th century. There are hands-on activities for children and reconstructions of a croft house room, a school room, a shop, and the inside of a local lighthouse. Evening demonstrations during July and August, spinning, baking, butter-making and net and creel making. A Millennium exhibition 'Garloch Parish from 1840-1999' incorporates hands-on activities.

Times: Open Apr-Sep, Mon-Sat 10-5; Oct, Mon-Fri 10-1.30
Fee: £2.50 (ch 50p & pen £2). Group 10+
P ☕ ✕ licensed ♿ shop

GLENCOE

Glencoe & North Lorn Folk Museum

PA39 4HS
☎ 01855 811664

Two heather-thatched cottages in the main street of Glencoe now house items connected with the Macdonalds and the Jacobite risings. A variety of local domestic and farming exhibits, dairying and slate-working equipment, costumes and embroidery are also shown.

Times: Open mid May-Sep, Mon-Sat 10-5.30.
Fee: £2 (ch free, concessions £1).
P ♿ shop

Glencoe Visitor Centre

PA39 4HX (on A82, 17m S of Fort William)
☎ 01855 811307 & 811729 📠 01855 811772

Glencoe has stunning scenery and some of the most challenging climbs and walks in the Highlands. Red deer, wildcats, eagles and ptarmigan are among the wildlife. It is, however, also forever known as a place of treachery and infamy. The Macdonalds of Glencoe were hosts to a party of troops who, under government orders, fell upon them, men, women and children, in a bloody massacre in 1692. The Visitor Centre tells the story.

Times: Open - Site all year, daily. Visitor Centre May-Aug, daily 9.30-5.30; Mar-Apr & Sep-Oct, daily 10-5; (last admission 30 mins before closing).
Fee: 50p (ch & pen 30p). Includes parking.
P ☕ ♿ (induction loop in video programme room) toilets for disabled shop (ex guide dogs)

Highland Mysteryworld

PA39 4HL (on A82, 10m S of Fort William)
☎ 01855 811660 📠 01855 821463
e-mail: monster@mysteryworld.co.uk

In a spectacular location at the foot of Glencoe, Highland Mysteryworld explores the myths and legends of the past, with actors and animatronic effects. The indoor attractions include the Astromyth Theatre, Clootie Well and Mysterymall. Other facilities are lochside trails, adventure playground and a leisure centre.

Times: Open Etr-Oct, daily, 10-5 (last entry 4.30).
Fee: £4.95 (concessions £3.50). Family (2 adults & 2 ch) £14.00.
P ☕ ✕ licensed ♿ toilets for disabled shop (ex guide dogs)

GLENFINNAN

Glenfinnan Monument

PH37 4LT (on A830, 18.5 miles W of Fort William)
☎ 01397 722250

The monument commemorates Highlanders who fought for 'Bonnie' Prince Charlie in 1745. It stands in an awe-inspiring setting at the head of Loch Shiel. There is a visitor centre with information (commentary in four languages) on the Prince's campaign.

Times: Open - Site all year. Visitor Centre, Apr-18 May & 1 Sep-Oct, daily 10-5; 19 May-Aug, daily 9.30-6.
Fee: £1.50 (ch £1). Family ticket £4. Includes parking.
P ☕ ♿ (information centre only) shop

GOLSPIE

Dunrobin Castle

KW10 6SF (1m NE on A9)
☎ 01408 633177 & 633268 📠 01408 633800

Times: Open Etr-15 Oct, Mon-Sat 10.30-5.30, Sun 12-5.30. Closes 1 hr earlier Etr, May & Oct. Last admission half hour before closing.
P ☕ ♿ (access by arrangement only) shop *Details not confirmed for 2001*

HELMSDALE

Timespan

Dunrobin St KW8 6JX (off A9 in centre of village, by Telford Bridge)
☎ 01431 821327

Times: Open Etr-mid Oct, Mon-Sat 9.30-5, Sun 2-5 (6pm Jul-Aug). Last admission one hour before closing.
P ☕ ♿ (lifts) toilets for disabled shop garden centre (ex guide dogs) *Details not confirmed for 2001*

KINCRAIG

Highland Wildlife Park

PH21 1NL (on B9152, 7m S of Aviemore)
☎ 01540 651270 📠 01540 651236
e-mail: wildlife@rzss.org.uk

As you drive through the main reserve, you can see awe-inspiring European bison grazing alongside wild horses, red deer and highland cattle plus a wide variety of other species. Then in the walk-round forest, woodland and moorland habitats prepare for close encounters with animals such as wolves, capercaillie, arctic foxes, wildcats, pine martens, otters and owls. Special events every weekend April to October.

Times: Open throughout the year, weather permitting. Apr-Oct, 10-6; Jun-Aug 10-7; Nov-Mar 10-4. last entry 2 hours before closing.
Fee: £6.30 (child £4.20, pen £5.25)
P ☕ ♿ toilets for disabled shop

KINGUSSIE

Highland Folk Museum

Duke St PH21 1JG (12m SW of Aviemore off A9 at Kingussie)
☎ 01540 661307 📠 01540 661631
Times: Open Mar-Oct, Mon-Sat 10-6, Sun 2-6.
P ♿ toilets for disabled shop (ex guide dogs) *Details not confirmed for 2001*

Ruthven Barracks

(0.5m SE of Kingussie)
☎ 0131 668 8800

Despite being blown up by 'Bonnie' Prince Charlie's Highlanders, these infantry barracks are still the best preserved of the four that were built after the Jacobite uprising. The considerable ruins are the remains of a building completed in 1716 on the site of a fortress of the 'Wolf of Badenoch'.

Times: Open at any reasonable time.
Fee: Free.
P

KIRKHILL

Moniack Castle (Highland Winery)

IV5 7PQ (7m from Inverness on A862, near village of Beauly, on S side of Beauly Firth)
☎ 01463 831283 📠 01463 831419

Commercial wine-making is not a typically Scottish industry, but nevertheless a wide range of 'country'-style wines is produced, including elderflower and silver birch; and mead and sloe gin are also made here. A selection of related products and tours of the production area are available at this unique attraction, situated in a 16th-century castle.

Times: Open all year, Mon-Sat 10-5. (11-4 in winter).
Fee: £2. Party 12+
P shop

NEWTONMORE

Clan Macpherson House & Museum

Main St PH20 1DE
☎ 01540 673332
Times: Open May-Oct, Mon-Sat 10-5.30, Sun 2.30-5.30. Other times by appointment.
P ♿ toilets for disabled shop *Details not confirmed for 2001*

POOLEWE

Inverewe Garden

IV22 2LG (6m NE of Gairloch, on A832)
☎ 01445 781200 📠 01445 781497
e-mail: aclipson@nts.scot.demon.co.uk

The influence of the North Atlantic Drift enables this remarkable garden to grow rare and sub-tropical plants. At its best in early June, but full of beauty from March to October, Inverewe has a backdrop of magnificent mountains and stands to the north of Loch Maree.

Times: Open - Garden all year, mid Mar-Oct, daily 9.30-9. Nov-mid Mar 9.30-5. Visitor Centre mid Mar-Oct, daily 9.30-5.30. Guided walks mid Apr-mid Sep Mon-Fri at 1.30.
Fee: £4.80 (concessions £3.20). Family ticket £12.80. Party.
P ✕ licensed ♿ (some paths difficult) toilets for disabled shop (ex guide dogs)

STRATHPEFFER

Highland Museum of Childhood

The Old Station IV14 9DH (take A9 N of Inverness, then the Tore rdbt, follow signs to Dingwall)
☎ 01997 421031
e-mail: info@hmoc.freeserve.co.uk

Located in a renovated Victorian railway station of 1885, the museum tells the story of childhood in the Highlands amongst the crofters and townsfolk; a way of life recorded in oral testimony, displays, and evocative photographs. An award-winning video, "A Century of Highland Childhood" is shown. There are also doll and toy collections.

Times: Open Apr-Oct, daily 10-5, (Sun 2-5) also Jul & Aug evenings open to 7pm. Other times by arrangement.
Fee: £1.50 (ch, pen & students £1). Family ticket (2 adults & 3 children) £3.50.
P ☕ ♿ shop (ex guide dogs) 

TORRIDON

TORRIDON COUNTRYSIDE CENTRE

The Mains IV22 2EZ (N of A896)
☎ 01445 791221 📠 01445 791378
e-mail: aclipson@nts.scoy.demon.co.uk.

Set amid some of Scotland's finest mountain scenery, the centre offers audio-visual presentations on the local wildlife. At the Mains nearby there are live deer to be seen.
Times: Open - Countryside Centre May-Sep, Mon-Sat 10-5, Sun 2-5. Estate and Deer Museum daily all year.
Fee: Audio-visual display & Deer Museum £1.50 (ch & concessions £1). Family ticket £4.
P ♿ toilets for disabled

WICK

CAITHNESS GLASS FACTORY & VISITOR CENTRE

Airport Industrial Estate KW1 5BP (on northern side of Wick, beside Airport on A99 to John O'Groats)
☎ 01955 602286 📠 01955 605200
Times: Open all year, Factory shop & Restaurant Mon-Sat 9-5 (Sun, Etr-Dec 11-5). Glassmaking Mon-Fri 9-4.30.
P ✕ licensed ♿ toilets for disabled shop *Details not confirmed for 2001*

CASTLE OF OLD WICK

(1m S)
☎ 0131 668 8800 📠 0131 668 8888

A ruined four-storey square tower that is probably from the 12th century. It is also known as Castle Oliphant.
Times: Open except when adjoining rifle range is in use.
Fee: Free.

WICK HERITAGE CENTRE

20 Bank Row KW1 5HS (close to the harbour)
☎ 01955 605393 📠 01955 605393

The heritage centre is near the harbour in a complex of eight houses, yards and outbuildings. The centre illustrates local history from Neolithic times to the herring fishing industry. In addition, there is a complete working 19th-century lighthouse, and the famous Johnston collection of photographs.
Times: Open Jun-Sep, daily 10-5. (Closed Sun).
Fee: £2 (ch 50p).
P ♿ toilets for disabled

INVERCLYDE

GREENOCK

McLEAN MUSEUM & ART GALLERY

15 Kelly St PA16 8JX (close to Greenock West Railway Station)
☎ 01475 715624 📠 01475 715626

James Watt was born in Greenock, and various exhibits connected with him are shown. The museum also has an art collection, and displays on shipping, local and natural history, Egyptology and ethnography. Temporary exhibition gallery. 2001 is the 125th anniversary of the museum – celebratory events are to take place throughout the year.

Times: Open all year, Mon-Sat 10-5. (Closed local & national PH).
Fee: Free.
P (200mtrs) ♿ (induction loop) toilets for disabled shop (ex guide & service dogs)

PORT GLASGOW

NEWARK CASTLE

☎ 01475 741858

The one-time house of the Maxwells, dating from the 15th and 17th centuries. The courtyard and hall are preserved. Fine turrets and the remains of painted ceilings can be seen, and the hall carries an inscription of 1597.
Times: Open Apr-Sep, daily 9.30-6.30.
Fee: £2 (ch 75p, concessions £1.50).
P shop

MIDLOTHIAN

CRICHTON

CRICHTON CASTLE

(2.5m SW of Pathhead, off A68)
☎ 01875 320017

The castle dates back to the 14th century, but most of what remains today was built over the following 300 years. A notable feature is the 16th-century wing built by the Earl of Bothwell in Italian style, with an arcade below.
Times: Open Apr-Sep, daily 9.30-6.30.
Fee: £1.80 (ch 75p, concessions £1.30).
P

DALKEITH

Edinburgh Butterfly & Insect World

Dobbies Garden World, Lasswade EH18 1AZ (0.5m S of Edinburgh city bypass at Gilmerton junct)
0131 663 4932 **0131 654 2774**
e-mail: ebiw@compuserve.com

Richly coloured butterflies from all over the world can be seen flying among exotic rainforest plants, trees and flowers. The tropical pools are filled with giant waterlilies and colourful fish, and are surrounded by lush vegetation. Also scorpions, leaf cutting ants, beetles, tarantulas and other remarkable creatures. There is a unique honeybee display and daily insect handling sessions.

Times: Open Summer daily 9.30-5.30; winter daily 10-5. (Closed 25-26 Dec & 1-2 Jan).

Fee: £3.95 (ch, concessions & students £2.85). Family ticket (2 adults & 2 ch) £12. Party 10+.

toilets for disabled shop garden centre (ex guide dogs)

NEWTONGRANGE

Scottish Mining Museum

Lady Victoria Colliery EH22 4QN (on A7)
0131 663 7519 **0131 654 1618**

Based at the Lady Victoria colliery, Scotland's National Coal Mining Museum offers entertaining tours led by ex-miners. Visit the pit-head, Scotland's largest steam winding engine, and a full-scale replica of a modern underground coalface.

Times: Open all year, daily 10-5.

Fee: £4 (ch & concessions £2.20). Family ticket £10. Party 20+.

toilets for disabled shop (ex guide dogs)

PENICUIK

Edinburgh Crystal Visitor Centre

Eastfield Industrial Estate EH26 8HB (on A701)
01968 675128 **01968 674847**
e-mail: scampbell@edinburgh-crystal.co.uk

A tour around the factory allows you to see craftsmen at work during the various stages in the art of glassmaking. An exhibition and video entitled 'Capturing the Light' explains the process further. There is also a large collection of Edinburgh Crystal and a factory shop.

Times: Open all year. Factory tours Mon-Fri 9-3.30. (Closed 25-26 Dec & 1 Jan). Visitor Centre Mon-Sat 9-5, Sun 11-5.

Fee: Tours £3 (concessions £2). Family ticket £7.50. Party 15+.

licensed (ramp to first floor) toilets for disabled shop (ex guide dogs)

MORAY

BALLINDALLOCH

The Glenlivet Distillery

AB37 9DB (off B9008 10m N of Tomintoul)
01542 783220 **01542 783218**

The visitor centre includes a guided tour of the whisky production facilities and a chance to see inside the vast bonded warehouses where the spirit matures. The new multimedia exhibition and interactive presentations communicate the unique history, and traditions of Glenlivet Scotch Whisky.

Times: Open: mid Mar-end Oct, Mon-Sat 10-4, Sun 12.30-4. Jul & Aug remains open until 6 daily.

Fee: £2.50 for over 18's which includes £2 voucher redeemable in distillery shop against the purchase of a 70cl bottle of whisky. This charge covers entry to exhibition, guided tour of Distillery & a free dram of whisky. (ch18 free, under 8's not admitted to production areas)

toilets for disabled shop (ex guide dogs) 

BRODIE CASTLE

Brodie Castle

IV36 2TE (4.5m W of Forres, off A96)
01309 641371 **01309 641600**

The Brodie family lived here for hundreds of years before passing the castle to the NTS in 1980. It contains many treasures, including furniture, porcelain and paintings. The extensive grounds include a woodland walk and an adventure playground. Wheelchairs for disabled visitors are available. Please telephone for details of recitals, concerts, open air theatre etc.

Times: Open Apr-Sep, Mon-Sat 11-5.30, Sun 1.30-5.30; wknds in Oct, Sat 11-5.30, Sun 1.30-5.30 (last admission 4.30). Grounds open all year, 9.30-sunset. Other times by appointment.

Fee: £4.20 (concessions £2.80). Grounds £1. Family ticket £11.20. Party.

(audio tape & information sheet in Braille) toilets for disabled shop (ex guide dogs)

BUCKIE

Buckie Drifter Maritime Heritage Centre

Freuchny Rd AB56 1TT (1m off A98 between Elgin and Fraserburgh, signposted)
01542 834646 **01542 835995**

An exciting maritime heritage centre, where you can discover what life was like in the fishing communities of Moray District during the herring boom years of the 1890s and 1930s. Sign on as a crew member of a steam drifter and find out how to catch herring. Try your hand at packing fish in a barrel.

Times: Open Apr-Oct, Mon-Sat 10-5, Sun 12-5.
Fee: £2.75 (concessions £1.75).
P ✕ licensed ♿ (car parking, touch display on lower floor) toilets for disabled shop (ex guide dogs)

CRAIGELLACHIE

Speyside Cooperage Visitor Centre

Dufftown Rd AB38 9RS (1m S of Craigellachie on A941)
☎ 01340 871108 🖷 01340 881437
e-mail: info@speyside-coopers.demon.co.uk

A working cooperage with unique visitor centre, where skilled coopers and their apprentices practise this ancient craft. Each year they repair around 100,000 oak casks which will be used to mature many different whiskies. The 'Acorn to Cask' exhibition traces the history and development of the coopering industry.
Times: Open all year, Mon-Fri 9.30-4.30, also Jun-Sep on Sat 9.30-4. (Closed Xmas & New Year).
Fee: £2.95 (ch £1.75 & pen £2.45). Family ticket £7.95. Party 15+.
P ♿ (Special picnic table) toilets for disabled shop (ex guide dogs)

DUFFTOWN

Balvenie Castle

AB55 4DH
☎ 01340 820121

The ruined castle was the ancient stronghold of the Comyns, and became a stylish house in the 16th century.
Times: Open Apr-Sep, daily 9.30-6.30.
Fee: £1.20 (ch 50p, concessions 90p).
P ♿ toilets for disabled

Glenfiddich Distillery

AB55 4DH (N of town, off A941)
☎ 01340 820373 🖷 01340 822083

Set close to Balvenie Castle, the distillery was founded in 1887 by William Grant and has stayed in the hands of the family ever since. Visitors can see the whisky-making process in its various stages, including bottling, and then sample the finished product.
Times: Open all year Mon-Fri 9.30-4.30, also Etr-mid Oct Sat 9.30-4.30, Sun 12-4.30. (Closed Xmas & New Year).
Fee: Free.
P ♿ (ramp access to production area & warehouse gallery) toilets for disabled shop (ex guide dogs)

DUFFUS

Duffus Castle

(off B9012)
☎ 0131 668 8800

The remains of the mighty motte-and-bailey castle are surrounded by a moat. Within the eight-acre bailey is a 15th-century hall, and the motte is crowned by a 14th-century tower.
Times: Open at all reasonable times.
Fee: Free.
P

ELGIN

Elgin Cathedral

North College St IV30 1EL
☎ 01343 547171

Founded in 1224, the cathedral was known as the Lantern of the North and the Glory of the Kingdom because of its beauty. In 1390 it was burnt, along with most of the town. Although it was rebuilt, it fell into ruin after the Reformation. The ruins are quite substantial, however, and there is still a good deal to admire, including the fine west towers and the octagonal chapter house.
Times: Open all year, Apr-Sep, daily 9.30-6.30; Oct-Mar, Mon-Sat 9.30-4.30, Sun 2-4.30. (Closed Thu pm, Fri in winter & 25-26 Dec).
Fee: £2.50 (ch £1, concessions £1.90).
P ♿ shop

Elgin Museum

1 High St IV30 1EQ (East end of High Street, opp 'Safeway'. Follow brown signs)
☎ 01343 543675 🖷 01343 543675
e-mail: curator@elginmuseum.demon.co.uk

This award-winning museum is internationally famous for its fossil fish and fossil reptiles, and for its Pictish stones. The displays relate to the natural and human history of Moray.
Times: Open Apr-Oct, Mon-Fri 10-5, Sat 11-4, Sun 2-5.
Fee: £2 (ch 50p, pen, students & UB40 £1). Family ticket £4.50.
P (50mtrs) ♿ (handrails inside & out. All case displays at sitting level) toilets for disabled shop (ex guide dogs)

Pluscarden Abbey

IV30 8UA (6m SW on unclass road)
☎ 01343 890257 🖷 01343 890258

The original monastery, founded by Alexander II in 1230, was burnt, probably by the Wolf of Badenoch who also destroyed Elgin Cathedral. It was restored in the 14th and 19th centuries, and reoccupied in 1948 by Benedictines from Prinknash. Once more a religious community, retreat facilities are available for men and

contd.

women. All services (with Gregorian chant) are open to the public. Pluscarden Pentecost Lectures held annually on Tuesday, Wednesday and Thursday after Pentecost.
Times: Open all year, daily 4.45-8.30pm.
Fee: Free.
P ♿ (induction loop, ramps to shop) toilets for disabled shop 

FOCHABERS

Baxters Highland Village

IV32 7LD (1m W of Fochabers on A96)
☎ 01343 820666 🖷 01343 821790
e-mail: highland.village@Baxters.co.uk

The Baxters food firm started here almost 130 years ago and now sells its products in over 60 countries. Visitors can see the shop where the story began, watch an audio-visual display, and visit four shops. See the great hall, audio-visual theatre and cooking theatre. A food tasting area is a new addition.
Times: Open all year, Apr-Oct 9-6; Nov-Dec 9-5; Jan-Mar 10-5.
Fee: Free. The cooking demonstration theatre will be by appointment & charged for.
P ✕ licensed ♿ (parking facilities) toilets for disabled shop (ex guide dogs)

Fochabers Folk Museum

High St IV32 7EP
☎ 01343 821204 🖷 01343 821291

This converted church exhibits the largest collection of horse-drawn vehicles in the North of Scotland. There are also displays of the many aspects of village life through the ages, including model engines, clocks, costumes, a village shop and a Victorian parlour.
Times: Open May-Sep 10.30-4.
Fee: Free.
P ♿ shop

FORRES

Dallas Dhu Distillery

(1m S of Forres, off A940)
☎ 01309 676548

A perfectly preserved time capsule of the distiller's art. It was built in 1898 to supply malt whisky for Wright and Greig's 'Roderick Dhu' blend. Visitors are welcome to wander at will through this fine old Victorian distillery, or to take a guided tour, dram included.
Times: Open all year, Apr-Sep, daily 9.30-6.30; Oct-Mar, Mon-Sat 9.30-4.30, Sun 2-4.30. (Closed Thu pm, Fri in winter & 25-26 Dec).
Fee: £3 (ch £1, concessions £2.30).
P ♿ toilets for disabled shop

Falconer Museum

Tolbooth St IV36 1PH (on A96)
☎ 01309 673701 🖷 01309 675863
e-mail: alasdair.joyce@techleis.moray.gov.uk

Founded by bequests made by two brothers, Alexander and Hugh Falconer. Hugh was a distinguished scientist, friend of Darwin, recipient of many honours and Vice-President of the Royal Society. On display are fossil mammals collected by him, and items relating to his involvement in the antiquity of mankind. Other displays are on local wildlife, geology, archaeology and history. Regular temporary exhibitions are held.
Times: Open all year - Apr-Oct, Mon-Sat 10-5; Nov-Mar, Mon-Thu 11-12.30 & 1-3.30. (Closed Good Fri & May Day).
Fee: Free.
P (100yds) ♿ (induction loop system) shop (ex guide dogs)

Suenos' Stone

☎ 0131 668 8800

The 20ft-high stone was elaborately carved in the 9th or 10th century, with a sculptured cross on one side and groups of warriors on the other. Why it stands here no one knows, but it may commemorate a victory in battle.
Times: Open - accessible at all times.
Fee: Free.
P

KEITH

Strathisla Distillery

Seafield Av AB55 5BS (follow A96 Aberdeen to Inverness road, Strathisla is signposted midway through the town)
☎ 01542 783044 🖷 01542 783039
e-mail: jeanett_grant@seagram.com

Tour the oldest distillery in the highlands, founded in 1786. Discover the art of the blender before sipping a dram in luxurious comfort.
Times: Open Feb-mid Mar, Mon-Fri 9.30-4; mid Mar-end Nov, Mon-Sat 9.30-4, Sun 12.30-4.
Fee: £4 including £2 voucher redeemable in the distillery shop against the purchase of 70cl bottle of whisky. (ch18 free, children under 8 are not admitted to production areas, but are welcome in the centre)
P (access is very limited) shop (ex guide dogs)

MARYPARK

Glenfarclas Distillery

AB37 9BD (4m W of Aberlour on A95 to Grantown-on-Spey)
☎ 01807 500245 & 500257 🖷 01807 500234
e-mail: J&GGrant@glenfarclas.demon.co.uk

Home of one of the finest Highland malt whiskies, this distillery provides visitors with comprehensive guided tours illustrating the whisky's history and production. In the cask-filling store visitors can watch new whisky being poured into oak casks when filling is in progress. A Spirit of Speyside Whisky Festival is held every April.
Times: Open Jun-Sep, Sat 9.30-4.30; Sun by appointment only.
Fee: £3.50 per adult. Free admission to under 18's.Party.
P ♿ (only visitor centre is accessible) toilets for disabled shop (ex guide dogs in vis. centre)

ROTHES

Glen Grant Distillery

AB38 7BS (On A941, in Rothes)
☎ 01542 783318/783303 🖷 01542 783304
e-mail: jenniferrobertson@seagram.com

Founded in 1840 in a sheltered glen by the two Grant

brothers. Discover the secrets of the distillery, including the delightful Victorian garden originally created by Major Grant, and now restored to its former glory, where you can enjoy a dram.

Times: Open mid Mar-end Oct, Mon-Sat 10-4, Sun 11.30-4. Jun-end Sept remains open until 5 daily.

Fee: £2.50 includes £2 voucher redeemable in the distillery shop against 70cl bottle of whisky. Inclusive charge for garden visit & distillery tour. A free dram is offered to over 18s. (ch18 free, children under 8 not admitted to production areas, but are welcome in centre & garden)

P ♿ (reception centre & still house) toilets for disabled shop (ex guide dogs)

SPEY BAY

Tugnet Ice House

Tugnet IV32 7PJ (8m E of Elgin on A96, then onto B9104 towards Spey Bay, establishment is 1m further)

☎ 01309 673701 📠 01309 675863

e-mail: alasdair.joyce@techless.money.gov.uk

The largest ice house in Scotland, built in 1830, containing exhibitions on the history and techniques of commerical salmon fishing on the River Spey. There are sections on the geography, wildlife and industries of the Lower Spey area, such as ship-building at nearby Kingston.

Times: Please phone for details.

Fee: Free.

P ♿ toilets for disabled (ex guide dogs)

TOMINTOUL

Tomintoul Museum

The Square AB37 9ET (on A939, 13m E of Grantown)

☎ 01309 673701 📠 01309 675863

e-mail: alasdair.joyce@techleis.moray.gov.uk

Situated in one of the highest villages in Britain, the museum features a reconstructed crofter's kitchen and smiddy, with other displays on the local wildlife, the story of Tomintoul, and the local skiing industry.

Times: Open Mon-Fri early Apr-late May & late Sep-late Oct 9.30-4; late May-late Aug 9.30-4.30. Closed 12-2 each day, Good Fri & May Day.

Fee: Free.

P ♿ (handling display for visually impaired) shop (ex guide dogs)

NORTH AYRSHIRE

HUNTERSTON

Hunterston Power Station

KA23 9QJ (off A78, S of Largs)

☎ 0800 838557 📠 01294 826008

Times: Open - Mar-Sep, daily, 9.30-4.30; Oct-Feb, Mon-Fri 9.30-4.30, Sat & Sun 1-4.30. Tours - Mar-Sep 10.30, 1.30 & 3.30; Oct-Feb 1.30 & 3.30 (Closed 10 Dec-10 Jan).

P ♿ (trained guides for visually impaired visitors) toilets for disabled shop (ex guide dogs) *Details not confirmed for 2001*

IRVINE

The Big Idea

The Harbourside KA12 8XX (follow tourist signs)

☎ 08708 404030 📠 08708 403130

e-mail: net@bigidea.org.uk

The Big Idea is a permanent Millennium exhibition on the Ardeer Peninsula linked to Irvine harbourside by a retractable pedestrian bridge. It features 100 years of Nobel Laureates, and 1,000 years of invention and creative genius. Visitors can explore the history of mankind's inventions, creations and innovations.

Times: Open all year, daily 10-6. (Closed 25 Dec & 1 Jan).

Fee: £7 (ch, pen & concessions £5). Family ticket (2 adults & 2 ch) £20. Parties 12+

P ♿ toilets for disabled shop (ex guide dogs)

Scottish Maritime Museum

Harbourside KA12 8QE (Follow AA signs from Irvine)

☎ 01294 278283 📠 01294 313211

The museum has displays which reflect all aspects of Scottish maritime history. Vessels can be seen afloat in the harbour and undercover. Experience life in a 1910 shipyard worker's tenement flat. Visit the Lighthouse Engine Shop originally built in 1872, which is being developed and holds a substantial part of the museum's collection in open store.

Times: Open all year, daily 10-5, except Xmas & New Year.

Fee: £2.50 (ch & pen £1.75). Family ticket £5.

P ♿ (audio tapes for blind) toilets for disabled shop (ex guide dogs)

Vennel Gallery

10 Glasgow Vennel KA12 0BD

☎ 01294 275059 📠 01294 275059

e-mail: vennel@globalnet.co.uk

The Vennel Gallery has a reputation for exciting and varied exhibitions, ranging from international artists to local artists. Behind the museum is the Heckling Shop where Robert Burns, Scotland's most famous poet, spent part of his youth learning the trade of flax dressing. In addition to the audio-visual programme on Burns, there is a reconstruction of his lodgings at No.4 Glasgow Vennel, Irvine.

Times: Open all year - Jun-Sep, Mon-Sat 10-5, Sun 2-5 (Closed Wed); Oct-May, Tue, Thu-Sat 10-5. Closed for lunch 1-2.

Fee: Free.

P (residential area) ♿ shop (ex guide dogs)

LARGS

Kelburn Castle and Country Centre

Fairlie KA29 0BE (on A78 2m S of Largs)

☎ 01475 568685 📠 01475 568121

e-mail: admin@kelburncountrycentre.com

Historic home of the Earls of Glasgow, Kelburn is famous for its romantic Glen, family gardens, unique trees and spectacular views over the Firth of Clyde. Glen walks, riding and trekking centre, adventure course, activity workshop, Kelburn Story Cartoon

contd.

Exhibition and a family museum. The "Secret Forest" at the centre, Scotland's most unusual attraction, is a chance to explore the Giant's Castle, maze of the Green Man and secret grotto.
Times: Open all year, Apr-Oct, daily 10-6; Nov-Mar, 11-5.
Fee: £4.50 (concessions £3). Family tickets £13.
licensed (Ranger service to assist disabled) toilets for disabled shop

VIKINGAR!
Greenock Rd KA30 8QL
01475 689777 01475 689444
e-mail: anyone@vikingar.co.uk

A multi-media experience that takes you from the first Viking raids in Scotland to their defeat at the Battle of Largs. Additional facilities include a swimming pool, a 500-seat theatre and cinema, cafe and theatre bar.
Times: Open daily, Apr-Sep 10.30-5.30; Oct & Mar, 10.30-3.30; Nov & Feb wknds only, 10.30-3.30 (Closed Dec & Jan).
Fee: £3.75 (ch 4-15 £2.85, pen £2.75). Family ticket £10.50 (2adults + 2 children or 1 adult + 3 children)
toilets for disabled shop (ex guide dogs)

SALTCOATS

NORTH AYRSHIRE MUSEUM
Manse St, Kirkgate KA21 5AA
01294 464174 01294 464174
e-mail: namuseum@globalnet.co.uk

This museum is housed in an 18th-century church, and features a rich variety of artefacts from the North Ayrshire area, including archaeological and social history material. There is a continuing programme of temporary exhibitions.
Times: Open all year, Mon-Sat (ex Wed) 10-1 & 2-5.
Fee: Free.
P (100 mtrs) toilets for disabled shop (ex guide dogs)

NORTH LANARKSHIRE

COATBRIDGE

SUMMERLEE HERITAGE TRUST
Heritage Way, West Canal St ML5 1QD (Follow main routes torwards town centre, adjacent to Coatbridge central station)
01236 431261 01236 440429
Times: Open daily 10-5pm. (Closed 25-26 Dec & 1-2 Jan).
(wheelchair available & staff assistance) toilets for disabled shop (ex guide dogs) *Details not confirmed for 2001*

MOTHERWELL

MOTHERWELL HERITAGE CENTRE
High Rd ML1 3HU (M74 junct 6, A723 for town centre. At top of hill, turn left, before railway bridge)
01698 251000 01698 268867
Times: Open daily 10-5, Sun noon-5pm. Closed Xmas/New Year.
toilets for disabled shop (ex guide dogs) *Details not confirmed for 2001*

PERTH & KINROSS

BLAIR ATHOLL

BLAIR CASTLE
PH18 5TL (7m NW of Pitlochry, off A9)
01796 481207 01796 481487
e-mail: office@blair-castle.co.uk

Home of the Dukes of Atholl and the Atholl Highlanders, the Duke's unique private army. The castle dates back to the 13th century but was altered in the 18th, and later given a castellated exterior. The oldest part is Cumming's Tower, built in about 1270. There are paintings, Jacobite relics, lace, tapestries, and Masonic regalia. The extensive grounds include a deer park, and a restored 18th-century walled garden and children's play area. Events held include the annual parade of the Duke's Private Army (ring for details).
Times: Open Apr-27 Oct, daily 10-6. Last admission 5pm.
Fee: £6 (ch £4 & pen £5). Family ticket £18. Party.
licensed (toilets, but not suitable for severely disabled) shop (ex guide dogs/in grounds)
See advert on p337.

BRUAR

CLAN DONNACHAIDH (ROBERTSON) MUSEUM
PH18 5TW (approx 4m N of Blair Atholl, on B8079)
01796 483264 01796 483338
e-mail: donkey3@freenetname.co.uk

Clan centre for Robertsons, Duncans, Reids and other associated names. Changing displays feature the history of the clan and its people, exhibits include Jacobite relics, maps, silver, tartan and archives.
Times: Open Apr-Oct, Mon-Sat 10-5, Sun 11-5 (Jun-Aug closes at 5.30).
Fee: £1 (concessions 50p)
shop (ex guide dogs)

CRIEFF

GLENTURRET DISTILLERY
The Hosh PH7 4HA (1.5m NW off A85)
01764 656565 01764 654366

The distillery dates from 1775 and is the oldest in Scotland.
Times: Open Feb-Dec, Mon-Sat 9.30-6 (last tour 4.30), Sun 12-6 (last tour 4.30); Jan, Mon-Fri 11.30-4 (last tour 2.30). (Closed 25-26 Dec & 1-2 Jan)
Fee: Guided tours and Audio visual exhibition £3.50 (ch 12-17 £2.30 ch under 12 free).
licensed toilets for disabled shop

INNERPEFFRAY LIBRARY
PH7 3RF (4.5m SE on B8062)
01764 652819

This is Scotland's oldest free lending library. It was founded in 1691 and is still open every day except Thursdays. It is housed in a late 18th-century building, and contains a notable collection of bibles and rare books. Adjacent is St Mary's Chapel, the original site for the library and the Drummond family burial place.

Times: Open all year, Mon-Wed & Fri-Sat 10-12.45 & 2-4.45, Sun 2-4. (Closed Thu).
Fee: £2 (ch & pen £1)
shop

DUNKELD

The Ell Shop & Little Houses

The Cross PH8 0AN (off A9, 15m N of Perth)
☎ 01350 727460

The National Trust owns two rows of 20 houses in Dunkeld, and has preserved their 17th/18th-century character. They are not open to the public, but there is a display and audio-visual show in the Information Centre.
Times: Open Ell Shop Jun-Aug, Mon-Sat 10-5.30, Sun 1.30-5.30; Apr-May & Sep, Mon-Sat 10-5.30; Oct-23 Dec, Mon-Sat 10-4.30. Exterior of Little Houses can be viewed all year.
Fee: Free.
P (300yds) toilets for disabled shop

GLENGOULANDIE DEER PARK

Glengoulandie Deer Park

PH16 5NL (8m NW of Aberfeldy on B846).
☎ 01887 830261 01887 830261

Various native birds and animals are kept in surroundings as similar to their natural environment as possible, and there are herds of red deer and Highland cattle. Pets must not be allowed out of cars.
Times: Open May-Oct, 9am-1hr before sunset.
Fee: £1. Cars £5.
shop

KILLIECRANKIE

Killiecrankie Visitor Centre

NTS Visitor Centre PH16 5LG (3m N of Pitlochry on B8079)
☎ 01796 473233 01796 473233
e-mail: aclipson@nts.scot.demon.ac.uk

The visitor centre features an exhibition on the battle of 1689, when the Jacobite army routed the English, although the Jacobite leader, 'Bonnie Dundee', was mortally wounded in the attack. The wooded gorge is a notable beauty spot, admired by Queen Victoria, and there are some splendid walks.
Times: Visitor Centre, Exhibition, shop & snack bar Apr-Oct, daily 10-5.30. Site all year daily.
Fee: £1 honesty box.
(visitor centre only) toilets for disabled shop

KINROSS

Kinross House Gardens

KY13 8ET (M90 Edinburgh to Perth, junct 6 to Kinross, and signposted in village)
☎ 01577 862900 01577 863372
e-mail: jm@kinrosshouse.com

Yew hedges, roses and herbaceous borders are the elegant attractions of these formal gardens. The 17th-century house was built by Sir William Bruce, but is not generally open to the public.
Times: Gardens only open May-Sep, daily 10-7.
Fee: £2 (ch 50p).

Loch Leven Castle

Castle Island (on an Island in Loch Leven accessible by boat from Kinross)
☎ 01786 450000

Mary, Queen of Scots was imprisoned here in this five-storey castle in 1567 - she escaped 11 months later and so gave the 14th-century castle its special place in history.
Times: Open Apr-Sep, daily 9.30-6.30.
Fee: £3 (ch £1, concessions £2.30). Charge includes ferry trip.
shop

RSPB Nature Reserve Vane Farm

By Loch Leven KY13 7LX (on southern shore of Loch Leven, entered off B9097 to Glenrothes, 2m E junct 5 M90)
☎ 01577 862355 01577 862013

Well placed beside Loch Leven, with a nature trail and hides overlooking the Loch. Noted for its pink-footed geese, the area also attracts whooper swans, greylag geese, long-eared owls and great spotted woodpeckers amongst others. Details of special events are available from the Visitors Centre.
Times: Open daily, Apr-Xmas, 10-5; Jan-Mar 10-4.
Fee: £3 (ch 50p, concessions £2) Family (2 adults + all children) £6.
(ramps into visitor centre) toilets for disabled shop (ex guide dogs)

MILNATHORT

Burleigh Castle

KY13 7XZ
☎ 0131 668 8800

Dating from 1582, this tower house has an enclosed courtyard and roofed angle tower.
Times: Open at all reasonable times.
Fee: Free.

MUTHILL

Drummond Castle Gardens

PH7 4HZ (2m S of Crieff on A822)
☎ 01764 681257 & 681433 01764 681550
Times: Open - Gardens May-Oct, daily 2-6 (Last admission 5pm). Also Etr for 4 days.
toilets for disabled shop (ex on leads in grounds) *Details not confirmed for 2001*
See advert on p337.

PERTH

Black Watch Regimental Museum

Balhousie Castle, Hay St PH1 5HR (Follow signs to Perth & signs to Black Watch Museum, the best approach is via Dunkeld Road)
☎ 0131 310 8530 01738 643245

The treasures of the 42nd/73rd Highland Regiment from 1739 to the present day are on show in this

contd.

museum, together with paintings, silver, colours and uniforms.
Times: Open all year. May-Sep, Mon-Sat 10-4.30 (Closed last Sat in Jun); Oct-Apr, Mon-Fri, 10-3.30 (Closed 23 Dec-6 Jan). Other times & Parties 16+ by appointment.
Fee: Donations.
P (parking for disabled) shop (ex guide dogs)

BRANKLYN GARDEN
116 Dundee Rd PH2 7BB (on A85)
☎ 01738 625535
e-mail: aclipson@nts.scot.demon.co.uk

The gardens cover two acres and are noted for their collections of rhododendrons, shrubs and alpines. Garden tours and botanical painting courses are held.
Times: Open Mar-Oct, daily 9.30-sunset.
Fee: £2.40 (ch £1.50). Family ticket £6.40. Party 20+ £1.90 (ch/concessions £1)
P (ex guide dogs)

CAITHNESS GLASS FACTORY & VISITOR CENTRE
Inveralmond Industrial Est PH1 3TZ (on Perth Western Bypass, A9, at Inveralmond Roundabout)
☎ 01738 637373 01738 622494
Times: Open all year, Factory shop & restaurant Mon-Sat 9-5, Sun 10-5 (Nov-Mar, Sun 11-5). Glassmaking Mon-Fri 9-4.30.
P licensed (wheelchair available) toilets for disabled shop (ex guide dogs) *Details not confirmed for 2001*

HUNTINGTOWER CASTLE
PH1 3JL (2m W)
☎ 01738 627231

Formerly known as Ruthven Castle and famous as the scene of the so-called `Raid of Ruthven' in 1582, this structure was built in the 15th and 16th centuries and features a painted ceiling.
Times: Open all year, Apr-Sep, daily 9.30-6.30; Oct-Mar, Mon-Sat 9.30-4.30, Sun 2-4.30. (Closed Thu pm, Fri in winter & 25-26 Dec).
Fee: £2 (ch 75p, concessions £1.50).
P shop

PERTH MUSEUM & ART GALLERY
78 George St PH1 5LB
☎ 01738 632488 01738 443505
e-mail: museum@pkc.gov.uk

This purpose-built museum houses collections of fine and applied art, social and local history, natural history and archaeology. Temporary exhibitions are held throughout the year.
Times: Open all year, Mon-Sat 10-5. (Closed Xmas-New Year).
Fee: Free.
P (adjacent) toilets for disabled shop (ex guide dogs)

PITLOCHRY

EDRADOUR DISTILLERY
PH16 5JP (2.5m E of Pitlochry on A924)
☎ 01796 472095 01796 472002
e-mail: lwilliamson@campbell-distillers.co.uk

It was in 1825 that a group of local farmers founded Edradour, naming it after the bubbling burn that runs through it. It is Scotland's smallest distillery and is virtually unchanged since Victorian times. Have a dram of whisky while watching an audio-visual in the malt barn and then take a guided tour through the distillery itself.
Times: Open, early Mar-end Oct, Mon-Sat 9.30-5, Sun 12-5. Winter months, Mon-Sat 10-4, shop only. Tours by arrangement in winter months.
Fee: Free.
P toilets for disabled shop (ex guide dogs)

HYDRO-ELECTRIC VISITOR CENTRE, DAM & FISH PASS
PH16 5ND
☎ 01796 473152

The visitor centre features an exhibition showing how electricity is brought from the power station to the customer, and there's access to the turbine viewing gallery. The salmon ladder viewing chamber allows you to see the fish as they travel upstream to their spawning ground.
Times: Open Apr-Oct, daily 10-5.30.
Fee: £2 (ch £1, concessions £1.20). Family ticket £4.
P (monitor viewing of salmon fish pass) toilets for disabled shop

QUEEN'S VIEW

QUEEN'S VIEW VISITOR CENTRE
PH16 5NR (7m W of Pitlochry on B8019)
☎ 01350 727284 01350 728635
Times: Open Apr-Oct, daily 10-6.
P (charged) toilets for disabled shop *Details not confirmed for 2001*

SCONE

SCONE PALACE
PH2 6BD (2m NE of Perth on A93)
☎ 01738 552300 01738 552588
e-mail: sconepalace@com.co.uk

Scottish kings were crowned at Scone until 1651; and it was the site of the famous coronation Stone of Destiny from the 9th century until it was seized by the English in 1296. The castellated edifice of the present palace dates from 1803 but incorporates the 16th-century and earlier buildings. The grounds include a pinetum, woodland garden and brilliant displays of rhododendrons and azaleas in spring.

Times: Open early Apr-mid Oct, daily 9.30-5.15 (last admission 4.45). Special parties outside normal opening hours & during winter by arrangement.

Fee: Palace & Grounds £5.60 (ch £3.30, students & pen £4.80). Grounds only £2.80 (ch £1.70) Family £17.

licensed toilets for disabled shop

WEEM

Castle Menzies

PH15 2JD (1.5m from Aberfeldy on B846)

01887 820982

Restored seat of the Chiefs of Clan Menzies, and a fine example of a 16th-century Z-plan fortified tower house. Prince Charles Edward Stuart stayed here briefly on his way to Culloden in 1746. The whole of the 16th-century building can be explored, and there's a small clan museum.

Times: Open Apr-14 Oct, wkdays 10.30-5, Sun 2-5. Last entry 4.30pm.

Fee: £3 (ch £1.50, pen £2.50).

toilets for disabled shop (ex guide dogs)

RENFREWSHIRE

KILBARCHAN

Weaver's Cottage

The Cross PA10 2JG (off A737, 12m SW of Glasgow)

01505 705588

e-mail: aclipson@nts.scot.demon.co.uk

The weaving craft is regularly demonstrated at this delightful 18th-century cottage museum, and there is a collection of weaving equipment and other domestic utensils.

Times: Open Good Fri-Sep, daily, 1.30-5.30; wknds in Oct, 1.30-5.30 (last admission 5).

Fee: £2 (ch & concessions £1.30). Family ticket £5.30 Party.

(ex guide dogs)

LANGBANK

Finlaystone Country Estate

PA14 6TJ (on A48 W of Langbank, 10m W of Glasgow Airport on A8)

01475 540285 & 540505 01475 540285

e-mail: info@finlaystone.co.uk

A charming exhibition of Victoriana displayed in a homely family house with historical connections to John Knox and Robert Burns. The house, though, is only a foil to the considerable natural beauty of the formal gardens, walled gardens and woodland walks. The 'Dolly Mixture', an international collection of dolls, can be seen in the Visitor Centre.

Times: Open all year. Woodland & Gardens daily, 10-5. House, open Sun: Jul: groups by appointment.

Fee: Garden & Woods £2.50 (ch & pen £1.50); Guided tour of house by appointment £1.50. 'The Dolly Mixture' Doll Museum 50p.

(lift to second floor pathways for wheelchairs) toilets for disabled shop (ex on lead)

LOCHWINNOCH

Lochwinnoch Community Museum

High St PA12 4AB
☎ 01505 842615 📠 0141 889 9240

Local agriculture, industry and village life are reflected in the series of changing exhibitions displayed in this enterprising museum. There is an annual art exhibition and occasional special exhibitions based on the district's varied collections.

Times: Open all year, Mon 10-1, 2-5 & 6-8; Sat 10-1 & 2-5.
Fee: Free.
P ♿ (ex guide dogs)

RSPB Nature Reserve

Largs Rd PA12 4JF (on A760, Largs road, opposite Lochwinnoch station)
☎ 01505 842663 📠 01505 843026
e-mail: Lochwinnoch@interramp.co.uk

The reserve, part of Clyde Muirshiel Regional Park and a Site of Special Scientific Interest, comprises two shallow lochs fringed by marsh which in turn is fringed by scrub and woodland. There are two trails leading to three hides and a visitor centre with an observation tower.

Times: Open all year, daily 10-5. (Closed Xmas & New Year).
Fee: £2 (ch 50p, concessions £1). Family ticket £4.
P ♿ (wheelchairs available,access 3 hides) toilets for disabled shop

PAISLEY

Coats Observatory

49 Oakshaw St West PA1 2DE (M8 junct 27, 28 or 29)
☎ 0141 889 2013 📠 0141 889 9240

Victorian astronomical observatory, built in 1883, designed by John Honeyman. Displays on earthquakes, weather, astronomy and astronautics.

Times: Open all year, Tue-Sat 10-5, Sun 2-5. Last entry 15 minutes before closing.
Fee: Free.
P 150yds (meters/limited street parking) shop (except guide dogs)

Paisley Museum & Art Galleries

High St PA1 2BA
☎ 0141 889 3151 📠 0141 889 9240

Pride of place here is given to a world-famous collection of Paisley shawls. Other collections illustrate local industrial and natural history, while the emphasis of the art gallery is on 19th-century Scottish artists and an important studio ceramics collection.

Times: Open all year, Tue-Sat 10-5, Sun 2-5. BH 10-5.
Fee: Free.
P (200yds) ♿ (parking on site) toilets for disabled shop (Specialises in Paisley goods) (ex guide dogs)

SCOTTISH BORDERS

BROUGHTON

Broughton Place

ML12 6HJ (N on A701)
☎ 01899 830234

Times: Open - Gallery 28 Mar-19 Oct & 21 Nov-21 Dec, daily (ex Wed) 10.30-6.
P ♿ shop garden centre (ex guide dogs) *Details not confirmed for 2001*

COLDSTREAM

Hirsel

Douglas & Angus Estates, Estate Office, The Hirsel TD12 4LP (0.5m W on A697)
☎ 01890 882834 & 882965 📠 01890 882834

The seat of the Home family, the grounds of which are open all year. The focal point is the Homestead Museum, craft centre and workshops. From there, nature trails lead around the lake, along the Leet Valley and into woodland noted for its rhododendrons and azaleas.

Times: Garden & Grounds open all year, daylight hours. Museum 10-5. Craft Centre Mon-Fri, 10-5, wknds noon-5.
Fee: Etr-Sep: £2 per car. Oct-Etr £1 per car.
P (charged) ♿ toilets for disabled shop (ex on lead)

DRYBURGH

Dryburgh Abbey

(5m SE of Melrose on B6404)
☎ 01835 822381

The abbey was one of the Border monasteries founded by David I, and stands in a lovely setting on the River Tweed. The ruins are equally beautiful, and the church has the graves of Sir Walter Scott and Earl Haig.

Times: Open all year, Apr-Sep, daily 9.30-6.30; Oct-Mar, Mon-Sat 9.30-4.30, Sun 2-4.30. (Closed 25-26 Dec).
Fee: £2.50 (ch £1, concessions £1.90).
P ♿ shop

DUNS

Jim Clark Room

44 Newtown St TD11 3AU
☎ 01361 883960 📠 01361 884104

The Jim Clark Room houses a fascinating collection of trophies, awards, photographs and memorabilia of twice World Motor Racing Champion, and local farmer, Jim Clark. The Room also has a video presentaion and a small shop.

Times: Open Etr-Sep, Mon-Sat 10.30-1 & 2-4.30, Sun 2-4; Oct, Mon-Sat 1-4.
Fee: £1 (ch & pen 50p, ch under 5 free). 1 ch free with each paying adult.
P (on street) ♿ (ramps, wheelchair space, large print notices etc) shop (ex guide dogs)

MANDERSTON
TD11 3PP (2m E of Duns on the A6105)
☎ 01361 883450 🖷 01361 882010
e-mail: palmer@manderston.co.uk

This grandest of grand houses gives a fascinating picture of Edwardian life above and below stairs. Completely remodelled for the millionaire racehorse owner Sir James Miller, the architect was told to spare no expense, and so the house boasts the world's only silver staircase. The state rooms are magnificent, and there are fine formal gardens, with a woodland garden and lakeside walks.

Times: Open 11 May-28 Sep, Thu & Sun 2-5.30 (also late Spring & Aug English BH Mons).
Fee: Telephone 01361 882636 for details.
P ☕ ♿ shop 🐕 (ex guide dogs & in gardens)

EYEMOUTH

EYEMOUTH MUSEUM
Auld Kirk, Manse Rd TD14 5JE
☎ 018907 50678

The museum was opened in 1981 as a memorial to the 129 local fishermen lost in the Great Fishing Disaster of 1881. Its main feature is the 15ft Eyemouth tapestry, which was made for the centenary. There are also displays on local history.

Times: Open Apr-Jun & Sep, Mon-Sat 10-5, Sun 11.30-1.30; Jul-Aug, Mon-Sat 9.30.5.30; Sun 11.30-4.30; Oct, Mon-Sat 10-4, (closed Sun).
Fee: £1.75 (concessions £1.25). 1 accompanied ch free with each adult. Party.
P (250yds) (45min on street outside) ♿ shop

GALASHIELS

LOCHCARRON OF SCOTLAND VISITOR CENTRE
Waverley Mill, Huddersfield St TD1 3BA
☎ 01896 752091 & 751100 🖷 01896 758833

The museum brings the town's past to life and the focal point is a display on the woollen industry. Guided tours of the mill take about 40 minutes.

Times: Open all year, Mon-Sat 9-5, Sun (Jun-Sep) 12-5. Mill tours Mon-Thu at 10.30, 11.30, 1.30 & 2.30, Fri am only.
Fee: Museum free. Mill tour £2.50 (ch 14 free).
P ♿ toilets for disabled shop

GORDON

MELLERSTAIN HOUSE
TD3 6LG (5m E of Earlston, on unclass road)
☎ 01573 410225 🖷 01573 410636
e-mail: mellerstain.house@virgin.net

One of Scotland's finest Georgian houses, begun by William Adam and completed by his son Robert in the 1770s. It has beautiful plasterwork, period furniture and pictures, terraced gardens and a lake.

Times: Open Etr, then 25 Apr-Sep, Sun-Fri 12.30-5 (Last admission 4.30pm).
Fee: £4.50 (ch £2, pen £3.50) Party 20+.
P ☕ ♿ shop 🐕 (ex guide dogs)

HAWICK

DRUMLANRIG'S TOWER
1 Tower Knowe TD9 7JL
☎ 01450 373457 🖷 01450 378526

Drumlanrig's Tower has a fascinating history, beginning in the 12th century when it served as a fortified keep - occupied by the Black Douglas of Drumlanrig, through to the 18th century when Anne, Duchess of Monmouth and Buccleuch transformed it into a glittering residence. Later the Tower served as a gracious hotel. Now visitors may see the historic room settings, costumed figures, dioramas and audio visual programmes.

Times: Open Mar-31 Oct, peak season Mon-Sat 10-6, Sun 12-6; other times Mon-Sat 10-5, Sun 12-5. Family research room open Wed-Fri 10-12 & 1-3.
P ♿ toilets for disabled shop 🐕 (ex guide dogs) *Details not confirmed for 2001*

HERMITAGE

HERMITAGE CASTLE
TD9 0LU (5.5m NE of Newcastleton, on B6399)
☎ 01387 376222

A vast, eerie ruin of the 14th and 15th centuries, associated with the de Soulis, the Douglases and Mary, Queen of Scots. Much restored in the 19th century.

Times: Open Apr-Sep, daily 9.30-6.30.
Fee: £1.80 (ch 75p, concessions £1.30).
P ♿

INNERLEITHEN

ROBERT SMAIL'S PRINTING WORKS
7/9 High St EH44 6HA
☎ 01896 830206

These buildings contain a Victorian office, a paper store with reconstructed waterwheel, a composing room and a press room. The machinery is in full working order and visitors may view the printer at work and experience typesetting in the composing room.

Times: Open Etr & May-Sep Mon-Sat 10-1 & 2-5, Sun 2-5; wknds in Oct: Sat 10-1 & 2-5, Sun only 2-5. (Last tour 45mins before closing morning & afternoon).
Fee: £2.40 (ch & concessions £1.60). Family ticket £6.40. Party.
P (300yds) ♿ shop 🐕 (ex guide dogs)

JEDBURGH

JEDBURGH ABBEY
☎ 01835 863925

Standing as the most complete of the Border monasteries (although it has been sacked and rebuilt many times) Jedburgh Abbey has been described as 'the most perfect and beautiful example of the Saxon and early Gothic in Scotland'. It was founded as a priory in the 12th century by David I and the remains of some of the domestic buildings have been uncovered during excavations.

Times: Open all year, Apr-Sep, daily 9.30-6.30; Oct-Mar, Mon-Sat 9.30-4.30, Sun 2-4.30. (Closed 25-26 Dec).
Fee: £3 (ch £1, concessions £2.30).
P ♿ (limited access) toilets for disabled shop 🐕

KELSO

Floors Castle

Roxburghe Estates Office TD5 7SF (from town centre follow Roxburghe Street to main gates)

☎ 01573 223333 📠 01573 226056
e-mail: roxburghe_estate@btconnect.com

The home of the 10th Duke of Roxburghe, the Castle's lived-in atmosphere enhances the superb collection of French furniture, tapestries and paintings. The house was designed by William Adam in 1721 and enjoys a magnificent setting overlooking the River Tweed and the Cheviot Hills beyond.

Times: Open mid Apr-late Oct, daily 10-4.30. (last admission 4)
Fee: £5 (ch 2-15 £3, pen £4.50). Family ticket £14. Grounds only £3. Group rates for 20+.
licensed ♿ (lift) toilets for disabled shop garden centre (ex on lead)

Kelso Abbey

☎ 0131 668 8800

Founded by David I in 1128 and probably the greatest of the four famous Border abbeys, Kelso became extremely wealthy and acquired extensive lands. In 1545 it served as a fortress when the town was attacked by the Earl of Hertford, but now only fragments of the once-imposing abbey church give any clue to its long history.

Times: Open at any reasonable time.
Fee: Free.
♿

LAUDER

Thirlestane Castle

TD2 6RU (off A68, follow signs on main road approaches)

☎ 01578 722430 📠 01578 722761
e-mail: thirlestane@great-houses-scotland.co.uk

One of the seven "Great Houses of Scotland" this fairy-tale castle has been the home of the Maitland family, the Earls of Lauderdale, since the 12th century. Some of the most splendid plasterwork ceilings in Britain may be seen in the 17th-century state rooms. The family nurseries house a sizeable collection of antique toys and dolls. The informal grounds, with their riverside setting and views of nearby grouse moors, include a woodland walk and picnic tables.

Times: Open mid Apr-Oct daily 11-5 except Sat. Last admission 4.15
Fee: £5. Family ticket £12. Grounds only £1.50. Party.
shop (ex guide dogs)

MELROSE

Abbotsford

TD6 9BQ (2m W off A6091, on B6360)

☎ 01896 752043 📠 01896 752916

Set on the River Tweed, Sir Walter Scott's romantic mansion remains much the same as it was in his day. Inside there are many mementoes and relics of his remarkable life and also his historical collections, armouries and library, with some 9000 volumes. The mansion was built by Scott between 1811 and 1822, and he lived here until his death ten years after its completion.

Times: Open daily from 3rd Mon in Mar-Oct, Mon-Sat 10-5. Sun in Mar-May & Oct 2-5. Sun Jun-Sep 10-5.
Fee: £3.80 (ch £1.90). Party.
♿ (parking at private entrance) toilets for disabled shop (ex guide dogs & hearing dogs)

Harmony Garden

St Mary's Rd TD6 9LJ

☎ 01721 722502 📠 01721 724700

Set around the early 19th-century Harmony Hall (not open to visitors), this attractive walled garden has magnificent views of Melrose Abbey and the Eildon Hills. The garden comprises lawns, herbaceous and mixed borders, vegetable and fruit areas, and a rich display of spring bulbs.

Times: Open Apr-Sep, Mon-Sat 10-5.30, Sun 1.30-5.30.
Fee: £1 (honesty box),
♿

Melrose Abbey & Abbey Museum

☎ 01896 822562

The ruin of this Cistercian abbey is probably one of Scotland's finest, and has been given added glamour by its connection with Sir Walter Scott. The abbey was repeatedly wrecked during the Scottish wars of independence, but parts survive from the 14th century. The heart of Robert the Bruce is buried somewhere within the church.

Times: Open all year, Apr-Sep, daily 9.30-6.30; Oct-Mar, Mon-Sat 9.30-4.30, Sun 2-4.30. (Closed 25-26 Dec).
Fee: £3 (ch £1, concessions £2.30).
♿ shop

Priorwood Garden & Dried Flower Shop

TD6 9PX (off A6091)

☎ 01896 822493
e-mail: aclipson@nts.scot.demon.co.uk

This small garden specialises in flowers suitable for drying. It is formally designed with herbaceous and everlasting annual borders, and the attractive orchard has a display of `apples through the ages'. Dried flowers are on sale in the shop.

Times: Open Garden & Shop; Apr-Sep, Mon-Sat 10-5.30, Sun 1.30-5.30; Oct-24 Dec, Mon-Sat 10-4, Sun 1.30-4. Shop in Abbey St only; 9 Jan-Mar, Mon-Sat 12-4; Apr-24 Dec, Mon-Sat 10-5.30, Sun 1.30-5.30. (Closed 31 Oct-7 Nov).
♿ shop *Details not confirmed for 2001*

PEEBLES

Kailzie Gardens

EH45 9HT (2.5m SE on B7062)

☎ 01721 720007 📠 01721 720007

These extensive grounds, with their fine old trees, provide a burnside walk flanked by bulbs,

rhododendrons and azaleas. A walled garden contains herbaceous, shrub rose borders, greenhouses and a formal rose garden. A garden for all seasons, don't miss the snowdrops.
Times: Open 25 Mar-Oct, daily 11-5.30. Grounds close 5.30pm. Garden open all year.
Fee: Mid Oct-mid Mar, honesty box; mid Apr-mid Oct £2.50 (ch 5-15 75p).
P licensed (ramps in garden & gravel paths) toilets for disabled shop

Neidpath Castle
EH45 8NW (1m W on A72)
☎ 01721 720333 01721 720333

Occupying a spectacular position on the Tweed, this 14th-century stronghold has been interestingly adapted to 17th-century living; it contains a rock-hewn well, a pit prison, a small museum, and a tartan display. There are fine walks and a picnic area.
Times: Open mid Apr-early May, Mon-Sat 11-5, Sun 11-5; Jul-mid Sep, Mon-Sat 11-6, Sun 1-5.
Fee: £3 (ch £1, concessions £2.50). Family ticket £7.50. Party 20+.
P (charged) shop

SELKIRK
Bowhill House and Country Park
TD7 5ET (3m W of Selkirk off A708)
☎ 01750 22204 01750 22204
e-mail: bht@buccleuch.com

An outstanding collection of pictures, including works by Van Dyck, Canaletto, Reynolds, Gainsborough and Claude Lorraine, are displayed here. Memorabilia and relics of people such as Queen Victoria and Sir Walter Scott, and a restored Victorian kitchen add further interest inside the house. Outside, the wooded grounds are perfect for walking.
Times: Open, Park: Apr-Aug 12-5 (ex Fri). House & park: Jul, daily 1-4.30.
Fee: House & grounds £4.50 (ch under 5 & wheelchair users free, pen & groups £4). Grounds only £2.
P licensed (guided tours for the blind) toilets for disabled shop (Jul) (ex in park)

Halliwells House Museum
Halliwells Close, Market Place TD7 4BC (off A7 in town centre)
☎ 01750 20096 01750 23282
Times: Open Apr-Oct, Mon-Sat 10-5 (Jul & Aug until 6), Sun 2-4.
P toilets for disabled shop (ex guide dogs) *Details not confirmed for 2001*

Sir Walter Scott's Courtroom
Market Place TD7 4BT (on A7 in town centre)
☎ 01750 20096 01750 23282
Times: Open May-Sep, Sat 10-4, Sun 2-4; Oct, Mon-Sat 1-4.
P (100mtrs) (time limit-onstreet, none for car park) shop (ex guide dogs) *Details not confirmed for 2001*

SMAILHOLM
Smailholm Tower
TD5 7RT (6m W of Kelso on B6937)
☎ 01573 460365

An outstanding example of a classic Border tower-house, probably erected in the 15th century. It is 57ft high and well preserved. The tower houses an exhibition of dolls and a display based on Sir Walter Scott's book *'Minstrels of the Border'*.
Times: Open Apr-Sep, daily 9.30-6.30; Oct-Mar, Sat-Sun only. (Closed 25-26 Dec).
Fee: £2 (ch 75p, concessions £1.50).
P shop

STOBO
Dawyck Botanic Garden
EH45 9JU (8m SW of Peebles on B712)
☎ 01721 760254 01721 760214

From the landscaped walks of this historic arboretum an impressive collection of mature specimen trees can be seen - some over 40m tall and including the unique Dawyck beech-stand. Notable features include the Swiss Bridge, a fine estate chapel and stonework/terracing produced by Italian craftsmen in the 1820s.
Times: Open Mar-Oct, daily 9.30-6.
Fee: £3 (ch £1, concessions £2.50). Family ticket £7.
P toilets for disabled shop garden centre (ex guide dogs)

TRAQUAIR
Traquair House
EH44 6PW (1m S of Innerleithen on B709)
☎ 01896 830323 & 830785 01896 830639
e-mail: enquiries@traquair.co.uk

Said to be Scotland's oldest inhabited house, dating back to the 12th century, 27 Scottish monarchs have stayed at Traquair House. William the Lion Heart held court here, and the house has associations with Mary, Queen of Scots and the Jacobite risings. The Bear Gates were closed in 1745, not to be reopened until the Stuarts should once again ascend the throne. There is croquet, a maze and woodland walks by the River Tweed, craft workshops and an art gallery.
Times: Open Etr-Oct daily, 12.30-5.30 (ex Jun, Jul & Aug 10.30-5.30). Last admission 5pm. Grounds open Apr-Sep, 10.30-5.30.
Fee: £5.20 (ch £2.60 pen £4.20) Family £14. Grounds only £2 (ch £1).
P licensed shop

SOUTH AYRSHIRE

ALLOWAY

Burn's Cottage

Burns National Heritage Park KA7 4PY (2m S of Ayr, M77/A77 from Glasgow))

☎ 01292 441215 📠 01292 441750
e-mail: dotmckay@aol.com

This thatched cottage was built in 1757, and Robert Burns was born here in 1759. The adjacent museum contains a large number of the poets' songs, poems, letters and personal relics. On display are the original manuscripts of *'Auld Lang Syne'* and *'Tam O'Shanter'*. Special events are held during Burns Week (18-25 Jan).

Times: Open all year, Apr-Oct 9-6; Nov-Mar 10-4 (Sun 12-4).

Fee: £2.80 (ch & pen £1.40). Group.

P ☕ ♿ toilets for disabled shop ✗ (ex guide dogs)

Burn's Monument

KA7 4PQ (2m S of Ayr, follow signs for Burns' National Heritage Park in Alloway)

☎ 01292 443700 📠 01292 441750
e-mail: dotmckay@aol.com

The monument was built in 1823 to a fine design by Thomas Hamilton Junior, with sculptures of characters in Burns' poems by a self-taught artist, James Thom.

Times: Open as for Burns' Cottage. (Closed Oct-Etr).

Fee: Admission included in entrance to Burns' Cottage

P ♿

Tam O'Shanter Experience

Burns National Heritage Park, Murdoch's Lone KA7 4PQ (2m S of Ayr)

☎ 01292 443700 📠 01292 441750
e-mail: dotmckay@aol.com

An introduction to the life of Robert Burns, with two audio-visual presentations one about the life of Robert Burns, the other being a multi-screen 3D experience of the *Tale of Tam O'Shanter*. There are also tranquil landscaped gardens.

Times: Open all year, Apr-Oct 9-6, Nov-Mar 9-5.

Fee: £2.80 (pen & ch £1.40).

P ☕ ✕ licensed ♿ (wheelchair available) toilets for disabled shop ✗ (ex guide dogs)

BARGANY

See Old Daillly

CULZEAN CASTLE

Culzean Castle & Country Park

KA19 8LE (4m W of Maybole, off A77)

☎ 01655 884455 📠 01655 884503

This 18th-century castle stands on a cliff in spacious grounds and was designed by Robert Adam for the Earl of Cassillis. It is noted for its oval staircase, circular drawing room and plasterwork. The Eisenhower Room explores the American general's links with Culzean. The 563-acre country park has a wide range of attractions - shoreline, woodland walks, parkland, an adventure playground and gardens.

Times: Country park open all year, daily 9.30-sunset. Castle & visitor centre open Apr-Oct, 10.30-5.30. Last admission 5pm. Other times by appointment.

Fee: Country Park £3.50 (concessions £2.40). Castle £4.20 (concessions £2.80). Combined ticket for castle and country park £6.50 (concessions £4.40) Family combined ticket £17. Party 20+

P ☕ ✕ licensed ♿ (wheelchairs available, lift in castle) toilets for disabled shop garden centre (ex castle, ex guide dogs)

See advert on opposite page.

KIRKOSWALD

Souter Johnnie's Cottage

Main Rd KA19 8HY (on A77, 4m SW of Maybole)

☎ 01655 760603
e-mail: aclipson@nts.scot.demon.co.uk

'Souter' means cobbler and the village cobbler who lived in this 18th-century cottage was the inspiration for Burns' character Souter Johnnie, in his ballad *Tam O'Shanter*. The cottage is now a Burns museum and life-size stone figures of the poet's characters can be seen in the restored ale-house in the cottage garden.

Times: Open Good Fri-Sep daily 11.30-5; wknds in Oct, 11.30-5. Last admission 4.30

Fee: £2 (ch & concessions £1.30). Family ticket £5.30. Party.

P (75yds) ♿ (only one small step into cottage) ✗ (ex guide dogs)

MAYBOLE

Crossraguel Abbey

(2m S)

☎ 01655 883113

The extensive remains of this 13th-century Cluniac monastery are impressive and architecturally important. The monastery was founded by Duncan, Earl of Carrick and the church, claustral buildings, abbot's house and an imposing castellated gatehouse can be seen.

Times: Open Apr-Sep, daily 9.30-6.30.

Fee: £1.80 (ch 75p, concessions £1.30).

P ✗

OLD DAILLY

Bargany Gardens

KA26 9PH (4m NE on B734 from Girvan)

☎ 01465 871249 📠 01465 871282

Woodland walks display snowdrops, daffodils and blubells in spring, and a fine show of azaleas and rhododendrons is to be seen around the lilypond in May and June. Ornamental trees give autumn colour, and visitors can buy plants from the gardens.

Times: Open Gardens Mar-Oct, daily to 7pm (or dusk).

Fee: Contribution Box, £1 per person requested.

P ♿

TARBOLTON

Bachelors' Club

Sandgate St KA5 5RB (on B744, 7.5m NE of Ayr)
☎ 01292 541940
e-mail: aclipson@nts.scot.demon.co.uk

In this 17th-century thatched house, Robert Burns and his friends formed a debating club in 1780. Burns attended dancing lessons and was initiated into freemasonry here in 1781. The house is furnished in the style of the period.

Times: Open Apr-Sep, daily 1.30-5.30; wknds in Oct 1.30-5.30.-last admission 5pm.
Fee: £2 (concessions £1.30) Family £5.30. Schools £1.
P (in village) (ex guide dogs)

SOUTH LANARKSHIRE

BIGGAR

Gladstone Court Museum

ML12 6DT (entrance by 113 High St)
☎ 01899 221573 & 221050 01899 221050
e-mail: margaret@bmtrust.co.uk

An old-fashioned village street is portrayed in this museum, which is set out in a century-old coach-house. On display are reconstructed shops, complete with old signs and advertisements - a bank, telephone exchange, photographer's booth and other interesting glimpses into the recent past.

Times: Open Etr-Oct, Mon-Sat 10-5, Sun 2-5.
Fee: £2 (ch £1, pen £1.25). Family ticket £4. Party.
P shop (ex guide dogs)

Greenhill Covenanters House

Burn Braes ML12 6DT
☎ 01899 221572 & 221050 01899 221050
e-mail: margaret@bmtrust.co.uk

This 17th-century farmhouse was brought, stone by stone, ten miles from Wiston and reconstructed at Biggar. It has relics of the turbulent 'Covenanting' period, when men and women defended the right to worship in Presbyterian style. Audio presentations.

Times: Open mid May-Sep, daily 2-5.
Fee: £1 (ch 50p, pen 70p). Family ticket £2.50. Party.
P shop (ex guide dogs)

Moat Park Heritage Centre

ML12 6DT
☎ 01899 221050 01899 221050
e-mail: margaret@bmtrust.co.uk

The centre illustrates the history, archaeology and geology of the Upper Clyde and Tweed valleys with interesting displays.

Times: Open all year, Apr-Oct, daily 10-5, Sun 2-5; Nov-Feb, wkdays during office hours. Other times by prior arrangement.
Fee: £2 (ch £1, pen £1.50). Family ticket £4. Party.
P (upper floor with assistance on request) toilets for disabled shop (ex guide dogs)

BLANTYRE

David Livingstone Centre

165 Station Rd G72 9BY (M74 junct 5 onto A725, to A724, take signs for Blantyre, right at lights, Centre is at foot of hill)
☎ 01698 823140 01698 821424

Share the adventurous life of Scotland's greatest explorer, from his childhood in the Blantyre Mills to his explorations in the heart of Africa, dramatically illustrated in the historic tenement where he was born. Various events are planned throughout the season.

Times: Open Mon-Sat 10-5, Sun 12.30-5. (Last admission 4.30). Opening hours may be reduced in winter (contact for details).
Fee: £3 (concessions £2). Up to 3 ch free when accompanied by an adult.
P toilets for disabled shop (ex guide dogs/lead grounds)

BOTHWELL

Bothwell Castle

G71 8BL (approach from Uddingston off B7071)
☎ 01698 816894

Besieged, captured and 'knocked about' several times in the Scottish-English wars, the castle is a splendid ruin. Archibald the Grim built the curtain wall; later, in

contd.

1786, the Duke of Buccleuch carved graffiti - a coronet and initials - beside a basement well.
Times: Open all year, Apr-Sep, daily 9.30-6.30; Oct-Mar, Mon-Sat 9.30-4.30, Sun 2-4.30. (Closed Thu pm, Fri in winter & also 25-26 Dec).
Fee: £2 (ch 75p, concessions £1.50).
P shop

HAMILTON

Chatelherault

Ferniegair ML3 7UE (2.5km SE of Hamilton on A72 Hamilton-Larkhall/Lanark Clyde Valley tourist route)
☎ 01698 426213 01698 421532

Times: Open all year, Mon-Sat 10-5, Sun 12-5. House closed all day Friday.
P (architect designed for disabled person) toilets for disabled shop garden centre (ex grounds & guide dogs) *Details not confirmed for 2001*

Low Parks Museum

129 Muir St ML3 6BJ
☎ 01698 283981 01698 283479

The museum tells the story of Hamilton and the Clyde Valley, created by linking the former District Museum and The Cameronians (Scottish Rifles) Museum. Housed in the town's oldest building, dating from 1696, the museum features a restored 18th-century assembly room and exhibitions on Hamilton Palace and The Covenanters.
Times: Open Mon-Sat (ex Fri) 10-5, Sun 12-5.
Fee: Free.
P shop (ex guide dogs)

UDDINGSTON

Glasgow Zoopark

Calderpark G71 7RZ
☎ 0141 771 1185, 771 1186 & 771 1187
0141 771 2615

Times: Open all year, daily 10-5 (or 6pm depending on season).
P (charged) (key for toilet at gate) toilets for disabled shop (ex guide dogs) *Details not confirmed for 2001*

STIRLING

BANNOCKBURN

Bannockburn Heritage Centre

Glasgow Rd FK7 0LJ (2m S of Stirling off M80/M9 junct 9)
☎ 01786 812664 01786 810892

The Heritage Centre stands close to what is traditionally believed to have been Robert the Bruce's command post before the 1314 Battle of Bannockburn, a famous victory for the Scots and a turning point in Scottish history.
Times: Open - Rotunda & site always open. Heritage Centre & Shop; Mar & Nov-23 Dec, daily 11-4.30; Apr-Oct daily 10-5.30. (Last audio-visual showing half hour before closing).
Fee: Admission to Heritage Centre incl. audio-visual presentation £2.40 (ch & concessions £1.60). Family £6.40. Party.
P (Induction loop for the hard of hearing) toilets for disabled shop (Closed 1-10 Nov) (ex site only)

BLAIR DRUMMOND

Blair Drummond Safari & Leisure Park

FK9 4UR (M9 exit 10, 4m along A84 towards Callander)
☎ 01786 841456 & 841396 01786 841491

Drive through the wild animal reserves where monkeys, zebras, North American bison, antelope, lions, tigers, white rhino and camels can be seen at close range. Other attractions include the sea lion show, a ride on the boat safari through the waterfowl sanctuary and around Chimpanzee Island, an adventure playground, giant astraglide, and pedal boats. There are also African elephants, giraffes and ostriches.
Times: Open Apr-2 Oct, daily 10-5.30. Last admission 4.30.
Fee: £8.50 (ch 3-14 & pen £4.50, ch under 3 free). Party 15+.
P licensed (special menus & waitress service if booked in advance) toilets for disabled shop (ex guide dogs)

CALLANDER

Rob Roy and Trossachs Visitor Centre

Ancaster Square FK17 8ED (on A84)
☎ 01877 330342 01877 330784

The fascinating story of Scotland's most famous outlaw, Rob Roy MacGregor is vividly portrayed through an exciting multi-media theatre and explained in the carefully researched 'Life and Times' exhibition. Also tourist information centre covering the beautiful Trossachs area. Traditional Scottish music evenings, celidhs and illustrated talks, are arranged 6 nights a week from June to October. School pack available.
Times: Open Mar-Dec daily; Mar-May & Oct-Dec 10-5; Jun 9.30-6; Jul-Aug 9-8, Sep 10-6. Jan & Feb wknds only 11-4.30.
Fee: £2.90 (ch £1.05, student £2.40 & pen £2.05). Family ticket £6.35
P toilets for disabled shop (ex guide dogs)

CAUSEWAYHEAD

National Wallace Monument

Abbey Craig, Hillfoots Rd FK8 2AD (reached from A907, Stirling to Alloa Rd)
☎ 01786 472140 01786 461322

The 220ft tower was completed in 1869, and Sir William Wallace's two-handed sword is preserved inside. Seven battlefields and a fine view towards the Highlands can be seen in one of the most awe inspiring views in Scotland. Exhibitions on three floors.
Times: Open all year daily. Jan-Feb & Nov-Dec, 10-4; Mar-May & Oct, 10-5; Jun & Sep 10-6; Jul-Aug 9.30-6.30.
Fee: £3.30 (ch & pen £2.30, student £3.05). Family ticket £9.70.
P (accessible visitors pavillion at foot of hill) shop (ex guide dogs)

DOUNE

Doune Castle

FK16 6EA (8m S of Callander on A84)
☎ 01786 841742

The 14th-century stronghold with its two fine towers has been restored. It stands on the banks of the River Teith, and is associated with 'Bonnie' Prince Charlie and Sir Walter Scott.

Times: Open all year, Apr-Sep, daily 9.30-6.30; Oct-Mar, Mon-Sat 9.30-4.30, Sun 2-4.30. (Closed Thu pm, Fri in winter & 25-26 Dec).
Fee: £2.50 (ch £1, concessions £1.90).
P shop

Doune Motor Museum

The Doune Collection, Carse of Cambus FK16 6HD (8m NW of Stirling on A84)
☎ 01786 841203 01786 842070
Times: Open 1 Apr-30 Nov, daily, 10am-5pm.
P (ramped areas to museum & cafeteria) toilets for disabled shop *Details not confirmed for 2001*

KILLIN

Breadalbane Folklore Centre

Falls of Dochart FK21 8XE (on A82, turn right at Crianlarich onto A85 towards Perth/Stirling. Then join A827 to Killin)
☎ 01567 820254 01567 820764

Overlooking the beautiful Falls of Dochart, the Centre gives a fascinating insight into the legends of Breadalbane - Scotland's 'high country'. Learn of the magical deeds of St Fillan and hear tales of mystical giants, ancient prophesies, traditional folklore and clan history. Housed in historic St Fillans Mill which features a restored waterwheel. Tourist Information and gift shop.

Times: Open Mar-May & Oct, daily 10-5; Jun & Sep, daily 10-6; Jul-Aug, daily 9.30-6.30. Feb wknds only 10-4 Closed Nov-Jan; Feb 10-4 wknds only.
Fee: £1.55 (concessions £1.05, ch under 5 free). Family £3.05
P (30 mtrs) toilets for disabled shop (ex guide dogs)

PORT OF MENTEITH

Inchmahome Priory

(4m E of Aberfoyle, off A81)
☎ 01877 385294

Walter Comyn founded this Augustinian house in 1238, and it became famous as the retreat of the infant Mary Queen of Scots in 1543. The ruins of the church and cloisters are situated on an island in the Lake of Monteith.

Times: Open Apr-Sep, daily 9.30-6.30. Ferry subject to cancellation in adverse weather conditions.
Fee: £3 (ch £1, concessions £2.30). Admission charge includes ferry trip.
P shop

STIRLING

Mar's Wark

Broad St FK8 1EE
☎ 0131 668 8800

Now partly ruined, this Renaissance-style mansion was built in 1570 by the lst Earl of Mar, Regent of Scotland. With its gatehouse enriched with sculptures, it is one of several fine buildings on the road to Stirling Castle. The Earls of Mar lived there until the 6th Earl fled the country after leading the 1715 Jacobite Rebellion.

Times: Open all reasonable times.
Fee: Free.

Museum of Argyll & Sutherland Highlanders

The Castle FK8 1EH (museum located in Stirling Castle)
☎ 01786 75165 01786 446038

Situated in the King's Old Building in Stirling Castle, the museum tells the history of the Regiment from 1794 to the present day. Displays include uniforms, medals, silver, paintings, colours, pipe banners, and commentaries.

Times: Open Etr-Sep, Mon-Sat 10-5.30, Sun 11-5; Oct-Etr, Mon-Sun 10-4.
Fee: Entry to museum free but entry fee to castle.
P (castle esplanade) shop

Old Town Jail

Saint John St FK8 1EA (follow signs for castle up the hill, jail on left at top of St John's St)
☎ 01786 450050 01786 471301
e-mail: otjva@aillst.ossian.net

Built in 1847 to replace the old Tolbooth jail, this is an outstanding example of Victorian architecture. A living history performance means the visitor can learn about the daily life of the prisoners and the strict regime practised in the prison.

Times: Open daily, Apr-Sep 9.30-5; Oct-Mar 9.30-3.30,
Fee: £3.30 (concessions £2.45). Family ticket £9.15.
P (lift to viewpoint) toilets for disabled shop (ex guide dogs)

Royal Burgh of Stirling Visitor Centre

Castle Esplanade FK8 1EH (next to Stirling Castle)
☎ 01786 479901 & 462517 01786 451881
Times: Open all year, Jan-Mar & Nov 9.30-5; Apr-Jun 9.30-6.30; Jul-Aug, 9-6.30; Sep-Oct 9.30-6.
P (Induction loop for the hard of hearing) toilets for disabled shop (ex guide dogs) *Details not confirmed for 2001*

Smith Art Gallery & Museum

Dumbarton Rd FK8 2RQ (junct 10 M9 follow town centre signs)

☎ 01786 471917 01786 449523
e-mail: museum@smithartgallery.demon.co.uk

This award-winning museum and gallery presents a variety of exhibitions drawing on its own rich collections and works from elsewhere. A range of programmes and events takes place.

Times: Open all year, Tue-Sat 10.30-5, Sun 2-5 (Closed Mon, Xmas day, Boxing day, New Years day).

Fee: Free.

(wheelchair lift, induction loop in theatre) toilets for disabled shop

Stirling Castle

Upper Castle Hill FK8 1EJ

☎ 01786 450000

Sitting on top of a 250ft rock, Stirling Castle has a strategic position on the Firth of Forth. As a result it has been the scene of many events in Scotland's history. James II was born at the castle in 1430. Mary, Queen of Scots spent some years there, and it was James IV's childhood home. Among its finest features are the splendid Renaissance palace built by James V, and the Chapel Royal, rebuilt by James VI.

Times: Open all year, Apr-Sep, daily 9.30-6; Oct-Mar, daily 9.30-5. Last ticket sold 45 mins prior to closing time.

Fee: £6 (ch £1.50, concessions £4.50).

(charged) licensed toilets for disabled shop

WEST DUNBARTONSHIRE

BALLOCH

Balloch Castle Country Park

G83 8LX (A82 for Dumbartonshire, Balloch from Glasgow. A811 for Balloch from Stirling)

☎ 01389 758216 01389 720922

Set at the southern end of Loch Lomond, the park encompasses varying habitats, a walled garden, and lawns for picnics giving wonderful views of the loch. Overlooking the lawns is Balloch Castle, built in 1808. Its visitor centre gives an introduction to local history and wildlife.

Times: Open: Visitor Centre, Apr-Oct daily 10-5.45. Country Park open all year, 8-dusk.

Fee: Free.

toilets for disabled shop

DUMBARTON

Dumbarton Castle

☎ 01389 732167

The castle, set on the 240ft Dumbarton Rock above the River Clyde, dominates the town (the capital of the Celtic kingdom of Strathclyde) and commands spectacular views. Most of what can be seen today dates from the 18th and 19th centuries, but there are a few earlier remains.

Times: Open all year, Apr-Sep, daily 9.30-6.30; Oct-Mar, Mon-Sat 9.30-4.30, Sun 2-4.30. (Closed Thu pm, Fri in winter & 25-26 Dec).

Fee: £2 (ch 75p, concessions £1.50).

shop

WEST LOTHIAN

LINLITHGOW

Blackness Castle

EH49 7AL (4m NE)

☎ 01506 834807

Once, this was one of the most important fortresses in Scotland. Used as a state prison during covenanting time and in the late 19th century as a powder magazine, it was one of four castles left fortified by the Articles of Union. Most impressive are the massive 17th-century artillery emplacements.

Times: Open all year, Apr-Sep, daily 9.30-6.30; Oct-Mar, Mon-Sat 9.30-4.30, Sun 2-4.30. (Closed Thu pm, Fri in winter & 25-26 Dec).

Fee: £2 (ch 75p, concessions £1.50).

shop

House of The Binns

EH49 7NA (4m E of Linlithgow off A904)

☎ 01506 834255
e-mail: aclipson@nts.scot.demon.co.uk

An example of changing architectural tastes from 1612 onwards, this house reflects the transition from fortified stronghold to spacious mansion. The original three-storey building, with small windows and twin turrets, evolved into a fine crenellated house with beautiful moulded plaster ceilings - the ancestral home of the Dalyell family. There is a magnificent display of snowdrops and daffodils in spring.

Times: Open: House, May-Sep, daily ex Fri, 1.30-5.30 (last admission 5). Parkland, Apr-Oct, daily 10-7; Nov-Mar, daily 10-4 (last admission 30 mins before closing).

Fee: £3.70 (ch & pen £2.50). Family tickets £9.90. Schools £1. Members of the Royal Scots Dragoon Guards, in uniform, admitted free.

(braille sheets) (ex guide dogs)

Linlithgow Palace

(off M9)

☎ 01506 842896

The magnificent ruin of a great Royal Palace, set in its own park or 'peel'. All the Stewart kings lived here, and work commissioned by James I, III, IV, and VI can be seen. The great hall and the chapel are particularly fine. James V was born here in 1512 and Mary, Queen of Scots in 1542.

Times: Open all year, Apr-Sep, daily 9.30-6.30; Oct-Mar, Mon-Sat 9.30-4.30, Sun 2-4.30. (Closed 25-26 Dec).

Fee: £2.50 (ch £1, concessions £1.90).

shop

The Scottish Islands

Both beautiful and daunting, the islands around the Scottish coast reward the braver traveller with incredible unspoilt landscapes, and the satisfaction of journeying to them.

Lewis, Skye and Mull are the largest of the islands, but there are countless others, some of them are tiny, like the sparsely populated Scarp (2500 acres) or the furthest south of the Outer Hebrides, Berneray, which is only 500 acres. The furthest north is Shetland, which is 110 miles north-east of Scotland's north coast. The traditions of this group of islands are more Viking than Scottish, as is demonstrated by Lerwick's annual celebration, the fire feast of 'Up-Helly-Aa'. Held on the last Tuesday of January, the festival is an adaptation of a Norse feast, Uphalliday, marking the end of Yule and the long winter nights. A replica of a 30ft Viking galley is hauled through the streets and ceremonially burned as a prelude to a night of revelry.

Lewis and Harris form a single island that, together with the Uists, Benbecula and Barra, provides a 150-mile long storm-break for the Inner Hebrides and the Western Highlands. Though thousands of people live on Lewis and Harris, the island nevertheless contains huge areas of emptiness. What is not peat-bog and water is mostly rock. The seas are cold, unsurprisingly, but the white sands are lovely to walk on, and there are a number of standing stones near Callanish.

From the sea, Skye's cloud-cap can be seen long before its dark mountains climb over the horizon; so the Norsemen called it Skuyo, 'Isle of Clouds'. Composed mainly of moutain and moor, Skye is a gathering of peninsulas, where crofting is still the main occupation.

Top: Loch Scridain on the Isle of Mull.

ARRAN, ISLE OF

BRODICK

Brodick Castle, Garden & Country Park

KA27 8HY

☎ 01770 302202 & 302462 📠 01770 302312

The site has been fortified since Viking times, but the present castle dating from the 13th century was a stronghold of the Dukes of Hamilton. Splendid silver, fine porcelain and paintings acquired by generations of owners can be seen. There is a magnificent woodland garden, world famous for its rhododendrons and azaleas.

Times: Open - Castle: Jul-Aug, daily 11-5 (last admission 4.30); Apr-Jun & Sep-Oct, daily 11-4.30 (last admission 4). Reception centre: 10-5. Walled garden: open all year, daily 9.30-5. Country park: open all year, daily 9.30-sunset.

Fee: Castle & Gardens £4.80 (concessions £3.20). Garden only £2.40. Family ticket £12.80. Party.

P ✕ ♿ (Braille sheets, motorised buggy, wheelchairs & stairlift) toilets for disabled shop (ex guide dogs)

BUTE, ISLE OF

ROTHESAY

Ardencraig

PA20 9HA (1m off A844, S of Rothesay)

☎ 01700 504225 📠 01700 504225

e-mail: p_weatherall@cqm.co.uk

Particular attention has been paid to improving the layout of the garden and introducing rare plants. The greenhouse and walled garden produce plants for floral displays throughout the district. A variety of fish is kept in the ornamental ponds and the aviaries have some interesting birds.

Times: Open May-Sep. **Fee:** Free. P ♿ (ex guide dogs)

See advert on opposite page.

Rothesay Castle

☎ 01700 502691

The focal point of Rothesay is this 13th-century castle. It has lofty curtain walls defended by drum towers that enclose a circular courtyard.

Times: Open all year, Apr-Sep, daily 9.30-6.30; Oct-Mar, Mon-Sat 9.30-4.30, Sun 2-4.30. (Closed Thu pm, Fri in winter & 25-26 Dec).

Fee: £2 (ch 75p, concessions £1.50). P shop

GREAT CUMBRAE ISLAND

MILLPORT

Museum of the Cumbraes

Garrison House KA28 0DG (Ferry to Millport, from Largs Cal-Mac Terminal. Bus meets each ferry.)

☎ 01475 531191 📠 01294 464174

e-mail: namuseum@globalinet.co.uk

A small museum which displays the history and life of the Cumbraes. Along with artefacts from the collection, the museum displays a major exhibition each summer.

Times: Open Jun-Sep, Mon-Sat 11-1 & 1.30-5.

Fee: Free. P (50m) ♿ (ex guide dogs)

LEWIS, ISLE OF

ARNOL

Black House Museum

PA86 9DB (11m NW of Stornoway on A858)

☎ 01851 710395

A traditional Hebridean dwelling, built without mortar and roofed with thatch on a timber framework. It has a central peat fire in the kitchen, no chimney and a byre under the same roof.

Times: Open all year, Apr-Sep, Mon-Sat 9.30-6.30; Oct-Mar, Mon-Thu & Sat 9.30-4.30. (Closed 25-26 Dec).

Fee: £2.50 (ch £1, concessions £1.90).

P ♿ toilets for disabled shop

CALLANISH

Callanish Standing Stones

PA86 9DY (12m W of Stornoway off A859)

☎ 01851 621422

An avenue of 19 monoliths leads north from a circle of 13 stones with rows of more stones fanning out to south, east and west. Probably constructed between 3000 and 1500BC, this is a unique cruciform of megaliths.

Times: Site accessible at all times. Visitor Centre open Apr-Sep, Mon-Sat 10-7; Oct-Mar, Mon-Sat 10-4.

Fee: £1.50 (ch 50p, concessions £1).

P ✕ ♿ toilets for disabled shop

CARLOWAY

Dun Carloway Broch

(1.5m S of Carloway)

☎ 0131 668 8800

Brochs are late-prehistoric circular stone towers, and their origins are mysterious. This is one of the best examples - the tower still stands about 30ft high.

Times: Open at all reasonable times. **Fee:** Free. P

MULL, ISLE OF

CRAIGNURE

Mull & West Highland Narrow Gauge Railway
Craignure (old pier) Station PA65 6AY
☎ 01680 812494 (in season) or 01680 300389 📠 01680 300595

The first passenger railway on a Scottish island, opened in 1984. Both steam and diesel trains operate on the ten-and-a-quarter inch gauge line, which runs from Craignure to Torosay Castle.
Times: Open 20 Apr-21 Oct.
Fee: Return £3.30 (ch £2.20); Single £2.20 (ch £1.40). Family ticket return £8.75, single £6.
P ♿ (provision to carry person seated in wheelchair on trains) shop

Torosay Castle & Gardens
PA65 6AY (1m S of Ferry Terminal at Craignure)
☎ 01680 812421 📠 01680 812470
e-mail: torosay@aol.com

The Scottish baronial architecture of this Victorian castle is complemented by the magnificent setting, and inside the house there are displays of portraits and wildlife pictures, family scrapbooks and a study of the Antarctic. The gardens include a statue walk and water garden, a Japanese garden, a narrow gauge steam and diesel railway.
Times: Open Etr-mid Oct, daily 10.30-5.30. Gardens all year.
Fee: £4.50 (ch £1.50, pen & students £3.50). Gardens only £3.50. Groups.
P ☕ ♿ toilets for disabled shop garden centre 🐕 (ex on leads in grounds only) 💳

ORKNEY ISLES

BIRSAY

Earl's Palace
KW15 1PD
☎ 0131 668 8800

The gaunt remains of the residence of the late-16th-century Earl of Orkney, constructed round a courtyard.
Times: Open at all reasonable times. **Fee:** Free. 🐕

DOUNBY

Brough of Birsay
(6m NW)
☎ 0131 668 8800

This ruined Romanesque church stands next to the remains of a Norse village. The nave, chancel, semicircular apse and buildings remain. Crossings must be made on foot at low-water - there is no boat.
Times: Open at all reasonable times. **Fee:** Free.

Click Mill
(NE of village,off B9057)
☎ 0131 668 8800

This is an example of the rare Orcadian horizontal watermill, and is in working condition.
Times: Open at all reasonable time. **Fee:** Free.

Skara Brae
(19m W of Kirkwall on B9056)
☎ 01856 841815

Engulfed in drift sand, this remarkable group of well-preserved Stone Age dwellings is the most outstanding survivor of its kind in Britain. Stone furniture and a fireplace can be seen.
Times: Open all year, Apr-Sep, daily 9.30-6.30; Oct-Mar, Mon-Sat 9.30-4.30, Sun 2-4.30. (Closed 25-26 Dec).
Fee: Summer: £4.50 (ch £1.30, concessions £3.30); Winter: £3.50 (ch £1.20, concessions £2.60). P ✕ ♿ toilets for disabled shop 🐕

FINSTOWN

Maes Howe Chambered Cairn
(9m W of Kirkwall, on A965)
☎ 01856 761606

The masonry of Britain's finest megalithic tomb is in a remarkable state of preservation. Dating from neolithic times, it contains Viking carvings and runes.
Times: Open all year, Apr-Sep, daily 9.30-6.30; Oct-Mar, Mon-Sat 9.30-4.30, Sun 2-4.30. (Closed Thu pm, Fri in winter & 25-26 Dec).
Fee: £2.50 (ch £1, concessions £1.90). P ✕ shop 🐕

Stenness Standing Stones
(3m SW off A965)
☎ 0131 668 8800

Dating back to the second millennium BC, the remains of this stone circle are near the Ring of Brogar - a splendid circle of upright stones surrounded by a ditch.
Times: Open at any reasonable time. **Fee:** Free.

HARRAY
Orkney Farm & Folk Museum
KW17 2JR
☎ 01856 771411 & 771268 01856 874615

The museum consists of two Orkney farmhouses with outbuildings. Kirbuster (Birsay) has the last surviving example of a `Firehoose' with its central hearth; Corrigall (Harray) represents an improved farmhouse and steading of the late 1800s.
Times: Open Mar-Oct, Mon-Sat 10.30-1 & 2-5, Sun 2-7.
Fee: £2 (ch, students, pen & UB40 free) .
shop (ex guide dogs)

KIRKWALL
Bishop's & Earl's Palaces
☎ 01856 871918

The Bishop's Palace is a hall-house of the 12th century, later much altered, with a round tower built by Bishop Reid in 1541-48. A later addition was made by the notorious Patrick Stewart, Earl of Orkney, who built the adjacent Earl's Palace between 1600 and 1607 in a splendid Renaissance style.
Times: Open Apr-Sep, daily 9.30-6.30.
Fee: £2 (ch 75p, concessions £1.50). shop

The Orkney Museum
Broad St KW15 1DH
☎ 01856 873191 01856 874616

One of the finest vernacular town houses in Scotland, this 16th-century building now contains a museum of Orkney history, including the islands' fascinating archaeology.
Times: Open all year, Mon-Sat 10.30-12.30 & 1.30-5 (May-Sep Sun 2-5). **Fee:** Free. (50yds) shop (ex guide dogs)

STROMNESS
Orkney Maritime & Natural History Museum
52 Alfred St KW16 3DF
☎ 01856 850025

The museum focuses on Orkney's broad maritime connections, including fishing, whaling, the Hudson's Bay Company, the German Fleet in Scapa Flow, and the award winning Pilot's House extension. The Natural History Gallery gallery is fully restored.
Times: Open May-Sep, Mon-Sun 10-5; Oct-Apr, Mon-Sat 10.30-12.30 & 1.30-5. (Closed Xmas, New Year & 3 wks Feb-Mar).
Fee: £2.50 (ch 50p). Family ticket £4.50.
(50yds) toilets for disabled shop (ex guide dogs)

Pier Arts Centre
KW16 3AA
☎ 01856 850209 01856 851462

The collection is housed in a warehouse standing on its own stone pier. There is a constantly changing programme of exhibitions.
Times: Open all year, Tue-Sat 10.30-12.30 & 1.30-5.
Fee: Free. (100 yds) shop (ex guide dogs)

WESTRAY
Noltland Castle
☎ 0131 668 8800

Started in the 16th century, this ruined castle was never completed. It has a fine hall, vaulted kitchen and a notable winding staircase.
Times: Open all reasonable times. Application to key keeper.
Fee: Free.

SHETLAND ISLES

LERWICK
Clickhimin
ZE1 0QX (1m SW)
☎ 0131 668 8800

The remains of a prehistoric settlement that was fortified at the beginning of the Iron Age with a stone-built fort. The site was occupied for over 1000 years. The remains include a partially demolished broch (round tower) which still stands to a height of 17ft.
Times: Open at all reasonable time. **Fee:** Free.

Fort Charlotte
ZE1 0JN (overlooking harbour)
☎ 0131 668 8800

An artillery fort, begun in 1665 to protect the Sound of Bressay during the Anglo-Dutch War. The fort was burned by the Dutch in 1673, together with the town of Lerwick. It was repaired in 1781 during the American War of Independence. The fort is pentagonal.
Times: Open at all reasonable time. **Fee:** Free.

Shetland Museum
Lower Hillhead ZE1 0EL
☎ 01595 695057 01595 696729
e-mail: shetland.museum@sic.shetland.gov.uk

The massive brass propeller blade outside the building is from the 17,000-ton liner *Oceanic*, wrecked off Foula in 1914. The archaeology gallery covers Neolithic burials, axe-making, Bronze Age houses, Iron Age farming and domestic life. There are also agricultural and social history displays, including peat-working, corn harvest, local businesses, medals, bootmaking and Shetland weddings.
Times: Open all year Mon, Wed, Fri 10-7, Tue, Thu, Sat 10-5.
Fee: Free. (lift, wheelchair available) toilets for disabled shop (ex guide dogs)

MOUSA ISLAND

Mousa Broch

(Accessible by boat from Sandwick)

☎ 0131 668 8800

This broch is the best-preserved example of an Iron Age drystone tower in Scotland. The tower is nearly complete and rises to a height of 40ft. The outer and inner walls both contain staircases that may be climbed to the parapet.

Times: Open at all reasonable time. **Fee:** Free.

SCALLOWAY

Scalloway Castle

☎ 0131 668 8800

The ruins of a castle designed on the medieval two-step plan. The castle was actually built in 1600 by Patrick Stewart, Earl of Orkney. When the Earl, who was renowned for his cruelty, was executed in 1615, the castle fell into disuse.

Times: Open at all reasonable time. **Fee:** Free.

SUMBURGH

Jarlshof Prehistoric Site

(At Sumburgh Head, approx 22m S of Lerwick)

☎ 01950 460112

One of the most remarkable archaeological sites in Europe. There are remains of Bronze Age, Iron Age and Viking settlements as well as a medieval farm. There is also a 16th-century Laird's House, once the home of the Earls Robert and Patrick Stewart, and the basis of 'Jarlshof' in Sir Walter Scott's novel *The Pirate*.

Times: Open Apr-Sep, daily 9.30-6.30.

Fee: £2.50 (ch £1, concessions £1.90). shop

SKYE, ISLE OF

ARMADALE

Armadale Castle Gardens & Museum of the Isles

IV45 8RS (1.5km from Armadale Pier)

☎ 01471 844305 & 844227 01471 844275

e-mail: office@cland.demon.co.uk

Armadale Castle and Gardens were built in 1815 as the home of Lord Macdonald. The warming effect of the Gulf Stream allows exotic trees and plants to flourish. Within the 40 acres of gardens is the Museum of the Isles, where visitors can discover the history of the Highlands.

Times: Open daily 9.30-5.30. Garden & Museum open Apr-Oct.

Fee: £3.85 (concessions £2.60). Family ticket £10. Group 8+

licensed (wheelchairs available, hearing loop in Audiovisual room) toilets for disabled shop garden centre (ex on leads)

DUNVEGAN

Dunvegan Castle

IV55 8WF

☎ 01470 521206 01470 521205

e-mail: info@dunvegancastle.com

This fortress stronghold set on the sea loch of Dunvegan has been the home of the Chief of Macleod for 790 years. On view are books, pictures, arms and treasured relics of the clan. Pedigree Highland Cattle, and boat trips to the nearby Seal Colony.

Times: Open 20 Mar-Oct, Mon-Sun 10-5.30 (last admission 5pm). Winter opening: Nov-Mar Castle & Gardens Mon-Sun 11-4, last admission 3.30pm.

Fee: Castle & Gardens: £5.50 (ch 5-15 £3, pen, students & disabled £4.80) Family ticket (2 adults & 3 ch) £15. Parties. Gardens only: £3.80 (ch £2)

licensed (restaurant has ramps for wheelchair access) shop (ex guide dogs & in grounds)

Precipice Walk, Dolgellau

Wales

EVENTS & FESTIVALS

March
16-25 Wrexham Science Week Event, Wrexham

April
tbc Country Music Festival, North Wales Theatre, Promenade, Llandudno, Conwy

May
tbc Wrexham Arts Festival, Wrexham
tbc St David's Cathedral Festival, St David's, Pembrokeshire

June
26-7 Beaumaris Festival, Beaumaris, Anglesey
30 Three Peaks Yacht Race, The Quay, Barmouth, Gwynedd

July
1-7 Cnapan Folk Festival, Ffoftrafol, near Llandysul
tbc Brecon County Show
6-8 North Wales Bluegrass Festival, Bodlondeb Field, Llandudno, Conwy
tbc Llangollen International Musical Eisteddfod, International Pavilion, Abbey Road, Llangollen, Denbighshire
tbc Fishguard International Music Festival (various venues), Fishguard, Pembrokeshire
tbc Welsh Proms, St David's Hall, The Hayes, Cardiff
tbc Royal Welsh Show, Royal Welsh Showground, Builth Wells
tbc Royal Welsh Show, Royal Welsh Showground, Llanelwedd, Powys

August
2-4 Welsh Sheepdog Trials, Anglesey
14-15 Anglesey County Show, Anglesey Showground, Gwalchmai, Mona, Anglesey
25 Denbighshire & Flintshire Show, Denbigh, Denbighshire
30 Monmouthshire Show, Vauxhall Fields, Monmouth, Monmouthshire
tbc Brecon Jazz Festival (various venues), Brecon, Powys
tbc Llandrindod Wells Victorian Festival, Llandrindod Wells, Powys
tbc Llangurig & District Show, Tynymaes, Llangurig, Powys
tbc Pembrokeshire County Show, County Showground, Withybush, Haverfordwest, Pembrokeshire
tbc Royal National Eisteddfod, Llanelli, Carmarthenshire
tbc World Bog Snorkeling Championship, Llanwrtyd Wells, Powys
tbc Conwy River Festival, Harbour, Conwy
tbc Victorian Week, Talyllyn Railway, Wharf Station, Tywyn, Gwynedd
tbc Chepstow Agricultural Show, Chepstow Racecourse, Chepstow
tbc Vale of Glamorgan Agricultural Show, Fonmon Castle Park, Fonmon

September
tbc Barmouth Art Festival, Dragon Theatre, Jubilee Road, Barmouth, Gwynedd
tbc Tenby Arts Festival (various venues), Tenby, Pembrokeshire
tbc Llangollen Hot Air Balloon Festival, International Pavilion, Abbey Road, Llangollen, Denbighshire
tbc North Wales International Music Festival, the Cathedral, St Asaph, Denbighshire
tbc Usk Show, Gwernesney, Monmouthshire

October
27 Oct-9 Nov Dylan Thomas - The Celebration, Dylan Thomas Centre, Somerset Place Swansea
28 Snowdonia Marathon, Llanberis, Gwynedd
tbc Anglesey Oyster Fair
tbc Bala Autumn Fair Day, Bala, Gwynedd
tbc Llandudno October Festival, Llandudno, Conwytbc Cardigan Festival of Walks, Theatr Mwldan, Cardigan, Pembrokeshire

November
tbc Gwyl Ffilm Ryngwladol Cymru - Welsh International Film Festival, Market House, Market Road, Cardiff

December
tbc Royal Welsh Agricultural Winter Fair, Royal Welsh Showground, Builth Wells

BRIDGEND

BRIDGEND

NEWCASTLE

☎ 01656 659515

The small castle dates back to the 12th century. It is ruined, but a rectangular tower, a richly carved Norman gateway and massive curtain walls enclosing a polygonal courtyard can still be seen.

Times: Open - accessible throughout the year. Key keeper arrangement.

Fee: Free.

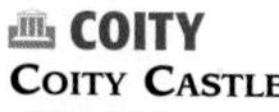

COITY

COITY CASTLE

CF35 6BG

☎ 01656 652021

A 12th to 16th-century stronghold, with a hall, chapel and the remains of a square keep.

Times: Open all year, at all times. Key keeper arrangement.

Fee: Free.

CAERPHILLY

CAERPHILLY

CAERPHILLY CASTLE

CF8 1JL (on A469)

☎ 029 20883143

The concentrically planned castle was begun in 1268 by Gilbert de Clare and completed in 1326. It is the largest in Wales, and has extensive land and water defences. A unique feature is the ruined tower - the victim of subsidence - which manages to out-lean even Pisa! The south dam platform, once a tournament-field, now displays replica medieval siege-engines.

Times: Open all year, late May-early Oct, daily 9.30-6; late Mar-late May & Oct, daily 9.30-5. Nov-late Mar, Mon-Sat 9.30-4, Sun 11-4. (Closed 24-26 Dec & 1 Jan).

Fee: £2.50 (ch 5-16, pen & students £2, disabled free). Family ticket £7.

shop

LLANCAIACH FAWR MANOR

Gelligaer Rd, Nelson CF46 6ER (M4 Jnct 32, A470 to Merthyr Tydfil. Towards Ystrad Mynach A472 follow brown tourist signs)

☎ 01443 412248 01443 412688

Step back in time to the Civil War period at this fascinating living history museum. The year is 1645 and visitors are invited into the Manor to meet the servants of 'Colonel' Edward Prichard - from the puritanical to the gossipy.

Times: Open Mon-Fri 10-3.30 (last admission), Sat 10-4.30 Sun 10-4.30. (Closed Mon, Nov-Feb).

Fee: £4.50 (ch & concessions £3). Family ticket £12.

licensed (lift in visitor centre to audio visual show) toilets for disabled shop (ex in grounds)

CWMCARN

CWMCARN FOREST DRIVE

Nantcarn Rd NP11 7FA (8m N of Newport on A467, M4 junct 28, follow brown tourist signs)

☎ 01495 272001 01495 272001

e-mail: tourism@caerphilly.gov.uk

A seven-mile scenic drive with spectacular views over the Bristol Channel and surrounding countryside. Facilities include barbecues, picnic and play areas, and forest and mountain walks. Special events are held throughout the year.

Times: Open Forest Drive: Etr-Oct. Visitor Centre: all year except between Xmas & New Year.

Fee: Cars & Motorcycles £3, Minibus fr £6, Coaches £20.

toilets for disabled shop

CARDIFF

CARDIFF

Cardiff Castle

Castle St CF1 2RB (City Centre)

☎ 029 2087 8100 📠 029 2023 1417

Times: Open all year, daily (ex 25-26 Dec & 1 Jan) including guided tours, Mar-Oct, 9.30-6 (last tour 5pm); Nov-Feb, 9.30-4.30 (last tour 3.15pm). Royal Regiment of Wales Museum closed Tue. Queen's Dragoon Guards Museum closed Fri.

P (200 yds) toilets for disabled shop (ex in grounds & guide dogs) *Details not confirmed for 2001*

Dyffryn Gardens

St Nicholas CF5 6SU (6m W of city centre off A48)

☎ 029 2059 3328 📠 029 2059 1966

One of Wales' finest Edwardian gardens, the beautiful grounds offer an endless variety of colour and form with many small garden rooms recently restored with the aid of a Heritage Lottery fund grant. Additional works are still ongoing and some areas may be subject to closure.

Times: Open all year, 10-dusk

Fee: £3 (ch & pen £2). Family ticket £6.50.

P (wheelchairs, parking) toilets for disabled shop garden centre

Llandaff Cathedral

Llandaff CF5 2YF (A48 off M4)

☎ 029 2056 4554 📠 029 2056 4554

Times: Open all year.

P (Wheelchair available) toilets for disabled shop (ex guide dogs) *Details not confirmed for 2001*

National Museum & Gallery Cardiff

Cathays Park CF10 3NP (Situated in Cathays Park in the heart of Cardiff's Civic Centre)

☎ 029 2039 7951 📠 029 2037 3219

This establishment is unique amongst British museums and galleries in its range of art and science displays. 'The Evolution of Wales' exhibition takes visitors on a spectacular 4600-million year journey, tracing the world from beginning of time and the development of Wales. There are displays of Bronze Age gold, early Christian monuments, Celtic treasures, silver, coins and medals, ceramics, fossils and minerals.

Times: Open all year, Tue-Sun 10-5. (Closed Mon (ex BHs), 24-26 Dec).

Fee: £4.50 (ch & concessions £2.65). Family ticket £10.25.

P (charged) licensed (wheelchair available) toilets for disabled shop (ex guide dogs)

Techniquest

Stuart St CF10 5BW (M4 jcnt 33, follow A4232 to Cardiff Bay)

☎ 029 2047 5475 📠 029 2048 2517

e-mail: gen@tquest.org.uk

Located in the heart of the Cardiff Bay redevelopment area, visitors of all ages will find science and technology made accessible at Britain's leading hands-on discovery science centre. Launch a hot air balloon, see yourself on television and write a Mozart piece with a pair of dice. Fascinating and educational fun.

Times: Open all year (ex Xmas), Mon-Fri 9.30-4.30; Sat-Sun & BH's 10.30-5.

Fee: £5.50 (ch 5-16 & concessions £3.80). Family ticket (2 adults & 3 ch) £15.75. Family season ticket £42.50

P (lift) toilets for disabled shop (ex guide dogs)

ST FAGANS

Museum of Welsh Life

CF5 6XB (4m W of Cardiff, 3m from M4 jnct 33, along A4232)

☎ 029 2057 3500 📠 029 2057 3490

A stroll around the indoor galleries and 100 acres of beautiful grounds will give you a fascinating insight into how people in Wales have lived, worked and spent their leisure hours since Celtic times. You can see people practising the traditional means of earning a living, the animals they kept and at certain times of year, the ways in which they celebrated the seasons.

Times: Open all year daily, Jul-Sep 10-6, Oct-Jun 10-5. Closed 24-26 Dec. Site may close Mon except BH Mon.

Fee: Etr-Oct: £5.50 (ch under 18 free, pen/students/UB40 £3.90). Nov-Etr: £4.50 (ch under 18 free, pen/students/UB40 £2.65).

P licensed (wheelchairs available on a 'first come-first served' basis) toilets for disabled shop (ex in grounds if on lead)

TONGWYNLAIS

Castell Coch

CF4 7YS (A470 to Tongwynlais junction, then B4262 to castle on top of hill)

☎ 029 2081 0101

Castell Coch is Welsh for red castle, an appropriate name for this fairy-tale building with its red sandstone walls and conical towers. The castle was originally built in the 13th century but fell into ruins, and the present castle is a late 19th-century creation. Inside, the castle is decorated in fantasy style.

Times: Open all year, late May-early Oct, daily 9.30-6; late Mar-late May & Oct, daily 9.30-5; Nov-late Mar, Mon-Sat 9.30-4, Sun 11-4. (Closed 24-26 Dec & 1 Jan).
Fee: £2.50 (ch 5-16, pen & students £2, disabled free). Family ticket £7.
P shop

CARMARTHENSHIRE

ABERGWILI

CARMARTHEN MUSEUM
SA31 2JG (2m E of Carmarthen, just off A40, at Abergwili rndbt)
☎ 01267 231691 📠 01267 223830
e-mail: cdelaney@carmarthenshire.gov.uk

Housed in the old palace of the Bishop of St David's and set in seven acres of grounds, the museum offers a wide range of local subjects to explore, from geology and prehistory to butter making, Welsh furniture and folk art. Temporary exhibitions are held.
Times: Open all year, Mon-Sat 10-4.30. (Closed Xmas-New Year).
Fee: Free.
P ♿ toilets for disabled shop (ex guide dogs)

CARREG CENNEN CASTLE

CARREG CENNEN CASTLE
SA19 6UA (unclassified road from A483 to Trapp village)
☎ 01558 822291

A steep path leads up to the castle, which is spectacularly sited on a limestone crag. It was first built as a stronghold of the native Welsh and then rebuilt in the late 13th century. Most remarkable among the impressive remains is a mysterious passage, cut into the side of the cliff and lit by loopholes. The farm at the site has a rare breeds centre.
Times: Open all year, Apr-late Oct, daily 9.30-7.30; late Oct-Mar, daily, 9.30-4. (Closed 24-26 Dec & 1 Jan).
Fee: £2.50 (ch 5-16, pen & students £2, disabled free). Family ticket £7.
P shop

DRE-FACH FELINDRE

MUSEUM OF THE WELSH WOOLLEN INDUSTRY
SA44 5UP (16m W of Carmarthen off A484, 4m E of Newcastle Emlyn)
☎ 01559 370929 📠 01559 371592

The museum is housed in the former Cambrian Mills and has a comprehensive display tracing the evolution of the industry from its beginnings to the present day. Demonstrations of the fleece to fabric process are given on 19th-century textile machinery.
Times: Open all year, Apr-Sep, Mon-Sat 10-5; Oct-Mar, Mon-Fri 10-5. (Closed 24-26 Dec & 1 Jan). The site may be closed Mondays (except Bank Holidays).
Fee: £2.60 (concessions £1.60).
P ♿ (Wheelchair access to ground floor & ample seating) toilets for disabled shop garden centre

DRYSLWYN

DRYSLWYN CASTLE
(on B4279)
☎ 029 2050 0200

The ruined 13th-century castle was a stronghold of the native Welsh. It stands on a lofty mound, and was important in the struggles between English and Welsh. It is gradually being uncovered by excavation.
Times: Open - entrance by arrangement with Dryslwyn Farm.
Fee: Free.
P

KIDWELLY

KIDWELLY CASTLE
SA17 5BQ (via A484)
☎ 01554 890104

This is an outstanding example of late 13th-century castle design, with its `walls within walls' defensive system. There were later additions made to the building, the chapel dating from about 1400. Of particular interest are two vast circular ovens.
Times: Open all year, late May-early Oct, daily 9.30-6; late Mar-late May & Oct, daily 9.30-5; Nov-late Mar, Mon-Sat 9.30-4 & Sun 11-4. (Closed 24-26 Dec & 1 Jan).
Fee: £2.20 (ch 5-16, pen & students £1.70, disabled free). Family ticket £6.10.
P ♿ toilets for disabled shop

KIDWELLY INDUSTRIAL MUSEUM
Broadford SA17 4LW (signposted from Kidwelly by-pass)
☎ 01554 891078

Two of the great industries of Wales are represented in this museum: tinplate and coal mining. The original buildings and machinery of the Kidwelly tinplate works, where tinplate was hand made, are now on display to the public. There is also an exhibition of coal mining with pit-head gear and a winding engine, while the more general history of the area is shown in a separate exhibition.
Times: Open Etr, Jun-Aug, PH wknds, Mon-Fri 10-5, Sat-Sun 2-5. Last admission 4pm (5pm Jul-Aug). Other times by arrangement for parties only.
Fee: Free.
P ♿ toilets for disabled shop (ex in grounds)

LAUGHARNE

DYLAN THOMAS' BOAT HOUSE
Dylans Walk SA33 4SD (14m SW of Carmarthen)
☎ 01994 427420 📠 01554 747501
Times: Open all year, May-Oct, daily 10-5; Nov-Apr, daily 10.30-3.
P (10mins walk) shop (ex guide dogs) *Details not confirmed for 2001*

Laugharne Castle
King St SA33 4SA (on A4066)
☎ 01994 427906

Newly opened to the public, picturesque Laugharne Castle stands on a low ridge overlooking the wide Taff Estuary. A medieval fortress converted into an Elizabethan mansion, it suffered a civil war siege and later became the backdrop for elaborate Victorian gardens, now recreated. Laugharne Castle has also inspired two modern writers - Richard Hughes and Dylan Thomas.

Times: Open late Apr-late Sep, daily 10-5.
Fee: £2 (ch 5-16, pen & students £1.50, disabled free). Family ticket £5.50.
P (150 mtrs) ♿ toilets for disabled shop

LLANDEILO

Dinefwr Park
SA19 6RT (off A40 Carmarthenshire, on the western outskirts of Llandeilo)
☎ 01558 823902 01558 822036

At the heart of Welsh history for a thousand years, the Park as we know it today took shape in the years after 1775 when the medieval castle, house, gardens, woods and deer park were integrated into one vast and breathtaking landscape. Access to Church Woods and Dinefwr Castle is through the landscaped park.

Times: Open Apr-Oct, daily (ex Tue & Wed) 11-4.30. Last admission 30 mins before closing.
Fee: Free.
P (charged) ♿ toilets for disabled (ex outer park on lead)

LLANELLI

WWT Llanelli
Penclacwydd, Llwynhendy SA14 9SH (3m E of Llanelli, off A484)
☎ 01554 741087 01554 741087
e-mail: wwtllanelli@aol.com

A wide variety of wild birds, including oystercatchers, redshanks, curlews, little egrets and occasionally ospreys, can be seen here during the right season. The grounds are beautifully landscaped, and include CCTV transmitting pictures of wild birds on the reserve, a wetland craft area and a flock of colourful Caribbean Flamingos. Facilities for the disabled include easy access on level paths, special viewing areas and wheelchair loan.

Times: Open summer 9.30-5.30, winter 9.30-4.30. Closed 24-25 Dec.
Fee: £5 (ch £3, pen £4). Family ticket £13. Party 10+.
P ✕ ♿ toilets for disabled shop

LLANARTHNE

National Botanic Garden of Wales
Middleton Hall SA32 8HG (8m E of Carmarthen on A48 (M4), dedicated intersection - signed)
☎ 01558 667134 01558 667138

The Garden of Wales is a model to a sustainable way of living in harmony with the natural world. Set in the 18th-century parkland of the former Middleton Hall, the garden is situated within a 568-acre estate on the edge of the beautiful Towy Valley with spectacular views. The garden's centrepiece is one of the largest single span glasshouses in the world, and houses a landscape filled with a living collection of threatened Mediterranean plants and 'Bioverse', a hands-on educational adventure aimed at unlocking the mysteries of plant life.

Times: Opening mid May 10-6.30, Jun-Aug 10-7. Sep-Oct 10-5.30, Nov-Dec 10-4.30. Last admission 1hr before closing time. Closed 25 Dec.
Fee: £6.50 (ch 5-16 £3, concessions £5). Family £16. Carer with wheelchair user/blind visitor free.
P ✕ licensed ♿ toilets for disabled shop garden centre (ex guide dogs)

LLANSTEFFAN

Llansteffan Castle
(off B4312)
☎ 01267 241756

The ruins of this 11th to 13th-century stronghold stand majestically on the west side of the Towy estuary.

Times: Open - access throughout the year.
Fee: Free.

PUMSAINT

Dolaucothi Gold Mines
SA19 8RR (on A482, signposted both directions)
☎ 01558 650359 01588 822036
e-mail: penpeb@Smpt.NTrust.org.uk

Here is an opportunity to spend a day exploring the gold mines and to wear a miner's helmet and lamp while touring the underground workings. The information centre and a walk along the Miners' Way disclose the secrets of 2000 years of gold mining. This is the only place in Britain where the Romans mined gold.

Times: Open 14 Apr-17 Sep, daily 10-5. Guided underground tours daily.
Fee: £2.60 (ch £1.30) Family ticket £6.50. NT members free. Guided underground tours £3.60 (ch £1.80) Family ticket £9. NT members: £2.60 (ch £1.30). Family ticket £6.50.
P ♿ toilets for disabled shop (ex on leads, but not on tours)

CEREDIGION

ABERAERON

Llanerchaeron
SA48 8DG (2.5m E of Aberaeron off A482)
☎ 01545 570200 01545 571759

A rare survivor of the core of a Welsh gentry estate. It was acquired by The National Trust in 1994 having received minimal maintenance in recent decades. Parts of the property are open to visitors.

Times: Open early Apr-late Oct, Thu-Sun & BH Mons 11-5. Last admission 30 mins before closing. Park open all year dawn to dusk.
Fee: £2 (ch £1). Family ticket £5. Party.
toilets for disabled (ex on lead)

ABERYSTWYTH
NATIONAL LIBRARY OF WALES
Penglais Hill SY23 3BU (off Penglais Hill, A487 N Aberystwyth)
01970 632800, 623834 & 623837 01970 615709
e-mail: holi@llgc.org.uk

This huge library is one of Britain's six copyright libraries, and specialises in Welsh and Celtic literature. It has maps, manuscripts, prints and drawings. A major permanent exhibition 'A Nation's Heritage' is on view and there is a programme of travelling exhibitions.
Times: Open all year, exhibitions, library & reading rooms Mon-Fri 9.30-6, Sat until 5. (Closed BH's & first wk Oct).
Fee: Free.
toilets for disabled shop

CAPEL BANGOR
RHEIDOL HYDRO ELECTRIC POWER STATION & VISITOR CENTRE
Cwm Rheidol SY23 3NF (off A44 at Capel Bangor)
01970 880667 01970 880670

A guided tour of the power station and fish farm can be taken. There is a visitor centre, nature trail and scenic drive.
Times: Open Apr-Oct, daily 10-4 for free tours of the Power Station, fish farm & visitor centre.
Fee: Free.
toilets for disabled

EGLWYSFACH
RSPB NATURE RESERVE
Cae'r Berllan SY20 8TA (6m S of Machynlleth on A487 in Eglwys-Fach. Signposted from main road)
01654 781265 01654 781328

Lying at the head of the Dyfi estuary, this grazed saltmarsh is bordered by freshwater marsh and some remnant peat bogs. In the oakwoods are pied flycatchers, redstarts, wood warblers, nut hatches, and both great spotted and lesser spotted woodpeckers. Buzzards, kestrels and sparrowhawks breed in the wood whilst redbreasted mergansers and common sandpipers frequent the river. Peregrines can be seen all year while Merlins and hen harriers hunt over the reserve during the winter. Badgers and polecats live here and there are many species of butterfly. Phone for an events leaflet.
Times: Open daily, 9am-9pm (or sunset if earlier). Visitor Centre: Apr-Oct 9-5 daily; Nov-Mar 10-4 (wknds only)
Fee: £3 (ch £1, concessions £2) Family £6.

FELINWYNT
FELINWYNT RAINFOREST & BUTTERFLY CENTRE
Rhosmaen SA43 1RT (from A487 Blaenannerch Airfield turning, turn onto B4333. Signposted)
01239 810882 01239 810882
e-mail: d.j.devereux@talk21.com

A chance to wander amongst free-flying exotic butterflies accompanied by the recorded wildlife sounds of the Peruvian Amazon. A waterfall, ponds and streams contribute to a humid tropical atmosphere and provide a habitat for fish and native amphibians. See the exhibition of rainforests of Peru and around the world. Free paper and crayons to borrow for children.
Times: Open daily mid Apr-Oct
Fee: £3.25 (ch 4-14 £1.25 pen £3)
shop

GWBERT-ON-SEA
CARDIGAN ISLAND COASTAL FARM PARK
SA43 1PR (off Cardigan bypass at Aberystwyth Road junct, into Cardigan, right at Gwbert junct, follow rd for 2.5m)
01239 612196 01239 612196
Times: Open: 9.30-7 daily till Nov 1st. Closed for Winter.
shop *Details not confirmed for 2001*

PONTERWYD
LLYWERNOG SILVER-LEAD MINE
Llywernog Mine SY23 3AB (11m E of Aberystwyth on A44)
01970 890620 01545 570823
Times: Open Etr-Oct, daily 10-6 (Oct 5pm). Nov-Dec by appointment.
shop *Details not confirmed for 2001*

STRATA FLORIDA
STRATA FLORIDA ABBEY
SY25 6BT (unclassified road from Pontrhydfendigaid, reached from B4340)
01974 831261

Little remains of the Cistercian abbey founded in 1164, except the ruined church and cloister. Strata Florida was an important centre of learning in the Middle Ages, and it is believed that the 14th-century poet Dafyd ap Gwilym was buried here.
Times: Open all year, late Apr-late Sep, daily 10-5; Site open rest of year.
Fee: £2 (ch 5-16, pen & students £1.50). Family ticket £5.50.
shop

CONWY

BETWS-Y-COED

Conwy Valley Railway Museum

Old Goods Yard LL24 0AL (signed from the A5 into Old Church Rd, adjacent to train station)

☎ 01690 710568 01690 710132

The two large museum buildings have displays on both the narrow-and standard-gauge railways of North Wales, including railway stock. There are working model railway layouts, a steam-hauled miniature railway in the grounds, which cover over four acres, and a 15in-gauge tramway to the woods. The latest addition is the quarter-size steam *'Britannia'* loco.

Times: Open Etr-Oct, daily 10-5.30, then weekends until Mar. Museum, large model & gift shop also open on Mon & Tue in winter period.

Fee: £1 (ch & pen 50p). Family ticket £2.50. Steam train ride 75p. Tram ride 60p.

(Ramps & Clearances for wheelchairs) toilets for disabled shop (ex in museum)

CERRIGYDRUDION

Llyn Brenig Visitor Centre

LL21 9TT (on B4501)

☎ 01490 420463 01490 420694

e-mail: llyn.brenig@hyder.com

The 1800-acre estate has a unique archaeological trail and round-the-lake walk of 10 miles. A hide is available. Disabled anglers are catered for with a specially adapted fishing boat and an annual open day. The centre has an exhibition on archaeology, history and conservation and an audio-visual programme.

Times: Open mid Mar-Nov, daily 9-5.

Fee: Free. (Charge made for water sports & fishing).

(charged) (boats for disabled & fishing open days) toilets for disabled shop (ex guide dogs)

CONWY

Aberconwy House

LL32 8AY (At junction of Castle St & High St)

☎ 01492 592246 01492 585153

This house dates from the 14th century; it is the only medieval merchant's house in Conwy to have survived the centuries of turbulence, fire and pillage in this frontier town. Furnished rooms and an audio-visual presentation show daily life in the house at different periods in its history.

Times: Open 29 Mar-Oct, Wed-Mon 11-5. Last admission 30 mins before closing.

Fee: £2 (ch £1). Family ticket £5. Party.

P (100yds & 0.5 mile) shop (ex guide dogs)

Conwy Castle

LL32 8AY (by A55 or B5106)

☎ 01492 592358

The castle is a magnificent fortress, built from 1283-7 by Edward I. There is an exhibition on castle chapels on the ground floor of the Chapel Tower. The castle forms part of the same defensive system as the extensive town walls, which are among the most complete in Europe.

Times: Open all year, late May-early Oct, daily 9.30-6; late Mar-late May & Oct, daily 9.30-5; Nov-late Mar, Mon-Sat 9.30-4, Sun 11-4. (Closed 24-26 Dec & 1 Jan)

Fee: £3.50 (ch 5-16, pen & students £2.50, disabled free). Family ticket £9.50.

toilets for disabled shop

Conwy Suspension Bridge

LL32 8LO (adjacent to Conwy Castle)

☎ 01492 573282

Designed by Thomas Telford, one of the greatest engineers of the late 18th and early 19th century, this was the first bridge to span the river at Conwy. The bridge has recently been restored and the toll house furnished as it would have been a century ago.

Times: Open Jul-Aug, daily 10-5; 29 Mar-Jun & Sep-Oct, Wed-Mon 10-5.

Fee: £1 (ch 50p).

P

Plas Mawr

High St LL32 8DE

☎ 01492 593413

Plas Mawr is an excellent example of an Elizabethan town mansion, and is practically the same as when it was built between 1570 and 1580. Temporary exhibitions are held.

Times: Open Apr-late May & early Sep-early Oct, daily 9.30-5; late May-early Sep, daily 9.30-6; Oct daily 9.30-4. Closed Mon ex BH weekends.

Fee: £4 (ch, pen & students £3). Family £11

shop

Smallest House

The Quay LL32 8BB (leave A55 at Conwy signpost, trough town, at bottom of High St towards quay, turn left)

☎ 01492 593484 01492 593484

The `Guinness Book of Records' lists this as the smallest house in Britain. Just 6ft wide by 10ft high, it is furnished in the style of a mid-Victorian Welsh cottage.

Times: Open Apr-end Oct daily 10-6 (10-9.30/9pm in Jul & Aug). In winter by arrangement.

Fee: 50p (ch under 16 30p, under 5yrs free admission).

P (100 yds) shop

DOLWYDDELAN

Dolwyddelan Castle

LL25 0EJ (on A470 Blaenau Ffestiniog to Betws-y-Coed)
01690 750366

The castle is reputed to be the birthplace of Llywelyn the Great. It was captured in 1283 by Edward I, who immediately began strengthening it for his own purposes. A restored keep of around 1200, and a 13th-century curtain wall can be seen. An exhibition on the castles of the Welsh Princes is located in the keep.

Times: Open all year, early Apr-late Oct, daily 9.30-6.30; late Oct-Mar, Mon-Sat 9.30-4 & Sun 11-4. (Closed 24-26 Dec & 1 Jan).

Fee: £2 (ch 5-16, pen & students £1.50, disabled free). Family ticket £5.50

P

LLANDUDNO JUNCTION

RSPB Nature Reserve

LL31 9XZ (off A55, signposted)
01492 584091 **01492 584091**

The visitor centre has a viewing area which overlooks the estuary and Conwy Castle, and there's a nature trail and 4 hides for viewing lapwings and shelduck amongst many others.

Times: Open daily, 10-5 (or sunset if earlier).

Fee: Free.

P (wheelchair available) toilets for disabled shop (ex guide dogs)

LLANRWST

Gwydyr Uchaf Chapel

(0.5m SW off B5106)
01492 640578

Built in the 17th century by Sir John Wynn of Gwydir Castle, the chapel is noted for its painted ceiling and wonderfully varied woodwork.

Times: Open any reasonable time.

Fee: Free.

P

PENMACHNO

Penmachno Woollen Mill

LL24 0PP (2m off A5, between Llangollen & Betws-Y-Coed)
01690 710545

Times: Open daily 10-5.30; Nov-Feb open 10-4.30.

P shop *Details not confirmed for 2001*

Ty Mawr Wybrnant

LL25 0HJ (From A5 3m S of Betws-y-Coed take B4406. House is 2.5m NW of Penmachno by forest road)
01690 760213

Situated in the beautiful, secluded Wybrnant Valley, Ty Mawr was the birthplace of Bishop William Morgan (1545-1604), the first translator of the entire Bible into Welsh. The house has been restored to its probable 16th-17th century appearance. The Wybrnant Nature Trail, a short walk, covers approximately one mile.

Times: Open 30 Mar-Sep, Thu-Sun & BH Mons 12-5; Oct, Thu, Fri & Sun 12-4. Last admission 30 mins before closing.

Fee: £2 (ch £1). Family ticket £5. Party 15+.

P (ex in grounds) (minibus access only)

TAL-Y-CAFN

Bodnant Garden

LL28 5RE (8m S of Llandudno & Colwyn Bay off A470. Also signposted from A55)
01492 650460 **01492 650448**

Set above the River Conwy with beautiful views over Snowdonia, these gardens are a delight. Five Italian style terraces were constructed below the house - on the lowest terrace is a canal pool with an open-air yew hedge stage and a reconstructed Pin Mill. The garden is renowned for its collections of magnolias, camellias, rhododendrons and azaleas and the famous Laburnum Arch. Contact for details of open air theatre.

Times: Open mid Mar-Oct, daily 10-5 (last admission half hour before closing)

Fee: £5 (ch £2.50). Party 20+

P (steep in places with many steps not easy for wheelchairs) toilets for disabled shop (ex guide dogs)

TREFRIW

Trefriw Woollen Mill

LL27 0NQ (on B5106 in centre of Trefriw, 5m N of Betws-y-Coed)
01492 640462 **01492 640462**

Established in 1859, the mill is situated beside the fast-flowing Afon Crafnant, which drives two hydro-electric turbines to power the looms. All the machinery of woollen manufacture can be seen here: blending, carding, spinning, dyeing, warping and weaving. In the Weaver's Garden, there are plants traditionally used in the textile industry, mainly for dyeing. Hand-spinning demonstrations.

Times: Mill open Etr-Oct, Mon-Fri 10-5. Weaving demonstrations & turbine house: open all year, Mon-Fri 10-5.

Fee: Free

P (35 yds) shop (in shop & grounds, not mill) 

DENBIGHSHIRE

BODELWYDDAN

Bodelwyddan Castle

LL18 5YA (adjacent to A55, near St Asaph)
01745 584060 01745 584563
e-mail: bolcastle@freeuk.com

Set in rolling parkland against the impressive background of the Clwydian Hills, this imposing Victorian country house has been magnificently restored. The lavish interiors reflect various design styles from the 19th century and provide a sumptuous setting for a collection of portraits on loan from the National Portrait Gallery, complemented by furniture from the Victoria and Albert Museum and sculptures from the Royal Academy of Arts.

Times: Open mid Apr-early Jul & early Sep-early Oct, Sat-Thu 10-5; early Jul-early Sep, daily 10-5; Oct-mid Apr 10-3.30 (ex Mon or Fri).
Fee: £4 (ch £2.50, pen, UB40, student, disabled £3.50). Family ticket £10.
(lift to first floor & Braille Guide) toilets for disabled shop (ex guide dogs)

CORWEN

Rug Chapel

Rug
01490 412025

Rug Chapel was built in 1637 for Colonel William Salusbury, famous Civil War defender of Denbigh Castle. A rare little altered example of a 17th-century private chapel, it reflects the Colonel's High Church religious views. Prettily set in a wooded landscape, the chapel's modest exterior gives little hint of the interior where local artists and carvers were given a free reign, with some spectacular results.

Times: Open late Apr-late Sep, Wed-Sun 10-2 & 3-5. (Closed Mon & Tue, ex BH wknds).
Fee: £2 (ch 5-16, pen & students £1.50). Family ticket £5.50.
toilets for disabled shop

DENBIGH

Denbigh Castle

(via A525, A543 & B5382)
01745 813385

The castle was begun by Henry de Lacy in 1282 and has an inspiring and impressive gatehouse, with a trio of towers and a superb archway, which is surmounted by a figure believed to be that of Edward I.

Times: Open early Apr-late Oct, Mon-Fri 10-5.30, Sat & Sun 9.30-5.30; Site open at all other times. (Closed 24-26 Dec & 1 Jan).
Fee: £2 (ch 5-16, pen & students £1.50, disabled free). Family ticket £5.50.
shop

LLANGOLLEN

Doctor Who Exhibition & Model Railway World

Lower Dee Exhibition Centre LL20 8RX (from Llangollen Bridge, 500yds along road towards Wrexham)
01978 860584 01978 861928
e-mail: dapol.drwho@btinternet.com

The world's largest collection of Doctor Who items direct from the BBC, original costumes, models and Hall of Monsters, also 'Bessie', the Doctor's car. Model Railway World illustrates the history of model railways, from the earliest hand made models of the 1920s up to the present day, as well as working layouts of various sizes, and examples of rolling stock from around the world. Dapol Toy Factory is also on site, visitors can watch toys being made.

Times: Open 10-5. Closed 25/26 Dec & 1 Jan.
Fee: Doctor Who Experience £5.75 (ch £3.50). Family ticket £15.50; Model Railway World £4.75 (ch £3.75). Family ticket £13.50; Combination ticket to all attractions £9 (ch £6). Family ticket £24.95.
shop (except guide dogs)

Horse Drawn Boats Centre

The Wharf, Wharf Hill LL20 8TA (A5 turn right at traffic lights over bridge)
01978 860702 & 01691 690322
01978 860702

Take a horsedrawn boat trip along the beautiful Vale of Llangollen, and visit the museum, which illustrates the heyday of canals in Britain. The displays include working and static models, photographs, murals and slides. There is also a narrowboat trip which crosses Pontcysyllte Aqueduct, the largest navigable aqueduct in the world.

Times: Open Mar, wknds; Apr-Oct, daily (limited opening in Oct).
Fee: Horse Drawn Boat Trip from £3.50 (ch £2.50). Family ticket £9. Narrowboat Trip £6 (ch £5).
(400 yds) licensed (alighting/pick-up point available) shop

Llangollen Station

(At the junction of A5 & A539)
01978 860979 & 860951 timetable
01978 869247
e-mail: office@llanrail.freeserve.co.uk

Locomotives and rolling stock are displayed, and passenger trains run on a fourteen-and-a-half-mile round trip between Llangollen and Carrog. A special coach for the disabled is available at times.

Times: Open - Station wknds, Steam hauled trains Apr-Oct Sun & daily in early May-late Oct, diesel trains for some off peak services.
Fee: Station Free, except for special event days when charge of £1 (ch 50p) this is deducted from fare if travelling; 2nd class return fare for full journey £7.50 (ch £3.80, pen £5.58) Family ticket £18 (2+2).
(special coach for disabled parties on some trains) toilets for disabled shop (at Llangollen only)

Plas Newydd

Hill St LL20 8AW (Follow brown signs from A5, close to Grapes public house in Llangollen)

☎ 01978 861314 01978 861906

The 'Ladies of Llangollen', Lady Eleanor Butler and Sarah Ponsonby, lived here from 1780 to 1831. The original stained-glass windows, carved panels, and domestic miscellany of two lives are exhibited along with prints, pictures and letters.

Times: Open Apr-Oct, daily, 10-5.

Fee: Adults £2.50 (children £1.25 Family £6. Party 20+.

P ♿ toilets for disabled (ex guide dogs or in grounds)

Valle Crucis Abbey

LL29 8DD (on B5103, off A5 W of Llangollen)

☎ 01978 860326

Set in a deep, narrow valley, the abbey was founded for the Cistercians in 1201 by Madog ap Gruffydd. Substantial remains of the church can be seen, and some beautifully carved grave slabs have been found. There is a small exhibition on the Cistercian monks and the abbey.

Times: Open all year, late Apr-late Sep, daily 10-5; Site open rest of year. (Closed 24-26 Dec & 1 Jan)

Fee: £2 (ch 5-16, pen & students £1.50). Family ticket £5.50.

P ♿ shop

RHUDDLAN

Rhuddlan Castle

LL18 5AD

☎ 01745 590777

The castle was begun by Edward I in 1277, on a simple 'diamond' plan with round towers linked by sections of 9ft thick curtain wall. The moat was linked to a deep-water canal, allowing Edward's ships to sail from the sea right up to the castle.

Times: Open late Apr-late Sep, daily 10-5.

Fee: £2 (ch 5-16, pen & students £1.50). Family ticket £5.50.

P ♿ shop

FLINTSHIRE

EWLOE

Ewloe Castle

(NW of village on B5125)

Standing in Ewloe Wood are the remains of Ewloe Castle. It was a native Welsh castle, and Henry II was defeated nearby in 1157. Part of the Welsh Tower in the upper ward still stands to its original height, and there is a well in the lower ward. Remnants of walls and another tower can also be seen.

Times: Open at all times.

Fee: Free.

FLINT

Flint Castle

CH6 5PH

☎ 01352 733078

The castle was started by Edward I in 1277 and overlooks the River Dee. It is exceptional for its great tower, or Donjon, which is separated by a moat. Other buildings would have stood in the inner bailey, of which parts of the walls and corner towers remain.

Times: Open at all times.

Fee: Free.

P

HOLYWELL

Basingwerk Abbey

Greenfield Valley Heritage Pk, Greenfield

☎ 01352 714172

The abbey was founded around 1131 by Ranulf de Gernon, Earl of Chester. The first stone church dates from the beginning of the thirteenth century. The last abbot surrendered the house to the crown in 1536. The Abbey is close to the Heritage Park Visitor Centre and access to the Museum and Farm Complex at Greenfield Valley.

Times: Open all year, daily 9-6.

Fee: Free.

P ✕ ♿ (disabled facilities in Heritage Park) toilets for disabled shop

GWYNEDD

BANGOR

Penrhyn Castle

LL57 4HN (1m E at Bangor, at Llandegai on A5122, just off A55)

☎ 01248 353084 01248 371281

e-mail: ppemsn@smtp.ntrust.org.uk

The splendid castle with its towers and battlements was commissioned in 1827 as a sumptuous family home. Notable rooms include the great hall, the library and the dining room, which is covered with neo-Norman decoration. Among the furniture is a slate bed weighing over a ton, and a decorated brass bed made for Edward VII at the then huge cost of £600.

Times: Open 22 Mar-5 Nov, daily (ex Tue) Castle 12-5pm. Grounds and stableblock exhibitions 11-5 (Jul & Aug 10-5.30). Last admission 4.30pm. Last audio tour 4pm.

Fee: All inclusive ticket: £5 (ch £2.50). Family ticket £12.50. Party 15+. Grounds & stableblock only £3.50 (ch £2).

P ✕ licensed ♿ (wheelchairs & golf buggies pre bookable) toilets for disabled shop

BEDDGELERT

Sygun Copper Mine

LL55 4NE (1m E of Beddgelert on A498)
☎ 01766 510100 📠 01766 510102
e-mail: SygunMine@cs.com

With the help of an expert guide, and an audio-visual underground tour, visitors can explore the workings of this 19th-century copper mine, where magnificent stalactite and stalagmite formations can be seen. The less energetic can enjoy a continuous audio-visual presentation and a display of artefacts found during excavations.

Times: Open most of the year, daily 10-6. (last tour 5pm).
Fee: £4.75 (ch £3, pen £4). Family ticket £14
P ♿ toilets for disabled shop

BLAENAU FFESTINIOG

Ffestiniog Pumped Storage Scheme

Ffestiniog Information Centre, First Hydro Company, Tan-Y-Grisiau LL41 3TP (off A496)
☎ 01766 830465 📠 01766 833472
e-mail: robertsb@fhc.co.uk

The scheme was the first hydro-electric pumped storage scheme, and was opened by Her Majesty the Queen in 1963. Water is released from an upper dam, through turbines, to generate electricity when needed, and then pumped back up when demand is low. Guided tours are available, and the information centre includes a café.

Times: Open Etr-Oct, Sun-Fri, 10-4.30. Other times by prior arrangement.
Fee: £2.75 (ch £1.50, students & pen £2), Family ticket (2 adults, 2 children) £7.25
P shop (ex guide dogs)

Llechwedd Slate Caverns

LL41 3NB (25m from A55 N Wales Expressway S on A470. 10m from A5 junct with A470. Beside A470 from Llandudno)
☎ 01766 830306 📠 01766 831260
e-mail: llechwedd@aol.com

The Miners' Underground Tramway carries visitors into areas where early conditions have been recreated, while the Deep Mine is reached by an incline railway and has an unusual audio-visual presentation. Free surface attractions include several exhibitions and museums, slate mill and the Victorian village which has Victorian shops, bank, Miners Arms pub, lock-up and working smithy.

Times: Open all year, daily from 10am. Last tour 5.15 (Oct-Feb 4.15). (Closed 25-26 Dec & 1 Jan).
Fee: Single Tour £6.95 (ch £4.80, pen £6.20). Double Tour £10.50 (ch £7.20, pen £9.50)
P ✕ licensed ♿ toilets for disabled shop (also Victorian shops in the Village) (ex on surface)

CAERNARFON

Caernarfon Castle

LL55 2AY
☎ 01286 677617

Edward I began building the castle and extensive town walls in 1283 after defeating the last independant ruler of Wales. Completed in 1328, it has unusual polygonal towers, notably the 10-sided Eagle Tower. There is a theory that these features were copied from the walls of Constantinople, to reflect a tradition that Constantine was born nearby. Edward I's son and heir was born and presented to the Welsh people here, setting a precedent that was followed in 1969, when Prince Charles was invested as Prince of Wales.

Times: Open all year, late May-early Oct, daily 9.30-6; late Mar-late May & Oct, daily 9.30-5; Nov-late Mar, Mon-Sat 9.30-4, Sun 11-4. (Closed 24-26 Dec & 1 Jan)
Fee: £4.20 (ch 5-16, pen & students £3.20, disabled free). Family ticket £11.60.
P shop

Segontium Roman Museum

Beddgelert Rd LL55 2LN (on A4085 leading to Beddgelert approx 1m from Caernarfon)
☎ 01286 675625 📠 01286 678416

Segontium Roman Museum tells the story of the conquest and occupation of Wales by the Romans and displays the finds from the auxiliary fort of Segontium, one of the most famous in Britain. You can combine a visit to the museum with exploration of the site of the Roman Fort, which is in the care of Cadw: Welsh Historic Monuments. The exciting discoveries displayed at the museum vividly portray the daily life of the soldiers stationed in this remote outpost of the Roman Empire.

Times: Open Etr-Oct, Mon-Sat 10-5, Sun 2-5. Nov-Mar, Mon-Sat 10-4, Sun 2-4. Opening hours may vary. (May be closed on Mon, ex BH's from Apr).
Fee: £1.25 (concessions & ch 75p).
P (ex guide dogs)

COED-Y-BRENIN

Coed-y-Brenin Forest Park & Visitor Centre

(Off A470 3m S of Trawsfynydd, 8m N of Dolgellau. Clearly signed from main road)

☎ 01341 422289 01341 423893

Times: Open Apr-Oct 10-5. Other dates by prior bookings.

P (charged) toilets for disabled shop *Details not confirmed for 2001*

CRICCIETH

Criccieth Castle

LL52 0DP (off A497)

☎ 01766 522227

The castle dates from the 13th century and was taken and destroyed by Owain Glyndwr in 1404. Evidence of a fierce fire can still be seen. The gatehouse leading to the inner ward remains impressive, and parts of the walls are well preserved.

Times: Open all year, late May-late Sep, daily 10-6; Apr-late May, daily 10-5; site can be viewed at all other times. (Closed 24-26 Dec & 1 Jan).

Fee: £2.20 (ch 5-16, pen & students £1.70, disabled free). Family ticket £6.10.

P shop

CYMER ABBEY

Cymer Abbey

(2m NW of Dolgellau on A494)

☎ 01341 422854

The abbey was built for the Cistercians in the 13th century. It was never very large, and does not seem to have been finished. The church is the best-preserved building, with ranges of windows and arcades still to be seen. The other buildings have been plundered for stone, but low outlines remain.

Times: Open all year, early Apr-Oct, daily 9.30-6; Nov-Mar, daily 9.30-4. (Closed 24-26 Dec & 1 Jan)

Fee: £1.20 (ch 5-16, pen & students 70p, disabled free). Family ticket £3.10.

P

FAIRBOURNE

Fairbourne Railway

Beach Rd LL38 2PZ (on A493 follow signs for Fairbourne, main terminus is just past level crossing on left)

☎ 01341 250362 01341 250240

e-mail: enquiries@fairbourne-railway.co.uk

One of the most unusual of Wales's 'little trains' - built in 1890 as a horse-drawn railway to carry building materials it was later converted to steam, and now covers two-and-a-half miles. Its route passes one of the loveliest beaches in Wales, with views of the beautiful Mawddach Estuary. An enjoyable round trip can be made from Barmouth in summer, crossing the Mawddach by ferry, catching the narrow gauge steam train to Fairbourne and then taking the British Rail train - or walking - across the Mawddach Viaduct. At Gorsaf Newydd terminus visitors can see locomotive sheds.

Times: Open early/mid Apr-mid/late Sep, times vary according to season and events. Trains will run during Oct half term holiday and Santa Specials at Xmas.

Fee: 2nd class return £4.30 (ch £2.75, pen £3.80). 1st class return £5.40 (ch £3.25, pen £4.30). Family £12.40 (2 adults + 3 children £12.40)

P shop

HARLECH

Harlech Castle

LL46 2YH (from A496)

☎ 01766 780552

Harlech Castle was built in 1283-81 by Edward I, with a sheer drop to the sea on one side. Owain Glyndwr starved the castle into submission in 1404 and made it his court and campaigning base. Later, the defence of the castle in the Wars of the Roses inspired the song *Men of Harlech*. Today the sea has slipped away, and the castle's great walls and round towers stand above the dunes.

Times: Open all year, late May-early Oct, daily 9.30-6; late Mar-late May & Oct, daily 9.30-5; Nov-late Mar, Mon-Sat 9.30-4 & Sun 11-4. (Closed 24-26 Dec & 1 Jan).

Fee: £3 (ch 5-16, pen & students £2, disabled free). Family ticket £8.

P (disabled spaces in car park) shop

LLANBEDR

Maes Artro Centre

LL45 2PZ (on A496)

☎ 01341 241467

Times: Open mid May-mid Sep, daily 10-5.30

P toilets for disabled shop *Details not confirmed for 2001*

LLANBERIS

Dinorwig Discovery

Oriel Eeyri LL55 4TU (on A4086, Llanberis by-pass)

☎ 01286 870636 01286 871331

Times: Open Mar-Oct, daily, 10-5 peak season, 10.30-3.30 mid-season & 11-3 low season. Booked tours at other times please ring.

P (charged) (vehicle with chair lift available for tour) toilets for disabled shop *Details not confirmed for 2001*

Dolbadarn Castle

LL55 4UD (A4086)

Built by Llywelyn the Great in the early 13th century, this Welsh castle overlooks Llyn Padarn in the Llanberis pass.

Times: Open any reasonable time.

Fee: £1 (reductions 60p).

P

Llanberis Lake Railway

Padam Country Park LL55 4TY (off A4086)

☎ 01286 870549 01286 870549

e-mail: llrdlake-railway.freeserve.co.uk

Steam locomotives dating from 1889 to 1948 carry passengers on a four-mile return journey along the

contd.

shore of Padarn Lake. The terminal station is adjacent to the Welsh Slate Museum, in the Padarn Country Park. The railway was formerly used to carry slate.
Times: Open Etr-late Oct. Trains run frequently Sun-Fri (Sat in Jul & Aug), 11-4.30 in peak season. Send for free timetable.
Fee: £4.20 (ch £2.50). Family ticket available.
(charged) (Disabled carriage available) toilets for disabled shop (train & shop)

Snowdon Mountain Railway

LL55 4TY (on A4086, Caernarfon to Capel Curig road. 7.5 miles from Caernarfon)
01286 870223 01286 872518
e-mail: enquiries@snowdonrailway.force9.co.uk

The journey of just over four-and-a-half miles takes passengers more than 3000ft up to the summit of Snowdon; breathtaking views include, on a clear day, the Isle of Man and the Wicklow Mountains in Ireland. The round trip to the summit and back takes two and a half hours including a half hour at the summit.
Times: Open 15 Mar-1 Nov, daily from 9am (weather permitting).
Fee: Return £15.80 (ch £11.30). Single £11.30 (ch £8.10). Family ticket £42. Llanberis to summit. Party 15+. Phone or write for special rates.
(charged) (some carriages suitable for wheelchairs - must notify) toilets for disabled shop (ex off peak)

Welsh Slate Museum

Gilfach Ddu, Padarn Country Park LL55 4TY (0.25m off A4086. The Museum is within Padarn Country Park at Llanberis)
01286 870630 01286 871906

Set among the towering quarries at Llanberis, the Welsh Slate Museum is a living, working site located in the original workshops of Dinorwig Quarry, which once employed 15,000 men and boys. You can see the foundry, smithy, workshops and mess room which make up the old quarry, and view original machinery, much of which is still in working order.
Times: Open Etr-Oct, daily 10-5; Nov-Etr, Sun-Fri 10-4. Last admission 1 hour before closing. The site may close Monday (except Bank Holidays).
Fee: £3.50 (ch & concessions £2) Family ticket £7.90.
(charged) (all parts accessible except patten loft) toilets for disabled shop

LLANFIHANGEL-Y-PENNANT

Castell-y-Bere

029 2050 0200

The castle was begun around 1221 by Prince Llewelyn ap Iorwerth of Gwynedd to guard the southern flank of his principality. It is typically Welsh in design with its D-shaped towers. Although a little off the beaten track, the castle lies in a spectacular setting, overshadowed by the Cader Idris range.
Times: Open all reasonable times.
Fee: Free.

LLANGYBI

St Cybi's Well

01766 810047

Cybi was a sixth-century Cornish saint, known as a healer of the sick, and St Cybi's Well (or Ffynnon Gybi) has been famous for its curative properties through the centuries. The corbelled beehive vaulting inside the roofless stone structure is Irish in style and unique in Wales.
Times: Open at all times.
Fee: Free.

LLANUWCHLLYN

Bala Lake Railway

The Station LL23 7DD (off A494 Bala to Dolgellau road)
01678 540666 01678 540666

Steam locomotives which once worked in the slate quarries of North Wales now haul passenger coaches for four-and-a-half miles from Llanuwchllyn Station along the lake to Bala. The railway has one of the few remaining double-twist lever-locking framed GWR signal boxes, installed in 1896. Some of the coaches are open and some closed, so passengers can enjoy the beautiful views of the lake and mountains in all weathers; the latest corridor coach has facilities for the disabled.
Times: Open Etr-1 Oct, daily (except certain Mon & Fri in Apr, May, Jun and Sep)
Fee: £6.50 return. Family ticket £14. Pen £6
(wheelchairs can be taken on train) shop

LLANYSTUMDWY

Lloyd George Museum & Highgate Victorian Cottage

LL52 0SH (on A497 between Pwllheli & Criccieth)
01766 522071 01766 522071
e-mail: emryswilliams@gwynedd.gov.uk

Explore the life and times of David Lloyd George in this museum. His boyhood home is recreated as it would have been when he lived there between 1864 and 1880, along with his Uncle Lloyd's shoemaking workshop.

Times: Open Etr, daily 10.30-5; May, Mon-Fri 10.30-5; June, Mon-Sat 10.30-5; Jul-Sep daily 10.30-5; Oct, Mon-Fri, 11-4. Other times by appointment, telephone 01286 679098 for details.
Fee: £3 (ch & pen £2). Family ticket £7.
(induction loop, audio visual theatre) toilets for disabled shop (ex guide dogs)

PENARTH FAWR

PENARTH FAWR
(3.5m NE of Pwllheli off A497)
01766 810880

The hall, buttery and screen are preserved in this house which was probably built in the 15th century.
Times: Open at all times.
Fee: Free.

PLAS-YN-RHIW

PLAS-YN-RHIW
LL53 8AB (12m from Pwllheli signposted from B4413 to Aberdaron)
01758 780219

This is a small manor house, part medieval, with Tudor and Georgian additions. The ornamental gardens have flowering trees and shrubs including sub-tropical specimens, divided by box hedges and grass paths. There is a stream and waterfall, which descends from the snowdrop wood behind.
Times: Open end Mar-mid May, Thu-Mon noon-5; mid May-Oct, Wed-Mon noon-5.
toilets for disabled shop *Details not confirmed for 2001*

PORTHMADOG

FFESTINIOG RAILWAY
Harbour Station LL49 9NF (SE end of town, on A487)
01766 512340 01766 514576
e-mail: info@festrail.demon.co.uk

A narrow gauge steam railway running for 13.5 miles through Snowdonia National Park, with breathtaking views and superb scenery. Buffet service on all trains including licensed bar (in corridor carriages).
Times: Open late Mar-early Nov, daily service and also 26 Dec-1 Jan. Limited service Nov-Dec (most days). Limited service Feb & Mar.
Fee: Full distance return £13.80 (1 child free with each adult, pen £10.35). Other fares available.
(charged) licensed (Wheelchair ramps recently installed) toilets for disabled shop (closed 24/25 Dec)

PORTMEIRION

PORTMEIRION
LL48 6ET (Off A487 at Minffordd)
01766 770000 01766 771331
e-mail: info@portmeirion-village.com

Welsh architect Sir Clough Williams Ellis built his fairy-tale, Italianate village on a rocky, tree-clad peninsula on the shores of Cardigan Bay. A bell-tower, castle and lighthouse mingle with a watch-tower, grottoes and cobbled squares among pastel-shaded picturesque cottages let as holiday accommodation. The 60-acre Gwyllt Gardens include miles of dense woodland paths and are famous for their fine displays of rhododendrons, azaleas, hydrangeas and sub-tropical flora. There is a mile of sandy beach and a playground for children.
Times: Open all year, daily 9.30-5.30.
Fee: £4.50 (ch £2.25, pen £3.30). Party 15+.
licensed toilets for disabled shop (ex guide dogs)

TYWYN

TALYLLYN RAILWAY
Wharf Station LL36 9EY (A493 Machynlleth to Dolgellau for Tywyn station, B4405 for Abergynolwyn)
01654 710472 01654 711755
e-mail: enquiries@talyllyn.co.uk

The oldest 27in-gauge railway in the world, built in 1865 to run from Tywyn on Cardigan Bay to Abergynolwyn slate mine some seven miles inland. The railway climbs the steep sides of the Fathew Valley with stops on the way at Dolgoch Falls and the Nant Gwernol forest. The return trip takes 2.5 hours. All scheduled passenger trains are steam hauled.
Times: Open mid Feb-end Mar, daily Apr-early Nov & 26 Dec-1 Jan. Ring for timetable.
Fee: £9 day rover (ch accompanied £2). Intermediate fares available.
(charged) (prior arrangement useful) toilets for disabled shop

ISLE OF ANGLESEY

BEAUMARIS

BEAUMARIS CASTLE
LL58 8AP
01248 810361

Beaumaris was built by Edward I and took from 1295 to 1312 to complete. In later centuries it was plundered for its lead, timber and stone. Despite this it remains one of the most impressive and complete castles built by Edward I. It has a perfectly symmetrical, concentric plan, with a square inner bailey and curtain walls, round corner towers and D-shaped towers in between. There are also two great gatehouses, but these were never finished.
Times: Open all year, late May-early Oct, daily 9.30-6; late Mar-late May & Oct, daily 9.30-5; Nov-late Mar, Mon-Sat 9.30-4, Sun 11-4. (Closed 24-26 Dec & 1 Jan).
Fee: £2.20 (ch 5-16, pen & students £1.70, disabled free). Family ticket £6.10.
shop

Beaumaris Gaol & Courthouse

Steeple Ln LL58 8EW
☎ 01248 810921 & 724444 🖷 01248 750282

With its treadmill and grim cells, the gaol is a vivid reminder of the tough penalties exacted by 19th-century law. The courthouse, built in 1614 and renovated early in the 19th century, is a unique example of an early Welsh court.

Times: Open Etr–end Sep, daily 10.30-5. Other times by arrangement only.

Fee: Gaol £2.75 (ch, pen £1.75). Courthouse £1.50 (ch, pen £1). Combined ticket £3.50 (ch £2.50 & pen £2.50). Family ticket £7.75.

P (500yds) ♿ (narrow gates may restrict some wheelchairs) shop (ex guide dogs)

Museum of Childhood

1 Castle St LL58 8AP (on A545. Opposite Beaumaris Castle)
☎ 01248 712498 🖷 01248 716869

Times: Open daily 10.30-5.30, Sun 12-5. Last admission 4.30, Sun 4. (Closed Nov-2nd wk Mar).

P (50yds) ♿ shop (ex guide dogs) *Details not confirmed for 2001*

BRYNCELLI DDU

Bryn Celli Ddu Burial Chamber

(3m W of Menai Bridge off A4080)
☎ 029 2050 0200

Excavated in 1865, and then again in 1925-9, this is a prehistoric circular cairn covering a passage grave with a polygonal chamber.

Times: Open at all times.

Fee: Free.

P

BRYNSIENCYN

Anglesey Sea Zoo

LL61 6TQ (follow Lobster signs along A4080 to zoo)
☎ 01248 430411 🖷 01248 430213
e-mail: fishandfun@seazoo.demon.co.uk

Nestling by the Menai Straits, this all-weather undercover attraction contains a shipwreck bristling with conger eels, hand-reared lobsters, exquisite seahorses, inquisitive rays to stroke and colourful invertebrates including octopi.

Times: Open 3 Jan-24 Mar, daily 11-3; 25 Mar-5 Nov, daily 10-5; 6 Nov-17 Dec. (Closed 18-26 Dec & 1 Jan).

Fee: £5.50 (ch, student & UB40 £4.50, pen £5). Family ticket £12.95-£19.95. Party 12+.

P ✕ licensed ♿ (wheelchair available) toilets for disabled shop (ex guide dogs)

HOLYHEAD

RSBP Nature Reserve South Stack

South Stack LL65 3HB (A5 to Holyhead then follow brown tourist signs)
☎ 01407 764973 🖷 01407 764973

Times: Open: Visitor Centre daily, Apr-mid Sep, 11-5. Reserve open daily at reasonable times.

Fee: Free.

P

LLANALLGO

Din Llugwy Ancient Village

(1m NW off A5025)

The remains of a 4th-century village can be seen here. There are two circular and seven rectangular buildings, still standing up to head height and encircled by a pentagonal stone wall some 4 to 5ft thick.

Times: Open at all times.

Fee: Free.

PLAS NEWYDD

Plas Newydd

LL61 6DQ (2m S of Llanfairpwll, on A4080)
☎ 01248 714795 🖷 01248 713673
e-mail: ppnmsn@smtp.ntrust.org.uk

In a spectacular parkland setting, this elegant 18th-century house was built by James Wyatt. The interior, re-styled in the 1930s, is famous for its association with Rex Whistler. A military museum contains campaign relics of the 1st Marquess of Anglesey who commanded the cavalry at the Battle of Waterloo. Historical cruises, boat trips on the Menai Strait, operate weather and demand permitting. The Rhododendron garden is open from April to early June.

Times: Open Apr-1 Nov, Sat-Wed. House 12-5pm, garden 11am-5.30pm. Last admission 30mins before closing.

Fee: £4.50 (ch £2.25). Family £11. Pre-booked groups (15+). Garden only: £2.50 (ch £1.25).

P ✕ licensed ♿ (Close parking, wheelchairs, stairclimber) toilets for disabled shop

MERTHYR TYDFIL

MERTHYR TYDFIL

Brecon Mountain Railway

Pant Station Dowlais CF48 2UP (2.5m NE to the N of A465)
☎ 01685 722988 🖷 01685 384854

Opened in 1980, this narrow-gauge railway follows part of an old British Rail route which closed in 1964 when the iron industry in South Wales fell into decline. The present route starts at Pant Station and continues for 3.5 miles through the beautiful scenery of the Brecon Beacons National Park, as far as Taf Fechan reservoir. The train is pulled by a vintage steam locomotive and is one of the most popular railways in Wales.

Times: Opening times on application to The Brecon Mountain Railway, Pant Station, Merthyr Tydfil.

Fee: Fares are under review, please ring for details.

P ♿ (adapted carriage) toilets for disabled shop

Cyfarthfa Castle Museum & Art Gallery
Cyfarthfa Park CF47 8RE (off A470, N towards Brecon, follow brown signs)
☎ 01685 723112 📠 01685 722146

The home of the Crawshay family, this imposing Gothic mansion was built in 1825 and the magnificent gardens, designed at around the same time, still survive. The state rooms are given over to a museum which covers the social and industrial life of the area, and also houses collections of fine and decorative art, natural history items, archaeology and Egyptology.
Times: Open Apr-Sep: Mon-Sun 10-5.30. Oct-Mar: Tue-Fri 10-4, Sat-Sun 12-4.
Fee: £1.90 (concessions £1).
(stair lift & wheelchair available) toilets for disabled shop (ex guide dogs)

MONMOUTHSHIRE

CAERWENT
Caerwent Roman Town
(off A48)
☎ 029 2050 0200

A complete circuit of the town wall of 'Venta Silurum', together with excavated areas of houses, shops and a temple.
Times: Open - access throughout the year.
Fee: Free.

CALDICOT
Caldicot Castle, Museum & Countryside Park
NP6 4HU (from M4 junct 23 or M48 junct 2. Signposted from both A48 and B4245)
☎ 01291 420241 📠 01291 435094

Times: Open Mar-Oct, Mon-Fri 10.30-5, Sat & BH 10.30-5, Sun 1.30-5.
toilets for disabled shop *Details not confirmed for 2001*

CHEPSTOW
Chepstow Castle
NP6 5EZ
☎ 01291 624065

Built by William FitzOsbern, Chepstow is the first recorded Norman stone castle. It stands in a strategic spot above the Wye. The castle was strengthened in the following centuries, but was not besieged (as far as is known) until the Civil War, when it was twice lost to the Parliamentarians. The remains of the domestic rooms and the massive gatehouse with its portcullis grooves and ancient gates are still impressive, as are the walls and towers.
Times: Open all year, late May-early Oct, daily 9.30-6; late Mar-late May & Oct, daily 9.30-5; Nov-late Mar, Mon-Sat 9.30-4, Sun 11-4. (Closed 24-26 Dec & 1 Jan).
Fee: £3 (ch 5-16, pen & students £2, disabled free). Family ticket £8.
shop

Chepstow Museum
Gwy House, Bridge St NP6 5EZ (opposite Chepstow Castle car park)
☎ 01291 625981 📠 01291 625983
Times: Open Jan-Jun & Oct-Dec, Mon-Sat 11-1 & 2-5, Sun 2-5; Jul-Sep, Mon-Sat 10.30-1 & 2-5.30, Sun 2-5.30.
(opposite) (Charged parking) toilets for disabled shop (ex guide dogs) *Details not confirmed for 2001*

GROSMONT
Grosmont Castle
(on B4347)
☎ 01981 240301

Grosmont is one of the 'trilateral' castles of Hubert de Burgh (see also Skenfrith and White Castle). It stands on a mound with a dry moat, and the considerable remains of its 13th-century great hall can be seen. Three towers once guarded the curtain wall, and the western one is well preserved.
Times: Open - access throughout the year.
Fee: Free.

LLANTHONY
Llanthony Priory
☎ 029 2050 0200

William de Lacey discovered the remains of a hermitage dedicated to St David. By 1108 a church had been consecrated on the site and just over a decade later the priory was complete. After the priory was brought to a state of siege in an uprising, Hugh de Lacey provided the funds for a new church, and it is this that makes the picturesque ruin seen today. Visitor can still make out the west towers, north nave arcade and south transept.
Times: Open - access throughout the year.
Fee: Free.
toilets for disabled

LLANTILIO CROSSENNY

Hen Gwrt

(off B4233)

☎ 029 2050 0200

The rectangular enclosure of the former medieval house, still surrounded by a moat.

Times: Open - access throughout the year.

Fee: Free.

MONMOUTH

Nelson Museum & Local History Centre

New Market Hall, Priory St NP5 3XA (Town centre)

☎ 01600 713519

e-mail: nelsonmuseum@monmouthshire.gov.uk

Commemorative glass, china, silver, medals, books, models, prints and Admiral Nelson's fighting sword feature here. The local history displays deal with Monmouth's past as a fortress market town, and include a section on the co-founder of the Rolls Royce company, Charles Stewart Rolls, who was also a pioneer balloonist, aviator and, of course, motorist.

Times: Open all year, Mon-Sat 10-1 & 2-5; Sun 2-5. (Closed Xmas & New Year).

Fee: £1 (pen, students 75p) accompanied ch under 18 free.

P (200yds) shop (ex guide dogs)

RAGLAN

Raglan Castle

NP5 2BT (signposted off A40)

☎ 01291 690228

This magnificent 15th-century castle is noted for its 'Yellow Tower of Gwent'. It was built by Sir William ap Thomas and destroyed during the Civil War, after a long siege. The ruins are still impressive however, and the castle's history is illustrated in an exhibition situated in the closet tower and two rooms of the gate passage.

Times: Open all year, late Mar-late May & mid Oct, daily 9.30-5; late May-early Oct, daily 9.30-6; late Oct-late Mar Mon-Sat 9.30-4 & Sun 11-4. (Closed 24-26 Dec & 1 Jan).

Fee: £2.40 (ch 5-16, pen & students £1.90). Family ticket £6.70.

P shop

SKENFRITH

Skenfrith Castle

☎ 029 2050 0200

This 13th-century castle has a round keep set inside an imposing towered curtain wall. It was built by Hubert de Burgh as one of three 'trilateral' castles to defend the Welsh Marches.

Times: Open - access throughout the year. Key keeper arrangement.

Fee: Free.

P

TINTERN

Tintern Abbey

NP6 6SE (via A466)

☎ 01291 689251

The ruins of this Cistercian monastery church are still surprisingly intact. The monastery was established in 1131 and became increasingly wealthy well into the 15th century. During the Dissolution, the monastery was closed and most of the buildings were completely destroyed. During the 18th century many poets and artists came to see the ruins and recorded their impressions.

Times: Open all year, late Mar-late May & mid Oct, daily 9.30-5; late May-early Oct, daily 9.30-6; late Oct-late Mar, Mon-Sat 9.30-4 & Sun 11-4. (Closed 24-26 Dec & 1 Jan).

Fee: £2.40 (ch 5-16, pen & students £1.90). Family ticket £6.70.

P toilets for disabled shop

USK

Usk Rural Life Museum

Malt Barn, New Market St NP15 1AU

☎ 01291 673777

An award-winning collection of farm tools, machinery, wagons and domestic items.

Times: Open Apr-Oct, daily 10-5 (ex Sat & Sun am) Last admission 4.30. Winter hours contact the Museum.

Fee: £2 (ch £1, pen £1.50). Party.

P (special tape recording of tour for deaf) shop

WHITE CASTLE

White Castle

NP7 8UD (7m NE of Abergavenny, unclass road N of B4233)

☎ 01600 780380

The impressive 12th to 13th-century moated stronghold was built by Hubert de Burgh to defend the Welsh Marches. Substantial remains of walls, towers and a gatehouse can be seen. This is the finest of a trio of castles, the others being at Skenfrith and Grosmont.

Times: Open all year, late Apr-late Sep, daily 10-5; site open rest of year.

Fee: £2 (ch 5-16, pen & students £1.50). Family ticket £5.50.

P

NEATH PORT TALBOT

ABERDULAIS

Aberdulais Falls

SA10 8EU (from M4 junct 43, take A465, signposted Vale of Neath)

☎ 01639 636674 🖷 01639 645069

For over 300 years this famous waterfall has provided energy to drive the wheels of industry. The Turbine House allows visitors access to the top of the falls, with views of the power equipment, fish pass and displays.

Times: Open: March: Sat & Sun 11am-4pm only. 1 Apr-Oct Mon-Fri 10am-5pm, Sat, Sun & Bank Hols 11am-6pm.

P ☕ ♿ (lifts for disabled to view falls) toilets for disabled shop *Details not confirmed for 2001*

CILFREW

Penscynor Wildlife Park

SA10 8LF (Leave M4 at Junction 43 onto A465. Park is 2.5 miles N of Neath)

☎ 01639 642189 🖷 01639 635152

Times: Open all year, daily 10-6, dusk in winter. (Closed 25 Dec).

P ☕ ♿ toilets for disabled shop *Details not confirmed for 2001*

CRYNANT

Cefn Coed Colliery Museum

SA10 8SN (1m S of Cryant, on A4109)

☎ 01639 750556 🖷 01639 750556

Times: Open daily, Apr-Oct 10.30-5; Nov-Mar, groups welcome by prior arrangement.

P ☕ ♿ toilets for disabled shop *Details not confirmed for 2001*

CYNONVILLE

South Wales Miners Museum

Afan Argoed Country Park SA13 3HG (on A4107 6 miles NE of Port Talbot, leave M4 at Junction 40)

☎ 01639 850564 & 850875 🖷 01639 850446

The picturesquely placed museum gives a vivid picture of mining life, with coal faces, pit gear and miners' equipment. Guided tours of the museum on request. The country park has forest walks and picnic areas, and a visitor centre.

Times: Open all year daily, Mar-Sep 10.30-5 (Sat & Sun 10.30-6); Oct-Mar 10.30-4 (Sat & Sun 10.30-5).

Fee: £1 (ch & pen 50p). Disabled free of charge. Concessionary rate for advance bookings.

P (charged) ☕ ✕ ♿ (mechanical & manual wheel chairs on request) toilets for disabled shop (except aid dogs)

MARGAM

Margam Park

SA13 2TJ (Junction 38 off M4, follow signs approx. 300 yards on A48 towards Pyle)

☎ 01639 881635 🖷 01639 895897

Times: Open all year, Apr-Sep daily 10-6 (last admission 5pm). Oct-Mar, Wed-Sun 10-5 (last admission 3pm).

P ☕ ✕ licensed ♿ (free wheelchair loan, garden for disabled) toilets for disabled shop *Details not confirmed for 2001*

NEATH

Gnoll Estate Country Park

SA11 3BS (follow brown tourist signs)

☎ 01639 635808 🖷 01639 635694

The extensively landscaped Gnoll Estate offers tranquil woodland walks, picnic areas, stunning views, children's play areas, adventure playground, 9-hole golf course, and coarse fishing. The visitor centre explores the history of the estate, which was originally owned by local industrialists, the Mackworths.

Times: Open all year - Country park; Vistor centre, daily from 10am, (closed Xmas wk).

Fee: Free.

P ☕ ♿ toilets for disabled shop (ex on lead)

Neath Abbey

SA10 7DW

☎ 01639 812387

These ruins were originally a Cistercian abbey founded in 1130 by Richard de Grainville.

Times: Open at all times. Key keeper arrangement.

Fee: Free.

P ♿

NEWPORT

CAERLEON

Caerleon Fortress Baths, Amphitheatre & Barracks

NP6 1AE (on B4236)

☎ 01663 422518

Caerleon was an important Roman military base, with accommodation for thousands of men. The foundations of barrack lines and parts of the ramparts can be seen, with remains of the cookhouse, latrines and baths. The amphitheatre nearby is one of the best examples in Britain.

Times: Open all year, late Mar-Oct, daily 9.30-5; Nov-late Mar, Mon-Sat 9.30-5, Sun 1-5. (Closed 24-26 Dec & 1 Jan).

Fee: £2 (ch 5-16, pen & students £1.50, disabled free). Family ticket £5.50.

P ♿ shop

Roman Legionary Museum

High St NP18 1AE (Situated 10mins from M4/Severn Bridge. Take Junction 25 from M4 onto B4596)

☎ 01633 423134 🖷 01633 422869

The museum illustrates the history of Roman Caerleon and the daily life of its garrison. On display are arms, armour and equipment, with a collection of engraved gemstones, a labyrinth mosaic and finds from the legionary base at Usk. Please telephone for details of children's holiday activities.

Times: Open all year, Apr-Oct, Mon-Sat 10-6, Sun 2-6; Nov-Mar, Mon-Sat 10-4, Sun 2-4.30. (May be closed on Mon from Apr, ex BH's).

Fee: £2.10 (ch & concessions £1.25). Joint ticket available with Roman Baths & Amphitheatre £3.30 (ch £2).

P (100yds) ♿ toilets for disabled shop (ex guide dogs) 

NEWPORT

Tredegar House & Park

Coedkernew NP1 9YW (2m W, signposted from A48/ M4 junct 28)

01633 815880 01633 815895

e-mail: tredegar.house@newport.gov.uk

Times: Open Good Fri-Sep, Wed-Sun & BHs 11-4.(All week in August. Wknds only in Oct. Special Hallowe'en & Xmas opening. Also open for group visits at other times.

(charged) licensed (wheelchairs for loan) toilets for disabled shop (ex grounds & guide dogs) *Details not confirmed for 2001*

PENHOW

Penhow Castle

NP6 3AD (on A48 between Newport & Chepstow. Use M4 Junction 24)

01633 400800 01633 400990

e-mail: castles@compuserve.com

Times: Open Good Fri-end Sep, Wed-Sun & BH 10-5.15 last admission; "Candlelit Tours" by arrangement; Aug open daily; Winter Wed 10-4 Sun 1-4. Closed Jan-Feb.

(refreshment bar) (audio-tours for blind) shop (ex guide dogs) *Details not confirmed for 2001*

PEMBROKESHIRE

AMROTH

Colby Woodland Garden

SA67 8PP (1.5 miles inland from Amroth beside Carmarthen Bay, follow brown signs from A477)

01834 811885

Tranquillity and seclusion abound in this sheltered valley. There are many pleasant meadow and woodland walks. From early spring to the end of June the garden is a blaze of colour, from the masses of daffodils to the rich hues of rhododendrons, azaleas and bluebells. Followed by hydrangeas in shaded walks through summer to glorious shades of autumn

Times: Open Apr-Oct, daily 10-5. Walled garden Apr-30 Oct 11-5.

Fee: £2.80 (ch £1.40). Family ticket £7. Pre-booked parties £2.30 (ch £1.15) NT members free.

(Limited due to terrain) toilets for disabled shop garden centre

CAREW

Carew Castle & Tidal Mill

SA70 8SL (on A4075, 4m E of Pembroke)

01646 651782 01646 651782

e-mail: tracy@carew-pcnp.freeserve.co.uk

This magnificent Norman castle has royal links with Henry Tudor and was the setting for the Great Tournament of 1507. Nearby is the Carew Cross (Cadw), an impressive 13ft Celtic cross dating from the 11th century. Carew Mill is one of only four restored tidal mills in Britain, with records dating back to 1558.

Times: Open Apr-Oct, daily 10-5.

Fee: £2.75 (ch & pen £1.80).Family ticket £7.30. Single ticket (castle or mill) £1.90 (ch £1.40).

(ramps) toilets for disabled shop

CILGERRAN

Cilgerran Castle

SA43 2SF (off A484 & A478)

01239 615007

Set above a gorge of the River Teifi - famed for its coracle fishermen - Cilgerran Castle dates from the 11th to 13th centuries. It decayed gradually after the Civil War, but its great round towers and high walls give a vivid impression of its former strength.

Times: Open all year, late Mar-late Oct, daily 9.30-6.30; late Oct-late Mar, daily 9.30-4. (Closed 24-26 Dec & 1 Jan).

Fee: £2 (ch 5-16, pen & students £1.50, disabled free). Family ticket £5.50.

shop

CRYMYCH

Castell Henllys Fort

Pant-Glas, Meline SA41 3UT (Off A487 between Eglwyswrw and Newport Pembrokeshire)

01239 891319 01239 891319

e-mail: celts@castellhenllys.freeserve.co.uk

This Iron Age hill fort is set in the beautiful Pembrokeshire Coast National Park. Excavations began in 1981 and three roundhouses have been reconstructed, another roundhouse has been completed and is the largest on the site. A Celtic roundhouse has been constructed in its original way using hazel wattle walls, oak rafters and a thatched conical roof. A forge, smithy, and looms can be seen.

Times: Open Apr-early Nov, daily 10-5. Last entry 4.30

Fee: £2.70 (ch & pen £1.80) Family £7

toilets for disabled shop

FISHGUARD

OceanLab

The Parrog, Goodwick SA64 0DE (close to Stena Line ferry terminal at harbour)

01348 874737 01348 872528

e-mail: ocean_lab01@hotmail.com

Overlooking the Pembrokeshire coastline, OceanLab is a multifunctional centre which aims to provide a fun filled experience for the family. A deep-sea adventure takes the visitor back in time to see marine creatures that lived in the distant past. There is also a hands on ocean quest exhibition, a soft play area and a cybercafe where visitors can surf the Internet.

Times: Open Etr-Oct 10-6, winter opening on request.

Fee: Telephone for details

toilets for disabled shop (ex guide dogs) 

LAMPHEY

Lamphey Palace

SA71 5NT (off A4139)

☎ 01646 672224

This ruined 13th-century palace once belonged to the Bishops of St Davids.

Times: Open all year, daily 10-5.

Fee: £2 (ch 5-16, pen & students £1.50, disabled free). Family ticket £5.50.

P toilets for disabled shop

LLANYCEFN

Penrhos Cottage

SA66 7XT (Near Maenclochog & Llanycefn, N of Haverfordwest)

☎ 01437 760460 01437 760460

Local tradition has it that cottages built overnight on common land could be claimed by the builders, together with the ground a stone's throw away from the door. This thatched cottage is an example, built with help from friends and family; and it gives an insight into traditional Welsh country life.

Times: Open mid May-Sep Mon-Fri, by appointment only. Tel: 01437 760460.

Fee: Free.

P (roadside) shop (ex in grounds or guide dogs)

LLAWHADEN

Llawhaden Castle

☎ 01437 541201

The castle was first built in the 12th century to protect the possessions of the bishops of St David's. The 13th and 14th-century remains of the bishops' hall, kitchen, bakehouse and other buildings can be seen, all surrounded by a deep moat.

Times: Open at all times. Key keeper arrangement.

Fee: Free.

NARBERTH

Oakwood Park

Canaston Bridge SA67 8DE (signposted off A40, between Carmarthen and Haverfordwest at Canaston Bridge. Take A4075 for 2m)

☎ 01834 891373, 891376 & 891484 (bookings) 01834 891408

The numerous activities offered here include treetops rollercoaster, pirate ship, waterfall and bobsleigh rides, miniature trains, go-karts, assault courses and a theatre show. There is a huge undercover Playland and an outdoor children's theme park. Plus 'Megafobia', UK's largest wooden rollercoaster, Vertigo, a 140 ft skycoaster, Snake River Falls, Europe's first watercoaster and Voodoo Mansion.

Times: Open 15 Apr-Sep, daily from 10am.

Fee: Adults & ch over 10 £11.50, ch 3-9 £10.50, under 2 free, pen & disabled £9.50. Party 20+. Family ticket £40.

P licensed toilets for disabled shop (ex guide dogs)

NEWPORT

Pentre Ifan Burial Chamber

(3m SE from B4329 or A487)

☎ 029 2050 0200

Found to be part of a vanished long barrow when excavated in 1936-37, the remains of this chamber include the capstone, three uprights and a circular forecourt.

Times: Open - access throughout the year.

Fee: Free.

PEMBROKE

The Museum of the Home

7 Westgate Hill SA71 4LB (Opposite Pembroke Castle)

☎ 01646 681200

A pleasant domestic setting provides an opportunity to view some of the objects that have been part of everyday life over the past three hundred years.

Times: Open May-Sep, Mon-Thu 11-5, other times by arrangement.

Fee: £1.20 (ch & pen 90p).

P (100 yards) (Public Pay & Display)

Pembroke Castle

SA71 4LA (west end of Main St)

☎ 01646 681510 01646 622260

This 12th to 13th-century fortress has an impressive 80ft-high round keep. There is also an Interpretative Centre with introductory video and Pembroke Yeomanry exhibition. Special events may include archery and falconry displays.

Times: Open all year, daily, Apr-Sep 9.30-6; Mar & Oct 10-5; Nov-Feb, 10.30-4.30; (Closed 24-26 Dec & 1 Jan).

Fee: £3 (ch under16 & pen £2, ch under5 & wheelchairs free). Family ticket £8.

P (200 yds) toilets for disabled shop

ST DAVID'S

St Davids Bishop's Palace

SA62 6PE (on A487)

☎ 01437 720517

These extensive and impressive ruins are all that remain of the principal residence of the Bishops of St Davids. The palace shares a quiet valley with the cathedral, which was almost certainly built on the site of a monastery founded in the 6th century by St David. The Bishop's Palace houses an exhibition: 'Lords of the Palace'.

Times: Open all year, late Mar-late May & mid Oct, daily 9.30-5; late May-early Oct, daily 9.30-6; Nov-late Mar, Mon-Sat 9.30-4 & Sun 12-2. (Closed 24-26 Dec & 1 Jan).

Fee: £2 (ch 5-16, pen & students £1.50). Family ticket £5.50.

P toilets for disabled shop

St Davids Cathedral
The Close SA62 6PE
☎ 01437 720202 📠 01437 721885
e-mail: adminstrator@stdavidscathedral.org.uk

Begun 1181 on the reputed site of St David's 6th century monastic settlement. The present building was altered during the 12th to the 14th centuries and again in the 16th. The ceilings of oak, painted wood and stone vaulting are of considerable interest.

Times: Open all year 8.30-6.

Fee: Suggested donation of £2.00.

P (300yds) ☕ ♿ toilets for disabled shop 🐕 (ex guide dogs)

ST FLORENCE

Manor House Wildlife & Leisure Park
Ivy Tower SA70 8RJ (on B4318 between Tenby & St Florence)
☎ 01646 651201 📠 01646 651201

The park is set in 35 acres of delightful wooded grounds and award-winning gardens. The wildlife includes exotic birds, reptiles and fish. Also a pets' corner, a children's playground with free rides on astraglide slide and roundabouts. Other attractions include a natural history museum, a go-kart track, model railway exhibition. Daily falconry displays.

Times: Open Etr-end Sep, daily 10-6. Please telephone for late opening Jul/Aug.

Fee: £4 (ch £3, pen £3.50, disabled/helpers £2.50) Family ticket (2 adults, 2 children) £12.50. Party 20+.

P ☕ ♿ toilets for disabled shop 🐕

SCOLTON

Scolton Visitor Centre
SA62 5QL (5m N of Haverfordwest, on B4329)
☎ 01437 731328 (Mus) & 731457 (Park)
📠 01437 731743

Scolton Manor Museum is situated in Scolton Country Park. The early Victorian mansion, refurbished stables and the exhibition hall illustrate the history and natural history of Pembrokeshire. There are new displays in the house and stables, plus a 'Pembrokeshire Railways' exhibition. The 60-acre grounds, partly a nature reserve, have fine specimen trees and shrubs. Environmentally friendly Visitor Centre, alternative energy and woodland displays, guided walks and children's play areas.

Times: Open; Museum Apr-Oct, Tue-Sun & BH's 10.30-5.30; Country Park all year ex 25 & 26 Dec, Etr-Sep 10-7, Oct-Etr 10-4.30.

Fee: Museum: £2 (ch £1, concessions £1.50). Country Park car park £1 all day.

P (charged) ☕ ♿ (disabled parking area near house) toilets for disabled shop 🐕 (ex guide dogs & in grounds)

TENBY

Tenby Museum & Art Gallery
Castle Hill SA70 7BP (Near the centre of town on Castle Hill, above the Harbour)
☎ 01834 842809 📠 01834 842809
e-mail: tenbymuseum@hotmail.com

The museum is situated on Castle Hill. It covers the local heritage from prehistory to the present in galleries devoted to archaeology, geology, maritime history, natural history, militaria and bygones. The art galleries concentrate on local associations with an important collection of works by Augustus, Gwen John and others.

Times: Open all year, Etr-Oct, daily 10-5; Nov-Etr, Mon-Fri 10-5.

Fee: £2 (ch £1, concessions £1.50). Family ticket £4.50.

P ♿ shop 🐕 (ex guide dogs)

Tudor Merchant's House
Quay Hill SA70 7BX
☎ 01834 842279

Recalling Tenby's history as a thriving and prosperous port, the Tudor Merchant's house is a fine example of gabled 15th-century architecture. There is a good Flemish chimney and on three walls the remains of frescoes can be seen. A small herb garden has been created.

Times: Open 2 Apr-Sep, Mon-Tue, Thu-Sat 10-5, Sun 1-5. Dec Mon-Tue, Thu-Fri 10-3, Sun 12-3.

Fee: £1.80 (ch 90p). NT members free.

P (500yds) (no coaches nearby) ♿ (garden could be accessed) 🐕 (ex guide or small dogs)

POWYS

ABERCRAF

Dan-Yr-Ogof The National Showcaves Centre for Wales
SA9 1GJ (M4 J45, midway between Swansea & Brecon on A4067)
☎ 01639 730284 & 730801 📠 01639 730293
e-mail: info@showcaves.co.uk

This award winning attraction includes three separate caves, dinosaur park, Iron Age Farm, museum, shire horse centre and covered children's play area.

Times: Open Apr-Oct, daily from 10am. Please telephone for Oct.

Fee: £7 (ch £4.20). Group rates 15+

P ☕ ♿ toilets for disabled shop

BERRIEW

GLANSEVERN HALL GARDENS

Glansevern SY21 8AH (on A483 between Welshpool and Newtown)

☎ 01686 640200 📠 01686 640829

Built in the Greek Revival style for Arthur Davies Owen, who chose a romantically positioned site on the banks of the River Severn. The current owners have developed the gardens, respecting the plantings and features of the past, and added a vast collection of new and interesting species. There are many fine and unusual trees, a lakeside walk, water gardens and a rock garden with lamp-lit grotto.

Times: Open May-Sep, BH Mon, Fri-Sat 2-6. Parties other dates by arrangement

Fee: £2 (pen £1.50, ch 15 free). Reduced rate £1.50 Fri & Sat. Party 20+

P ☕ ♿ (most areas accessible) shop garden centre

BRECON

BRECKNOCK MUSEUM

Captain's Walk LD3 7DW (Near centre of town on junction of The Watton & Glamorgan St.)

☎ 01874 624121 📠 01874 611281

e-mail: brecknock.museum@powys.gov.uk

A wealth of local history is explored at the museum, which has archaeological and historical exhibits, with sections on folk life, decorative arts and natural history. There is a 19th-century Assize Court and one of the finest collections of Welsh Lovespoons.

Times: Open all year, Mon-Fri 10-5, Sat 10-1 & 2-5, closed 4 Nov-Feb. (also open Sun 12-5 Apr-Sep) . Closed Good Fri.

Fee: Free.

P ♿ (limited parking, must be accompanied by able-bodied) toilets for disabled shop 🐕 (ex guide dogs)

SOUTH WALES BORDERERS (24TH REGIMENT) MUSEUM MUSEUM

The Barracks, The Watton LD3 7EB (close to town centre, well signed)

☎ 01874 613310 📠 01874 613275

e-mail: swb@rrw.org.uk

The museum of the South Wales Borderers and Monmouthshire Regiment, which was raised in 1689 and has been awarded 23 Victoria Crosses. Amongst the collections is the Zulu War Room, devoted to the war and in particular to the events at Rorke's Drift, 1879, when 121 men fought 4500 Zulus.

Times: Open all year, Apr-Sep daily; Oct-Mar, Mon-Fri 9-5. (Closed Xmas & New Year).

Fee: £2 (ch 16 £1).

P (town centre) ♿ toilets for disabled shop 🐕 (ex guide dogs) 🎫

LLANFAIR CAEREINION

WELSHPOOL & LLANFAIR LIGHT RAILWAY

SY21 0SF (beside A458, Shrewsbury-Dolgellau road)

☎ 01938 810441 📠 01938 810861

The Llanfair Railway is one of the Great Little Trains of Wales. It offers an 8-mile trip through glorious scenery by narrow-gauge steam train. The line is home to a collection of engines and coaches from all round the world.

Times: Open Etr-Oct, phone for timetable enquiries.

Fee: £7.90 return (ch £1, pen £6.90).

P ☕ ♿ (two coachs adapted for wheelchairs) toilets for disabled shop 🎫

MACHYNLLETH

CELTICA

Y Plas, Aberystwyth Rd SY20 8ER (2 minutes walk S of town clock. Car park entrance off Aberystwyth Rd)

☎ 01654 702702 📠 01654 703604

e-mail: celtica@celtica.wales.com

Located in a restored mansion house, Celtica is an exciting heritage centre introducing the history and culture of the Celtic people. The sights and sounds of Celtic life are brought alive as you go on a journey portraying the Celtic spirit of the past, present and future. There's an interpretive centre dedicated to Welsh and Celtic history, a children's indoor play area, and conference rooms. Education resources are available and groups are welcome. Storytelling, lectures, music and craft events take place.

Times: Open daily 10-6 (last show starts 4.40). Evening opening for pre-booked groups. (Closed 24-26 Dec & 17-22 Jan).

Fee: £4.95 (concessions £3.80). Family ticket £13.75.

P ☕ ✕ licensed ♿ (Lift & ramps to public areas; Induction loop) toilets for disabled shop 🐕 (ex guide dogs)

CENTRE FOR ALTERNATIVE TECHNOLOGY

SY20 9AZ (2.5m N on A487)

☎ 01654 702400 📠 01654 702782

e-mail: help@catinfo.demon.co.uk

The Centre for Alternative Technology promotes practical ideas and information on sustainable technologies. The exhibition includes displays of wind, water and solar power, organic gardens, low-energy dwellings, and a unique water-powered railway which ascends a 200ft cliff from the car park. The Wave Tank

contd.

and the underground 'Mole-Hole' are particularly popular with children.

Times: Open Mar-Oct; 10-5.30; Nov-Feb; 11-4. Closed 23-26 Dec & 5-23 Jan.

Fee: Dec-Mar £4.90 (ch £2.50, concessions £3.50). Family ticket £13.40; Apr-Oct £6.90 (ch £3.50, concessions £4.90). Family ticket £19.50. Discounted admission for those arriving by train, bus, cycle & on foot.

(wheelchair available) shop (ex guide dogs) 

MONTGOMERY

Montgomery Castle

029 2050 0200

Initially an earth and timber structure guarding an important ford in the River Severn, Montgomery was considered a 'suitable spot for the erection of an impregnable castle' in the 1220s. Building and modifications continued until 1251-53, but the final conquest of Wales by Edward I meant the castle lost much of its role.

Times: Open all year, any reasonable time.

Fee: Free.

PRESTEIGNE

The Judge's Lodging

Broad St LD8 2AD (on B4362)

01544 260650/1 01544 260652

A restored Victorian town house with integral courtroom, cells and service areas - step back into the 1870s, accompanied by an 'evesdropping' audiotour of voices from the past.

Times: Open daily, Mar-Apr 10-4; May-Oct 10-6. Closed Nov-Feb.

(lift, disabled pack for inaccesible items) shop *Details not confirmed for 2001*

TRETOWER

Tretower Court & Castle

NP8 2RF (3m NW of Crickhowell, off A479)

01874 730279

The castle is a substantial ruin of an 11th-century motte and bailey, with a three-storey tower and 9ft-thick walls. Nearby is the Court, a 14th-century fortified manor house which has been altered and extended over the years. The two buildings show the shift from medieval castle to more domestic accommodation over the centuries.

Times: Open early-late Mar, daily 10-4; Late Mar-late May & early Sep-late Oct, daily 10-5; late May-early Sep, daily 10-6.

Fee: £2.20 (ch 5-16, pen & students £1.70). Family ticket £6.10.

toilets for disabled shop

WELSHPOOL

Powis Castle

SY21 8RF (1m S of Welshpool, signposted off A483)

01938 554338 01938 554336

e-mail: ppcmsn@smtp.ntrust.org.uk

Laid out in the Italian and French styles, the Garden retains its original lead statues, an Orangery and an aviary on the terraces. The medieval castle contains one of the finest collections of paintings and furniture in Wales and a beautiful collection of treasures from India.

Times: Castle & museum open: Apr-Jun and Sep-Oct, Wed-Sun 1-5; Jul-Aug Tue-Sun 1-5; Open all Bank Hol's in season. Garden is open same days as castle and museum 11-6. Last admission to all parts is 30 mins before closing.

Fee: Castle, Museum & Gardens £7.50, (ch under 17 £3.75) Family ticket £18.75. Group member £6.50. Garden only: £5 (ch £2.50) Family £12.50, Group member £4. NT members & ch under 5 free.

licensed shop garden centre (ex guide dogs) 

RHONDDA CYNON TAFF

TREHAFOD

Rhondda Heritage Park

Lewis Merthyr Colliery, Coed Cae Rd CF37 7NP (between Pontypridd & Porth, off A470; follow brown tourist signs from M4 junct 32)

01443 682036 01443 687420

e-mail: rhonpark@netwales.co.uk

Based at the Lewis Merthyr Colliery, the Heritage Park is a fascinating 'living history' attraction. You can take the Cage Ride to 'Pit Bottom' and explore the underground workings of a 1950's pit, guided by men who were miners themselves. There are children's activities, an exhibition gallery and a museum illustrating living conditions in the Rhondda Valley. Special events throughout the year.

Times: Open all year, daily 10-6. Closed Mon from Oct-Etr. Last admission 4.30pm. Closed 25 & 26 Dec.

Fee: £5.60 (ch £4.30, pen £4.95). Family ticket £16.50.

licensed (Wheelchair available, accessible parking, lifts) toilets for disabled shop (ex guide dogs)

SWANSEA

LLANRHIDIAN

Weobley Castle

SA3 1HB (from B4271 or B4295)

☎ 01792 390012

A 12th to 14th-century fortified manor house with an exhibition on the history of Weobley and other historic sites on the Gower peninsula.

Times: Open all year, Apr-Oct, daily 9.30-6; Oct-Mar daily 9.30-5. (Closed 24-26 Dec & 1 Jan).

Fee: £2 (ch 5-16, pen & students £1.50). Family ticket £5.50.

P ♿ shop

OXWICH

Oxwich Castle

SA3 1NG (A4118 from Swansea)

☎ 01792 390359

Situated on the Gower peninsula, this Tudor mansion is a striking testament in stone to the pride and ambitions of the Mansel dynasty of Welsh gentry. The E-shaped wing houses an exhibition on historical Gower and 'Chieftains and Princes of Wales'.

Times: Open late Apr-late Sep, daily 10-5.

Fee: £2 (ch 5-16, pen & students £1.50). Family ticket £5.50.

P ♿ (Radar key toilet) toilets for disabled

PARKMILL

Gower Heritage Centre

Y Felin Ddwr SA3 2EM (Follow signs for South Gower on A4118 W from Swansea. W side of Parkmill village)

☎ 01792 371206 📠 01792 371471

e-mail: gower.heritage.centre@compuserve.com

Based around a 12th-century water-powered cornmill, the site also contains a number of craft workshops, a museum and a miller's cottage, all set in attractive countryside in an Area of Outstanding Natural Beauty.

Times: Open daily, Mar-Oct 10-7; Nov-Feb 10-5. Closed 25 Dec.

Fee: £2.60 (ch, students & pen £1.60). Family ticket £6.80. Party.

P ♿ toilets for disabled shop

SWANSEA

Glynn Vivain Art Gallery

Alexandra Rd SA1 5DZ

☎ 01792 655006 & 651738 📠 01792 651713

A broad spectrum of visual arts form the original bequest of Richard Glynn Vivian, including old masters and an international collection of porcelain and Swansea china. The 20th century is also well represented with modern painting and sculpture by British and foreign artists, with the emphasis on Welsh artists.

Times: Open all year, Tue-Sun & BH Mon 10-5. Closed 25, 26 Dec & 1 Jan.

Fee: Free.

P (200 yards, NCP) ♿ also sculpture court toilets for disabled shop (ex guide dogs, hearing dogs)

Swansea Maritime & Industrial Museum

Museum Square, Maritime Quarter SA1 1SN (M4 junct 42, on main rd into Swansea city centre)

☎ 01792 650351 & 470371 📠 01792 654200

Times: Open all year, Tue-Sun 10-5.(last admission 4.45pm). Closed Mon except BH Mon, 25, 26 Dec & 1 Jan.

P (50yds) (charged) ♿ shop (ex guide dogs) *Details not confirmed for 2001*

TORFAEN

BLAENAVON

Big Pit Mining Museum

NP4 9XP (M4 J26/25, follow signs along A4042 & A4043 to Pontypool & Blaenavon. Signposted off A465)

☎ 01495 790311 📠 01495 792618

e-mail: pwllmawr@aol.com

The `Big Pit' closed as a working mine in 1980, but today you can don safety helmets and cap lamps, and descend the 300ft shaft to find out what life was like for Welsh miners. There is also an exhibition in the old pithead baths and a reconstructed miner's cottage. Stout shoes and warm clothes are recommended for tours of the mine.

Times: Open Mar-Nov, daily 9.30-5, last tour 3.30. Dec-Feb telephone for opening details.

Fee: Underground & surface £5.75 (ch £3.95, pen £5.50). Family ticket £17. Surface only £2 (ch £1, pen £1.75)

P ♿ (underground tours by prior arrangement) toilets for disabled shop (Welsh crafts, books & publications)

Blaenavon Ironworks

North St

☎ 01495 792615

The Blaenavon Ironworks were a milestone in the history of the Industrial Revolution. Constructed in 1788-99, they were the first purpose-built, multi-furnace ironworks in Wales. By 1796, Blaenavon was the

contd.

second largest ironworks in Wales, eventually closing down in 1904.
Times: Open Etr-Oct, daily 9.30-4.30. (Closed 24-26 Dec & 1 Jan). For details of opening outside this period, telephone 01633 648081.
Fee: £1.50 (ch 5-16, pen & students £1, disabled free). Family ticket £4.

CWMBRAN

Greenmeadow Community Farm

Greenforge Way NP44 5AJ (Follow signs for Cwmbran then brown tourist signs (with sheep on) to farm)
☎ 01633 862202 01633 489332
e-mail: greenmeadow_community_farm@compuserve.com
Times: Open summer 10-6, winter 10-4. Closed 25 Dec.
licensed (tractor & trailer rides for wheelchair users) toilets for disabled shop *Details not confirmed for 2001*

VALE OF GLAMORGAN

BARRY

Welsh Hawking Centre

Weycock Rd CF62 3AA (on A4226)
☎ 01446 734687 01446 739620

There are over 200 birds of prey here, including eagles, hawks, owls, buzzards and falcons. They can be seen and photographed in the mews and some of the breeding aviaries. There are flying demonstrations at regular intervals during the day. A variety of tame, friendly animals, such as donkeys, goats, pigs, lambs and rabbits will delight younger visitors.
Times: Open end Mar-end Sep, daily 10.30-5, 1hr before dusk in winter. **Fee:** £3 (ch & pen £2).
toilets for disabled shop

OGMORE

Ogmore Castle

☎ 01656 653435

Standing on the River Ogmore, the west wall of this castle is 40ft high. A hooded fireplace is preserved in the 12th-century, three-storey keep and a dry moat surrounds the inner ward.
Times: Open - access throughout the year. Key keeper arrangement.
Fee: Free.

PENARTH

Cosmeston Lakes Country Park & Medieval Village

Cosmeston Lakes Country Park, Lavernock Rd CF64 5UY (on B4267 between Barry and Penarth, close to M4 junct 33)
☎ 029 2070 9141 & 2070 1678
029 2070 8686

Deserted during the plagues and famines of the 14th century, the original village was rediscovered through archaeological excavations. The buildings have been faithfully reconstructed on the excavated remains, creating a living museum of medieval village life.
Special events throughout the year include re-enactments and Living History.
Times: Open all year, daily 11-5 in Summer, 11-4 in Winter. Closed 25 Dec. Country park open at all times.
Fee: Entry to Village £3, (concessions £2) Family ticket £6.50. Entry to Country Park is free. toilets for disabled shop

ST HILARY

Old Beaupre Castle

(1m SW, off A48)
☎ 01446 773034

This ruined manor house was rebuilt during the 16th century. Its most notable features are an Italianate gatehouse and porch. The porch is an unusual three-storeyed structure and displays the Basset arms.
Times: Open - access throughout the year. Key keeper arrangement.
Fee: Free.

WREXHAM

CHIRK

Chirk Castle

LL14 5AF (8m S of Wrexham, signposted off A483)
☎ 01691 777701 01691 774706
e-mail: pcwmsn@smtp.ntrust.org.uk

Chirk Castle is one of a chain of late 13th-century Marcher castles. Its high walls and drum towers have hardly changed, but the inside shows the varied tastes of 700 years of occupation. One of the least altered parts is Adam's Tower. Many of the medieval-looking decorations were by Pugin in the 19th century. Varied furnishings include fine tapestries.
Times: Open 29 Mar-Sep, Wed-Sun & BH Mon 12-5 (castle), 11-6 (gardens); Oct, Wed-Sun 12-4 (castle), 11-5 (gardens). Last admission 30 mins before closing.
Fee: £5 (ch £2.50). Family ticket £12.50. Party. Garden only £2.80 (ch £1.40) National Trust members free.
licensed (stairclimber) toilets for disabled shop (ex guide dogs)

WREXHAM

Erddig

LL13 0YT (off A525, 2m S of Wrexham and A483/A5152 Oswestry road)
☎ 01978 355314 01978 313333

Built in 1680, the house was enlarged and improved by a wealthy London lawyer with a passion for gilt and silver furniture. Original furnishings remain, including a magnificent state bed in Chinese silk. The house is notable for the view it gives of both 'upstairs' and 'downstairs' life. The gardens, unusually, have been changed very little since the 18th century.
Times: Open 25 Mar-1 Nov, Sat-Wed (open Good Fri), house 12-5, garden 11-6 (Jul-Aug gardens 10-6); Oct-1 Nov, Sat-Wed, house 12-4, garden 11-5.
Fee: All inclusive tickets inc: Family rooms, below stairs, outbuildings & gardens £6 (ch £3). Party 15+. Below stairs, outbuildings & garden £4 (ch £2) Family ticket £10.00. National Trust members free.
licensed toilets for disabled shop garden centre (ex guidance dogs)

Northern Ireland

The six counties of Ulster are part of the United Kingdom. The greater part of its 1.6 million inhabitants are Protestants, descendants of an influx of settlers from England and Scotland in the 17th century.

Despite recent tensions, the province has consistently drawn tourists, not so much to the cities which are more interesting than attractive, but for the scenery.

The most popular landscapes are linked by the 430 mile (700km) Ulster Way, which would take an intrepid walker though all six counties, taking in the Glens of Antrim with its woods, waterfalls and ruins, and the remarkable Giant's Causeway. Further south near the border with the Republic, the Ulster Way meanders through the Mountains of Mourne, rather gaunt, steep granite hills (highest point Slieve Donard, 2795 ft (852m)). Less strenuous stretches explore the beautiful Lough Erne.

After Belfast, the second city is Londonderry, or Derry, depending on your perspective. The city walls stand virtually complete, a reminder of the siege of 1688 when the Apprentice Boys locked out James II's army. From the walls you can view the sweep of the River Foyle.

Downpatrick, the market town of Down, claims to be the burial place of St Patrick, the patron saint of Ireland. His life is commemorated in the cathedral, and in the converted jail.

For lakes, islands, caves, castles and grand houses, Enniskillen is the place to go. Perched on an island between the Upper and Lower Lough Erne, it offers boat trips, angling, water sports and easy rambling.

EVENTS & FESTIVALS

March
17 St Patrick's Day Parade, 22-31 Between the Lines Literary Festival, Belfast

April
tbc World Irish Dancing Championships, Belfast

May
25-27 Portrush Raft Race

June
tbc Fleadh Amhram Agus Rince, Co Antrim
tbc Ulster Scottish Pipe Band Championships, Belfast

July
13 The Sham Fight, Scarva (William of Orange vs James II)

August
27-28 Oul' Lammas Fair, Ballycastle, Co Antrim

September
tbc Oyster Festival, Hillsborough, Co Down

October
tbc Coleraine Community Arts Festival, Co Derry

November
29 Nov-9 Dec Cinemagic International Film Festival for Young People, Belfast

Top: Murlough Bay, Co Antrim

It should be noted that telephone codes in Northern Ireland have changed for entries where details have not been confirmed for 2001.

BELFAST

BELFAST

Belfast Castle

Antrim Rd BT15 5GR (2.5m from city centre, take Antrim road towards Glengormley then left into Innisfayle Park, signed)

☎ 028 9077 6925 📠 028 9037 0228

Times: Open all year, daily. Castle open to public viewing. Food & drink available all day & evening. (closed only 25 Dec)

P licensed ♿ (lift to all floors, ramps being installed early '98) toilets for disabled shop (ex guide dogs) *Details not confirmed for 2001*

Belfast Zoological Gardens

Antrim Rd BT36 7PN (6m N, on A6)

☎ 028 9077 6277 📠 028 9037 0578

e-mail: strongej@belfastcity.gov.uk

The 50-acre zoo has a dramatic setting on the face of Cave Hill, enjoying spectacular views. Attractions include the award-winning primate house (gorillas and chimpanzees), penguin enclosure, free-flight aviary, African enclosure, and underwater viewing of sealions and penguins. There are also red pandas, free-ranging lemurs and a group of very rare spectacled bears.

Times: Open all year (ex 25 Dec), daily Apr-Sep 10-5; Oct-Mar 10-2.30.

Fee: Admission charged (ch under 4, pen & disabled free). Party. (Prices under review)

P ♿ (free admission & reserved parking) toilets for disabled shop (ex guide dogs)

Botanic Gardens

Stranmillis Rd BT7 1JP

☎ 028 9032 4902 📠 028 9023 7070

One highlight of the park is the beautiful glass-domed Victorian Palm House, built between 1839-52. This palm house predates the one in Kew Gardens and is one of the earliest curved-glass and iron structures in the world. Another feature is the Tropical Ravine - stand on a balcony to get a wonderful view through a steamy ravine full of exotic plants.

Times: Open all year, Park daily 8-dusk. Tropical ravine and palmhouse Mon-Fri 10-12.30 & 1-5 (summer), closes 4.30 (winter); wknds open 1-5 (summer), 1-4 (winter).

Fee: Free.

P (street) ♿

Giant's Ring

(0.75m S of Shaws Bridge)

☎ 01232 235000 📠 01232 310288

Times: Open all times.

P *Details not confirmed for 2001*

Ulster Museum

Botanic Gardens BT9 5AB (M1/M2 to Balmoral exit)

☎ 028 9038 3000 📠 028 9038 3003

Both a national museum and an art gallery, the collections are Irish and international in origin and cover antiquities, art, botany and zoology, geology and local history (including industrial archaeology). An annual programme of changing temporary exhibitions and events takes place.

Times: Open all year, Mon-Fri 10-5, Sat 1-5, Sun 2-5. Tel for details of Xmas closures.

Fee: Free.

P (100yds on street) (Clearway 0800-0930 & 1630-1800) ♿ (all galleries except one. Loop system, wheelchair lifts) toilets for disabled shop (ex guide dogs)

CO ANTRIM

ANTRIM

Antrim Round Tower

(N of town)

☎ 01232 235000 📠 01232 310288

Times: Open all year.

P ♿ *Details not confirmed for 2001*

BALLYCASTLE

Bonamargy Friary

(E of town, at golf course)

☎ 01232 235000 📠 01232 310288

Times: Open all year.

P ♿ *Details not confirmed for 2001*

BALLYLUMFORD

Ballylumford Dolmen

(on B90 on NW tip of Island Magee)

☎ 01232 235000 📠 01232 310288

Times: Open all year.

♿ *Details not confirmed for 2001*

BALLYMENA

Harryville Motte

(N bank of river Braid)

☎ 01232 235000 📠 01232 310288

Times: Open all year.

P ♿ *Details not confirmed for 2001*

BALLYMONEY

Leslie Hill Open Farm

Leslie Hill BT53 6QL (1m NW of Ballymoney on MacFin Rd)

☎ 028 2766 6803 📠 028 2766 6803

An 18th-century estate with a Georgian house, magnificient period farm buildings, and fine grounds with paths, lakes and trees. Attractions include an extensive collection of rare breeds, poultry, horsedrawn machinery and carriages, exhibition rooms, a museum, working forge, walled garden and an adventure playground.

Times: Open Jul-Aug Mon-Sat 11-6, Sun 2-6; Jun Sat-Sun & BH's 2-6; Etr-May & Sep Sun & BH's 2-6, open all Etr wk 11-6.

Fee: £2.90 (ch £1.90). Family ticket £8.50.

(ramps) toilets for disabled shop garden centre (ex on leads)

BUSHMILLS

Old Bushmills Distillery

BT57 8XH (on the Castlecatt road)

028 2073 1521 028 2073 1339

e-mail: s.croskery@idl.ie.com

Old Bushmills was granted its licence in 1608 and is the oldest licenced whiskey distillery in the world. There's a guided tour, and afterwards you can take part in a comparative tasting session and become a whiskey expert!

Times: Open Apr-Oct, Mon-Sat 9.30-5.30, Sun 12-5.30, last tour 4pm; Nov-Mar, Mon-Fri 5 tours daily, from 10.30 until 3.30.

Fee: £3.50 (pen & student £3, accompanied ch £1.50) Family ticket £9.

toilets for disabled shop (ex guide dogs)

CARRICK-A-REDE

Carrick-a-rede Rope Bridge and Larrybane Visitors Centre

(E of Ballintoy on B15)

028 2076 9839 & 2073 1159

028 2073 2963

e-mail: unavsm@smtp.ntrust.org.uk

This shaky rope bridge, 80ft above the sea, bridges the 60ft gap between cliffs and a small rocky island. It owes its existence to the salmon who regularly make the dash through the chasm and get netted for their efforts. The bridge has been put across the gap each spring and dismantled every autumn for the last 300 years.

Times: Bridge open Spring-early Sep, daily 10-6; Jul-Aug, daily 10-8. Visitor centre & Tea room open May, wknds & BHs 1-5; Jun-Aug daily 12-6.

Fee: £2.50 per car, coaches £6.

(charged) (information centre) toilets for disabled (NT Ireland)

CARRICKFERGUS

Carrickfergus Castle

(on N shore of Belfast Lough)

01960 351273 01960 365190

Times: Open all year, Apr-Sep, weekday 10-6, Sun 2-6; Oct-Mar closes at 4.

toilets for disabled shop *Details not confirmed for 2001*

Town Walls

01232 235000 01232 310288

Times: Visible at all times.

Details not confirmed for 2001

CHURCHTOWN

Cranfield Church

(3.75m SW of Randalstown)

01232 235000 01232 310288

Times: Open all year.

Details not confirmed for 2001

GIANT'S CAUSEWAY

Giant's Causeway Centre

44 Causeway Rd BT57 8SU (2m N of Bushmills on B146)

028 2073 1855 028 2073 2537

Times: Open all year, daily 10-4 (6pm Jun & Sep-Oct; 7pm Jul-Aug).

(charged) (mini bus transport with wheelchair hoist, reserved parking) toilets for disabled shop (ex guide dogs) *Details not confirmed for 2001*

LARNE

Olderfleet Castle

01232 235000 01232 310288

Times: Open at all times.

Details not confirmed for 2001

LISBURN

Duneight Motte and Bailey

(2.3m S beside Ravernet River)

01232 235000 01232 310288

Times: Open all year.

Details not confirmed for 2001

Irish Linen Centre & Lisburn Museum

Market Square BT28 1AG (signposted both in and outside the town centre)

028 9266 3377 028 9267 2624

Times: Open all year, Monday-Saturday, 9.30am-5pm.

(200m) (limited for disabled and coaches) (lift, induction loop, staff trained in sign language) toilets for disabled shop (ex guide dogs) *Details not confirmed for 2001*

PORTBALLINTRAE

Dunluce Castle

(off A2)

012657 31938 01232 318288

Times: Open all year, Apr-Sep, weekdays 10-7, Sun 2-7; Oct-Mar, Tue-Sat 10-4, Sun 2-4.

toilets for disabled shop *Details not confirmed for 2001*

TEMPLEPATRICK

Pattersons Spade Mill

751 Antrim Rd BT39 0AP (2m SE of Templepatrick on A6)

☎ 028 9443 3619 🖹 028 9443 3619

This is the last surviving water-driven spade mill in Ireland. It has been completely restored by the National Trust and is now back in production.

Times: Open Etr, Apr-May & Sep, wknds 2-6; Jun-Aug, daily (ex Tue) 2-6, also on BHs.

Fee: £3 (ch £1.25). Family Ticket £6.25. Party.

P ♿ (ramps wheelchair available) toilets for disabled (NT Ireland)

Templetown Mausoleum

BT39 (in Castle Upton graveyard on A6, Belfast-Antrim road)

Situated in the graveyard of Castle Upton, this family mausoleum is in the shape of a triumphal arch and was designed by Robert Adam.

Times: Open daily during daylight hours.

Fee: Free.

(NT Ireland)

CO ARMAGH

ARMAGH

Armagh County Museum

The Mall East BT61 9BE (on the Mall, in the centre of Armagh City)

☎ 028 3752 3070 🖹 028 3752 2631

Housed in a 19th-century schoolhouse, this museum contains an art gallery and library, as well as a collection of local folkcrafts and natural history. Special events are planned thoughout the year.

Times: Open all year, Mon-Fri 10-5, Sat 10-1 & 2-5.

Fee: Free.

P ♿ toilets for disabled shop (ex guide dogs)

Armagh Friary

(SE edge of town)

☎ 01232 235000 🖹 01232 310288

Times: Open all year.

P ♿ *Details not confirmed for 2001*

Armagh Planetarium

College Hill BT61 9DB (on main Armagh-Belfast road close to mall, Armagh City centre)

☎ 028 3752 3689 & 3752 4725 🖹 028 3752 6187

e-mail: ktl@armagh-planetarium.co.uk

The Planetarium is home to The Star Theatre, a multi-media environment equipped with the latest technology including a virtual reality digital system. Also featured are The Hall of Astronomy, the new Eartharium Building and surrounding the Planetarium is the Astropark, a 25-acre 'hands on' park.

Times: Open all year, Hall of Astronomy Mon-Fri 10-4.45, shows daily at 3. Also open Sat & Sun 1.15-4.45, shows every Sat & Sun 2, 3 & 4. Additional shows during Etr, Xmas & BH's.

Fee: £3.75 (ch, pen & students £2.75). Family ticket £11. Exhibition area £1.

P ♿ (Loop system in theatre) toilets for disabled shop (ex guide dogs)

Navan Centre

Killylea Rd BT60 4LD (2m W on A28)

☎ 028 3752 5550 🖹 028 3752 2323

Times: Open all year, Apr-Jun & Sep, Mon-Sat 10-6, Sun 11-6; Jul-Aug, Mon-Sat 10-7, Sun 11-7; Oct-Mar, Mon-Fri 10-5, Sat 11-5, Sun noon-5.

P ♿ (loop for hearing aids) toilets for disabled shop (ex guide dogs) *Details not confirmed for 2001*

Palace Stables Heritage Centre

The Palace Demesne BT60 4EL (located off Friary Road beside council offices)

☎ 028 3752 9629 🖹 028 3752 9630

e-mail: stables@armagh.gov.uk

This picturesque Georgian building, set around a cobbled courtyard, has been lovingly restored and now houses a heritage centre. A daily Georgian interpretation is provided by authentic costumed characters.

Times: Open all year, May-Aug, Mon-Sat 10-5.30, Sun 1-6; Sep-Apr, Mon-Sat 10-5, Sun 2-5. Last tour 1hr before closing.

Fee: £3.50 (ch £2, pen £2.75). Family ticket £9.50.

P ✕ licensed ♿ (ramps & Lift in stables) toilets for disabled shop (courtyard only)

St Patrick's Trian

40 English St BT61 7BA

☎ 028 9252 1801 🖹 028 9251 0180

An exciting complex in the city centre illustrating the development of Armagh from prehistoric times to the present day and showing Armagh's importance as a world ecclesiastical centre. The development also houses The Land of Lilliput (based on *Gulliver's Travels*); The Craft Courtyard; Pilgrim's Table Conservatory Restaurant and educational and conference facilities.

Times: Open all year, Mon-Sat 10-5, Sun 2-5; Jul-Aug, Mon-Sat 10-5. Last tour 1hr before closing.

Fee: £3.75 (ch £2, pen & student £2.75). Family ticket £9.50.

P (charged) ✕ ♿ (specially designed for disabled) toilets for disabled shop

CAMLOUGH

Killevy Churches

(3m S lower eastern slopes of Slieve Gullion)

☎ 01232 235000 🖹 01232 310288

Times: Open all year.

♿ *Details not confirmed for 2001*

JONESBOROUGH

KILNASAGGART INSCRIBED STONE

(1.25m S)

☎ 01232 235000 01232 310288

Times: Open all year.

P *Details not confirmed for 2001*

MOY

ARGORY

Derrycaw Rd BT71 6NA (3m NE)

☎ 028 8778 4753 028 8778 9598

e-mail: uagest@smtp.ntrust.org.uk

Originally the home of the McGeough family, this Regency house is situated on a hillside overlooking the Blackwater River. The house is full of period furniture and bric-a-brac. Of particular interest is the very unusual acetylene lighting, installed by the family in 1906.

Times: Open Etr, daily; Apr-May & Sep, wknds & BH; Jun-Aug, daily (ex Tue) 2-6. Open from 1pm on BHs. Last tour 5.15.

Fee: House & grounds £3 (ch £1.30). Family ticket £6.75. Car park £1.50. Party.

P (charged) (special parking facilities, wheelchair available) toilets for disabled shop (ex guide dogs) (NT Ireland)

NEWRY

MOYRY CASTLE

(7.5m S)

☎ 01232 235000 01232 310288

Times: Open all year

Details not confirmed for 2001

OXFORD ISLAND

LOUGH NEAGH DISCOVERY CENTRE

Oxford Island National Nature, Reserve BT66 6NJ (signposted from M1, exit 10)

☎ 028 3832 2205 028 3834 7438

e-mail: oxford.island@craigavon.gov.uk

Learn about the history and wildlife of the Lough through a series of exciting audio-visual shows, interactive games and exhibition. Then experience the Island for yourself: natural history, wildlife, family walks and much more, in a spectacular setting on the water's edge.

Times: Open Apr-Sep, daily 10-7; Oct-Mar, Wed-Sun 10-5.

Fee: £2 (ch £1.50, concessions £1.80). Family ticket £5.

P (grounds accessible in part, bird watching hides) toilets for disabled shop (ex guide dogs)

PORTADOWN

ARDRESS HOUSE

Annaghmore BT62 1SQ (7m W on B28)

☎ 028 3885 1236 028 3885 1236

A plain 17th-century house, transformed around 1770 by its visionary architect-owner George Ensor, who added elegant wings and superb Adamesque plasterwork. The house has a fine picture gallery on loan from the Earl of Castlestewart. The grounds are beautifully unspoilt and there is a farmyard with livestock and a display of farm implements.

Times: Open Etr, daily; Apr-May & Sep, wknds & BH's; Jun-Aug, daily (ex Tue) 2-6.

Fee: House, grounds & farm £2.70 (ch £1.35). Family ticket £6.75. Farmyard only £2.40 (ch £1.20). Family ticket £6. Party.

P toilets for disabled shop (ex guide dogs) (NT Ireland)

TYNAN

VILLAGE CROSS

☎ 01232 235000 01232 310288

Times: Open all year

P *Details not confirmed for 2001*

CO DOWN

ARDGLASS

JORDAN'S CASTLE

☎ 01232 235000 01232 310288

Times: Open Jul-Aug; Tue-Sat 10-7, Sun 2-7. Other times on request.

Details not confirmed for 2001

BALLYWALTER

GREY ABBEY

(on east edge of village)

☎ 01232 235000 01232 310288

Times: Open Apr-Sep; Tue-Sat 10-7, Sun 2-7.

P toilets for disabled *Details not confirmed for 2001*

CASTLEWELLAN

DRUMENA CASHEL

(2.25m SW)

☎ 01232 235000 01232 310288

Times: Open all times

P *Details not confirmed for 2001*

COMBER

WWT CASTLE ESPIE

Ballydrain Rd BT23 6EA (3m S of Comber, 13m SE of Belfast. Signed from the A22 Comber-Killyleagh-Downpatrick road)

☎ 028 9187 4146 028 9187 3857

e-mail: castleespie@wwt.org.uk

Home to the largest collection of wildfowl in Ireland. Comfortable hides enable you to watch the splendour of migratory waders and wildfowl. Beautiful landscaped gardens, a taxidermy collection and fine paintings by wildlife artists can also be seen. Thousands of birds migrate to the reserve in winter and birdwatch mornings are held on the last Thursday of every month. The Centre's effluent is treated in a reed bed filtration system which can be seen on one walk.

Times: Open all year; summer, Mon-Sat 10.30-5, Sun 11.30-6; winter Mon-Fri 11.30-4.15, Sat 11.30-4.30, Sun 11.30-5. (Closed 24 & 25 Dec).

Fee: £3.50 (ch under 4 free, ch £2.25, pen & concessions £2.75). Family ticket £9.25. Party 12+

P (hides have wheelchair platforms) toilets for disabled shop

DONAGHADEE

Ballycopeland Windmill

(1m W, on B172)

01247 861413 01232 310288

Times: Open all year Apr-Sep, Tue-Sat 10-7, Sun 2-7; Oct-Mar, Sat 10-4, Sun 2-4.

shop *Details not confirmed for 2001*

DOWNPATRICK

Down County Museum

The Mall BT30 6AH (follow brown signs)

028 4461 5218 028 4461 5590

e-mail: museum@downdc.gov.uk

The museum occupies the old county gaol built between 1789 and 1796. The Saint Patrick Heritage Centre in the former gatehouse tells the story of Ireland's patron saint, and the governor's residence has galleries relating to the human and natural history of County Down.

Times: Open all year, Jun-Aug, Mon-Fri 10-5, wknds 2-5; rest of year, Tue-Fri 10-5 & Sat 2-5. Also open all BH's.

Fee: Free.

(100yds) (wheelchair available, handling boxes on application) toilets for disabled shop (ex guide dogs)

Inch Abbey

(0.75m NW off A7)

01232 235000 01232 310288

Times: Open Apr-Sep 10-7, Sun 2-7. Oct-Mar free access.

Details not confirmed for 2001

Loughinisland Churches

(4m W)

01232 235000 01232 310288

Times: Open all times

Details not confirmed for 2001

Mound of Down

(on the Quoile Marshes, from Mount Crescent)

01232 235000 01232 310288

Times: Open all times

Details not confirmed for 2001

Struell Wells

(1.5m E)

01232 235000 01232 310288

Times: Open all times

Details not confirmed for 2001

DROMARA

Legananny Dolmen

(4m S)

01232 235000 01232 310288

Times: Open at all times

Details not confirmed for 2001

HILLSBOROUGH

Hillsborough Fort

01846 683285 01232 310288

Times: Open all year; Apr-Sep, Tue-Sat 10-7, Sun 2-7; Oct-Mar, Tue-Fri 10-4, Sat 10-4, Sun 2-4.,

Details not confirmed for 2001

KILKEEL

Greencastle

(4m SW)

01232 235000 01232 310288

Times: Open Jul-Aug, Tue-Sat 10-7, Sun 2-7.

Details not confirmed for 2001

KILLINCHY

Sketrick Castle

(3m E on W tip of Sketrick Islands)

01232 235000 01232 310288

Times: Open at all times.

Details not confirmed for 2001

NEWCASTLE

Dundrum Castle

(4m N)

01232 235000 01232 310288

Times: Open Apr-Sep, Tue-Sat 10-7, Sun 2-7.

toilets for disabled *Details not confirmed for 2001*

Maghera Church

(2m NNW)

01232 235000 01232 310288

Times: Open all year.

Details not confirmed for 2001

NEWTOWNARDS

Mount Stewart House, Garden & Temple of the Winds

Greyabbey BT22 2AD (5m SE off A20)

028 4278 8387 & 4278 8487

028 4278 8569

e-mail: umsest@smtp.ntrust.org.uk

On the east shore of Strangford Lough, this 18th-century house was the work of three architects. In the inspired gardens, which are now a nominated world heritage site, many rare and subtropical trees thrive. Located by the shore is the Temple of the Winds, built by James 'Athenian' Stuart in 1782 for the first Marquess.

Times: Open House Etr, daily; May-Sep daily (ex Tue); Apr & Oct wknds, 1-6. Garden: Mar, Sun 2-5 & St Patrick's Day 11-6; Apr-Sep, daily & Oct, wknds 11-6. Temple of the Winds Apr-Oct, wknds 2-5.

Fee: House Garden & Temple: £3.50 (ch £1.75). Family ticket £8.75. Garden: £3 (ch £1.50) Family ticket £7.50. Group 15+.

(4 wheelchairs(2 electric) available) toilets for disabled shop (NT Ireland)

Scrabo Tower

Scrabo Country Park, 203A Scrabo Rd BT23 4SJ (1m W)

01247 811491 01247 820695

Times: Open Etr, May-Sep, Sat-Thu 11-6.30. Country park open all year, daily, 11-6.30.

shop *Details not confirmed for 2001*

PORTAFERRY

Exploris Aquarium

The Rope Walk, Castle St BT22 1NZ (A20 or A2 or A25 to Strangford Ferry Service)

028 4272 8062 028 4272 8396

e-mail: susan.moore@ards-council.gov.uk

Exploris Aquarium is Northern Ireland's only public aquarium and now includes a seal sanctuary. Situated in Portaferry on the shores of Strangford Lough it houses some of Europe's finest displays. The Open Sea Tank holds 250 tonnes of sea water, and the Shoal Ring, where visitors are surrounded by hundreds of shoaling fish, is 6m in diameter. The complex includes a park with duck pond, picnic area, children's playground, caravan site, woodland and bowling green.

Times: Open all year, Mon-Fri 10-6, Sat 11-6, Sun 1-6. (Sep-Feb closing 1 hr earlier).

Fee: £3.95 (concessions £2.80). Family £12.30.

(lift available) toilets for disabled shop (ex guide dogs)

SAINTFIELD

Rowallane Garden

BT24 7LH (1m S of Saintfield on A7)

028 9751 0131 028 9751 1242

Beautiful and exotic 52-acre gardens, started by the Rev John Moore in 1860, containing exquisite plants from all over the world. They are particularly noted for their rhododendrons and azaleas and for the wonderful floral displays in spring and summer. There are monthly demonstrations on The Art of the Gardener.

Times: Open Apr-Oct, Mon-Fri 10.30-6, Sat & Sun 2-6; Nov-Mar, Mon-Fri 10.30-5. (Closed 25-26 Dec & 1 Jan)

Fee: Apr-Oct £3 (ch £1.25); Nov-Mar £1.50 (ch 75p).

(parking facilities) toilets for disabled (must be on leads) (NT Ireland)

STRANGFORD

Audley's Castle

(1.5m W by shore of Strangford Lough)

01232 230560 01232 310288

Times: Open Apr-Sep, daily 10-7.

Details not confirmed for 2001

Castle Ward

BT30 7LS (0.5m W of Strangford Village on A25)

028 4488 1204 028 4488 1729

The curious diversity of styles in this house is due to the fact that its owner and his wife could never agree; so classical themes and a more elaborate Gothic look were both incorporated. The servants' living quarters are reached by an underground passage. Gardens, complete with a small lake and classical summerhouse, are richly planted and especially beautiful in spring.

Times: House open Jun-15 Sep, Fri-Wed 1-6; Apr-May & 18 Sep-Oct, wknds 1-6.

(charged) (wheelchair available, may be driven to house) toilets for disabled shop (NT Ireland) *Details not confirmed for 2001*

Strangford Castle

01232 235000 01232 310288

Times: Visable from outside.

Details not confirmed for 2001

WARRENPOINT

Narrow Water Castle

(1m NW)

01232 235000 01232 310288

Times: Open Jul-Aug, Tue-Sat 10-7, Sun 2-7.

Details not confirmed for 2001

CO FERMANAGH

BELLEEK

Belleek Pottery

3 Main St BT93 3FY

028 6865 9300 028 6865 8625

e-mail: visitorcentre@belleek.ie

Known worldwide for its fine Parian china, Ireland's oldest pottery was started in 1857 by the Caldwell family. Meet the craftspeople at work whilst touring the Pottery and visit the museum, which has exhibits dating back over 140 years.

Times: Open all year, Apr-Sep, Mon-Fri 9-6, Sat 10-6; also Apr-Jun, Sun 2-6 & Jul-Aug, Sun 11-6. Oct-Mar, Mon-Fri 9-5.30.

Fee: Guided tours £2.00 (ch under 12 free, pen £1).

(wheelchairs can be provided) toilets for disabled shop (small dogs allowed) 

CASTLE ARCHDALE BAY

White Island Church

(in Castle Archdale Bay; ferry from marina)
☎ 01232 235000 01232 310288
Times: Open Jul-Aug, Tue-Sat 10-7, Sun 2-7.
Details not confirmed for 2001

DERRYGONNELLY

Tully Castle

(3m N, on W shore of Lower Lough Erne)
☎ 01232 235000 01232 310288
Times: Open Apr-Sep Tue-Sat 10-7, Sun 2-7; Oct-Mar 10-4.(2-4 Sun).
Details not confirmed for 2001

ENNISKILLEN

Castle Coole

BT74 (1.5m SE on A4)
☎ 028 6632 2690 028 6632 5665
e-mail: UCASCO@smtp.ntrust.org.uk

No expense was spared in the building of this mansion. James Wyatt was the architect, the lovely plasterwork ceilings were by Joseph Rose, and the chimneypieces the work of Richard Westmacott. Vast amounts of Portland stone were specially imported, together with an Italian expert in stonework. The house is filled with beautiful Regency furniture.
Times: Open Jun-Aug, Fri-Wed 1-6 (last tour 5.15); Apr-May & Sep, wknds & BH's.
Fee: £3 (ch £1.50). Family ticket £8.
(may be driven to house) toilets for disabled shop (ex in park & guide dogs) (NT Ireland)

Devenish Island

(2m N)
☎ 028 9023 5000 028 9031 0288
Times: Open Apr-Sep, Tue-Sat 10-7, Sun 2-7.
shop *Details not confirmed for 2001*

Enniskillen Castle

☎ 01365 322711
Times: Open all year Mon 2-5, Tue-Fri 10-5 (closed 1-2, Oct-Apr), Sat 2-5 May-Aug, Sun 2-5 Jul-Aug, all day BH's.
shop *Details not confirmed for 2001*

Florence Court

BT92 1DB (8m SW via A4 & A32)
☎ 028 6634 8249 028 6634 8873
e-mail: UFCEST@smtp.ntrust.org.uk

An 18th-century mansion overlooking wild and beautiful scenery towards the Mountains of Cuilcagh. The interior of the house, particularly noted for its flambuoyant rococo plasterwork, was gutted by fire in 1955, but has been miraculously restored. There are pleasure grounds with an Ice House, Summer House, Water Powered Sawmill and also a walled garden.
Times: Open Etr, daily 1-6; Apr, May & Sep wknds & BH's 1-6; Jun-Aug, daily (ex Tue) 1-6.
Fee: £3 (ch £1.50). Family ticket £8. Estate only £2 per car.
(charged) (electric wheelchair available) toilets for disabled shop (NT Ireland)

Marble Arch Caves

Marlbank Scenic Loop BT92 1EW (off A4 Enniskillen-Sligo road)
☎ 028 6634 8855 028 6634 8928
e-mail: mac@fermanagh.gov.uk

A magical cave system, one of Europe's finest, under the Mountains of Cuilcagh. Visitors are given a tour of a wonderland of stalagmites, stalactites and underground rivers and lakes, starting with a boat trip on the lower lake. The streams, which feed the caves, flow down into the mountain then emerge at Marble Arch, a 30ft detached limestone bridge.
Times: Open late Mar-Sep. From 10 daily.
Fee: £6 (ch £3, concessions £4). Family ticket (2 adults & 3 ch) £14. Party 10+
toilets for disabled shop (ex guide dogs)

Monea Castle

(6m NW)
☎ 028 9023 5000 028 9031 0288
Times: Open at any reasonable time.
Details not confirmed for 2001

LISNASKEA

Castle Balfour

☎ 01232 235000 01232 310288
Times: Open at all times.
Details not confirmed for 2001

NEWTOWNBUTLER

Crom Estate

BT92 8AP (3m W)
☎ 028 6773 8174 & 6773 8118
028 6773 8174
e-mail: ucromw@smtp.ntrust.org.uk

Featuring 770 hectares of woodland, parkland and wetland, the Crom Estate is one of Northern Ireland's most important conservation areas. Nature trails are signposted through woodlands to the ruins of the old castle, and past the old boat house and picturesque summer house. Day tickets for pike fishing and boat hire are available from the Visitor Centre.
Times: Open Apr-Sep, daily 10-6, Sun 12-6.
Fee: Parking £3
(charged) toilets for disabled shop (NT Ireland)

CO LONDONDERRY

COLERAINE

Hezlett House

Castlerock BT51 4TN (5m W on Coleraine/Downhill coast road)

☎ 028 7084 8567

A low, thatched cottage built around 1690 with an interesting cruck truss roof, constructed by using pairs of curved timbers to form arches and infilling around this frame with clay, rubble and other locally available materials.

Times: Open Etr, daily; Apr & Sep wknds & BH's; Jun-Aug, daily (ex Tue) 12-5.

(ex in gardens) (NT Ireland) *Details not confirmed for 2001*

Mount Sandel

(1.25m SSE)

☎ 01232 230560 01232 310288

Times: Open at all times.

Details not confirmed for 2001

COOKSTOWN

Tullaghoge Fort

(2m S)

☎ 01232 235000 01232 310288

Times: Open at all times.

Details not confirmed for 2001

Wellbrook Beetling Mill

Corkhill BT80 9RY (4m W in Co Tyrone, 0.5m off A505)

☎ 028 8675 1735

This 18th-century water-powered linen mill was used for bleaching and, until 1961, for finishing Irish linen. Beetling was the name given to the final process in linen making, when the material was beaten by 30 or so hammers (beetles) to achieve a smooth and slightly shiny finish.

Times: Open Etr, daily; Apr-Jun & Sep, wknds & BH's; Jul-Aug, daily (ex Tue) 2-6.

shop (NT Ireland) *Details not confirmed for 2001*

DOWNHILL

Mussenden Temple Bishop's Gate and Black Glen

Mussenden Rd BT51 4RP (1m W of Castlerock off A2)

Spectacularly placed on a cliff edge overlooking the Atlantic, this perfect 18th-century rotunda was modelled on the Temple of Vesta at Tivoli. Visitors entering by the Bishop's Gate can enjoy a beautiful glen walk up to the headland where the temple stands.

Times: Open Temple: Etr, daily, noon-6; Apr-Jun & Sep, wknds & BH's noon-6; Jul-Aug, daily noon-6.

(NT Ireland) *Details not confirmed for 2001*

DUNGIVEN

Banagher Church

(2m SW)

☎ 01232 235000 01232 310288

Times: Open at all times.

Details not confirmed for 2001

Dungiven Priory

(SE of town overlooking River Roe)

☎ 01232 235000 01232 310288

Times: Open - Church at all times, chancel only when caretaker available. Check at house at end of lane.

Details not confirmed for 2001

LIMAVADY

Rough Fort

(1m W off A2)

Early Christian rath.

Times: Open at all times.

(NT Ireland) *Details not confirmed for 2001*

LONDONDERRY

City Walls

☎ 01232 235000 01232 310288

Times: Open all times.

(charged) *Details not confirmed for 2001*

Foyle Valley Railway Museum

Foyle Rd BT48 6SQ

☎ 028 7126 5234 028 7137 7633

A collection of relics from the four railway companies which served Londonderry are displayed at the Foyle Valley Railway Heritage Centre. Steam locomotives, diesel railcars and all the paraphernalia of a station can be seen and the Railway Gallery tells the story of the railways. Travel in the historic County Donegal railcars for a trip to the historic mill.

Times: Open all year, Apr-Sep Mon-Sat 10-5, Sun 2-5; Oct-Mar Mon-Sat 10-4.

Fee: Museum free. Train rides £2.50 (ch & concessions £1.25).

toilets for disabled shop garden centre

Tower Museum

Union Hall Place BT48 6LU

☎ 028 7137 2411 028 7137 7633

e-mail: towermuseum@dnet.co.uk

This exhibition recounts the history of Londonderry from pre-historic times to the present day using real artefacts, theatrical displays and eleven audio-visual programmes showing the spread of Irish monasticism, the famous Siege of Derry and the road to the partition of Ireland.

Times: Open all year, Sep-Jun Tue-Sat 10-5. Jul-Aug Mon-Sat 10-5, Sun 2-5. Also open all BH Mons.

Fee: £3.75 (pen, UB40s, students £1.25) Family ticket £7.50.

P (300 yds) toilets for disabled shop (ex guide dogs)

MAGHERA

Maghera Church
(E approach to the town)
☎ 01232 235000 ▯ 01232 310288
Times: Key from Leisure Centre.
P ♿ *Details not confirmed for 2001*

MONEYMORE

Springhill
BT45 7NQ (1m from Moneymore on B18)
☎ 028 8674 8210 ▯ 028 8674 8210

This pleasingly symmetrical manor house dates back to the 17th century. Today much of the family furniture, books and bric-a-brac have been retained. Outside, the laundry, stables, brewhouse, and old dovecote make interesting viewing, as does the excellent costume museum.
Times: Open Etr, Apr-Jun & Sep, wknds & BH's 2-6; Jul-Aug, daily (ex Thu) 2-6.
P ♿ toilets for disabled shop (must be on leads) (NT Ireland) *Details not confirmed for 2001*

CO TYRONE

ARDBOE

Ardboe Cross
(off B73)
☎ 01232 235000 ▯ 01232 310288
Times: Open at all times.
P ♿ *Details not confirmed for 2001*

BALLYGAWLEY

U S Grant Ancestral Homestead & Visitor Centre
Dergenagh, 190 Ballygawley Rd BT70 1TW (off A4, 3m on Dergenagh road, signposted)
☎ 028 8555 7133 ▯ 028 8576 7911
Times: Open Etr-Sep, Mon-Sat 12-5, Sun 2-6. Other times by arrangement. (Closed 25-26 Dec & 1 Jan).
P ♿ (wide doorway to audio-visual area/entrances/exits) shop (ex guide dogs) *Details not confirmed for 2001*

BEAGHMORE

Beaghmore Stone Circles and Alignments
☎ 01232 235000 ▯ 01232 310288
Times: Open at all times.
P ♿ *Details not confirmed for 2001*

BENBURB

Benburb Castle
☎ 01232 235000 ▯ 01232 310288
Times: Castle grounds open at all times. Special arrangements, made in advance, necessary for access to flanker tower.
P ♿ *Details not confirmed for 2001*

CASTLECAULFIELD

Castle Caulfield
☎ 01232 235000 ▯ 01232 310288
Times: Open at all times.
P ♿ *Details not confirmed for 2001*

NEWTOWNSTEWART

Harry Avery's Castle
(0.75m SW)
☎ 01232 235000 ▯ 01232 310288
Times: Open at all times.
Details not confirmed for 2001

OMAGH

Ulster American Folk Park
BT78 5QY (5m NW Omagh)
☎ 028 8224 3292 ▯ 028 8224 2241
Times: Open Etr-Sep, daily 11-6.30, Sun & BH 11.30-7; Oct-Etr Mon-Fri 10.30-5. Last admission 1hr 30mins before closing.
P ✕ ♿ toilets for disabled shop (ex guide dogs) *Details not confirmed for 2001*

Ulster History Park
Cullion BT79 7SU (7m on B48)
☎ 028 8164 8188 ▯ 028 8164 8011
e-mail: uhp@omagh.gov.uk

The story of settlement in Ireland, told with the aid of full-scale models of the houses and monuments built through the ages. Exhibitions and audio-visual presentations expand the theme.
Times: Open all year, Jul-Aug daily 10-6.30; Apr-Jun & Sep, daily 10-5.30; Oct-Mar, Mon-Fri 10-5.
Fee: £3.75 (ch, students, pen & registered disabled £2.50). Family ticket (2 adults & 2 ch) £12. Group 15+
P ♿ toilets for disabled shop (ex guide dogs)

STEWARTSTOWN

Mountjoy Castle
Magheralamfield (3m SE, off B161)
☎ 01232 235000 ▯ 01232 310288
Times: Open at all times.
P *Details not confirmed for 2001*

STRABANE

Gray's Printing Press
49 Main St BT82 8AU
☎ 028 7188 4094

Strabane was once an important printing and book-publishing centre, the only relic of this is a small shop in Main Street which now houses a museum illustrating the history of Strabane. The Print Museum, in a separate building, contains three 19th-century presses and shows the development of printing techniques over one hundred and fifty years.
Times: Open Apr-Sep, Tue-Sat 2-5. Other times by prior arrangement.
Fee: £2 (ch 90p). Family ticket £4.50. Party.
P (100yds) ♿ (ex guide dogs) (NT Ireland)

Republic of Ireland

No visitor comes here without preconceptions, and while some of these will be confirmed, there are always plenty of surprises, and more to discover.

To be sure it is green - the Emerald Isle is no misnomer - and you're never far from water, from the craggy Atlantic coast, the countless loughs, rivers and bogs, to the regular falls of rain, or Irish mist. And then there are the people.

Certainly this country with its tiny population has brought us an abundance of world-class literary figures, and you will meet the same love of words and ideas in any street, shop or pub. Music too seems to run in the veins - listening to an Irish band, it soon becomes clear that the musicians are playing as much for their own pleasure as for the tourist's. However, this is no quaint backwater; the Republic has enthusiastically embraced its European identity.

Where to go? It would be hard to miss out on elegant, cosmopolitan Dublin, and in the south there's Cork, vying with the capital for business and cultural supremacy. To explore the west, head for Galway, where Gaelic is still spoken by many inhabitants as a first language, and inland you will not be disappointed by the craft studios and restaurants of Kilkenny.

Further afield there is no end of opportunity for fishing, golfing, walking and relaxing. You can find a quiet charm everwhere you visit, but there are some strikingly unique attractions. The Burren is a naturalist's joy, with exotic flora in every crevice of its strange rockscape, and Newgrange is one of Europe's most important and mysterious prehistoric sites.

EVENTS & FESTIVALS

March
St Patrick's Festival, Dublin

April
17-22 April Pan Celtic International Festival, Tralee
19 Mar-1 Apr Feis Ceoil, Dublin
tbc Dublin Film Festival

May
25 May-3 Jun Dundalk International Maytime Festival
24-28 Fleadh Nua, Co Clare

June
16 Bloomsday, Dublin
tbc The Cat Laughs, international comedy festival, Kilkenny, Co Kilkenny

July
17-29 Galway International Arts Festival, Co Galway

August
16 Connemara Pony Show, Clifden, Co Galway
Dublin Horse Show, Ballsbridge, Dublin
24-26 Fleadh Ceoil na hEireann, venue to be confirmed
10th-19th Kilkenny Arts Festival

September
tbc Galway International Oyster Festival, Galway City, Co Galway

October
1-13 Dublin Theatre Festival
15-22 Cork Film Festival, Co Cork

Top: County Kerry

CO CLARE

BALLYVAUGHAN

AILLWEE CAVE

(3m S)

☎ 065 7077036 & 7077067 📠 065 7077107

e-mail: aillwee@eircom.net

An underground network of caves beneath the world famous Burren. Guided tours take you through large caverns, over bridged chasms and alongside thunderous waterfalls. There is a craftshop, dairy speciality food shop and tea room.

Times: Open mid Mar-Nov, 10-5.30 (Jul-Aug 6.30pm); Nov-mid Mar 11.30-3. **Fee:** IR£4.75 (ch IR£2.75). Family ticket IR£13.50-IR£15.50 licensed toilets for disabled shop (in cave)

BUNRATTY

BUNRATTY CASTLE & FOLK PARK

(8 miles from Limerick city on N18 road to Ennis)

☎ 061 361511 & 360788 📠 061 361020

e-mail: oconnorm@shannon-dev.ie

Times: Open all year, daily 9.30-5.30 (last admission 4.15pm). Folk Park also open Jun-Aug 9-6.30 (last admission 5.30pm). licensed toilets for disabled shop *Details not confirmed for 2001*

LISCANNOR

O'BRIEN'S TOWER & CLIFFS OF MOHER

(6m NW of Lahinch)

☎ 065 81565 & 061 360788 📠 061 361020

e-mail: oconnorm@shannon-dev.ie

Times: Open daily Mar-Oct, 10-6 (subject to weather conditions). Visitor centre open all year daily 10am-6pm. (charged) toilets for disabled shop *Details not confirmed for 2001*

QUIN

THE CRAGGAUNOWEN BRONZE AGE PROJECT

(signed from N18, 10km N from Sixmilebridge)

☎ 061 367178 & 360788 📠 061 361020

e-mail: oconnorm@shannon-dev.ie

Times: Open Apr-Oct daily 10-6 (last admission 5pm). Mid May-mid Aug 9-6. toilets for disabled shop *Details not confirmed for 2001*

CO CORK

BALLINCOLLIG

BALLINCOLLIG GUNPOWDER MILLS HERITAGE CENTRE

(on Cork/Killarney road)

☎ 021 4874430 📠 021 4874836

e-mail: ballinco@indigo.ie

An amazing industrial complex on the banks of the River Lee. The mills supplied vast quantities of explosives for the British military forces throughout the world from 1794 to 1903.

Times: Open daily, 25 Apr-Sep 10-6. Last tour at 5.15pm.

Fee: IR£3 (ch IR£1.80, pen & students IR£2.50). Family ticket IR£8. toilets for disabled shop (ex guide dogs)

BLARNEY

BLARNEY CASTLE & ROCK CLOSE

(5m from Cork on main road towards Limerick)

☎ 021 385252 & 385669 📠 021 381518

The site of the famous Blarney Stone, known the world over for the eloquence it is said to impart to those who kiss it. The stone is in the upper tower of the castle, and, held by your feet, you must lean backwards down the inside of the battlements in order to receive the gift of the gab.

Times: Open - Blarney Castle & Rock Close, Jun-Jul Mon-Sat 9-7.30; Aug Mon-Sat 9-7.30; May Mon-Sat 9-7; Sep Mon-Sat 9-6.30; Apr & Oct Mon-Sat 9-sunset; summer Sun 9.30-5.30; winter Sun 9.30-sunset. Blarney House & Gardens Jun-mid Sep Mon-Sat noon-6.

Fee: Blarney Castle & Rock Close IR£3.50 (ch IR£1, pen & students IR£2.50). shop (ex guide dogs)

CARRIGTWOHILL (CARRIGTOHILL)

FOTA ARBORETUM & GARDENS

Fota Estate

☎ 021 4812728 📠 021 4812728

Located in the sheltered harbour of Cork, Fota Arboretum and Gardens are of international importance, containing one of the finest collections of rare and tender trees and shrubs grown outdoors in Ireland and Britain. The gardens were created by the Smith-Barry family in the mid-19th century.

Times: Open Mar-Oct, daily 10-6; Nov-Feb, daily 10-5. (Closed 25 Dec). **Fee:** Free. (charged) toilets for disabled (ex on lead)

FOTA WILDLIFE PARK

Fota Estate (situated 10km E of Cork City. Take the Cobh road from the N25 Cork - Waterford road)

☎ 021 4812678 📠 021 4812744

e-mail: info@fotawildlife.ie

Established with the primary aim of conservation, Fota has more than 90 species of exotic wildlife in open, natural surroundings. Many of the animals wander freely around the park. Giraffes, zebras, ostriches, antelope, cheetahs and a wide array of waterfowl are among the species here.

Times: Open all year 17 Mar-Sep daily, 10-6 (Sun 11-6) Oct-17 Mar wkends only. Last admission 5.
Fee: IR£4.80 (ch, pen & students IR£2.70). Family day ticket IR£18.
(charged) (Ramps where required) toilets for disabled shop

CLONAKILTY

West Cork Model Village Railway

Inchydoney Rd (signposted at road junction. Village is at Bay side of Clonakilty)
023 33224 023 34843

Times: Open Feb-Oct Mon-Fri 11-5, Sat & Sun 1-5; Jul-Aug, daily, extended hours 10.30-6.
toilets for disabled (ex guide dogs) *Details not confirmed for 2001*

COBH

The Queentown Story

Cobh Railway Station
021 813591 021 813595
e-mail: cobhher@indigo.ie

A dramatic exhibition of the origins, history and legends of Cobh. Between 1815 and 1950 over 3 million Irish people were deported from Cobh on convict ships. Visitors can explore the conditions onboard these vessels and learn about the harbour's connections with the Lusitania and the Titanic.
Times: Open all year 10-6. Last admission 5pm.
Fee: IR£3.50 (ch12 IR£2, pen & students IR£3). Family ticket IR£10.
toilets for disabled shop (ex guide dogs)

CORK

Cork City Gaol

Convent Av, Sundays Well (2km from Patrick St. Cork, off Sunday's Well Rd)
021 305022 021 307230

A restored 19th century prison building. Furnished cells, lifelike characters and sound effects combine to allow visitors to experience day-to-day life for prisoners and gaoler. There is an audio-visual presentation of the social history of Cork City. Individual sound tours are available in a number of languages. A new permanent exhibition, the Radio Museum Experience, is located in the restored 1920's broadcasting studio, home to Cork's first radio station, 6CK.
Times: Open Mar-Oct, daily 9.30-6; Nov-Feb, daily 10-4. Last admission 1hr before closing.
Fee: IR£3.50 (ch IR£2, pen & student IR£3). Family ticket (2 adult & 3 children) IR£10.
(customer care policy - individual attention) toilets for disabled shop (ex guide dogs)

Cork Public Museum

Fitzgerald Park, Mardyke (N of University College)
021 270679 021 270931
Times: Open all year, Jun-Aug Mon-Fri 11-1 & 2.15-6, Sun 3-5; Sep-May Mon-Fri 11-1 & 2.15-5, Sun 3-5. (Closed Sat, BH wknds & PH)
(100 yds) shop (ex guide dogs) *Details not confirmed for 2001*

GLENGARRIFF

Garinish Island

(1.5km boat trip from Glengarriff)
027 63040 027 63149

An Italianate garden, designed by Harold Peto, bathed in the warm waters of the Gulf Stream provides an ideal setting for the collection of tender plants which thrive here. A Martello Tower, Clock Tower, a Grecian Temple overlooking the sea and magnificent pedimented gateways are some of the architectural features of the garden.
Times: Open Jul-Aug, Mon-Sat 9.30-6.30, Sun 11-7; Apr-Jun & Sep, Mon-Sat 10-6.30, Sun 1-7; Mar & Oct, Mon-Sat 10-4.30, Sun 1-5. Last landing 1 hour before closing. Charge made by boat operators.
Fee: IR£2.50 (ch IR£1 & pen IR£1.75) Family ticket IR£6.
(minimal due to boat access) toilets for disabled (must be on leads)

KINSALE

Charles Fort

☎ 021 772263 📠 021 774347
e-mail: info@heritageireland.ie

Built as part of the fortifications of the Irish coast in the late 17th century, Charles Fort was named after King Charles II. After the Battle of the Boyne in 1690, Williamite forces attacked and successfully besieged Charles Fort and the nearby James Fort, both of which held out for King James. The Fort also played a role in the Napoleonic Wars and was made a National Monument in 1973.

Times: Open all year, mid Mar-Oct, daily 10-6; Nov-mid Mar, Sat-Sun 10-5, wkdays by arrangement. Last admission 45 minutes before closing.
Fee: IR£2.50 (pen IR£1.75 & student IR£1). Family ticket IR£6.
P ☕ ♿ toilets for disabled 🐕 (ex guide dogs)

Desmond Castle

Cork St
☎ 021 774855

Built by the Earl of Desmond around the beginning of the 16th century, this tower was originally a custom house, but has also served as an ordnance office, prison, workhouse, stable and meeting place for the Local Defence Force during World War II. In 1938 it was declared a National Monument and restored.

Times: Open mid Jun-early Oct, daily 10-6; mid Apr-mid Jun, Tue-Sun & BH Mon 10-6. Last admission 45 mins before closing.
Fee: IR£2 (pen IR£1.50 & student IR£1). Family ticket IR£5.
P 🐕 (ex guide dogs)

MIDLETON

Old Midleton Distillery

(15m E of Cork towards Waterford.)
☎ 021 613594 & 613596 📠 021 613642

A tour of the Old Midleton Distillery consists of a 15 minute audio/visual presentation, then a 35 minute guided tour of the Old Distillery and then back to the Jameson Bar for a whiskey tasting - minerals are available for children. The guided tour and audio-visual aids are available in five languages.

Times: Open Mar-Oct, daily 10-6. Last tour 4. Nov-Feb Mon-Fri, two tours 12 & 3. Sat-Sun, two tours 2 & 4. (Closed Xmas).
Fee: IR£3.95 (ch IR£1.50). Family ticket IR£9.50
P ☕ ✕ licensed ♿ toilets for disabled shop 🐕 (ex guide dogs)

CO DONEGAL

ARDARA

Ardara Heritage Centre

The Diamond
☎ 075 41704 📠 075 41381

Times: Open Apr-Sep, 10-6.
P ☕ ✕ ♿ toilets for disabled shop 🐕 (ex guide dogs) *Details not confirmed for 2001*

BALLYSHANNON

The Water Wheels

Abbey Assaroe (cross Abbey River on Rossnowlagh Rd, next turning left & follow signs)
☎ 072 51580

Abbey Assaroe was founded by Cistercian Monks from Boyle Abbey in the late 12th century. The Cistercians excelled in water engineering and canalised the river to turn water wheels for mechanical power. Two restored 12th-century mills, one is used as coffee shop and restaurant; the other houses a small museum related to the history of the Cistercians.

Times: Open Etr week & May-Aug, Mon-Sat 10.30-6.30, Sun 1.30-dusk. **Fee:** Free.
P ☕ ✕ licensed ♿ toilets for disabled shop garden centre

DONEGAL

Donegal Castle

☎ 073 22405 📠 073 22436

This restored 15th-century castle and adjoining 17th-century ruined English manor house contain exhibitions of Irish historical events. Guided tours are available.

Times: Open mid Mar-mid Oct, daily 9.30-6.30 (last admission 5.45).
Fee: IR£3 (ch & students IR£1.25, pen IR£2). Family ticket (2 adults & 3 ch) IR£7.50. P 🐕 (ex guide dogs)

LETTERKENNY

Glebe House & Gallery

Churchill (signposted from Letterkenny)
☎ 074 37071 📠 074 37521

This Regency house set in beautiful woodland gardens along the shore of Lough Gartan, was given to the nation, along with his art collection, by the artist Derek Hill. The interior of the house is decorated with original wallpapers and textiles by William Morris.

Times: Open Etr & mid May-Sep, Sat-Thu 11-6.30. (Last tour of house 5.30). **Fee:** IR£2 (ch & student IR£1, pen IR£1.50). Family ticket IR£5.
P ☕ ♿ toilets for disabled 🐕 (ex guide dogs)

Glenveagh National Park & Castle

Churchill
☎ 074 37090 📠 074 37072

Over 40,000 acres of mountains, lakes, glens and woods. A Scottish-style castle situated in one of Ireland's finest gardens that contrasts dramatically with the rugged scenery that surrounds it.

Times: Open daily mid Mar-early Nov, 10-6.30
Fee: Park: IR£2(ch & students IR£1, pen IR£1.50, family ticket IR£5. Castle: IR£2 (ch & students IR£1, pen IR£1.50, family ticket IR£5.
P ☕ ✕ ♿ toilets for disabled

LIFFORD

Cavanacor Historic House & Craft Centre

Ballindrait (1.5m from town off N14 Strabane/Letterkenny road)
☎ 074 41143 📠 074 41143

Times: Open Etr-Aug, Tue-Sat 12-6, Sun 2-6. Closed Mon ex BH's.
P ☕ ✕ ♿ shop garden centre (on leads) *Details not confirmed for 2001*

CO DUBLIN

BALBRIGGAN

Ardgillan Castle

(on R127)

☎ 01 8492212 📠 01 8492786

A large and elegant country manor house built in 1738, set in 194 acres of parkland, overlooking the sea and coast as far as the Mourne Mountains. There is a permanent exhibition of the 17th century 'Down Survey' maps and various temporary exhibitions. Tours of the Gardens (June, July and August) begin at 3.30pm every Thursday.

Times: Open Apr-Sep, Tue-Sun & BH's 11-6 (daily Jul-Aug); Oct-Mar, Wed-Sun & BH's 11-4.30. (Closed 23 Dec-1 Jan).

Fee: IR£3 (pen & students IR£2). Family ticket IR£6.50. Party.

P ☕ ♿ toilets for disabled shop 🚫🐕 (ex guide dogs)

DONABATE

Newbridge House and Traditional Farm

☎ 01 8436534 & 8462184 📠 01 8462537

Newbridge House was designed by George Semple and built in 1737 for Charles Cobbe, Archbishop of Dublin. The house contains many splendidly refurbished rooms featuring plasterwork, furniture and paintings. Special events throughout the year include demonstrations of sheep shearing, weaving, dying, pottery and harness making.

Times: Open Apr-Sep Tue-Sat 10-5, Sun & PH 2-6; Oct-Mar Sat-Sun & PH 2-5. Parties at other times by arrangement.

Fee: House IR£3 (ch IR£1.65, concessions IR£2.60). Family ticket IR£8.25. Combined ticket for related attractions available.

P ☕ shop 🚫🐕

DUBLIN

The Casino

off Malahide Rd, Marino (5km N of City Centre)

☎ 01 8331618 📠 01 8331618

The Casino was designed in 1757 by Sir William Chambers to look like a one-roomed, one-storied Greek temple containing 16 rooms. Possibly one of the finest 18th-century neo-Classical buildings in Europe.

Times: Open Jun-Sep, daily 10-6; May & Oct, daily 10-5; Apr, Sun, Thu & BH's 12-5; Feb, Mar & Nov, Sun, Thu & BH's 12-4. Last admission 45 mins before closing. (Closed Dec & Jan).

Fee: IR£2 (ch & students IR£1, pen IR£1.50). Family ticket IR£5.

P ♿ 🚫🐕 (ex guide dogs)

The Chester Beatty Library

Clock Tower, Dublin Castle

☎ 01 4070750 📠 01 4070760

e-mail: info@cbl.ie

A rare collection of oriental manuscripts and miniatures, including New Testament manuscripts and Chinese jade books are on display in this fascinating gallery. The gallery was bequeathed to Ireland by its first honorary citizen, American mining engineer and collector, Sir Alfred Chester Beatty (1875-1968).

Times: Open all year, daily. (Closed Good Fri & 25 Dec).

Fee: Free.

P ☕ ✕ ♿ toilets for disabled shop garden centre 🚫🐕 (ex guide dogs)

Christ Church Cathedral

Christchurch Place (at the top end of Dame St)

☎ 01 6778099 📠 01 6798991

e-mail: cccdub@indigo.ie

Founded in 1038, the present building dates from 1180 with a major restoration in the 1870s. The crypt is the second largest medieval crypt in Britain or Ireland. There are daily services and choral services during the week.

Times: Open 10-5.30.

Fee: Requested donation IR£2 (children IR£1)

P (100yds) ♿ shop 🚫🐕 (ex guide dogs)

Drimnagh Castle

Long Mile Rd, Drimnagh

☎ 01 4502530 📠 01 4505401

The last surviving medieval castle in Ireland with a flooded moat, Drimnagh dates back to the 13th century and was inhabited until 1954. The Castle consists of a restored Great Hall and medieval undercroft, a tall battlement tower and lookout posts, and other separate buildings including stables, an old coach house and a folly.

Times: Open Apr-Sep, Wed & wknds 12-5; Oct-Mar, Sun 12-5. Last tour 4.15. Other times by arrangement.

Fee: IR£1.50 (ch IR50p, pen & students IR£1). Party.

P ☕ ♿ (gravel courtyard and garden. steps) 🚫🐕 (ex guide dogs)

Dublin Castle

Dame St

☎ 01 6777129 📠 01 6797831

With two towers and a partial wall, this is the city's most outstanding legacy of the Middle Ages. Of interest are the Record Tower, state apartments, Church of the Most Holy Trinity and Heraldic Museum. The inauguration of the President of Ireland and related ceremonies are held in St. Patrick's Hall, an elegant state apartment.

Times: Open all year, Mon-Fri 10-5, Sat-Sun & BH 2-5. (Closed 24-26 Dec & Good Fri).

Fee: IR£3 (ch IR£1, students & pen IR£2)

P ✕ ♿ toilets for disabled

Dublinia

St Michael's Hill, Christ Church

☎ 01 6794611 📠 01 6797116

The story of medieval Dublin. Housed in the former Synod Hall beside Christ Church Cathedral and developed by the Medieval Trust, DVBLINIA recreates the period from the arrival of Strongbow and the Anglo-Normans in 1170 to the closure of the monasteries by Henry VIII in 1540.

contd.

Times: Open Apr-Sep 10-5; Oct-Mar, Mon-Sat 11-4, Sun & BH 10-4.30. (Closed 24-26 Dec).
Fee: IR£3.95 (ch/pen/student/unwaged IR£3). Family ticket IR£10.
P (100yds) (2 floors accessible, but bridge and tower are not) toilets for disabled shop (ex guide dogs)

Dublin Writers Museum

18 Parnell Square North
☎ 01 8722077 01 8722231
e-mail: writers@dublintourism.ie

The Dublin Writers Museum is housed in a restored 18th-century building and a modern annexe with lecture rooms and exhibition spaces. Dublin's rich literary heritage can be followed, through displays, tracing the written tradition in Ireland from the Book of Kells in the 8th century to the present day. An audio tour, available in several languages, is included in the admission price.
Times: Open all year, Mon-Sat 10-5 & Sun & BH 11-5. Jun-Aug, Mon-Fri 10-6pm.
Fee: IR£3.10 (ch IR£1.45, concessions IR£2.60). Family ticket IR£8.50. Combined ticket for related attractions available.
P (200 yds) (Metered) licensed shop (ex guide dogs)

Guinness Hop Store

St James's Gate
☎ 01 4084800 01 4084965
Times: Open all year, daily (Closed 25-26Dec & Good Fri) Jan-Mar & Oct-Dec, Mon-Sat 9.30-4 (Sun & PH 12-4) Apr-Sep Mon-Sat 9.30-5 (Sun & PH 10.30-4.30)
P toilets for disabled shop *Details not confirmed for 2001*

Howth Castle Rhododendron Gardens

Howth (9m NE of Dublin city centre, via Fairview Clontarf & Sutton)
☎ 01 8322624 & 8322256 01 8392405
e-mail: sales@deerpark.iol.ie
Times: Open all year, daily 8am-dusk. (Closed 25 Dec).
P licensed (ramped entrance) toilets for disabled (ex guide dogs) *Details not confirmed for 2001*

Hugh Lane Municipal Gallery of Modern Art

Charlemont House, Parnell Square
☎ 01 8741903 01 8722182
e-mail: info@hughlane.ie

Situated in Charlemont House, a fine Georgian building, the gallery's collection includes one of the most extensive collections of 20th century Irish art. A superb range of international and Irish paintings, sculpture, works on paper and stained glass is also on show. There are public lectures every Sunday and regular concerts (at noon on Sundays) throughout the year.
Times: Open all year, Tue-Thu 9.30-6, Fri-Sat 9.30-5, Sun 11-5. Late night opening Thu until 8, Apr-Aug only. (Closed Mon, Good Fri & 24-25 Dec).
Fee: Free.
P (100 metres) (meter parking) (Ramp & reserved parking) toilets for disabled shop (ex guide dogs)

Irish Museum of Modern Art

Royal Hospital, Kilmainham (from City Centre pass Heuston Station, 1st left on St John's Rd)
☎ 01 612 9900 01 612 9999
e-mail: info@modernart.ie

Housed in the Royal Hospital Kilmainham, an impressive 17th-century building, the museum presents a wide-ranging programme of Irish and International 20th-century art from its own collections. There are also temporary exhibitions, talks, seminars and musical events.
Times: Open all year Tue-Sat 10-5.30, Sun & BH's 12-5.30. (Closed 24-26 Dec & Good Fri).
P (wheelchair available) toilets for disabled shop (ex guide dogs)

James Joyce Centre

35 North Great George's St
☎ 01 8788547 01 8788488
e-mail: joycecen@iol.ie

Situated in a beautifully restored 18th-century Georgian town house, the Centre is dedicated to the promotion of a greater interest in, and understanding of, the life and works of Joyce. There is a library open to visitors, exhibition rooms, videos and tapes.
Times: Open all year, Mon-Sat 9.30-5, Sun 12.30-5. (Closed Good Fri & 24-26 Dec).
Fee: IR£3 (ch IR75p, pen & students IR£2). Family ticket IR£6.
P (200 mtrs) toilets for disabled shop (ex guide dogs)

Kilmainham Gaol

Inchicore Rd
☎ 01 4535984 01 4532037

An unparalleled historical resource in the understanding of Ireland's emergence as a modern nation. Touching in many ways on the people and forces that shaped modern Ireland, Kilmainham Gaol offers a panoramic insight into some of the most profound, disturbing and inspirational themes of modern Irish history.
Times: Access by guided tour only. Open Apr-Sep, daily 9.30-6 (last tour 4.45); Oct-Mar, Mon-Fri 9.30-5 (last tour 4pm), Sun 10-6 (last tour 4.45).
Fee: IR£3.50 (ch/student IR£1.50, pen IR£2.50). Family ticket IR£8.
P (on street parking only) (tours available by prior appointment) toilets for disabled

Marsh's Library

St Patrick's Close
☎ 01 4543511 01 4543511
e-mail: marshlib@iol.ie

The first public library in Ireland, dating from 1701. Designed by William Robinson, the interior has been unchanged for nearly 300 years. The collection is of approximately 25,000 volumes of 16th, 17th and early 18th century books.
Times: Open Mon & Wed-Fri, 10-12.45 & 2-5; Sat 10.30-12.45.
Fee: IR£2 (students & pen IR£1, ch free).
P

National Botanic Gardens
Glasnevin (on Botanic Road, between N1 and N2)
☎ 01 8374388 & 8377596 🖷 01 8360080

Established in 1795, covering an area of 48 acres, the gardens contain fine collections of trees, shrubs and renowned herbaceous borders. Separate areas are devoted to annuals and vegetables, and to native Irish plants, arranged according to habitats. The glasshouses feature collections of palms, rare cycads, tropical ferns, cacti and alpines.

Times: Open all year, summer Mon-Sat 9-6, Sun 11-6; winter Mon-Sat 10-4.30, Sun 11-4.30.

Fee: Free entry. Guided tours by arrangement.

P ♿ (Wheelchair available) toilets for disabled (ex guide dogs)

National Gallery of Ireland
Merrion Square (situated 5 mins walk from Pearse Station)
☎ 01 6615133 🖷 01 6615372
e-mail: artgall@eircom.net

The gallery, founded in 1854, houses the national collections of Irish art and European Old Masters from the 14th to the 20th centuries. A Yeats museum has recently opened and a new wing to the existing building will be completed by Summer 2001.

Times: Open Mon-Sat 10-5.30 (Thu 10-8.30), Sun 2-5. (Closed 24-26 Dec & Good Fri).

Fee: Free.

P (5 mins walk) (meter parking, 2hrs max) licensed ♿ (braille/audio tours, lifts, ramps, parking bay) toilets for disabled shop

National Library of Ireland
Kildare St
☎ 01 6030200 🖷 01 6766690
e-mail: info@nli.ie

In 1877 a large portion of the Royal Dublin Society was bought by the State to establish the National Library of Ireland. The Library administers the Genealogical Office. Passes or tickets are required to use the Library, these can be obtained on application.

Times: Open: Mon-Wed 10-9, Thu-Fri 10-5 & Sat 10-1. (Closed Sun, Xmas-New Year, Etr & BH's).

Fee: Free.

♿ toilets for disabled shop (ex guide dogs)

National Photographic Archive
Meeting House Square, Temple Bar
☎ 01 6030200 🖷 01 6777451
e-mail: photoarchive@nli.ie

Up to 250,000 images are held in this archive, which is part of the National Library of Ireland. The collections are of Irish interest and cover areas such as postcard views of the country and political and social events. The glass plate archive includes the Lawrence, Poole, Valentine and Eason collections.

Times: Open all year, Mon-Fri 10-5; Sat 10-2 exhibition area only. (Closed BH's).

Fee: Free.

♿ toilets for disabled shop (ex guide dogs)

Natural History Museum
Merrion St
☎ 01 6777444 🖷 01 6766116

Founded by the Royal Dublin Society in 1792, the museum has occupied its present premises since 1857. There are extensive zoological exhibitions and geological specimens, including the world famous Blaschka glass models of marine animals. The museum is also an important research institute.

Times: Open Tue-Sat 10-5, Sun 2-5.

Fee: Free.

P (parking meters wkdays) ♿

Newman House
University College Dublin, 86 St Stephens Green (South side of St Stephen's Green)
☎ 01 7067422 & 4757255 🖷 01 7067211

Newman House consists of two superb Georgian town houses, containing some of Ireland's finest 18th-century plasterwork and decoration. As the founding home of University College Dublin in 1854, the house has been associated with many famous literary and historical figures, including John Henry Newman, Gerard Manley Hopkins and James Joyce.

Times: Open Jun-Aug, Tue-Fri 12-5, Sat 2-5, Sun 11-1. At other times tours by prior arrangement only.

Fee: IR£3 (concessions IR£2).

P (100yds) licensed (ex guide dogs)

Number Twenty Nine
29 Lower Fitzwilliam St (on the corner of Lower Fitzwilliam St & Upper Mount Sq)
☎ 01 7026165 🖷 01 7027796
e-mail: numbertwentynine@mail.esb.ie

Number Twenty-Nine is an exhibition of the home life of a middle-class merchant family in Dublin, in the late 18th and early 19th century.

Times: Open all year, Tue-Sat 10-5, Sun 2-5. (Closed Mon & 2 wks prior to Xmas).

Fee: IR£2.50 (ch under 16 free, other concessions IR£1).

P (charged) shop

Phoenix Park Visitor Centre
Phoenix Park
☎ 01 6770095 🖷 01 8205584

Situated in Phoenix Park the Visitor Centre provides an historical interpretation of the park from 3500BC, through a series of attractive displays. Part of the building is devoted to nature and there is a colourful film of Phoenix Park. The castle, probably dating from the early 17th century has been restored to its former glory.

Times: Open all year; Jun-Sep, daily 10-6; Apr-May, daily 9.30-5.30; mid-end Mar & Oct, daily 9.30-5; Jan-mid Mar & Nov-Dec, Sat & Sun 9.30-4.30. Last admission 45 mins before closing.

Fee: IR£2 (ch & students IR£1, pen IR£1.50). Family ticket IR£5.

P ♿ toilets for disabled (ex guide dogs)

George Bernard Shaw House

33 Synge St
☎ 01 4750854 & 8722077 01 8722231
e-mail: Dublin-Tourism@msn.com

Times: Open May-Oct, Mon-Sat 10-5, Sun & PH's 11-5.
P (charged) shop garden centre (ex guide dogs) *Details not confirmed for 2001*

DUN LAOGHAIRE

James Joyce Tower

Joyce Tower, Sandycove (1m SE Dun Laoghaire by coast road to Sandycove Point or turn off main Dun Laoghaire-Dalkey road)
☎ 01 2809265 & 8722077 2809265
e-mail: enterprises@dublintourism.ie

Times: Open Apr-Oct Mon-Sat 10-5, Sun & PHs 2-6; Nov-Mar by arrangement.
P (100 yds) shop (ex guide dogs) *Details not confirmed for 2001*

MALAHIDE

Fry Model Railway

Malahide Castle Demesne
☎ 01 8463779 & 8462184 01 8463723
e-mail: fryrailway@dublintourism.ie

The Fry Model Railway is a rare collection of '0' gauge trains and trams, depicting the history of Irish rail transport from the first train that ran in 1834. Cyril Fry began to build his model collection in his attic, in the late 1920s. All the models are built to scale, and they are now housed in a purpose-built setting adjacent to Malahide Castle.

Times: Open all year, Apr-Oct, Mon-Sat 10-5, Sun & PH 2-6; Nov-Mar Sat-Sun & PH 2-5. Parties at other times by arrangement.
Fee: IR£2.90 (ch IR£1.70, concessions IR£2.20). Family ticket IR£7.75. Combined ticket for related attractions available.
P shop

Malahide Castle

☎ 01 8462184 & 8462516 01 8462537
e-mail: malahidecastle@dublintourism.ie

One of Ireland's oldest castles, this romantic and beautiful structure, set in 250 acres of grounds, has changed very little in 800 years. Tours offer views of Irish period furniture and historical portrait collections. Additional paintings from the National Gallery depict Irish life from the last few centuries.

Times: Open all year, Apr-Oct, Mon-Sat 10-5, Sun & PH 11-6; Nov-Mar, Mon-Fri 10-5, Sat-Sun & PH 2-5. (Closed for tours 12.45-2pm).
Fee: IR£3.15 (ch IR£1.75, concessions IR£2.65). Family ticket IR£8.75. Combined tickets for related attractions available.
P licensed shop

CO GALWAY

GALWAY

Galway City Museum

Spanish Arch
☎ 091 567641 091 567641

Galway City Museum is devoted to the city's history, featuring examples of medieval stonework, stone axe heads and scrapers dating from 3,500 years BC, a peat fire, a large map of the city in 1651, photographs of 19th-century traditional dress and memorabilia of Connaught Rangers Regiment.

Times: Open all year daily, Mar-Oct 10-5.15. Nov-Feb 2-4, times under review.
Fee: IR£1. (concessions IR50p).
P (100yds) (parking discs required) (ex guide dogs)

Nora Barnacle House Museum

Bowling Green (close to St Nicholas Collegiate Church)
☎ 091 564743

The smallest museum in Ireland, this tiny turn-of-century house was the home Nora Barnacle, companion, wife and lifelong inspiration of James Joyce. It was here in 1909, sitting at the kitchen table that Joyce first met his darling's mother. Letters, photographs and other exhibits of the lives of James Joyce & Nora Barnacle make a visit here a unique experience.

Times: Open Jun-mid Sep, Mon-Sat 10-1 & 2-5. Opening times may vary.
Fee: IR£1
P 100yds shop

Royal Tara China Visitor Centre

Tara Hall, Mervue (off N17 opp Trappers Rest or left off N6 after Ryan's Hotel)
☎ 091 751301 091 757574
e-mail: visitorcentre@royal-tara.com

Royal Tara China is the country's leading manufacturer of fine bone china, cold cast bronze, miniature pubs, castles, cottages and handpainted pieces. Tours every hour from 9.30am-3.30pm.

Times: Open all year, 9-6 (9-8 Jul-Sep, 9-9 Dec). Guided factory tours Mon-Fri 9.30-3.30.
Fee: Free.
P toilets for disabled shop (ex guide dogs) 

GORT

Thoor Ballylee

(1km off N18, 1km off N66)
☎ 091 631436 091 565201

This tower house is the former home of the poet William Butler Yeats and this is where he completed most of his literary works. The tower, which has been restored to appear exactly as it was when he lived there, houses an Interpretative Centre with audio-visual presentations and displays of his work.

Times: Open Etr-Sep, daily 10-6.
Fee: IR£3.50 (ch IR£1, pen & students IR£3). Family ticket IR£7. Party.
P (audio-visual presentation) toilets for disabled shop

KINVARRA

Dunguaire Castle

☎ 091 37108 & 061 360788 📠 061 361020
e-mail: oconnorm@shannon-dev.ie

Times: Open May-Oct, daily 9.30-5.30 (last admission 5pm).
P shop (ex guide dogs) *Details not confirmed for 2001*

PORTUMNA

Portumna Castle & Gardens

☎ 0509 41658

Built by Richard Burke around 1618, this castle was intended to replace the family's previous castle at Loughrea. Situated on a magnificent site adjacent to Lough Derg on the River Shannon, it had lain in ruins since a fire in 1826 until restoration work began in 1968.

Times: Open mid Apr-Sep, daily 9.30-6.30.
Fee: IR£1.50 (ch & students IR60p, pen IR£1). Family ticket IR£3.
P ♿ (access limited) (ex guide dogs)

ROUNDSTONE

Roundstone Musical Instruments

Craft Centre
☎ 095 35875 📠 095 35980
e-mail: bodhran@iol.ie

Times: Open all year daily 9-6.
P ♿ toilets for disabled shop *Details not confirmed for 2001*

CO KERRY

CASTLEISLAND

Crag Cave

(1m N, signposted off N21)
☎ 066 7141244 📠 066 7142352
e-mail: cragcave@eircom.net

Crag Cave is one of the longest surveyed cave systems in Ireland, with a total length of 3.81km. It is a spectacular world, where pale forests of stalagmites and stalactites, thousands of years old, throw eerie shadows around vast echoing caverns complemented by dramatic sound and lighting effects. Tours lasts about 30 minutes.

Times: Open daily, Mar-Nov 10-6 (Jul-Aug until 6.30). Last tour 30 minutes before closing time.
Fee: IR£4 (ch IR£2, pen & students IR£3). Family ticket IR£12.
P ✕ licensed ♿ (ramp to visitor centre) toilets for disabled shop (ex guide dogs)

DUNQUIN

The Blasket Centre

(10m W of Dingle town, on Slea Head Drive)
☎ 066 9156444 & 9156371 📠 066 9156446
e-mail: demordha@indigo.ie

In the early part of this century a small group of writers from the remote Blasket Island, just off the coast of County Kerry, achieved world renown. They told their own story in their own language and the centre describes the lives of the Islanders before the sad abandonment of the island in 1953. Research and conference facilities also available.

Times: Open daily, Etr-late Oct 10-6 (7 Jul-Aug). Open on request all year for groups over 30.
Fee: IR£2.50 (ch & student IR£1, pen IR£1.75). Family ticket IR£6.
P ✕ licensed ♿ (reserved parking) toilets for disabled (ex guide dogs)

KENMARE

Kenmare Heritage Centre

The Square
☎ 064 31633 📠 064 34506

Times: Open Apr-Sep, Mon-Sat 9.30-5.30 (also Sun Jul-Aug)
P (400mtrs) ♿ toilets for disabled shop (ex guide dogs) *Details not confirmed for 2001*

KILLARNEY

Killarney Transport Museum

Scotts Hotel Gardens (centre of town, opposite railway station)
☎ 064 34677 📠 064 32638

A unique collection of Irish veteran, vintage and classic cars, motorcycles, bicycles, carriages and fire engines. Exhibits include the 1907 Silver Stream, reputed to be the rarest car in the world, it was designed and built by an Irishman and he only made one!

Times: Open Apr-Oct, daily 10-6. Open at other times by appointment
Fee: IR£3 (ch IR£1.50, students & pen IR£2). Family ticket IR£7. Wheelchair visitors free. Party.
P ✕ licensed ♿ shop

Muckross House, Gardens & Traditional

Muckross (4m on Kenmare Road)
☎ 066 31440 & 35571 📠 066 33926
e-mail: mucros@iol.ie

The 19th century mansion house of the formerly private Muckross Estate. It now houses a museum of Kerry folklife. In the basement craft centre, a weaver, blacksmith and potter demonstrate their trades. The

contd.

grounds include Alpine and bog gardens, rhododendrons, azaleas and a rock garden.
Times: Open Jul-Aug, daily 9-7; 17 Mar-Jun & Sep-Oct, 9-6; Nov-16 Mar 9-5.30.
Fee: House: IR£4 (pen IR£3, ch & students IR£1.60). Family ticket IR£10. House & Farm: IR£6 (ch & students IR£2.75). Family ticket IR£15.
licensed toilets for disabled shop (ex guide dogs) 

VALENTIA ISLAND
The Skellig Experience
(Ring of Kerry Road, signed after Cahersiveen town then Valentia bridge or ferry from Rena Rd Point)
066 9476306 066 9476351

The Skellig Rocks are renowned for their scenery, sea bird colonies, lighthouses, Early Christian monastic architecture and rich underwater life. The two islands - Skellig Michael and Small Skellig - stand like fairytale castles in the Atlantic Ocean, rising to 218 metres and their steep cliffs plunging 50 metres below the sea. The Heritage Centre, (on Valentia Island, reached from the mainland via a bridge), tells the story of the Skellig Islands in an exciting multimedia exhibition.
Times: Open 25 Mar-Jun & Sep 10-7, Jul-Aug 9.30-7 (last tour 6.15). Oct-mid Nov, Sun-Thu 10-5.30.
Fee: IR£3 (ch IR£1.50, pen & student IR£2.70). Family ticket IR£7.
toilets for disabled shop (ex guide dogs)

CO KILDARE

CELBRIDGE
Castletown
(13m from Dublin, follow signs to Celbridge from N4)
01 6288252 01 6271811

Ireland's largest and finest Palladian country house, begun c1722 for William Conolly, Speaker of the Irish House of Commons. The state rooms include the 'Pompeian' Long Gallery with its Venetian chandeliers, green silk drawing room and magnificent staircase hall with Lafranchini plasterwork. There is a fine collection of 18th-century Irish furniture and paintings.
Times: Open Etr Day-Sep Mon-Fri 10-6, Sat-Sun & BH 1-6; Oct Mon-Fri 10-5, Sun & BH 1-5; Nov Sun 1-5. Restoration continues.
Fee: IR£3 (ch & students IR£1.25, pen IR£2). Family ticket IR£7.50.
toilets for disabled (ex guide dogs)

KILDARE
Japanese Gardens
Irish National Stud, Tully (Off N7)
045 521617 & 522963 045 522964
e-mail: stud@IRISH-national-stud.ie

Situated in the grounds of the Irish National Stud, the gardens were established by Lord Wavertree between 1906 and 1910, and symbolise 'The Life of Man' in a Japanese-style landscape. You can also visit the Horse Museum which includes the skeleton of Arkle. The Commemorative Millennium Garden of St Fiachra seeks to capture the power of the Irish landscape in its rawest state, that of rock and water.
Times: Open 12 Feb-12 Nov, daily 9.30-6, last admission 5.
Fee: IR£6 (ch 12 IR£3, students & pen IR£4.50). Family ticket IR£14.
licensed (all parts of stud accessible, only small part of gardens) toilets for disabled shop (ex on lead)

CO KILKENNY

KILKENNY
Kilkenny Castle
056 21450 056 63488

Situated in a beautiful 50-acre park, the castle dates from 1172. The first stone castle was built 20 years later by William Marshall, Earl of Pembroke. It was home of the very powerful Butler family, Earls and Dukes of Ormonde from 1391 to 1935. In state care since 1969, to date two wings have been restored and opened to the public. Within the next two years the final phase of restoration should be complete.
Times: Open all year - Jun-Sep, daily 10-7; Apr-May, daily 10.30-5; Oct-Mar, Tue-Sat 10.30-12.45 & 2-5, Sun 11-12.45 & 2-5. Last tour 45mins before closing. (Closed Xmas & Good Fri).
Fee: IR£3.50 (ch, students IR£1.50 & pen IR£2.50). Family ticket IR£8.
(charged) shop (ex guide dogs)

CO LIMERICK

FOYNES
Foynes Flying Boat Museum
(on N69)
069 65416 069 65416
e-mail: famm@eircom.net

The museum recalls the era of the flying boats during the 1930s and early 1940s when Foynes was an important airport for air traffic between the United States and Europe. There is a comprehensive range of exhibits, graphic illustrations and a 1940s style cinema featuring a 17 minute film - all original footage from the 30s and 40s. Where Irish coffee was first invented by chef, Joe Sheridan, in 1942.
Times: Open 31 Mar-Oct, daily 10-6. Last admissions 5.15pm
Fee: IR£3.50 (ch IR£2, student IR£3). Family ticket IR£9.
toilets for disabled shop (ex guide dogs)

HOLYCROSS
Lough Gur Stone Age Centre
Bruff Rd (17 km S of Limerick City, off R512 rd to Kilmallock)
061 385186 & 061 360788 061 361020
e-mail: oconnorm@shannon-dev.ie
Times: Open May-Sep, daily 10-6 (last admission 5pm)
shop (ex guide dogs) *Details not confirmed for 2001*

KILCORNAN

CELTIC PARK & GARDENS

(N69 Limerick to Tralge rd)

☎ 061 394243 Fax 353 69 64257

Times: Open daily, Mar-Oct 9-7. Last entry 6pm.

shop (on lead) *Details not confirmed for 2001*

LIMERICK

HUNT MUSEUM

The Custom House, Rutland St (a short walk from Arthur's Quay)

☎ 061 312833 Fax 061 312834

e-mail: info@huntmuseum.com

Three floors of galleries exhibit a collection of 2000 pieces of art and antiquity. It includes statues in stone, bronze and wood, crucifixes, panel paintings, metalwork, jewellery, enamels and ceramics. There are drawings by Picasso and da Vinci, and a gold cross worn by Mary, Queen of Scots.

Times: Open daily Mon-Sat 10-5, Sun 2-5.

Fee: IR£4.20 (ch IR£2, concwssions IR£3.20). Family ticket IR£10. Party.

(50 mtrs) (parking discs for street parking) licensed toilets for disabled shop (ex guide dogs)

KING JOHN'S CASTLE

Nicholas St

☎ 061 411201 & 360788 Fax 061 361020

e-mail: oconnorm@shannon-dev.ie

Times: Open Apr-Oct daily 9.30-5.30 (last admission 4.30); Nov-Apr, Sun 11-4 (last admission 3pm).

(lifts and ramps) toilets for disabled shop (ex guide dogs) *Details not confirmed for 2001*

KEENAGH

CORLEA TRACKWAY VISITOR CENTRE

(Off R397, 3km from village)

☎ 043 22386 Fax 043 22442

Times: Open Apr-1 Oct, daily 10-6. Last admission 45 mins before closing.

Fee: IR£2.50 (ch & students IR£1, pen IR£1.75). Family ticket IR£6.

toilets for disabled (ex guide dogs)

BALLYCASTLE

CÉIDE FIELDS

(5m W on R314)

☎ 096 43325 Fax 096 43261

Preserved beneath the wild blanket bogland on the dramatic North Mayo coast is a 5,000 year old Stone Age landscape of stone-walled fields, dwellings and megalithic tombs. Guided tour on request.

Times: Open Jun-Sep, daily 9.30-6.30; mid Mar-May & Oct, daily 10-5; Nov, daily 10-4.30; other times by arrangement.

Fee: IR£2.50 (ch, student IR£1 & pen IR£1.75). Family ticket IR£6.

toilets for disabled (ex guide dogs)

CO MONAGHAN

INNISKEEN

PATRICK KAVANAGH RURAL & LITERARY RESOURCE CENTRE

Candlefort (between Carrickmacross N2 & Dundalk N1)

☎ 042 78560 Fax 042 78560

e-mail: infoatpkc@tinet.ie

Birthplace of Patrick Kavanagh, one of Ireland's foremost 20th-century poets. The village grew around the ancient monastery of St Daig MacCairill, founded by 562, and its strong, 10th-century round tower still stands. The centre, housed in the former parish Church, chronicles the ancient history of the region and its role in developing Kavanagh's work.

Times: Open all year, Mon Fri 11-5, wknds & BH's 2-6. (Closed Oct-May, wknds & BH's Dec-16 Mar)

Fee: IR£2 (ch 12 free, concessions IR£1). Kavanagh trail guide map available IR50p. Kavanagh Country Tours - a guided tour with live performances lasting 90 mins, advance booking essential IR£5 including admission to centre.

toilets for disabled shop

MONAGHAN

Monaghan County Museum

1-2 Hill St (near town centre, opposite Tourist Information office)
☎ (047) 82928 047 71189
e-mail: moncomuseum@eircom.net

This is an award-winning museum of local archaeology, history, arts and crafts. Throughout the year various special exhibitions take place.
Times: Open all year, Tue- Sat 11-1 & 2-5.
Fee: Free.
P (near town centre) (restricted on street parking)

CO OFFALLY

BIRR

Birr Castle Demesne

☎ 0509 20336 0509 21583
e-mail: info@birrcastle.com

A large landscaped park with a lake, rivers and waterfalls, with important plant collections including magnolias, maples, limes and oaks. The Demesne is particularly colourful in the spring and autumn, and is noted for its formal gardens, containing the tallest box hedges in the world. The Demesne is also home to the Great Birr Telescope, built in 1844. Ireland's Historic Science Centre, a series of galleries focusing on Ireland's scientific past.
Times: Open all year, 9am-6pm.
Fee: IR£5 (ch IR£2.50, pen & students IR£3.50). Family ticket (2 adults & 2 ch) IR£12.
P toilets for disabled shop garden centre 

CO ROSCOMMON

BOYLE

King House

(in town centre, 1km from N4)
☎ 079 63242 079 63243
e-mail: kinghouseboyle@hotmail.com

Built around 1730, King House is of unique architectural and historical importance. Home to the King family until 1788, it then became a military barracks and was home to the famous Connaught Rangers Regiment and latterly the national army. Now magnificently restored, exhibitions tell the stories of the ancient kings of Connaught and explore the Gaelic way of life.
Times: Open Apr-mid Oct, daily 10-6 (last admission 5pm). All other times by appointment.
Fee: IR£3 (ch IR£2, pen/student IR£2.50). Family ticket IR£8. Party.
P (lift to all areas) toilets for disabled shop garden centre (ex guide dogs)

STROKESTOWN

Strokestown Park House Garden & Famine Museum

Strokestown Park
☎ 078 33013 078 33712
e-mail: info@strokestownpark.ie

A fine example of an early 18th-century gentleman farmer's country estate. Built in Palladian style the house reflects perfectly the confidence of the newly emergent ruling class. The pleasure garden has also been restored, and the Famine Museum, located in the stable yard, commemorates the Great Irish Famine of the 1840s.
Times: Open Apr-Oct, daily 11-5.30. All other times, group bookings only.
Fee: House, museum & garden IR£8.50, house & museum IR£6, house & garden IR£6, house only/museum only/garden only IR£3.25. Concessions.
P licensed (Access for ramps) toilets for disabled shop 

CO TIPPERARY

CAHIR

Swiss Cottage

Kilcommon (1m from town on Ardfinnan road)
☎ 052 41144 052 42324

A delightful thatched "cottage orné" built in the early 1800s on the estate of the Earls of Glengall to a design by the famous Regency architect John Nash.
Times: Open mid Mar-Apr & Oct-Nov, Tue-Sun 10-1 & 2-4.30; May-Sep, daily 10-6. Last admission 30mins before closing.
Fee: IR£2 (ch & student IR£1, pen IR£1.50). Family ticket IR£5. Party 20+
P (ex guide dog)

CASHEL

Br' Bor' Heritage Centre

☎ 062 61122 062 62700
e-mail: bruboru@comhaltas.com
Times: Open Jan-May & Oct-Dec, Mon-Fri 9.30-5.30; Jun-Sep Tue-Sat 9.30-11, Sun-Mon 9.30-5.30.
P (charged) licensed (wheelchair bay in theatre) toilets for disabled shop *Details not confirmed for 2001*

CO WATERFORD

LISMORE

Lismore Castle Gardens

☎ 058 54424 058 54896
e-mail: lismoreestates@eircom.net

Lismore castle is the Irish home of the Duke of Devonshire. The beautifully situated walled and woodland gardens contain a fine collection of camellias, magnolias and other shrubs and a

remarkable Yew Walk. It is said that Spenser wrote part of his *Faerie Queene* in these gardens.
Times: Open 22 Apr-15 Oct, daily 1.45-4.45.
Fee: IR£3 (ch 16 IR£1.50). Party 20+.
P

WATERFORD

WATERFORD CRYSTAL VISITOR CENTRE

(on N25, 1m from city centre)
☎ 051 73311 📠 051 78539
Times: Tours of factory: Apr-Oct, daily 8.30-4, gallery daily 8.30-6; Nov-Feb,Mon-Fri 9-3.15, gallery 9-5.
P ☕ ✕ ♿ (special tours on request) toilets for disabled shop 🐕
Details not confirmed for 2001

CO WEXFORD

FERRYCARRIG

IRISH NATIONAL HERITAGE PARK

(3m from Wexford, on N11)
☎ 053 20733 📠 053 20911
e-mail: info@inhp.com
Times: Open Apr-Oct daily 9.30-6.30. Last admission 5. Allow 1.5 hour for visit (closing time subject to seasonal change).
P ☕ ✕ licensed ♿ toilets for disabled shop 🐕 (ex guide dogs)
Details not confirmed for 2001

NEW ROSS

DUNBRODY ABBEY VISITORS CENTRE

Dunbrody Abbey, Campile (10 miles from New Ross at the base of the Hook Peninsular)
☎ 051 88603
Times: Open Apr-Sep 10-6 (7pm Jul-Aug).
P ☕ ♿ shop garden centre (specialising in conifers & shrubs)
Details not confirmed for 2001

JOHN F KENNEDY ARBORETUM

(12km S of New Ross, off R733)
☎ 051 388171 📠 051 388172

The Arboretum covers 623 acres across the hill of Slievecoiltia which overlooks the Kennedy ancestral home at Dunganstown. There are 4,500 types of trees and shrubs representing the temperate regions of the world, and laid out in botanical sequence. There's a lake and a visitor centre.
Times: Open daily, May-Aug 10-8; Apr & Sep 10-6.30; Oct-Mar 10-5. Last admission 45 mins before closing. (Closed Good Fri & 25 Dec).
Fee: IR£2 (ch & student IR£1, pen IR£1.50). Family ticket IR£5. Party 20+. Heritage card (12month) visits all Heritage Service sites. Adult IR£15 (pen IR£10, ch/student IR£6). Family ticket IR£36
P ☕ ♿ toilets for disabled shop (on lead)

WEXFORD

THE IRISH AGRICULTURAL MUSEUM

Johnstown Castle Old Farmyard (4m SW, signposted off N25)
☎ 053 42888 📠 053 42213

This museum has displays on rural transport, farming and the activities of the farmyard and farmhouse; and includes a large exhibition on the history of the potato and the Great Famine (1845-49). Large scale replicas of different workshops, including a blacksmith, cooper and basket worker, and include displays on dairying, cycling, and sugar-beet harvesting and a collection of Irish country furniture.
Times: Open all year, Jun-Aug Mon-Fri 9-5 & Sat-Sun 11-5; Apr-May & Sep-14 Nov Mon-Fri 9-12.30 & 1.30-5, Sat-Sun 2-5; 15 Nov-Mar Mon-Fri 9-12.30 & 1.30-5 (Closed 25 Dec-2 Jan).
Fee: IR£2.50 (ch & students IR£1.50). Family ticket IR£8. Parking charge May-Sep.
P (charged) ☕ ♿ toilets for disabled shop 🐕 (ex small dogs)

JOHNSTOWN CASTLE GARDENS

Johnstown Castle (4m SW, signposted off N25)
☎ 053 42888 📠 053 42004
Times: Open all year, daily 9-5-30. (Closed 25 Dec).
P ☕ ♿ toilets for disabled shop *Details not confirmed for 2001*

WEXFORD WILDFOWL RESERVE

North Slob (take coast road over bridge for 3km, signs show turning on right)
☎ 053 23129 📠 053 24785
e-mail: cjwilson@esatclear.ie

The reserve is of international importance for Greenland white-fronted geese, brent geese, Bewick's swans and wigeon. The reserve is a superb place for birdwatching and there are hides and a tower hide available as well as a visitor centre.
Times: Open all year, 15 Apr-Sep 9-6; Oct-14 Apr 10-5.
Fee: Free.
P ♿ 🐕 (ex guide dogs)

CO WICKLOW

ENNISKERRY

POWERSCOURT GARDENS EXHIBITION

Powerscourt Estate (just off N11 S of Bray, next to Enniskerry village)
☎ 01 2046000 📠 01 2863561
e-mail: gardens@powerscourt.ie

Begun by Richard Wingfield in the 1740s, the gardens are a blend of formal plantings, sweeping terraces, statuary and ornamental lakes together with secret hollows, rambling walks and walled gardens. The house itself incorporates an exhibition which traces the history of the estate, and tells the story of the disastrous fire of 1974 which gutted the house.

contd.

Times: Open - Gardens Mar-Oct daily 9.30-5.30; Nov-Feb daily 9.30-dusk. Waterfall Mar-Oct daily 9.30-7; Nov-Feb daily 10.30-dusk.(Please check winter opening times as they are subject to change. Closed 25-26 Dec).

Fee: Gardens & House exhibition: IR£5 (ch IR£3, students IR£4.50) House only IR£1.50 (ch IR£1, students IR£1.30) Gardens only IR£3.50 (ch IR£2, students IR£3.50) Waterfall IR£2 (ch IR£1, students IR£1.50) (Winter rates are cheaper)

licensed (Lift to first floor, Wheelchair available) toilets for disabled shop garden centre (ex guide dogs)

KILQUADE

National Gardens Exhibitions Centre

Calumet Nurseries (7m S of Bray - turn off the N11 at Kilpedder)

01 2819890 01 2810359

e-mail: calumet@clubi.ie

There are 17 different gardens designed by some of Ireland's leading landscapers and designers. There are lectures during the year and guided tours during summer. Ring for details and a calender of events.

Times: Open Feb-22 Dec, Mon-Sat 10-6, Sun 1-6.

Fee: IR£2.50 (ch under 16 free, pen IR£2). Party IR£2.

shop garden centre (ex guide dogs)

RATHDRUM

Avondale House & Forest Park

(1.6km S of town. R752 off N11)

0404 46111 0404 46111

e-mail: costelloe_j@coillte.ie

It was here in 1846 that one of the greatest political leaders of modern Irish history, Charles Stewart Parnell, was born. Parnell spent much of his time at Avondale until his death in October 1891. The house is set in a magnificent forest park with miles of forest trails.

Times: House: 17 Mar-Oct, 11-6. Outside of these dates group bookings by appointment. Last admission 1 hour before closure. (Closed Good Fri). Park: Open daily.

Fee: House IR£3 (pen & students IR£2.75). Family ticket IR£8.50, extra ch IR£1.50 each. Parking; car IR£3, minibus IR£6, coach IR£12 (if pre booked, no charge).

(charged) licensed (Special carpark & one forest trail accessible) shop (ex guide dogs & on lead)

KEY TO ATLAS

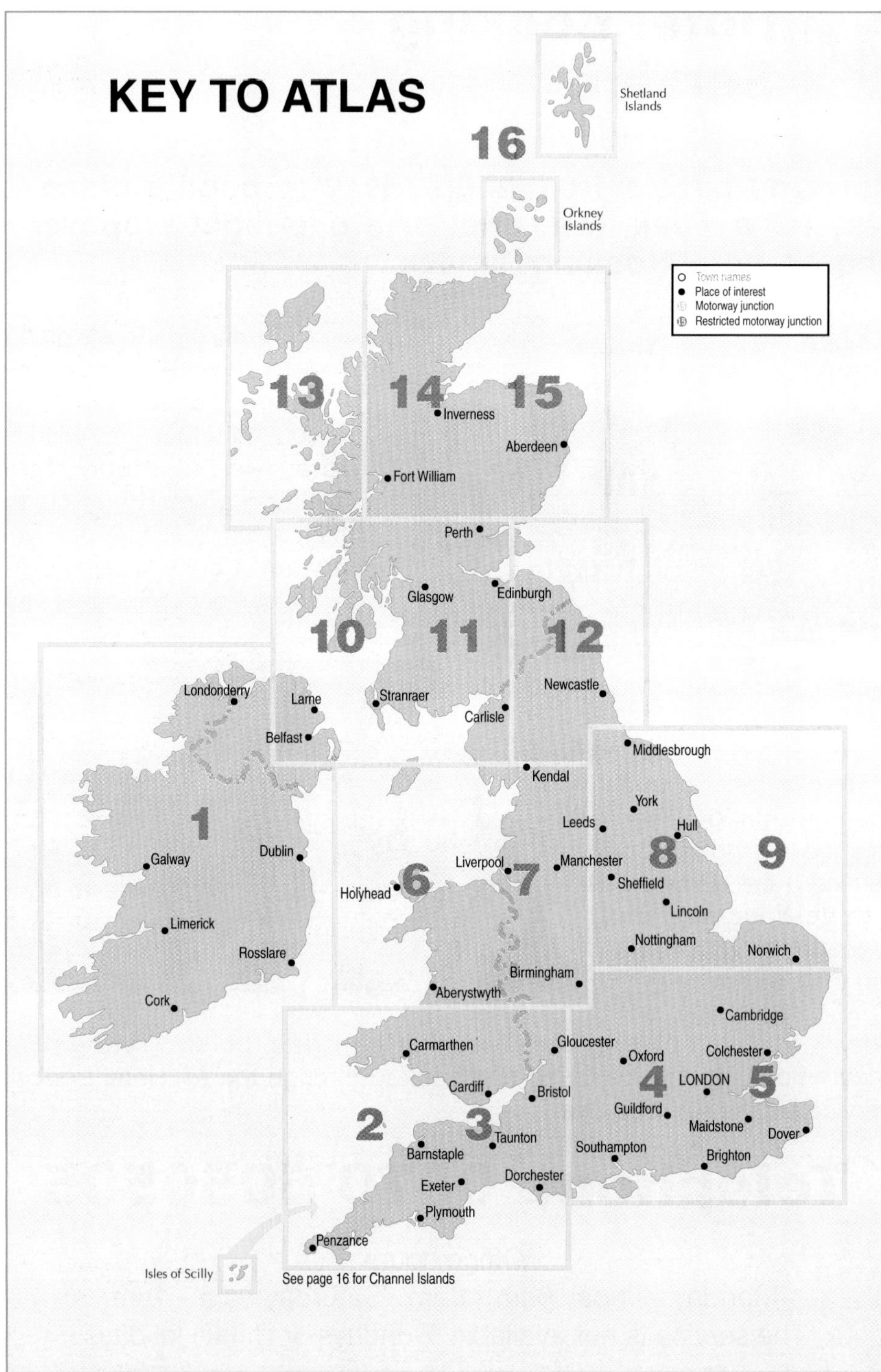

See page 16 for Channel Islands

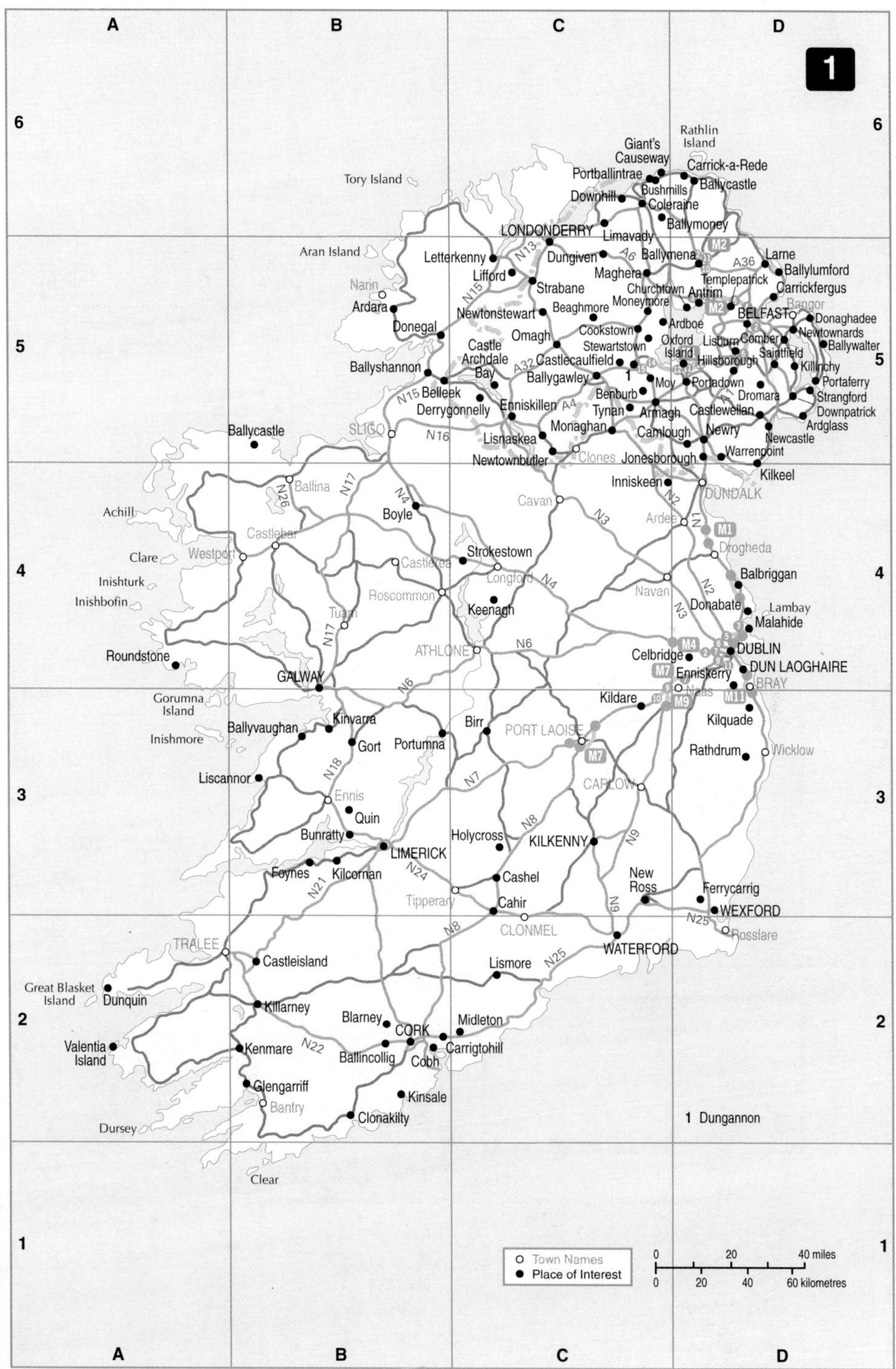

1
A
B
C
D
6
5
4
3
2
1
Rathlin Island
Giant's Causeway
Carrick-a-Rede
Portballintrae
Bushmills
Ballycastle
Downhill
Coleraine
Ballymoney
Tory Island
LONDONDERRY
Limavady
Aran Island
Letterkenny
Dungiven
Ballymena
Larne
Ballylumford
Lifford
Maghera
Templepatrick
Narin
Strabane
Churchtown
Antrim
Carrickfergus
Ardara
Moneymore
Bangor
Newtownstewart
Beaghmore
BELFAST
Donaghadee
Donegal
Ardboe
Cookstown
Newtownards
Omagh
Oxford Island
Lisburn
Comber
Stewartstown
Ballywalter
Castle Archdale Bay
Saintfield
Ballyshannon
Castlecaulfield
Hillsborough
Killinchy
Ballygawley
Moy
Portadown
Portaferry
Belleek
Benburb
Dromara
Strangford
Derrygonnelly
Enniskillen
Tynan
Armagh
Castlewellan
Downpatrick
Ardglass
Monaghan
Camlough
Newry
Ballycastle
SLIGO
Lisnaskea
Newcastle
Warrenpoint
Clones
Jonesborough
Newtownbutler
Kilkeel
Inniskeen
Ballina
DUNDALK
Achill
Boyle
Cavan
Ardee
Castlebar
Drogheda
Clare
Westport
Strokestown
Castlerea
Longford
Balbriggan
Inishturk
Navan
Roscommon
Lambay
Inishbofin
Donabate
Keenagh
Tuam
Malahide
ATHLONE
Celbridge
DUBLIN
Roundstone
DUN LAOGHAIRE
Enniskerry
GALWAY
BRAY
Naas
Gorumna Island
Kildare
Kilquade
Kinvarra
Ballyvaughan
Birr
Inishmore
PORT LAOISE
Gort
Portumna
Rathdrum
Wicklow
Liscannor
CARLOW
Ennis
Quin
Holycross
Bunratty
KILKENNY
LIMERICK
Foynes
Kilcornan
New Ross
Cashel
Ferrycarrig
Tipperary
Cahir
WEXFORD
CLONMEL
Rosslare
TRALEE
WATERFORD
Castleisland
Lismore
Great Blasket Island
Dunquin
Killarney
Blarney
Midleton
CORK
Valentia Island
Kenmare
Ballincollig
Carrigtohill
Cobh
Glengarriff
Kinsale
Bantry
Clonakilty
Dursey
1 Dungannon
Clear
Town Names
Place of Interest
0
20
40 miles
0
20
40
60 kilometres
N13
N15
A6
A36
M2
A32
A4
A1
N16
N26
N17
N4
N3
N2
M1
M4
M7
M9
M11
N6
N18
N7
N8
N9
N24
N21
N25
N22

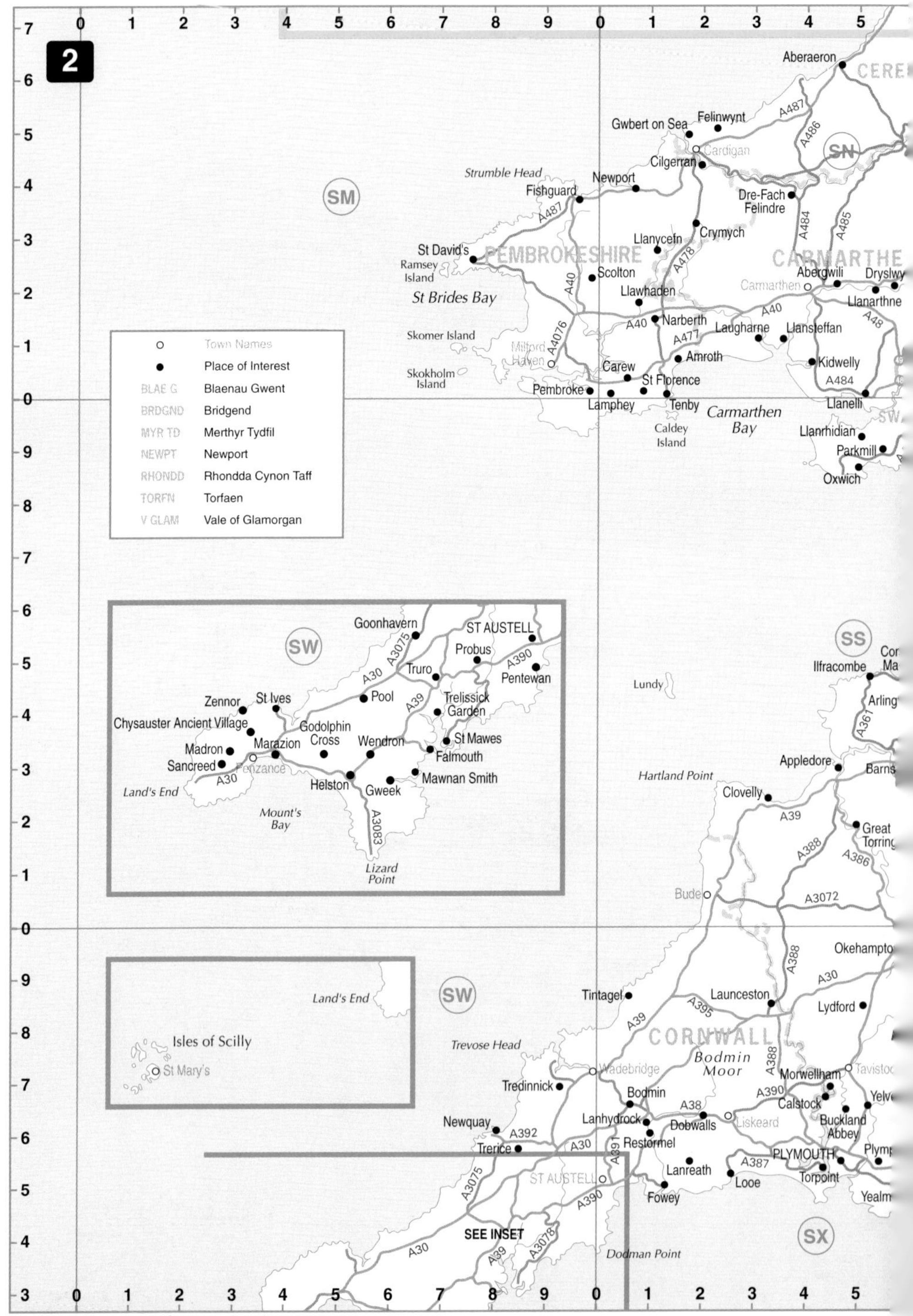

For continuation pages refer to numbered arrows

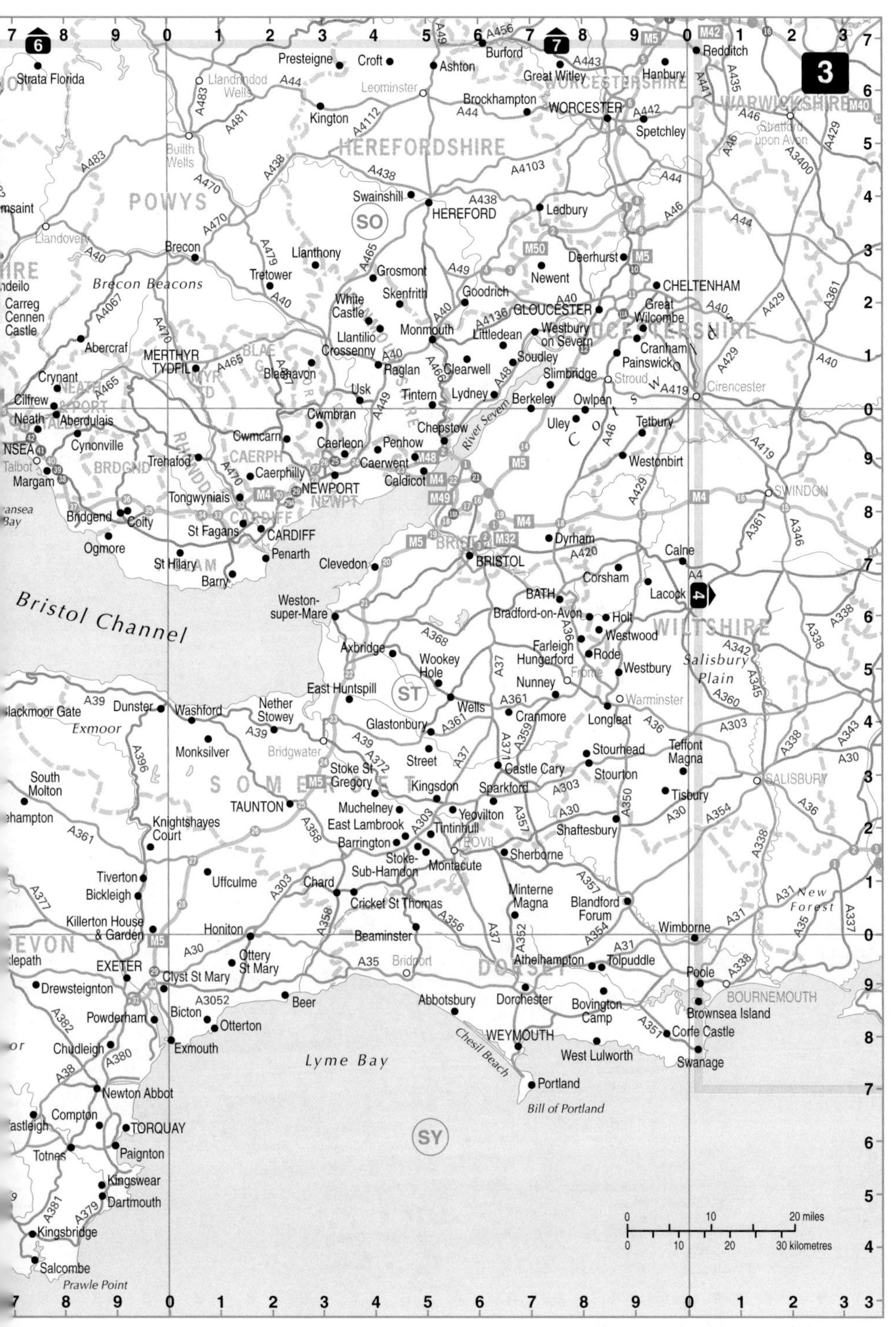

3
Strata Florida
Presteigne
Croft
Ashton
Burford
Great Witley
Hanbury
Redditch
Llandrindod Wells
Leominster
Kington
Brockhampton
WORCESTER
Spetchley
WORCESTERSHIRE
WARWICKSHIRE
Stratford upon Avon
Builth Wells
HEREFORDSHIRE
POWYS
Swainshill
HEREFORD
Ledbury
Llandovery
Brecon
Llanthony
Deerhurst
Newent
CHELTENHAM
Brecon Beacons
Tretower
Grosmont
Skenfrith
Goodrich
GLOUCESTER
Great Witcombe
Carreg Cennen Castle
White Castle
Llantilio Crossenny
Monmouth
Littledean
Westbury on Severn
Cranham
Painswick
Abercraf
MERTHYR TYDFIL
Blaenavon
Raglan
Clearwell
Soudley
Slimbridge
Stroud
Cirencester
Crynant
Usk
Tintern
Lydney
Berkeley
Owlpen
Cilfrew
Neath
Aberdulais
Cwmbran
River Severn
Chepstow
Uley
Tetbury
Cynonville
Cwmcarn
Caerleon
Penhow
Trehafod
Caerphilly
Caerwent
Caldicot
Westonbirt
Talbot
Margam
NEWPORT
Tongwyniais
SWINDON
Bridgend
Coity
St Fagans
CARDIFF
Dyrham
Ogmore
Penarth
BRISTOL
Calne
St Hilary
Barry
Clevedon
Corsham
BATH
Lacock
Bristol Channel
Weston-super-Mare
Bradford-on-Avon
Holt
Westwood
WILTSHIRE
Axbridge
Farleigh Hungerford
Rode
Wookey Hole
Frome
Westbury
Salisbury Plain
East Huntspill
Nunney
Wells
Warminster
Blackmoor Gate
Dunster
Washford
Nether Stowey
Cranmore
Longleat
Exmoor
Glastonbury
Monksilver
Bridgwater
Street
Stourhead
Teffont Magna
South Molton
Stoke St Gregory
Castle Cary
Stourton
SOMERSET
Kingsdon
Sparkford
SALISBURY
TAUNTON
Muchelney
Yeovilton
Tisbury
Knightshayes Court
East Lambrook
Tintinhull
Shaftesbury
Barrington
YEOVIL
Sherborne
Stoke-Sub-Hamdon
Montacute
Tiverton
Uffculme
Chard
Minterne Magna
Bickleigh
Cricket St Thomas
Blandford Forum
New Forest
Killerton House & Garden
Honiton
Beaminster
Wimborne
DEVON
EXETER
Ottery St Mary
Bridport
Athelhampton
Tolpuddle
Poole
Clyst St Mary
DORSET
Drewsteignton
Beer
Abbotsbury
Dorchester
Bovington Camp
BOURNEMOUTH
Brownsea Island
Bicton
Powderham
Otterton
Chesil Beach
WEYMOUTH
Corfe Castle
Chudleigh
Exmouth
Lyme Bay
West Lulworth
Swanage
Newton Abbot
Portland
Bill of Portland
Compton
TORQUAY
Totnes
Paignton
Kingswear
Dartmouth
Kingsbridge
Salcombe
Prawle Point
SO
ST
SY
0 10 20 miles
0 10 20 30 kilometres

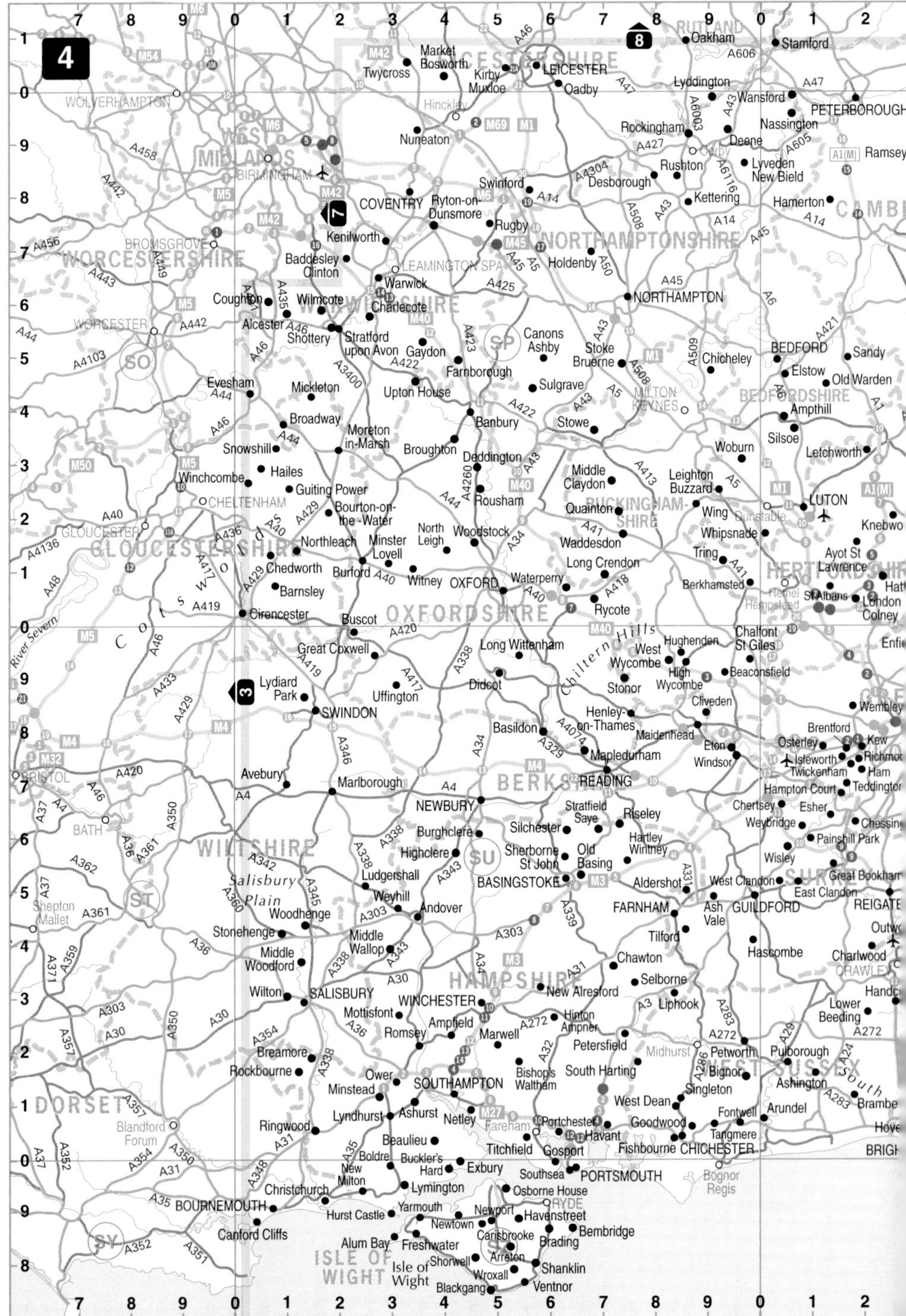

For continuation pages refer to numbered arrows

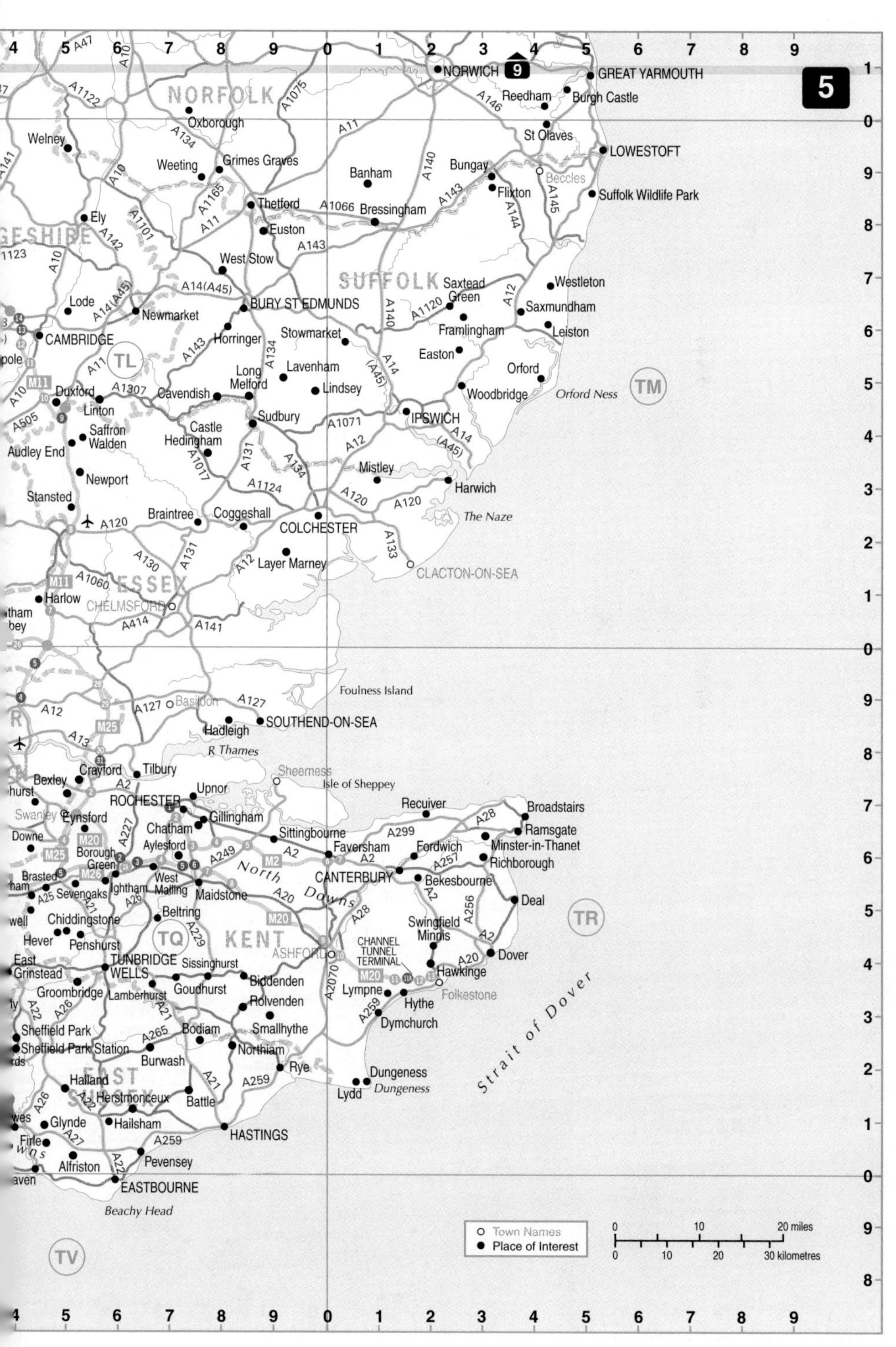
5
NORFOLK
NORWICH
GREAT YARMOUTH
Reedham
Burgh Castle
Oxborough
St Olaves
LOWESTOFT
Welney
Weeting
Grimes Graves
Banham
Bungay
Beccles
Flixton
Suffolk Wildlife Park
Thetford
Bressingham
Ely
Euston
West Stow
SUFFOLK
Saxtead Green
Westleton
Saxmundham
Leiston
Lode
Newmarket
BURY ST EDMUNDS
Framlingham
CAMBRIDGE
Horringer
Stowmarket
Easton
TL
Lavenham
Orford
Long Melford
Lindsey
Woodbridge
Orford Ness
TM
Duxford
Cavendish
Linton
Sudbury
IPSWICH
Saffron Walden
Castle Hedingham
Audley End
Mistley
Newport
Harwich
Stansted
The Naze
Braintree
Coggeshall
COLCHESTER
Layer Marney
CLACTON-ON-SEA
ESSEX
Harlow
CHELMSFORD
Foulness Island
Basildon
SOUTHEND-ON-SEA
Hadleigh
R Thames
Bexley
Crayford
Tilbury
Sheerness
Isle of Sheppey
Upnor
ROCHESTER
Gillingham
Recuiver
Broadstairs
Eynsford
Chatham
Ramsgate
Sittingbourne
Faversham
Fordwich
Minster-in-Thanet
Aylesford
Richborough
North Downs
CANTERBURY
Bekesbourne
Borough Green
West Malling
Maidstone
Deal
Sevenoaks
Ightham
Chiddingstone
Beltring
TR
Swingfield Minnis
Hever
Penshurst
TQ
KENT
CHANNEL TUNNEL TERMINAL
ASHFORD
Dover
East Grinstead
TUNBRIDGE WELLS
Sissinghurst
Hawkinge
Groombridge
Lamberhurst
Goudhurst
Biddenden
Lympne
Folkestone
Hythe
Rolvenden
Dymchurch
Strait of Dover
Sheffield Park
Bodiam
Smallhythe
Sheffield Park Station
Northiam
Burwash
Rye
Dungeness
Halland
Lydd
EAST SUSSEX
Herstmonceux
Battle
Glynde
Hailsham
HASTINGS
Firle
Pevensey
Alfriston
EASTBOURNE
Beachy Head
TV
Town Names
Place of Interest
0 10 20 miles
0 10 20 30 kilometres

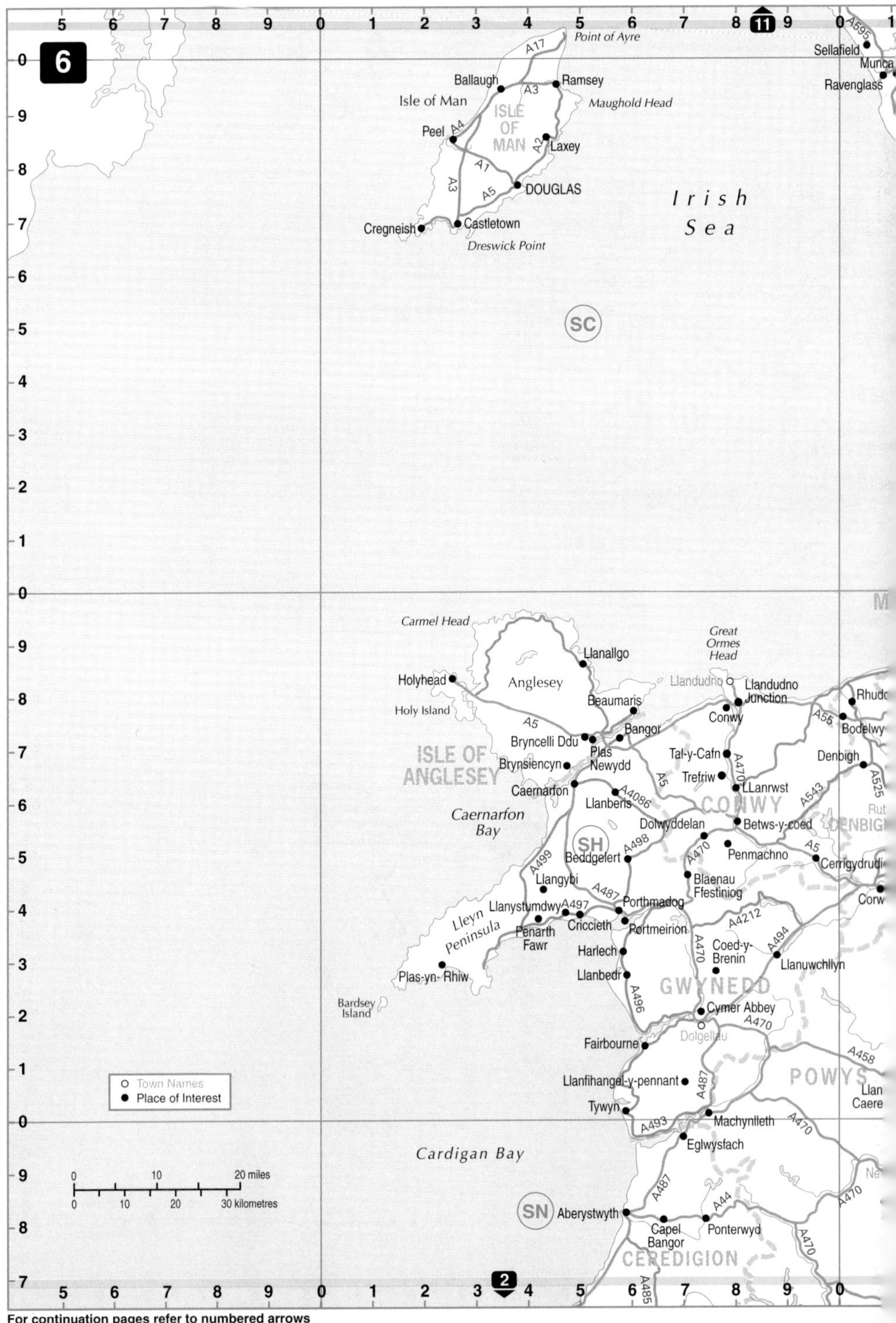

For continuation pages refer to numbered arrows

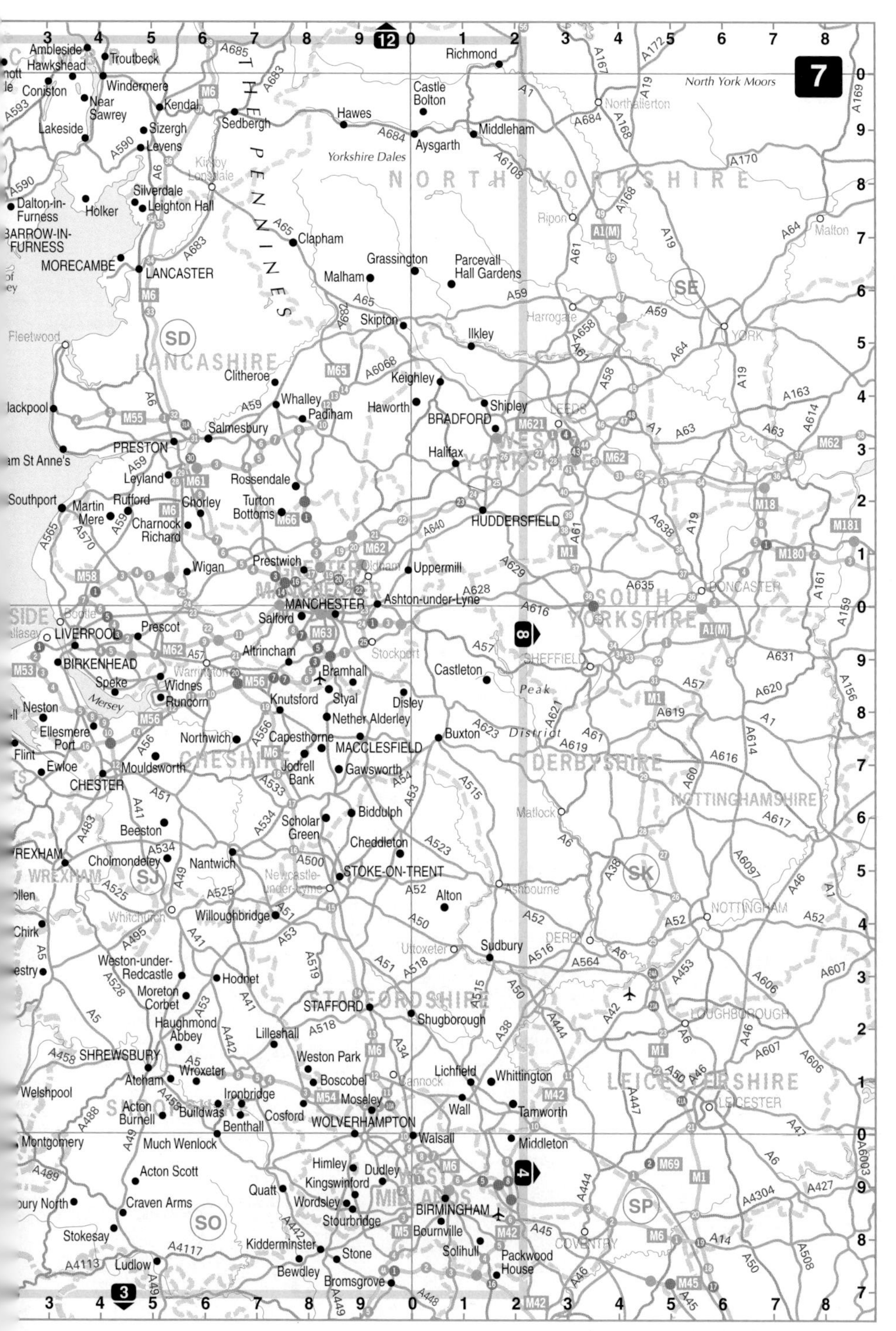

7
North York Moors
NORTH YORKSHIRE
THE PENNINES
Yorkshire Dales
LANCASHIRE
WEST YORKSHIRE
SOUTH YORKSHIRE
GREATER MANCHESTER
CHESHIRE
DERBYSHIRE
NOTTINGHAMSHIRE
STAFFORDSHIRE
LEICESTERSHIRE
WEST MIDLANDS
SHROPSHIRE
WREXHAM
Peak District
Mersey
SD
SE
SJ
SK
SO
SP
Ambleside
Troutbeck
Hawkshead
Coniston
Windermere
Near Sawrey
Kendal
Lakeside
Sizergh
Levens
Kirkby Lonsdale
Silverdale
Leighton Hall
Holker
Dalton-in-Furness
BARROW-IN-FURNESS
MORECAMBE
LANCASTER
Fleetwood
Sedbergh
Hawes
Clapham
Richmond
Castle Bolton
Middleham
Aysgarth
Northallerton
Ripon
Malton
Grassington
Parcevall Hall Gardens
Malham
Skipton
Ilkley
Harrogate
YORK
Clitheroe
Whalley
Padiham
Keighley
Haworth
Shipley
BRADFORD
LEEDS
Halifax
HUDDERSFIELD
Blackpool
Salmesbury
PRESTON
Lytham St Anne's
Leyland
Rossendale
Southport
Martin Mere
Rufford
Chorley
Turton Bottoms
Charnock Richard
Wigan
Prestwich
Oldham
Uppermill
DONCASTER
MANCHESTER
Ashton-under-Lyne
Salford
Bootle
LIVERPOOL
Prescot
BIRKENHEAD
Altrincham
Warrington
Stockport
SHEFFIELD
Castleton
Bramhall
Speke
Widnes
Runcorn
Styal
Disley
Neston
Knutsford
Nether Alderley
Ellesmere Port
Buxton
Flint
Northwich
Capesthorne
MACCLESFIELD
Ewloe
Mouldsworth
Jodrell Bank
Gawsworth
CHESTER
Matlock
Biddulph
Beeston
Scholar Green
Cheddleton
WREXHAM
Cholmondeley
Nantwich
Newcastle-under-Lyme
STOKE-ON-TRENT
Ashbourne
Alton
NOTTINGHAM
Whitchurch
Willoughbridge
Chirk
DERBY
Uttoxeter
Sudbury
Weston-under-Redcastle
Hodnet
Moreton Corbet
STAFFORD
Shugborough
LOUGHBOROUGH
Haughmond Abbey
Lilleshall
Weston Park
SHREWSBURY
Lichfield
Whittington
Atcham
Wroxeter
Boscobel
Cannock
Welshpool
Ironbridge
Moseley
Wall
Acton Burnell
Buildwas
Cosford
Tamworth
LEICESTER
Benthall
WOLVERHAMPTON
Montgomery
Walsall
Middleton
Much Wenlock
Himley
Dudley
Acton Scott
Kingswinford
Quatt
Wordsley
Craven Arms
BIRMINGHAM
Stourbridge
Bournville
Stokesay
COVENTRY
Kidderminster
Solihull
Packwood House
Stone
Ludlow
Bewdley
Bromsgrove

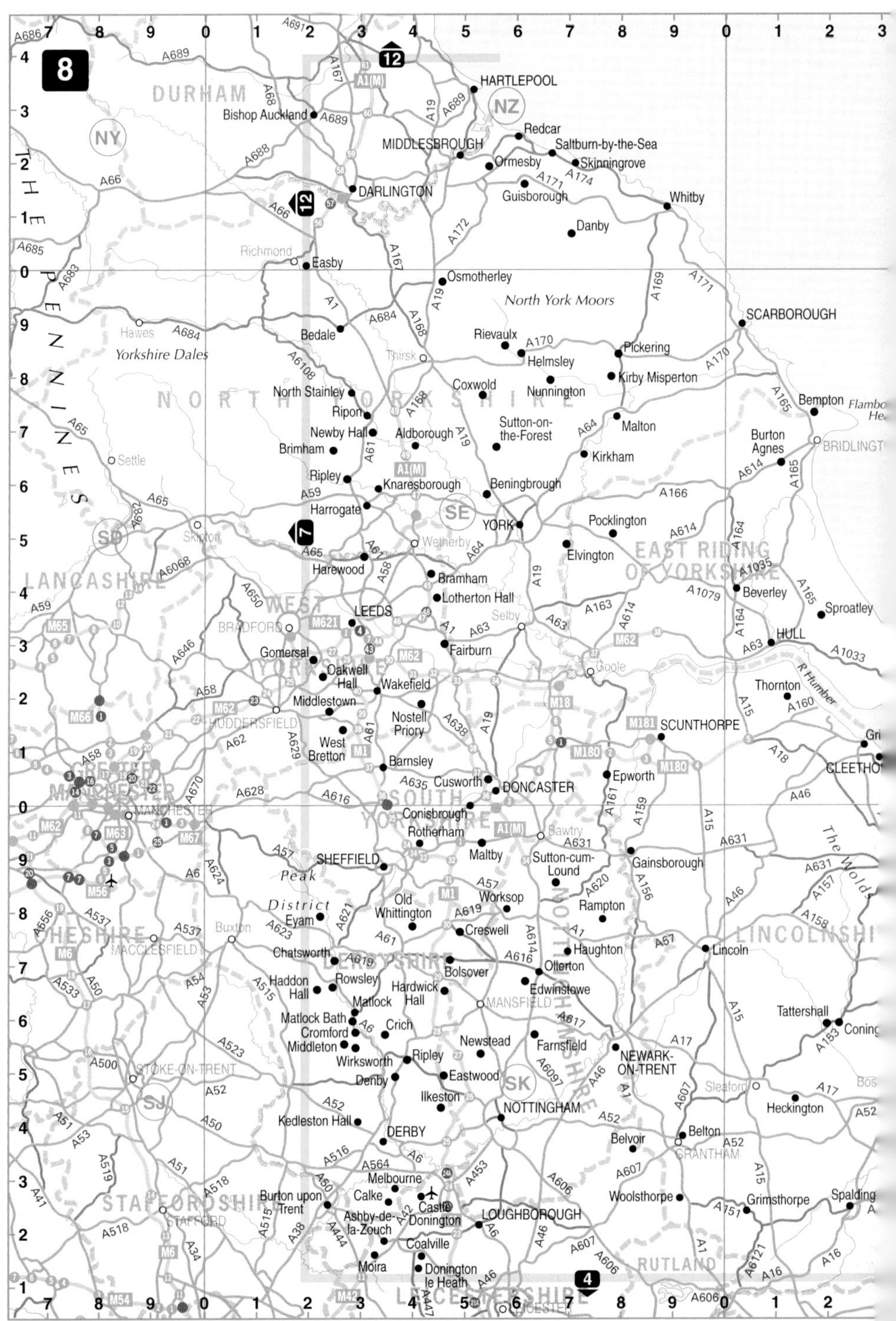

For continuation pages refer to numbered arrows

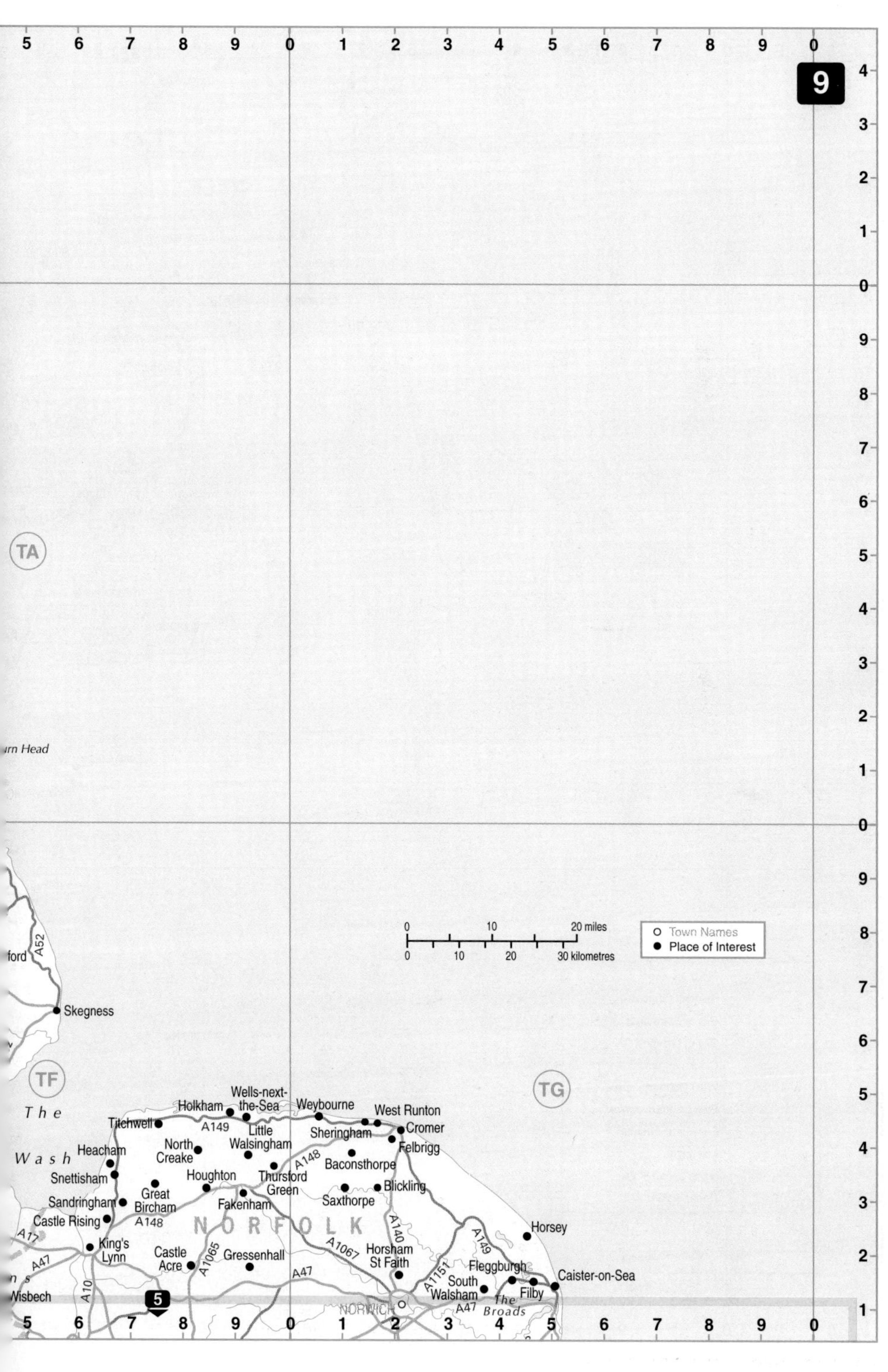
9
TA
TF
TG
urn Head
ford
A52
Skegness
The Wash
Titchwell
Holkham
Wells-next-the-Sea
Weybourne
West Runton
Cromer
Sheringham
Felbrigg
A149
Little Walsingham
North Creake
Heacham
Snettisham
Houghton
Thursford Green
A148
Baconsthorpe
Blickling
Saxthorpe
Great Bircham
Sandringham
Fakenham
Castle Rising
A148
NORFOLK
A140
A149
Horsey
A17
King's Lynn
A47
Castle Acre
A1065
Gressenhall
A1067
Horsham St Faith
Fleggburgh
Caister-on-Sea
A47
A1151
South Walsham
Filby
Wisbech
A10
5
NORWICH
A47
The Broads
0 10 20 miles
0 10 20 30 kilometres
Town Names
Place of Interest

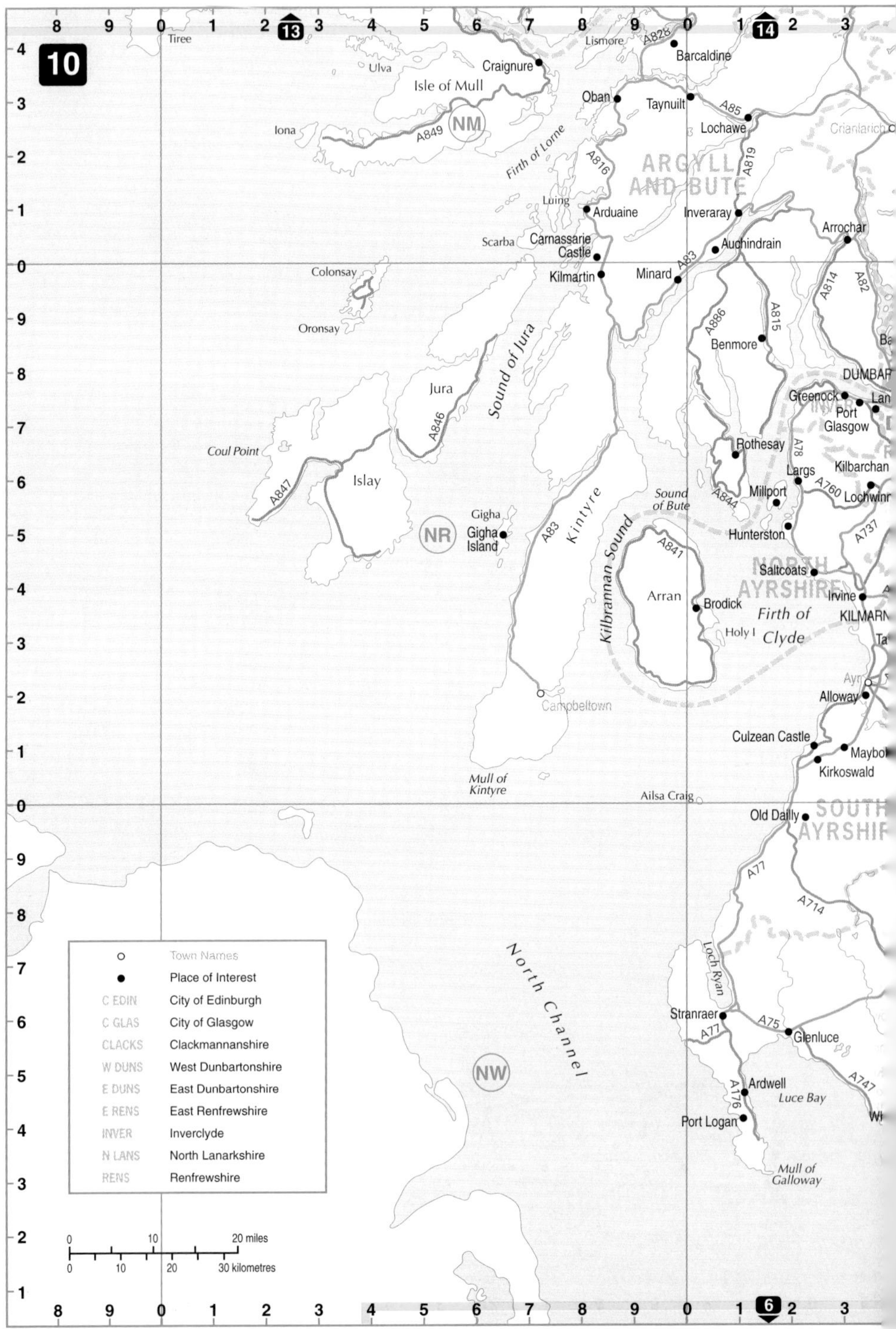
10
13
14
6
Tiree
Ulva
Craignure
Isle of Mull
Iona
A849
NM
Lismore
A828
Barcaldine
Oban
Taynuilt
A85
Lochawe
Crianlarich
Firth of Lorne
A816
ARGYLL AND BUTE
A819
Luing
Arduaine
Inveraray
Arrochar
Scarba
Carnassarie Castle
Auchindrain
Kilmartin
Minard
A83
Colonsay
Oronsay
A886
A815
A814
A82
Benmore
Sound of Jura
Jura
A846
DUMBAR
Greenock
Port Glasgow
INVER
Rothesay
A78
Largs
Kilbarchan
A760
Lochwinn
Coul Point
A847
Islay
Kintyre
Sound of Bute
A844
Millport
Gigha
Gigha Island
NR
A83
Kilbrannan Sound
Hunterston
A737
A841
NORTH AYRSHIRE
Saltcoats
Arran
Brodick
Irvine
Firth of Clyde
KILMARN
Holy I
Ayr
Alloway
Campbeltown
Culzean Castle
Maybol
Kirkoswald
Mull of Kintyre
Ailsa Craig
Old Dailly
SOUTH AYRSHIR
A77
A714
North Channel
Loch Ryan
Stranraer
A77
A75
Glenluce
NW
Ardwell
A716
Luce Bay
A747
Port Logan
Mull of Galloway
Town Names
Place of Interest
C EDIN City of Edinburgh
C GLAS City of Glasgow
CLACKS Clackmannanshire
W DUNS West Dunbartonshire
E DUNS East Dunbartonshire
E RENS East Renfrewshire
INVER Inverclyde
N LANS North Lanarkshire
RENS Renfrewshire
0 10 20 miles
0 10 20 30 kilometres
For continuation pages refer to numbered arrows

11
15
Dunkeld
PERTH AND KINROSS
DUNDEE CITY
DUNDEE
Scone
PERTH
Firth of Tay
NO
St Andrews Bay
St Andrews
Crieff
Muthill
Cupar
FIFE
Fife Ness
Callander
Milnathort
Falkland
Kinross
NORTH
SEA
Isle of May
Doune
Blair
Drummond
Alva
Dollar
Port of Menteith
Causewayhead
STIRLING
Alloa
Bannockburn
Dunfermline
KIRKCALDY
Aberdour
Burntisland
Culross
Firth of Forth
Birkhill
Bo'ness
North Queensferry
South Queensferry
Falkirk
Linlithgow
Ingliston
EDINBURGH
Prestonpans
Dunbar
Gogar
Inveresk
EAST LOTHIAN
St Abb's Head
Dalkeith
GLASGOW
Coatbridge
Balerno
Newtongrange
Uddingston
Bothwell
Penicuik
Crichton
Lammermuir Hills
Blantyre
Motherwell
Hamilton
Berwick-upon-Tweed
Holy Island
NT
SOUTH LANARKSHIRE
Biggar
Broughton
Peebles
Innerleithen
12
Galashiels
Stobo
Traquair
Uplands
BORDERS (SCOTTISH)
Kelso
Jedburgh
Hawick
The Cheviot Hills
Wanlockhead
Sanquhar
Thornhill
Otterburn
Moniaive
Southern
DUMFRIES AND GALLOWAY
NORTHUMBERLAND
DUMFRIES
Drumcoltran Tower
New Abbey
Caerlaverock
Ruthwell
Castle Douglas
Palnackie
Hexham
Tongland
CARLISLE
Kirkcudbright
Dundrennan
NY
Abbey Head
Solway Firth
WORKINGTON
Cockermouth
Penrith
DURHAM
Keswick
CUMBRIA
North Head
Lake District
Grasmere
Rydal
7
A827
A826
A822
A94
A92
A90
A85
A84
A9
A823
A91
A914
A915
A917
M90
M9
M80
A811
A198
A1
M73
M8
A71
A8
A1107
A70
A706
A702
A68
A703
A7
A6105
A6112
A697
A698
A726
A73
M74
A721
A72
A6089
A701
A708
A74(M)
A76
A6088
A709
A712
A713
A711
A75
A710
A69
A689
A695
A696
A596
A595
A6
M6
A686
A691
A66
A5086
A591
A688

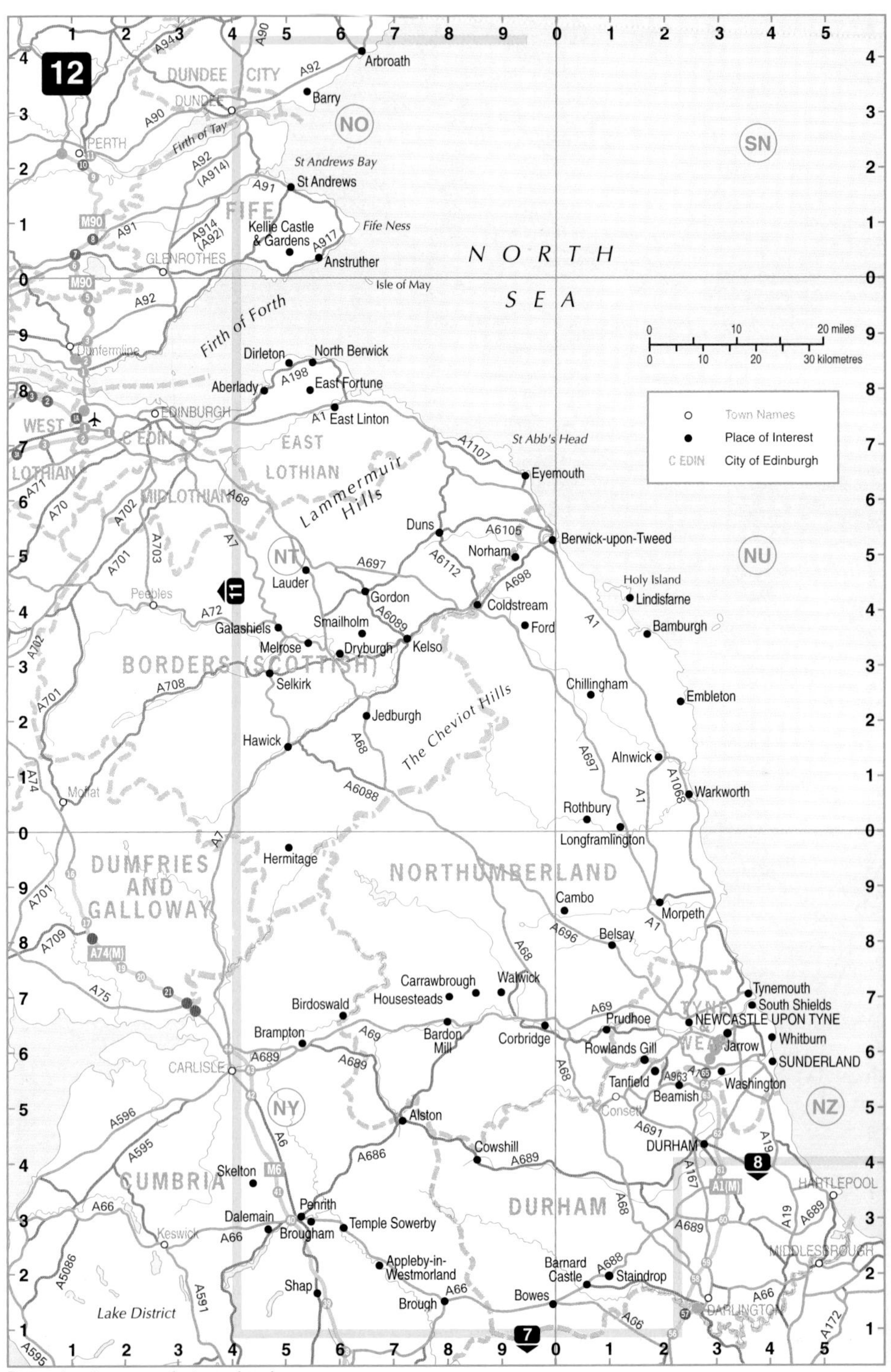

For continuation pages refer to numbered arrows

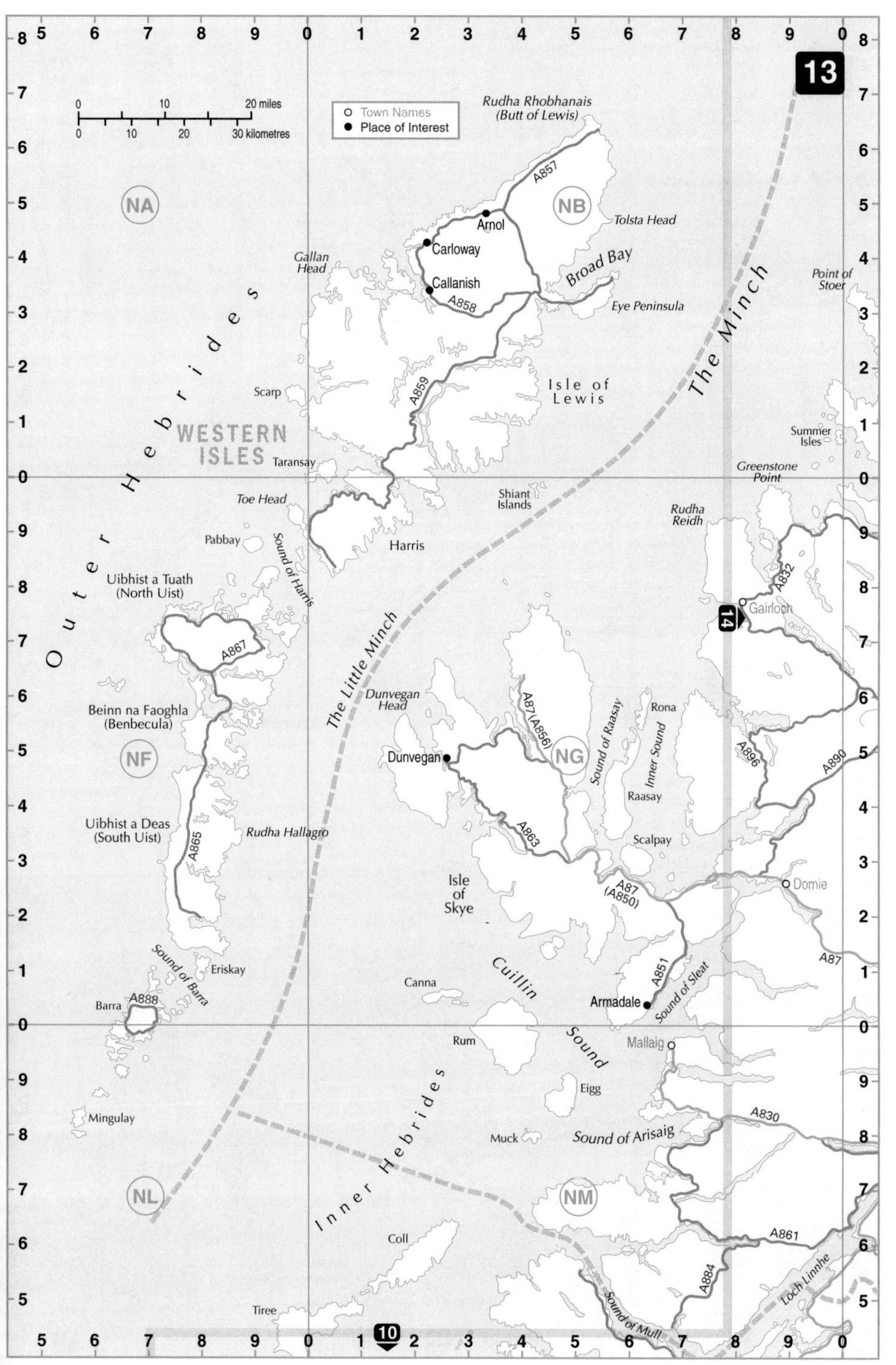
13
Town Names
Place of Interest
0 10 20 miles
0 10 20 30 kilometres
Rudha Rhobhanais (Butt of Lewis)
A857
Arnol
Carloway
Callanish
A858
Tolsta Head
Broad Bay
Eye Peninsula
Gallan Head
Outer Hebrides
WESTERN ISLES
Scarp
Taransay
A859
Isle of Lewis
The Minch
Point of Stoer
Summer Isles
Greenstone Point
Toe Head
Shiant Islands
Harris
Rudha Reidh
Pabbay
Sound of Harris
Uibhist a Tuath (North Uist)
A867
A832
Gairloch
14
The Little Minch
Dunvegan Head
Dunvegan
A87 (A856)
Sound of Raasay
Inner Sound
Rona
Raasay
Scalpay
Beinn na Faoghla (Benbecula)
A865
Uibhist a Deas (South Uist)
Rudha Hallagro
A863
A896
A890
Dornie
Isle of Skye
A87 (A850)
A87
A851
Cuillin
Armadale
Sound of Sleat
Eriskay
Sound of Barra
Barra
A888
Canna
Rum
Sound
Mallaig
Eigg
A830
Mingulay
Muck
Sound of Arisaig
Inner Hebrides
Coll
A861
A884
Loch Linnhe
Sound of Mull
Tiree
10
NA
NB
NF
NG
NL
NM

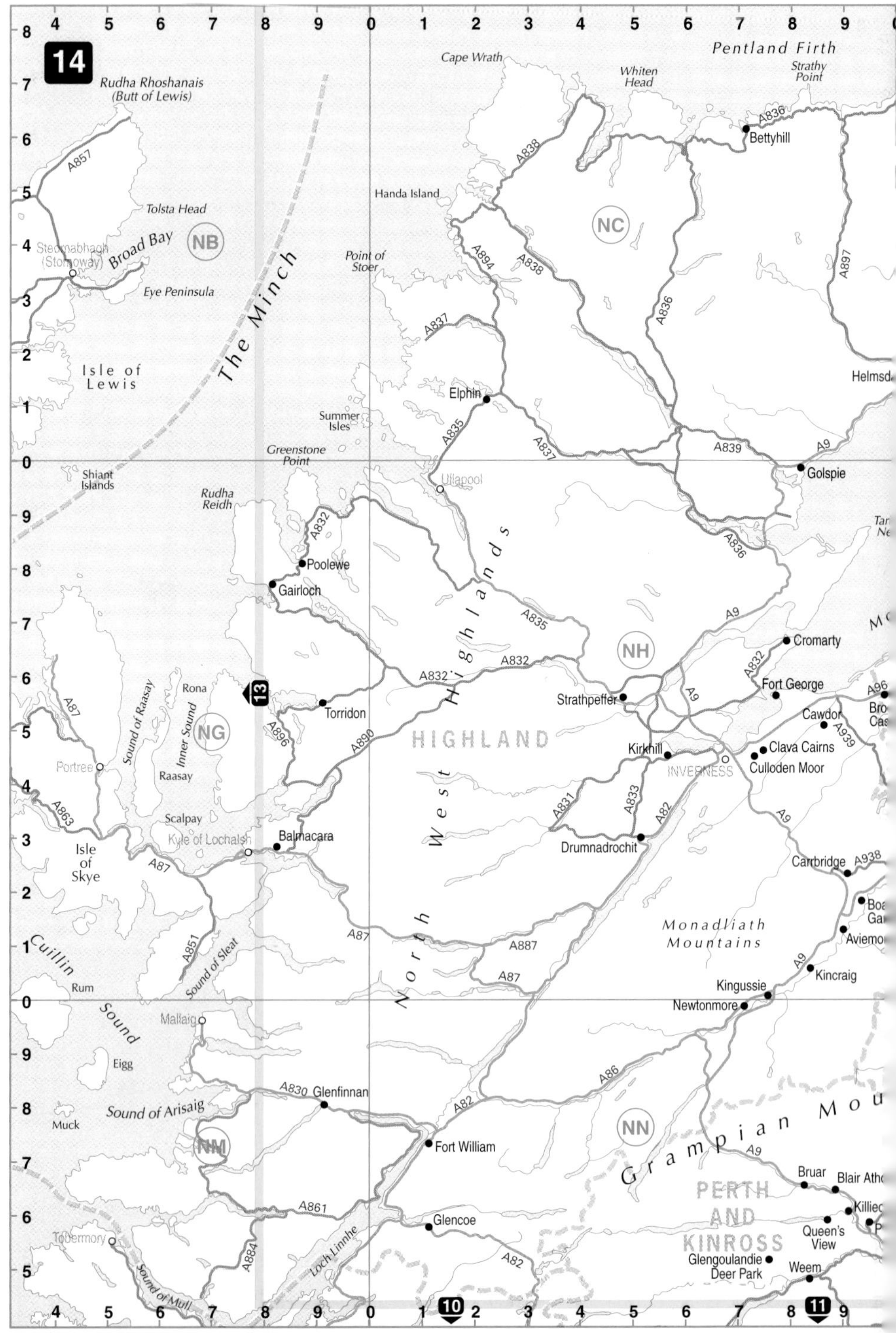

For continuation pages refer to numbered arrows

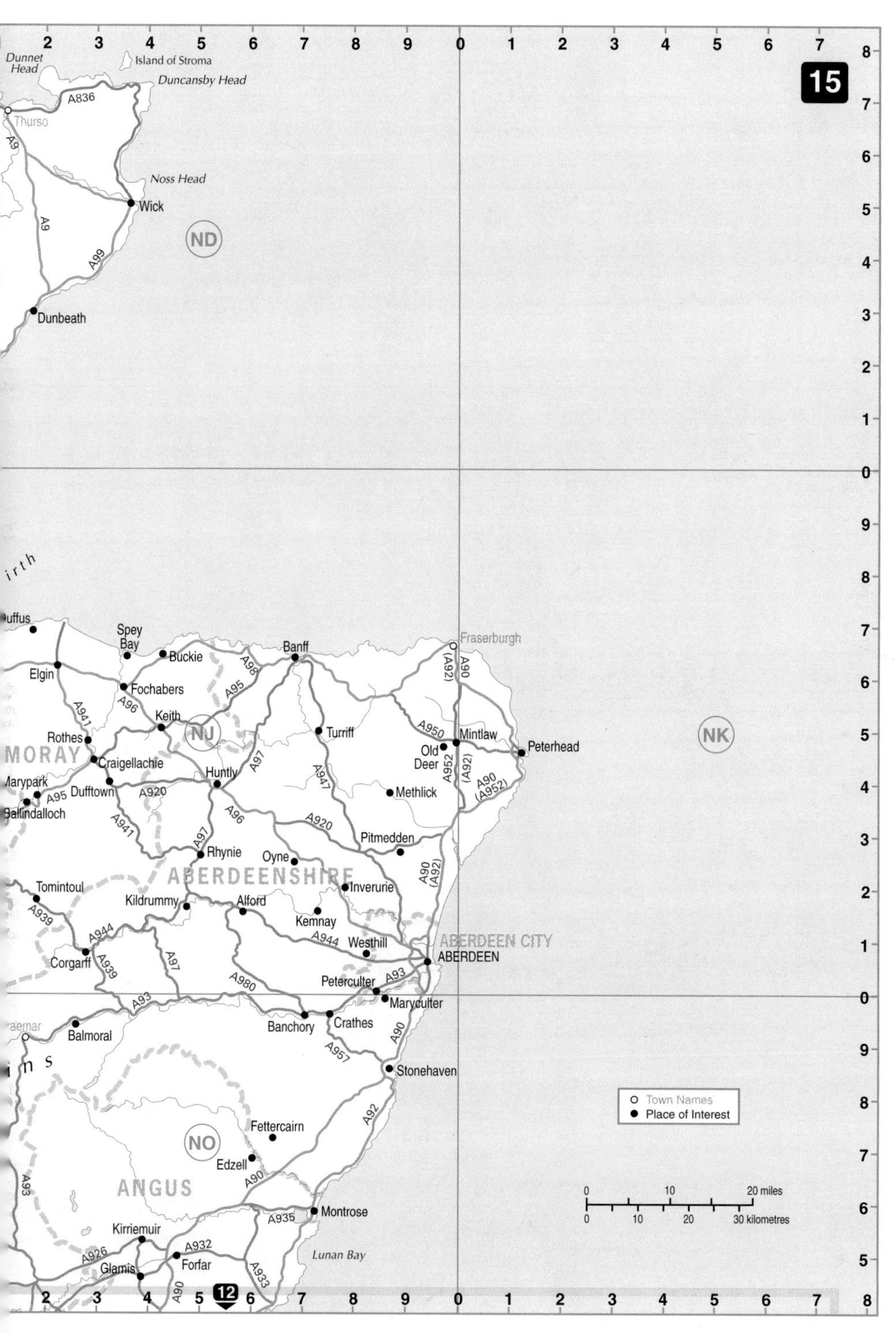
15
Dunnet Head
Island of Stroma
Duncansby Head
Thurso
Noss Head
Wick
ND
Dunbeath
Duffus
Spey Bay
Buckie
Banff
Fraserburgh
Elgin
Fochabers
Keith
NJ
Rothes
MORAY
Craigellachie
Turriff
Mintlaw
Peterhead
Old Deer
NK
Marypark
Dufftown
Ballindalloch
Huntly
Methlick
Pitmedden
Rhynie
Oyne
ABERDEENSHIRE
Tomintoul
Kildrummy
Alford
Inverurie
Kemnay
Westhill
ABERDEEN CITY
ABERDEEN
Corgarff
Peterculter
Maryculter
Braemar
Balmoral
Banchory
Crathes
Stonehaven
Town Names
Place of Interest
Fettercairn
NO
Edzell
ANGUS
Montrose
Kirriemuir
Forfar
Glamis
Lunan Bay
20 miles
30 kilometres

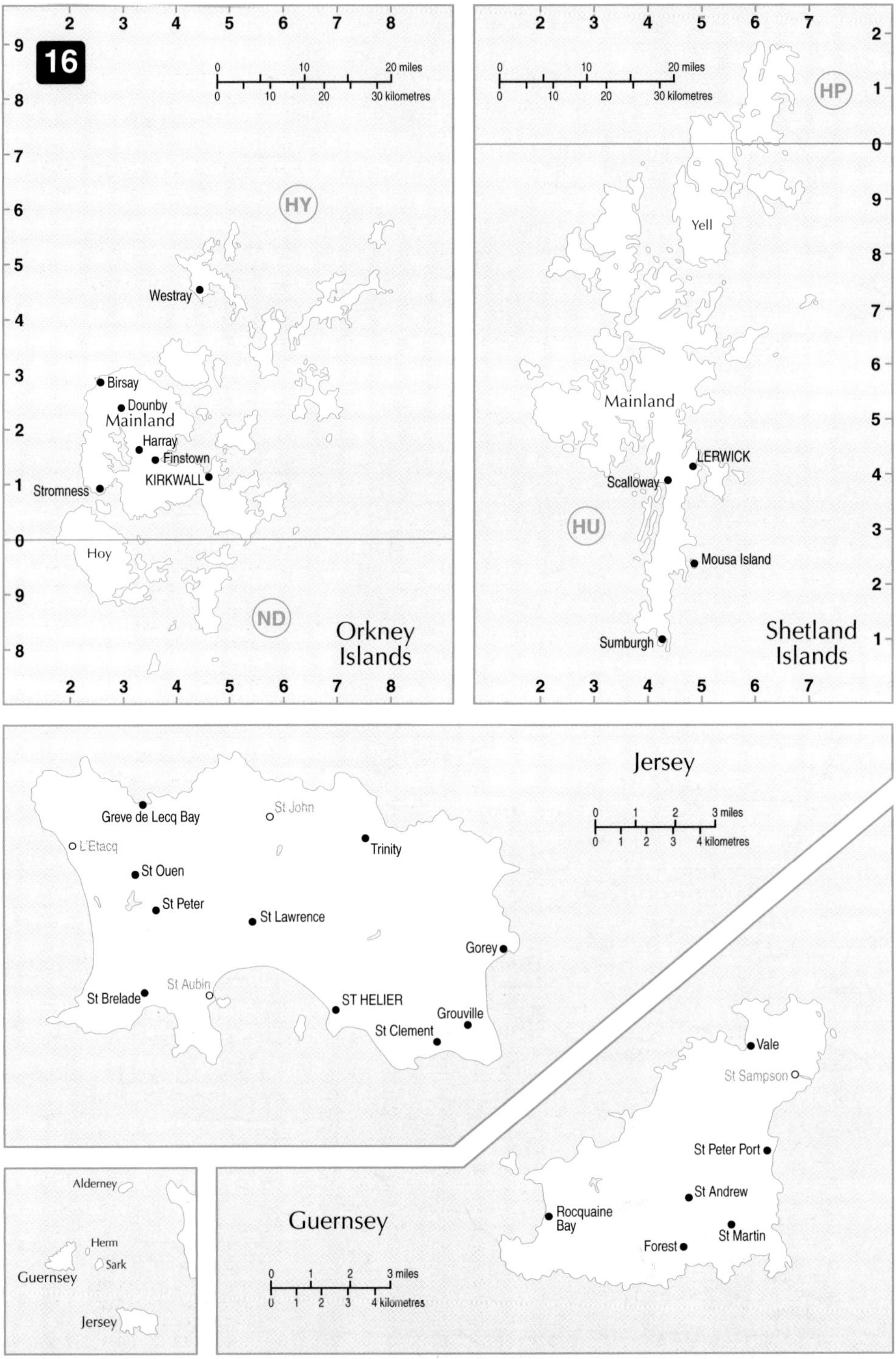

16

2 3 4 5 6 7 8

9 8 7 6 5 4 3 2 1 0 9 8

0 10 20 miles

0 10 20 30 kilometres

HY

Westray

Birsay

Dounby

Mainland

Harray

Finstown

KIRKWALL

Stromness

Hoy

ND

Orkney Islands

2 3 4 5 6 7 8

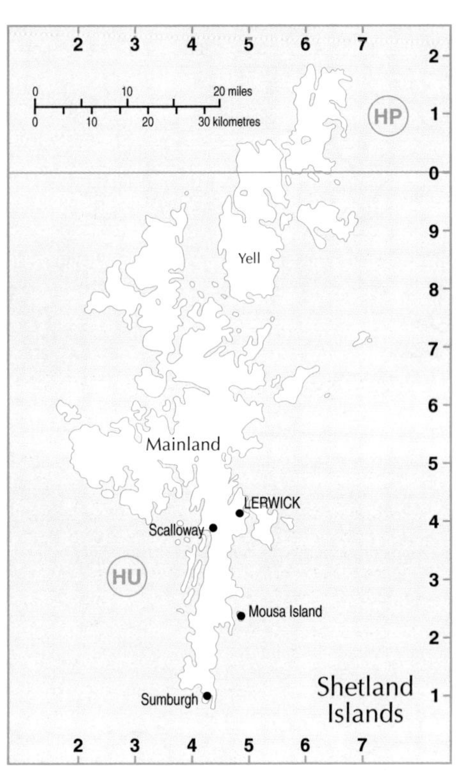

Jersey

0 1 2 3 miles

0 1 2 3 4 kilometres

Greve de Lecq Bay

St John

L'Etacq

Trinity

St Ouen

St Peter

St Lawrence

Gorey

St Aubin

St Brelade

ST HELIER

Grouville

St Clement

Alderney

Herm

Sark

Guernsey

Jersey

Guernsey

0 1 2 3 miles

0 1 2 3 4 kilometres

Vale

St Sampson

St Peter Port

St Andrew

Rocquaine Bay

St Martin

Forest

Index

The figures in bold are map references. These denote the map page number, followed by the National Grid Reference. To find the location, read the first figure across and the second figure vertically within the lettered square.

Due to space limitations, some abbreviations have been used.

Gdn = Garden
Mus = Museum
Cas = Castle
Ctr = Centre
Gly = Gallery
Hse = House
Pk = Park
Rwy = Railway
Stn = Station
Vtr = Visitor
Ch = Church

A

B

C

D

H

I

J

K

L

M

N

Index

O

P

Q

R

S

T

U

V

W

Acknowledgements

The main photographs in this book were supplied by AA Photo Library and were taken by the following photographers:

AA PHOTOLIBRARY 135b, 173b 213a, 254a; STUART ABRAHAMS 291b; 294; MARTYN ALDEMAN 92b, 264a; ADRIAN BAKER 8c, 223a; PETER BAKER 244a; VIC BATES 295a; JEFF BEAZLEY 76a, 177a; JAMIE BLANDFORD 387a; M BIRKITT Front Cover, 1, 3b, 6a, 8b, 9b, 13a, 13b, 21b, 25a, 25b, 50b, 79b, 111a, 131a, 131b, 174a, 174b, 192a, 192b; E A BOWNESS 5b; IAN BURGUM 5c, 194b, 354b; DEREK CROUCHER 352a; STEVE DAY 42a, 83a, 91, 161a, 161b, 187a, 213b, 238a, 282a; ROBERT EAMES 29a; RICHARD ELLIOT 347a; 347b; ROBIN FLETCHER 96a; DEREK FORSS 16b, 127a, 219a, 223b, 249b, 253; STEVE GREGORY 278; JIM HENDERSON 297a; STEPHEN HILL 387b; CAROLINE JONES 21a, 29b, 111b, 260a; S KING 42b; ANDREW LAWSON 35a, 57a, 57b; CAMERON LEES 76b; S & O MATHEWS 79a, 83b, 96b, 115a, 115b, 165a, 177b, 135a, 254b; JENNY McMILLAN 160; ERIC MEACHER 19a; C MELLOR 9a; COLIN MOLYNEAUX 92a; JOHN MORRISON 50a; ROGER MOSS 35b, 199a, 199b; JOHN MOTTISHAW 127b; GEORGE MUNDAY 377a; 377b; RICH NEWTON 69b, 182a, 182b, 264b; KEN PATERSON 5a, 6b, 297b; NEIL RAY 3a, 10a, 10b, 11b; MICHAEL SHORT 187b, 238b; ANTONY SOUTER 230a; FORBES STEPHENSON 260b; RICK STRANGE 16a; DAVID TARN 267a; MARTIN TRELAWNY 230b; PETER TRENCHARD 289b, 291a; ANDREW TRYNER 2, 11a; WYN VOYSEY 8a, 19b, 69a, 219b, 249a, 289b, 295b; JONATHON WELSH 194a, 207a, 207b, 244b, 248; LINDA WHITWAM 288; HARRY WILLIAMS 108a, 108b; PETER WILSON 139a, 279a, 279b, 281, 282b; TIM WOODCOCK 139b, 165b, 235b, 267b